Montesquieu's Science of Politics

Essays on *The Spirit of Laws*

EDITED BY DAVID W. CARRITHERS, MICHAEL A. MOSHER, AND PAUL A. RAHE

ROWMAN & LITTLEFIELD PUBLISHERS, INC.
Lanham • Boulder • New York • Toronto • Oxford

ROWMAN & LITTLEFIELD PUBLISHERS, INC.

Published in the United States of America
by Rowman & Littlefield Publishers, Inc.
A wholly owned subsidary of The Rowman & Littlefield Publishing Group, Inc.
4501 Forbes Boulevard, Suite 200, Lanham, Maryland 20706
www.rowmanlittlefield.com

PO Box 317
Oxford
OX2 9RU, UK

British Library Cataloguing in Publication Information Available

Library of Congress Cataloging-in-Publication Data

Montesquieu, Charles de Secondat, baron de, 1689-1755.
    Montesquieu's science of politics : essays on *the spirit of laws* / edited by David W.
    Carrithers, Michael A. Mosher, and Paul A. Rahe.
        p. cm.
    Includes index.
    ISBN 0-7425-1180-4 (alk. paper) – ISBN 0-7425-1181-2 (pbk. : alk, paper)
        1. Political science. 2. State, The. 3. Law—Philosophy. 4. Jurisprudence.
    I. Carrithers, David Wallace. II. Mosher, Michael A., 1944- III. Rahe, Paul Anthony.
    IV. Title.

    JC179 .M74 2001
    320—dc21
    Printed in the United States of America   00-059226

Montesquieu's Science of Politics

For Mary Carrithers, Mieko Ogawa, and Laura Rahe

Contents

Note on Bibliographical References

I.   Citations of Complete Works of Montesquieu

Œuvres complètes de Montesquieu, Roger Caillois, ed., 2 vols. (Paris: Bibliothèque de la Pléiade, 1949-1951)

Citations of this edition are abbreviated: e.g., Pléiade, I and II. We have routinely cited this edition since it is much more widely available than the one listed below.

Œuvres complètes de Montesquieu, André Masson, ed., 3 vols. (Paris: Nagel, 1950-1955)

Citations of this edition are abbreviated: e.g., Nagel, I, II, and III. The first volume is a photographic reprint of the 1758 edition of the *Œuvres complètes*, Amsterdam and Leipzig (=Paris). It has three sequences of pagination, referred to as A, B, and C.

II.   Citations of *The Spirit of Laws* (1748)

The title of this work is cited in the English translation employed between 1750 and 1900 in all editions of Thomas Nugent's classic translation of 1750, i.e., without a second definite article before the word Laws. Where brief chapters are cited, no pagination is included: e.g. (I, 1). Where lengthy chapters are cited, the relevant page number from the Pléiade edition is included: e.g. (XI, 6, 397 or XI, 6, 397-98). The Roman numeral refers to the Book number of *The Spirit of Laws*, and the arabic numeral refers to the chapter number.

III.   Citations of *Persian Letters* (1721)

Citations are to the Pléiade edition: e.g., Persian Letter 83, in Pléiade, I, 236.

IV.   Citations of *Considerations on the Greatness of the Romans and Their Decline* (1734)

Citations are to the Pléiade edition: e.g., *Considerations*, chap. 9, in Pléiade, I, 119.

V.   Citations of Montesquieu's *Mes Pensées*

Citations reflect both the original ordering of Montesquieu's *Pensées* and the rearranged, topical order published in *Pensées et fragments inédits*, Henri Barckhausen, ed., 2 vols. (Bordeaux, 1899-1901): e.g. *Pensée* 1802 (32), in Pléiade, I, 1431. The first number is the re-ordered numbering of Barckhausen. The second number within parentheses is the original order of composition of the *Pensées*, printed in Nagel.

The volume number is cited since those *Pensées* whose content is closely related to *The Spirit of Laws* are printed in vol. 2 of the Pléiade edition: e.g., *Pensée* 192 (1866), in Pléiade, II, 1038.

VI.   Citations of *Spicilège*

Citations are to the Pléiade edition: e.g., *Spicilège* 604, in Pléiade, II, 1390.

VII. Citations of Correspondence

Citations are to the Nagel edition of the *Œuvres complètes*: e.g., Montesquieu to Durey de Meinières, July 9, 1753, in Nagel, III, 1467-68.

Introduction

An Appreciation of *The Spirit of Laws*

David W. Carrithers

Montesquieu's *The Spirit of Laws* (1748) is one of those classic works long ago elevated into the pantheon of Western political philosophy. Clearly one reason for its acknowledged status is that in Books II through VIII, which constitute (along with Book XI) the most widely read portions of the work, Montesquieu chose to dwell on the fundamental concern of all human beings to comprehend the full range of political choices regarding regime types available to mankind. The classification of governmental types from Plato down to Montesquieu's day had remained relatively constant, as if to suggest that there are only so many possibilities open for political invention. Had Montesquieu done nothing more than re-define and re-conceptualize the basic types of government, while adding important information on the accompanying psychologies motivating the subjects, or citizens, of each type, he would have secured for himself an important place in the history of political thought. That he did substantially more than this makes it easy to appreciate the lasting significance of his achievement and the steady interest that has been shown in his work since its original publication in 1748.

Immediately upon its initial publication, *The Spirit of Laws* evoked an extraordinary amount of discussion, praise, and commentary. If David Hume's *Treatise of Human Nature* (1739), by his own admission, "fell *dead-born from the press*," Montesquieu's work was widely noticed and unleashed a torrent of controversy, becoming one of the hot topics of its day. Fifteen editions appeared by 1757, and twenty-eight editions were published before 1789.[1] Many readers believed the work merited the highest praise. In his *Enquiry Concerning the Principles of Morals* (1751) Hume labeled Montesquieu an "author of great genius, as well as extensive learning," while categorizing *The Spirit of Laws* as "the best system of political knowledge that, perhaps, has ever yet been communicated to the world."[2] Earlier, in a letter to Montesquieu dated April 10, 1749, Hume had predicted that Montesquieu's work would be considered "the wonder of all centuries."[3] Hume's contemporary, Horace Walpole, was similarly smitten and went so far as to call Montesquieu's treatise "the best book that ever was written."[4] Edmund Burke, whose outlook was substantially influenced by Montesquieu, referred to him as "the greatest genius, which has enlightened this age."[5] Montesquieu was, in Burke's judgement, "a genius not born in every country, or every time; a man gifted by nature with a penetrating, aquiline eye; with a judgement prepared with the most extensive erudition; with an Herculean robustness of mind, and nerves not to be broken with labour; a man who could spend twenty years in one pursuit."[6] Burke's contemporary, William Blackstone, paid Montesquieu the highest possible compliment by copying the main lines of his analysis of the English constitution into his own depiction of the English system in his *Commentaries on the Laws of England* (1765-69).

In France many readers were similarly moved to praise the brilliance of *The Spirit of Laws*. The Chevalier d'Aydie wrote to Montesquieu to congratulate him on "discovering for mankind the ways to become more just and consequently happier." The Marquis de Breille considered T*he Spirit of Laws* "a beacon light for princes or heads of Republics . . . who wish to govern well." In a similar vein Monseigneur Cerati, a prelate and close friend of Montesquieu, wrote to praise him for "having used the superiority of your genius, the quintessence of your great wisdom, and the grounds of your laconic eloquence to turn European minds towards a very great number of truths useful to the human race." Montesquieu had done no less than save mankind, Cerati concluded, "from the ravages of arbitrary power."[7] No less generous with accolades was Mme de Tencin who remarked that "philosophy, reason, [and] humanity have been brought together to compose this work, and the Graces have taken care to adorn it with erudition."[8] For Rousseau, Montesquieu was a "celebrated author" and a "glorious genius (*beau génie*)."[9] For D'Alembert, who composed a eulogy and an analysis of *The Spirit of Laws* for the fifth volume of Diderot's *Encyclopédie* (1755), it was the spirit of a good citizen that shone through *The Spirit of Laws*. The reader will encounter "love of the public good" and "the desire to see men happy" throughout the whole of the work, D'Alembert asserted, in labeling Montesquieu nothing less than "the benefactor of humanity" and the "legislator of nations."[10] For Jean-Paul Marat, Montesquieu was "the greatest man that the century had produced," owing to his "love for humanity," his "hatred for despotism," his "respect for the laws," and his "zeal for the public good."[11]

In France even Montesquieu's harshest critics felt duty bound to balance their criticisms with praise in order not to unfairly denigrate the worth of Montesquieu's monumental achievement. Certainly the need felt by both Voltaire and Antoine Destutt de Tracy to pen lengthy, critical appraisals of *The Spirit of Laws* attests to the extraordinary importance of the work. In addition to writing a dialogue entitled *L'ABC, On Hobbes, Grotius and Montesquieu* (1768), Voltaire also composed a *Commentary on Some Important Maxims of The Spirit of Laws* (1777) in which, in spite of advancing multiple criticisms, he affirmed the overall worth of Montesquieu's efforts. "The works of Grotius and Pufendorf were only compilations," Voltaire asserted. "Montesquieu's appeared to be that of a statesman, a *philosophe*, a man of wit, a citizen. Almost all those who were the natural judges of such a book," Voltaire continued, "men of letters and of the law in all countries . . . regard it as the code of reason and liberty."[12] Destutt de Tracy, though highly critical of what he perceived as Montesquieu's tendency to accept whatever political and social order had developed gradually over time, nonetheless had extremely flattering things to say in the preface he wrote for Thomas Jefferson's translation of his commentary. Destutt de Tracy acknowledged that "Montesquieu's immortal work on the Spirit of Laws, could not fail, of course, to furnish matter for profound consideration. I have admired his vivid imagination, his extensive reading, and dextrous use of it," he asserted, "and I have thought the errors of his book, the more important to be corrected as its truths are numerous, and of powerful influence on the opinions of society."[13]

For some readers the long-awaited access to the result of Montesquieu's arduous labors stretching out over nearly twenty years brought nothing less than intense pleasure and delight. Consider, for example, the reaction of another very prominent provincial magistrate of the first half of the eighteenth century, Président Charles de Brosses, author of interesting works both on the psychological origins of religious consciousness and on travels in Italy. "Oh how beautiful this is," de Brosses exclaimed to a friend. "What ideas, what fire (*feu*), what precision (and much more!) what new and luminous thoughts." De Brosses vows that he intends to read *The Spirit of Laws* not just once but twice, and then reflect on it, and learn it by heart. Only then, he remarked, would he feel ready to discuss this great work.[14] In Italy, Stefano Bertolini, city auditor of Florence and the author of an *Analyse de L'Esprit des lois* (1771), was so taken with the work that he placed Montesquieu in the select company of Plato and Cicero and complimented him for displaying "a profound genius, a virile and vigorous spirit and exquisite discernment, comprehensive and sublime viewpoints, a marvelous sequence and concentration of ideas, a steady and confident course, [and] love and zeal for the welfare of humanity."[15] It was little wonder, Bertolini asserted, that upon hearing of Montesquieu's death in 1755, Louis XV "publicly remarked that this was a man impossible to replace."

Across the Atlantic the initial reaction was equally positive. An enthusiastic James Madison praised Montesquieu as the Francis Bacon of political studies and concluded that he "had lifted the veil from the venerable errors, which enslaved opinion and pointed the way to those luminous truths of which he had but a glimpse himself."[16] Meanwhile, Thomas Jefferson and John Adams were both compiling careful notes on Montesquieu's work since it was widely regarded as the most authoritative work on politics of its time. Jefferson would eventually

sharply criticize Montesquieu for his putative zeal in defending monarchy, but
there is no denying his youthful enthusiasm for Montesquieu. In a letter to
Robert Skipwith, penned in 1771, he twice recommended *The Spirit of Laws* as
indispensable reading, as he outlined the crucial subject heads and book titles
that should be known by a properly educated man of his time. In addition, Jefferson compiled notes from twenty-five of the thirty-one books of *The Spirit of
Laws*, giving more space in his *Commonplace Book* to Montesquieu than to any
other political philosopher.[17] Furthermore, even as late as 1790, Jefferson wrote
to Edmund Randolph, acknowledging that if the most important work in the
field of economics was Adam Smith's *The Wealth of Nations* (1776), Montesquieu's *The Spirit of Laws* should be deemed similarly authoritative in politics.[18]

Even those readers who attributed organizational flaws and factual shortcomings to Montesquieu's massive treatise could not help but marvel at the
scope and ambition of his project. The Marquis de Mirabeau, for example,
termed *The Spirit of Laws* a "profound meditation . . . where all the ideas on all
types of law can be found assembled."[19] As was characteristic of such other
Enlightenment classics as Voltaire's *Essay on Customs* (1756), Raynal's six
volume *A Philosophical and Political History of the Settlements and Trade of
the Europeans in the East and West Indies (1770)*, and Smith's *Wealth of Nations* (1776), the scope of *The Spirit of Laws* is indeed truly remarkable. Montesquieu took nothing less than the whole domain of government and lawmaking past and present as his subject. Like Aristotle before him, to whose work
Montesquieu's own treatise may be fruitfully compared,[20] he set out to address
the overall nature and prospects of government, while adding much that was
new to our understanding of the complex origins of laws that men fashion for
themselves. Anyone who picks up Montesquieu's weighty tome comprising no
less than 757 pages in its most recent English translation,[21] feels by its very heft
the impressive range of Montesquieu's interests and explanations. Not just the
specific laws, or specific legal system, of any one country but rather the "spirit
of laws" in general serves as his focus, freeing him to posit the macro connections between physical and moral causes and laws for which he is so justly famous. Specific laws and legal systems he does of course mention, as he moves
through his work, but only as particular examples to render more concrete his
more general investigations into the "spirit" of laws in general.

No educated intellectual of the latter half of the eighteenth century could ignore the content of Montesquieu's conclusions and speculations without appearing to be uninformed. To have been ignorant of Montesquieu's new classificatory scheme of governments, including his attribution of virtue to republics,
honor to monarchies, and fear to despotisms, not to speak of his appreciation for
the crucial role of commerce in contributing to national wealth while simultaneously fostering peace, and his striking attribution of substantial influence to climate and other "physical causes" (*causes physiques*) on human behavior, would
have been to be thought a veritable political dunce cut off from the most ad-

vanced currents of modern thought. The tireless propagation of Montesquieu's ideas by the Chevalier de Jaucourt in his numerous contributions to the *Encyclopédie* ensured that Montesquieu's political ideas would become the common coin of the French world of letters. Those who preferred to imbibe their Montesquieu in somewhat distilled and simplified form had only to turn to the articles of Jaucourt, which did little more than repeat his great master's *dicta*.

It is certainly not difficult to comprehend the intense interest and admiration that Montesquieu's work evoked among his contemporaries. *The Spirit of Laws* is nothing less than the most fertile and enduring work of political thought produced during the entire French Enlightenment. Montesquieu's *chef d'œuvre* is a veritable compendium of liberal principles, including the need to temper political power to avoid despotic rule; the necessity to abolish slavery and other forms of oppression incompatible with the needs of the human spirit; the requirement to oppose brutal, dehumanizing conquest and colonialism; the mandate to establish toleration for the sake of preserving peace; and the imperative to radically lessen the severity of punishments while also decriminalizing offenses against religious orthodoxy. All of the major Enlightenment conceptions regarding the freedom and dignity of human beings can be found in Montesquieu's great and abiding work. Thus even Voltaire, who was extremely critical of the organization of the work and of Montesquieu's accuracy on specific points, had to acknowledge the key role of *The Spirit of Laws* in the advancement of the cause of human liberty. Montesquieu, Voltaire acknowledged, "reminds men that they are free; he shows mankind the rights it has lost in most of the world, he combats superstition, he inspires good morals."[22]

In spite of Montesquieu's enormous prestige in his own time, and in spite of the keen interest shown in him by numerous others down to our own time, including Rousseau, Voltaire, Beccaria, Herder, Sieyès, Condorcet, Robespierre, Filangieri, Bentham, Burke, De Lolme, Bonald, de Maistre, Constant, Hegel, Tocqueville, Durkheim, Pitirim Sorokin, Albert Mathiez, Friedrich Meinecke, Raymond Aron, and Hannah Arendt, to name just a few, his chief work is now more often mentioned than read and is only infrequently taught in American classrooms. Montesquieu's treatise is all too rarely included in even the standard courses surveying the history of political philosophy. This has much to do, no doubt, with the extraordinary range of subjects, massive size, and degree of complexity of *The Spirit of Laws*, which we cite throughout this volume in what we take to be the proper English translation of its French title, *De l'esprit des lois*.[23] The difficulties in teaching such a complex text too often preclude the attempt, but the effort is worthwhile because Montesquieu's disquisitions continue to enlighten on matters of perennial concern. Indeed, the last decade has seen something of a revival in Montesquieu studies, perhaps in part because of growing awareness that the very complexity of his work points beyond the tired antipathies that have dominated political theory in recent years—between liberals and communitarians, for instance, and between normative theory and intellectual history, and even between Left and Right.

The Rational Explicability of Human Phenomena

The defining characteristic of *The Spirit of Laws* is Montesquieu's unrelenting search for the basic causes underlying what exists. He believed that very little in the world of man is the product of pure chance, and this perspective opened up for him the prospect of a new science of man modeled on the natural philosophy that had so demystified the realm of nature.[24] Clearly where chance recedes, science may enter. "Everything is tied together extremely closely," Montesquieu concluded (XIX, 15),[25] and for him, human science involves finding the principles and paradigms bestowing explanatory order on what human beings have designed and fashioned for themselves in distinct settings. For understanding his contributions to human science there is perhaps no more important sentence in the whole of his work than the triumphant assertion in his Preface that his painstaking investigations of an "infinite diversity of laws and manners" had fully convinced him that mankind had not been led along merely by capricious whim. He explains that following years of study and observation he had finally arrived at basic explanatory principles illuminating the structure and viability of the various governmental forms and had finally realized that individual situations are explicable by means of those principles. "The histories of all nations," he asserts, "are only the consequences of them; and each particular law is linked to another law, or depends on another more general law."

The more Montesquieu gathered details about how human beings have acted in different historical settings, the more he saw his purpose as demonstrating the validity of these underlying explanatory principles. The practitioner of human science, he explains, must seek nothing less than the veritable "chain" linking one fact to all the others. Once this chain is perceived, truths will emerge. Human blinders will fall away, and what formerly appeared arbitrary and capricious—and therefore not at all subject to scientific analysis—will be seen as conforming to "natural reasons" (*les raisons naturelles*) rendering explanation not only fully possible, but even, at times, self-evident. "Here," writes Montesquieu in his Preface to *The Spirit of Laws*, "a great many truths will not be made to appear until we have seen the chain that links them to the others. The more we will reflect on details, the more we will sense the certainty of our principles."

The significance of the explanatory potential of Montesquieu's new human science was quickly recognized by at least some among his contemporaries. Charles Bonnet, for example, wrote to him in November of 1753 to say, "Newton discovered the laws of the material world. You, Monsieur, have discovered the laws of the intelligent world."[26] It was Montesquieu's belief in underlying causes that has so fascinated those theorists inventing the new, nineteenth-century science of sociology. Hence we find Emile Durkheim remarking in his doctoral dissertation devoted to the methodology of *The Spirit of Laws* that Montesquieu regarded laws as interconnected with "all of social life." Therefore, Durkheim explained, Montesquieu "necessarily deals with almost all aspects of society. Thus in order to explain the nature of domestic law, to show how laws harmonize with religion, morality, etc., he is obliged to investigate religion, morality and the family, with the result that he has actually written a treatise dealing with social phenomena as a whole."[27]

With the appearance of Montesquieu's two most serious and noteworthy works, his Roman history and his treatise on laws, the first brilliantly evaluating the causes of Roman decline and the second investigating the spirit, or genesis, of positive laws, modern human science was launched. The normative outlook of previous political philosophy is certainly evident in Montesquieu's strong preferences for political and civil freedom and in his opposition to such evils as slavery, the colonial exploitation of subject peoples, aggressive wars, despotism, and religious intolerance. It should be apparent to any reader of *The Spirit of Laws*, however, that he approaches political and social phenomena with an eye to description and understanding that rests alongside his liberal reform agenda and bestows on his treatise a tone of objectivity reminiscent of a work like Aristotle's *Politics*, which in similar fashion combines description with prescription.

The Spirit of Laws, then, combines a normative, prescriptive mode of analysis with a contrasting positivist approach emphasizing description of human behavior. As Cecil Courtney points out in the opening chapter of this volume, Montesquieu regarded certain absolute values stemming from natural law as providing the proper parameters for determining what is just. At the same time, however, he displayed a remarkable appreciation for pluralism and diversity as revealed by the numerous facts he gathered about the vast world beyond Europe. Therefore, Auguste Comte was certainly not completely wrong—though he surely exaggerated the point—when he attributed to Montesquieu the first attempt to treat politics as a science of facts rather than dogmas.[28] Nor was Emile Durkheim incorrect in identifying Montesquieu's *The Spirit of Laws* as the key work inaugurating the new social science that Comte had labeled "sociology" even though, by Durkheim's own admission, Montesquieu had not completely abandoned the older method of relying primarily on reason and deduction rather than letting the facts speak for themselves.[29] Although in Montesquieu's work values ultimately prevail over facts, few classics of political theory are so suffused with such a torrent of diverse facts as *The Spirit of Laws*. At times the reader is likely to feel completely overwhelmed by what Bertrand Binoche has aptly referred to as "the unceasing mobilization of facts" in a work that sharply contrasts with that of Rousseau, who in his *Social Contract* suggested that the best way to begin the study of "political right" (*droit politique)* is to "lay aside the facts."[30] In Montesquieu's lengthy work, references to the laws of classical antiquity, to the early Germanic law of the Ostrogoths, the Ripuarian Franks, and the Lombards, to Roman marriage law, to the Roman law of succession, and to the feudal law of the medieval period, to mention but a few of Montesquieu's interests, seem at times to overwhelm any main points he might have been trying to make. The attentive and patient reader, however, will surely be successful in perceiving that Montesquieu marshaled his facts in support of the principles he adopted to explain the spirit of laws and the functioning of governments in a method, which, in the opinion of Emile Durkheim and several other commentators, is more deductive than inductive.[31]

Montesquieu's Goals in *The Spirit of Laws*

What exactly was Montesquieu seeking to accomplish in *The Spirit of Laws*? As is transparent in its very title, he set out to explore the myriad influences that shape the content of the system of political, civil, and criminal laws that every people must devise for itself. His search for what constitutes the "spirit of laws" is the central quest that bestows order on his treatise. Clearly he believed that it is the form of government that will have the greatest influence on the content of any given legal system, a conclusion that, as Paul Rahe observes in the second chapter of this volume, makes him more of a traditional political philosopher than a sociologist, however much certain aspects of his work may also forecast the future. Government, for Montesquieu, remains paramount among the influences on the laws that will prove appropriate for a given society. Not only political laws, but also civil laws, including sumptuary laws and criminal laws, will necessarily reflect the institutional structure and underlying principles of whatever governmental type is established.

According to Montesquieu, however, it is not just the regime type that will substantially influence the content of both civil and criminal laws since all such laws will have to be designed to suit the overall conditions and needs of a particular society. Therefore the diverse influences that constitute the "spirit of laws," which he first sketches out in the third chapter of Book I, extend well beyond governmental forms and include, in the order of Montesquieu's own enumeration, the physical-material conditions of climate and terrain; the amount of liberty the constitution can sustain; the dominant modes of subsistence and the professional occupations established in a given society; the nature and strength of religious beliefs; the wealth, population level, and inclinations of a nation's people; and, finally, the mode and extent of commerce and the nature of the mores and manners dominant in a particular political society. All of these diverse influences on legislation constitute what Montesquieu referred to as "the spirit of laws" (I, 3). Most appropriately, the full title that he bestowed on his work was: *The Spirit of Laws, or the Relation Laws Should Bear to the Constitution of Each Government, the Customs, the Climate, the Religion, the Commerce etc. to which the Author Has Added Some New Examinations on Roman Laws concerning Inheritances, on French Laws, and on Feudal Laws.*

In addition to embarking on a quest for the "spirit" of laws, Montesquieu was also motivated by a less detached, less scientific motive, which was to instruct those who rule with useful lessons regarding how best to promote peace and well-being. Although rather modest and unassuming by nature, Montesquieu clearly believed he was setting forth much that would be of use to "the education of young princes" who would profit much more, he believed, from study of his observations than from hearing "vague exhortations to govern well and to be great princes and render their subjects happy."[32] Indeed there is evidence that the future Louis XVI read *The Spirit of Laws* and was inspired to write a brief essay entitled "On Moderate Monarchy" ("De la monarchie tempérée").[33] In addition, when Catherine the Great sent a long list of *Instructions* to an assembly meeting from 1766 to 1768 to codify and reform Russian laws, many of them were simply copied verbatim from *The Spirit of Laws*. Frederick the Great of Prussia was also a student of *The Spirit of Laws*, as were several other European rulers of the late eighteenth century.[34]

Disenchanted in his youth with the prospects for politics to have much influence on the unfolding of events,[35] Montesquieu self-consciously set out in his later years to elevate the study of politics to the status it had enjoyed in Greek antiquity when contemplation of what constitutes moral good and moral evil had been regarded as man's highest calling. Therefore he envisioned his work, at least in part, as an enlightened breviary designed to explain to princes, or other lawmakers, how they could best compose laws to achieve the moderation of power necessary for the protection of liberty and security. "It is in seeking to instruct mankind," he wrote in the Preface to *The Spirit of Laws*, "that one can practice that general virtue which comprehends the love of all." And like other Enlightenment-era thinkers, Montesquieu had no doubt that human beings were in need of substantial instruction. He believed that very little pertaining to the realm of human science, as compared to natural science, had been properly understood, and if he by no means attempted to subsume the whole of human history under one overarching explanatory paradigm, as did such later, even more ambitious "totalizing" philosophers of history as Condorcet, Hegel, Comte, Marx, Spengler, and Toynbee, he did nonetheless aim to be a political sociologist identifying certain "necessary" relations, or "chains" of connection between all of the distinct components of a given society.[36]

Aspects of Novelty in *The Spirit of Laws*

Montesquieu's chosen motto for his treatise, *Prolem sine matre creatum* (A Work with No Mother), taken from Ovid's *Metamorphoses*, was no idle boast. Rather it was an apt description of a work that is substantially innovative. Not without good reason did Montesquieu write in one of his *Pensées*: "The bent of my mind is not to retrace what everyone knows."[37] Similarly, he remarked in an explanatory note inserted in the posthumous edition of 1757, "I have had new ideas; it has been very necessary to find new words, or to give new meanings to old ones." Most appropriate, then, was Mme de Tencin's remark in a letter to Montesquieu praising the work, "I know of nothing that can compare to it."[38]

Montesquieu's treatise is noteworthy, among other things, for its display of intense curiosity regarding non-European customs and habits. Interest in such exotic areas as Asia, Africa, and the Americas was sharply on the rise as travel accounts poured into Europe from previously unknown parts of the globe throughout the seventeenth and eighteenth centuries, and it was Montesquieu, among others, who gave key emphasis to this important trend, thereby substantially broadening the hitherto much more parochial vision of modern Europeans. He was very much aware of the significance of the vast scope of his project, remarking in his *Defense of the Spirit of Laws* (1750) that his work "has for its object the laws, customs, and diverse usages of all the peoples of the earth. One can say its subject is immense," he acknowledged, "since it embraces all the institutions created by mankind."[39]

Certainly not all readers approved of Montesquieu's new, non-Western gaze. Voltaire, for one, has the character "B" in his dialogue *L'ABC* lampoon the eclectic range of Montesquieu's curiosity. "When, after quoting the laws of the Greeks and the Romans, he talks solemnly about the laws of Bantam, Cochin, Tonkin, Borneo, Jakarta, Formosa, as if he had accurate reports on the governments of these countries, I keep on laughing," says "B."[40] In spite of his own intense interest in China and other non-European parts of the world Voltaire audaciously contends in his critique of Montesquieu that non-Western practices may be irrelevant to the European experience. "Montesquieu claims that at Tonkin all the magistrates and the principal military officers are eunuchs, and that among the lamas the law permits women to have several husbands," says this same participant "B" in Voltaire's dialogue. "Suppose these fables were true—what would follow from that? Would our magistrates want to become eunuchs, and be only a fourth or fifth of a husband to our lady councilors?"[41]

According to Voltaire, Montesquieu would have been better advised to concentrate on explaining thoroughly and accurately those things within his more narrow, European frame of reference rather than being carried so far afield by his strong desire for more exotic information. Complaining that Montesquieu failed to discuss in his historical treatment of French laws and institutions the bloody tribunal of Charlemagne called the *Vehmgericht,* Voltaire has "B" assert, "What! Montesquieu talks to me about the laws of Bantam, and he doesn't even know the laws of Charlemagne, although he calls him a good legislator!"[42] Nor was Voltaire alone in the eighteenth century in failing to appreciate the significance of Montesquieu's interest in exploring the parameters of human diversity. "Whenever he wants to support a strange opinion," complained Dr. Johnson, "he quotes you the practice of Japan or of some other distant country, of which he knows nothing. To support polygamy, he tells you about the island of Formosa, where there are ten women born for one man."[43]

It would appear that neither Voltaire nor Samuel Johnson comprehended the true nature and purpose of Montesquieu's project, which in addition to all its other methodological novelty launched the study of comparative law and politics. When a shift in emphasis radically restructures an existing mode of discourse, it takes time for understanding, followed by appreciation, to take hold. Readers are at first more likely to be bewildered than enlightened. As Voltaire's response indicates, novelty is likely to be distrusted when it first appears on the scene, and it is little wonder that Montesquieu's work both perplexed and irritated some among its first consumers. Thus it took some time before Montesquieu's interest in the manners, morals, and customs of non-European nations could be seen as launching a new type of social science that blended politics and history with emerging lines of thought best described as comparative, anthropological, ethnological and sociological.

The novelty of Montesquieu's perspective went well beyond his intense interest in non-European cultures. As was typical of most other *philosophes* of the Enlightenment, he adopted a mode of analysis and explanation at odds with religious orthodoxy. Far from resorting to Providential explanations of human actions and achievements, he pointedly explained to his readers, as Rebecca Kingston reminds us in her chapter on Montesquieu and religion, that he was a political writer rather than a theologian, adding, however, as a sop for the orthodox, that however true theological exploration might be in an ultimate, metaphysical sense, he was purposefully adopting a secular mode of analysis independent of the exegesis of any divine plan for human beings (XXIV, 1). Machiavelli had long since adopted a similarly non-religious mode of explanation in both *The Prince* and *The Discourses on Livy*, but the lack of complete novelty in Montesquieu's approach by no means negates its singular importance in a world so suffused with religious meanings and symbolism.

As important as was Montesquieu's interest in non-European societies and his secular perspective to what he set out to achieve in *The Spirit of Laws*, those aspects of his work alone cannot fully explain the innovative nature of his investigations. Certainly the importance of his discussions of climate and other physical causes in Books XIV through XVIII deserve emphasis as well. If Montesquieu was by no means the first political philosopher to explore the influence of climate and other physical-material influences on human cultures— one thinks of both Bodin and Chardin as key predecessors, not to mention Hippocrates and Aristotle much earlier—he was certainly the first to do so in such a bold and comprehensive fashion, carefully delineating the strong influence of climate, topography, and terrain on the nature of the human possibilities that may be realized in a given polity.[44] If his conclusions in *The Spirit of Laws* were certainly not deterministic, and if he explicitly disavowed determinist conclusions in his posthumously published *Essay on Causes Affecting Minds and Characters*

(1736-43),[45] he was nonetheless suggesting, at a minimum, that in certain environments human beings will be rowing against the current if they seek to establish a particular governmental form or custom that does not harmonize with the prevailing environmental conditions. It may not be impossible for human beings to produce political liberty in hot, southern climates where energy levels are low, but it will be more difficult, Montesquieu concluded, and there will have to be incentives devised for work that will not be necessary in colder regions where energy levels are higher.

Montesquieu's Philosophy of Politics

As careful readers of The Spirit of Laws will surely appreciate, Montesquieu championed important liberal causes while nonetheless displaying a profound distrust of wrenching, ill-considered change, an attitude toward politics that explains the interest that Edmund Burke and other like-minded individuals have shown in his thought.[46] He was certainly not opposed to implementing enlightened reforms where human freedom can thereby be advanced, but this essentially liberal outlook was balanced by his awareness that changing one aspect of a government or legal system can have extremely destabilizing consequences. Pull out just one thread, and the whole political fabric may begin to unravel.

Certainly it would be incorrect to assess Montesquieu as an alienated or disaffected writer who believed that something radically new should be introduced into the French political system, or for that matter into the stable mix of institutions, laws, and customs likely to undergird any political system that has developed gradually over time. We do not encounter in Montesquieu's philosophy advocacy of sudden breaks with the past. Perhaps the most revelatory sentence, in the whole of The Spirit of Laws, therefore, is the passage in Book XIV where he likens politics to a "smooth file" (lime sourde), which arrives only slowly at its ends (XIV, 13). Not surprisingly, Montesquieu was often cited during the French Revolution by those who thought events were moving too swiftly, as when the author of the Nouvelles éphémerides de l'Assemblee Nationale lectured his readers on August 14, 1789 that "Innovations, Montesquieu says, are dangerous in a monarchical state."[47]

A most intriguing Pensée is Montesquieu's autobiographical assertion, "I am the first man in the world to believe that those who govern do so with good intentions."[48] Unlike others writing later in the century, particularly as the final financial crisis loomed menacingly over the French state in 1788 and 1789, he did not envision politics as a path toward revolutionary change. That is why he was moved to assert in his preface to The Spirit of Laws, "I write not to censure anything established in any country whatsoever. Every nation will here find the reasons on which its maxims are founded."[49] He pointed out in this preface that reformers with a partisan agenda to pursue often see "only one side of the subject" rather than focusing on the inner logic of a given political and legal system so as to comprehend why things are arranged along certain patterns that ought to be respected and retained. The contrast between Montesquieu and Rousseau on this point is instructive. We would not find Montesquieu remarking, as Rousseau was to assert in *Emile*, "We are approaching a state of crisis and a century of revolutions. The great monarchies of Europe will not survive much longer."[50]

Montesquieu appreciated that the complex relations between all of a society's component elements represent a process of mutual adjustment over time and must be respected and preserved. The very reformation of abuses, he explained, may give rise to greater abuses. Hence it is wisest to be content with a "lesser good" when we doubt that a "greater" good can be obtained.[51] The proper manner of judging and assessing a political system, he explains in the Preface to *The Spirit of Laws,* is "to examine into the parts" in order "to judge them in connection." When one adopts this approach, one will end up offering "new reasons to every man to love his prince, his country, his laws." Montesquieu proclaims that he will be the "happiest of mortals" if he can be the vehicle for making men aware of the blessings they enjoy "in every nation and government." This conservative aspect of his outlook was widely noticed in his day. As is often pointed out, Rousseau complained in *Emile* that Montesquieu had failed to deal with political right (*droit politique*), owing to his penchant for appreciating and accepting what had sprung up naturally in a given environment. Less commonly mentioned are similar laments of Gaetano Filangieri, who remarked in his *The Science of Legislation* (1784) that Montesquieu "reasoned rather on what *has been* done than on what *ought* to be done" and of Bertrand Barère, who asserted that Montesquieu was too attentive to "facts" and not enough concerned with "right."[52]

Certainly Montesquieu believed that there are some governments so despotic and abusive of human nature as to be in need of transformation, but identifying abuses to be repaired or purged, like a cancer or gangrene out of the body, was not his particular orientation or emphasis. He saw himself as much more of an analyst of how things are linked together in a particular political, social, and scientific system to produce what he termed a "general spirit" than as a firebrand reformer setting out to identify and change every abuse that existed. It is certainly not surprising that the former finance minister, Charles-Alexandre de Calonne, would remark, once he had become an émigré fleeing the French Revolution, that Montesquieu "was prone to thinking, and all reasonable men must think, that wisdom and strength imply regulating and restraining (*contenir*), whereas weakness and tyranny are connected with changing and overturning."[53] This does not mean, however, that there are not strong elements of a liberal reform agenda present in Montesquieu's work, particularly in the matter of blunting despotic power, reforming excessively Draconian punishments, and avoiding the cruel excesses of both religious intolerance and colonial exploitation. Still, as pointed out in chapter 7 of this volume, Montesquieu stopped short of recommending radical changes in the manner in which French criminal trials were conducted, and his satisfaction with existing legal procedures prompted some harsh criticism from later reformers of a more radical persuasion. Montesquieu's cautious attitude toward change is well summed up in his statement in his *Persian Letters* (1721) that "it is occasionally necessary to change certain laws. But such cases are rare, and when they occur, the law must be treated with trembling hands."[54] Thus Montesquieu remarks in *The Spirit of Laws* that "It is up to the legislator to follow the spirit of the nation when it isn't contrary to the principles of government" (XIX, 5).

Montesquieu gave voice to his explanatory rather than revolutionary goals with great lucidity and self-awareness in one of his *Pensées*. "I know that there is such and such country that is poorly governed and that it would be very difficult for it to be governed better," he wrote. "In short, I see more than I judge; I reason about everything, and I criticize nothing."[55] This rather detached aspect of his persona was swiftly acknowledged and often quite sharply criticized by his more reform-minded contemporaries. Justly famous is Condorcet's attack on Book XXIX of *The Spirit of Laws* which Montesquieu had devoted to the subject of how best to compose laws. "Why, in *The Spirit of Laws*," Condorcet asked, "has Montesquieu never spoken of the justice and injustice of the laws that he has cited, but only of the purposes that he has attributed to these laws? Why hasn't he established a principle for learning to distinguish, among the laws emanating from legitimate power, those which are unjust and those which are in conformity to justice?"[56] Obviously Condorcet favored the delineation of a formulaic, categorical guide to the legal codes of mankind constituting a veritable syllabus of good and bad laws whereas Montesquieu preferred to demonstrate the relation laws bear to the panoply of governmental, societal, economic, and geographical influences that shape their content.

Unlike those later caught up in the momentum of events swirling beyond their control after 1789, Montesquieu was no revolutionary reformer seeking to hack through the dense underbrush of the present, imperfect world in order to completely weed out existing practices not in keeping with a radical blueprint whose superimposition on the present would require dislocating changes. Nor was he a strident, doctrinaire thinker pushing for any single set of institutions or laws regarded as so perfectly designed as to be appropriate for all peoples regardless of their distinct histories, material circumstances, and aspirations. Rather, he was prone to believing that there exist multiple paths to the ultimate goal of politics, which he conceived as political moderation. "Good sense," he proclaimed in his *Defense of The Spirit of Laws* (1750), written in the wake of stinging attacks on the work as amoral and blind to religious orthodoxy, "very much consists in comprehending the nuances of things."[57]

As he remarked in Book XXIX, chapter 18 of *The Spirit of Laws*, what matters above all is that citizens be law-abiding. They need not necessarily obey exactly the same laws. What matters is that they obey. He includes this telling observation, which is so revealing of his abhorrence of anarchy and tumultuous change, in one of the most important chapters of his whole treatise entitled "On ideas of uniformity." This is the very chapter that so irritated Condorcet. Here Montesquieu ridicules those "small intellects" who crave uniformity. One should be willing, he asserts, to tolerate not just a diversity of laws and religions within different portions even of the same state, but even different weights and measures! It is not always appropriate, he insists, to strive for uniformity because achieving sameness where diversity presently reigns will require radical, wrenching alterations of the complex array of societal influences that have become balanced and mutually adjusted to one another over time. His rejection of the geometrical spirit sets Montesquieu apart from the later, more doctrinaire, reformist *philosophes* who sought to define a more perfect world and get there—whatever the cost. As his attack on uniformity helps us to understand, Montesquieu possessed a conservative bent of mind that caused him to prefer a known present—even one containing some known abuses—to an uncharted future involving dislocating, unpredictable, and potentially destructive changes whose consequences cannot be predicted. Politics, he observed, is not like mathematics, since in arithmetic one can foresee the effect of adding or subtracting. In politics, on the other hand, the results of change are very difficult to predict.[58]

Montesquieu's functionalist perspective, that is, his conviction that things are ultimately linked together, as in a chain, caused him to seek to explain the "spirit" of various legal systems, or the complex connections between a given set of laws and all of the diverse influences operating over time to produce that particular system. He was more concerned to explain the necessary relations between all of the diverse physical and moral influences on a given society than to suggest root and branch reforms based on some abstract conception of political right. This proto-sociological orientation certainly did not prevent him from proposing certain basic, liberal reforms where injustice was most glaring, as with despotism, slavery, intolerance, and harshly punitive punishments. He did not envision reform, however, as essentially trumping explanation as far as the purposes of his work are concerned.

Montesquieu's cautious attitude toward change was not just a product of his own particular character and vision. It was also partly a product of the times in which he lived. He was a first generation *philosophe*, and he died shortly after mid-century before levels of discontent with the French political system had come anywhere close to reaching revolutionary proportions. Many have concluded that the French obsession for politics as a tool of fundamental change was a product of the last few decades of the eighteenth century. Daniel Mornet long ago observed, for example:

In the final period (of the ancien régime), it was chiefly politics that occupied men's minds. They hardly thought of it before 1748. Everything that had been said or published concerning politics before that date was, with a few exceptions, merely academic. Whenever writers sought specific, practical remedies for evil

and abuses, they did not for an instant consider changing the principles of government. . . . From 1748 to 1770, discussions became much more numerous, less
abstract and much bolder. . . . After 1770, works appeared which even questioned the order of the state, sometimes savagely. But these works were not numerous.[59]

Furthermore, Mornet concluded, "In politics, neither Voltaire, Montesquieu,
Rousseau, nor Diderot was a revolutionary nor even the boldest reformer."[60]
More recently, Robert Wokler has advanced a similar conclusion, observing that

> the diverse policies put forward by eighteenth-century political theorists had
> been designed to stave off rather than promote revolution, to safeguard and not
> subvert authority, or, rather, through drastic reform to thwart an uprising that
> would otherwise explode the governments of their day. Not one of the major po-
> litical thinkers of the Enlightenment advocated revolution before 1789, whatever
> debt their more incendiary disciples later professed to owe to them, and what-
> ever might in fact have been the practical implications of their doctrines.[61]

The Structure and Style of *The Spirit of Laws*

Few books reward their readers with more brilliant insights than Montesquieu's
Spirit of Laws. But few books, it may also be said, require more patience on the
reader's part. Perhaps the key factor rendering full comprehension of Montesquieu's ideas by no means readily achievable is his tendency to employ an elliptical style where meanings and lines of thought are merely hinted at rather than
being fully explored and elaborated. Montesquieu's meaning often has to be
teased out of elliptical texts, and Bertrand Binoche has gone so far as to say that
"at all levels, the discourse is in a state of constant rupture."[62] Hence Montesquieu's contemporary, the Abbé Coyer, found it appropriate to refer to Montesquieu as "this genius too philosophical to be enamoured of a dogmatic tone,"
while also commenting that the result is at times a lack of clarity that leaves the
reader somewhat in doubt as to the precise meaning intended by Montesquieu.[63]
But Montesquieu had a distinct purpose in adopting such a style—or so it has
been argued. Binoche reminds us of D'Alembert's suggestion that Montesquieu
blunted or even masked his direct arguments in order to avoid wounding the
objects of his scorn or criticism.[64] Thus it is useful to observe, as Cecil Courtney, Sharon Krause, and Iris Cox remind us in their chapters written for this
volume, that all authors writing under the risks imposed by ancien régime censorship had to mask their meanings somewhat, and Montesquieu was certainly
no exception.[65]

Whatever the reasons, Montesquieu often merely scratched the surface of
important subjects without fully explaining his point of view. Indeed, part of the

very fascination of *The Spirit of Laws* for many readers is its enigmatic quality. Points are often hinted at without full elaboration so that readers have to puzzle long and hard to decipher Montesquieu's intended meanings. There is certainly evidence that he was aware of the epistemological consequences of his aphoristic style. In Book XXVIII, chapter 45, for example, he asserts that he could easily have gone into greater detail to make his arguments concerning the historical development of French civil law more clear. Instead of doing so, however, he chose to act, by his own admission, like an antiquarian who might travel all the way to Egypt only to take one quick glimpse at the pyramids before promptly turning around and heading home.

Montesquieu bestowed a good deal of thought on how he should compose his work, and there is strong evidence that his elliptical and enigmatic style of presentation was at least partly intentional. He was determined not to bore his readers by spelling everything out in such detail that they did not need to think for themselves. He advertises this approach in the final chapter of Book XI, where he asserts that he could take time to go through, one by one, all of the moderate governments that might be identified in order to lay out the extent of their distribution of powers and hence their degree of liberty. He opts not to do so, however. "One must not always so exhaust a subject, however, that there is nothing left for the reader to do," he suggests. "It is not a question of making him read but of making him think" (XI, 20). Quite similarly, he asserts in one of his *Pensées* that "to write well, one must skip over (*sauter*) the intermediate ideas just enough to avoid being boring, but not too much for fear of not being understood."[66]

Many have suggested that Montesquieu's somewhat sprawling treatise lacks a systematic, sustained argument. Rather than encountering clearly delineated themes, the reader of Montesquieu's work continuously comes upon chapters of often very miscellaneous contents that often seem arbitrarily grouped under only very general headings. Many of the chapters are simply labeled "Continuation of the Same Subject." A few others are called "Reflections," signaling a point Montesquieu regards as particularly important, as where, for example, he cautions against considering moral vices political vices, and vice versa (XIX, 11). Sometimes even the chapter title seems misapplied to the content of what follows, as in Book XII, chapter 29, where, after announcing that he will discuss the civil laws likely to introduce a modicum of liberty in despotic governments, he speaks only of the role of religion, custom, manners, and prejudices.

The structure of Montesquieu's text impedes the weaving of a sustained narrative. The numerous short chapters interrupt the reader's progress in search of a central thread. Thus Michel de Servan, a criminal law reformer of the generation immediately after Montesquieu, compared *The Spirit of Laws* to "an ancient temple, where in spite of large fractures, mangled beauty, (and) disunity between the parts, one still senses, with religious reverence, the presence of the genius who fashioned it."[67] Many later commentators have agreed with Servan that Montesquieu's masterpiece lacks the order and coherence achieved by many other writers. As Emile Faguet once observed, *The Spirit of Laws* is less a text than an existence, and many readers of Montesquieu's justly famous work have seen within it the unplanned forays and jagged edges one would expect to find in a human life unfolding without a preordained plan of existence or development.[68] Jean Ehrard, the *doyen* of Montesquieu studies in France, has also spoken of "the extreme fragmentation of the text."[69] Furthermore, in a statement that will resonate for many readers, Franz Neumann once referred to "the initial bewilderment, which is the inevitable fate of every reader of *The Spirit of Laws*."[70] Similarly, Isaiah Berlin has remarked regarding *The Spirit of Laws* that "on the face of it is a shapeless amalgam of disquisitions on various topics, in no apparent order." Nor, thought Berlin, could that disorder be explained away by any amount of cleverness on the critic's part. Only "misdirected ingenuity," he concluded, can impose an ordered pattern on the work.[71]

Some critics have gone too far in their criticisms of the perceived lack of structure in *The Spirit of Laws*. "It cannot be said," observed George Sabine in a textbook once widely used in teaching political theory in America, "that Montesquieu's *Spirit of the Laws* has any arrangement; it has been saved from the fate suffered by Bodin's *Republic* mainly by superior style. . . . But there is not in truth much concatenation of subject-matter, and the amount of irrelevance is extraordinary."[72] Whatever the obvious exaggeration in this remark, some contemporary reactions were very much in the same mode. Perhaps no one reacted quite so negatively to the perceived lack of structure and continuity in the work as did Voltaire, who clearly regarded Montesquieu as a rival for contemporary adulation and who in his dialogue *L'ABC* has one of the three participants in a conversation on Grotius, Hobbes, and Montesquieu lament:

> I looked for a thread through this labyrinth; the thread is broken at almost every article; I was deceived: I found the spirit of the author—and he has a great deal!—but rarely the spirit of the laws; he hops more than he walks; he amuses more than he enlightens; sometimes he satirizes more than he judges; and he makes us wish that so noble a mind had tried to instruct rather than to shock.[73]

Later in the dialogue this same speaker "B" asserts that *The Spirit of Laws* "seems to me like an ill-constructed building, built irregularly in which there are many beautiful apartments, polished and gilded."[74]

Certainly Montesquieu's treatise was not the sort of work that could be finally finished, or perfected. There was always more that could be said, and always the potential for greater clarity and thoroughness in the treatment of the points covered. Montesquieu himself, in fact, expressed this realization very poignantly in a *Pensée* revealing some of the anguish he felt in having to publish the work before he had given it its final touches. "I had conceived the idea of giving greater breadth and depth to certain areas of this work," he explained. "I have became incapable of it. My reading has weakened my eyes. . . . In the deplorable state in which I find myself, it has not been possible for me to give this work the final finish, and I would have burned it a thousand times, if I had not thought it noble to make oneself useful to men up until one's very last sighs."[75]

Whatever the views of Voltaire and other critics, Montesquieu's treatise can hardly be said to lack at least a rudimentary structure. He divided *The Spirit of Laws* into six distinct parts, each designed to achieve a somewhat different purpose. Part One begins with a brief opening book explaining the various types of laws to which men are subject. Books II through VII address the basic types of government and their appropriate structures, underlying psychologies, laws, and policies. Montesquieu's overriding concern for regime stability in this first part of his work involves him in discussions of principles of government (Book III), educational policy (Book IV), political laws suited to each regime's constitutional system (Book V), civil and criminal laws (Book VI), and sumptuary laws (Book VII), followed by a discussion of how each of the basic regime types he has identified is corrupted and ceases to be viable as a stable governmental form (Book VIII). This first part of *The Spirit of Laws* is by far the most studied portion of the work, setting forth the justly famous republic/monarchy/despotism typology that so greatly influenced the political discourse of its day in both Europe and America. Just these first eight books of Montesquieu's treatise alone, would have made a worthy contribution to political philosophy. But in composing Part One of his massive treatise Montesquieu had barely begun to lay out the essentials of what he wished to accomplish.

Books IX through XIII comprise Part Two of *The Spirit of Laws* and deal with offensive force, defensive force, liberty of the constitution, liberty of the citizen, and taxation policy. This second part displays a somewhat more arbitrary arrangement of subject matter. The themes addressed, however, are certainly no less important than those covered in Part One. Discussions of international relations (Book IX) and national defense (Book X) are crucial to any comprehensive treatise on politics. Furthermore, no government void of liberty for its institutions (Book XI), or its citizens (Book XII), will be properly directed toward the human goods of constitutional liberty and personal security, and no government without an adequate stream of revenue to support its various operations will prove long sustainable (Book XIII).

In Part Three, spanning Books XIV through Book XIX, Montesquieu analyzes the influence of such physical and environmental factors as climate, topography, terrain, and soil quality on such societal practices as slavery and polygamy and on the likely presence of despotism or liberty in a society's constitution. In this third part, which is filled with exceedingly bold speculations, he also focuses on the means of subsistence supporting various peoples at different stages of their development and substantially influencing the content of the laws and legal systems that will be set in place (XVII, 8-17). This portion of *The Spirit of Laws* was much commented upon by Montesquieu's contemporaries who were intrigued to see climate related to political and civil law (Book XIV) and also to slavery (Book XV) and to marriage customs and polygamy (Book XVI). A bold and speculative seventeenth book posits a thesis of North/South dominance based on the superior energy and courage of northern peoples while also explaining the relative liberty enjoyed by European states as compared to Asian states in terms of the roughly similar climates of contiguous countries and the relatively small size of European states as compared to the sprawling despotic empires of Asia. An eighteenth book correlates soil quality, topography, and terrain and the extent of liberty a people may expect to enjoy.

In an especially striking and important nineteenth book, which ends the first volume as the work was set up in the first edition of 1748, Montesquieu explores the relation between positive laws and customs, manners, and religion along with other components of a nation's "general spirit" (*esprit général*). Here he demonstrates better than anywhere else in his treatise what he meant by asserting that "laws are the necessary relations deriving from the nature of things" (I, 1). To a great extent, he suggests, the content of a given nation's laws will necessarily reflect the situation, both materially and psychologically, in which it finds itself, which will in turn give rise to "the principles forming the general spirit, the mores, and the manners of a nation." The final result, Montesquieu concludes, will be "a nation's way of thinking" (XIX, 3).[76]

This third part of *The Spirit of Laws* spanning Books XIV through XIX contains many of the speculations that fascinated such figures of the Scottish Enlightenment as Adam Ferguson, Dugald Stewart, David Hume, Lord Kames, Lord Monboddo, and John Millar and greatly contributed to their interest in broadly defined stages of history based on the underlying form of economic organization or modes of subsistence prevalent at a given time. And these are also the portions of Montesquieu's work often derided by contemporary authors who failed to understand what he was attempting to do in the work, which was not to describe codes of particular laws the way a legal historian might do but rather to seek out the "spirit of laws" by which he meant the relation laws bear to all the diverse influences shaping their content, some constituting what he terms *causes morales* and others what he terms *causes physiques*.

Part Four of *The Spirit of Laws*, comprising Books XX to XXIII, contains some of the most carefully crafted books of the whole treatise. In these books Montesquieu presents a learned account of the rise and progress of commerce, the usage of money, and the relation laws should bear to population size as part of an attempt to make others aware that commerce is not only a matter of professional interest for those engaged in it but also a matter of general, philosophical, and political interest. Never before had such issues of commerce, population, and money been included in such a major work of political philosophy as *The Spirit of Laws*. This aspect of Montesquieu's work was nearly as novel as his concern to include numerous facts about non-European countries previously of interest mainly to the writers of travel books. As Catherine Larrère explains in chapter 8 of this volume, it is in Part Four of Montesquieu's work that Rome emerges as an anti-model, the exemplar of the militaristic state excessively concerned with destructive conquests and paying too little attention to peaceful commercial exchange with people who may rightly expect constancy, accuracy, and honesty from those with whom they deal. Once commerce is placed squarely in the center of political analysis, Rome ceases to be the paradigmatic political reference point it had long been in more traditional political thought.

Part Five of *The Spirit of Laws* consists of only three books and is by far the shortest of the six parts into which Montesquieu divided his work. Books XXIV and XXV are devoted to what we would now call the sociology and psychology of religion, respectively, and Book XXVI defines the various types, or orders of laws both divine and human, while contending that they relate to quite different aspects of human existence and must, therefore, be kept distinct if human freedom is to flourish unburdened by overly punitive and ultimately unworkable legal constraints. The grouping of these two books on the sociology and psychology of religion and on types of law seems quite arbitrary, though there is no denying the importance of the subjects Montesquieu covers.

The sixth and final part of *The Spirit of Laws* is the longest, and it contains a wealth of detail on the history of both Roman and French laws as well as important observations, in Book XXIX, on how laws should be composed. This twenty-ninth book might better have been made the concluding book to the whole treatise, or perhaps the concluding book of Part One. The importance of this concluding series of books in Part Six, however, should not be underestimated. There is clear textual evidence that they were not simply the product of last minute thoughts, even though Montesquieu placed the results of his historical researches in the concluding books, while explaining to his Genevan printer, Jacob Vernet, that they had turned his hair gray.[77]

Whatever the merits of Montesquieu's somewhat rough-hewn organizational scheme for his work, other idiosyncrasies bordering on weaknesses have been identified. It has struck many readers that rather than having one particular thought or theme to develop, one particular *idée fixe* to follow to its logical conclusion, Montesquieu's great work is something of a miscellany of thoughts. Hence readers have frequently expressed frustration at their inability to discern any central message. Servan spoke of looking for the body (*corps*) while admiring the parts.[78] "To summarize Montesquieu's conclusions," George Sabine has much more recently complained, "is quite impossible; they are mainly episodic and as a rule they have little dependence on what he alleges to be evidence."[79] Often critics have been sensitive to certain unresolved tensions and even contradictions within Montesquieu's work. Hence Melvin Richter, a close student of Montesquieu's texts on despotism and also of his comparative method, remarks that "despite his claims to having developed a logically coherent system, in practice, Montesquieu characteristically refused to resolve ambivalence and contradictions; he seldom chose among mutually exclusive intellectual options. By loose definitions, by availing himself to the full of his extraordinary intellectual imagination, he generated tensions among a plurality of overlapping and often contradictory explanations, models, and perspectives."[80]

In spite of these reservations about the clarity of Montesquieu's assertions and conclusions, it is certainly not true that there is no central message that he meant to convey in his work. Surely the need for political moderation to avoid the extremes of both radical democracy and despotism, which he identifies as antithetical to liberty, emerges as the clear, central teaching of *The Spirit of Laws*.[81] It was the excesses that unlimited, unchecked sovereignty gives rise to that led Montesquieu to argue so consistently for the need to partition and moderate power to produce both political and civil liberty. Those who wield power will always abuse it, he concluded, unless obstacles are placed in their path. It is precisely this timeless lesson in liberal constitutionalism that is currently sparking an interest in Montesquieu's thought, even in places where, first Jacobinism and then, somewhat later, and for a substantially longer period, Marxism had an extremely strong hold on the intelligentsia.[82]

The presence of Montesquieu's underlying message of the need for moderation in politics is by no means readily transparent, and few, if any would say that *The Spirit of Laws* is an easy, or an unchallenging read. In fact, there is evidence that Montesquieu was himself aware that he was laying before the world a work that very few individuals would sit down and read from start to finish. "If I may be permitted to predict the fortune of my work, he wrote in one of his *Pensées*, "it will be more approved than read: such reading can be pleasurable; it can never be amusing."[83] He feared that not many readers would take the time that would be required for comprehension of his ideas. In the Preface to *The Spirit of Laws* he asks "one favor" of his readers, which is "not to judge by a quick reading the work of twenty years" and to judge "the entire work" rather than assessing its merits owing to just "several phrases." He had no illusions in this matter, however, and guessed that he was not likely to be granted this favor, a prediction that has proved all too true.

Voltaire, for example, failing to perceive the methodological innovations of *The Spirit of Laws*, rather pettily complained about all the errors it contained—"erroneous digressions" he called them—lamenting contemptuously, for example, in his lengthy dialogue *L'ABC* that Montesquieu had taken, as fact, what Pufendorf had only guessed to be the population of France under Charles IX and, as fact, based on an overly hastily reading of the French Jesuit Chardin's reporting, that the Cyrus was the only navigable river in Persia whereas Chardin had said something else altogether. Similarly, Voltaire complained that Montesquieu had completely ignored the presence of numerous mountain ranges in Persia in asserting that great, long-lasting empires endure because of their large plains. So, too, had Montesquieu failed miserably, Voltaire contended, in his attempts, again influenced by Chardin, to establish linkages between climate and religion. How could Montesquieu treat climate as the key to the explanation of religious belief and practices, Voltaire wondered, when Islam had taken root in areas of the Middle East, Africa, and Europe so very different in climate and terrain?

One would make a great mistake in regarding *The Spirit of Laws* as important only for the accuracy, or lack thereof, of the facts it reports. Certainly Montesquieu relied too uncritically on the traveler's reports that formed the substance of his knowledge of distant parts of the world, as Sharon Krause explains in her chapter on Montesquieu's theory of despotism, and admittedly he sometimes misread or misquoted these accounts. But it was Montesquieu's craving for information concerning the world beyond Europe that makes his perspective so important. The importance of Montesquieu's factual errors, then, should not be exaggerated. Part of the significance of his great work is its tendency to inspire others to speculate further along the lines of thought he has left incomplete or even gotten wrong. This tendency of his work to serve as a catalyst for other theorists was appreciated soon after its original publication. Hence we find Antoine Pecquet observing in his *Analyse raisonnée de L'Esprit des lois* (Paris, 1757) that Montesquieu is valuable "less as a sure guide in all the subjects covered" than as a thinker whose work contains "big ideas" and "opens up large prospects" requiring some correction by others.[84] Similarly, we encounter the appreciative comment in Volume IX of the *Encyclopédie méthodique* (1782-90) that "even when he erred, he made the reader think and showed him the path leading to the truth."[85]

The Legacy of *The Spirit of Laws*

What, then, are some of these "big ideas" and "large prospects" that captured the imagination of many of Montesquieu's contemporaries and still warrant careful consideration today? First off, Montesquieu shifted the focus of political theory away from attention mainly to the behavior of individual rulers or members of the ruling class and onto the broader question of the structure and principles of the underlying regime as well as the customs and manners supportive of each regime type. In so doing, he did nothing less than transform the science of politics from a psychological orientation to a sociocultural emphasis, thereby helping to launch the sciences of anthropology, sociology, and comparative politics as we know them. Montesquieu sensed, better than any of his contemporaries, that the comparative perspective provides the highest level of understanding and self-awareness. It is in contemplating difference that we come best to know ourselves.

Montesquieu's contributions and perspectives are also of crucial significance in the history of Western political thought because one will rarely, if ever, encounter a fuller appreciation of the importance of human freedom than one discovers in his various writings. "Liberty," he remarked in an important *Pensée*, "(is) that good that renders us capable of enjoying other goods."[86] Long before

the boom times of the late twentieth century, Montesquieu understood the connection between liberty and national wealth, contending that "countries are not
cultivated in proportion to their fertility but in proportion to their liberty"
(XVIII, 3). It is liberty, which he understood primarily in the negative sense of
freedom from unwelcome constraints—whether stemming from immoderate,
despotic governments or from errors of misguided, unenlightened law-makers
drafting immoderate, oppressive laws—that creates the conditions for human
flourishing. "The law," he remarked in a memorable phrase, "is not an act of
pure power. Things indifferent by their nature are not within its jurisdiction"
(XIX, 14). Whether human beings use or misuse their liberty in their pursuit of
private goals in the civil realm, the beneficial aspect of such freedom is the absence of either the painful self-renunciation that had been required in the republics of classical antiquity or the external constraints imposed by despots in nations where political freedom is completely unknown. To the extent that the
quest for political and personal freedom has proven to be the driving force of
modern politics, Montesquieu may justly be regarded as the patron saint of the
modern city.

Furthermore, Montesquieu bequeathed to later generations a definition of
freedom that is still of crucial importance for the liberal tradition. Rather than
assuming the existence of a governmental prerogative to regulate human conduct in all areas not fenced off from interference by explicit legal protections, he
preferred to adopt the view that citizens may only be compelled to do what the
law obliges. Beyond that, they are by definition free. Where the law is silent, the
citizen has only right reason and conscience to guide his actions (XI, 3). Furthermore, freedom, Montesquieu believed, has an ethical dimension. "Freedom
can only consist in having the power to do what one ought to wish (*ce que l'on
doit vouloir*)" (XI, 3). And, above all, freedom must not be considered independent of law. Freedom is law bound and must not to be confused with total
independence. It is "the right to do what the laws permit" (XI, 3).

Montesquieu understood that free states necessarily possess complex constitutional structures that arise only as the result of the conscious effort of lawgiv-
ers informed by a thorough understanding of past failures and successes. Erudition and politics must go hand in hand if the all-important goal of moderation is
to be achieved. Despotic governments spring up all too spontaneously from the
common human instinct to dominate (XXVIII, 4).[87] The route to freedom, on the
other hand, can only be paved with human artifice consciously working to partition and balance powers in constitutional frameworks reflecting the very best
inventions of human political wisdom. Hence we find Montesquieu remarking in
the Preface to *The Spirit of Laws* that "It is not an indifferent matter that the
people be enlightened. The prejudices of magistrates have started out as being
the prejudices of the nation." Above all, it is the makers of law who need to be
enlightened, but the people, too, must be well informed since no free government can rest its foundations only on an hereditary class exercising political

power commensurate with its wealth, status, experience, and wisdom. Montesquieu was substantially more prescient than many of his fellow *philosophes* who naively looked towards "legal" or "enlightened" despotism as the preferred condition for mankind, as if reason alone can guarantee just rule. Despotism can never be anything other than abhorrent in Montesquieu's judgment and, like Tocqueville at a later point, he had no more patience for the despotism of the many, exercised in an unmixed democratic regime where excessive regard for equality has put all on the same level, than for the despotism of a single individual pretending to a monopoly of wisdom.

Owing in large part to the influence of Montesquieu, the politics of modern liberty has rightly stressed the key importance of an independent judiciary insulated from both threats and favors. As a titled member of France's own judicial elite, enjoying judicial office as a property right in France's system of venality of offices, Montesquieu was well positioned to trumpet the importance of a judiciary capable of speaking truth to power, a presumed role for the French Parlements that Michael Mosher explores in substantial detail in chapter 4 of this volume. Many among Montesquieu's contemporaries attacked the French system of judicial office-holding, and, not surprisingly, the system of venality was one of the first aspects of the ancien régime to be eliminated in the French Revolution. Montesquieu understood, however, that the presence of independent judges owing their offices neither to royal favor nor popular election was the crucial aspect of the French constitution averting full-blown despotism. The American conception of judicial review of legislative acts for a determination of their constitutionality is not specifically traceable to *The Spirit of Laws*. The idea of testing laws to assess their conformity to the higher law of the constitution, however, is certainly akin to the role Montesquieu envisioned for the French Parlements as depositories of laws that even the king is not free to violate once his edicts have been registered and announced as law by judges serving on the highest courts of the realm.

Still another aspect of the modern liberal tradition to which Montesquieu made important contributions is the creation of a system of criminal punishment that is fair to the accused at the same time that its modes of punishment conform to the state's need to deter criminal acts. It was Montesquieu who initiated the intense public discussions in France regarding a proper scale of punishments. No *philosophe* so substantially influenced Cesare Beccaria in his composition of his influential *On Crimes and Punishments* (1764) as Montesquieu, and owing to the enormous influence of both Beccaria and Montesquieu, liberals ever since have argued for reducing the severity of grossly disproportionate, cruel, and arbitrary punishments. Furthermore, Montesquieu's decriminalization agenda, which included an absolute prohibition on offenses against religion being judged criminal, found important echoes not only in the French Declaration of the Rights of Man and of the Citizen (1789), but also in the writings of such American Founders as Jefferson and Madison, who envisioned religion as essentially a matter of individual conscience independent of state power.

Owing to his conceptualization of despotism as what Sharon Krause aptly labels in chapter 5 of this volume "an entrenched possibility of politics," Montesquieu displayed a keener appreciation for the need to divide and separate executive, legislative, and judicial powers than any of his contemporaries. Clearly the influence of his views regarding the need to separate and balance powers on the basic structure of the American Constitution, as well as his much more recent influence on the structure of new constitutions that have been drafted in Eastern Europe since the collapse of communism, render his place in the pantheon of modern liberal thought fully secure.[88] No political philosopher has voiced greater appreciation of the threat of despotism than Montesquieu. "Monarchy ordinarily degenerates into the despotism of one," he lamented, and "aristocracy into the despotism of several" whereas "democracy ordinarily degenerates into the despotism of the People."[89] It is not at all surprising, then, that French revolutionaries asserting the relevance of *The Spirit of Laws* to France's republican ambitions in the 1790s routinely dwelled on Montesquieu's implacable opposition to despotism as his finest achievement. Hence we find Bertrand Barère responding to the excesses of the Revolution by asserting that Montesquieu's discovery of the need to partition powers made him the Kepler of "political constitutions."[90]

Montesquieu's views on toleration are also of crucial significance to the liberal project of modernity. His scalding denunciation of the Spanish Inquisition in *The Spirit of Laws* and his general argument that competing religious viewpoints should be tolerated once they are present in a state render him a key figure in the development in Europe of conceptions of religious freedom. Although he believed the presence of only one religion may be preferable in terms of achieving stability, he was just as firmly convinced that wherever more than one religion has taken root, toleration of difference is the only just policy and the only approach capable of averting turmoil and even civil war. Instrumental in creating a brand of post-Enlightenment liberalism that does not shun religion is Montesquieu's strong belief that although politics and religion occupy separate spheres, they both occupy the same "public" space, so that the presence of religious beliefs supporting moral conduct should be welcomed as contributing to the achievement of the public goals of peace and order.[91]

Montesquieu's ideas on commerce and economics are equally important to understanding his contributions to modern liberal theory. He is justly famous for his conviction that commercial exchanges will contribute to peace between nations, and he struck an important blow for economic liberalism in warning of the dangers of excessive taxation. Just as rulers will abuse power in general, he suggested, they will also tend to regard their own, personal ambitions as equivalent to real and legitimate state needs requiring exorbitant levels of taxation (XIII, 1). As Catherine Larrère suggests in chapter 8 of this volume, Montesquieu reverses previously dominant attitudes regarding work as an unwelcome burden required to energize lethargic individuals by conceptualizing work as an activity willingly adopted for the sake of accumulating wealth. We find, then, in Montesquieu's theory the important liberal tenet that individual interest is the best incentive for activating citizens to undertake activities that benefit, first themselves, and then the state of which they are a part. Self-interest is the surest and the freest path to the achievement of common goals.

Surely the modern liberal state elevating liberty and autonomy above classical conceptions of the good owes as much to the legacy of Montesquieu as to any other single figure in the history of liberalism, just as Constant and other French liberals reacting to France's revolutionary excesses well understood. If Locke was the most important liberal thinker of the seventeenth century, superceding Hobbes in importance because of the untenable nature of Hobbes' conclusions, Montesquieu was clearly the most important European liberal theorist of the next century. Who today would read Voltaire, or even Rousseau, rather than Montesquieu, to gain prudential understanding of ways to structure an actual regime? Long before the purges, exterminations, and ethnic cleansings of the twentieth century, Montesquieu was exquisitely aware of the corrupting influences of political power that too often reduce human reason to a mere reflex of human will. The crucial need to check unbridled power runs along as a steady and strong undercurrent in *The Spirit of Laws* and has continually inspired liberal constitution makers intent on restraining power.

To his credit, Montesquieu was able to stress the importance of liberty's triumph over despotism without resorting to a value-neutral version of liberalism (as if one were even possible) leaving no role for moral absolutes as guide posts for legal enactments. As Cecil Courtney contends in the opening chapter of this volume, Montesquieu's political thought teaches the still crucial lesson that contemplating and even respecting diversity need not result in extreme relativism. Human diversity is inevitable, but so, too, is the continued presence in the human mind (whatever their ultimate source), of certain core values that must be respected, including reason, modesty, decency, humanitarianism, freedom, and toleration. Evidence abounds in *The Spirit of Laws* that Montesquieu believed in the existence of basic tenets of justice and basic human values that are universal and should be maintained regardless of any society's particular physical or cultural setting. It is for this reason that he made his famous proclamation in Book XIV of his work that good legislators oppose the effects of climate, topography, and terrain when they incline towards slavery or despotism whereas bad legislators regard themselves as impotent before the forces of nature (XIV, 5).

Similarly useful in comprehending Montesquieu's continual concern to prioritize not just "facts" but "values" is his caveat in Book XVI, chapter 4, following his discussion of polygamy, "In all this, I do not justify these practices, but only express the reasons for them." No philosopher lacking strong normative preferences would have defined liberty as "the power to do what one ought to wish" (XI, 4) rather than the power to do whatever one wishes. Even prior to Kant, Montesquieu was suggesting that the best measure of the legitimacy of what an individual may desire is his willingness to see the same prescription, practice, custom, or law that he himself prefers universalized so that it applies equally to all (XV, 9). Montesquieu was quite perturbed that some critics of his work had misconstrued his interest in certain *bizarreries* as somehow expressing approval of them. Thus he laments in the explanatory note added to the 1757 edition of *The Spirit of Laws* that those who had failed to comprehend his "new meanings" had sometimes attributed "absurd" and "revolting" ideas to him that conflicted with the good morals favored by every country.

In addition to contributing to many important strands of liberalism, Montesquieu was one of those rare figures in the history of human thought who only occasionally come along to reveal to us the new lenses through which we need to gaze in order to perceive the true relations among things. If he is often difficult to interpret, and if he often leaves matters ambiguous, he never fails to add novel perspectives to whatever subjects he addresses, while fathoming interconnections between laws, customs, beliefs, and physical and moral causes that other theorists did not envision.

There is a sociology of knowledge in Montesquieu's work suggesting, as his greatest student of the nineteenth century, Alexis de Tocqueville, also appreciated, that no culture can be understood without comprehending its spirit, or what Dilthey would later term its "lived experience," visible only to someone who thoroughly immerses himself in all of the various aspects of a culture, including laws, politics, religion, political economy, customs, manners, and morals. Montesquieu understood that *verstehen* involves more than just the marshalling of one fact after another. True understanding of human behavior, he believed, requires the sympathetic appreciation of the "spirit" of a given culture culled from what we would now term an anthropological quest for the customs and practices signifying the values that a given people hold dear, as in his explorations of the principles of virtue and honor providing the psychological springs, respectively, for republican and monarchical governments.[92]

The Purpose of this Volume

Somewhat surprisingly, this volume is the very first English-language collection of essays devoted to exploring the various contributions Montesquieu made to the science of politics in *The Spirit of Laws* (1748). In planning the volume, we have been motivated by the conviction that, given the complexity of the issues raised by Montesquieu's thought, most readers will benefit from, if not require, assistance in comprehending the import, significance, and even at times the very meaning, of many of his assertions. At a minimum, therefore, each contributor to the volume seeks to explicate Montesquieu's often enigmatic texts by means of incisive analysis of precisely what he intended to say on a given subject. This is by no means a difficult task in interpreting some authors, but, as mentioned above, Montesquieu often poses substantial challenges in this regard, in part because he often veils his meanings and in part because he often places his comments on the same subject in very disparate parts of his work.

A second aspect of our common approach has been to develop important aspects of the intellectual and historical context that can assist in rendering Montesquieu's thoughts, intimations, and even intuitions intelligible. We make no claims to dogmatic certainty, however. As Jean Ehrard recently observed concerning the difficulty of interpreting *The Spirit of Laws*, "If the text and its history remain for us sometimes enigmatic, we can and must try to clarify them by means of the context consisting of facts and events to which he alluded, which will lead to certain or possible readings."[93] Ehrard's emphasis on "possible readings" strikes us as very appropriate. On certain interpretative points, there will never be perfect agreement, or even rough consensus. Claims of dogmatic certainty in interpreting Montesquieu must, then, be even more suspect than when dealing with other major figures in the history of political thought.

Was he, for example, a political philosopher for whom the dictates of natural law continued to function as the underlying postulates of politics, as Cecil Courtney contends in this volume, or did he merely give perfunctory voice to a few natural law concepts in Book I of his *œuvre* without paying substantial heed to the natural law approach in the remainder of his text?[94] Was he a staunch monarchist who saw substantial promise for liberty in a reformed French monarchy where the legislative role of the Parlements might be elevated and the role of the tax farmer substantially diminished, as both Michael Mosher and David Carrithers contend in this volume? Or was he a critic and satirist of monarchy who thought France was inclining inevitably toward despotism and displayed little potential for liberty?[95] Did he envision honor as the exclusive possession of the French nobility, or did he present a substantially democratic vision of honor that reaches across social boundaries, as Michael Mosher suggests in chapter 4 of this volume? Did he substantially admire the republics of antiquity—and even wish to emulate them—or did he, as suggested by David Carrithers in chapter 3 of this volume, see mainly the darker side of Athens, Sparta, and Rome based on a sober realization of the need in egalitarian republics for the suppression of ego and individual desire?[96]

Did his eighteen-month visit to England in 1729-31 turn him into the Anglophile some of his compatriots thought they perceived, or did he, as both C. P. Courtney and Paul Rahe contend in this volume, harbor serious reservations about the English approach to politics? Did he believe the English government was animated by a specific "principle," as with republics, monarchies, and despotisms, or was his discussion of "principles" intended only to describe the ideal types of states rather than mixed regimes? And precisely what did Montesquieu mean when he described England as "a republic disguised as a monarchy?" Did he regard England as a new, modern form of republic—a commercial republic—or did he consider England a species of constitutional monarchy, very different from the French monarchy, but a monarchy nonetheless?

Can we find in Montesquieu's work the same high level of dissatisfaction with existing criminal law procedures one encounters later in Beccaria and Voltaire and other legal reformers of the second half of the eighteenth century, or did he mainly object to the severity of the punishments being employed, while regarding the procedures as adequate, as suggested by David Carrithers in chapter 7 of this volume? Should he be regarded as primarily a mercantilist, or was he a classic economic liberal, and did he contribute to economic science in the same substantial way that Hume and Smith, and even Quesnay did? Did he adhere to the mercantilist belief that commerce is a zero-sum activity with only one winner, or was he able, as Catherine Larrère suggests in chapter 8 of this volume, to break away from mercantilism in order to conceptualize commerce as a mutual sum game where two trading partners can benefit nearly equally from commercial exchanges?

Was he a proponent of religious toleration purely and simply, or did he believe there are advantages to uniformity and orthodoxy when a state is able to avoid the clash of competing religious viewpoints? Furthermore, with regard to his views on religion, is Montesquieu to be most accurately assessed as a defender of natural religion, or as a deist, or an Erastian, or a Machiavellian? And was his advocacy of toleration based on a strong conviction of the need for public order, on a skeptical view of the uncertainty of religious truths, on a conviction that individual conscience is impervious to legal constraints, or, rather, on utilitarian concerns of a quite different sort, as Rebecca Kingston suggests in chapter 9 of this volume? And finally, how do Montesquieu's historical views compare to the dominant interpretations of early French history put forth by the Comte de Boulainvilliers and Abbé Dubos earlier in the eighteenth century? Did he develop a viewpoint, as Iris Cox suggests in chapter 10 of this volume, different from that of both Boulainvilliers and Dubos? And, finally, what is the general relevance of theories of the Frankish conquest of Gaul to the later political history of France?

These and other questions are not easy ones to answer, and at times even the contributors to this volume do not fully agree in their interpretations. Our goal nonetheless has been to shed light on how best to approach these important issues. As mentioned, we have tried to situate Montesquieu's thought in a broad context, both theoretical and historical. Thus C. P. Courtney in chapter 1 pleads with readers to study Montesquieu in the intellectual context of his own times rather than projecting him ahead into a world he did not inhabit. He then proceeds to demonstrate how reflection on the early modern proponents of natural law theory helps us to understand Montesquieu's fundamental mission in *The Spirit of Laws*. In chapter 2 Paul Rahe discusses Montesquieu's overall regime typology while also comparing Montesquieu's mode of conceptualizing governmental forms to the classical approaches of Plato and Aristotle and suggesting parallels and antitheses between the viewpoints of Machiavelli and Montesquieu. He includes the English regime in this discussion and boldly suggests what Montesquieu may have considered the unspecified principle of English government. David Carrithers in chapter 3 explicates Montesquieu's views on the essential features and policies of both democratic and aristocratic republics with attention to where Montesquieu agrees with or diverges from assertions made by other theorists both ancient and modern. He also argues for the presence in Montesquieu's depiction of classical democracy of two distinct models, the first based on Athens and anticipating commercial activity on the part of citizens, and the second based on Sparta and much more closely resembling a closed society where commercial exchange with foreigners is viewed as incompatible with the successful practice of political virtue.

Michael Mosher in chapter 4 explicates Montesquieu's views on monarchy by means of a comparison to Bodin's views, while also delineating key facts regarding French political history and the French constitution that illuminate Montesquieu's often veiled and enigmatic meanings. He detects a tension between the juridical structure of monarchy and the aristocratic culture of monarchy summed up by the term honor, which is not found in Bodin and which introduces possibilities of "civil disobedience" that Montesquieu considered a necessary supplement to monarchical authority. In chapter 5 Sharon Krause analyzes Montesquieu's concept of despotism, tracing the origins of his terminology and the use of his sources, while explaining what his account of despotism reveals about the rest of his philosophy, including his views on human nature and human freedom. Cecil Courtney in chapter 6 analyzes Montesquieu's views on England and dwells on certain negative attitudes Frenchmen displayed toward England in order to avoid the common error of exaggerating the extent of Montesquieu's admiration for the English people and their government.

In chapter 7 David Carrithers focuses on the French Criminal Ordinance of 1670 as the essential background to consideration of Montesquieu's views on crime and punishment in order to demonstrate that it was the punishment scheme and not the judicial procedures of ancien régime criminal justice that he found so suspect and unfair to the accused. Catherine Larrère, in analyzing Montesquieu's views on commerce, taxation, money, and population in chapter 8, compares Montesquieu's conceptions to those of numerous earlier writers on these subjects, while suggesting that he developed a critique of mercantilism in advancing some of the main arguments of economic liberalism, including a conception of economics as at least partly a self-regulating process. Paying close attention to the relevant historical developments in early modern France, Rebecca Kingston in chapter 9 demonstrates how Montesquieu's views on religion, rather than being developed abstractly as a matter of pure philosophy, derived from and reflected the Jesuit/Jansenist tensions of the ancien régime. She also explains how and why Montesquieu avoided a strictly separationist approach to religion and the state. Iris Cox reminds us in chapter 10 that the constitutional struggle between the Crown and the Parlements during the eighteenth century cannot be understood without proper attention to the historical debate that raged in Montesquieu's day over the influence of the Frankish invasion of Gaul in the late fifth century on the powers wielded by early Frankish kings and noblemen, and, by implication, their legal heirs right down to Montesquieu's day. She analyses his views on France's ancient constitution while at the same time comparing his perspective to the views expressed by Boulainvilliers and Dubos, the two authors whose opinions best encapsulated, respectively, the *thèse nobiliaire* and the *thèse royale*.

We hope, above all, that this volume will make completely apparent the richness and complexity of Montesquieu's thought in order to encourage others to engage this great and enlightened mind with the same level of interest that his writings have generated among the contributors to this volume. Throughout the volume, the focus has been kept largely on *The Spirit of Laws*, but other works by Montesquieu are at times brought into the picture to aid comprehension of his major work. As mentioned, the interpretative questions posed by Montesquieu's texts are often complex, and the answers at times necessarily too indefinite for all readers to reach the same conclusions. Whatever disagreements will necessarily exist concerning Montesquieu's precise meanings and the implications of his arguments, anyone who has studiously pondered Montesquieu's text knows that, like other great works in the history of Western political philosophy, *The Spirit of Laws* reflects the issues of a particular time and place while also transcending them in such a manner as to greatly contribute to shaping the political and philosophical debates of subsequent generations.

Notes

I would like to thank Cecil Courtney, Catherine Larrère, Rebecca Kingston, Sharon Krause, Michael Mosher, and Paul Rahe for reading an earlier draft of this introduction and offering useful comments.

1. There were also twenty-three editions of Montesquieu's *Œuvres complètes* that incorporated *The Spirit of Laws* published between 1758 and 1789. See Cecil Patrick Courtney, "L'Esprit des lois dans la perspective de l'histoire du livre (1748-1800)," in *Le temps de Montesquieu*, Michel Porret and Catherine Volpilhac-Auger, eds. (Geneva: Droz, 2000 forthcoming).

2. Hume, *Enquiry*, cited in Robert Shackleton, *Montesquieu. A Critical Biography* (Oxford: Clarendon Press, 1961), 245.

3. Quoted by Louis Desgraves, "Aspects de la correspondance de Montesquieu en 1749," in *Lectures de Montesquieu*. Actes de colloque de Wolfenbüttel, 26-28 octobre 1989, Edgar Mass and Alberto Postigliola, eds. (Naples: Liguori Editore, 1993), 66.

4. H. Walpole to H. Mann, January 10, 1750, in *Letters of Horace Walpole* (Oxford, 1903-05), II, 419, cited in Shackleton, *Montesquieu*, 357.

5. *Abridgment of English History* (1757), in *Works* (London, 1854-59), VI, 297, quoted by C. P. Courtney, *Montesquieu and Burke* (Westport, Conn.: Greenwood Press; org. ed., 1963), 165.

6. Edmund Burke, *Appeal from the New to the Old Whigs* (1791), in Burke, *Works* (London, 1854-59), III, 113, cited in Cecil Courtney, "Montesquieu and Revolution," in *Lectures de Montesquieu*, Mass and Postigliola, eds., 49.

7. See Desgraves, "Aspects de la correspondance de Montesquieu," in *Lectures de Montesquieu*, Edgar Mass, ed., 64-65.

8. Mme de Tencin to Montesquieu, December 2, 1748, in Nagel, III, 1148-49.

9. *Social Contract*, III, 4, cited by Brethe de La Gressaye, "Montesquieu jugé par les philosophes, ses contemporaines," in *Académie nationale des sciences, belles lettres, et arts de Bordeaux*. Actes 4th series, XVII (1960-61): 48.

10. Jean Brethe de La Gressaye, "Montesquieu jugé par les philosophes," 61.

11. Jean-Paul Marat, *Projet de déclaration des droits de l'homme. . .* (1789), 2-5 cited in Roger Barny, *"Montesquieu patriote?"* in *Dix-huitième siècle, revue annuelle publiée par la société française d'étude du 18ème siècle* 21 (1989): 90.

12. Voltaire, *Commentaire sur L'Esprit des Lois* (1777), "Avant-Propos," in *Œuvres complètes de Voltaire*, Louis Moland, ed., 52 vols. (Paris: Garnier frères, 1877-85), IX, 405-6.

13. The quotation is from a brief author's note Destutt de Tracy wrote for his *A Commentary and Review of Montesquieu's Spirit of Laws. Prepared for Press from the Original Manuscript*, Thomas Jefferson, trans. (Philadelphia: Duane, 1811; reprt. New York: Burt Franklin, 1969), 1. The first French edition of the commentary was not published until 1819.

14. De Brosses to Gemeaux, February 24, 1749, cited in Shackleton, *Montesquieu*, 357.

15. Stefano Bertolini, *Analyse raisonnée de L'Esprit des lois* (Geneva, 1771), I, and Avertissement.

16. Madison, "Spirit of Governments" (1792), cited in Paul M. Spurlin, *Montesquieu in America, 1760-1801* (New York: Octagon Books; 1969; orig. ed. 1940), 241.

17. See Gilbert Chinard, ed., *The Commonplace Book of Thomas Jefferson. A Repertory of his Ideas on Government* (Baltimore: Johns Hopkins University Press, 1926). For an analysis of Montesquieu's influence on the shaping of Jefferson's republican thought, see David W. Carrithers, "Montesquieu, Jefferson and the Fundamentals of Eighteenth-Century Republican Theory," *The French American Review* 6, no. 2 (Fall 1982): 160-88.

18. Jefferson to Randolph, New York, May 30, 1790, in *The Writings of Thomas Jefferson* (Memorial ed.), VIII, 31, cited by Paul M. Spurlin, *Montesquieu in America*, 96.

19. Marquis de Mirabeau, *L'Ami des Hommes* (Hambourg, 1758), I, chap. 7, 194-95, cited in Elie Carcassonne, *Montesquieu et le problème de la constitution française au XVIIIe siècle* (Geneva: Slatkine Reprints, 1978; orig. ed., 1927), 236.

20. A thorough comparison and contrast of the political philosophy of these two ancient and modern theorists, however, has yet to be undertaken, though one finds many useful observations on this subject in Thomas Pangle's *Montesquieu's Philosophy of Liberalism. A Commentary on The Spirit of the Laws* (Chicago: University of Chicago Press, 1973) and also in Harvey C. Mansfield, Jr., *Taming the Prince. The Ambivalence of Executive Power* (Baltimore: Johns Hopkins University Press, 1993, orig. ed., 1989) and in David Lowenthal, "Montesquieu," in *History of Political Philosophy*, Leo Strauss and Joseph Cropsey, eds. (Chicago: Rand McNally, 1972), 487-509.

21. See Montesquieu, *The Spirit of the Laws*, Anne Cohler, Basia Miller, and Harold Stone, trans. and eds. (Cambridge: Cambridge University Press, 1989).

22. Voltaire, *L'ABC*, in *Philosophical Dictionary*, Peter Gay, trans. (New York: Harcourt, Brace and World, Inc., 1962), 509.

23. We use this once favored translation of the title instead of the now more commonly used *The Spirit of the Laws* both because the definite article is often used in French where it is not welcome in English, and because refraining from using the second definite article properly suggests that Montesquieu was seeking the method of exploring the spirit of laws in general and not just the spirit of the laws of any one particular government. *The Spirit of Laws* had always been the preferred English translation until the rendering was changed, without explanation, in a 1900 printing of the classic Thomas Nugent translation dating from 1750.

24. On the influence of achievements in natural philosophy on the emergence of the human sciences, see especially Peter Gay, *The Enlightenment: An Interpretation*, vol. II: *The Science of Freedom* (New York: Knopf, 1969); Georges Gusdorf, *Introduction aux sciences humaines* (Paris: Ophrys, 1974); Sergio Moravia, "The Enlightenment and the Sciences of Man," *History of Science* 18 (1980): 247-68; Christopher Fox, Roy Porter, and Robert Wokler, eds., *Inventing Human Science. Eighteenth-Century Domains* (Berkeley: University of California Press, 1995), and Richard Olson, *The Emergence of the Social Sciences, 1642-1792* (New York: Twayne Publishers, 1993).

25. All references to *The Spirit of Laws* in this introduction and in the rest of the volume are cited in this manner with the Roman numeral corresponding to the Book number and the Arabic numeral corresponding to the chapter number.

26. Charles Bonnet to Montesquieu, November 14, 1753, in Nagel, III, 1478.

27. Emile Durkheim, *Montesquieu and Rousseau as Forerunners of Sociology*, Ralph Manheim, trans. (Ann Arbor: University of Michigan Press, 1960), 1-2.

28. See Auguste Comte, "Plan des travaux scientifiques necéssaires pour réorganiser la société" (May, 1822), in *Système de politique positive. . .* 4 vols. (Paris, 1851-54), IV, Appendix.

29. Durkheim, *Montesquieu and Rousseau,* 52-53.

30. Bertrand Binoche, *Introduction à De l'esprit des lois de Montesquieu* (Paris: Presses Universitaires de France, 1998), 6.

31. Durkheim, *Montesquieu and Rousseau,* 52-53; Paul Vernière, "Montesquieu et le monde musulman, d'après *L'Esprit des Lois,*" in *Actes du Congrès Montesquieu réuni à Bordeaux du 23 mai au 26 mai 1955 pour commémorer le deuxième centenaire de la mort de Montesquieu* (Bordeaux: Delmas, 1956), 175-90; Muriel Dodds, *Les récits de voyages. Sources de L'Esprit des Lois* (Paris: Champion, 1929). The contention is, of course, debatable, and other students of Montesquieu's thought have placed substantial stress on his empiricism. See, for example, Isaiah Berlin, "Montesquieu," in *Against the Current. Essays in the History of Ideas*, Henry Hardy, ed. (Harmondsworth: Penguin Books, 1982), 137. For a view seeking to develop the strengths of both perspectives, see Montesquieu, *The Spirit of Laws. A Compendiun of the First English Edition. . .* David Wallace Carrithers, ed. (Berkeley: University of California Press, 1977), 40-44.

32. *Pensée* 200 (1864), in Pléiade, II, 1040.

33. For Louis XVI's essay, see Soulavie, *Mémoires historiques et politiques du règne de Louis XVI depuis son mariage jusqu'à sa mort,* 6 vols. (Paris, 1801), II, 52-53, cited by Ran Halévi, *"La modération à l'épreuve de l'absolutisme de l'Ancien Régime à la Révolution française"* in *Le Débat* 109 (March-April, 2000), 87. Soulavie reports that Louis XVI had written the work "according to the taste of and following the forms of Montesquieu" and that he composed chapters entitled "De la personne du prince, De l'autorité des corps dans l'état, Du caractère de l'execution de la monarchie, etc. etc."

34. For the Empress Catherine's use of Montesquieu, see Jean Brethe de La Gressaye, "Montesquieu jugé par les philosophes," 50. For Diderot's opinions on Catherine's proposed reforms (and therefore indirectly on Montesquieu), see Diderot, *Observations on the Instructions of the Empress of Russia to the Deputies for the Making of the Laws* (1774-1780), in Diderot, *Political Writings*, John Hope Mason and Robert Wokler, eds. (Cambridge: Cambridge University Press, 1992), 81-164.

35. See Montesquieu's flirtations with determinist readings of history in his *On Politics* (1716), in Pléiade, I, 112-19 and also David Carrithers, "Montesquieu's Philosophy of History," *Journal of the History of Ideas* 47, no. 1 (Jan.-Mar., 1986), 61-80.

36. For stress on his sociological method, see in addition to Durkeim's classic study cited in note 27 above, Robinet de Clery, "Montesquieu sociologue," *Revue internationale de sociologie* 47 (1939), 221-32; Franz Neumann, "Editor's Introduction," in Montesquieu, *The Spirit of the Laws* (New York: Hafner, 1949), xxxvi-xlvii; Sergio Cotta, *Montesquieu e la scienza della società* (Turin: Ramella, 1953); Werner Stark, *Montesquieu: Pioneer of the Sociology of Knowledge* (Toronto: University of Toronto Press, 1960);

David Carrithers, "The Enlightenment Science of Society," in *Inventing Human Science. Eighteenth-Century Domains,* 232-70; Pierre Manent, "The Sociological Viewpoint," in *The City of Man,* Marc A. LePain, trans. (Princeton: Princeton University Press, 1998), 50-85.

37. *Pensée* 192 (1866), in Pléiade, II, 1038.

38. Mme de Tencin to Montesquieu," December 2, 1748, in Nagel, III, 1148-49.

39. *Defense of the Spirit of Laws,* in Pléiade, II, 1137.

40. The initial cause of Voltaire's mirth, enunciated by participant "B" in the dialogue, had been the division of the work into so many, extremely short chapters.

41. *L'ABC* in Voltaire, *Philosophical Dictionary,* Peter Gay, trans., 507.

42. *L'ABC* in Voltaire, *Philosophical Dictionary,* Peter Gay, trans., 508.

43. Boswell, *The Tour of the Hebrides,* G. B. Hill and L. F. Powell, eds. (Oxford, 1950), 209, cited in Shackleton, *Montesquieu,* 234. Montesquieu was not, it need be said, "supporting" polygamy. He regarded giving the reasons for things very different from approving of them, whatever Johnson may have thought.

44. For a useful discussion of Montesquieu's precursors on this subject see Roger Mercier, "La théorie des climats des *Réflexions critiques* à *L'Esprit des lois,* in *Revue d'histoire littéraire de la France* 53 (1953): 17-37; 159-174.

45. For a translation of this work see *The Spirit of Laws, a Compendium of the First English Edition together with an English Translation of An Essay on Causes Affecting Minds and Characters* (1736-1743), David Wallace Carrithers, ed. (Berkeley: University of California Press, 1977), 417-63.

46. See C. P. Courtney, *Montesquieu and Burke* (Oxford: Basil Blackwell, 1963).

47. Cited in Pierre Rétat, "1789: Montesquieu Aristocrate," *Dix-huitième siècle* 21 (1989): 79 (italics in original).

48. *Pensée* 194 (1873), in Pléiade, II, 1039.

49. Whatever its general validity, this pronouncement cannot be taken completely literally. In Book XIII, chapters 19 and 20 of *The Spirit of Laws,* Montesquieu, for example, sharply criticized the system of tax farming in France, and in Books VI and XII he attacked the excessive punishment scale embodied in the King's edicts, to mention just two areas of French policy where he proposed substantial reforms. It remains true, nonetheless, as Condorcet and others contended, that his overall goal was to explicate the reasons why a given set of sociopolitical, economic, governmental practices had arisen in a given country while also exploring their interconnections.

50. *Emile,* Book III, quoted in Robert Wokler, "The Enlightenment Science of Politics," in *Inventing Human Science,* Fox, Porter, and Wokler, eds., 326.

51. *Pensée* 1920 (1436), in Pléiade, I, 1461.

52. Filangieri is quoted in "Montesquieu," in *Against the Current,* 146. For Barère's comment, see his *Montesquieu peint d'après ses ouvrages* (an V-VII), 62, 66, cited in Roger Barny, "Montesquieu patriote?" in *Dix-huitième siècle* 21 (1989): 92.

53. Charles-Alexandre de Calonne, *Lettre adressée au Roi. . .le 9 février 1789* (London, 1789), cited by Courtney, "Montesquieu and Revolution," in *Lectures de Montesquieu*, Mass and Postigliola, eds., 48.

54. Letter 129 in Montesquieu, *The Persian Letters* (1721), George R. Healey, trans. (Indianapolis: Bobbs-Merrill, 1964), 217.

55. *Pensée* 194 (1873), in Pléiade, II, 1039.

56. Catherine Larrère cites the French text in her *Actualité de Montesquieu* (Paris: Presses de Sciences Po, 1999), 9.

57. *Defense of The Spirit of Laws*, in Pléiade, II, 1138.

58. *Pensée* 1918 (941), in Pléiade, I, 1461.

59. Daniel Mornet, *Les Origines intellectuelles de la Révolution française* (Paris: A. Colin, 1933), in *The Influence of the Enlightenment on the French Revolution: Creative, Disastrous or Non-Existent?* William F. Church, ed. (Boston: D.C. Heath, 1964), 79-80.

60. Mornet, *Les Origines intellectuelles*, in *The Influence of the Enlightenment*, Church, ed., 81.

61. Wokler, "The Enlightenment Science of Politics," in *Inventing Human Science*, Fox, Porter, and Wokler, eds., 326.

62. Binoche, *Introduction à De l'esprit des lois*, 10.

63. Abbé Coyer, *Noblesse commerçante* (1756), 56, cited in Carcassonne, *Montesquieu et le problème de la constitution française*, 224.

64. Binoche, *Introduction à De l'esprit des lois*, 13.

65. On this subject, see Leo Strauss, *Persecution and the Art of Writing* (Chicago: University of Chicago Press, 1988; orig. ed., 1952), 28-29.

66. *Pensée* 1970, in Pléiade, I, cited in Bertrand Binoche, *Introduction à De l'esprit des lois*, 10.

67. *Discours sur le progrès des connaissances humaines en général, de la morale et de la législation en particulier. Lu dans une Assemblée publique de l'Académie de Lyon*, s.l., 1781, 28, cited in Michel Porret, "Montesquieu pénaliste à l'épreuve des réformateurs du droit pénal: la perfectabilité de *l'Esprit des lois* (1750-1790)," *Actes du Colloque international tenu à Bordeaux, de 3 au 6 décembre 1998 pour commémorer le 250ème anniversaire de la parution de* L'Esprit des lois *réunis et présentés par Louis Desgraves* (Bordeaux: Académie de Bordeaux, 1999), 336.

68. See Emile Faguet, *Dix-huitième siècle; études littéraires*, 28th ed. (Paris, 1890), 156.

69. Jean Ehrard, "La Chaîne de *L'Esprit des lois*," in *L'Esprit des mots. Montesquieu en lui-même et parmi les siens* (Geneva: Droz, 1998), 179.

70. Franz Neumann, "Editor's Introduction," in Montesquieu, *The Spirit of the Laws* (New York: Hafner, 1949), xxxi.

71. Isaiah Berlin, "Montesquieu," in *Against the Current*, 137.

72. George Sabine, *A History of Political Theory*, 3rd ed. (New York: Holt, Rinehart and Winston, 1961) 551, 556.

73. Voltaire, *L'ABC*, in *Philosophical Dictionary*, 508.

74. Voltaire, *L'ABC*, in *Philosophical Dictionary*, 512. Jean Brethe de La Gressaye, one of the eminent editors of Montesquieu's chief work concluded that "The plan of *The Spirit of Laws* is not clear, it's true, but it definitely exists, and Voltaire would have been able to discover it if he had focused on the whole rather than the details of the work." And Brethe de La Gressaye was no doubt correct in asserting that Voltaire "never grasped the profound intention of Montesquieu" in his quest for the spirit of laws since he "reads quickly, is not a jurist and is even less a sociologist." (Brethe de La Gressaye, "Montesquieu jugé par les philosophes," 46.) There is certainly no reason to dissent from J. H. Brumfitt's assertion that Voltaire often "went out of his way to criticize him (Montesquieu), finding ways to introduce Montesquieu's arguments into discussions only in order to have occasion to pillory them." Furthermore, Brumfitt observes, by the time Voltaire composed his own *Essai sur les mœurs* and his *Philosophical Dictionary*, he was ready to pay Montesquieu the ultimate compliment of imitating some of the very same climatological explanations of human behavior and government he had earlier ridiculed. See Brumfitt, *Voltaire Historian* (Oxford: Oxford University Press, 1958), 119-120.

75. *Pensée* 206 (1805), in Pléiade, II, 1041.

76. For a detailed exposition of the genesis in Montesquieu's writings of his concept of the "general spirit," see Montesquieu, *The Spirit of Laws. A Compendium of the First English Edition*, David W. Carrithers, ed., 23-30.

77. Certainly not all critics agree, however. Hence Franz Neumann remarks in his "Editor's Introduction" (see note 71) that "Books XXVII, XXVIII, XXX, and XXXI add fragmentary observations, which are not related to the rest of *The Spirit of the Laws*" (at xlvii).

78. Servan, *Discours sur le progrès*, 65, in Porret, "Montesquieu pénaliste," 336.

79. Sabine, *History of Political Theory*, 556-57.

80. Melvin Richter, "Montesquieu's Comparative Analysis of Europe and Asia: Intended and Unintended Consequences," in Cahiers Montesquieu 2: *L'Europe de Montesquieu. Actes du colloque de Gênes (26-29 mai 1993)*, Alberto Postigliola and Maria Grazia Bottaro Palumbo, eds. (Naples: Liguori Editore, 1995), 342.

81. Moderation emerges as the key theme in the following studies of Montesquieu's thought and influence: Anne Cohler, *Montesquieu's Comparative Politics and the Spirit of American Constitutionalism* (Lawrence, Kans.: University Press of Kansas, 1988); Pierre Manent, *An Intellectual History of Liberalism*, Rebecca Balinski, trans. (Princeton: Princeton University Press, 1994); and Ran Halévi, "La modération à l'épreuve de l'absolutisme."

82. See Catherine Larrère, *Actualité de Montesquieu*, which develops the continuing importance of Montesquieu to certain key issues of modern, liberal forms of states.

83. *Pensée* 188 (1723), in Pléiade, II, 1038.

84. Michel Porret cites the French text in his "Montesquieu pénaliste," 335.

85. *Encyclopédie méthodique*, IX, "La Police et les municipalités," clvii-clviii, cited in Porret, "Montesquieu pénaliste," 339. Emile Durkheim advanced this same argument, asserting, "By this I do not mean to say that Montesquieu's work contains very many propositions that modern science can accept as well-demonstrated theorems. . . . He did not always interpret history correctly, and it is easy to prove him wrong. But no one before him had gone so far along the way that led his successors to true social science. No one had perceived so clearly the conditions necessary for the establishment of this discipline. . . . Montesquieu's science is really social science. It deals with social phenomena and not with the mind of the individual." See Durkheim, *Montesquieu and Rousseau*, 2, 17.

86. *Pensée* 1797 (1574), in Pléiade, I, 1430.

87. See also *Pensée* 633 (935), in Pléiade, I, 1153.

88. For an example of Montesquieu's influence on emerging regimes in eastern Europe, see Péter Lászaló, "Montesquieu's Paradox on Freedom and Hungary's Constitutions 1790-1990," *History of Political Thought* 16, no. 1 (Spring, 1995): 77-104. For a whirlwind tour of the overall importance of Montesquieu in the aftermath of all the revolutions of 1989, see M. Steven Fish, "Postcommunist Subversion: Social Science and Democratization in East Europe and Eurasia," *Slavic Review* 58, no. 4 (Winter, 1999): 794-823. "The theorists who furnish the surest guidance," Fish asserts, "turn out to be Montesquieu and James Madison" (at 805). Fish credits Montesquieu and Madison, and also Tocqueville and Durkheim, with furnishing "profound and useful insights into the difficulties and advantages of dispersing state power and of controlling executive authority" while also comprehending the importance of "intermediary associations for democracy" (at 821-22).

89. *Pensée* 235 (1893), in Pléiade, II, 1048.

90. See Barère, *Montesquieu peint d'après ses ouvrages*, in Barny, "Montesquieu patriote?" (at 91).

91. Rebecca Kingston ably sketches out this point of view in chapter 9 of this volume.

92. For an intriguing and insightful exploration of the linkages between Montesquieu and both Tocquevelle and Dilthey, see Roger Boesche "Why could Tocqueville predict so well?" *Political Theory* 2, no. 1 (February, 1983): 79-103.

93. Jean Ehrard, "Comment lire *L'Esprit des lois*?" in *Actes du Colloque international commémorant le 250ème anniversaire de la parution de 'L'Esprit des lois'*, 494. Although the French failed to translate the theory of separate powers into practice during their revolutionary struggles, they did not fail to write into Article 16 of the Declaration of the Rights of Man and of the Citizen the following axiom: "Every society in which the guarantee of rights is not assured nor the separaton of powers determined, has no constitu-

tion." Translated from *Droits de l'homme et philosophie. Une anthologie, textes choisis et présentés par Frédéric Worms* (Paris: Presses Pocket, 1993), 75.

94. In addition to Cecil Courtney's forceful presentation of this theme in chapter 1 of this volume, see Mark Waddicor, *Montesquieu and the Philosophy of Natural Law* (The Hague: Martinus Nijhoff, 1970).

95. See Mark Hulliung, *Montesquieu and the Old Regime* (Berkeley: University of California Press, 1976).

96. During the Revolution Bertrand Barère interpreted Montesquieu as a republican at heart and treated his account of monarchy as satirical. See Barère, *Montesquieu peint d'après ses ouvrages*, s.1, an V, 71-72, cited in Shackleton, *Montesquieu*, 276. Destutt de Tracy, on the other hand, read him as a fierce critic of democracy, asserting that Montesquieu describes democracy as just as "insupportable and almost as absurd" as despotism. See Destutt de Tracy, *A Commentary and Review of Montesquieu's Spirit of Laws*, 25.

Chapter One

Montesquieu and Natural Law

C. P. Courtney

Montesquieu's proud insistence on the originality of the *Spirit of Laws*, the title page of which carries the epigraph "Prolem sine matre creatam"[1] was certainly justified; no one before him had ever undertaken a work devoted to quite the same project which, in his own words from the preface, was to demonstrate that "I have first of all considered mankind; and the result of my thoughts has been, that, amidst such an infinite diversity of laws and manners, they were not solely conducted by the caprice of fancy."[2] That is to say, that underlying the apparently chaotic variety of laws and customs in human societies, past and present, it was possible to find an intelligible pattern.

To acknowledge Montesquieu's originality does not mean of course that we should study him in isolation from his predecessors or, like so many of his commentators from Comte and Durkheim to Althusser, assume that he was a man so much ahead of his time that he can only be understood in the light of the principles of nineteenth- or twentieth-century positivist sociology or Marxism.[3] On the contrary, to appreciate his originality we need to study him, at least initially, in the context of the intellectual debate of the period concerning the kind of problem to which he proposes a solution. This is essentially the problem of whether, in the study of jurisprudence, it makes sense to speak of natural law, that is to say of a law which defines an immutable and universal standard of justice by which all positive laws should be judged, or whether in fact there is no such thing as natural law (at least not in the sense of a moral law) and that positive laws are simply to be seen as a matter of convention.[4]

This was a debate with a long history that can be traced back through the Middle Ages to ancient Greece and Rome. Plato, the Stoics, and Cicero were among those who in the ancient world had upheld the idea of a universal and absolute law of justice. Aquinas had redefined it in a form acceptable to the teachings of the Roman Catholic Church, and in the seventeenth century Grotius had founded the modern school of natural law, the main achievement of which was to free jurisprudence from the theology of the medieval Schoolmen and to base it on unaided human reason. Opposed to this was a long tradition of skeptical thought represented in the ancient world by the Sophists, Carneades, and Sextus Empiricus and, among the moderns, by Montaigne, Charron, and Pascal. These thinkers argued that speculations about natural law were not exempt from their general belief in man's incapacity to establish anything with intellectual certainty. Cultural diversity, it was argued, illustrated not only human illogicality (why should laws be different, sometimes even from one village to the next or one year to the next?) but also, if one takes into account that many laws and customs are revolting and cruel, that any talk of a higher universal standard of justice relevant to human behavior is no more than metaphysical nonsense. It should be accepted, therefore, that men are governed, not by reason, but by prejudice, self-interest, or indeed, by mere caprice.

Montesquieu was certainly familiar with the traditional skeptical argument, particularly as it was reported (with abundant repetitions of the key terms "diversity" and "the caprice of fancy") in the pages of the standard authorities on modern natural law, Grotius, Pufendorf, and Barbeyrac.[5] He was also familiar with the opposition to the natural law jurists by Hobbes and Spinoza. Hobbes was interpreted as an author who asserted boldly that the only laws were positive laws; Spinoza as a philosopher whose naturalism simply dissolved all moral distinctions.[6]

To counter skepticism and relativism was one of the aims of the modern natural law jurists. This they did, at least to their own satisfaction, by setting out to prove that the precepts of natural law and natural right were propositions which, if we use our God-given reason correctly, we can deduce by the rules of logic from "the nature of things" (that is to say from their ideal nature) and which therefore have the same certainty as the propositions of mathematics. Thus Grotius wrote:

> To begin with Natural Right, it consists in certain principles of Right Reason, which enable us to know whether an action is morally honest or dishonest, according to the necessary fitness or unfitness it has with a reasonable and sociable nature, and consequently whether God, who is the Author of Nature, orders or forbids such an action (I, i, §10).

Similar definitions can be found in Pufendorf and Barbeyrac. Pufendorf speaks, for example, of "the honest and the dishonest character of human actions which result from the fitness or unfitness of these actions judged by a certain rule or the law" (I, ii, §6). Barbeyrac states that the principles of natural law "have their basis in the nature of things, in the very constitution of mankind, from whence there result certain relations between such and such an action and the nature of a reasonable and sociable animal."[7] It would be easy to give further examples. Variations on the same definition, in terms of "necessary relations," "relations of fitness and unfitness" and "the nature of things" can be found not only in the later followers of Grotius and Pufendorf (for example Cumberland and Burlamaqui), but also in most of the rationalist philosophers of the period, particularly Malebranche, Leibniz, and Clarke.[8] Mention should also be made of Locke, who was frequently quoted in this context on account of his assertion that it was possible to "place morality amongst the sciences capable of demonstration."[9]

This optimistic view of the possibility of establishing ethics as an exact science is based on the presupposition that the universe has a rational structure and that the relations things bear to one another within this structure can be discerned by means of logical deduction. Thus from the nature of a triangle one can deduce that the sum of the angles equals two right angles, and from the nature of a circle that the circumference bears a certain set relation to the radius. Likewise, from the nature of man, defined as "a reasonable and sociable being" ("un être raisonnable et sociable"), we can deduce necessary relations ("rapports nécessaires") of fitness and unfitness ("convenance et disconvenance"), which are moral relations analogous to the relations of mathematics.[10]

It would be misleading, however, to give the impression that, among those who accepted the general principles of natural law, there was agreement on every point. Rationalists in the realist tradition might argue with Grotius that the principles of justice are inherent in the nature of things and are not therefore to be understood as the command of a superior, so that even if God did not exist, they would still remain valid. Others, like Pufendorf and Barbeyrac, might argue that Grotius had misleadingly implied that God was not free to will what was good and that in any case there could be no obligation to pursue what was morally good (even if it were perceived by unaided reason) unless it had been commanded by God.[11] It is unnecessary, however, to examine in detail these somewhat scholastic discussions, except to note that Montesquieu would find himself attacked by religious critics as a "Spinosiste" on account of his defining laws in a way very similar to Grotius.

Another point on which there was disagreement concerned Grotius' conviction that the principles of natural law could be proved, not only by logical deduction from the nature of things, but from the fact of universal consent.[12] This second method was rejected in no uncertain terms by Pufendorf, Barbeyrac, and their followers, who pointed out that, in the first place, there simply was no universal consent on questions of morals and, secondly, that even if there were, this was no guarantee of truth. Moral philosophers and natural law jurists should therefore only accept as true those propositions that were clearly demonstrable *a priori* according to agreed rational and logical criteria.[13]

Where, in this kind of philosophical enquiry, one may ask—and this was the question Montesquieu would ask—do positive laws fit in? By accepting the criterion of universal consent, Grotius had, in a way, attempted to make positive laws, or at least some of them, respectable; but the authority attributed to universal consent had been rejected by his successors. What we are left with, then, is the somewhat stark affirmation that since natural law provides the standard by which positive laws are to be judged, no positive law ought to deviate from this standard. And if whole nations have positive laws which do so deviate, this can be accounted for by ignorance or by the fact that in some countries people misguidedly prefer vice to virtue. Whatever the skeptics may say, however, as far as the natural lawyers are concerned, this no more invalidates the rules of eternal justice than the inability of some people to count invalidates the rules of mathematics.[14]

It would be easy to think of the natural law jurists as metaphysicians who have lost contact with empirical reality, especially if one follows the various ways in which some of them develop and elaborate their theories of the state of nature and the social contract. It would also be possible to stress the subversive and revolutionary potential of these theories. There can be no doubt, however, that, with the exception of Locke, natural law thinkers were interpreted, at least in the eighteenth century, as expressing fairly conservative opinions. As for the perception of their being lost in the clouds of metaphysics or distancing themselves from empirical reality, they may indeed give this impression when attempting to refute the skeptics, but generally speaking they saw the task of the legislator as a practical one, a matter of framing laws which, while respecting the basic rules of justice, must take into account such diverse matters as time, place and general circumstances and the general character of the people.[15] The natural law jurists did not normally pronounce on whether monarchy, aristocracy, or democracy is, in the abstract, the best form of government. For each form, they believe, may be compatible with good laws. Nor did they overlook the fact that in every state there are laws concerning purely practical arrangements (such as weights and measures) or that there are matters (such as divorce and polygamy) where natural law does not give unequivocal guidance. In such cases, they believed, the best solution was simply to conform to the established laws of one's country. Legislators should be practical-minded persons guided by prudence, which Pufendorf defined as "a habit of acting in conformity with right reason in those things which we perceive as good or bad."[16]

A careful reading of Pufendorf and Barbeyrac reveals that in certain passages of their writings there is apparent what might be described as a drift toward a charitable view of what human beings have achieved in the course of history. Without going as far as Grotius in basing natural law on consent, they expressed rather tentatively the opinion that existing positive laws embody at least the rudiments of natural law. Pufendorf believed that human beings have implanted in them "an internal restraint" which is designed to discourage them from wickedness. He expressed this point as follows:

For all civil laws presuppose, or contain, at least the principal heads of Natural Law, without the observation of which the human species could not be preserved, and which are in no way destroyed by the particular laws which the interest of each civil society requires to be added to them (II, iii, §11).

Barbeyrac, who had an optimistic outlook on human nature, stated that knowledge of the precepts of natural law, far from being reserved for the meditations of profound philosophers, is inscribed on the hearts of all human beings, to whom the Creator has given naturally virtuous inclinations.[17] It is not surprising then, that he believed that positive laws embodied something of this God-given moral awareness: "History appears to show," he wrote, "that the peoples who seem to have had no sentiment of virtue, are very few in number." He follows this with a quotation from Bayle to the effect that "no legislator has been able to pass laws which were all bad."[18]

While we find in these writers a tendency to judge positive laws with considerable sympathy and also a readiness to anticipate Montesquieu in believing that men are not invariably governed by "the caprice of fancy," there is no suggestion that man-made laws might be treated systematically in the same way as natural laws. Grotius had stated this in a way which must have seemed unanswerable:

> For Natural Laws being always the same, can easily be brought under the rules of art: but those which owe their origin to some human establishment being different according to place, and changing often in the same place, do not lend themselves to systematic treatment, any more than other ideas of particular things.[19]

Pufendorf agreed and contended that positive law cannot be deduced from the nature of things:

> Positive Law is law which is not founded on the general constitution of human nature, but purely and simply on the will of the legislator. . . . The reasons on which positive laws are based are derived, not from the universal constitution of the human species, but from the particular advantage of each society and from an advantage which sometimes is only a short-term one (I, vi, §18).

Barbeyrac shared this view, asserting that positive law

> concerns things indifferent in themselves, or which are not based on the constitution of our nature, and which consequently can be regulated in different ways according to time, place and other circumstances; all this, as it is judged appropriate by a superior, whose will is the only basis of this kind of law which, for this reason, is called arbitrary.[20]

One can conclude from such statements that the natural lawyers had not really provided a convincing refutation of the skeptics. In the final analysis, positive laws, it would seem, are arbitrary. Accordingly, there was no possibility of setting up a science of positive law since, unlike natural law, this was something which could not be deduced from "the nature of things," that is to say from the constitution of human nature.

It is against this background provided by discussion among natural law theorists that we should read Montesquieu's bold statement in the preface to *The Spirit of Laws* that he will demonstrate, in the light of principles drawn "from the nature of things," that he has discovered how positive laws in all their diversity can be made the object of systematic study:

> I have laid down the first principles, and have found that the particular cases apply naturally to them; that the histories of all nations are only consequences of them; and that every particular law is connected with another law, or depends on some other of a more general extent.

Montesquieu was clearly proposing to do something which had never been done before and which had been pronounced impossible by the greatest authorities on natural jurisprudence.

Natural Law in Montesquieu's Early Writings

Before passing to *The Spirit of Laws* it will be of interest to examine briefly Montesquieu's views on natural law as expressed in some of his earlier works. There can be no doubt that, from the beginning, he was drawn to the problem posed by the skeptics. Within the *Persian Letters* he constructs the fable of the Troglodytes (Letters 11-14) to examine the question of whether human beings were born to be virtuous and whether justice is a quality as natural to them as their existence. The first part of the fable, describing a community where individuals follow their selfish interest without regard to any moral principles, was designed to show that a society lacking in justice will inevitably perish. The second part describes a community where individuals are naturally virtuous and where the result is idyllic perfection. The story has a continuation[21] which introduces a more realistic note: even if people are naturally virtuous, it is unrealistic to expect them to live forever in an idyllic society where everyone conforms spontaneously and effortlessly to the rules of justice; it is necessary, therefore, to introduce the legal apparatus of civil society. The fable is usually interpreted, probably correctly, as a variation on the theme of the state of nature. It rejects the theory of Hobbes that this is a state where people are naturally wicked. If they are not naturally wicked, however, neither are they morally perfect, and this imperfection, along with the fact that, as time passes, society will become more complex, requires that the rules of justice should be given concrete embodiment in laws and political institutions.[22]

More interesting than this rather tentative exploration of certain aspects of the theory of the state of nature and the establishment of civil society is Letter 83, written by Usbek, where we find a discussion of the nature of justice. First there is the argument that God, if he exists, must necessarily be just: "If there is a God . . . he must necessarily be just: for if he were not just, he would be the most wicked and most imperfect of all beings." Justice is then defined as "a relation of fitness, which really exists between two things" and this relationship "is always the same, whichever being considers it, whether God, an angel or a man."[23] This definition, as has been seen, was a commonplace of seventeenth- and eighteenth-century rationalist ethical thought.

Judging from his reference to English liberty in Letter 104, Montesquieu was also familiar with the more radical implications of the natural law jurists' theory of the state of nature and the social contract. Usbek writes in this letter:

> But, if a prince, far from making his subjects happy, wants to overwhelm and destroy them, the basis for obedience ceases: nothing binds them, nothing attaches them to the prince: and they re-enter the state of natural freedom.[24]

It would be a mistake, on the evidence of the letters, which have been quoted, to assume that Montesquieu at this stage was completely convinced by the arguments of the modern natural law thinkers. In Letter 83 which, as we have seen, opens with the words, "If there is a God," Usbek is not quite certain whether God actually exists, and the principle of justice is presented as no more than an hypothesis which we ought to accept even if there is no God:

> So, if there were no God, we should still love justice; that is to say do our utmost to resemble that being of whom we have such a beautiful idea and who, if he existed, would necessarily be just.[25]

Nor does Usbek exactly convince us that he has overcome these obvious intellectual doubts when, in the same letter, he states complacently that it is consoling for us to know that the rules of justice are inscribed on the hearts of all men,[26] for the reader will not have forgotten that this self-proclaimed apologist for absolute standards of justice is a domestic tyrant, the owner of a harem where, for his personal pleasure and in defiance of anything remotely resembling natural justice, men are physically mutilated and women enslaved. In fact, the only person in the *Persian Letters* who follows the rules of justice is Usbek's favourite wife, Roxane, who leads a revolt in the harem and justifies it by an appeal to nature: "I have reformed your laws on the model of those of Nature," she writes defiantly in the final letter to her absent husband,[27] to whom, needless to say, it had never occurred that the theory of the right of resistance would have been heard of in the harems of Persia or had any relevance to his private affairs. Roxane rebels and finds herself in the state of natural liberty. This is no more than an heroic gesture, however, and since there is obviously no way forward, she commits suicide.

The *Persian Letters* should be read as work of moral satire, not as a treatise on morals or jurisprudence, and obviously one should beware of attributing to Montesquieu every opinion expressed by his Persians or their correspondents. However, it is probably true to say that at this stage he was by no means convinced by the arguments against the skeptics. In its very conception the work is a variation on the skeptical theme of satirizing irrational behavior, and the device of playing off against each other the conflicting and incommensurable opinions of East and West had implications subversive of all accepted values. This, along with the doubts attributed to Usbek and the suicide of the only real ethical rationalist in the work, suggests that, at the time he composed the *Persian Letters,* Montesquieu remained within the tradition of skepticism.[28]

The next work of Montesquieu's relevant to his interest in natural law is the *Treatise on Duties,* which dates from 1725. Unfortunately, it is known to us only from a contemporary report, from a list of the chapter headings and from certain fragments preserved in the *Pensées.*[29] From this fragmentary material, however, it is possible to reconstruct the plan of the work which, although allegedly inspired by Cicero's *De Officiis,* is actually closely modelled on Pufendorf's *De Officio hominis et civis,* first published in 1673.[30] There is no doubt that, at this stage, Montesquieu had become an unequivocal supporter of natural law, both in its early form as elaborated by the Stoics and by Cicero, as well as in its more modern form as presented by Grotius, Pufendorf and Barbeyrac. A section of the *Treatise* expresses his admiration for the Stoics. As for the moderns, his debt to them is particularly obvious when he reproduces their standard formula that justice "is based on the existence and the sociability of rational beings" and when he follows them in attacking Hobbes and Spinoza.[31]

The *Treatise on Duties* is particularly interesting in that some parts of it display parallels with certain passages in the first chapter of *The Spirit of Laws.*[32] There can be no doubt that, at this stage, Montesquieu had made up his mind about the main principles of natural justice. He was still a long way from having anything new to say about positive law, however. Indeed, he seemed at times to speak like the skeptics, for example when he devoted a chapter to demonstrating how natural law had been ignored by the Spaniards in their conquest of South America or when he declared that the course of history is unintelligible (or at least totally unpredictable) since human beings are governed mainly by caprice.[33] As for the question of different forms of government, what we find in the *Treatise* is no more than a repetition of the opinion generally accepted by the natural law jurists:

Chance and the character of those who were in agreement have established as many different forms of government as there are peoples: all good, since they represent the will of the parties to the contract.[34]

The *Treatise on Duties* was left unfinished, as were several other projected works of this period, a period when Montesquieu seems to have been interested in an enormous array of subjects (scientific, philosophical, political, and literary), but without any clearly defined aim.[35] Eventually he turned his attention to the history of Rome and in 1734 published the *Considerations on the Causes of the Greatness of the Romans and on their Decline*. By then he had clearly changed his mind on the subject of history. Rejecting his earlier assertion that it is composed of unintelligible events, he maintained that it could be explained in terms of physical and moral causation. There can be no doubt that this methodology is relevant to *The Spirit of Laws*, as are various ideas expressed in the *Treatise on Duties* and other unfinished works of the period. From this it would be easy to assume that Montesquieu was now ready to write what would become his major work. There is no evidence, however, that this was so. He had not yet discovered the "principles" which would enable him to make sense of cultural diversity. But once he was in possession of these principles, he tells us in the preface to *The Spirit of Laws*, his researches over a period of twenty years, often ill-focused and apparently leading nowhere, were seen in a new perspective and everything fell into place: "But when I had once discovered my first principles," he asserted, "everything I sought for appeared."

Book I of *The Spirit of Laws*

The first book of the *The Spirit of Laws* opens with a definition of laws in general:

Laws, in their most general signification, are the necessary relations arising from the nature of things. In this sense, all beings have their laws; the Deity his laws, the material world its laws, the intelligences superior to man their laws, the beasts their laws, man his laws (I, 1).

This definition, in terms of "the nature of things" and "necessary relations" is a variant of the standard natural law definitions to which reference has already been made.[36] Modern readers may be puzzled by the fact that Montesquieu obviously expected his definition to apply to both the laws of science and to those of morals, thus giving the impression that he is confusing the descriptive and the normative. It was not unusual in the eighteenth century, however, to use the expression "laws of nature" in this way. The assumption which made this possible is that the laws of morals are analogous to those of physics and mathematics because they all refer to the rational order of the cosmos.[37] Montesquieu made it clear, however, in a section at the end of the chapter, that he was perfectly aware of the difference between the laws of the natural scientist and those of the moralist.[38]

As far as moral laws are concerned, Montesquieu's implication is that even God is bound by the laws of reason:

> Thus the creation, which seems an arbitrary act, supposes laws as invariable as those of the fatality of the atheists. It would be absurd to say that the Creator might govern the world without those rules, since without them it could not subsist (I, 1).

He may have chosen this anti-voluntarist formulation to stress that the inquiry he meant to conduct is along strictly rationalist lines and that laws (including positive laws) are not merely the product of the will of the legislator. The choice of this formulation, however, laid him open to the kind of objections that Pufendorf and Barbeyrac had made to Grotius' definitions and to violent attacks from some contemporary critics (including ecclesiastics) for whom any apparent limitations placed on God's will indicated a form of "fatalisme" or "Spinosisme."[39] Montesquieu, had little patience with this kind of accusation which he obviously regarded as irrelevant to his enterprise (a work on political theory, not on theology) and which, with indignation and contempt, as well as reasoned argument, he brushed aside in the *Defense of The Spirit of Laws* (1750).[40]

After his preliminary definitions Montesquieu devoted a brief paragraph to the invariable laws of nature as they apply to the physical universe, and he then moved on to consideration of the laws governing the world of intelligent beings, stressing (with Hobbes in mind) what he considers the absurdity of supposing that there are no laws but positive laws:

> Before laws were made, there were relations of possible justice. To say that there is nothing just or unjust, but what is commanded or forbidden by positive laws, is the same as saying that, before the describing of a circle, all the radii were not equal (I, 1).

This is followed by a number of textbook examples similar to those which any reader can find in the pages of Grotius, Pufendorf, and Barbeyrac:

> We must therefore acknowledge relations of justice antecedent to the positive law by which they are established: as for instance, that, if human societies existed, it would be right to conform to their laws; if there were intelligent beings that had received a benefit of another being, they ought to show their gratitude; if one intelligent being had created another intelligent being, the latter ought to continue in its original state of dependence; if one intelligent being injured another, it deserves a retaliation; and so on (I, 1).

This logical pattern in relations of justice is subject to disruption, however, because human beings belong to two worlds. As physical beings we are subject to the invariable laws of the material universe, but as intelligent beings we do not always obey the laws of morals, partly on account of ignorance or weakness, but also because we are endowed with free will and often choose to follow the promptings of the non-rational side of our nature. Hence Montesquieu's conclusion to the chapter:

> Such a being might every instant forget his Creator; God has therefore reminded him of his duty by the laws of religion. Such a being is liable every moment to forget himself; philosophy has provided against this by the laws of morality. Formed to live in society, he might forget his fellow-creatures; legislators have, therefore, by political and civil laws, confined him to his duty (I, 1).

After presenting these largely traditional definitions and reflections in the first chapter of Book I, Montesquieu devoted a second chapter to "The Laws of Nature," by which he meant, in this context, laws "which derive from the constitution of our being," that is to say, the basic laws of human nature which can be deduced logically from the definition of what (ideally) we are. To arrive at an understanding of these laws he uses the fiction of the state of nature. The essential problem which he examines here has not changed since he had written the story of the Troglodytes: was man, in the state of nature, fundamentally wicked, as Hobbes would have it? Or was he, as described by Pufendorf and Locke, a sociable creature equipped with reason and moral awareness? Once again, Montesquieu rejected the Hobbesean theory, arguing that Hobbes had made a mistake in logic and psychology by attributing to natural man the kind of aggressive behavior (going about armed and always locking the door of his house) which presupposed that civil society was already in existence. As for the picture of the state of nature found in Pufendorf and Locke, Montesquieu implied that they had made a similar mistake when they assumed that pre-social man was a fully developed "reasonable and sociable being" equipped with a rational awareness of the higher moral law.

Montesquieu's description of the state of nature is original. Anticipating Rousseau's *Discourse on the Origins of Inequality among Mankind* (1754) and *The Social Contract* (1762),[41] he transformed the implications of the theory of the state of nature by introducing the dimension of time and the concept of development:

> Man, in a state of nature, would have the faculty of knowing before he had acquired any knowledge. Plain it is that his first ideas would not be of a speculative nature: he would think of the preservation of his being before he would investigate its origin (I, 2).

This means that natural man was governed, not by reason, but by instinct, an instinct which induced him, not to attack others, but simply to seek to preserve himself and the species. For Montesquieu peace, feeding oneself and attraction to the opposite sex are the basic laws of nature. Since natural law in the state of nature refers to instinct, it has been argued that throughout *The Spirit of Laws* it is a law without normative content and that Montesquieu has assimilated it to purely descriptive law.[42] Indeed, if we read no further in this second chapter we might be convinced that this is so. However, if we read on, we shall find that while it is true that pre-social man is governed by instinct, there comes a point where, having become a sociable creature endowed with reason, he becomes aware of natural law[43] (and also, Montesquieu tells us, of the existence of God).[44] That this is the correct interpretation is confirmed by a later passage of *The Spirit of Laws* where Montesquieu distinguished "the law of nature, which makes everything tend to the preservation of the species," from "the law of natural reason, which teaches us to do to others what we would have done to ourselves" (X, 3). He had a similar distinction in mind when he wrote, in his fragmentary *Essay on the Causes Affecting Minds and Characters*: "Those who are born among an uncivilized people have only, strictly speaking, ideas relating to self-preservation; they live in an eternal night with regard to the rest."[45]

In the final chapter of Book I we learn that the development of man's social instinct leads to conflict: "As soon as mankind enter into a state of society, they lose the sense of their weakness; equality ceases, and then commences the state of war" (I, 3). Now that man has become a rational and sociable creature, however, it is unnatural (against the higher moral law) for him to live in a state of anarchy. He therefore creates civil society.[46] This transition to civil society, however it comes about (there is no direct mention of social contract in Montesquieu)[47] is, as in Rousseau, a transition in which the independence and equality appropriate to the state of nature are exchanged for the liberty and equality of the citizen. This is reinforced in later parts of the work:

> In the state of nature indeed, all men are born equal; but they cannot continue in this equality: society makes them lose it, and they recover it only by the protection of the laws (VIII, 3).

> As men have given up their natural independence to live under political laws, they have given up the natural community of property to live under civil laws. By the first, they acquired liberty; by the second, property (XXVI, 15).

Montesquieu classifies these different kinds of laws as follows: the law of nations, political laws, and civil laws. One thing all these forms of laws have in common is that they are applications of human reason to circumstances: "Law in general is human reason, inasmuch as it governs all the inhabitants of the earth;

the political and civil laws of each nation ought to be only the particular cases in which human reason is applied" (I, 1). None of the natural law jurists would have disagreed with this definition, nor would they have been surprised at the content of the next short paragraph: "They should be adapted in such a manner to the people for whom they are framed, that it is a great chance if those of one nation suit another" (I, 1).

However, the next section outlines a project, which is new and unprecedented:

> They should be relative to the nature and principle of each government; whether they form it, as may be said of political laws; or whether they support it, as is the case of civil institutions.
>
> They should be relative to the climate of each country, to the quality of its soil, to its situation and extent, to the principal occupation of the natives, whether husbandmen, huntsmen or shepherds; they should have a relation to the degree of liberty which the constitution will bear, to the religion of the inhabitants, to their inclinations, riches, numbers, commerce, manners, and customs. In fine, they have relations to each other, as also to their origin, to the intent of the legislator, and to the order of things on which they are established; in all which different lights they ought to be considered.
>
> This is what I have undertaken to perform in the following work. These relations I shall examine, since all these together constitute what I call THE SPIRIT OF LAWS (I, 3).

To understand the full meaning of this program we must read the books that follow, first those that are devoted to the different forms of government (II-XIII), then those on environmental and other factors (XIV-XXVI). However, it is useful to note at this stage that Montesquieu considered the first series more important than the second:

> I shall first examine the relations which laws have to the nature and principle of each government: and, as this principle has a strong influence on laws, I shall make it my study to understand it thoroughly; and, if I can but once establish it, the laws will soon appear to flow from thence as from their source. I shall proceed afterwards to other more particular relations (I, 3).

The Nature and Principle of Governments

Books II and III, devoted to Montesquieu's classification of three different forms of government (republic, monarchy, and despotism,) can be summarized rapidly. Each is first defined in terms of its "nature" or essential characteristics which make it what it is. A republic is a form of government where power is in the hands of the few (aristocracy) or the many (democracy). In a monarchy it is in the hands of one man, but there are fixed laws, and the power of the monarch is limited by the existence of intermediary bodies and a repository of laws. In despotism, power is in the hands of one man who rules according to his personal whim. Each of these three forms of government has what Montesquieu calls its "principle," which can be deduced from its "nature." In republics the principle is virtue, that is to say good citizenship and love of one's country. In monarchy it is honor, which is respect for ranks and distinctions, and in despotism the principle is fear. The next eight books (III-X) are devoted to further deductions from the nature and principle of each form, covering such areas as education, criminal law, luxury, the position of women in society, and relations with other countries; these are followed by three books (XI-XIII) on laws related to political and civil liberty.

What Montesquieu offers in this typology is a kind of logical grammar of forms of government. Each is defined as a kind of geometrical figure composed of "necessary relations." For example, beginning with a definition of democracy as a form of government in which the body of the people has the supreme power, he argues that it follows logically that the laws that establish the right of suffrage are fundamental. It also follows logically that there should be laws defining the number of citizens who are to form the public assemblies and, since some matters must be delegated to ministers, it is logical that they should be chosen by the people. Again, from the definition of democracy one can deduce that the "principle" must be virtue, which means a high sense of civic responsibility and a willingness to participate in public affairs, without which democracy would be meaningless. It is logical that in a democracy education should encourage commitment to public life. It is likewise logical that in this form of government encouragement should be given to equality and frugality, and this has implications for a vast area of laws, including those covering such matters as distribution of wealth, taxation, and inheritance.

As for monarchy, Montesquieu demonstrates that by the rules of logic certain consequences follow from its very definition. Monarchy implies an hierarchical society based on respect for rank (honor) and, since the king rules in accordance with established laws, it follows that there must be a repository of laws. Needless to say, education in monarchies should encourage respect for social rank. In addition, in this form of government neither social equality nor frugality is to be encouraged. Indeed the production of luxury goods is necessary to satisfy the rich and to provide work for the poor. As for despotism, which is the rule of naked power, it implies by definition no stable political institutions and no restraint on the despot. All that is required from the citizen is obedience based on fear.

A striking aspect of these books is how Montesquieu, drawing on his reading of history as well as travel literature and his own first-hand experience, shows a remarkably wide knowledge of the customs of primitive peoples and of regimes ancient and modern. It is no doubt this wealth of factual information that has led many commentators to suppose that he is writing here as a positivist sociologist, whose method consists in working from facts to principles. However, this is a serious misunderstanding: Montesquieu's typologies of the different forms of government, though obviously inspired by what he knew about real republics, monarchies, and despotisms, have the status of abstract models or ideal types, not of factual accounts or descriptive generalizations.[48] Thus, he writes at the end of Book III:

> Such are the principles of the three sorts of government: which does not imply, that, in a particular republic, they actually are, but that they ought to be, virtuous: nor does it prove, that, in a particular monarchy, they are actuated by honor; or, in a particular despotic government, by fear; but that they ought to be directed by these principles. Otherwise the government is imperfect (III, 11).

In this respect Montesquieu remains faithful to the *a priori* method of the natural law jurists, who were familiar with the use of models, such as natural man and the state of nature, and knew that these models were abstractions. However, it does not seem to have occurred to them that from the definition of the nature of different forms of government it would be possible to deduce systematically the political and civil laws appropriate to each. Montesquieu's originality lies in his understanding of this possibility. Deductions drawn merely from each form of government would not have taken him very far, however, if he had not arrived at the idea of the "principle" and replaced the traditional monolithic view of man as a rational and social being by a more flexible view corresponding to different possibilities of human nature: man governed by virtue, by honor, or by fear. Once he had grasped the necessary relation of the form of each kind of government to its principle, Montesquieu could construct models describing in considerable detail the political and social life of each of his three kinds of man.[49]

These models made it possible for Montesquieu to explain and evaluate laws and political institutions of the past and of his own day. He could see, for example, the logic that lies behind the traditional French monarchy with its nobility and clergy (intermediary powers) and its Parlements (repositories of laws). He could also see that this form of government is subject to corruption if the monarch reduces the powers of the intermediary bodies and the Parlements or undermines the principle of honor. And such, he implies, had been the policy of Louis XIV, so that France was well on the way to despotism. The models also help to explain to the contemporary reader certain laws of other cultures which seem bizarre. Why, for example, should the Athenians have inflicted the death penalty on a foreigner who attempted to take part in the legislative assembly? The answer is that, in the context of democracy, this was a usurpation of sovereignty and therefore, quite logically, liable to the most severe punishment.[50]

Such examples demonstrate (and it is one of the key themes of *The Spirit of Laws*) that men are not governed entirely by caprice and that in the real world positive laws often approximate to the logic which the philosopher can deduce from the nature of things. Montesquieu finds that logic and historical examples are frequently in agreement and thus, on occasion, he can write: "What I have here advanced is confirmed by the unanimous testimony of historians, and is extremely agreeable to the nature of things" (III, 3). He does not go so far as Adam Smith, however, according to whom "Every system of positive law may be regarded as a more or less imperfect attempt towards a system of natural jurisprudence, or towards an enumeration of the particular rules of justice."[51] If Montesquieu did not share this optimism, at least not quite in this form, it was because he was aware of the existence of the unnatural, particularly as embodied in despotism, a form of government by which the majority of the earth's population were governed. For even despotism had its own terrifying logic[52] and could be seen (to adapt Adam Smith) as an attempt toward a system of the unnatural.

It is obvious that Montesquieu's typologies, like all typologies, offer only simplified models. All that they tell us is how "pure" republics, monarchies, or despotisms would function, if there were no other factors influencing them. But, of course, he is aware that there are other factors, to which he refers at the end of Book I, chapter 3, and which include climate, geography, demography, religion, trade, customs, manners, and the "general spirit."

It is especially when Montesquieu is discussing these factors that he gives the reader the impression that he is a positivist sociologist, and indeed he certainly attempts a scientific approach when, in the first chapters of Book XIV, he reports on his experiment on the effects of hot and cold on a sheep's tongue. However, it is a long way from this rather crude experiment to the new series of abstract models based on his conviction that there is a "necessary relation" between, for example, liberty in the north and servitude in the south, large territories and despotism and small territories and republics, or that Protestantism is more compatible than Roman Catholicism with the liberty of the citizen.

These models have often been criticized because of their alleged factual inaccuracy.[53] Once again, however, one must distinguish between an abstract model and a factual description. This was understood by Jean-Jacques Rousseau, who remarked in defense of Montesquieu in *The Social Contract:*

> Let us always distinguish general laws from particular causes, which can alter their effect. If the whole of the South were covered with republics, and the whole of the North with despotic states, it would be no less true that, by the effect of climate, despotism is best suited to hot countries, barbarism to cold countries, and good government to the intermediate regions.[54]

And Rousseau added the following important methodological statement:

I can see that in accepting the principle, there can be disagreement about how it is to be applied: it can be said that there are cold countries which are very fertile and southern ones that are very arid. But this is a difficulty only for those who do not take all the different relations between things into account.

Rousseau, who at the beginning of his *Discourse on the Origins of Inequality* wrote, "Let us begin by setting aside all the facts," fully understood the explanatory and evaluative power of simplified models, such as his own model of natural man. He also understood that they are valid only for pure cases and that it is essential to study "the thing in all its relations." This was precisely what Montesquieu proposed to do, examining several factors in succession and then finally, in Book XIX, chapter 4, attempting a synthesis in his theory of the "general spirit":

Mankind are influenced by various causes: by the climate, by the religion, by the laws, by the maxims of government, by precedents, morals, and customs; from whence is formed a general spirit of nations.

Natural Law as the Proper Guide for Human Actions

Montesquieu's theory, culminating in Book XIX, that life in civil society is shaped by a multitude of factors, physical and moral, might suggest that we have now come a long way from anything related to natural law. But this is not so. In fact it is especially in the chapters devoted to climate and environment that he speaks of the duties of the legislator, who is by no means seen as a mere instrument dominated by factors beyond his control. Significantly, chapter 5 of Book XIV is entitled, "That those are bad legislators who favour the vices of the climate, and good legislators who oppose those vices," a useful reminder that, while Montesquieu believed that the various factors that make up the "general spirit" have an enormous influence on our lives, he was not an environmental determinist, if by this one means that human beings have absolutely no freedom of choice. His considered view on such factors is that environmental factors, particularly the basic ones of climate and geographical situation, are most influential on primitive and unenlightened peoples. It is in this sense that he writes in chapter 14 of Book XIX: "the empire of climate is the first of all empires."

If Montesquieu believed, however, that it is possible for people in some way to override environmental factors, or at least the more basic ones, does it follow that he believed they do so in order to conform to the norms of natural law? There may seem to be some ambiguity here, since he usually insisted that the legislator should respect the "general spirit" and, if this spirit is merely the sum of environmental factors, it might be argued that this is still a form of determinism. But it is essential not to overlook the fact that human intelligence (which implies awareness of the rational principles of natural law) is part of the equation. Awareness of the factors that shape our life in society enables us to act in such a way that we can manipulate these factors or even oppose them. Montesquieu's ideal legislator is one who like Solon, while realizing that he cannot legislate against the grain and must take the "general spirit" into account, at the same time strives to introduce enlightened reforms:

> Solon being asked if the laws he had given to the Athenians were the best, he replied, "I have given them the best they were able to bear." A fine expression that ought to be perfectly understood by all legislators! (XIX, 21).

The kind of reforms Montesquieu refers to here must of course be gradual and acknowledge the existence of all the relevant circumstances. This has led to the misunderstanding that he is not really a reformer, but rather a relativist, who always finds arguments to justify existing institutions. This was a common interpretation of Montesquieu's thought during the period of the French Revolution, when it was not unusual to argue that, since justice is the same everywhere, laws and institutions ought to be uniform. Thus Condorcet criticized Montesquieu's perspective as follows:

> Since truth, reason, justice, the rights of man, the interest of property, of liberty, of security, are the same everywhere, it is difficult to see why all the provinces of a state, or even all states, should not have the same criminal laws, the same civil laws, the same commercial laws, etc. A good law should be good for all men, just as a true proposition is true for all.[55]

Montesquieu anticipated this kind of criticism when he wrote in Book XXIX, chapter 18 ("Concerning ideas of uniformity"):

> There are certain ideas of uniformity, which sometimes strike great geniuses, (for they even affected Charlemagne) but infallibly make an impression on little souls. They discover therein a kind of perfection, because it is impossible for them not to discover it; the same weights in the *police*, the same measures in commerce, the same laws in the state, the same religion in all its parts. But is this always right, and without exception? Is the evil of changing always less than that of suffering? And does not a greatness of genius consist rather in distinguishing between those cases in which uniformity is requisite, and those in which there is a necessity for differences? In China, the Chinese are governed by the Chinese ceremonial; and the Tartars by theirs: and yet there is no nation in the world that aims so much at tranquillity. If the people observe the laws, what signifies it whether these laws are the same?

In fact Montesquieu (unlike Condorcet) said nothing here that would have surprised the natural lawyers who, as has been seen, believed it was perfectly legitimate for laws to vary. The only stipulation was that they should not be out of line with the general precepts of natural law.

While Montesquieu may at times appear ultra-conservative in the way he recommends that the legislator should respect the "general spirit," it should be noted that this recommendation is not unconditional: "It is the business of the legislature to follow the spirit of the nation," he wrote, but with the important proviso: "when it is not contrary to the principles of government" (XIX, 5). He might also have added, "when it is not contrary to natural law."

An example of an institution which Montesquieu sees as contrary to natural law is slavery. This was a topic on which there had been some disagreement among thinkers in the natural law tradition.[56] It had been argued that the existence of slaves could be justified by the fact of conquest in war, or that there could be a contract whereby men had the right to sell themselves into slavery. In addition, it was argued that it was legitimate to treat as slaves the children of slaves. Grotius and Pufendorf, for example, allowed that some forms of slavery were legitimate. Others, like Locke (and later, Rousseau), rejected any argument supporting slavery. As for Montesquieu, his approach to the problem, which involved taking into account environmental factors, convinced him that it was possible to find a logical explanation for the existence of slavery. It is "natural" in the sense that there is a "necessary relation" between slavery and the form of government (despotism) and climate (in hot countries). It is "unnatural," however, for intelligent beings to allow themselves to be dominated by the influence of climate or to be the instruments of the immoral power of a despot. In this sense slavery is contrary to natural law and cannot therefore be condoned even though it can be explained by "natural causes":

But, as all men are born equal, slavery must be accounted unnatural, though, in some countries, it be founded on natural reason; and a wide difference ought to be made between such countries and those in which even natural reason rejects it, as in Europe, where it has been so happily abolished (XV, 8).

Another example of how breaches of natural law are not to be condoned can be found in the following passage where, referring to how certain spontaneous moral promptings of nature have been distorted and corrupted, he recommended that the legislator should take vigorous action to introduce the necessary reforms:

All nations are equally agreed in fixing contempt and ignomy on the incontinence of women. Nature has dictated this to all: she has established the attack, and she has established too the resistance; and having implanted desires in both, she has given to the one boldness, and to the other shame. To individuals she has granted a long succession of years to attend to their preservation; but, to continue their species, she has granted only a moment.

It is, then, far from being true, that to be incontinent is to follow the laws of nature; on the contrary, it is a violation of these laws, which can be observed only by behaving with modesty and discretion.

Besides, it is natural for intelligent beings to feel their imperfections; nature has therefore fixed shame in our minds, a shame of our imperfections.

When, therefore, the physical power of certain climates violates the natural law of the two sexes, and that of intelligent beings, it belongs to the legislator to make civil laws, with a view to opposing the nature of the climate and re-establishing the primitive laws (XVI, 12).

What lies behind this passage, and the previous passage on slavery is the theory of man's dual nature which Montesquieu had developed in Book I. When man's physical nature (the "passions" and other amoral tendencies, or even instinct unguided by reason) takes over, or when man allows himself to be dominated by physical factors, such as climate, the result is "unnatural." This is because (at the risk of belaboring the obvious) man's physical nature is, by definition, inferior to his intelligent nature. This was a commonplace of natural law thought; Barbeyrac, for example, had written in a footnote to Grotius:

> From whence it appears that the author does not intend to say that natural instinct alone is the rule of Natural Law, but that he joins to it reason, to direct this instinct and that inclination, which otherwise could mislead us and lead us to seek, in satisfying it, only our private interest. From whence also, in describing the characteristics of natural law, he makes it consist in a necessary fitness or unfitness with a reasonable and sociable nature.[57]

There is at least one passage in *The Spirit of Laws* where Montesquieu expressed the opinion that when there is an affront to natural law, in the form of tyranny or slavery, it may even be necessary to think in terms of violent, indeed, revolutionary, action:

> Jornandez the Goth called the North of Europe the forge of the human race. I should rather call it the forge where those weapons were framed which broke the chains of southern nations. In the North were formed those valiant peoples who sallied forth and deserted their countries to destroy tyrants and slaves, and to teach men, that, nature having made them equal, reason could not render them dependent, except where it was necessary to their happiness (XVII, 5).

This outburst is, however, unique in *The Spirit of Laws*. If Montesquieu hopes for a revolution, it is a revolution in ideas, of the kind expressed in the following passage: "Knowledge humanizes mankind, and reason inclines to mildness, but prejudices eradicate every tender disposition" (XV, 3). Perhaps the modern reader may feel there is an unacceptable amount of eighteenth-century optimism in this declaration, but Montesquieu was convinced that it is a fact that enlightenment has brought about more humane laws. Thus, when he discussed the law of nations with regard to the treatment of conquered nations, he wrote:

> The inhabitants of a conquered country are treated by the conqueror in one of the four following ways: either he continues to rule them according to their own laws, and assumes to himself only the exercise of the political and civil government; or he gives them new political and civil government; or he destroys and disperses the society; or, in fine, he exterminates the people.
>
> The first way is conformable to the law of nations now followed; the fourth is more agreeable to the law of nations followed by the Romans; in respect to which, I leave the reader to judge how far we have improved upon the ancients. We must give due commendations to our modest refinements in reason, religion, philosophy, and manners (X, 3).

Montesquieu's reflections on the duties of legislators, which was one of his major themes, makes it difficult to accept the judgement of Jean-Jacques Rousseau, who wrote:

> The discipline of political law [*le droit politique*] has not yet been born. . . . The only modern capable of creating this great and useless discipline was the illustrious Montesquieu. But he was careful not to deal with the principles of political law; he was content to deal with the positive law of established governments. And nothing in the world is more different than these two disciplines. But whoever wants to form a sound judgement on existing governments must join these two disciplines; he must know what ought to be in order to judge what is (*Emile*, Book V).

In fact Montesquieu would have agreed with the last sentence from this quotation, which, *pace* Rousseau, describes his practice in *The Spirit of Laws*. Perhaps what Rousseau is saying is simply that Montesquieu did not set out to write yet another treatise on natural law. No doubt he could have done so if he had wished. The result would have been a work which was more humane and which had a higher respect for human dignity than anything in Grotius or Pufendorf. However, Montesquieu's aim was different, and more original: it was to do for positive law what Grotius had achieved for the law of nations and natural law. What this achievement was, as it appeared to readers in the eighteenth century, was admirably summarized by Barbeyrac who wrote, "It is impossible to refuse the author [Grotius] the glory of being original in his genre. It is the characteristic of this treatise, the first ever written to make a systematic presentation of the finest and most useful of the human sciences, but unfortunately the most neglected." After referring to "the frightful chaos" of natural law and the law of nations before Grotius, he continued:

Such was the state of that first jurisprudence, which was to be the basis of all others, when Grotius conceived the noble plan of founding it on its authentic principles, and of showing it as it really is, stripped of the rags in which it had been decked out.[58]

Having rescued the study of positive law from an equally disreputable state, Montesquieu was not unmindful of his debt to his predecessors; in one of his *Pensées* he wrote: "I thank Messieurs Grotius and Pufendorf, for having carried out so well the task that a large part of this work required from me, with an excellence of genius which I could never have equalled."[59]

Montesquieu's affinity with Grotius, Pufendorf and the natural law tradition has often been overlooked, or indeed denied, by later interpreters, who identify him with "the decadence of natural law"[60] and assimilate his work to the discipline of positivist sociology. His aim, in *The Spirit of Laws*, we are given to understand, is to formulate value-free empirical generalizations based on his study of the facts of man's life in society, past and present. However, those who propose this approach have difficulty in making sense of the definitions of law in the first Book;[61] they also have to explain away Montesquieu's condemnation of despotism, torture, and slavery as being inconsistent with his method, and they can hardly fail to note that, instead of basing his theories on observed facts, he examines factual material in the light of his theories.[62] These theories, which have always been valued for their explanatory power, are deduced in geometrical fashion from "the nature of things," and in the final analysis, from a theory of the nature of man. They are essentially Montesquieu's response to the phenomenon of diversity. Just because the real is so bafflingly manifold, he felt the need for abstract models which would serve as a standard by which the laws of regimes past and present might be classified and explained. These models explain not only constitutional differences, but deeper differences at the level of the "general spirit" and moral values involved. It is here, at this deeper level, and thanks to this ethical approach, that Montesquieu finds the vital meaning of laws and political institutions.

Notes

1. The reference to an "offspring engendered without a mother" is from Ovid, *Metamorphoses*, II, v, 553.

2. *The Spirit of Laws*, Preface. All references to this work are hereafter cited by Book and chapter number within parentheses inserted in the main body of the text. Translations are from the classic Thomas Nugent translation of the eighteenth century, although I have occasionally altered or corrected the text as necessary.

3. The relevant works are: Auguste Comte, *Cours de philosophie positive,* 4 vols. (Paris: Bachelier, 1835-52), IV, Leçon 47, 243-63; Émile Durkheim, *Quid Secundatus politicae scientiae instituendae contulerit* (Bordeaux, 1892); English translation in Durkeim, *Montesquieu and Rousseau, Forerunners of Sociology,* Foreword by Henri Peyre (Ann Arbor: University of Michigan Press, 1960); Louis Althusser, *Montesquieu, la politique et l'histoire* (Paris: PUF, 1964). For a useful account of the positivists' misunderstanding of Montesquieu, see Mark H. Waddicor, *Montesquieu and the Philosophy of Natural Law* (The Hague: Nijhoff, 1970), 18-21.

4. For general studies of natural law see A. P. d'Entrèves, *Natural Law, an Introduction to Legal Philosophy* (London: Hutchinson, 1951), and Knud Haakonssen, *Natural Law and Moral Philosophy, from Grotius to the Scottish Enlightenment* (Cambridge: Cambridge University Press, 1996). See also the relevant chapters of *The Cambridge History of Political Thought 1450-1700,* J. H. Burns and Mark Goldie, eds. (Cambridge: Cambridge University Press, 1991). For Montesquieu and natural law see the study by Waddicor quoted in the previous note; see also the following, of which the present chapter is essentially an expanded version: C. P. Courtney, "Montesquieu and the problem of *la diversité,*" *Enlightenment Essays in Memory of Robert Shackleton,* Giles Barber and C. P. Courtney, eds. (Oxford: Voltaire Foundation, 1988), 61-81; "Montesquieu dans la tradition du droit naturel," *La Fortune de Montesquieu: Montesquieu écrivain: Actes du colloque international de Bordeaux (18-21 janvier 1989),* Louis Desgraves, ed. (Bordeaux: Bibliothèque municipale, 1995), 27-40.

5. The relevant works are the following: Grotius, *De jure belli ac pacis* (Paris: Brion, 1625); Pufendorf, *De jure naturae et gentium,* (Lund: Junghaus, 1672); and the translations by Barbeyrac; Grotius, *Le Droit de la guerre et de la paix,* nouvelle traduction par Jean Barbeyrac (Amsterdam: P. de Coup, 1724); Pufendorf, *Le Droit de la nature et des gens,* traduit du latin par Jean Barbeyrac (Amsterdam: Vve P. de Coup, 1734). Quotations are adapted from the following English translations: Grotius, *The Rights of War and Peace, in three books. Wherein are explained, the Law of Nature and Nations, Written in Latin by the learned Hugo Grotius, and translated into English. To which are added, all the large notes of Mr. J. Barbeyrac* (London: printed for W. Innys and R. Manby, J. and P. Knapton, D. Brown, T. Osborn, and E. Wicksteed, 1738); Pufendorf, *Of the Law of Nature and Nations, Eight books, done into English by Basil Kennet. To which is prefix'd M. Barbeyrac's Prefatory Discourse, containing An Historical and Critical Account of the Science of Morality, done into English by Mr. Carew,* 5th ed. (London, 1749).

6. For Hobbes and Spinoza in this context, see Simone Goyard-Fabre, *Montesquieu adversaire de Hobbes* (Paris: Les Lettres modernes, 1980), 192 and Paul Vernière, *Spinoza et la pensée française avant la Révolution,* 2 vols. (Paris: Presses universitaires de France, 1954).

7. Grotius, "Preliminary Discourse," §11, note 1.

8. Richard Cumberland, *De legibus naturae* (1672); Burlamaqui, *Principes du droit naturel* (1747); *Principes du droit politique* (1751); Malebranche, *Traité de morale*

(1684); Leibniz, *Essai de Théodicée* (1710); Samuel Clarke, *Discourse concerning the Being and Attributes of God* (1728).

9. Pufendorf, "Translator's Preface," vi. The refererence is to Locke's *Essay concerning Human Understanding,* IV, iii, 18.

10. For a useful discussion of the rationalist theory of ethics, see Locke, *Essays on the Law of Nature,* W. von Leyden, ed. (Oxford: Clarendon Press, 1954), Introduction, 43-60.

11. See, for example, Grotius, "Preliminary discourse," §11, with notes by Barbeyrac; Grotius, I. i, §10, note 4; Pufendorf, I, ii, §6, note 1.

12. Grotius, I, i, §12.

13. Grotius, I, i, §12, and note 1; Pufendorf, II, iii, §§7-8. See also Jean-Jacques Rousseau's observation on Grotius: "His most constant method of reasoning is always to base what is right on matters of fact. One could use a method which is more logical, but not more favorable to tyrants" (*The Social Contract,* I, i).

14. Pufendorf, I, ii, §5, note 2. Cf. Grotius, "Translator's Preface," p. xxii.

15. Pufendorf ,VII, ii, §5.

16. Pufendorf, I, ii, §4.

17. "But though none had ever yet discovered, in the principles and rules of morality, so high a degree of evidence, and that they are so duly adjusted to all capacities, one might still appeal, in this matter, to the very nature of the thing itself; and, in some measure, to experience. We have here no business to inquire into the impenetrable secrets of nature, to discover those imperceptible springs that produce in the world so many phenomena and such a variety of wonderful events, to measure the magnitude and distance of the stars and observe their motions, to search into the bowels of the earth and even pierce the centre; no more have we here any occasion to bury ourselves in metaphysical speculation, to turn over a vast number of volumes, to learn several languages, to penetrate through the darkness of remote antiquity, in a word, to be very learned. We shall scarce have occasion to carry our thoughts beyond ourselves, or consult any other master besides our own heart. The most common experience of life, and a little reflection on ourselves and the objects that surround us on every side are sufficient to furnish even the most ordinary capacities with general ideas of the Law of Nature and the true foundations of all our moral duties" (Pufendorf, "Translator's Preface," pp. iii-iv).

18. Pufendorf, "Translator's Preface," p. xix.

19. Grotius, "Preliminary Discourse," §31.

20. Grotius, I, i, §13, note 1.

21. For this continuation in the *Pensées,* see Pléiade, I, 377-79.

22. For the interpretation of the fable of the Troglodytes, see A. S. Crisafulli, "Montesquieu's Story of the Troglodytes: its Background, Meaning, and Significance," *Publications of the Modern Language Association of America* 58 (1943): 372-92; Robert Shackleton, *Montesquieu, a Critical Biography* (Oxford University Press, 1961), 37-38; Waddicor, *Montesquieu,* 69-86.

23. Persian Letter 83, in Pléiade, I, 256.

24. Persian Letter 104, in Pléiade, I, 284.

25. Persian Letter 83, in Pléiade, I, 256.

26. "We are surrounded by men stronger than ourselves; they can harm us in a thousand different ways; three quarters of the time they can do it with impunity. How reassuring for us to know that in the hearts of all these men there is an internal principle which fights in our favour and shelters us from their attacks!" (Persian Letter 83, in Pléiade, I, 256-57).

27. Persian Letter 161, in Pléiade, I, 372.

28. For a fuller development of this argument regarding the skepticism of the *Persian Letters*, see C. P. Courtney, "Montesquieu and the problem of *la diversité,*" 69-72.

29. See Shackleton, *Montesquieu*, 72-73.

30. *Des Devoirs de l'homme et du citoyen, tels qu'ils lui sont prescrits par la Loi Naturelle*, Amsterdam: Schelte,1707. A copy of the French translation by Barbeyrac was owned by Montesquieu; see Louis Desgraves et Catherine Volpilhac-Auger, *Catalogue de la bibliothèque de Montesquieu à La Brède, Cahiers Montesquieu*, 4 (1999): 117, n° 802.

31. "Analysis of the Treatise on Duties," in Pléiade, I, 109-10; *Pensée* 615 (1266), in Pléiade, I, 1138-40.

32. See Shackleton, *Montesquieu,* 72-73.

33. See *Pensée* 1260 (614), in Pléiade, I, 1134-37: "Exemples particuliers des conquêtes des Espagnols dans les Indes."

34. *Pensée,* 616 (1267), in Pléiade, I, 1141.

35. See Shackleton, *Montesquieu,* 68-76.

36. The definition of law in terms of "necessary relations" or "relations of fitness or unfitness" deduced from the "nature of things" has puzzled generations of commentators unfamiliar with the natural law tradition. It is strange that this unfamiliarity should have been shared by Shackleton, who wrote, with reference to the opening sentence of *The Spirit of Laws*: "This was a surprising attitude to law, and a surprising definition, to come from the pen of one who had been a celebrated magistrate and who was still known by the title of President" (*Montesquieu,* 245). There is a vast literature on the possible sources of Montesquieu's definition. Most commentators, overlooking the obvious, quote Malebranche, Leibniz, and Clarke. See Shackleton, 245-46. See also Sheila M. Mason, *Montesquieu's Idea of Justice* (The Hague: Nijhoff, 1975), which in its examination of "Montesquieu's definition of justice: precursors and parallels" (1-109), barely even mentions Grotius, Pufendorf, or Barbeyrac.

37. Cf. Voltaire, "La lumière est uniforme pour l'astre de Sirius et pour nous; la morale doit être uniforme" in *Dictionnaire philosophique*, Julien Benda et Raymond Naves, eds. (Paris: Garnier), 608. See, on the ambiguity of the concept of nature, Jean Ehrard, *L'idée de nature en France dans la première moitié du XVIIIème siècle* (Paris: SEVPEN, 1963).

38. See the final paragraph of Book I, chapter 1.

39. See, for the contemporary attacks on *The Spirit of Laws*, Shackleton, *Montesquieu*, 357-77, and *De l'esprit des lois*, Robert Derathé, ed., 2 vols. (Paris: Garnier, 1973), I, xviii-xlvi.

40. For an analysis of the *Defense*, see Shackleton, *Montesquieu*, 361-62.

41. See Robert Derathé, "Montesquieu et Jean-Jacques Rousseau," *Revue internationale de philosophie* 9 (1955): 366-86.

42. Shackleton, *Montesquieu*, 253-61.

43. Cf. Rousseau, of whose theory Robert Derathé writes perceptively: "In passing from the state of nature to the state of civil society, natural law changes in the same way as natural man. In the state of nature natural law was nothing more than instinct and goodness; in the state of civil society it becomes justice and reason." See Derathé, *Jean-Jacques Rousseau et la science politique de son temps* (Paris: Presses universitaires de France, 1950), 168.

44. "The law which imprinting in our minds the idea of a Creator inclines us to him, is the first in importance, though not in order, of natural laws" (*Laws*, I, 2). See also, on the idea of (natural) religion, Montesquieu's letter of c. May 1754 to William Warburton: "It is not impossible to attack a revealed religion, because it is founded on particular facts, and the facts, by their very nature can be disputed. But it is not so with natural religion: it is based on the nature of man, about which there can be no dispute, and on man's inner sentiment, about which likewise there can be no dispute" (Nagel, III, 1509).

45. Pléiade, II, 53.

46. Cf. *Pensée* 883 (1935), in Pléiade, I, 1467: "The authority of princes and magistrates is founded not only on civil law, but also on natural law; for, since anarchy is contrary to natural law, the human species being unable to subsist in an anarchic state, it is necessary that the authority of the magistrates, which is opposed to anarchy, should be in conformity to natural law."

47. However, there appears to be a tacit assumption on his part that there is in fact a contract; see below the two brief quotations from *The Spirit of Laws*, VIII, 3 and XXVI, 15. See also Waddicor, *Montesquieu*, 86-99.

48. See Ernst Cassirer, *The Philosophy of the Enlightenment* (Boston: Beacon Press, 1960), 209-16 and Alan Baum, *Montesquieu and Social Theory* (Oxford: Pergamon Press, 1979). See also Courtney, "Montesquieu and the problem of *la diversité*," 76-78.

49. The inspiration for Montesquieu's theory can possibly be found in *The Republic*, Book VIII, where Plato describes four different forms of government, each with its inner principle. See Courtney, "Montesquieu and the problem of *la diversité*," 78. Commentators have also pointed out the debt to Machiavelli; see Shackleton, *Montesquieu*, 268.

50. See *Laws*, II, 2: "Libanius says that in Athens a stranger who intermeddled in the assembly of the people was punished with death. This is because such a man was usurping the right of sovereignty" (II, 240).

51. *Theory of Moral Sentiments* (1757), VII, iv, §36.

52. See, for example, *Laws* VI, 17, where Montesquieu writes, with reference to torture: "I was going to say that it might be appropriate in despotic governments, where everything that inspires fear is the proper spring of government."

53. On this topic see the following: Muriel Dodds, *Les récits de voyages, sources de l'Esprit des lois de Montesquieu* (Paris: Champion, 1929) and Paul Vernière, "Montesquieu et le monde musulman d'après *l'Esprit des lois*," *Actes du Congrès Montesquieu réuni à Bordeaux pour commémorer, le deuxième centenaire de la mort de Montesquieu* (Bordeaux: Delmas, 1956), 176-90.

54. See *Social Contract*, Book III, chapter 8.

55. *Observations sur le vingt-neuvième livre de l'Esprit des lois*, in Destutt de Tracy, *Commentaire sur l'Esprit des lois de Montesquieu* (Paris: Desoer, 1819), 418.

56. See, for a useful discussion of this topic, Waddicor, *Montesquieu*, 149-62.

57. "Preliminary discourse," §8, note 1.

58. Grotius, "Translator's Preface," pp. ii-iii.

59. *Pensée* 191(1863), in Pléiade, II, 1038.

60. This is the title of the chapter in which Montesquieu is discussed in George H. Sabine's influential *History of Political Thought*, 3rd edition (London: Harrap, 1963), 551-60.

61. See for an interesting example of blank misunderstanding of Montesquieu's key concepts and methodology, the following (disarmingly honest) statement by John Plamenatz: "I shall not go minutely into Montesquieu's definitions of law or try to weigh carefully what he said about the laws of nature or the rules of equity. He spoke so loosely that his words will bear several different and equally plausible interpretations. And yet it is not this looseness which makes me reluctant to take these parts of his theory seriously. Confusion is often worth unraveling, especially in political and social theory, because the most original and suggestive writers are not always the most lucid. But in this case the attempt is not worthwhile, simply because Montesquieu makes no use, in the body of his work, of his preliminary definitions and classifications." See Plamenatz, *Man and Society, Political and Social Theories from Machiavelli to Marx*, revised edition (London: Longman, 1992), 11. See also, for the argument that the definitions in Book I are irrelevant to Montesqueiu's enquiry, Pierre Martino, "De quelques résidus métaphysiques dans *L'Esprit des lois*," *Revue d'histoire de la philosophie et de l'histoire générale de la civilisation*, 43 (1946): 235-43.

62. See particularly the article by Paul Vernière, note 53 above.

Chapter Two

Forms of Government: Structure, Principle, Object, and Aim

Paul A. Rahe

In *The Spirit of Laws*, Montesquieu introduces for the first time his novel typology of political forms.[1] His purpose in doing so is to trace the logic underlying the "infinite diversity of laws and mores" found in the larger world: his aim thereby is to demonstrate to the satisfaction of all that there is a method to this apparent madness and that human beings "are not conducted solely (*uniquement*) by their fantasies" (Preface).[2]

To this end, at the beginning of the second book of this great work, Montesquieu distinguishes, with regard to "nature," three species of government—republics, in which "the people as a body, or only a part of the people, hold the sovereign power"; monarchies, in which "one governs alone, but by laws fixed and established"; and despotisms, in which "one alone, without law and without regulation (*règle*), draws everything in train by his will and by his caprices" (II, 1). As Montesquieu's argument unfolds in the course of that book (II, 2-3), he complicates this assertion, by further differentiating aristocratic republics, in which a part of the people hold the sovereignty, from democratic republics, in which the people hold the sovereignty themselves.

The typology deployed by Montesquieu is peculiar in two regards.[3] On the one hand, it abstracts from questions of moral character.[4] Where Xenophon, Plato, Aristotle, Polybius, and their medieval admirers had distinguished kingship from tyranny, aristocracy from oligarchy, and well-ordered popular government from the regime variously called democracy, anarchy, or mob rule and had done so chiefly with an eye to the character of the ruling individual or group,[5] Montesquieu insists that "the form of the constitution" is alone determinative; and when discussing one-man rule, he therefore treats as "accidental" matters such as "the virtues or vices of the prince" and as "external" questions such as "usurpation" and "the succession" (XI, 9).

At the same time, however, that Montesquieu jettisons the contrast between aristocracy and oligarchy and that between well-ordered and ill-ordered popular government, he reasserts that between well-ordered monarchy and tyranny.[6] Where Thomas Hobbes had explicitly rejected all such distinctions as not just illusory but dangerous in the extreme,[7] Montesquieu insists on restoring in this one case something like the classical understanding. But where the ancients and their medieval admirers had juxtaposed the lawful rule of an individual over willing subjects in the interest of those ruled with the lawless rule of an individual over unwilling subjects solely in the interest of the ruler himself, Montesquieu abandons the focus on interest and consent while re-emphasizing the rule of law. If he eschews political moralism, he is nonetheless a constitutionalist of sorts; and although he appears at one stage to have been inclined to criticize Machiavelli for confusing depotism and well-ordered one-man rule,[8] in the end, it is from the Florentine, who teaches that one should attend solely to "the effectual truth of the matter," that he takes his cue.[9] As he sees it, monarchical government is distinguished from despotism solely by the presence of "powers intermediate, subordinate, and dependent" which cause the monarch to "govern by the fundamental laws." There is, he contends, a sense in which "the nobility . . . enters . . . into the essence of monarchy," for the "fundamental maxim" of this form of government is: "*no monarch, no nobility; no nobility, no monarch.*"[10] Where there is one-man rule in the absence of such a nobility, "one has a despot" on one's hands (II, 4).[11]

Principles

In the third book of his encyclopedic work, Montesquieu puts flesh on these constitutional bones. There is, he suggests, a "difference between the nature of the government and its principle: its nature is that which makes it such as it is, and its principle, that which makes it act. The one is its particular structure, and the other is the human passions that set it in motion" (III, 1). The principle of democracy is virtue; that of aristocracy is moderation; that of monarchy is honor; and that of despotism is *la crainte* or fear (III, 2-11). If Montesquieu rivals Aristotle as an analyst of political regimes, it is because he attends to the procedure followed by Plato in the eighth and ninth books of *The Republic* and supplements his strictly institutional analysis with an attention to political psychology which gives to his political science a suppleness, a flexibility, a subtlety, and range elsewhere unexcelled in modern times.[12] The bulk of the first part of *The Spirit of Laws* is devoted to a consideration of the manner in which the laws and customs reigning within a polity must be framed with an eye not only to the structure of that polity but to the passions setting it in motion (IV-

VIII). As Montesquieu explains when he first introduces the notion, the "principle" of a polity has "a supreme influence over the laws," and one can see them "flow from it as from their source" (I, 3).[13]

We would therefore expect that, when Montesquieu suddenly and without warning complicates his typology further by introducing yet another species of government,[14] he would not only discuss the structure of that government but take care to specify its principle and examine in detail the consequences that arise therefrom. But when the time comes and Montesquieu turns his attention to the question of "political liberty" in the eleventh book, he has nothing of the sort to say. He prefaces his discussion of what he terms elsewhere "a republic concealed under the form of a monarchy" (V, 19, 304) by introducing a new category of distinction: the "object" of the polity. He concedes that "all states have the same object in general, which is to maintain themselves"; then, he suggests that "each state has an object that is particular to it."

> Aggrandizement was the object of Rome; war, that of Lacedaemon; religion, that of the Jewish laws; commerce, that of Marseilles; public tranquillity, that of the laws of China; navigation, that of the laws of the Rhodians; natural liberty was the object of the police of the savages; in general, the delights of the prince, that of despotic states; his glory and that of the state, that of monarchies; the independence of each individual is the object of the laws of Poland, and what results from this is the oppression of all.

"There is also," he then adds, "one nation in the world which has for the direct object of its constitution political liberty," and he promises "to examine the principles (*les principes*) on which" this constitution "is founded" (XI, 5). This promise he keeps in the very next chapter by launching into an elaborate discussion of the pertinent nation's constitution and laws.[15] But neither here nor anywhere else does he tell us what is *the* "principle" and what are "the human passions that set in motion" what turns out to be the government of England.

It is difficult to know what to make of this. It is possible that, when he deals with England's constitutional monarchy in the eleventh book, Montesquieu abandons the mode of analysis that he had made extensive use of earlier when he discussed democracy, aristocracy, monarchy, and despotism. He may, in fact, be implying that it makes no sense to analyze the English polity in terms of "the human passions that set it in motion." But it is equally possible that Montesquieu has deliberately left it to his readers to discover on their own "the principle" exercising "a supreme influence over the laws" of England, which he had himself left unmentioned. At the end of the eleventh book, Montesquieu remarks that "it is not necessary always to so exhaust a subject that one leaves nothing for the reader to do. The task is not to make him read but to make him think" (XI, 20).[16] At the very least, Montesquieu's silence on the subject of the English polity's "principle" is an invitation to ponder whether it has one and, if it does, just what this "principle" might be. To properly address these two questions, we will have to explore Montesquieu's political typology as a whole.

Virtue as a Principle

On the face of it, if the English polity really is "a republic concealed under the form of a monarchy," it should be set in motion by virtue—the principle that animates democratic republics.[17] But this seems not to be the case. To begin with, Montesquieu never attributes political virtue to the English: he touches on the subject only in referring to the brief republican experiment that took place after the execution of Charles I. The "impotent efforts" of the English "to establish among themselves democracy" on this occasion he regards as "a fine spectacle," noting that those "who took part in affairs had no virtue" and that the ambition that fueled their rivalries and gave rise to faction produced so "much of movement" and so "many shocks and jerks" that "the people," unable "to find anywhere" the democracy that "they were seeking," eventually "found repose" in the monarchical "government that had been proscribed" (III, 3).

Moreover, Montesquieu nowhere suggests that political liberty is the object pursued by democracies and aristocracies. Indeed, he contends that these republics "are not in their nature free states" (XI, 4). Moreover, he warns that it is a mistake to look for liberty "in democracies" where "the people seem pretty much to do what they wish" since to do so would be to "confound the power of the people with the liberty of the people" (XI, 2), for "political liberty does not at all consist in doing what one wants" (XI, 3). It is, in any case, "not to be found except" in what he calls "moderate governments"—and not always there. Political liberty, he observes, "is not present except where there is no abuse of power, and it is an eternal experience that every man who has power is drawn to abuse it; he proceeds until he finds the limits." It is in alluding to the human propensity for the abuse of power that he pointedly adds, "Who would say it! Even virtue has a need for limits" (XI, 4).

This claim should give us pause. If virtue has a need for limits, it is because the principle of democratic republicanism can itself become a motive for the abuse of power. It is "a misfortune attached to the human condition," Montesquieu later observes, but one cannot deny the fact:

> Great men who are moderate are rare; and as it is always easier to follow one's momentum (*force*) than to arrest it, within the class of superior people, one may perhaps with greater facility find people extremely virtuous than men extremely wise.
>
> The soul tastes so much delight in dominating other souls; even those who love the good love themselves so strongly that there is no one who is not so unfortunate as to still have reason to doubt his own good intentions: and, in truth, our actions depend on so many things

that it is a thousand times easier to do good than to do it well (XXVIII, 41).

In this passage, Montesquieu describes one dimension of the problem: there is something inherently immoderate and perhaps even tyrannical at the heart of all forms of political idealism and public spiritedness. The other dimension of the problem stems from the nature of political virtue itself.

When Montesquieu speaks of democratic republics, he nearly always has foremost in his mind ancient Rome and the cities of classical Greece. His analysis of these communities and of their customs and laws in terms of constitutional structure and political psychology is, in one crucial regard, at odds with their self-understanding. As I have tried to demonstrate in fine detail elsewhere, the Greeks—and the Romans as well—took political rationality to be the fundamental principle of the classical republican regime. To be precise, their institutions and practices embodied the presumption that, with the proper civic education, human beings can rise to the task of sorting out through public deliberation the character of the advantageous, the just, and the good; and a quarter of a millennium before Aristotle fully articulated what this entailed, they evidenced that they were quite conscious of the fact.[18] Montesquieu stands opposed to the ancients and to those of their civic-minded, humanist admirers in the communes of Renaissance Italy who entertained similar presumptions concerning man's capacity for rational, public speech—for, like Machiavelli, he has next to nothing to say concerning public deliberation. When he speaks of virtue, he is not interested in those qualities of character and intellect that enable the very best citizens (and perhaps even the ordinary citizens at their very best) to transcend petty, private concerns and engage in public deliberation concerning the dictates of justice and the common good. Nor is he concerned with the liberation of reason from passion. In stark contrast with the citizens of the ancient republics, the classical philosophers, and their disciples the Christian theologians, he doubts whether "reason" ever "produces any great effects on the minds of men" (XIX, 27, 577).[19] In consequence, when he mentions virtue, he has in mind the fostering of an irrational, unreasoning passion for equality—for, in his judgment, it is this passion that sets the democratic republic in motion (V, 2-7).

This passion in no way depends on, gives rise to, or is subordinate to anything resembling moral, Christian, or even philosophical virtue as interpreted by Aristotle and his Christian successors,[20] and it is at odds with what Montesquieu calls "moderate" government. It is perfectly possible for a republic to adopt some of the institutional safeguards that the French *philosophe* considers essential to "political liberty"; and as he demonstrates, something of the sort actually happened in classical Rome (XI, 12-19). But this cannot alter the fact that the democratic republic is not in its "nature" moderate. Popular government is rendered problematic by the fact that, in such a polity, the rulers are subjects at the same time: "he who causes the laws to be executed senses that he must submit to them himself and that he will bear their weight." In consequence, where civic virtue is lacking among the populace as a whole, the laws will not be enforced—for, in the absence of self-discipline, there will be no discipline at all (III, 3).

The difficulty arises from the fact that self-discipline is, in Montesquieu's judgment, unnatural. Virtue is not onerous at the outset and, then, somehow satisfying in the end. It is not what it was for Aristotle—a completion of nature's work, a perfection of the soul.[21] Nor is virtue anything like what Homer and his successors took it to be: the product of self-assertion on the part of a man who strives "always to be the best (*aristeúein*) and to be superior to others."[22] It, in fact, requires doing violence to oneself: "political virtue" is not an assertion; it "is a renunciation of self"—and this is never pleasant, never satisfying. Virtue is "always a very painful thing" (IV, 5).

According to Montesquieu, republican virtue is grounded in a "love of the laws and the fatherland"; it demands "a continual preference for the public interest over one's own"; in its emphasis on equality, which Montesquieu describes as "the soul" of the democratic state, it "restricts ambition to a single desire, to the sole happiness of rendering to the fatherland greater services than the other citizens." To produce this love, to so restrict the scope of ambition, and to inspire in the citizens of a republic the requisite spirit of self-renunciation, one must deploy "the complete power of education" (IV, 5; V, 3, 5). In practice, this requires what Montesquieu calls "singular institutions"—of the sort established by the Spartans in Lacedaemon, by William Penn in Pennsylvania, by the Jesuits in Paraguay, and by Plato in his *Republic* (IV, 6). Such institutions are incompatible with "the confusion, the negligence, the extended affairs of a great people"; they find their "place" only "in a petty state" like the cities of ancient Greece where "one can provide a general education and rear a people as a family" (IV, 7).

In a large republic, Montesquieu adds, "interests become particular; a man senses then that he can be happy, great, glorious without his fatherland; and soon that he can be great solely on the ruins of his fatherland." One consequence of such a republic's size is that "the common good is sacrificed to a thousand considerations; it is subordinated to the exceptions; it depends on accidents." The situation "in a small" republic is more favorable: there, "the public good is more fully felt, better known, closer to each citizen; the abuses are less extensive there and as a consequence less well protected" (VIII, 16). Republics, if they are successfully to deploy shame as a reinforcement for the spirit of self-renunciation, must be comparatively simple and exceedingly small.

Montesquieu takes care to underline the alien character of classical republican institutions; and like Machiavelli,[23] he traces the change to the rise of Christianity. When the virtue of the ancients was "in full force," he reports, "they did things that we no longer see and which astonish our little souls." If his contemporaries are unable to rise to the same level, it is, he suggests, because the "education" given the ancients "never suffered contradiction" while "we receive three educations different" from and even "contrary" to one another: "that of our fathers, that of our masters, that of the world. What we are told in the last overthrows the first two." In short, there is now "a contrast between the engagements" which arise "from religion" and "those" which arise "from the world" that "the ancients did not know." This is apparently why the moderns possess such "little souls" (IV, 4).

As should be obvious, Montesquieu has much in common with his Florentine predecessor. Like Machiavelli, he wants his readers to stand in awe of the magnanimity of the ancients.[24] "One can never leave the Romans behind," he writes. "So it is that still today, in their capital, one leaves the new palaces to go in search of the ruins; so it is that the eye which has taken its repose on the flower-strewn grasslands loves to look at the rocks and mountains" (XI, 13). But, in contrast to the author of the *Discourses on Titus Livy*, Montesquieu is also intent that his readers recoil in horror and distaste at the price that the ancients paid for having great souls.[25] "It is necessary," he observes in one chapter, "to regard the Greeks as a society of athletes and warriors." The exercises that they engaged in were "suited to making men harsh and savage." They "excited" in the citizens "but one species of passion: severity, anger, cruelty" (IV, 8). Later, he may begin by remarking that the "love of the fatherland" fostered by the ancient republics "is conducive to goodness in mores" and that "goodness in mores leads to a love of the fatherland," but he goes on to clarify what "goodness in mores" involves by invoking a disturbing analogy:

> The less we are able to satisfy our private passions, the more we abandon ourselves to those of a more general nature. Why are monks so fond of their order? Precisely because of those things which make it insupportable. Their rule deprives them of all the things on which the ordinary passions rest: there remains, then, only that passion for the rule which torments them. The more austere the rule, that is, the more it curbs their inclinations, the more momentum (*force*) it gives to the one inclination which it leaves them with (V, 2).[26]

Classical virtue has something in common with Christian virtue: in both cases, the self-renunciation required contains within itself the seeds of an ugly fanaticism.[27] Montesquieu may accept in its broad outlines Machiavelli's account of ancient citizenship—but that does not make him an unabashed admirer of the severity, the cruelty, and the ferocity to which it gives rise. In this particular, he has much more in common with his fellow Frenchman Michel de Montaigne.[28] Both men enjoy contemplating "rocks and mountains," but both would prefer to reside in "flower-strewn grasslands."[29] The form of government admired by Montesquieu for its dedication to political liberty is not to be sought among those distinguished by their lack of moderation.

Moderation in Government

When he speaks of "moderate government," Montesquieu insists that it "is able, as much as it wishes and without peril, to relax its springs. It maintains itself by its laws and even by its momentum *(force).*"[30] Such is not the case, he points out, with despotism, the quintessence of immoderate government—for when "the spring" of that species of government, "which is fear," is no longer present, "all is lost" and "the people no longer have a protector." In such a polity, "it is necessary that the people be judged by the laws and the great ones by the whimsy of the prince; that the head of the least subject be secure while that of the pasha is always exposed." If, when contemplating republics, Montesquieu betrays the same inclination "to shudder" that he displays when "speaking of these monstrous governments" (III, 9), it is because republics can only within limits approximate moderation: they cannot without danger relax their springs as much as they wish. Republics and despotic governments thus have this in common: they are fragile; they require apprehension; they must remain tense. "It is necessary," Montesquieu asserts, "that a republic dread something. The fear *(crainte)* of the Persians maintained the laws among the Greeks. Carthage and Rome threatened one another and rendered one another firm. It is a thing singular: the more these states have of security, the more, like waters excessively tranquil, they are subject to corruption" (VIII, 5).

Moderate governments can profit from success and relax their springs because they encounter less friction than polities not in their nature moderate. Once set in motion, they possess a momentum all their own; like perpetual-motion machines, they do not run down. "To form a moderate government," Montesquieu tells us, "it is necessary to combine powers, to regulate them, to temper them, to make them act, to give, so to speak, a ballast to one in order to put it in a condition to resist another; this is a masterpiece of legislation, which chance rarely produces and prudence is rarely allowed to produce." It may be more difficult to sustain and stabilize the government of any given despot but it is much easier to institute despotic government in the first place. Despotism is, in a sense, natural. It "jumps up, so to speak, before our eyes; it is uniform throughout: as the passions alone are necessary for its establishment, the whole world is good enough for that" (V, 14, 297).

In his initial discussion of moderate governments, Montesquieu is coy. For this, there is a reason. "I say it," he will later confess, "and it seems to me that I have composed this work solely to prove it: the spirit of moderation ought to be that of the legislator; the political good, like the moral good, is always to be found between two limits" (XXIX, 1). Political moderation is, in a sense, Montesquieu's cause; and his purpose is not simply to describe the political phenomena. Description is subordinate to prescription throughout: his purpose is to teach legislators just how the spirit of moderation can be encouraged within each form of government. Thus, when treating despotism, he is quick to remark that religion, which may be otherwise politically malign, is useful as a check on arbitrary power: "as despotism subjects human nature to frightful evils, the very evil that limits it is a good" (II, 4).[31] And when speaking of moderate governments, he implies that various polities may qualify. He even treats republics as moderate states (VIII, 8), for to suggest that this is so is to justify and encourage their evolution in this direction.

Honor as a Principle

Where Montesquieu is direct and clear from the outset is in his contention that monarchy, as exemplified by his native France, is moderate. In fact, monarchy would appear to be moderate government par excellence.[32] This polity's moderation is not, however, a consequence of the moderation of the monarch and his nobility. As a "principle," moderation is peculiar to aristocratic republics: it is "the soul of these governments," and it is "founded on virtue"; it does not "come from a cowardice and a laziness of soul." Virtue is required in an aristocracy for the same reasons that it is required in a democracy: "those who are charged with the execution of the laws against their colleagues will sense that they then act against themselves. . . . The nature of this constitution is such that it seems to place the same people under the power of the laws that it exempts from them" (III, 4). Because inequality militates against the inculcation of virtue in such a polity, Montesquieu has nothing to say concerning the education given the citizen in an aristocracy.[33] In that polity, one must rely on the laws, which must themselves instill "a spirit of moderation" in its rulers. In an aristocratic republic, the nobles must display "modesty and simplicity of manners": they must "affect no distinction"; they must "confound themselves with the people"; they must "dress like them"; they must "partake of their pleasures"—and thereby make the people "forget their weakness." Since all of this is contrary to the natural instincts of the well-born, there has to be within an aristocracy, "for a time or forever, a magistrate who makes the nobles tremble." Put bluntly, "this government has need of quite violent springs." In Venice, Montesquieu tells us, "it is necessary that there be a hidden magistracy," for the conspiracies "that it punishes, always profound, are formed in secret and in silence." For the letters of anonymous accusers, there is "a mouth of stone open in Venice; you could say that it is the mouth of tyranny" (II, 3; V, 8). The state that inculcates and enforces the virtue of moderation is anything but moderate itself.[34]

Monarchy can be moderate because within it no one need be such himself. "In monarchies," Montesquieu observes, "policy makes great things happen with as little of virtue as it can, just as in the most beautiful machines, art also employs as little of movement, of forces, of wheels as is possible. The state subsists independently of love of the fatherland, of desire for true glory, of self-renunciation, of the sacrifice of one's dearest interests, and of all those heroic virtues which we find in the ancients and know only from hearing them spoken of." If virtue and moderation can be discarded, it is because in a monarchy "the laws take the place of all these virtues, for which there is no need; the state confers on you a dispensation from them." It is a good thing that monarchies have no need for the virtuous because therein "it is very difficult for the people to be so." Consider, Montesquieu urges, "the miserable character of courtiers.... Ambition in idleness, baseness in pride, desire to enrich oneself without work, an aversion for truth, flattery, treason, perfidy, the abandonment of all one's engagements, contempt for the duties of the citizen, fear of the virtue of the prince, hope looking to his weaknesses, and, more than that, the perpetual ridicule cast on virtue form, I believe, the character of the greatest number of courtiers, as is remarked in all places and times" (III, 5).

If monarchy can nonetheless produce good government, it is because honor "takes the place of the political virtue" found in republics. The honor that Montesquieu has in mind is artificial: if it gives rise not to civic virtue but to the vices characteristic of courtiers, it is because it is a "false honor," which demands artificial "preferences and distinctions" and is grounded in "the prejudice of each person and condition." The consequences of this all-pervasive "prejudice" are paradoxical but undeniable. "In well-regulated monarchies," Montesquieu contends, "everyone will be something like a good citizen while one will rarely find someone who is a good man." Monarchy he compares to Newton's "system of the universe, where there is a force which ceaselessly repels all bodies from the center and a force of gravity which draws them to it. Honor makes all the parts of the body politic move; it binds them by its own actions; and it happens that each pursues the common good while believing that he is pursuing his own particular interests" (III, 6-7; XXIV, 6). Monarchies are ruled by something like Adam Smith's "invisible hand."[35]

On the face of it, monarchical government would appear to be absolute: such was certainly the English view of France.[36] But, according to Montesquieu, monarchical rule is far from arbitrary.[37] "In states monarchical and moderate," he explains, "power is limited by that which is its spring; I mean to say honor, which reigns, like a monarch, over the prince and over the people." Honor reigns and limits monarchical power because "honor has its laws and regulations and knows not how to bend" and because "it depends on its own caprice and not on that of another." For this reason, honor is linked with constitutional government: its rules and laws may be as irrational and capricious as honor is itself artificial and false, but, reinforced as they are by human vanity, they do persist; and honor, though it may be replete with "whimsicalities (*bizarreries*)," can therefore "be found only in states where the constitution is fixed and the laws are certain." This explains why a monarchy can relax its springs without danger as much as it wants: it is not fragile; it does not require apprehension; it need not remain tense; "it maintains itself by its laws"; and like a well-made machine, it possesses a "momentum" all its own (III, 8-10), for the honor that sets it in motion is in no way painful: it "is favored by the passions and favors them in its turn" (IV, 5).

This false honor is taught "not in the public establishments where one instructs children" but in "the world," and it teaches "three things: 'that it is necessary to introduce into the virtues a certain nobility, into mores a certain frankness, and into manners a certain politeness.'" The pertinent virtues arise from honor itself. They are "always less what one owes others than what one owes oneself: they are not so much what summons us towards our fellow citizens as what distinguishes us from them." With regard to monarchical government, it can be said that "honor, mixing itself through everything, enters into all the modes of thinking and all the manners of feeling and directs even the principles" governing conduct. Under its influence, these become a matter of fashion: "this whimsical honor causes the virtues to be only what it wishes and to exist in the manner in which it wishes; on its authority, it sets down rules for everything that is prescribed for us; it extends or limits our duties in accord with its fancy— even though they have their origin in religion, in policy, or in morals." Laws, religion, and honor emphatically prescribe "obedience to the will of the prince," but this same honor restricts royal power—for it "dictates to us that the prince should never prescribe to us an action which dishonors us since that would render us incapable of serving him" (IV, 2).[38]

Above all else, false honor is significant because it contributes to the rule of law. Monarchy is distinguished from despotism by the presence of "powers intermediate, subordinate, and dependent" constituted principally by the nobility. These sustain "the fundamental laws" of the kingdom "against the momentary and capricious will of one alone" by forming "intermediate channels through which power flows." In France, the most essential of these are the Parlements, which serve as a "depository for the laws" independent of the royal council and "the momentary will of the prince." These exercise the right of remonstrance: they "announce the laws when they are made"; they "recall them when they are forgotten"; and they "ceaselessly cause the laws to come forth from the dust where they are buried" (II, 4). These bodies, Montesquieu emphasizes, prevent the prince's salutary promptness in executing the laws from degenerating into haste. They "never better obey than when they proceed tardily and carry into the affairs of the prince that reflection that one can hardly expect from the lack of enlightenment in the court concerning the laws of the state and from the precipitancy of its councils" (V, 10).

The existence of a depository for the laws independent of the prince does much more than encourage rational policy making on his part. These bodies serve as "tribunals." They "render decisions," and these decisions, Montesquieu asserts, "ought to be preserved; they ought to be a subject for teaching and learning in order that one may judge here today as one judged here yesterday and the property and the lives of citizens here may be as secure and fixed as the constitution of the state itself." It is this that Montesquieu celebrates: the "fastidiousness (*délicatesse*)" of the judges, the manner in which jurisprudence becomes its own peculiar "art of reasoning," even the fact that confusion creeps in as different judges rule and suits are ably or poorly defended. Montesquieu admits that in the end there will be "an infinity of abuses," for these "creep into all that passes through the hands of men." But he dismisses this as "a necessary evil that the legislator will correct from time to time as contrary to the spirit of moderate government" (VI, 1). The crucial fact is that "the formalities of justice" give rise to "the liberty and security of the citizens," for "the pains, the expenses, the delays, even the dangers attendant on justice are the price that each citizen pays for his liberty." In "moderate states," Montesquieu insists, "the head of the least citizen is valued (*considérable*)," and "one does not relieve him of his honor and goods except after an extended examination: one does not deprive him of his life except when the fatherland itself attacks it; and it does not launch such an attack without leaving him every possible means for defending" that life (VI, 2). Montesquieu makes much of the fact that monarchy is distinguished from despotism by "the security" that it confers on "the great" (VI, 21). Where Machiavelli was concerned chiefly with the integrity of the state and its success in conquest and war, Montesquieu gives priority to "the security of individuals."[39] It is "in moderate governments," where the obstacles to the abuse of power are many, that "gentleness reigns" (VI, 9).[40]

It would be tempting, then, to suppose that the government of England was conceived by Montesquieu as a variant form of monarchy. In more than one passage, he seems to take this for granted (IX, 9; XI, 7), and the notion is by no means patently absurd.[41] After all, England possessed a king, and Montesquieu associates monarchy not only with political moderation but with liberty as well. To this hypothesis, however, there are two insuperable objections. Quite early on, Montesquieu remarks in passing that "the English, in order to favor liberty, have eliminated all the intermediate powers that formed their monarchy" (II, 4); and he nowhere even intimates that honor is the passion that sets the English polity in motion.[42] England may be, as he puts it, monarchical in disguise—but it is monarchical neither in its nature and structure nor in its principle.[43] It would appear, then, to be *sui generis*.[44]

Object and Principle

To determine what is "the principle" of England's government, one must consider what is revealed by the fact that "political liberty" is that polity's particular "object." Monarchies may give rise to liberty but not in the course of pursuing it. As Montesquieu demonstrates, liberty is an accidental by-product of their pursuit of that polity's "direct object," which is "the glory of the citizens, of the state, and of the prince" (XI, 7). Monarchies may achieve moderation by combining, regulating, and tempering powers so that one power possesses the ballast to resist another—but moderation is not that at which they aim. Thus, if the government of France is, in this regard, "a masterpiece of legislation" (V, 14, 297), this fact is largely a matter of chance. After confessing, "I do not believe that there has ever been on this earth a government as well-tempered as that which existed in each part of Europe during the [feudal] period in which" the Gothic monarchy "subsisted," Montesquieu adds that he finds it "a matter for wonder (*admirable*) that the corruption of the government of a conquering people has formed the best species of government that men have been able to imagine" (XI, 8).[45] One consequence of the fortuitous origin of Europe's monarchies is that they only "approach political liberty more or less." England's government would appear to be different: if it actually provides for "political liberty," it is because it aims directly at it. English liberty is, at least in some measure, a product of "prudence" rather than "chance" (V, 14, 297; XI, 7).

Montesquieu prefaces his initial discussion of the English polity with an account of the nature of "liberty," which he carefully distinguishes from "independence" of the sort possessed by those in the state of nature. His point is that the former is much more valuable than the latter. "Liberty," properly understood, "is the right to do what the laws permit."[46] It is incompatible with genuine independence, for if a man is "able to do what the laws forbid, he no longer has liberty since the others would likewise possess this same power" and obstruct his freedom to do what the laws allow (XI, 3).[47] To prevent those most likely to strive for this species of independence from being "able to abuse power," he soon adds, "it is necessary that in the disposition of things power check power." It is his contention that "a constitution can be such that no one will be constrained to do things that the law does not require or prevented from doing those which the law permits him to do" (XI, 4). This is the object of the English polity, and it constitutes what Montesquieu has in mind when he devotes the eleventh book of his tome to the laws which form "political liberty in its relation with the constitution." The government of England pursues this end chiefly through what came to be called the separation of powers. In its relation with the constitution, political liberty "is formed by a certain distribution of the three powers" (XII, 1).[48]

Montesquieu distinguishes "political liberty in its relation with the constitution" from "political liberty in its relation with the citizen." The latter is the subject of the twelfth book of *The Spirit of Laws*. But because it is the central focus of Montesquieu's concern, it intrudes on that book's immediate predecessor as well. "In a citizen," Montesquieu explains therein, "political liberty is that tranquillity of mind (*esprit*) which comes from the opinion that each has of his security." If he is to possess "this liberty, it is necessary that the government be such that one citizen be unable to fear (*craindre*) another citizen" (XI, 6, 397). The separation of powers is as essential to the elimination of this fear as it is to the guarantee that "no one will be constrained to do things that the law does not require or prevented from doing those which the law permits him to do."[49]

On the face of it, the two forms of liberty would appear to be inseparable. Where the executive and the legislative power are united, as they are in despotisms and tend to be in republics, one has reason "to fear (*craindre*)" that the individual or body that "makes tyrannical laws" will "execute them in a tyrannical manner." In similar fashion, if "the power of judging" is not somehow "kept separate from the legislative power and the executive power, there is no liberty." If it is united with the legislative power, "the judge would be the legislator" and the citizen's life and property would be subject to "arbitrary power." If it is united with the executive power, "the judge would have the strength (*force*) of an oppressor." If the power "of making the laws" were united with "that of executing public resolutions and with that of judging crimes or the disputes of particular citizens," Montesquieu exclaims, "all would be lost" (XI, 6, 397).

After having set up this standard, Montesquieu applies it to the polities he has earlier described. If "the kingdoms of Europe" tend to be "moderate," we are told, it is because the prince, who exercises the legislative and the executive power, leaves the power of judging to his subjects. The unity of the three powers in the Turkish Sultan produces "a frightful despotism"; that same unity causes there to be "less liberty in the republics of Italy" than in Europe's monarchies: these governments can sustain themselves only with "means as violent" as those used by the government of the Turks. As a "witness" Montesquieu summons the example of Venice with its "state inquisitors and the lion's mouth into which every informer can at any time throw his accusation by letter," and he mentions the "tyrannical magistracy of the ephors" at Sparta in the same regard. It was generally true of "the ancient republics," he later notes, that "there was this abuse: that the people were at the same time judge and accuser." Republics can be "despotic" in more than one way (XI, 6, 397-99, 404).[50]

Montesquieu's account of the English constitution has an odd tone. Instead of describing, he resorts repeatedly to the language of prescription;[51] and he underlines the point by issuing a disclaimer at the end: "It is not for me to examine whether the English actually enjoy this liberty or not." All that he will assert is that "it is established by their laws" (XI, 6, 407). One is left with the impression that his England is less a reality than an ideal type suggestive of the potential inherent in England's laws: one is given the same impression later by his persistent resort to the conditional in describing the contribution of England's laws in forming "the mores, the manners, and the character" of the nation (XIX, 27). He is far more concerned with what is likely to happen than with what does. "I will be," he warns, "more attentive to the order of things than to the things themselves" (XIX, 1).

Moreover, like Tocqueville in *Democracy in America*, Montesquieu seems to have his eye as much on the future as on the present or past—and though he betrays an enthusiasm for the political liberty embodied in England's laws, he qualifies this with a denial that it is his intention "to disparage the other governments or to say that this extreme political liberty should serve to mortify those who possess none but one that is moderate." "How could I say that," he exclaims, "I who believe that an excess even of reason is not always desirable and that men better accommodate themselves nearly always to middling things than to extremities" (XI, 6, 407)?

Montesquieu's refusal to issue a blanket endorsement of the English example should give us pause—for, however valuable political liberty may be, there may be something wrong with a polity that makes that liberty its "direct object." There is much in his description of the structure of that polity which deserves discussion: his defense of the principle of representation, his endorsement of a bicameralism that leaves the initiative to the popularly elected branch and a veto to the hereditary nobility that stands in for the well-to-do, the case that he makes on behalf of a unitary executive armed with a veto and accountable to the legislature for his deeds solely through the principle of ministerial responsibility, the emphasis that he places on the linkage between taxation and representation, and the argument that he advances on behalf of an army of citizen soldiers commanded by the executive but ultimately dependent on the legislature (XI, 6).[52] More revealing of the source of Montesquieu's reservations concerning the English polity, however, is the fact that, when he discusses the English constitution, he singles out for particular attention the power of judging and the criminal law.[53] He argues for fixed judgments determined by statute, and he praises the practice by which defendants help select their panel of jurors.[54] Security and fairness are obviously a concern. But repeatedly another theme thrusts itself into the limelight: Montesquieu's interests seem to be largely psychological.[55] Thus, in praising the jury system, he initially exclaims that "the power of judging" is "so terrible among men," and he then recommends that this power "be attached neither to a certain condition nor to a certain profession" and that it "become, so to speak, invisible and null." If this is the practice, "one does not continually have one's judges before one's eyes; and one fears (*craint*) the magistracy and not the magistrates." In much the same spirit, he adds that the jury should be made up of the peers of the accused so that "he cannot be of the mind that he has fallen into the hands of those inclined to do him violence" (XI, 6, 398-99).

The emphasis placed on "fear" and on the defendant's state of mind is that which should catch and hold our attention. If Montesquieu can distinguish the liberty of the people from the power of the people, it is because he defines "political liberty in its relation with the citizen" in terms of "security, or, at least, the opinion that one has of one's security" (XII, 1-2). If anything, he seems more concerned with sustaining the citizen's "tranquillity of mind" than with sustaining his capacity "to do what the laws permit" him to do (XI, 3-4; XI, 6, 397). This explains why, in the end, he asks his readers to contemplate a paradoxical conclusion: that "it can happen that the constitution will be free and the citizen not" and that "the citizen will be free and the constitution not"; that while "only the disposition of the laws, and even the fundamental laws," can "form liberty in its relation with the constitution," liberty "in its relation with the citizen" can be made to arise "from the mores, from the manners, and from the received examples" prevalent within a political community and that it is less effectively promoted by political arrangements than by "certain civil laws" (XII, 1). It also clarifies why he can claim that "the knowledge which one has acquired in some countries and which one will acquire in others with regard to the surest regulations that one can hold to in criminal judgments interests human kind more than anything else that there is in the world" (XII, 2). And it makes sense of his otherwise inexplicable concern with the psychological impact of taxation and his association of "duties," such as those "on commodities," that "the people least feel" with both "moderate government" and "the spirit of liberty" (XIII, 7-8, 14).[56] If he claims that, "in our monarchies, all felicity consists in the opinion that the people have of the gentleness (la douceur) of the government" (XII, 25), it is because human happiness and, therefore, "political liberty in its relation with the citizen" is a state of mind.[57]

All of this suggests something about human nature and something about the "principle" of the "republic concealed under the form of a monarchy" that Montesquieu investigated during his extended sojourn in England. In contrast with its ancient counterpart, this modern republic requires little or no virtue. Nowhere does Montesquieu suggest that "self-renunciation" is required to sustain it. Nor can one claim that it demands anything "very painful." This is because what Montesquieu says of monarchy can be said of England's government as well: it "is favored by the passions and favors them in its turn" (IV, 5). But though the passion that it favors and is favored by is as solid and reliable as the "principle" of monarchy, if not more so, this passion is not the longing for distinction. The "principle" of the modern republic is not honor; it is something very much like fear.[58]

English Inquiétude

The government of England is not a despotism comparable to the oriental states that Montesquieu so vehemently despised, but it has an undeniable kinship with despotism. It has as its object "political liberty," not "the delights of the prince." But it comprehends that political liberty in terms of the citizen's "opinion of his security." Where the "despotic state" in China takes as its object "public tranquillity" and other despotisms pursue "tranquillity" as their "aim (but)," if not their "object," England's government pursues the individual citizen's "tranquillity of mind."[59]

If one were to examine the English constitution solely with regard to its "nature" or "structure," one would have to conclude that its three separated powers "form a condition of repose or inaction." But, of course, England's government is rarely, if ever, at rest (XI, 6, 405). In interpreting this fact, Montesquieu evidences a Heraclitean understanding of the human condition comparable to that of Machiavelli.[60] The foundation of the latter's teaching concerning politics is his claim that "all the things of men are in motion and cannot remain fixed." By this he meant to convey something closely akin to what Thomas Hobbes and David Hume had in mind when they asserted that reason is the slave of the passions. As Machiavelli put it by way of explanation, "the human appetites" are "insatiable"; "by nature" human beings "desire everything" while "by fortune they are allowed to secure little"; and since "nature has created men in such a fashion" that they are "able to desire everything" but not "to secure everything," their "desire is always greater than the power of acquisition (*la potenza dello acquistare*)."[61]

In writing of England, Montesquieu follows Machiavelli's lead—contending that "this nation" is "always inflamed" and that "it is more easily conducted by its passions than by reason, which never produces any great effects on the minds of men" (XIX, 27, 577). And in speaking of "the three powers," he argues that when, "by the necessary motion of things, they are constrained to move (*aller*), they are forced to move in concert" (XI, 6, 405). One cannot say of the English constitution what Montesquieu says of despotism: that it "jumps up, so to speak before our eyes"; that "it is uniform throughout"; that "the passions alone are necessary for its establishment." The modern republic is, after all, "a master-piece of legislation," a product not just of chance but of prudent artifice as well. One can say of it, instead, what he says of monarchy: that, in it, "policy makes great things happen with as little of virtue as it can" and that, "just as in the most beautiful machines, art also employs as little of movement, of forces, of wheels as is possible. The state subsists independently of love of the fatherland, of desire for true glory, of self-renunciation, of the sacrifice of one's dearest interests, and of all those heroic virtues which we find in the ancients and know only from hearing them spoken of." Moreover, one can say that, once a modern republic is instituted, "the human passions that set it in motion" are "alone" necessary to sustain it—and that the ruling passion that does so is closely akin to the very passion that is responsible for the "establishment" of despotism (III, 5; V, 14, 297).

This helps explain, among other things, the tenor of Montesquieu's description of the contribution made by England's "laws" in forming "the mores, the manners, and the character" of the English "nation" (XIX, 27).[62] One consequence of the laws' provision of liberty is that "all the passions there are free: hatred, envy, jealousy, the ardor to enrich and distinguish oneself appear to their full extent; and if things were otherwise, the state would be like a man struck down by a malady who has no passions because he has no strength (*forces*)." In a sense, the English citizen is unaccommodated man: like the individual trapped within the state of nature, he is "always independent."[63] He therefore follows "his caprices and his fantasies"; he and his countrymen are inclined "not to care to please anyone," and so "they abandon themselves to their own humors." And frequently, they switch parties and abandon one set of friends for another, having forgotten "the laws of love and those of hatred" (XIX, 27, 575).

Precisely because the laws make no distinctions among men, each Englishman "regards himself as a monarch; and men, in that nation," are, in a sense,
"confederates rather than fellow citizens." The fact that "no citizen ends up fearing (*craignant*) another" gives the Englishman a king-like "independence" that
makes the English as a nation "proud." But, at the same time, "living," as they
do "much among themselves" in a state of "retirement" or "retreat (*retraite*),"
they "often find themselves in the midst of those whom they do not know." This
renders them "timid," like those men in the state of nature truly graced with independence, but the recognition of "reciprocal fright (*une crainte réciproque*)"
does not have on them the effect that it has on men in their natural state: it does
not cause them to draw near, to take "pleasure" in the approach of "an animal"
of their "own sort," and to become sociable.[64] Instead, "one sees in" the "eyes"
of these Englishmen, "the better part of the time, a bizarre mixture of ill-
mannered shame and pride." Their "character" as a "nation" most clearly appears in the products of their minds—which reveal them as "people collected
within themselves" who are inclined to "think each entirely on his own" (XIX,
27, 582-83). In short, Montesquieu's Englishman is very much alone.

That so solitary a man should have an "uneasy spirit (*esprit inquiet*)" stands
to reason (XIX, 27, 582). Nor is it surprising that, unprompted by genuine peril
or even by false alarm, he should nonetheless "fear (*craint*) the escape of a
good" that he "feels," that he "hardly knows," and that "can be hidden from us,"
and that this "fear (*crainte*)" should "always magnify objects" and render him
"uneasy (*inquiet*) in his situation" and inclined to "believe" that he is "in danger
even in those moments when" he is "most secure" (XIX, 27, 575-76). The liberation of the passions does not give rise to joy. "Political liberty in its relation
with the constitution" may well be "established" for the English "by their laws,"
but this does not mean that they "actually enjoy" what Montesquieu calls "political liberty in its relation with the citizen"—for the latter is constituted by
"that tranquillity of mind which comes from the opinion that each has of his security," and the English are anything but tranquil of mind (XI, 1; XI, 6, 397,
407)

"Uneasiness (*inquiétude*)" without "a certain object" would appear to be the
Englishman's normal state of mind. He is rarely given reason to fear another
citizen: fear is not deployed to secure his obedience as it is in a despotism. But
he is anxious and fearful nonetheless. Moreover, in such a country, "the majority of those who possess wit and intelligence (*esprit*) would be tormented by that
very *esprit*: in the disdain or disgust" that they would feel with regard "to all
things, they would be unhappy with so many reasons not to be so" (XIX, 27,
576, 582).

In singling out *inquiétude* as the peculiar disposition of the English, Montesquieu is obliquely addressing a contemporary debate. In his *Essay Concerning
Human Understanding*, John Locke had argued "that the Philosophers of old did
in vain enquire, whether *Summum bonum* consisted in Riches, or bodily De-

lights, or Virtue, or Contemplation," observing that "they might have as reasonably disputed, whether the best Relish were to be found in Apples, Plumbs, or Nuts; and have divided themselves into Sects upon it." His point was that "Men may chuse different things, and yet all chuse right, supposing them only like a Company of poor Insects, whereof some are Bees, delighted with Flowers, and their sweetness; others, Beetles, delighted with other kind of Viands." What men have in common, Locke argued, is not an orientation towards the good defined in any concrete way but "a constant succession of *uneasinesses*" such that "very little part of our life is so vacant from these *uneasinesses*, as to leave us free to the attraction of remoter absent good." "*Uneasiness*" was for Locke the distinguishing characteristic of all mankind: it was, in fact, the motive for all human action.[65]

In the French translation of *An Essay Concerning Human Understanding* that Pierre Coste produced in collaboration with Locke, *uneasiness* was rendered by *inquiétude*. "By *uneasiness*," Coste remarked, "the author means *the state of a man who is not at ease, the lack of ease & tranquillity in the soul,* which is in this regard purely passive." When he deployed *inquiétude* to translate *uneasiness*, Coste added, he had consistently italicized the French word. Unless one kept in mind precisely what Locke meant by the term, he explained, "it would not be possible to comprehend exactly the matters treated in" his crucial chapter "Of Power"—matters which Coste considered "the most important and difficult (*délicates*) in the entire work."[66] Locke's broad claims in this regard stirred up considerable discussion, especially among those who spoke French,[67] and Montesquieu's strategic deployment of the pertinent term in *The Spirit of Laws* is intended to suggest three conclusions: that Locke had mistakenly presumed that his countrymen were representative of all mankind; that, as a settled disposition, *inquiétude* is specific to the citizens who live under a particular form of government; and, most important of all, that the form of government "which has for the direct object of its constitution political liberty" characteristically fails to produce in its citizens the "tranquillity of mind" which constitutes "political liberty in its relation with the citizen."

Montesquieu's point becomes obvious when one reads his extended description of the character of the English nation in the context of what he has just written a few pages before concerning his native France. "If there were in the world," Montesquieu observes, "a nation which had a sociable humor, an openness of heart, a joy in living, a taste, a facility for communicating its thoughts, which was lively, agreeable, playful, sometimes imprudent, often indiscreet; and which had along with this courage, generosity, frankness, a certain sensitivity to honor, it would be necessary not to trouble, by the laws, its manners lest one trouble its virtues" as well (XIX, 5). One could certainly not say of the French what Montesquieu says concerning the English: that they evidence so great "a disgust for all things" that "they kill themselves without one being able to imagine any reason that would cause them to do so, that they kill themselves when in the bosom of happiness" (XIV, 12-13).[68] *Inquiétude* is the distinguishing feature of modern republican man.

Partisanship

Inquiétude is not, however, the principle of Montesquieu's modern republic, for in and of itself uneasiness can do little more than keep a polity on edge. It cannot animate it and give it a definite direction and orientation. *Inquiétude* is too shapeless: it is too plastic, too protean, too apt to succumb to whimsy and fashion, too much a creature of circumstance. If it is to assume the status of a political principle, *inquiétude* must undergo a metamorphosis giving it a more precise and stable form.[69] In Montesquieu's England, as we have seen, the laws are primary: they are themselves almost sufficient to give form to the nation's mores, manners, and character (XIX, 26-27, 574). In practice, then, it must be the separation of powers itself, the fundamental law of the English constitution, that transforms the characteristic uneasiness of the English into a passion capable of setting their polity in motion.

England's constitution works this transformation by providing a focus for the *inquiétude* that makes modern republican man so inclined to "fear the escape of a good" that he "feels," that he "hardly knows," and that "can be hidden from us," and so prone to "believe" that he is "in danger even in those moments when" he is "most secure" (XIX, 27, 575-76). In the political realm, Montesquieu observes, the characteristic uneasiness of the English gives rise to occasional panic, and the separation of powers gives direction to these popular fears. It does so by way of the partisanship that it fosters.

Partisanship is, in Montesquieu's judgment, the fundamental fact of English life. In consequence, it is with this fact that he begins his analysis of the influence of the laws on English mores, manners, and character: partisanship is the premise from which his argument unfolds. "Given that in this state, there would be two visible powers, the legislative and the executive power," he observes at the outset, "and given that every citizen would have a will of his own and would value his independence according to his own pleasure, the majority of people would have more affection for one of these powers than for the other, since the great number is not ordinarily equitable or sensible enough to hold the two in equal affection." This propensity would only be exacerbated by the fact that the executive had offices in his gift, for his dispensing of patronage would alienate those denied favor as it turned those employed into adherents (XIX, 27, 575).

"The hatred" existing between the two parties "would endure," Montesquieu tells us, "because it would always be powerless," and it would forever be powerless because "the parties" would be "composed of free men" who would be inclined to switch sides if one party or the other appeared to have "secured too much." The monarch would himself be caught in the toils of partisan strife: "contrary to the ordinary maxims of prudence, he would often be obliged to give his confidence to those who have most offended him and to disgrace those who have best served him, doing out of necessity what other princes do by choice." Not even the historians would escape with their judgment intact: "in states extremely free, they betray the truth on account of their liberty itself, which always produces divisions" such that "each becomes as much the slave of the prejudices of his faction as he would be of a despot" in an absolute monarchy (XIX, 27, 575, 583).

Montesquieu finds this spectacle droll but in no way distressing. In a polity so caught up in partisanship, he notes, "every man would, in his way, take part in the administration of the state," and "the constitution would give to everyone . . . political interests." One consequence of this widespread political participation would be that "this nation would love its liberty prodigiously since this liberty would be true." To "defend" its freedom, "it would sacrifice its well-being, its ease, its interests," subjecting itself to taxes that no prince, however absolute, would dare impose, and deploying against its enemies in the form of a national debt owed its own citizens "an immense fictional wealth that the confidence and nature of its government would render real." Another side-effect of the party struggle would be that everyone "would speak much of politics," and some would "pass their lives calculating events which, given the nature of things and the caprice of fortune, . . . would hardly submit to calculation." It matters little, Montesquieu intimates, whether "particular individuals reason well or ill" concerning public affairs: in a nation that is free, "it suffices that they reason," for from their reasoning arises "the liberty" that provides them with protection against the unfortunate "effects of this same reasoning" (XIX, 27, 577, 582).

In a country governed in this manner, Montesquieu hastens to add, the charges lodged by the party inclined to oppose the executive "would augment even more" than usual "the terrors of the people, who would never know really whether they were in danger or not." The modern republic is, however, superior to its ancient predecessor in that "the legislative power," which is distinct from the people, "has the confidence of the people" and can in times of crisis render them calm.[70] "In this fashion," Montesquieu observes, when "the terrors impressed" on the populace lack "a certain object, they would produce nothing but vain clamors and name-calling (injures); and they would have this good effect: that they would stretch all the springs of government and render the citizens attentive" (XIX, 27, 576).

In circumstances more dire, however, the English would comport themselves in a manner reminiscent of the various peoples of ancient Crete–who showed how "healthy principles" can cause even "bad laws" to have "the effect of good." In their zeal "to keep their magistrates in a state of dependence on the laws," the Cretans are said to have "employed a means quite singular: that of insurrection." In a procedure "supposed to be in conformity with the law," Montesquieu reports, "one part of the citizenry would rise up, put the magistrates to flight, and oblige them to re-enter private life." One would naturally presume

that "such an institution, which established sedition for the purpose of preventing the abuse of power, would . . . overturn (*renverser*) any republic whatsoever," but Montesquieu insists that this was not the case in Crete because "the
people possessed the greatest love for the fatherland" (VIII, 11).

In England, where the citizens exhibit a love of liberty as prodigious as the
patriotism of the citizens of Crete, something quite similar transpires. If the terrors fanned by the party opposed to the executive were ever "to appear on the
occasion of an overturning (*renversement*) of the fundamental laws," Montesquieu observes, "they would be muted, lethal, excruciating and produce catas-
trophes: before long, one would see a frightful calm, during which the whole
would unite itself against the power violating the laws." Moreover, if such "disputes took shape on the occasion of a violation of the fundamental laws, and if a
foreign power appeared," as happened in 1688, "there would be a revolution,
which would change neither the form of the government nor its constitution: for
the revolutions to which liberty gives shape are nothing but a confirmation of
liberty" (XIX, 27, 576). As Montesquieu remarks elsewhere, the "impatience"
characteristic of such a people, "when it is joined with courage," gives rise to an
"obstinacy (*l'opiniâtreté*)" that makes a "free nation" well suited "to disconcert
the projects of tyranny." Their characteristic restlessness renders the English incapable of taking repose, and it renders them vigilant at the same time (XIV,
13).[71]

Paradoxically, then, the fact that Englishmen do not "actually enjoy" the
sense of "security" and "tranquillity of mind" which Montesquieu describes as
"political liberty in its relation with the citizen" helps account for the ethos of
political distrust and the spirit of watchfulness and wariness which guarantee
that "political liberty in its relation with the constitution" remains "established
by their laws" (XI, 6, 397, 407). The partisan conflict inspired by the separation
of powers transforms the *inquiétude* characteristic of the English into a vigilance
directed against all who might be tempted to encroach on their liberty. This vigilance is the passion that sets the English polity in motion.

Corruption in Republics

To grasp fully the implications of what Montesquieu has in mind when he intimates that underlying the principle of political vigilance animating the English
polity is the profound uneasiness that Locke had erroneously taken to be the distinguishing attribute of all mankind, one needs to consider the maladies to which
the various forms of government are prone. Montesquieu had brought his initial
account of political typology to an end with an examination of the phenomenon
of corruption. Throughout this discussion, he insisted that what counts as corruption in political affairs is relative to the form of government. "The corruption
of each government," he explains, "begins nearly always with that of its principles," and "once the principles of the government are corrupted, the best of its

laws become the worst and turn against the state . . . for the strength of the principle drives everything" (VIII, 1, 11-12).

The source of the pertinent species of corruption need not be internal to each form of government as such, but frequently it is. Thus, Montesquieu tells us, "the principle of democracy is corrupted not only when the spirit of equality is lost"—as it nearly always is in a republic situated on an extended territory in which "interests become particular" and "a man senses . . . that he can be happy, great, glorious without his fatherland and soon that he can be great solely on the ruins of his fatherland." Democracy's principle is corrupted also "when the spirit of extreme equality is seized on and each wishes to be equal to those chosen for command." If Montesquieu devotes considerable attention to the latter of the two possibilities, it is because "the spirit of extreme equality" reflects proclivities inherent within democratic republicanism. It is only natural that a democratic people should find "insufferable even the power that they confide" and that they should "wish to do everything on their own hook: to deliberate for the senate, to execute for the magistrates, and to strip all the judges" of their functions (VIII, 2, 16).

When a democratic people give way to "the spirit of extreme equality," the magistrates, the senators, the old, and fathers all lose respect; husbands are denied deference and masters, submission. Instead of being satisfied to have "for masters only one's equals," one seeks to have no master at all. All will then be equal not only in their capacity as citizens but regardless of the fact that a particular citizen may be "a magistrate, senator, judge, father, husband, or master." "Everyone will come to love this libertine life (*libertinage*)," Montesquieu laments. "The difficulty of command will be as fatiguing as that of obedience. The women, the children, the slaves will submit to no one. No longer will there be mores (*mœurs*) and love of order, and in the end there will be virtue no more" (VIII, 2-3).

The process of dissolution begins when "those to whom the people have entrusted themselves, wishing to conceal their own corruption, seek to corrupt the people." That their own ambition and avarice be not seen, these demagogues "speak to the people of their grandeur alone," and "they flatter their avarice without cessation." Thereafter, "corruption will grow among the corruptors, and it will grow among those who are already corrupted. The people will distribute all the public moneys to themselves. And just as they will have joined to their idleness the administration of affairs, they will join to their poverty the amusements of luxury." Given the taste that they have developed for idleness and luxury, the people will then make the public treasury their "object" and sell their votes for silver. But "the more they seem to draw advantage from their liberty, the more they approach the moment when they will lose it." At first, within the republic, there will be "petty tyrants possessing all of the vices of a single tyrant." In time, even "the remains of liberty become insupportable, a single tyrant

arises, and the people lose everything—even the advantages of their corruption"
(VIII, 2).[72]

Montesquieu's account of aristocratic corruption is similar. In its republicanism, after all, his aristocracy is quite like his democracy: it knows no restraint
but self-restraint (III, 3-4), and it can be sustained only if its territory is small
(VIII, 16). Even then, however, it becomes "corrupted when the power of the
nobles becomes arbitrary" and "the ruling families" no longer "observe" the
laws. What had been a monarchy with many monarchs then becomes a despotism with many despots. The republic may continue to exist with regard to and
among the nobles but it will be "despotic" with regard to "the governed." Moreover, when nobility becomes hereditary, "extreme corruption" is the natural result, for then the nobles "can hardly possess moderation." If they are few in
number, their power may be great but they will be insecure; if they are numerous, as they are in Venice, their power will be diminished and their security
augmented. The fact that a large membership in the ruling order renders their
"government less violent" does not, however, alter the fact that this government
will evidence "little in the way of virtue," for hereditary aristocracies are prone
to fall prey to "a spirit of nonchalance, idleness, and abandon," and a state under
the control of the dissolute will "possess neither strength (*force*) nor spring (*ressort*)." For an aristocracy to "sustain the strength (*force*) of its principle," Montesquieu insists, the laws must be such as to "make the nobles sense the dangers
and tiresomeness of command more than its delights" and the state must be "in
such a situation that it has something to dread." Security must "come from
within and uncertainty from without" (VIII, 5).

In this last regard, democracies and aristocracies are again alike. "Confidence" subverts them, for it is necessary that "a republic dread something." The
more successful a democracy is, the more the people have contributed to its success, the more prone they are to an "arrogance" that renders it impossible "to
guide them." It is in this context that Montesquieu remarks that the more democracies and aristocracies "have of security, the more, like waters excessively
tranquil, they are subject to corruption" (VIII, 4-5).

Corruption in Monarchies and Despotisms

In Montesquieu's estimation, monarchies are less vulnerable to corruption than
are democracies and aristocracies: the principle of honor that governs them is
far less fragile than the virtue required of democratic citizens and the moderation demanded from their aristocratic counterparts. In consequence, monarchies
are suited to territories of a considerable, if not unlimited size. If they become as
large as the empires of Alexander and Charlemagne, they either break apart or
succumb to despotic rule—but only then (VIII, 17). Of dread, morever, they
have no need. In fact, the "confidence" that tends to be fatal to republics "consti-

tutes the glory and security of a monarchy" (VIII, 5). The ruin of monarchies derives from another source.

If democracies succumb to corruption "when the people strip the senate, the magistrates, and the judges of their functions," monarchies suffer the same fate "when, little by little, they deprive the corporations (*des corps*) of their preroga-tives or the towns of their privileges" and thereby eliminate the intermediary powers. It is obvious that Montesquieu has in mind here the policy devised by Cardinal Richelieu—of whom he writes, "When this man did not have despot-ism in his heart, he had it in his head"—a policy systematically implemented at the first opportunity by Louis XIV. It is Montesquieu's contention that

> a monarchy is lost when the prince believes that he demonstrates his power more in changing the order of things than in following it; when he deprives one group of its natural functions in order to give them arbitrarily to others, and when he loves his fantasies more than what he wills.
>
> A monarchy is lost when the prince, ascribing everything solely to him-self, summons the state to his capital, the capital to his court, and the court to his person alone.
>
> Finally, it is lost when a prince misapprehends his authority, his situation, the love of his peoples; and when he does not sense that a monarch ought to judge himself secure just as a despot ought to believe himself in peril (V, 10; VIII, 6).

With an eye to Tacitus' depiction of imperial Rome, Montesquieu subsequently adds that monarchy's "principle" has itself been corrupted when "pre-eminent (*les premières*) dignities are marks of a pre-eminent servitude, when one de-prives the great of popular respect, and when one renders them the vile instru-ments of arbitrary power. It has been corrupted even more when honor has been set in contradiction with honors and when one is able to be covered at the same time with infamy and with dignities." In such circumstances, honor as a political principle ceases to be a force (VIII, 7).

There is an irony in this, which seems to have been lost on the courtiers and monarchs of the time. "If it is true (as one can see in every age) that to the de-gree that the power of the monarch becomes immense, his security diminishes," Montesquieu asks, "is it not a crime of *lèse-majesté* to corrupt this power to the extent of causing its nature to change" (VIII, 7)? Montesquieu openly worries that "a long abuse of power" or "a great conquest" will undermine "the mores" that sustain liberty and that there will be established on the continent of Europe a "despotism" such that "human nature" there will "suffer at least for a time the insults to which it is subject" elsewhere (VIII, 8). "Nothing," Montesquieu as-serts, "would have been more fatal to Europe, to his original subjects, to him-self, to his family" than the success of Louis XIV's putative "project" for the es-tablishment of a "universal monarchy" in the West. This king of France was better served by his "defeats" on the field of battle than he would have been "by victories" (IX, 7).

Montesquieu finds it difficult to speak of corruption within a despotism without resorting to paradox. The "principle" of this form of government, he explains, "is ceaselessly corrupted because it is in its nature corrupt. The other governments perish because particular accidents violate their principle; this one perishes by its own interior vice when accidental causes fail to impede its principle of self-corruption." Despotism can sustain itself without a frequent collapse into anarchy "only when circumstances drawn from its climate, religion, situation, or from the genius of its people force it to follow some order and to submit to some regularity (*souffrir quelque règle*). These things force its nature without altering it; its ferocity remains; for a certain time, it is tamed" (VIII, 10). Circumstances of just this sort, he soon adds, provide an explanation for the remarkable stability of the despotic polity that governs the Chinese (VIII, 21).[73]

English Corruption and the Separation of Powers

Just as Montesquieu nowhere explicitly discussed "the principle" informing the English polity, so nowhere in his book did he address the question of its "corruption." In one cryptic passage buried at the end of the chapter dealing with England as an exemplar of "political liberty in its relation with the constitution," however, he did acknowledge the vulnerability of England's government, and in that passage he deployed the pertinent adjective. "Just as all human things have an end," he wrote, "the state of which we speak will lose its liberty; it will perish. Rome, Lacedaemon, and Carthage have indeed perished. This state will perish when the legislative will be more corrupt than the executive power" (XI, 6, 407). On what he meant by the final sentence in the passage Montesquieu did not further elaborate—at least not in *The Spirit of Laws*.

Few appear to have taken notice of Montesquieu's puzzling aside. But, within a year of the book's publication, an English acquaintance named William Domville did write to its author to express dismay at the licentiousness of his own compatriots and to ask whether Montesquieu thought that England was in any immediate danger of succumbing to corruption and losing its liberty in the process.[74] In the course of preparing a reply designed both to reassure his English correspondent that "in Europe the last sigh of liberty will be heaved by an Englishman" and to draw his attention to the intimate connection between English liberty and English commerce,[75] Montesquieu sketched out in his notebooks a series of reflections that cast light on the brief remarks in his book.[76]

Montesquieu begins by remarking that it is "good" that England's monarch believes in the stability of the polity and "that the people believe that the foundations on which it is established are subject to disturbance (*peuvent être ébranlés*)": that "the prince renounces the idea of augmenting his authority" while "the people dream of preserving the laws." "I believe, sir," he then explains, "that what will conserve your government is the fact that the people basically have more of virtue than those who represent them." In England, "the soldier is worth more than his officers, and the people are worth more than their magistrates and those who govern them." The pay given officers is so great that it seems as if the English wanted to corrupt them, and there are so many ways in which one might make one's fortune in and through government that it seems as if the English wanted to corrupt their magistrates and representatives. "It is not the same with the whole body of the people," Montesquieu then adds, "and I believe that I have noticed a certain spirit of liberty that always flares up and is not readily extinguished."

Montesquieu acknowledges that corruption plays a role in Parliamentary elections but he denies that it affects the whole—for this species of corruption is limited to localities. Even more to the point: what Parliament lacks in probity, it possesses in enlightenment. The attempts of the executive to corrupt individual members of Parliament cannot successfully be covered up; and however much a given member may wish to be a rogue, he wishes as well to pass as a good man. Indeed, "those who betray their duty hope that the evil that they do will not extend so far that the members of the contrary party will wish to make them fear." In consequence, the evil that flows from this corruption is severely constrained.

From Montesquieu's perspective, the crucial fact is that within the populace there is a large and vigorous "middle class (*l'état moyen*)" that "still loves its laws and its liberty." As long as these "middling men (*gens médiocres*) preserve their principles," he insists, "it will be difficult" for England's "constitution to be overthrown." The steadfastness of these middling men is made possible by the fact that England is a mercantile society in which the chief "sources" of "wealth are commerce and industry," which are "of such a nature that he who draws on them is unable to enrich himself without enriching many others." Rome was more vulnerable to corruption because it was a martial society and the principal "sources" of its wealth were "the profits from the levying of tribute and the profits from the pillaging of the subject nations." That which enriched an individual Roman impoverished an infinite number of others. In consequence, Rome was distinguished by extreme wealth and extreme poverty. It lacked not only "middling men" but "the spirit of liberty" that, characteristically, they and they alone display. In England, Montesquieu concludes, liberty will be secure as long as "great fortunes . . . are not drawn from military employment and as long as those drawn from civil employment (*l'état civil*) remain moderate."[77]

To grasp the import of the observations that Montesquieu sketched out in preparation for writing back to his English correspondent, one must keep in mind that he is elaborating on his cryptic claim that England will continue to exemplify "political liberty in its relation with the constitution" as long as its legislature is less corrupt than its executive, and that he is doing so in a manner easily understood by someone conversant, as he and his correspondent were, with the principles espoused by the English Whigs. In this context, Montesquieu does what he pointedly refrains from doing in his book: he attributes "virtue" to the English middle classes. Nowhere, however, does he specify what constitutes this virtue: nowhere does he attribute to these Englishmen a passion for equality or a spirit of self-renunciation; nowhere does he describe the "singular institutions" by which the English provide for their education. Nor could he do so: as we have already noted, the "singular institutions" necessary for the production of virtue of this sort are inconsistent with "the confusion, the negligence, the extended affairs of a great people" and can be found only in "petty" states, such as the cities of ancient Greece, where "one can provide a general education and rear a people as a family" (IV, 7). The virtue that Montesquieu celebrates in his discussion of the English middle class is not republican virtue: it amounts to little more than the watchfulness typical of spirited men who are wary lest they be robbed of a prize possession.[78] Diminished though it may seem, this virtue deserves respect, for, as a political principle, vigilance is compatible with political moderation,[79] and this spirit is sufficient as a safeguard for the liberty established by England's laws.[80]

As Montesquieu and his English correspondent are both aware, the source of the pertinent corruption can be found in the military and civil offices and honors that are in the gift of England's executive.[81] These are, as Montesquieu confesses, exceedingly lucrative, and they can be used to influence voting in Parliament. But this public largesse is nothing, he insists, in comparison with the money to be made by private initiative in industry and commerce; and given the fact that this corruption extends to only a few members of Parliament, that the press and the opposition are poised to expose it,[82] and that the multitude of those within the electorate who are of middling wealth are beyond corruption's reach, fearful of executive encroachment, and vigilant in the Constitution's defense,[83] there is no immediate danger that the legislature will fully succumb to executive influence and that there will for all practical purposes cease to be a separation of powers. Such a danger would present itself only in the unlikely event that the management of commerce and industry were entrusted to the executive. In such a polity, should the populace in general and the middle class in particular ever be beholden to government for their economic well-being, the situation of the citizens would indeed be grim.[84]

All of this helps explain why, on the very first occasion in which Montesquieu mentions England, he makes two surprising observations: that if you "abolish in a monarchy the prerogatives of the lords, the clergy, the nobility, and the towns," as England's Parliament did, "you will soon have a state popular—or, indeed, one despotic"; and that the English who, "in order to favor liberty, have eliminated all the intermediate powers which formed their monarchy, . . . have good reason to conserve that liberty"—for, "if they should come to lose it, they would be one of the most fully enslaved peoples on the earth" (II, 4).[85] The principle of the English polity, the passion that sets it in motion, is by no means unnatural, and it is generally reliable—but it is not utterly impervious to corruption. The uneasiness, the fear, the anxiety, the impatience, and the restlessness that contribute to the spirit of obstinacy and vigilance which enables the English to defend their liberty might take another, less salutary, and quite ominous form should they fail, by chance, to succeed in that defense and should their failure in this particular deprive them thereafter of the sense of sturdy independence that had hitherto sustained their courage. Because the modern republic and despotism are in the passions that set them in motion akin, the former can easily degenerate into the latter.

This recognition caused Montesquieu's successors—Adam Ferguson and Adam Smith in Scotland, James Madison and Thomas Jefferson in America, and Benjamin Constant and Alexis de Tocqueville in his native France—to reflect on the laws and institutions that might be deployed within a modern republic to reinvigorate the despondent, to reduce timidity and reinforce pride, to transform impatience and anxiety into a form of public spiritedness unknown to the ancient republics, and to introduce within that polity a simulacrum of the sense of honor that had made monarchical France so attractive and so resistant to tyranny at the same time.[86] Their reflections were grounded in Montesquieu's analysis of the various "principles" or "human passions that set in motion" democracy, aristocracy, monarchy, despotism, and the peculiar form of government which he had found in England.

Notes

This essay was originally drafted for presentation at a conference on "Civic Humanism," sponsored by the Program on Constitutional Government in the Department of Government at Harvard University and held in Boulder, Colorado, 17-19 August 1995. It was subsequently presented: at a conference on "Republicanism and Liberalism in America and the German States, 1750-1850," sponsored by the German Historical Institute and held in Madison, Wisconsin, 3-5 October 1996; to gatherings of political scientists, historians, and students at Yale University, Columbia University, Johns Hopkins University, Dartmouth College, Boston College, St. Vincent's College, the University of California at Davis, Cambridge University, the Southern Political Science Association, the Society for Historians of the Early American Republic, the American Political Science Association, and the Centre de Recherches Politiques Raymond Aron at the École des Haute Études en Sciences Sociales in Paris—as well as at a conference on "*The Spirit of the Laws*, 1748-1998: Montesquieu's Enlightenment Science at the Millennium," held at the University of Tulsa, 19-20 February 1998. An earlier version was published as Paul A. Rahe, "Soft Despotism: Democracy's Drift," in *Foundations of American Civilization*, T. William Boxx and Gary M. Quinlivan, eds. (Latrobe, Pa: Center for Economic and Policy Education, 1999), 15-54. The overlapping paragraphs are reprinted here with permission. The final revisions were completed while I was a Visiting Fellow at Clare Hall, Cambridge.

I am especially indebted to Robert Dahl and to Bruce Ackerman, who by their own example brought home to me the degree to which Montesquieu's argument is less familiar in scholarly circles today than it should be; to James W. Muller and Michael Mosher—with whom, over the years, I have had innumerable conversations concerning *The Spirit of Laws*; and to Catherine Larrère, Istvan Hont, Cecil Courtney, and David Carrithers for concrete suggestions.

In citations, I have used the standard abbreviations for classical texts and for the books of the Bible provided in *The Oxford Classical Dictionary*, 3rd edition, Simon Hornblower and Antony Spawforth, eds. (Oxford: Oxford University Press, 1996), and in *The Chicago Manual of Style*, 14th edition (Chicago: University of Chicago Press, 1993), 474-75. Where possible, the ancient texts and more recent works of similar stature are cited by the divisions and subdivisions employed by the author or introduced by subsequent editors (that is, by book, part, chapter, section number, paragraph, act, scene, line, Stephanus page, or by page and line number). All of the translations are my own.

1. All of the interlinear references in the text are to the Pléiade edition of Montesquieu's *Œuvres complètes*. Where I found that I could not do better myself, I have not been hesitant to borrow phraseology from Montesquieu, *The Spirit of the Laws*, Thomas Nugent, trans. (New York: Hafner, 1949), and from Montesquieu, *The Spirit of the Laws*, Anne M. Cohler, Basia Carolyn Miller, and Harold Samuel Stone, ed. and trans. (Cambridge: Cambridge University Press, 1989).

2. See C. P. Courtney, "Montesquieu and the Problem of 'La Diversité,'" in *Enlightenment Essays in Memory of Robert Shackleton*, Giles Barber and C. P. Courtney, eds. (Oxford: The Voltaire Foundation, 1988), 61-81, and Chapter 1, above.

3. See Marcel Prélot, "Montesquieu et les formes de gouvernement," in *La pensée politique et constitutionnelle de Montesquieu: bicentenaire de L'Esprit des lois*, 1748-1948 (Paris: Recueil Sirey, 1952), 110-32; Simone Goyard-Fabre, "La typologie des gouvernements selon Montesquieu," *L'Ecole des lettres* (28 April 1973): 39-43; Thomas L. Pangle, *Montesquieu's Philosophy of Liberalism: A Commentary on The Spirit of the Laws* (Chicago: University of Chicago Press, 1973), 48-52, 70-71; Paul Vernière, *Montesquieu et "L'Esprit des lois" ou la raison impure* (Paris: Société d'édition d'enseignement supérieur, 1977); Catherine Larrère, "Les typologies des gouvernements chez Montesquieu," *in Études sur le XVIIIe siècle*, Jean Ehrard, ed. (Clermont-Ferrand: Association des publications de la Faculté des Lettres, 1979), 87-103; and Tzvetan Todorov, "Droit naturel et formes de gouvernement dans *L'Esprit des lois,"* *Esprit* n.s. 75 (March, 1983): 35-48. Note also Michael A. Mosher, "The Particulars of a Universal Politics: Hegel's Adaptation of Montesquieu's Typology," *American Political Science Review* 78 (1984): 179-88.

4. For a penetrating, if not in all respects persuasive discussion of this propensity on Montesquieu's part, see Louis Althusser*, Politics and History: Montesquieu, Rousseau, Hegel and Marx*, Ben Brewster, trans. (London: NLB, 1972), 17-42.

5. Cf. Polyb. 6.3.5-10.14 with Xen. *Mem.* 4.6.12, *Oec.* 21.9-12; Pl. *Pol.* 291d-303b, *Leg.* 3.689e-702d, 4.712c-715d, 8.832b-d; Arist. *Eth. Nic.* 1160a31-1161b10, *Pol.* 1278b30-1280a5, 1284b35-1285b33, 1295a7-24, *Rh.* 1365b21-1366a22, and see Pl. *Leg.* 6.756e-758a, Arist. *Pol.* 1281b22-38 (esp. 28-31), 1295a25-1297a12 (esp. 1296b14-16), 1297b1-27, 1329a2-17, 1332b12-41. Note, in this connection, Pind. *Pyth.* 2.86-88, Hdt.

3.80-83, and Thuc. 8.97.2. In Montesquieu's day, with the exception of a few fragments, the pertinent passages of Cicero's *Republic* (1.20.33-2.44.70, 3.13.23, 25.37-35.48) were as yet undiscovered.

6. Although he is perfectly aware of the possibility that an aristocracy will degenerate into a "despotism of the few" and a democracy into a "despotism of the people," Montesquieu is persuaded that these are unstable and will quickly enough collapse into a "despotism of one alone": consider "Dossier de *L'Esprit des lois*," 235 (1893), in Pléiade, II, 1048, in light of Larrère, "Les typologies des gouvernements chez Montesquieu," 87-103.

7. See Thomas Hobbes, *The Elements of Law Natural and Politic*, 2nd edition, Ferdinand Tönnies, ed. (London: Frank Cass, 1969), II.i.3; *De Cive: The Latin Version*, Howard Warrender, ed. (Oxford: Clarendon Press, 1983), II.vii.1-17, x.2; and *Leviathan*, Edwin Curley, ed. (Indianapolis: Hackett, 1994), II.xix.1-2.

8. The pertinent passage was initially included in and eventually excised from *Spirit of Laws* III, 9: see "Dossier de *L'Esprit des lois*," in Pléiade, II, 996.

9. For the most part, Machiavelli is content to juxtapose republics with principalities: consider *Il principe* 1 with an eye to the implications of 15-19. He makes it clear, however, that in the end even this distinction is illusory: cf. *Discorsi sopra la prima deca de Tito Livio* 1.20 with *Il principe* 9; see Harvey C. Mansfield, Jr., "Machiavelli and the Modern Executive," in *Understanding the Political Spirit: Philosophical Investigations from Socrates to Nietzsche*, Catherine H. Zuckert, ed. (New Haven: Yale University Press, 1988), 88-110 (esp. 97-102), and Mansfield, *Taming the Prince: The Ambivalence of Modern Executive Power* (New York: The Free Press, 1989), 1-149. And yet, in his discussion of Ottoman Turkey and of France, he insists on the crucial importance of the very features that are determinative for Montesquieu's denial that monarchy and despotism are one and the same: see *Il principe* 4 and 19. Note, more generally, Machiavelli, *Discorsi sopra la prima deca de Tito Livio* 1.2-8, 16, 19, 55, 58, 3.1, in light of Mansfield, *Machiavelli's New Modes and Orders: A Study of the Discourses on Livy* (Ithaca: Cornell University Press, 1979), 32-62, 79-83, 88-90, 160-64, 168-74, 299-305 (esp. 304-5), and see Elena Fasano Guarini, "Machiavelli and the Crisis of the Italian Republics," in *Machiavelli and Republicanism*, Gisela Bock, Quentin Skinner, and Maurizio Viroli, eds. (Cambridge: Cambridge University Press, 1990), 17-40. In citing Machiavelli, I have employed Niccolò Machiavelli, *Tutte le opere*, Mario Martelli, ed. (Florence: Sansoni, 1971). Note Robert Shackleton, "Montesquieu and Machiavelli: A Reappraisal," *Essays on Montesquieu and on the Enlightenment*, David Gilson and Martin Smith, eds. (Oxford: The Voltaire Foundation, 1988), 117-31. For an overview, see Etorre Levi-Malvano, *Montesquieu and Machiavelli*, A. J. Pansini, trans. (Kopperl, Tex.: Greenvale Press, 1992), 13-87 (esp. 33).

10. Precisely because he distinguished monarchy from despotism and did so in this fashion, historians, especially in France, have tended to treat *The Spirit of Laws* as a partisan tract written in defense of the order into which Montesquieu was himself born. Some take him to be a reactionary aristocrat: see Albert Mathiez, "La place de Montesquieu dans l'histoire des doctrines politiques du XVIIIe siècle," *Annales historiques de la Révolution française* 7 (1930): 97-112, and Franklin L. Ford, *Robe and Sword: The Regrouping of the French Aristocracy After Louis XIV* (Cambridge, Mass.: Harvard University Press, 1953), 222-45. Others treat him as an aristocratic liberal: see Elie Carcassonne, *Montesquieu et le problème de la constitution française au XVIIIe siècle* (Paris: Presses Universitaire de France, 1927). For a more nuanced approach, see Harold A.

Ellis, "Montesquieu's Modern Politics: *The Spirit of the Laws* and the Problem of Modern Monarchy in Old Regime France," *History of Political Thought* 10 (1989): 665-700. In their eagerness to make of Montesquieu a man of his own time, however, very few scholars are inclined even to contemplate the possibility that he wrote *The Spirit of Laws*, as he said that he had, with an eye to being "useful" to people "seven or eight centuries" after his own time: "Dossier de *L'Esprit des lois*," 198 (1940), in Pléiade, II, 1039-40.

11. In this connection, see R. Koebner, "Despot and Despotism: Vicissitudes of a Political Term," *Journal of the Warburg and Courtauld Institutes* 14 (1951): 275-302; Melvin Richter, "Despotism," in *Dictionary of the History of Ideas*, Philip P. Wiener, ed. (New York: Scribners, 1973-74), II, 1-18; and Franco Venturi, "Oriental Despotism," *Journal of the History of Ideas* 24 (1963): 133-42. Then, see Françoise Weil, "Montesquieu et le despotisme," in *Actes du Congrès Montesquieu réuni à Bordeaux du 23 au 26 mai 1955* (Bordeaux: Impriméries Delmas, 1956), 191-215; Badreddine Kassem, *Décadence et absolutisme dans l'oeuvre de Montesquieu* (Paris: Librairie Minard, 1960); David Young, "Montesquieu's View of Despotism and His Use of Travel Literature," *Review of Politics* 40 (1978): 392-405; and Chapter 5, below.

12. Bernard Manin, "Montesquieu et la politique moderne," *Cahiers de philosophie politique* 2-3 (1984-85): 157-229 (esp. 182-229), does much to clarify what it is that links Montesquieu with Aristotle and distinguishes these two exponents of political prudence from Plato, Hobbes, Rousseau, and the like—but he errs in suggesting that both are somehow pluralists with regard to political ends. His discussion of Plato and Aristotle should be contrasted with that to be found in Arlene W. Saxonhouse, *Fear of Diversity: The Birth of Political Science in Ancient Greek Thought* (Chicago: University of Chicago Press, 1992). As will become clear in the course of this essay, Montesquieu's appreciation for political and cultural diversity derives from the emphasis he gives to a unitary principle of political psychology. For further exploration of the links between Montesquieu and Aristotle, see Judith N. Shklar, "Virtue in a Bad Climate: Good Men and Good Citizens in Montesquieu's *L'Esprit des lois*," in *Enlightenment Studies in Honour of Lester G. Crocker*, Alfred J. Bingham and Virgil W. Topazio, eds. (Oxford: The Voltaire Foundation, 1979), 315-28, and Simone Goyard-Fabre, *Montesquieu: La nature, les lois, la liberté* (Paris: Presses Universitaires de France, 1993). That Montesquieu is best read as a sociologist I am persuaded neither by Émile Durkheim, "Montesquieu's Contribution to the Rise of Social Science," *Montesquieu and Rousseau: Forerunners of Sociology*, Ralph Mannheim, trans. (Ann Arbor: University of Michigan Press, 1965), 1-64, nor by Pierre Manent, *The City of Man*, Marc A. LePain, trans. (Princeton: Princeton University Press, 1998), 11-85 (esp. 50-85). As Tzvetan Todorov demonstrates in *On Human Diversity: Nationalism, Racism, and Exoticism in French Thought*, Catherine Porter, trans. (Cambridge, Mass.: Harvard University Press, 1993), 353-83, in Montesquieu, political analysis is inseparable from moral reflection.

13. See Althusser, *Politics and History*, 43-60. Unfortunately, Althusser's heavy-handed and clumsy attempt to depict Montesquieu as a partisan of his own class (26-29, 96-106) mars his otherwise perceptive discussion of the latter's analysis of republicanism, monarchy, and despotism (61-86).

14. For an extended meditation on the significance of this unexpected shift, see Manent, *The City of Man*, 11-85 (esp. 11-49, 82-85).

15. That he has discussed "the principles" of England's "constitution" in *Spirit of Laws* XI, 6 Montesquieu specifies at XIX, 27, 574. In XI, 5 and at XIX, 27, 574, he is evidently employing the plural term *principes* in the loose, non-technical sense in which

he had used it in the preface to his book (Preface), in the title of XIX, and with some frequency elsewhere (IV, 2, 264; IV, 8; V, 9; VIII, 14; XI, 16; XVII, 7; XIX, 5, 16-17; XXVIII, 6). As is suggested by Montesquieu's choice of words in V, 18; VIII, 11-12; XI, 13 and 16, the plural term as used in these passages quite often includes what he has in mind when he uses the singular term in its technical sense.

16. See Pangle, *Montesquieu's Philosophy of Liberalism*, 1-19. Note also Anne M. Cohler, "Montesquieu's Perception of his Audience for the *Spirit of the Laws*," *Interpretation* 11:3 (September, 1983): 317-32.

17. For an argument along these lines, see Mark Hulliung, *Montesquieu and the Old Regime* (Berkeley: University of California Press, 1976), 1-3, 14, 212-21. Cf., however, Giuseppe Cambiano, "Montesquieu e le republiche greche," *Rivista di filosofia* 45 (1974): 93-144.

18. I first set out much of the pertinent evidence in Paul A. Rahe, "The Primacy of Politics in Classical Greece," *The American Historical Review* 89 (1984): 265-93; I restate and amplify my argument and then explore its consequences for our understanding of classical civilization in Rahe, *Republics Ancient and Modern*, vol. I: *The Ancien Régime in Classical Greece* (Chapel Hill: University of North Carolina Press, 1994).

19. Cf. Pl. *Rep.* 443d-e, Rom. 6:17-18, and Thomas Aquinas, *Summa theologiae*, Thomas Gilby, O.P., et al., eds. (New York: McGraw and Hill, 1964-76) Ia q.77 a.4, and note Paul A. Rahe, "Situating Machiavelli," in *Renaissance Civic Humanism Reconsidered*, James Hankins, ed. (Cambridge: Cambridge University Press, 2000), 270-308.

20. See Pangle, *Montesquieu's Philosophy of Liberalism*, 50-70, who juxtaposes Aristotle's exploration of the character of political virtue, its defects, and the manner in which it points beyond itself to moral and philosophical virtue with Montesquieu's quite different account. See also Manent, *The City of Man*, 12-49 (esp. 12-34).

21. Consider Arist. *Eth. Nic.* 1103a4-b25 in light of 1097b28-1098a18, 1098b22-99a21.

22. Hom. *Il.* 6.208, 9.443.

23. Cf. Machiavelli, *Discorsi sopra la prima deca di Tito Livio* 1 Proemio, 4, 3.27, 31, 43—all of which should be read in light of 2.2.

24. For further evidence suggesting the depth of Montesquieu's admiration for the ancients, see *Pensées* 444 (110), 589 (1607), 598 (221), and 604 (1253), in Pléiade, I, 1018, 1081-82, 1127, 1129-31.

25. See Pangle, *Montesquieu's Philosophy of Liberalism*, 52-106 (esp. 72-106, 112-13). In this connection, see also Roger B. Oake, "Montesquieu's Analysis of Roman History," *Journal of the History of Ideas* 16 (1955): 44-59, and David Lowenthal, "Montesquieu and the Classics: Republican Government in *The Spirit of the Laws*," in *Ancients and Moderns: Essays on the Tradition of Political Philosophy in Honor of Leo Strauss*, Joseph Cropsey, ed. (New York: Basic Books, 1964), 258-87.

26. Cf. *Spirit of Laws* VII, 2.

27. One cure for this disease is provided by commerce: see Manent, *The City of Man*, 36-49, 80-85.

28. Consider Montaigne, "De la cruauté" and "De la vertu," in *Les essais de Michel de Montaigne*, Pierre Villey and V.-L. Saulnier, eds. (Paris: Presses Universitaires de France, 1978) 2.11, 29, in light of Paul A. Rahe, *Republics Ancient and Modern,* vol. II: *New Modes and Orders in Early Modern Political Thought* (Chapel Hill: University of North Carolina Press, 1994), 30-44.

29. Because Montesquieu's discussion of classical republicanism is so vigorous, so exciting, and so replete with admiration, the severity of his criticism of this form of government was lost on many of his early readers—who took him for a partisan: on this, see Robert Shackleton, *Montesquieu: A Critical Biography* (Oxford: Oxford University Press, 1961), 276-77; Wyger R. E. Velema, "Republican Readings of Montesquieu: *The Spirit of the Laws* in the Dutch Republic," *History of Political Thought* 18 (1997): 43-63; and Chapter 3, below: all of which correct this misinterpretation. This propensity is still very much evident in the scholarship, however: see, for example, Nannerl O. Keohane, "Virtuous Republics and Glorious Monarchies: Two Models in Montesquieu's Political Thought," *Political Studies* 20 (1972): 383-96; "The President's English: Montesquieu in America, 1976," *Political Science Reviewer* 6 (1976): 355-87; and *Philosophy and the State in France: The Renaissance to the Enlightenment* (Princeton: Princeton University Press, 1980), 392-419 (esp. 408-19). Some try to reconcile Montesquieu's admiration with his criticism of classical republicanism by suggesting that his book reflects an evolution in his thought from an enthusiasm for the ancients to a hostility to them: see Joseph Dedieu, *Montesquieu et la tradition politique anglaise en France: les sources anglaises de l'Esprit des lois* (Paris: Gabalda, 1909), 131-39, and Robert Shackleton, "La genèse de 'L'Esprit des lois,'" *Essays on Montesquieu and on the Enlightenment*, 49-63. Few appreciate the degree to which his assessment of each of the non-despotic polities is similarly balanced and nuanced.

30. In this connection, see Manin, "Montesquieu et la politique moderne," 182-229, and Anne M. Cohler, *Montesquieu's Comparative Politics and the Spirit of American Constitutionalism* (Lawrence, Kans.: University Press of Kansas, 1988), 66-97. Note also Walter Kuhfuss, *Mässigung und Politik: Studien zur politischen Sprache und Theorie Montesquieus* (Munich: Wilhelm Fink Verlag, 1975), 94-229. The argument advanced by Donald A. Desserud, "Virtue, Commerce and Moderation in the 'Tale of the Troglodytes': Montesquieu's *Persian Letters*," *History of Political Thought* 12 (1991): 605-26, though intriguing, is not justified by the textual evidence on which it is putatively based.

31. See also *Spirit of Laws* III, 10; XII, 29; XXVI, 2.

32. See Keohane, *Philosophy and the State in France*, 392-415; Cohler, *Montesquieu's Comparative Politics and the Spirit of American Constitutionalism*, 85-94; and Chapter 4, below. Cf. Pangle, *Montesquieu's Philosophy of Liberalism*, 64-69, 98-100, 102-3, 113-14, 151-53, 212-39, 301-3, who is so intent on situating Montesquieu within the tradition of modern natural right (20-47) and on making of him a partisan of the English polity (104-60, 197-200, 219-39) that he fails to do justice to Montesquieu's appreciation of the advantages that monarchy has to offer, with Manin, "Montesquieu et la politique moderne," 157-229, who goes too far in the opposite direction by failing to give due emphasis to the unitary principle of political psychology that underpins Montesquieu's subtle analysis of the defects and advantages associated with the diverse political and cultural forms. In contrast with Pangle, Pierre Manent emphasizes Montesquieu's rejection of doctrinaire politics—but he then follows Pangle in devoting his attention almost solely to the opposition between classical republicanism and the commercial polity established in England: *The City of Man*, 11-85. To get a sense of the obstacles that stand in the way of reducing Montesquieu's argument to a straightforward endorsement of liberal democracy, one should consider the critique of Montesquieu advanced from that point of view by Antoine Louis Claude Destutt de Tracy, *A Commentary and Review of Montesquieu's Spirit of Laws*, Thomas Jefferson, trans. (Philadelphia: William Duane, 1811).

33. Consider Montesquieu's failure to discuss the aristocratic republic in *Spirit of Laws* IV in light of the first paragraph of V, 8.

34. See David W. Carrithers, "Not So Virtuous Republics: Montesquieu, Venice, and the Theory of Aristocratic Republicanism," *Journal of the History of Ideas* 52 (1991): 245-68. Note also David Wootton, "Ulysses Bound? Venice and the Idea of Liberty from Howell to Hume," in *Republicanism, Liberty, and Commercial Society: 1649-1776*, David Wootton, ed. (Stanford: Stanford University Press, 1994), 341-67.

35. Cf. Adam Smith, *The Theory of Moral Sentiments* IV.i.10 and *An Inquiry into The Nature and Causes of the Wealth of Nations* IV.ii.9, with "The History of Astronomy" III.2, in *Essays on Philosophical Subjects*—all to be found in *The Glasgow Edition of the Works and Correspondence of Adam Smith* (Oxford: Oxford University Press, 1976).

36. Everyone who read *The Character of a Trimmer* understood that Lord Halifax was referring to the example set for James II of England by Louis XIV of France: see *The Works of George Savile, Marquis of Halifax*, Mark N. Brown, ed. (Oxford: Clarendon Press, 1989), I, 195-96. For the opinion of France prevalent in England in the 1720s, see [John Trenchard and Thomas Gordon], *Cato's Letters*, Ronald Hamowy, ed. (Indianapolis: Liberty Press, 1995), I, 11, 15, 59-60, 234-35, 308-9, 395, II, 525-44 (esp. 539-43), 661-69, 888-89, 910-18. Cf. *A Character of King Charles II*, in *The Works of George Savile*, II, 484-505 (esp. 504).

37. Cf. Hulliung, *Montesquieu and the Old Regime*, 15-107 (esp. 15-53), 173-230, who presents Montesquieu as a radical critic of monarchy inclined to see it as an ugly and unstable polity destined to become ever more despotic if it does not evolve in the direction taken by England, with Chapter 4, below, which, by way of examining the distinction between *pouvoir absolu* and *pouvoir arbitraire*, shows that monarchy is absolute in the French but not in the English sense of the word.

38. For an extended and valuable meditation on this important passage, see Sharon Krause, "The Politics of Distinction and Disobedience: Honor and the Defense of Liberty in Montesquieu," *Polity* 31 (1999): 469-99

39. Cf. *Spirit of Laws* VI, 5 with Niccolò Machiavelli, *Discorsi sopra la prima deca di Tito Livio* 1.7.

40. See also *Spirit of Laws* XII, 25.

41. Nowhere, however, does Montesquieu resort to the traditional language and refer to England's polity as "a mixed monarchy (*monarchie mixte*)." But, in his notebooks, he does refer to it on one occasion as a "monarchy blended (*mêlée*)," and he elsewhere describes it as a "government" that has been "moderated": *Pensée* 1795 (918) and "Dossier de L'Esprit des lois," 238 (1744), in Pléiade, I, 1429-30, II, 1048-49. For an exploration of this theme, see Chapter 4, below. Montesquieu's allusion to England as "a republic concealed under the form of a monarchy" was apparently a very late addition to the manuscript of *The Spirit of Laws*: see Keohane, "Virtuous Republics and Glorious Monarchies," 393 n. 3, with Shackleton, *Montesquieu*, 236.

42. In his notebooks, Montesquieu remarks that "money is" in England "accorded sovereign esteem" while "honor and virtue" are accorded but "little." See *Notes*, in Pléiade, I, 878.

43. See Hulliung, *Montesquieu and the Old Regime*, 46-48. See also 14, 85-88, 208-11.

44. Cf. Louis Althusser, "Despote et monarque chez Montesquieu," *Esprit* 267 (November, 1958): 595-614, and *Politics and History*, 65-95—who is so eager to fit Mon-

tesquieu into the procrustean bed of Marxist historical analysis and therefore to make of him a simple partisan of the class from which he hailed (26-29, 96-106) that he allows his own partisanship to blind him to the manner in which the latter's discussion of England is revealing of far deeper concerns which cannot be explained in terms of the interests of the French nobility—with Judith N. Shklar, "Montesquieu and the New Republicanism," in *Machiavelli and Republicanism*, 265-79, and see Georg Wilhelm Friedrich Hegel, *The Philosophy of Right*, T. M. Knox, trans. (Oxford: Oxford University Press, 1942), 177-78 (no. 273), and Manent, *The City of Man*, 11-49 (esp. 12-17).

45. Montesquieu devotes the last part of his book to an examination of the convoluted, internal logic governing the evolution over a period of centuries of the monarchical constitution and law in his native land: consider *Spirit of Laws* XXVII-XXXI in light of the passage cited. See Iris Cox, *Montesquieu and the History of French Laws* (Oxford: The Voltaire Foundation, 1983) and Chapter 10, below.

46. For an example of the confusion to which Montesquieu's discussion of liberty has given rise, see David Spitz, "Montesquieu's Theory of Freedom," *Essays in the Liberal Ideal of Freedom* (Tucson: The University of Arizona Press, 1964), 28-35. Cf. Pierre Manent, *An Intellectual History of Liberalism*, Rebecca Balinski, trans. (Princeton: Princeton University Press, 1994), 60-63.

47. See also *Spirit of Laws* XXVI, 15, 20. Cf. XXIV, 2.

48. On this, see Pangle, *Montesquieu's Philosophy of Liberalism*, 117-38; Manent, *An Intellectual History of Liberalism*, 53-64; and Mansfield, *Taming the Prince*, 213-46.

49. "Liberty," Montesquieu writes in his notebooks, "is that good which makes it possible to enjoy the other goods." It can be found in "well-regulated monarchies" and wherever one finds "good laws" functioning in the manner of "large nets" in which "the subjects" are like fish who "believe themselves free" because they do not "sense that they have been caught." For the pleasures associated with political participation, Montesquieu has little esteem: "I count," he writes, "as a very small thing the happiness of disputing furiously over the affairs of state and not ever saying one hundred words without pronouncing the word *liberty* as well as the privilege of hating half of the citizens." See *Pensées* 1797 (1574), 1798 (943), 1800 (597), and 1802 (32), in Pléiade, I, 1430-32. If Montesquieu considers England "the freest country that there is in the world"—freer than "any republic"—it is not because there are elections in that country and debates in its Parliament but because "a man in England" can have "as many enemies as he has hairs on his head" and yet "nothing" will "on this account befall him." This last observation Montesquieu glosses with the remark that "this fact matters much because the health of the soul is as necessary as that of the body." See *Notes*, in Pléiade, I, 884.

50. The remaining chapters of the eleventh book analyze in much greater detail the various polities with an eye to the separation of powers: consider *Spirit of Laws* XI, 7-19 in light of XI, 20.

51. Shackleton, *Montesquieu*, 288, took note of this fact but failed to detect its import (288-301); Judith N. Shklar, *Montesquieu* (Oxford: Oxford University Press, 1987), 86-88, was, characteristically, more perceptive. See also Hulliung, *Montesquieu and the Old Regime*, 214-15.

52. For an extended commentary on *Spirit of Laws* XI, 6, see Jean-Jacques Granpré Molière, *La théorie de la constitution anglaise chez Montesquieu* (Leyden: Presse Universitaire de Leyde, 1972), esp. 271-313.

53. He returns to the latter theme with a vengeance soon after: consider *Spirit of Laws* XII, 3-30 in light of XII, 2, and see Chapter Seven, below.

54. On the latter point, see also *Spirit of Laws* XI, 18.

55. See Pangle, *Montesquieu's Philosophy of Liberalism*, 139-42.

56. See Pangle, *Montesquieu's Philosophy of Liberalism*, 142-45.

57. To assimilate Montesquieu's thinking on the question of liberty to that of Rousseau and Kant, one must assume, as does Sheila Mason, that, when the author of *The Spirit of Laws* defines "liberty in its relation with the citizen" solely in terms of the citizen's "security" and "tranquillity of mind," he could not possibly mean what he actually says. Cf. Mason, "Montesquieu on English Constitutionalism Revisited: A Government of Potentiality and Paradoxes," *Studies on Voltaire and the Eighteenth Century* 278 (Oxford: The Voltaire Foundation, 1990), 105-46 (esp. 116-20); then, consider, in addition to the evidence to the contrary presented in the text of this essay, that cited in notes 49, above, and 68, below. In pursuit of this assimilation, Mason ("Montesquieu on English Constitutionalism Revisited," 116-28) also ignores Montesquieu's remarks justifying the restriction of the suffrage in England to men with tangible property (*Spirit of Laws* XI, 6, 400); and then, by neglecting the all-important difference between "is thought to have" and "has," she misconstrues as a call for universal suffrage and an assertion of the rational dignity of the autonomous individual Montesquieu's rather more prosaic observation (XI, 6, 399) that the logic of the legal order in "a free state" dictates that "every man who is thought to have a free soul ought to be governed by himself."

58. Cf. Keohane, "Virtuous Republics and Glorious Monarchies," 393, who describes the English government as "a political bumblebee which, according to [Montesquieu's] principles, was not supposed to fly" and who suggests that "it might best be regarded as a fourth type of regime, in which not virtue, honour or fear, but liberty, was the motive principle," with Pangle, *Montesquieu's Philosophy of Liberalism*, 116-17, who argues that, where liberty reigns and "there is the least 'modification' of man's soul, it is the course of nature for the selfish passions for security to become dominant." Consider also the brief but penetrating discussion buried within Keith Michael Baker, "Politics and Public Opinion Under the Old Regime: Some Reflections," in *Press and Politics in Pre-Revolutionary France*, Jack R. Censer and Jeremy D. Popkin, eds. (Berkeley: University of California Press, 1987), 204-46 (at 214-21). There is an Hegelian flavor, alien to Montesquieu, in the suggestion of Alan Gilbert, "'Internal Restlessness': Individuality and Community in Montesquieu," *Political Theory* 22 (1994): 45-70 (esp. 54-66), that the principle of the English polity is "*individuality*—the passion of each to live a life of her own"—and that the species of individuality which he found in England was also somehow at the same time "*liberal*" and "*communitarian*." For yet another view opposed to mine, see Chapter 6, below.

59. After considering *Spirit of Laws* XI, 6 and XII, 1-2 with an eye to V, 6 and XX, 5, see V, 14; VIII, 21; XI, 5; XVI, 9; XVIII, 1; XIX, 16, 19-20; XXV, 15; XXIX, 18.

60. In his notebooks, Montesquieu remarks that "the political world sustains itself by the internal, uneasy (*inquiet*) desire that each has to depart from the location in which he is placed. It is in vain that an austere morality should wish to efface the traits which the greatest of all the workers has impressed on our souls." See *Pensée* 69 (5), in Pléiade, I, 993.

61. Cf. Machiavelli, *Discorsi sopra la prima deca di Tito Livio* 1.6, 37, 2 Proemio, with Hobbes, *Leviathan* I.iii.3-5, viii.14-16, and with David Hume, *A Treatise of Human Nature*, L. A. Selby-Bigge, ed. (Oxford: Clarendon Press, 1888) II.iii.

62. Perhaps because he attributes to commerce what Montesquieu attributes to England's "laws" and explicitly associates with that country's "liberty," Pangle, *Montes-*

quieu's Philosophy of Liberalism, 146-60, fails to discern the degree to which *Spirit of Laws* XIX, 27 expresses grave reservations on Montesquieu's part with regard to the English form of government. Note, in this connection, Montesquieu's *Philosophy of Liberalism*, 104-6, 197-200, 219-39, and see Manent, *The City of Man*, 11-85 (esp. 46-49). Cf. Baker, "Politics and Public Opinion Under the Old Regime: Some Reflections," 214-21.

63. See Manent, *An Intellectual History of Liberalism*, 60-63.

64. Cf. *Spirit of Laws* I, 2.

65. See John Locke, *An Essay Concerning Human Understanding*, Peter H. Nidditch, ed. (Oxford: Clarendon Press, 1979) I.vii.1-2, II.xx.6, 15, xxi.29-71.

66. John Locke, *Essai philosophique concernant l'entendement humain: où l'on montre quelle est l'étendue de nos connoissances certaines, et la manière dont nous y parvenons*, Pierre Coste, trans. (The Hague: Pierre Husson, 1714), 267n. This edition was originally published in 1700.

67. See Jean Deprun, *La Philosophie de l'inquiétude en France au XVIIIe siècle* (Paris: Librairie philosophique J. Vrin, 1979). Note in this connection the response of Leibniz, who defended Coste's use of *inquiétude* to convey what Locke had in mind when he spoke of man's characteristic uneasiness: see Gottfried Wilhelm Leibniz, *Nouveaux essais sur l'entendement humain*, André Robinet and Heinrich Schepers, eds., in *Sämtliche Schriften und Brief*e VI:6 (Berlin: Akademie-Verlag, 1962), 162-212 (esp. 163-66).

68. In a series of remarks jotted down in his notebooks for his own use, Montesquieu observed that "the sole advantage that a free people has over another is the security wherein each is in a position in which the caprice of one alone will not deprive him of his goods or his life." He then adds that "a subject people, which has this security, well or badly founded, would be as happy as a free people, the mores otherwise [being] equal: for mores contribute still more to the happiness of a people than the laws." It is in this context that he continues, "This security of one's condition (*état*) is not greater in England than in France." See *Pensée* 1802 (32), in Pléiade, I, 1431, and consider the argument advanced in Chapter 4, below.

69. This fact explains why Locke speaks of "uneasiness" in *An Essay Concerning Human Understanding* and not in his *Two Treatises of Government*: see Manent, *The City of Man*, 111-55.

70. Cf. Machiavelli, *Discorsi sopra la prima deca di Tito Livio* 1.4.

71. In a much earlier work, Montesquieu has a character observe that in England's historians "one sees liberty constantly spring forth from the fires of discord and sedition" and that one finds "the Prince always tottering on a throne" which is itself "unshakeable." If the "nation" is "impatient," this character remarks, it is nonetheless "wise in its very fury." Consider *Persian Letter* 136, in Pléiade, I, 336, in light of Neal Wood, "The Value of Asocial Sociability: Contributions of Machiavelli, Sidney and Montesquieu," in *Machiavelli and the Nature of Political Thought*, Martin Fleisher, ed. (New York: Athenaeum, 1972), 282-307 (esp. 298-305).

72. In *Spirit of Laws* VIII, 2-3, Montesquieu draws heavily on the classical Greek descriptions of democratic Athens as it existed in the late fifth and fourth centuries: for the evidence, see Rahe, *Republics Ancient and Modern*, vol. I: *The Ancien Régime in Classical Greece*, 174-78 (with the attendant notes).

73. Elsewhere Montesquieu treats China's tempered despotism as an example of monarchy (*Spirit of Laws* VIII, 6; XII, 25); once he even calls it a monarchy and republic

(VI, 9, n. a). But he suffers no illusions in this regard: see VII, 7; X, 15-16; XI, 5; XVI, 9; XVIII, 6; XIX, 4, 10, 13, 16-20; XXV, 15. For a detailed analysis of the particular form of corruption intrinsic to despotic regimes, see Chapter 5, below.

74. William Domville to Montesquieu, 4 June 1749, in Nagel, III, 1235-37.

75. Montesquieu to William Domville, 22 July 1749, in Nagel, III, 1244-45.

76. See *Pensée* 1883 (1960) [Lettre à Monsieur Domville], in Pléiade, I, 1447-50. For an extended discussion of this fragment, see Lando Landi, *L'Inghilterra e il pensiero politico di Montesquieu* (Padua: CEDAM, 1981), 244-369. See also Chapter 6, below.

77. See *Pensée* 1883 (1960) [Lettre à Monsieur Domville], in Pléiade, I, 1447-50.

78. After reading note 42, above, see note 71.

79. In his aversion to classical virtue, understood as heroic self-sacrifice, and in his preference for this more modest form of virtue, understood as a spirited assertion of the long-term self-interest of a commercial people, Montesquieu was in the Whig mainstream: see Paul A. Rahe, "Antiquity Surpassed: The Repudiation of Classical Republicanism," in *Republicanism, Liberty, and Commercial Society*, 233-69.

80. In consequence, it would be completely inappropriate for an admirer of English liberty to share the disdain that, in his guise as a Roman republican, Cicero quite rightly expressed for "men of commerce . . . for whom all governments are equal as long as they are tranquil": cf. *Spirit of Laws* XVIII, 1 with *Pensée* 1883 (1960) [Lettre à Monsieur Domville], in Pléiade, I, 1450.

81. Montesquieu touches on the question of executive patronage in *Spirit of Laws* XIX, 27, 575.

82. See *Spirit of Laws,* XIX, 27, 576-77.

83. Elsewhere in his discussion of England Montesquieu treats elections as an antidote to corruption: *Spirit of Laws,* XI, 6, 402.

84. Cf. Sharon Krause, "The Spirit of Separate Powers in Montesquieu," *Review of Politics* 62 (2000): 231-65, who ignores the letter that Montesquieu wrote to William Domville and the notes that he penned in preparation for composing it and then argues that Montesquieu's worries concerning the long-term prospects for liberty in England arose from a conviction that the commercial spirit would gradually subvert the separation of powers: first, by eroding the residual distinction between peer and commoner needed to underpin it; second, by undercutting the inclination of the English to treat the person of their prince as sacred; and, third, by undermining their willingness to make sacrifices for the sake of retaining their liberty. There is warrant within *The Spirit of Laws* for supposing that commerce will promote social equality but none for attributing to Montesquieu the fear that a diminution in aristocratic deference would seriously threaten the separation of powers. Instead, as we have seen, he was persuaded that England's monarchical executive would eventually find the means with which to corrupt the legislative power. Krause's third claim has even less to recommend it. As should be evident from what has already been said in this chapter, it runs counter to the tenor of *Spirit of Laws* XIX, 27, which describes the English as a commercial people fervently involved in partisan politics, ferociously vigilant in defense of its liberties, and more than willing to "sacrifice its well-being, its ease, its interests" to defend its "freedom." Her third claim is similarly inconsistent, as we have now seen, with the observations elicited from Montesquieu by William Domville's question—which suggest on his part an exceedingly sanguine assessment of commerce's role.

85. See also *Spirit of Laws,* VIII, 6.

86. See Adam Ferguson, *An Essay on the History of Civil Society*, Duncan Forbes, ed. (Edinburgh: Edinburgh University Press, 1966), passim, and Adam Smith, *The Wealth of Nations* V.i.f-g; consider Paul A. Rahe, *Republics Ancient and Modern*, vol. III: *Inventions of Prudence: Constituting the American Regime* (Chapel Hill: University of North Carolina Press, 1994), 31-74, in light of Cohler, *Montesquieu's Comparative Politics and the Spirit of American Constitutionalism*, 85-94, 115-19, 148-69, and see Paul A. Rahe, "Thomas Jefferson's Machiavellian Political Science," *Review of Politics* 57 (1995): 449-81; then, see Stephen Holmes, *Benjamin Constant and the Making of Modern Liberalism* (New Haven: Yale University Press, 1984); and Alexis de Tocqueville, *De la Démocratie en Amérique*, Eduardo Nolla, ed. (Paris: Librairie philosophique J. Vrin, 1990) II.i.5, 15, ii.1-17, iii.8-13, 16-21, iv.1-7.

Chapter Three

Democratic and Aristocratic Republics: Ancient and Modern

David W. Carrithers

In May, 1793 there appeared in the *Chronique de Paris* two articles bearing the title "Montesquieu républicain" and containing extracts from *The Spirit of Laws*. The author's intent, in the period of Jacobin revolutionary ascendancy, was to demonstrate the crucial role played by political virtue in republics.[1] There was little danger, however, that French revolutionaries could legitimately read Montesquieu as an advocate for their cause.[2] As far as contemporary French politics was concerned, he was an advocate of monarchy designed on *thèse nobiliaire* lines, and he was convinced that the virtue and the intensive political participation required by democratic republicanism made such governments impractical in the modern world. Therefore his study of republicanism was more academic than partisan. By birth, profession, and personal predilection, he was inclined to favor monarchy over republicanism. Where France was concerned, he favored a monarchy tempered by time-honored privileges for the nobility and clergy and anchored by a host of local rights and liberties whose exercise served as a counterweight to the centralization of power in the King's Council and in the cadre of *intendants* reporting directly to the king's ministers. Montesquieu envisioned for France a reformed monarchy capable of avoiding despotism by means of Parlements functioning as depositories of stable laws and provincial estates handling taxation and regional affairs while communicating local and regional needs to a benevolent monarch.[3] Montesquieu greatly admired both the French and the English monarchies, and he believed that the power of kings could be moderated to produce liberty, not just in England as had occurred after the revolutionary settlement of 1689, but in France as well. As compared to England,

France did not have liberty as its "direct object," but "the spirit of liberty" none-theless permeated the French constitution.[4]

It was well understood by most of his contemporaries that Montesquieu was *not* a republican partisan. So identified was he with the cause of monarchy, in fact, that when the Revolution reached its more radical phases, he was just as sharply criticized in France for supporting a system based on privilege as he was attacked by Jefferson in America on similar grounds.[5] During the trial of Louis XVI in late 1792, for example, the Toulouse lawyer Jean-Baptiste Maihle, re-porter for the Convention's Committee on Legislation, remarked that "had he not prostituted his pen to apology for monarchy and nobility" he would have been "the greatest of men."[6] A few years earlier, owing to his expressed sympa-thies for the privileged elites of France, Montesquieu had been accused of "no-blemania" (*nobilmanie*) by an anonymous author complaining that his "soph-isms in favor of the nobility have struck mortal blows to the third estate."[7] Clearly there was little likelihood that the revolutionaries in France so interested in honoring Rousseau and in removing his remains to the Pantheon in 1794 would see fit to honor Montesquieu in similar fashion.[8] Unlike the Abbé Mably, who moved from support of monarchy in his *Parallèle des Romains et des François, par rapport au gouvernement* (1740) to equally fervent republicanism in his *Observations sur les Grecs* (1740) and his *Observations sur les Romains* (1751), Montesquieu experienced no republican moment. Furthermore, his lack of advocacy of republicanism is certainly not surprising. He died in 1755, and republicanism remained a very tough sell prior to its successful implementation in state constitutions in America in 1776, which were widely studied and praised in Europe. Montesquieu had no high regard for aristocratic republics such as Venice, which relied on tyrannical methods to impose moderation on the ruling class, and he considered pure democracy a relic of a long since vanished classi-cal past.[9] Unlike the American Founders, he did not conceive of republicanism along representative lines, and he was therefore convinced that in such large countries as France, England, or Spain, monarchy was the only viable form of government.

During the decades prior to mid-century that Montesquieu was composing his texts on republics, few, if any, dreamed that a veritable rage for republican-ism would one day become the pivotal force defining the political future not just of France but, later, of other European polities as well. And this is one reason why Rousseau's *Social Contract* (1762) found little in the way of immediate, partisan readership in France with its uncompromising and seemingly irrelevant formula, "no democracy, no legitimate state" contrasting so sharply with Mon-tesquieu's more timely formula, "no nobility, no monarchy."[10] Even at the time of the drafting of the *cahiers de doléances* of 1789 designed to set the agenda for the Estates General, the consensus was still that monarchy should be re-formed rather than rejected. And even on the occasion of the tennis court oath drafted on June 17, 1789 creating the National Assembly following the withdrawal of the Third Estate from the Estates-General, that new assembly's own written summary of its purposes (June 20, 1789) included the intention to "uphold the true principles of monarchy." In fact, it was only late in 1792 when the Convention was debating whether Louis XVI should be executed for his treachery in attempting to flee the realm that a critical mass of Frenchmen began to envision republicanism as a possible path for France.[11]

The political instincts underlying republicanism ran counter to the habits of life ingrained in the monarchies of Europe down through the eighteenth century. The principle of political equality deeply embedded in the republican ethos readily appealed to Americans without noble or aristocratic status or pretensions, but it certainly didn't come naturally to those accustomed to (or benefiting from) political arrangements thought to reflect the underlying hierarchies of both the natural and spiritual worlds. We have become so accustomed since the American and French revolutions to the ascendancy of republican principles that we have difficulty recalling a world in which the structures of monarchy seemed to mirror the hierarchies of nature and of religion, creating a political world where kings were considered agents of God and received awe and respect as inheritors of the power and glory of the Creator. Monarchical habits of deference were not easy to break, and given the nature of French society as it had evolved since the early Frankish conquests, republicanism could be grafted onto the French body politic, as subsequent events were to show, only by spilling noble blood on the altar of democratic ideals.

It is certainly not surprising, then, that Montesquieu shared with such eighteenth-century writers as Hume, Smith, De Lolme, and numerous others, strong reservations regarding the suitability and viability of the republican project under modern conditions. It was well understood that Athens, Sparta, and Rome, whatever their remarkable achievements, had all displayed serious flaws. As David Hume remarked concerning such ancient republics, "their wars were more bloody and destructive (than ours), their governments more factious and unsettled, commerce and manufactures more feeble and languishing, and the general police more loose and irregular."[12] Many thought that the republics of antiquity had failed to display proper standards of civilized behavior. Thus we find Hume complaining that ancient peoples lacked both "humanity and moderation."[13] When money was needed, he noted, such republics simply resorted to putting to death rich citizens or foreigners so that they could confiscate their money.[14] For Adam Smith it was the practice of infanticide that epitomized ancient barbarity. "When custom can give sanction to so dreadful a violation of humanity," he asserted, "we may well imagine that there is scarce any particular practice so gross which it cannot authorize." Much more valuable than some ancient, heroic form of virtue, Smith concluded, was "the general security and happiness which prevail in ages of civility and politeness," leaving the mind "more at liberty to unbend itself, and to indulge its natural inclinations."[15]

The intense militarism of the ancient republics was a particularly common source of modern disdain for their ethos. In the words of Hume, "the ancient republics were almost always in perpetual war, a natural effect of their martial spirit, their love of liberty, their mutual emulation, and that hatred which generally prevails among nations that live in close neighborhood."[16] In a similar vein, Jean-Louis De Lolme remarked in his *Constitution de l'Angleterre* (1771) that the Spartans and the Romans had been far too militaristic to be happy. It is not "the only proper employment of a free Citizen," he asserted, "to be either incessantly assembled in the forum or preparing for war."[17]

Many similar reservations can be found in Montesquieu's treatment of the democratic republics of antiquity. It is certainly true that he included in his texts on democracy just enough seemingly positive commentary to contribute to inspiring a love for republics in Rousseau among others, but close analysis of his discussions of democracy in *The Spirit of Laws* reveals a subterranean current of distaste for the self-renunciation and restraint of individual ambition that he identified as the anchors of republican stability based on classical models. One important reason why Montesquieu declined to advocate republicanism as superior to monarchy is that he did not hold in high regard the brand of liberty mimicking antique models and requiring political participation by large numbers of citizens.[18] He preferred as a model of political life productive of liberty what has become known, thanks to Bentham's original formulation, Constant's reemphasis, and discussion by a host of recent explicators,[19] as "negative" liberty, i.e., a form of liberty positing the right of individuals to be left alone and protected in the exercise of those freedoms producing personal safety and security while leaving the business of governing to elected representatives. Montesquieu was convinced that republics have no special claim to liberty. Laws and court procedures designed to produce civil liberty can exist in monarchies just as readily as in republics, provided kings properly understand that the true basis of their power and authority lies in the approval of their subjects.[20]

Unlike Rousseau and Mably, and, later, those caught up in the republican furor of the revolutionary years, Montesquieu never envisioned republicanism as the wave of Europe's political future. He presents no *new* republican theory in *The Spirit of Laws* designed to redesign Europe's political future. Instead, after identifying republics as one of the three basic types of government, he proceeds to discuss not republicanism in general as a prospect for the future but rather democracy and aristocracy as the two sub-types of republics, each having a long historical pedigree. Democracy rather than republicanism becomes the focal point of his analysis with somewhat lesser attention paid to aristocracy. We might say, then, that Montesquieu, was not so much a republican theorist per se as he was a prudent analyst of ancient democracies and ancient and modern aristocracies. He was much more a codifier of what had existed in the past than he was a prophet of the future. His views on republics were backward looking rather than forward looking, perhaps in part because, unlike such republican theorists as Madison, Jefferson, Paine, and Rousseau, he did not benefit from the efflorescence of republican thinking following the emergence of representative republicanism in America

Although he was clearly not a republican partisan, Montesquieu's extensive attention to the nature and principles of democratic and aristocratic republics nonetheless greatly contributed to the revival of interest in such governments in the late eighteenth century and even provided much of the key vocabulary for those discussions, particularly where virtue was concerned. To his contemporaries, *The Spirit of Laws* possessed the appeal of a complete compendium of political knowledge ancient and modern, a comprehensive encyclopedia of political forms with insightful discussions of the political psychology, laws, and customs appropriate for each distinctive governmental type. And Montesquieu's laying out in the opening books of *The Spirit of Laws* of two distinct models of republicanism, one democratic and the other aristocratic, supplemented by his discussion in Book IX of the advantages of confederate republics, no doubt played a key role in bringing the subject of republicanism to the forefront. Ironically, then, his discussion of republics eventually served the cause of republicanism even though he was not himself committed to that ideological dispensation.[21]

Fundamental Laws of the Democratic Republic

In depicting republics, Montesquieu followed Machiavelli in subsuming both democracies and aristocracies within the broad category of republics rather than following Aristotle's time-honored classificatory scheme of monarchies, aristocracies, and polities with their corresponding debased forms of tyrannies, oligarchies, and democracies. "When the body of the people possess the sovereign power in a republic," Montesquieu asserts, "it is a democracy." When only a portion of the people have a part in rule, it is an aristocracy (II, 2, 3). The identification of these two types of republics stemmed from what René Duhac rightly refers to as "the necessity of reducing historical multiplicity to a certain degree of theoretical unity."[22] There was enough data to swamp a mere mechanical compiler of historical minutiae, and Montesquieu sought to impose order on disparate materials by identifying the quintessence, or ideal type of each regime, whether democratic republic, aristocratic republic, monarchy, or despotism. None of his models directly corresponds to any particular government, historical or contemporary. There are certainly strong elements of empirical description present, but each remains his own theoretical creation. His vision of democracy is extraordinarily eclectic, juxtaposing democratic practices lifted from quite distinct classical settings (mainly Athens, Sparta, and Rome). He picks and chooses from among the various institutional, economic, and educational arrangements and policies of these three classical city-states in order to distill what he considers the essential elements of democratic republicanism.

Montesquieu presents the essential features of the democratic republic in the densely packed second chapter of Book II of *The Spirit of Laws*. In democracies, he asserts, the citizens combine the roles of monarch and subjects. When they cast their votes in a popular assembly, they are, collectively speaking, akin to a monarch expressing his will. Since those very same citizens who are sovereign in the making of laws are also subject to the laws they make, they are at once the rulers and the ruled. Nothing is more important in the democratic state than defining precisely which individuals among the populace will be regarded as eligible to attend and cast votes in the popular assembly as well as choose senators and magistrates. Such a determination will define the very identity of the citizens of the state, presumably so as to exclude slaves and resident aliens, although Montesquieu does not refer to such non-citizens in this discussion in Book II laying out the essentials of democracy. He does emphasize, however, the importance of strictly adhering to whatever definition of citizenship the state chooses, citing Libanius' statement that a foreigner who might insert himself illegally into the popular assembly in Athens would be punished with death for usurping the right of sovereignty (II, 2).

Once it is established which individuals will be recognized as citizens participating in the joint exercise of ruling and being ruled, attention can turn to the equally important question of whether voting will be by order or by head. In smaller democracies there will be a popular assembly in which all citizens will meet together, and voting will be by head. In larger democracies, however, as in ancient Rome, Montesquieu recommends that the people be divided into different tribes, or centuries. Praising Servius Tullius' division of the citizenry of Rome into 193 centuries, he recommends the use of such class divisions based on wealth to ensure that the poorest citizens will not be able to outvote the wealthier citizens.[23] So important does he regard the division of the citizenry into such classes to dilute the power of the poor that he labels this necessity the first "fundamental law" of the democratic state.

The second fundamental law of the democratic state governs the mode of electing magistrates. Following classical examples, Montesquieu asserts that voting by lot is natural to democracy whereas voting by choice is more appropriate to aristocracy. The advantage of choice by lot is that all citizens will feel that they are equally likely to be chosen, and this will reduce friction and competition (II, 2). The method of lot, or sortition will not produce candidates incapable of serving since the only citizens eligible for the lottery will be those who step forward and offer themselves for various posts, knowing full well that judges will ascertain their worthiness for service before they can actually become official candidates, and knowing full well that, should they be selected to serve, their conduct in office will be carefully scrutinized, and they will have to answer for any wrongdoing they have committed. Thus, only those truly competent to serve will volunteer for public office. Though he deems choice by lot natural to democracy, Montesquieu stipulates, by way of qualification to his argument, that not every type of office in the democratic state should be chosen in this fashion. Generals needing to display military expertise and magistrates holding offices requiring the expenditure of private resources should be selected by choice (II, 2).

Montesquieu's third fundamental law of the democratic republic stipulates that all voting will be conducted openly rather than by a secret ballot so that "the lesser people" will be guided by the "principal people" and will be properly "subdued by the gravity of certain eminent men." It was the failure of the Roman republic to stick to public voting, he believes, that became one of the chief causes of its ruin.[24]

Montesquieu rounds out his discussion of the basic constitutional features of the democratic state by focusing on the issue of eligibility for office. He considers it very wise for Solon, the legendary sixth century B. C. lawgiver of Athens, to have divided the citizenry into four economic classes, stipulating that only those in the top three classes would be eligible to serve as magistrates.[25] All citizens regardless of wealth, or lack thereof, should be allowed to participate in the popular assembly, vote for elected magistrates, and serve on juries, but eligibility to serve in various executive capacities should be restricted to the wealthier citizens since, presumably, they will possess superior ability and judgment. Clearly, then, Montesquieu was a supporter of what Aristotle called moderate rather than extreme democracy. He makes no reference to the decisions at Athens to pay citizens first for jury duty and later even for attendance at the popular assembly, but it is certainly likely that he shared Aristotle's disdain for these radical democratic developments. The formula Montesquieu proposes for the democratic republic represents a combination of political *inequality* and economic *equality* reminiscent of Aristotle's recommendations. In fact, in Book II of *The Politics* Aristotle had stressed that "the masses become revolutionary when the distribution of property is unequal. Men of education become revolutionary when the distribution of office is equal."[26] Hence, as Montesquieu well understood, the proper goal for the legislator in the democratic republic will be to placate both masses and elites by giving each what they desire most: economic equality ensuring security for the masses and political inequality ensuring greater power for the better educated, wealthier and more capable citizens.

The fourth fundamental law of the democratic state suggested by Montesquieu is that the power to make laws must be vested in a popular assembly. Since the people are sovereign in democratic republics, it would make no sense to locate lawmaking authority elsewhere. He does suggest, however, in keeping with his attraction to moderate rather than extreme democracy, that the democratic constitution should also establish a senate empowered to pass decrees that have the force of law for one year. A powerful senate, he clearly understood, will go a long way toward moderating the excesses of extreme democracy.

Basic Institutions of the Democratic Republic

Montesquieu's account of the nature of democracy in Book II, chapter 2 of *The Spirit of Laws* is rather sketchy and incomplete. Fortunately, however, he adds important details in Book V, which is devoted to explication of the political laws appropriate to each form of government. Here we learn that the popular assembly, senate, and executive magistracies are to be supplemented by other, equally important institutions designed to protect ancient customs and guard against the collapse of morality. Hence the democratic republic will make use of a senate of elders modeled on the Athenian Council of the Areopagus. He calls this a "senate made to be a rule, and, in a manner of speaking, the depository of morals" so that it will not be confused with the other "senate established to plan public business" (V, 7). This senate of elder statesmen overseeing morals and customs will be open only to those distinguished by "age, virtue, gravity, and service," and its function will be to preserve time-honored institutions, recall men to virtue, and maintain the established customs conducive to the heroic deeds that corrupt people rarely attempt or accomplish (V, 7). Such senators will serve for life, as they did in Rome and Sparta, and in the Council of the Areopagus at Athens.

Also watching over the morals of citizens in the properly constructed democratic state will be a body of censors. Their purpose will be to "keep their eyes on the people and the senate. They must reestablish all that has become corrupted in the republic, notice slackness, judge oversights, and correct mistakes just as the laws punish crimes" (V, 7). Substantially later, in Book XXIII, chapter 21, Montesquieu adds the important observation that censors can be effective only when moral corruption has not become so extensive as to be beyond repair. He leaves us in no doubt that morality is crucial to stability in such states. "Corrupt peoples," he asserts, "rarely do great things," whereas those possessing "simple and austere morals (*mœurs*)" establish societies, build cities and write codes of law (V, 7). Measures that will preserve ancient customs and institutions in their original vitality are therefore indispensable:

> It is not only crimes that destroy virtue, but also negligence, mistakes, a certain tepidness in love of country, dangerous examples, the seeds of corruption, that which does not offend the laws but eludes them, that which does not destroy them but weakens them: all this must be corrected by censors (V, 19).[27]

It is abundantly clear from Montesquieu's analysis of the need for both a senate of elders and a body of censors devoted to the maintenance of originally austere morals and discipline that in his model democratic republic there is no room for licentious behavior or for a private sphere of action deemed independent of the needs of the state. Instead, there is to prevail watchful surveillance of the citizenry both by the special senate and by censors. If it is the purpose of criminal laws to punish actual infractions of the laws, it is the function of cen-sors to guard against destructive conduct that may not be regulated by law, but which may nonetheless prove prejudicial to the maintenance of a democratic constitution and ethos. In contrast to what we have come to expect by way of freedom, independence, and even license in the liberal democratic states of modern times, the democratic republic as depicted by Montesquieu, modeled from ancient materials, is rigidly moral and austere. Although, as he explained in the 1757 edition of his work, it was mainly *political* virtue rather than *moral* virtue that he was attributing to republics, it should be clear to any reader of *The Spirit of Laws* that he nonetheless placed very heavy emphasis on moral virtue as well. He never meant to suggest that democratic citizens can be as immoral as they like in their private lives without undermining public virtue. Instead, he en-visioned moral virtue and political virtue as mutually supportive. Bernard Man-deville's suggestion that private vice could actually contribute to public virtue might prove true in luxurious monarchical states where honor was the motive force of behavior, but it would surely not apply to democratic states as Montes-quieu conceived them.

It is difficult to see how Montesquieu can be misinterpreted on this point. In a chapter entitled "What Virtue is in the Political State" he spells out in no un-certain terms the connection between moral virtue and political virtue, contend-ing that energy not expended in the private sphere is left over for the conduct of public business. "Love of the homeland leads to goodness in mores, and good-ness in mores leads to love of the homeland," he writes. "The less we can satisfy our particular passions, the more we give ourselves up to passion for the general order" (V, 2). This is the very same reason, he wryly concludes, why monks display strong attachments to the very monastic orders that rule their ordinary passions out of bounds. "Their rule deprives them of everything upon which or-dinary passions rest; what remains, therefore, is the passion for the very rule that afflicts them. The more austere it is, that is, the more it curtails their inclina-tions, the more force it gives to those that remain" (V, 2). The democratic repub-lic, then, if it is to function well, must operate on the basis of the same sort of repressive instinctual renunciation that keeps monasticism going. Needless to say, this would hardly recommend such a governmental form to those devoted to luxury and licentiousness and generally dissolute living. As subsequent events in France were all too clearly to reveal, however, such a repressive model of a moral state based on both political and moral virtue possessed extraordinary appeal to Robespierre and his followers committed to establishing a new repub-lican order for France.

Montesquieu's stress on the need for moral virtue in democratic republics is also very apparent in his discussion of the proper behavior of women in repub-lics. The loss of virtue in women, he asserts, will presage nothing less than the subversion of the democratic constitution. When women are no longer chaste, men will be drawn away from public business, and they will no longer devote themselves primarily to the needs of the state. Since the overall moral tone will be set by women, the constitution of Athens very wisely made use of "a particular magistrate who watched over the conduct of women." Women in republics, Montesquieu concludes, need to be "free by the laws and captured by the mores" (VII, 9). So important did he consider the preservation of moral virtue in women to the stability of the democratic state that he fully approves the Roman practice of giving husbands authority to judge the conduct of their wives and impose penalties for immoral conduct. For serious offenses where the penalty might be severe, Montesquieu explains, five of the wife's relatives would join the husband in the act of judging. Although normally an advocate, where republics are concerned, of fixed penalties written into law, he here supports more flexible penalties on the grounds that "all that concerns the rules of modesty can scarcely be included in a code of laws" (VII, 10). The laws will not be able to describe in advance all conduct that proper morals should punish, and therefore some flexibility in penalties must be tolerated, if republican morality is to be enforced.

The Political Economy of Democratic Republics

Just as important to establishing stable democracies as proper political institutions designed to ensure broad participation and preserve morals are economic policies intended to support the equality and frugality on which democratic republics must be based. On this subject, Montesquieu gathers his information from a large number of ancient sources, seeking out details of ancient practices not just from Aristotle's *Politics*, but also from Plato's *Republic* and *Laws*, Plutarch's *Lives* and *Moralia*, Philo's *De specialibus legibus*, Strabo's *Geographica*, Seneca's various writings, Xenophon's *Constitution of the Lacedaemonians*, Dionysius of Halicarnassus' *Antiquitates Romanae,* Livy's Roman history, Tacitus' *Annals*, *Germania*, and *Agricola*, Cicero's *On Legislation*, and Cornelius Nepos' *Liber de excellentibus ducibus exterrarum gentium*. Relying on all these classical sources, he sketches out a model for democratic republicanism just as economically austere as anything to be found later in the writings of Mably or Rousseau. The key concept is equality. We have seen that *political* equality in eligibility for office holding in democratic republics was not something Montesquieu desired. But economic equality was something else altogether. He firmly believed that no democratic republic can long survive amidst extremes of wealth. The reason is that economic inequality will inevitably lead to economic factions pitting themselves against one another in the legislative arena. Hence whether a democratic republic is based primarily on war or primarily on commerce,[28] economic equality and frugality must be the goals of public policy. Banish equality from the democratic republic, Montesquieu suggests, and there will be no frugality. Banish frugality, and equality will disappear (V, 6).

Montesquieu describes the appropriate economic policies of the democratic state in the lengthy fifth chapter of Book V of *The Spirit of Laws*. It will be particularly conducive to stability, he asserts, if the lands can be divided up equally either at the point of founding or amidst a crisis so severe that rich and poor alike will accept a new economic order. The absence of equal distribution of the land will not automatically preclude stability, but such equality will greatly strengthen a democracy, and its absence will render all the more important a senate of elders committed to preserving the same austere morals that equal land division will also engender (V, 7). Whether or not lands are equally divided, civil laws will need to be drafted so as to ensure that dowries, gifts, inheritances, and all contracts support economic equality. Hence both Solon and Lycurgus erred, Montesquieu asserts, in allowing individuals dying without heirs to leave their property to whomever they wished. Far better would it have been to mandate that such inheritances could pass only to the needy and that no one would receive more than one portion. So convinced was Montesquieu of the need for economic equality that he also recommends that the rich be made to give dowries to the poor, as undertaken by Phaleas of Chalcedon (V, 5).[29] In addition, he praises the requirement approved by Plato in his *Laws* that a father of several children should retain only one child to inherit from him and give up the rest, one by one, for adoption into families without children "in order that the number of citizens can always be kept equal to the number of shares" to be inherited (V, 5).[30]

It is certainly apparent that the political economy of Montesquieu's democratic republic constructed as an ideal type would not suit an economic liberal of the Smithian sort. As previously stressed, Montesquieu's model is an historical one, based exclusively on classical materials, and it is truly extraordinary that so many of his contemporary readers, Rousseau included, could combine intense appreciation for Montesquieu's wisdom with equally intense advocacy of democracy in the modern world. Only individuals willing to support extensive regulation of economic freedom for the presumed common good could read Montesquieu on the subject of democracy with any sense of approval. Far from advocating laissez-faire policies and market autonomy, Montesquieu recommends the strictest possible sorts of laws curtailing individual freedom to leave by will and testament the fruits of one's labor to whomever one pleases (V, 5). Policies designed to level wealth seemed nothing less than axiomatic to Montesquieu where democracy is concerned. "For if it were permissible to give one's wealth to whomever one wished as one wished," he asserts, "each particular would upset the disposition of the fundamental law" (V, 5). Montesquieu's views on the need for economic equality in democratic republics went even deeper than his concern for proper laws on inheritance. More fundamentally, there must be a census to classify people according to their degree of wealth so that economic differences can be reduced by laws burdening the rich while providing relief to the poor (V, 5).

Clearly, then, economic equality must be achieved at all costs. The reason is that wealth corrodes the political virtue that constitutes the very principle of the democratic republic. Hence Montesquieu concludes that the laws must "divide fortunes in proportion as commerce increases them, must make each poor citizen comfortable enough to be able to work as the others do, and must bring each rich citizen to a middle level such that he needs to work in order to preserve or to acquire" (V, 6). The novelty of this emphasis on achieving economic equality, as compared to the ancient model he was mainly following, is worth noting. This aspect of Montesquieu's model does not reflect the emphasis Aristotle and other ancient writers had placed on slaves performing the useful labor in order to free the citizens for a life devoted to both gymnastic exercise as training for war and a political life of deliberation in popular assemblies and courts of law. Rather, it is fair to say that the ancient philosophers would hardly have recognized the model of Montesquieu's creation where all must toil so that no citizens will be corrupted by luxury and indolence. Montesquieu was clearly convinced that maintaining purity of morals will depend on citizens not being allowed to enjoy idleness as the reward for wealth gained in commerce. Hence he asserts that in the democratic state no one should be allowed to hire agents to conduct their business for them since all must be employed in the active endeavors that foster the controlled and austere temperament of a hard working, democratic people capable of self-government (V, 6). Rather than government being placed in the hands of wealthy citizens who are devoted exclusively to politics and are freed by the presence of slaves from the need to engage in productive labor, the democratic citizenry populating Montesquieu's democratic state will be devoted to both work and politics.

Virtue in Democratic States

As every reader of Montesquieu becomes quickly aware, he distinguishes between the fundamental form of each regime type and the human passions that set it in motion. He labels the fundamental form of each type the "nature of government." To the human passions needed to energize each regime he gives the label "principles of government." Such passions constitute what, in our current political language, would be termed the "political psychology" of the citizens, or the "political culture" of the society. Montesquieu regards the underlying political culture as even more important for regime stability than the institutional structures set in place by the constitution. Without a pervasive attitude closely attuned to and supporting the needs of a particular type of regime, the institutions and laws will be lifeless relics of once energetic states. When the principle of government remains strong, on the other hand, even imperfect laws will not prevent the achievement of stability (VIII, 11).

It was Montesquieu's emphasis on virtue as the principle of democracy that his European and American readers returned to again and again, even as they contended that his detailed discussions of the political, economic, military, and educational policies of the classical republican states of Athens, Sparta, and Rome were largely irrelevant to modern situations.[31] And it was his association of virtue with *republican* rather than *monarchical* governments that offended both Jansenist and Jesuit religious authorities in France who were appalled at the implication that whereas republican citizens were to be deemed virtuous, the subjects of French kings were not. His critics believed he was driving a stake into the heart of monarchy by linking virtue to republican governments. His suggestion that in aristocratic republics such virtue takes the form of moderation displayed by the ruling patriciate did nothing to take the sting out of the implication that subjects of monarchs lack virtue. It only added the further implication that they might also lack moderation.

As with his discussions of both honor and fear as the principle of monarchical and despotic governments, it is difficult to overstate the importance Montesquieu attributed to the practice of virtue in successful democratic states. In one text he even suggests that virtuous love of country and of the laws must so permeate the consciousness of all democratic citizens that all the other virtues, however they might be conceived, are actually traceable to this overarching love of country. "One can define this (political) virtue," he writes, as love of the laws and of the homeland. This love, requiring a continuous preference of the public interest over one's own, produces all the individual virtues; they are only that preference" (IV, 5).[32]

Montesquieu's depiction of the virtue of democratic republics represents a radical departure from classical conceptions of virtue. In sharp contrast to the ancient theorists he so closely studied, Montesquieu depicted virtue as the instrumental means for achieving republican freedom rather than as a quality of the soul to be cultivated for its own intrinsic worth.[33] Rather than treating virtue as the achievement and condition of a well ordered soul with reason properly controlling spirit and appetites, he expanded on French conceptions of charity in order to construct a definition of virtue that emphasized placing the needs of the republic ahead of personal, individual needs. Hence, as Pierre Manent has aptly remarked, virtue itself, as the Greeks understood it, was not on trial in Montesquieu's analysis.[34]

Far from suggesting that virtue is accessible only to a select few men of exceptional intelligence, philosophical temperament, and proper training, as both Plato and Aristotle had believed, Montesquieu transforms virtue into a feeling of patriotic self-abnegation and devotion to the state attainable by *all* good republican citizens. Furthermore, he suggests that the very viability of the Greek republics and the Roman republic had hinged on the pervasiveness of such political virtue. When virtue ceases to exist in the democratic republic, he asserts, a veritable transvaluation of democratic values is set into motion, leading to a pervasive corruption of the regime. What was once loved and instinctively venerated is now suddenly despised. The very laws formerly applauded as producing liberty are now vilified by citizens whose lust for unregulated freedom Montesquieu likens to the frenzied elation experienced by slaves suddenly freed from their master's bondage. Where virtue is in full retreat, an irreversible downward spiral sets in. The path then lies open to raw ambition and avarice, as best exemplified by English developments in the period of the Cromwellian ascendancy. Where virtue is extinguished, soon frugality will be despised along with all constraints of law. Either anarchy or despotic rule will become the only alternatives to formerly well-regulated liberty (III, 3).

Virtue is clearly one of those protean concepts whose meaning shifts dramatically from context to context. Not only was Montesquieu's definition very different from classical usages, it was also very different from the *virtù* associated by Machiavelli with Roman manliness and military prowess and from Robespierre's later usage of the same word where it was always linked to terror inflicted by a repressive state seeking to extirpate presumed enemies of the Revolutionary cause.[35] What precisely, then, did Montesquieu mean by virtue? As is often the case with Montesquieu's political philosophy, one must consult a substantial variety of texts in *The Spirit of Laws* in order to adequately answer this question. His very first discussion of the human passions he identifies as "virtue" is contained in Book III, chapter 3 entitled "On the Principle of Democracy." In this chapter he underscores the importance of virtue to the continued viability of democracies by using not just Cromwellian England but also the Athens of the period of Demosthenes as two examples of states where proper virtue was lacking. In this initial discussion, however, he does not define virtue. Then in chapter 5 of the same Book III he begins to define virtue by contrasting it with the principle of monarchical government. Monarchies, he explains, do not rely for their energizing spirit on "love of country, the desire for true glory, self-renunciation, the sacrifice of one's dearest interests, and all those heroic virtues we find in the ancients." In chapter 6 of the same Book III he continues to sketch in the contours of virtue by contrasting it with the honor that motivates subjects in a monarchy, explaining that virtue involves loving the state, not for the benefits the state can provide, but for itself, a perspective that elevates the altruism of the democratic citizen to a higher plane than the substantially more self-interested motivation of monarchical subjects energized by a sense of honor. The virtuous democratic citizen self-consciously intends to be a "good man" (*homme de bien*) seeking the "general good" rather than pursuing self-interest that just happens to end up benefiting the monarchial state by providing limits to what the king can command (III, 6). Such democratic devotion to the common good, Montesquieu concludes, precludes all personal ambition. Hence in democracies one needs to be ambitious for the state rather than for oneself. And such conduct implies and requires the complete opposite of the hubris appropriate in monarchical states. In democracies the young must look up to and revere the elderly. Furthermore, all citizens must obey the laws and even "run when the magistrate calls them," as was common in Sparta according to Xenophon. In addition, paternal authority must be accorded great respect so that fathers can aid in preserving morals by prohibiting conduct that, while legal, may nonetheless prove destructive to the austere conduct needed to support the democratic republic (V, 7).

In Book IV of *The Spirit of Laws,* devoted to education, Montesquieu continues to sketch in the contours of virtue by contrasting the appropriate republican mental disposition with the honor characteristic of subjects of monarchical states. Virtue, he now suggests, has communitarian connotations and entails thinking of what we owe to others and what we have in common with others. Virtue also implies self-restraint and the avoidance of excessively grandiose or utopian aspirations. The actions of the virtuous man, Montesquieu explains, are "good," "just," and "reasonable" whereas the actions of men motivated by honor in monarchical states are "illustrious" (*belles*), great, and extraordinary. Hence in republican states, as contrasted with monarchies, mores are pure, and politics is not based on deceit (IV, 2).

It is only when one reaches Book IV, chapter 5 that the reader of Montesquieu's text finally encounters a full definition of political virtue. "This virtue can be defined," he now asserts, "as love of the laws and of country." Such love, he continues, is singularly associated with democracies because only there is "the government entrusted to each citizen." Kings may certainly be expected to love monarchy "since they are its direct beneficiaries, but it is only in democracies that all citizens may be induced, through appropriate education and training, to love the laws and their native land" (IV, 5).[36]

In Book V, chapter 3 of *The Spirit of Laws* Montesquieu broadens his earlier definition of virtue as love of laws and country to include love of equality and frugality. Any proper democratic republic, we are now informed, will be based on equality, defined as an equal desire to serve the state, and on frugality, which he describes in a manner reminiscent of Plato's ideal republic as the sole means to ensure that every citizen of the democratic state will experience "the same happiness and the same advantages" and "taste the same pleasures and form the same expectations" (V, 3). In a sublime act of political myth-making pregnant with meaning for Rousseau and numerous other republican enthusiasts soon to follow, Montesquieu attributes such political virtue above all to Sparta. And as he saw it, the contrast with modern times could hardly have been more marked. "Greek politicians," he writes, "who lived under popular government acknowledged no other force than virtue to sustain such government. Today, on the other hand, virtue is silent and one hears only of manufacturing, commerce, financial affairs, wealth, and luxury" (III, 3). The possession of this political virtue bestowed on the Greeks and Romans a certain "nobility" not found in current times. Today, he suggests, men are energized by "less than grandiose motives," base means of achieving them and avarice and ambition that is in marked contrast to the "love of glory" that stirred the Greeks and Romans to such noteworthy actions.[37]

As extensive as were Montesquieu's discussions of virtue in Books III through VII of *The Spirit of Laws*, what he understood by that principle of government only becomes fully apparent in those texts where he discusses its corruption. Virtue is corrupted, he explains in the second chapter of Book VIII entitled "On the Corruption of the Principle of Democracy," when extreme equality sets in, and those chosen to command are denigrated and ignored, so that there is no longer any "love of order" in the state. Magistrates, senators, fathers, husbands, masters, and elders then cease to enjoy the respect to which they are entitled. Moral laxness (*libertinage*) soon follows, and attachment to the hierarchical arrangements crucial to sustaining public order quickly atrophies (VIII, 2). Virtue is also corrupted when those wielding authority seek to retain their positions through bribery rather than merit. This happens when they transform the people into mirror images of their own corrupt selves and allow them to pilfer the public treasury (VIII, 2). Once they are corrupted in this fashion, they will scarcely notice the abuse of power by those who have found a way to rule them. Instead of being hard working and remaining dedicated to the proper conduct of public business, such corrupt democratic citizens desire only to live at the public trough (VIII, 2). All capacity for good and honest work is soon eviscerated.

A dominant motif in Montesquieu's discussion of political virtue suggests that the self-annihilating patriotic sentiment characterizing such emotion relies on self-renunciation as the engine driving its passionate commitments. Virtue, he remarks, involves self-renunciation and is "a very painful (*pénible*) thing" (IV, 5). Loving frugality rather than luxury will not, at first, come easily to democratic citizens. Only actual immersion in frugality will enable democratic citizens to find an austere existence palatable, and even pleasurable (V, 4). To love frugality, in other words, one must first experience it and grow accustomed to it. However difficult it may be to achieve, Montesquieu leaves no doubt that frugality must displace all taste for luxury. When satiating private appetites grown excessive under a regimen of luxury becomes the chief good individuals seek, as with the Romans in the period of their inexorable decline, each individual will seek private comforts, caring no longer for common needs. Implicit in Montesquieu's definition of virtue, then, is a critique of what we now term liberal individualism. Individuals turning inward to satisfy their own private needs and envisioning others only as instruments for the maximization of their own pleasures will soon corrupt the democratic republic where all notions of self-interest must be absent. Economic equality and frugality will only be found tolerable by individuals vigilant to the common interest rather than their own private interest.

If both Rousseau and Robespierre concluded that such a democratic regime was well within reach, and worth seeking, many other contemporary readers, Voltaire pre-eminent among them, believed that Montesquieu had gone so far in the direction of recommending sublimation of individual ego and desire that he had created a mere democratic utopia bearing no connection whatsoever to anything that was actually attainable by real human beings. Instead of properly comprehending the true springs of human behavior, Voltaire complained, Montesquieu had substituted a phantasmagorical portrait of self-abnegating altruism. "A republic is not founded on virtue at all," Voltaire contended. "It is founded on the ambition of each citizen, which keeps in check the ambition of all the others; on pride which curbs pride; on the wish to dominate which does not allow anyone else to dominate."[38] Voltaire was equally dismissive of any possible altruism underlying the quest for equality in republics. "It is the need to prevent some one individual from dominating all the rest," he asserts, "that provides the true motive for instituting equality in republics." This equality arises from a common need to guard against the role potentially played by "a powerful, greedy man" who would disrupt the common meal of equal citizens dining at the same table by helping "himself to everything, leaving them the crumbs."[39] So much, then, according to Voltaire, for any hopes of breeding a new race of republican men whether in some remote colony like William Penn's Pennsylvania or the remote Jesuit settlements in Paraguay, two modern experiments mentioned approvingly by Montesquieu.

Voltaire was certainly not alone in ridiculing utopian aspirations for the abrupt transformation of *l'homme* into *citoyen,* as Rousseau was later to recommend. For some other eighteenth-century critics of ancient democratic practices, the very practice of ostracism that Montesquieu found it necessary to praise as a tool of democratic equality (XII, 19) proved that the self-restraint he attributed to properly trained and educated democratic citizens can never be attained.[40] "Generosity, Self-denial, and private and personal Virtues," wrote Trenchard and Gordon in *Cato's Letters*, "are in Politics but mere Names, or rather Cantwords, that go for nothing with wise Men, though they may cheat the Vulgar. The Athenians knew this; and therefore appointed a Method of punishing Great Men, though they could prove no other crime against them but that of being Great men. . . . They would not trust to the Virtue and Moderation of any private Subject."[41] To such English liberals as the authors of the widely-read *Cato's Letters*, extreme skepticism regarding the capacity of those wielding power to control their domineering impulses suggests the fictitious nature of political virtue and the necessity of the checks and balances Montesquieu praises so strongly in his account of the English constitution.

Cultivating Political Virtue

Montesquieu recognized that the governments of antiquity made extraordinary demands on their citizens. Direct involvement in the day to day business of governing was anticipated even from the very poorest of those of citizen rank. Hence in Athens, even those too poor to be eligible for public-office under Solon's class based, moderate democracy were expected to attend meetings of the *ekklesia*, serve on juries, and participate in the selection of those executive magistrates not selected by lot—not to mention their all important role of serving in the citizen army required to defend a state often at war.[42] One of the central messages of Montesquieu's discussion of democracy is that to produce citizens capable of the sacrifices required by self-government great attention has to be placed on "education," by which he means not the formal imparting of knowledge per se, but rather the training up of citizens for a life of political virtue involving devotion to the needs of the state and a willingness to sublimate private desires for the sake of achieving public goals.[43] The purpose of such "education" is to instill love of the republic in all citizens. "Everything depends on establishing this love," he writes, "and education should attend to inspiring it" (IV, 5). Though we tend to lose sight of this point, republican mores are largely learned habits. The ability to sustain republican constitutions has much to do with conditioning, as the Spartans had understood best, and as Montesquieu explained in the relevant texts of Book IV of his classic work.[44]

Proper conditioning, or education, is crucial since political virtue must be an instinctual response to the needs of the republican state, deriving not from understanding but from sentiment and passion. It is not something, therefore, that can be learned by rote like a catechism or a list of battles. Rather, virtue must be an ingrained disposition and habit of the heart. Democratic citizens have to be trained to place the needs of the state ahead of private needs. Such altruism and sublimation of personal motive, far from being ingrained in human nature, is unnatural, and that is why all those philosophers who have conceived of virtue as stemming from a practice of self-denial, whether this be Plato in his *Republic*, or Bolingbroke in *The Idea of a Patriot King*, or Montesquieu in *The Spirit of Laws*, have emphasized education as the necessary means for inculcating virtue. If the subjection of passion to interest is undeniably difficult to achieve, then the subjection of both passions and interests to duty will require even more discipline.

In modern times, Montesquieu suggests, where the unity of life achieved in the ancient republics is only a rapidly fading cultural memory, family life, schooling, and the general ambiance of society push and pull individual psyches in different directions, resulting in a lack of harmony within individuals and, by extension, within societies as well. In the tight knit community of the democratic republic, on the other hand, fathers, schoolmasters, and the world at large will not work at cross purposes. All three influences, family, school, and world, will radiate the same strong message of the need for individuals to seek their own identities only within the common needs of the democratic state. This will result in a common identity being forged among citizens whose every waking thought will focus on the state and its needs for survival in a precarious world (IV, 4). Only then can the fragile republican moment be preserved. One of the best ways to sustain virtue, Montesquieu concludes, is to have it pass from fathers to sons. If fathers love the democratic republic, so too will their sons. It is only when grown men become corrupt that children fail to imbibe that instinctual regard for the needs of the state that sustains democratic governments (IV, 5). As explained below, such uniformity of outlook can only be achieved in a very small state functioning much like an extended family.

The Scale of Democracy

As is readily apparent from everything he says on the subject, Montesquieu's discussion of the institutions, laws, psychology, morals, and customs of the democratic republic presupposes a government that presides over an extremely small extent of territory. None of his recommendations would prove suitable for a territory larger than that possessed by the small city-states of classical antiquity whose histories he so painstakingly studied. This assumption of small size is implicit in his primary use of Athens and Sparta as his point of reference for democratic republics and also in his famous depiction of Roman republican collapse as the original small republic evolved, through conquest, into a vast empire. It is in Book VIII, chapter 16 that he makes this size assumption fully explicit, observing that "it is the nature of a republic to have only a small territory. Otherwise it can hardly subsist." A large republic, he contends, will include men of such wealth that they will be unable to display virtue and moderation. In addition, a large republic will require the presence of governmental power too extensive to be safely lodged in the hands of citizens. Distant provinces will need their own governors, and the creation of such strong regional executives will threaten liberty by setting up power centers competing with the central authority (X, 6). Furthermore, the uniformity of outlook that must characterize the unified, small republic will be split asunder by the emergence in a large republic of many diverse and conflicting interests. In large republics, Montesquieu asserts, individuals will divorce the very notions of happiness, grandeur, and glory from the needs of their country and begin to envision these conditions along personal lines having nothing to do with the overall welfare of the state. A desire for individual glory will displace virtuous identifications of human happiness with love of country. The very sentiment of the common good that was once readily perceived by all will cease to be felt in the extended republic (VIII, 16).

These are the classic texts that James Madison so painstakingly rebutted in *Federalist Paper* 10 in order to make the case for ratification of the American Constitution. Madison took it upon himself to turn Montesquieu's argument on its head in order to argue that, to the contrary, it is only in a large republic that the ever present factions associated with free states can be properly contained and diluted. The larger the republic, the more diverse the various factions will be and the less likely it will be that a permanent majority faction will arise to oppress the rest. Madison was certainly correct that the large, pluralist American republic could better endure the effects of factional strife than the classical democracies that formed the models for Montesquieu's discussion. It was only Madison's willingness to accept a representative republic in place of a pure democracy, however, that made possible the extension of republican rule over a large territory. Deriving his inspiration from the classical models of Greek and Roman antiquity, Montesquieu never actually contemplated the prospect of representative republicanism, except for his famous reference to England as "a republic disguised as a monarchy" (V, 19), suggesting that the presence of the elective House of Commons gave the English form of monarchy a marked republican turn. As commonplace as the notion of representative republicanism was soon to become, one finds no hint of its possibilities in the discussion of classical democracy in *The Spirit of Laws*. Clearly Montesquieu was not so much an architect of new republican theories as he was a codifier of past practices.

Even in Montesquieu's well-known analysis of confederate republics in Book IX, we find no clear model for the American or French representative republics that emerged later in the eighteenth century since what he discusses in these texts is simply a loose union of component states such as existed in the Dutch, Swiss, and German confederations of the eighteenth century, or in the Greek and Roman associations of the classical period. Athens herself, he notes, had been head of a confederate league of states in ancient times, but the formation of loose alliances among co-equal or largely co-equal states suggests nothing in particular about the nature of the central government that would keep order among the component states. Montesquieu says very little concerning the relationship between the political center and the periphery in such confederate republics. Thus Americans could find in *The Spirit of Laws* no substantial blueprint for what they wished to create.

The Spartan Model

Although Montesquieu does not display the distinction prominently in his work, he does suggest that democratic republics are divisible into two distinctive subtypes, one military and war-like and modeled on Sparta, and the other more focused on commerce and modeled on Athens.[45] He lavishes most of his attention on the Spartan, military model rather than the Athenian commercial model, particularly in Book IV devoted to education, and it is in these texts that he comes closest to approximating a view of democratic citizenship akin to what we moderns would find most distasteful. The citizens of military democratic republics, Montesquieu notes, will spend most of their time exercising and preparing for war and will consider all remunerative work done for a wage "unworthy of a free man" (IV, 8). When a man has to work for a wage, he has no time for his friends and no time for the republic (IV, 8). Hence, "a good republic will never give them (craftsmen) citizenship" (IV, 8). The productive work done in military democratic republics will have to be accomplished not by citizens, but rather by slaves and by resident aliens. This will leave the citizens free to engage in the governmental business expected of citizens while also providing them sufficient time to engage in a gymnastic regimen preparing them for war—a routine, Montesquieu notes, likely to turn the citizens into cold and unfeeling athletes and fighters with a marked tendency toward "roughness, anger, and cruelty" that can only be counteracted by listening to appropriate types of music that soften the soul (IV, 8).

In such military republics as Sparta, Montesquieu observes, there will be substantial regimentation designed to produce uniformity of outlook and opinion. It will be necessary that "citizens pay a singular attention to each other" and be raised up and educated nearly as if they were all one family (IV, 7). Harmony of interests will be carefully cultivated by means of conditions so frugal and so economically equal that when citizens come together to deliberate on the great questions of the day, they will not be influenced by different perspectives based on different life situations. "As each there should have the same happiness and the same advantages, each should taste the same pleasures and form the same expectation; this is something that can be anticipated only from the common frugality" (V, 3). As in Crete and Sparta, and as recommended by Plato for his ideal republic, there should be no money in circulation since the military democracy will encompass a very small territory and will be insular and withdrawn from worldly contacts and engagements with other countries. Self-sufficiency will preclude the need for trade with other peoples, and therefore there will be no need for money to serve as a common measure of things. A primitive form of barter will suffice.

It was not just Sparta that provided Montesquieu with a model for the democratic republic of the military type. Rome, too, fit the model, and in his history of Rome Montesquieu attributes to the Romans the same distaste for commerce that he attributes to the Spartans:

> Roman citizens regarded commerce and the arts as the occupation of slaves: they did not practice them. If there were any exceptions, it was only on the part of some freedmen who continued their original work. But, in general, the Romans knew only the art of war, which was the sole path to magistracies and honors.[46]

In *The Spirit of Laws* it was Sparta that Montesquieu utilized as the chief model for the military democratic republic. Although he was by no means as captivated by all things Spartan as was Rousseau, the tone of his discussion is largely positive since his goal was to explain what produces stability and longevity in the democratic republic rather than to comment on the desirability of the democratic republic as a governmental form. Montesquieu was struck by the existence of obvious paradoxes and cross currents in Spartan life, and he concludes that the overall result of such contrasts was the strengthening of the state. Using Plutarch as his source, he depicts Lycurgus as having combined seemingly incompatible tendencies that nonetheless worked well to help train up a population remarkably capable of both self-government and self-defense. Refer-

ring to the famous Spartan requirement that young males steal a significant portion of their food from gardens and from the state mess halls, he notes that Lycurgus had mixed larceny with the spirit of justice (IV, 6). Referring to the presence of the class of helots who served as slaves, he says Lycurgus had combined
"the harshest slavery with extreme liberty." Alluding, it would seem, to the
practice of the state raising male children once they reached the age of seven,
and to the Spartan practice of infanticide, and also, perhaps, to the siring of children by men other than husbands where Spartan stock could thus be improved,
he says they mixed "the most atrocious feelings with the greatest moderation"
(IV, 6).[47] He also notes, as another example of a striking paradox within Spartan
life, that they had combined chastity with immodesty, a reference, very likely, to
the Spartan custom of young men and women parading nude in state proces-
sions and festivals.[48] Montesquieu by no means ridicules what he terms the "singular institutions" of the Spartans. At one point in his text, in fact, he presents a
brief list of the key features of Spartan life as glossed by Plutarch and then adds
the following flattering appraisal of Spartan achievements: "He (Lycurgus)
seemed to remove all the resources, arts, commerce, money, walls." As a result,
ambition took a positive course, and natural feelings were not extinguished (IV,
6). Far from heaping scorn on the "singular" Spartan institutions, Montesquieu
concludes that "Down these paths Sparta was led to greatness and glory" (IV,
6). He refers to the "breadth of genius" and "wisdom" of Lycurgus while at the
same time acknowledging that the customs he devised for Sparta ran counter to
the existing "usages" and "confounded all the virtues" (IV, 6).

Had Montesquieu wished to criticize the Spartans, he could have turned for
inspiration and arguments to Aristotle's *Politics*. Far from emphasizing the
moral rectitude of the Spartans, Aristotle had called attention to the licentiousness, intemperance, and luxurious living of the Spartan women as well as their
resistance to all of Lycurgus' laws. Far from believing, furthermore, that Lycurgus had performed flawlessly as legislator for Sparta, Aristotle criticized his
failure to prohibit the sorts of dowries and gifts and inheritances of land and
property that undermined equality. And, finally, Aristotle further detracted from
the reputation of Sparta by claiming that, at its low point, the population had actually fallen to less than 1,000 citizens.[49] Rather than relying on Aristotle as his
source, Montesquieu drew his information from Plutarch, and this explains the
panegyrical tone of much of what he asserts.

Montesquieu was certainly not alone among the *philosophes* of the Enlightenment in finding reasons to admire what the Spartans had achieved. Prior to the
excesses of the Revolution exposing the dangers of a reign of virtue attempted
in modern times, enthusiasm for Sparta ran so rampant as to seem truly astonishing to us now. The anonymous author of the *Encyclopédie* article "Sparte, ou
Lacédémone" (very likely Diderot) fully understood that Lycurgus had intended
nothing less than to radically change human nature. Lycurgus understood, said
this author, "up to what point the laws, education, and society could change man

. . . and render him happy by bestowing habits on him that were seemingly opposed to his instinct and his nature." Such habits included dancing, poetry, witty
conversation, and elaborate festivals.[50]

As is well known, Rousseau went substantially farther than Montesquieu in
his praise for Sparta. If Sparta's unusual institutions seemed unnatural to some,
Rousseau concluded, it was only because modern peoples had erred in abandoning nature:[51]

> Here (in Sparta) one sees men who resemble us almost in nothing, who seem
> to us to be outside of nature—perhaps as much because we are in that state our-
> selves as because they are in fact there. Their crimes inspire in us horror. Some-
> times their virtues themselves make us shiver. Because we are weak and pusil-
> lanimous in good times and in bad, everyone that bears a certain character of
> force and vigor seems to us impossible. The incredulity that we parade is the
> work of our cowardice rather than that of our reason.[52]

Rousseau was attracted to Sparta's legendary image of moral purity. He
praised the absence of theater there,[53] and he expressed the wish that Geneva
could become a modern day Sparta, remarking to the people of Geneva in the
dedication of his *Discourse on the Origin and Foundations of Inequality among
Men* (1755): "Let dissolute youth go to seek easy pleasures and long lasting repentance elsewhere; let the supposed men of taste admire in other places the
grandeur of palaces, the beauty of carriages, the superb furnishings, the pomp of
spectacles, and all the refinements of softness and luxury. In Geneva one will
find only men."[54]

If Sparta greatly appealed to Rousseau, and also to Robespierre, others were
more critical. Hence we find Voltaire, that great appreciator of advancing "civilization," criticizing the absence of politeness and the arts in Sparta.[55] Like Voltaire, Turgot also greatly preferred Athens to Sparta, and admired Solon much
more than Lycurgus, whom he blamed for destroying all family ties and property in Sparta.[56] It was only substantially later, however, after the excesses of the
French Revolution had been weathered, that a strong reaction set in against all
that Sparta represented. The classic texts are in Benjamin Constant's "The Liberty of the Ancients compared with that of the Moderns" (1819). Even more
than the Athenians, the people of Sparta practiced what Constant termed, with
considerable disapproval, "the complete subjection of the individual to the authority of the community."

> All private actions were submitted to a severe surveillance. . . . In the do-
> mains which seem to us the most useful, the authority of the social body inter-
> posed itself and obstructed the will of individuals. Among the Spartans, Therpan-
> drus could not add a string to his lyre without causing offense to the ephors. In
> the most domestic of relations the public authority again intervened. The young

Lacedaemonian could not visit his new bride freely. . . . There among the ancients the individual, almost always sovereign in public affairs, was a slave in all his private relations. As a citizen, he decided on peace and war, as a private individual, he was constrained, and watched in all his movements.[57]

The Athenian Model

Montesquieu's keen interest in the agrarian, military government of Sparta is well known. Much less noticed is that he also posits a second sub-type of the democratic republic resembling Athens rather than Sparta and based on commerce rather than farming and the spoils of war. Aware that Athens maintained a far-flung commercial empire, and erroneously attributing the conduct of Athenian commerce to the citizens themselves rather than to resident aliens, he suggests that love of democracy, love of equality, and love of frugality are actually compatible with the spirit of commerce in such commercial democratic republics as Athens.[58] In spite of what he says regarding the strengths of the Spartan version of democracy, he now contends that the existence of wealth deriving from commerce need not necessarily corrode the virtue of republican citizens.

> This is because the spirit of commerce carries along with it the spirit of frugality, economy, moderation, work, wisdom, tranquillity, order and rule. Thus, as long as this spirit remains in existence, the wealth it produces has no ill effects. The harm comes when the excess of wealth destroys the spirit of commerce; one suddenly sees the disorders of inequality arise, which had not previously been experienced (V, 6).

There is certainly no denying the importance of this text, which seems to presage the viewpoint of Max Weber expressed in his classic work, *The Protestant Ethic and the Spirit of Capitalism* (1904-05). In addition to reminding us that Athenian conditions are readily distinguishable from Spartan ones, Montesquieu's appreciation for the beneficial effects of commerce may help to explain his enthusiasm for the English devotion to commercial enterprises within their "republic disguised as a monarchy" (V, 19). One can easily find other texts, however, suggesting that in spite of what he says in the context of explaining how the Athenian people combined commerce with frugality and virtue, Montesquieu believed there was a fundamental tension between devotion to commerce and single-minded devotion to the needs of the republican state. If commerce unites nations by forcing them to agree on rules that make commerce practicable and profitable, as he explains in Book XX of *The Spirit of Laws*, commerce also has a disunifying effect on the individuals within any one state, causing them to put a price on all things while seeking to maximize their own interest rather than the common interest (XX, 2).

Where democratic republics do rely extensively on commerce, the best that can be done is to make involvement in commercial ventures completely pervasive among the citizens while also dividing up commercial profits in as egalitarian a manner as possible. Solon was certainly correct, then, in prohibiting idleness in Athens and requiring that each citizen account for how he earns his living (V, 6). In stable commercial democracies the laws will ensure that any and all profits made in commerce will be divided among the populace so that no one will be so weakened by poverty that he cannot work and no one will be so rich that he does not need to work. Wealth must be leveled in order to prevent it from bestowing too much power on individuals (V, 4). Even where imbalances of wealth exist, all is not lost, however, if those who possess that wealth can be made to spend it for public purposes. Hence at both Athens and Rome "magnificence and abundance had their source in frugality itself" since the citizens were poor and the republic was wealthy (V, 3). There was no luxury "among the first Romans," Montesquieu asserts, and "none among the Lacedaemonians." Once luxury abounds, self-interest corrodes the altruistic virtue that sustains republics. "For people who have to have nothing but the necessities, there is nothing left to desire but the glory of the homeland and one's own glory. But a soul corrupted by luxury has many other desires; soon it becomes an enemy of the laws that hamper it" (VII, 2).

The absorption of individuals in the pursuit of luxury is incompatible with the austerity and self-sacrifice necessary to sustain democratic states, whether they are military or commercial democracies. Rome will ever be the paramount example of the corrupting effects of luxury, best chronicled by Livy, Sallust, Machiavelli, Montesquieu, and Gibbon. Montesquieu points out that Roman immorality eventually reached such epic proportions that few desired to marry, so that the emperor Augustus had to use the penal code to induce marriage among a citizenry preferring to live dissolute lives as bachelors and wenches (XXXI, 21). By now, the thesis set down by Montesquieu and others on Roman decline is quite familiar. The Roman people were originally virtuous and uncorrupted and displayed intense devotion to the needs of their small republican state. Gradually, however, as conquest destroyed the small scale required for democratic states, while also subjecting Rome to foreign influences and foreign wealth, Roman republicanism was corroded from within by increasing desire for wealth and luxury as the formerly austere Romans became the victims of immense and immoderate desires. "When everyone by a common impulse, was carried to voluptuousness," Montesquieu asked, "what became of virtue" (VII, 2)? It was a similar addiction to luxury, Montesquieu asserts, that had ruined the military ardor and discipline of the Greeks. By the time Philip of Macedonia, father of Alexander the Great, threatened Athens and other Greek city states in the fourth century B. C., the Greeks had already lost their resolve to defend themselves. "Athens feared Philip, not as the enemy of liberty, but of her pleasures." The Athenians, in fact, became so addicted to luxury and pleasure that they passed a law making it a capital offense to propose that money appropriated for the theaters of Athens be spent instead on the military. The result was that the Athenians were so ill-prepared for battle that they were easily routed at Chaerona in 338 B. C. and forced to humbly accept the terms of alliance offered by Philip (III, 3).

The Democratic Republic Measured on a Normative Scale

Thus far our discussion of Montesquieu's views on democratic republics has been restricted to consideration of those texts in Books II through VIII of *The Spirit of Laws* defining the needs of such republics considered as idealized political types structured to achieve a maximum degree of stability, longevity, and liberty. In those texts Montesquieu sets out to thoroughly analyze and explain the inner rationale of each governmental type he identifies, without indicating whether or not he actually thinks very highly of the type he is analyzing. Understanding the structure and political culture underlying each regime type is Montesquieu's goal in the early Books of his treatise rather than evaluating the worth of the various governmental types he identifies. It was not that he had no criticisms of democratic republics to advance, however. It was rather that his goal of depicting the inner rationale of each governmental type caused him to be as fair-minded as possible in explicating the nature and principle of each type. Hence he could assert in his Preface to *The Spirit of Laws*: "I write not to censure what is established in any country whatsoever. Each nation will find here the reasons for its maxims, and the consequence will naturally be drawn from them that changes can be proposed only by those who are born fortunate enough to fathom by a stroke of genius the whole of a state's constitution."

Turning to the normative side of Montesquieu's assessment of the democratic republic as a political type, one finds scant evidence that he held this type in high regard. One has only to turn to his famous discussion of the English constitution to find a pointed critique of democratic republics amidst his depiction of the superiorities of the English form of government. One of the great advantages of representatives, he asserts while praising the House of Commons, is that "they are capable of discussing political business. The people are not at all suited for that, which constitutes one of the great inconveniences of democracy" (XI, 6). Several paragraphs later he remarks that the right of the people in "most ancient republics" to rule was doubly misguided since this placed the very same makers of the laws in the role of executors of the law while dangerously vesting power in the whole body of the people rather than restricting political decision making to the more able representatives of the people. Montesquieu believed the English had taken a superior route to political stability by entrusting lawmaking to a select few, while leaving the execution of the laws in the hands of a king (XI, 6). Representatives capable of gaining a place in the legislature, he asserts, will be much less likely to have their judgment swayed by clever demagogues than would the people as a whole (XIX, 27). Thus the modern English republic disguised as a monarchy offers many advantages over the classical type whether based on Athens or Sparta or Rome.

There seems little doubt that Montesquieu opted for modern times as providing, on the whole, a superior atmosphere for human flourishing. Commerce, trade, and finance, leading to a penchant for luxurious living had softened and civilized mankind as compared to ancient times. Furthermore, the strong connection between commerce and peace among nations rendered the modern spirit far superior to the war-mongering bellicosity and harshness characteristic of the Spartan and Roman republics. Urbane, witty, irreverent, engaged in the wine trade, and solicitous of a comfortable lifestyle many in his day would have envied, Montesquieu seems unlikely to have been a happy Greek or a happy Roman citizen or warrior, however fond was Mme de Tencin of calling him "*mon petit Romain.*" Montesquieu was very much aware of the gulf separating ancients from moderns. However much he remained in awe of what human beings had achieved in classical time, he ultimately regards the prospects for humanity and peace as far superior to the record of cruelty and war compiled by the ancients. Hence on balance he finds modern times clearly superior.

There is little evidence that Montesquieu would have liked to live in the sort of democratic states whose contours he so carefully sketches. It is certainly true that in some of his *Pensées* he expresses nostalgia for a former, more heroic time when the achievements of men were so great as "to astonish our small souls" (III, 3).[59] And it is also true that he expressed the idea in various *Pensées* that the modern attachment to profit and luxury is less enobling than attachment to some higher state purpose implied by political virtue. But any such thoughts were tempered by his revulsion at the cruelty and barbarism that had characterized the Greeks, and particularly the Romans, as compared to modern times.[60] He explicitly portrays the ancient republic as an inhospitable abode where modern, enlightened views were nowhere to be found. In Book XXIII, devoted to population, for example, he depicts the ancient republics as so threatened by overpopulation that they resorted to infanticide and abortion and homosexuality to ensure that the free population did not outstrip the food supply. So greatly offended was he by the means employed by the people of Crete to control population, namely the provision of homosexual relations, that he protests to his readers that modesty precludes filling in the details, and he decides to simply footnote the relevant discussion in Aristotle's *Politics* without reviewing its contents (XXIII, 17).[61]

In focusing on Montesquieu's normative assessment of the democratic republic, one encounters the great divide between Montesquieu and Rousseau, the two giants of French political thought of the eighteenth century. Rousseau yearned to re-create in modern times what Montesquieu only described in order to reject as a viable prospect for modernity. Rousseau would have been a happy ancient whereas Montesquieu would have felt constricted and repressed by ancient mores and customs and by the need to function, not just as an active citizen deliberating in the public assembly but also as part of an armed citizenry ready for war. Montesquieu depicted democracy as entailing an element of surveillance and coercion that few moderns would find appealing. He was well aware that the heavily regulated democratic state was one that individuals would have to learn to love (V, 4), instructed perhaps by the likes of a fanatic like Robespierre. In time, Montesquieu suggests, people might cease to feel the restraints such a system imposes (V, 4). Far more in keeping with natural human inclinations, however, is the monarchical state where self-interest flourishes.

We may rightly conclude, then that in depicting the democratic republic in *The Spirit of Laws*, Montesquieu was by no means recommending that modern peoples attempt to resurrect ancient conceptions of virtue in small democratic states. In general, he believed that the unity of will characterizing the ancient city-states of Greece could no longer be achieved, though he does point both to William Penn's experiment in Pennsylvania and to the Jesuit settlements in Paraguay as evidence that even in the modern world people may sometimes be set on a course of living that vanquishes prejudices, subdues passions, sets religion on the proper course of serving humanity, and inspires mankind to the most extraordinary industry and concern for their fellow citizens (IV, 6). Of this much he was certain: only a system completely at odds with the free expression of human drives and desires could so transform the human materials of which politics is made as to produce the love of laws and country crucial to strong democracy on the ancient model. Lest we overstate his antipathy to the democratic model, however, it is important to reiterate that there are contrasting images of democratic republicanism in *The Spirit of Laws*. Athenian, Spartan, and Roman democracy were by no means all of a piece, and in contemplating Roman republicanism prior to the excesses of the period of the civil wars, Montesquieu was fully capable of asserting that moderation can be the natural spirit of the republic. It is surely not Sparta, he suggests in this intriguing text, that can be considered the exemplar of the moderate democratic state. Rather, it is Rome at a particular point in time that provides the model of republican moderation following the expulsion of the Decemvirs, the architects of the harsh Law of the Twelve Tables. In the aftermath of the Decemvirs, Montesquieu points out, the death penalty was abolished, and Roman law was revised in order to enable accused parties to depart prior to sentence being pronounced. Hence Montesquieu concludes that the Romans followed "that spirit of moderation that I have said is natural for a republic" (VI, 15). Such moderation existed in Rome, he suggests, until the time of Sulla who invented new crimes and increased the penalties for existing crimes, producing an atrocious blend of "tyranny, anarchy, and liberty" (VI, 15).

We will misinterpret Montesquieu on democracy if we fail to distinguish his descriptive exposition of the laws and customs that will support the self-renunciation required by political virtue from his normative assessment of classical democracy. He tended to mask his preferences, and this caused Condorcet and others to protest mightily that he was simply describing and thereby praising what existed.[62] But he does communicate, however subtlety, his distaste for pure democracy. Tucked away in Book XIX, chapter 16, for example, are revealing comments comparing Sparta to China, which he considered a despotic state. Both China, with its heavy reliance on Confucian rites, and Sparta with its "singular" institutions, confused laws, mores, and manners," which in liberal states desirous of augmenting personal liberty should be kept separate (XIX, 16-20; XXVI, 1-25). Tranquillity, respect for fathers, elders, and magistrates, and a capacity for hard work (XIX, 16-20) are all admirable goals. Not all means to achieve such goals are legitimate, however. Both Sparta and China undervalued personal freedom by failing to recognize a private realm shielded from the prying eyes of the state. In Sparta, Montesquieu remarks, Lycurgus failed to teach the citizens to have proper regard for one another (XIX, 16). The Spartan way of life, and the republican way of life in other democratic states, made a fetish of citizens always correcting and instructing one another in order to foster and preserve virtue. That is why both the Athenians and the Romans were finally moved to pass laws ensuring that the right of citizens to accuse one another not be abused. Very praiseworthy, Montesquieu contends, were the Athenian law stipulating that an accuser whose case failed to muster a fifth of the jury's votes suffer a heavy fine and the Roman practice of stamping the letter "K" for *Kalumnia* on the forehead of any false accuser (XII, 20). Montesquieu clearly regarded such laws as admirable, in the context of the states in which they existed, but they would not have been necessary had it not been for the inherent danger to individual liberty posed by life in democratic states whose very survival was thought to depend on all citizens carefully monitoring one another's personal and public conduct.

It was in the monarchial states of modern times that Montesquieu placed his hopes for the fuller development of civil liberty. He makes this very clear in the revealing eleventh chapter of Book V of *The Spirit of Laws* entitled "Concerning the Excellence of Monarchical Government." Here he lavishly praises the stability achieved by monarchical government, which he attributes primarily to the presence of subordinate, dependent powers capable both of upholding the constitutional forms of the state and moderating the political influence of the common people who act too impulsively. The presence in monarchies of subordinate, dependent powers possessing "wisdom and authority" results, Montesquieu asserts, in moderating and correcting policies that would otherwise be too extreme and in calling back to life laws that are forgotten or ignored (V, 11). Monarchies, then, possess a crucial power balancing mechanism absent from both aristocratic and democratic republics. As Hume so aptly expressed this point in his exposition of the superiority of modern states to ancient ones, "In those [ancient] days there was no medium between a severe, jealous Aristocracy, ruling over discontented subjects, and a turbulent, factious, tyrannical Democracy."[63]

Far from desiring to resurrect the politics and ethos of the ancient democratic republics, Montesquieu emphasizes the harshness of life in those republics that transformed self-interested human beings into dutiful citizens attentive to common needs. "One must regard the Greeks," he writes, "as a society of athletes and fighters" (IV, 8), and he by no means meant to bestow a compliment. The emphasis on physical exercise required to prepare male citizens for war necessarily led to a hardening of human sensibilities. The Greeks discovered an antidote, however, as Plato, Aristotle, Theophrastus, Plutarch, and Strabo had all emphasized in the use of music to "soften the mores" of the ancient peoples and in homoerotic love (IV, 8). A life spent in exercise and on the battlefield could engender cruelty, Montesquieu observes, and the Greeks cultivated music and love to soften the soul.

We have stressed that Montesquieu concluded that democratic republics must heavily regulate the conduct of citizens in political, economic, and social domains in order to achieve stability. To appreciate the novelty and importance of this particular reading of democracy, we have only to recall that both Plato and Aristotle depicted democratic regimes as loose and unregulated rather than well ordered and stable. For Plato, the heart of democracy was "freedom and free speech" so that "each will pursue a way of life to suit himself." The democratic constitution, Plato contended, may be compared to a cloak of many bright colors that will clash with one another.[64] The contrast with Montesquieu's perspective could hardly have been much greater. Rather than following Plato and Aristotle in emphasizing the degree to which those freed from the yoke of monarchy or oligarchy would demand both political and personal freedom, Montesquieu adopts the contrasting position that the anarchic potential of democracy can only be counteracted by cultivating dutiful, well-trained, disciplined citizens so devoted to the state that their every waking thought involves serving the common interest rather than seeking their own pleasures or profit. Montesquieu presents an austere model of democracy, to say the least, and, seemingly, it is not one designed to lend itself to the argument that modern peoples should attempt to emulate the ancients, a conclusion that renders all the more perplexing subsequent developments in France leading up to and including revolutionary events through Thermidor, which finally released France in 1794 from bondage to antique models not well suited to the modern epoch, though the achievement of liberal constitutionalism in France still remained in the distant future.

The Definition and Structure of the Aristocratic Republic

Up to this point it has been the democratic republic that has been the focus of our attention. There was a second type of republic, however, the aristocratic republic, on which Montesquieu bestowed ample, if somewhat lesser attention in the first eight books of *The Spirit of Laws*. When he discusses this second model, the aristocratic republic, as an ideal type, he relies most heavily upon Venice as his model.[65] In the seventy paragraphs he devotes to aristocratic republics, in fact, no less than seventeen either explicitly allude to Venice, or refer, without explicit identification, to a Venetian law or custom.[66] Montesquieu's heavy reliance on Venice should not be deemed surprising. Few governments in the history of the world have been so extravagantly praised by so many observers. Among her sixteenth- and seventeenth-century admirers Venice could count, among numerous others, Machiavelli, Guicciardini, Giannotti, Botero, and Boccalini in Italy; Wotton, Howell, Harrington, and Neville in England; and Van Cootwijck, Thysius, Heinsius, and Valkenier in Holland.

As was also true of the democratic republic, Montesquieu provides only the sketchiest account of the basic institutions of aristocratic republics in Book II of his treatise. Normally, as in Venice with its Great Council and smaller Pregadi, or Senate, there will be two legislative assemblies controlled by the nobility. Where "there are a great number of noblemen," he explains, "there should be a senate to regulate the affairs which the body of the nobles cannot decide, and to prepare the matters they will resolve" (II, 3). The senate is to have, at least in part, a probouleutic function, preparing business for the larger assembly composed of all noblemen within the state. Montesquieu does not actually describe the various types of business each assembly should consider. Nor does he discuss eligibility for either this larger assembly or the smaller senate, except to say that the senate should not select its own members. Furthermore, in spite of the widespread fame of the complex Venetian method of balloting for office,[67] he remains silent concerning the electoral procedures the full assembly of all noblemen should utilize in filling various political offices. He says only that all offices in an aristocratic republic should be filled through election rather than sortition and that all magistrates should serve brief terms since "it is necessary to counteract the greatness of the power by means of a brief tenure." (II, 3) As a rough rule of thumb, he recommends a year's term for all magistrates since "a longer period would be dangerous, and a shorter term would be contrary to the nature of the thing" (II, 3).

The only magistrates Montesquieu discusses in any detail are the Venetian state inquisitors and the Roman temporary dictators. On the important question of a chief magistrate he is completely silent. Hence he alludes neither to the Venetian doge, nor to the Florentine gonfaloniere of justice, nor to the Roman consuls. As has often been pointed out, the delineation of properly structured executive power was a weak point of republican theory in the early modern period, leaving Americans at the Constitutional Convention of 1787 with what many times seemed an intractable problem and providing them with an opportunity to break new theoretical ground in establishing the presidency.[68]

The Principle of Aristocratic Republics

As discussed above in the treatment of democratic republics, Montesquieu never tired of repeating that no republic can endure without political virtue inducing those entrusted with rule to place the needs of the state above their individual needs. And he meant this admonition concerning virtue to apply not just to democratic republics but to aristocratic republics as well. "As virtue is necessary in a popular government," he asserts, "it is also required in an aristocracy" (III, 4). Montesquieu sees such virtue as critical to moderating the power of the nobility. "But how are the nobility to be restrained?" he asks. "They who are to execute the laws against their colleagues will immediately perceive that they are acting against themselves. Virtue is therefore necessary in this body, from the very nature of the constitution" (III, 4).

Whether such political virtue must characterize the whole populace or only those who rule in the aristocratic republic is a somewhat vexing question. Sometimes Montesquieu suggests that the whole populace should display this virtue, as when he remarks, "If the people are virtuous in an aristocracy, they enjoy very nearly the same happiness as in a popular government" (V, 8). Similarly he remarks, "Aristocracy is corrupted when the power of the nobles becomes arbitrary. Neither those who govern or those who are governed can retain any virtue" (VIII, 5). In other texts, however, he implies that it is only members of the ruling class who need to possess virtue. The common people, he observes in one text, will be restrained by the laws the nobility make and will therefore have less need for virtue than the rulers (III, 4).

Whether or not virtue has to be displayed by all inhabitants or only by the ruling nobility of an aristocratic republic, such virtue certainly cannot be equated with the love of equality and frugality characteristic of the democratic republic since in the aristocratic republic only the nobility are equal among themselves. Furthermore, whatever frugality is achieved in aristocratic republics stems not from the natural way of life of the people but rather from sumptuary laws limiting luxury and ostentatious displays of wealth. Hence Montesquieu indicates that in aristocratic republics virtue normally presents itself in the diluted form of moderation, stemming from the same virtuous love of country and devotion to the common good characteristic of properly constituted democratic republics (III, 4; V, 3).

The more that the moderation displayed in aristocratic republics resembles the pure form of political virtue characterizing democratic republics, the more success the aristocratic republic will enjoy. In fact, Montesquieu can imagine a situation where the body of the nobles who wield legislative and executive power in an aristocratic republic displays what he terms "a great virtue which means the nobility find themselves equal in some fashion to the people." This would result, he concludes, in the formation of "a great republic" (III, 4). He leaves no doubt, however, that "a lesser amount of virtue," which he labels "moderation," is more likely to be attained, and he therefore terms moderation "the soul of these governments" (III, 4). The chief purpose of moderation in aristocratic republics is to ensure the preservation of political equality among the nobility themselves. Moderation will incline patricians from the most ancient and exalted families not to scorn and despise their more recently ennobled patrician associates, and this will contribute to harmony and order within the ruling class (III, 4). Furthermore, as the experience of Venice so clearly revealed, the presence of a spirit of moderation can also prompt the ruling patriciate to disguise as much as possible their political and social superiority over the rest of the populace. This, in turn, will contribute to the common people's love for and loyalty to their government, thereby enabling aristocratic republics to avoid substantial friction between rulers and the ruled (V, 8).

We will not adequately comprehend Montesquieu's thinking on aristocratic republics unless we realize that he was too much of a realist to count on either virtue or moderation alone to achieve liberty, equality, and stability. Ultimately he chose to rely on something substantially more concrete than a psychological disposition toward virtue or moderation to ensure constitutional stability in aristocratic republics. "An aristocracy can maintain the strength of its principle," he asserts, "if the laws are drafted so that they make the nobles feel the perils and fatigues of command more than its pleasures" (VIII, 5). Hence the nobility in aristocratic republics are to be forced to be free, not exclusively by motivating them toward political virtue or moderation, and certainly not by some Rousseauian *volonté générale*, but rather by the presence of "tyrannical magistracies" whose awesome power reduces the nobility to a state of continual dread. "It is necessary to have," Montesquieu writes, "either temporarily or permanently, a magistrate who makes the nobles tremble, like the ephors of Sparta and the state inquisitors of Venice, magistrates not subject to any formalities," (V, 8) that is, officials who act wholly on their own authority as did the censors at Rome. Such tyrannical magistracies, Montesquieu contends, must be present in aristocratic republics in order to keep in check the inflated sense of pride that tends to develop among a noble patriciate monopolizing power (V, 8).

For the sake of achieving stability, the ancient Roman republic had resorted to a temporary dictatorship to provide a sudden means of conferring awesome authority on one individual when it became necessary to put down a threat to liberty. In Venice, on the other hand, the institutional safeguard ensuring liberty and tranquillity was the Council of Ten, first created in 1310 to quell a conspiracy, and supplemented in 1539 by the creation of three state inquisitors. Montesquieu speaks approvingly of both institutions in the context of describing the need within aristocratic republics to humble proud and powerful patricians. The temporary dictatorship well suited Rome where the common people presented the most substantial threat to liberty, whereas Venice required a more permanent institution since the threat to liberty lay within the noble class itself whose designs were more cloaked and hidden from view (II, 3).

Montesquieu describes the Venetian state inquisitors as "formidable magistrates who through violent means lead the state back to liberty" (II, 3). Although
their methods were violent, their goal of preserving liberty was admirable.
Without such a "formidable magistracy," he concludes, some among the ruling
class will inevitably abuse their power or even attempt to subvert the established
constitution. Hence he concludes: "This government needs rather violent
springs. A mouth of stone is open to all informers at Venice—you could say it is
a mouth of tyranny" (V, 8). The inquisitors act tyrannically, but such tyranny directed at upstart noblemen seeking to subvert the established constitution is
completely necessary in the defense of republican liberty in aristocratic republics. The purpose of the inquisitors, Montesquieu observes, is not to subdue the
general populace but rather to check the ruling class itself in order "to preserve
her aristocracy against the nobles" (II, 3). This no doubt explains why the Venetian people regarded the inquisitors and the Council of Ten in such a favorable light, whereas noblemen at various times sought to reduce the power and
influence of both institutions.[69]

The Problem of Equality in Aristocratic Republics

If instilling moderation in those who rule is a critical problem every aristocratic
republic has to face, and a problem best solved by including a tyrannical institution within an otherwise moderate, limited constitution, so too is the maintenance of a sufficient degree of equality, both among the ruling nobility themselves and between this nobility and the subject population a key goal. Aristocratic republics single out a distinct corps of patricians for rule. Therefore only
the spirit of moderation can temper the designs of the ruling class within such
republics. And to be sure, noblemen in aristocratic republics must comport
themselves very differently from noblemen in monarchical states. The honorific
sense of self-importance coupled with pride of place that characterizes the nobility in monarchical government would be entirely inappropriate in such republics. "If the ostentation and splendor which surrounds kings contributes to their
power," Montesquieu writes, "modest and simple manners constitute the
strength of nobles in aristocratic governments" (V, 8).

Montesquieu was fully convinced of the political ends served by such moderation of manners among the nobility within aristocratic republics. The chief
goal is placating the disenfranchised commoners so that political stability can be
achieved. "When they (the nobility) affect no distinction, when they mix with
the people, when they dress like them, when they share with them all their
pleasures, the people forget their weakness" (V, 8). In fact, as the example of
Venice clearly reveals, successfully masking and concealing the true extent of
their power and superiority is crucial to the survival of narrowly based hereditary patriciates within aristocratic republics. If the nobility are bitterly resented
and envied, Montesquieu contends, then the two basic elements of the aristo-

cratic republic will be in tension, and there will be two warring states instead of just one. Under such circumstances the nobility will constitute a republic, and the ruled will constitute a despotic state. When this happens, unity becomes unattainable (VIII, 5). To avoid such a breakdown of one unified state into two warring states, the nobility in an aristocratic republic, unlike the nobility in a monarchy, must minimize any pride they feel in their rank so as not to stand out as a political and social group wholly distinct from and superior to the people. As in Venice, the patricians should dress like the people, or at least like the highest-ranking commoners, and they should mix with the people as much and as often as possible, a result achieved in Venice in part through residential housing patterns that put noblemen and commoners in close proximity to one another.[70]

It was precisely this strong emphasis upon the nobility minimizing their political and social superiority that led Montesquieu to suggest that aristocracies reach perfection along a path that has more in common with democracy than with monarchy. "The more an aristocracy approaches democracy," he writes, "the more perfect it will be; and it will become less perfect to the extent that it approaches monarchy" (II, 3). Clearly, then, if an aristocratic government is to achieve stability, its nobility must refrain from all conduct that would resemble an imperious monarch reveling in political and social superiority. Hence Montesquieu remarks that "The most imperfect of all (aristocracies) is that where the portion of the people that obeys is in a condition of civil servitude to those who command, like the aristocracy of Poland, where the peasants are slaves to the nobility" (II, 3). Inevitably, there will be political and social differences between patricians and plebeians in aristocratic republics, and unless these differences are masked from public view, tranquillity will be short-lived. The ruling nobility must disguise their political and social superiority so that their rule will not prove obnoxious to the governed. Certainly Montesquieu does not expect the ruling class in an aristocratic republic to actually lay aside their political superiority, announce a policy of political leveling and act like reformed democrats. Rather, what is required is that the distance between rulers and ruled be masked and moderated as much as possible. The gap cannot be made to disappear altogether, however, without the aristocratic republic being literally transformed into a democratic republic, a prospect Montesquieu does not consider in *The Spirit of Laws*.

As important as Montesquieu regards moderation in regulating the conduct of the nobility to create at least the appearance, if not the reality, of equality, he also recommends, as a supplement to this policy, various political and economic measures designed to augment the power and prosperity of the commoners. He praises the Bank of St. George of Genoa, for example, since the common people administer it, and this "gives them a certain influence in the government, whence their whole prosperity is derived" (II, 3). He also praises the Venetian government for barring the nobility from participating in commerce.[71] Without such a policy, the patricians, who would command substantially more credit than commoners, might soon drive the commoners out of business (V, 8). This in turn would lead to a destabilizing concentration of wealth in the hands of an elite patriciate while leaving the populace as abject economically as they are politically.

Another economic measure designed to produce equality between rulers and ruled in aristocratic republics is a properly structured taxation system. Montesquieu identifies four particular taxation situations to be avoided. The first is where the noblemen are not subject to any taxes at all. The second is where they are legally subject to taxation but avoid paying taxes through fraud. The third is where the nobles pay taxes but devise ways to compensate themselves for the economic loss this entails, often by arranging excessive remuneration for their public services. And the fourth situation to be avoided is where the nobles not only pay no taxes but also regard the taxes paid by others as their private patrimony. "This last case is rare," Montesquieu asserts, and "an aristocracy, following such a policy, is the harshest of all governments" (V, 8).

Montesquieu finds Rome rather than Venice the most admirable model for taxation policy in the aristocratic republic. When Rome inclined toward aristocracy, he observes, the magistrates received no salaries. Furthermore, the chief men of the state were taxed more heavily than the rest. The Romans had been able to adopt such policies because it was the second order of the state, rather than the patricians themselves, who determined the mode and level of taxation, a situation Montesquieu heartily approves. When the patricians themselves levy the taxes, he asserts, an important check on their power is removed. In such cases, "The nobles would be like the princes of despotic states, who confiscate the property of whomever they please" (V, 8).

A second type of inequality to be avoided within aristocratic republics is excessive inequality within the ruling class itself. Substantial inequality among the patricians who rule will give rise to hatreds and jealousies destructive of the solidarity required to consolidate noble rule. Montesquieu points out that Venice had done particularly well on this score. To achieve equality among noblemen, Venetian lawmakers had wisely rejected primogeniture as a system of inheritance. This prevented gross economic inequality between an eldest son, inheriting everything, and the dispossessed, younger sons[72] (V, 8). Montesquieu judged it similarly important to avoid poverty among the nobility by obliging noblemen to promptly repay their debts. Furthermore, he suggests that a proper degree of equality among the ruling class should be fostered by avoiding the feeling that some noble families are more noble, more revered, or more ancient than others. Such distinctions will only lead to quarrels that will quickly spread unless a mechanism for arbitrating disputes is provided (V, 8).

It should be clear that although Montesquieu believed aristocratic republics face much greater hurdles than democratic republics in both concealing and compensating for the degree of inequality that necessarily exists, he believed that intelligent legislators can successfully devise ways both to moderate and mask the dominance of the ruling class and to minimize inequality within the ruling class in aristocratic republics. As will be argued below, however, the concentration of power in the hands of one privileged class in such republics hardly recommended those governments to Montesquieu as a matter of personal preference.

Aristocratic Republics Measured on a Normative Scale

Thus far our discussion of Montesquieu's views on aristocratic republics has been restricted to consideration of those texts in Books II through VIII of *The Spirit of Laws* defining the needs of the aristocratic republic considered as an idealized political type structured to achieve a maximum degree of stability, longevity, and liberty. In those texts quite substantial objectivity is apparent. If, as mentioned above in assessing his views on democratic republics, his primary goal in the first eight books of *The Spirit of Laws* was description rather than criticism, there exists substantial evidence that his attitude toward aristocratic republics in general and Venice in particular was actually substantially more negative than his analytical commentary in those books implies. Certainly his first impression of Venice's system of government during his extensive travels on the continent in the late 1720's had been thoroughly negative. Although predisposed at the time of his travels to favor republics over monarchies,[73] he was clearly disappointed by what he observed in Venice. He saw people confusing licentiousness with liberty in a state experiencing such a condition of political and economic decline that no quantity of opera and carnival could conceal it from view. Furthermore, he saw self-interest rather than devotion to the common good prevalent among a Venetian nobility seeking to avoid paying even the low level of taxes they had assessed on themselves.[74] "The republics of Italy," he wrote in his travel notebooks, "are nothing more than miserable aristocracies that subsist merely on account of the pity accorded them and where the nobles, lacking all sense of grandeur or glory, have no ambition other than maintaining their idleness and prerogatives."[75]

Clearly, then, following close personal observation in the late 1720's, Venice did not strike Montesquieu as quite the republican paradise his previous ruminations on republicanism had predisposed him to expect. As was typical of French commentary beginning with Seyssel and Bodin in the sixteenth century, he clearly admired Venice as epitomizing the best that could be done with the aristocratic republic as a political type. There is ample evidence, however, that he did not have a high regard for this type of government. In Book XI, chapter 6 where he was substantially concerned with the theme of separating powers to achieve liberty, he leaves little doubt that Venice—and aristocratic governments in general—fall far short of the admirable English model. His line of thought deserves explanation.

Montesquieu's chief target in Book XI, chapter 6 is not actually Venetian but rather Turkish despotism. Hence he works up to his criticism of Venice gradually. He begins by contrasting the extent of separation of powers in the continental monarchies of Europe to Turkish despotism. "In Turkey," he writes, "where these three powers (executive, legislative, and judicial) are united in the Sultan's person, a frightful despotism reigns." The continental European monarchies such as France, on the other hand, while they do not display nearly the extent of separation evident in England, at least leave the judicial power in separate hands. Hence those states enjoy, Montesquieu asserts, a "moderate government." Aristocratic republics such as Venice present a very different and far less satisfactory situation. The Italian republics unite governmental power to a wholly inadmissible extent so that prospects for liberty diminish and despotic practices are sanctioned. Those same Venetian state inquisitors he had earlier praised as an essential stabilizing element within the aristocratic republic he now forthrightly condemns. "In the republics of Italy," he observes, "where these three powers are united, there is less liberty than in our monarchies. Hence in order to preserve itself their government needs mechanisms as violent as those employed by the Turkish government; witness the state inquisitors, and the trunk into which every informer may at any moment cast his accusatory note" (XI, 6). The difference in tone between this comment and earlier allusions to the Venetian state inquisitors is striking. Montesquieu has clearly moved from sympathetically explicating the inner rationale of the Venetian constitution as the epitome of the aristocratic republic to criticizing the tyrannical results of that same constitution as compared to a far more praiseworthy England.

Montesquieu readily acknowledges that in the Venetian constitution the three types of power, executive, legislative, and judicial, are at least distributed among "several tribunals that temper each other. The evil is that these different tribunals (Great Council, Senate, and Forty) are made up of magistrates from the same group" (XI, 6). The result is that Venice lacks England's truly mixed constitution where monarchical, aristocratic, and democratic parts of the constitution, embodied in Crown, Lords, and Commons, represent distinct orders of society whose institutionalized conflicts prevent any one class from subverting the common good for the sake of their own particular interests, needs, or desires.

The absence of real mixture in aristocratic republics has dire consequences, Montesquieu concludes, for those who are subject to the power of such governments. "Consider what the situation of a citizen in these republics would be. The same body of the magistracy possesses, as executor of the laws, all the power it has bestowed on itself as legislator." It can plunder the state as a whole through an expression of its general will while at the same time it can destroy each particular citizen since it also possesses the judicial power (XI, 6). Instead of any hint of a sympathetic appreciation for the Venetian constitution, Montesquieu now proclaims that government despotic. "All power there is united," he asserts, "and although there is none of the exterior pomp, which alerts us to a despotic prince, the subjects feel the brunt of this power every moment. Hence," he continues, "princes who have wished to become despots have always begun by joining in their person all the magistracies, and several kings of Europe have begun by uniting all the great offices of their state" (XI, 6). In these texts accompanying his eulogy of the English constitution and the liberty it embodies, Montesquieu expresses strong disdain for the same aristocratic republic of Venice he had seemed to be praising in Books II through VIII. It is little wonder, then, that Montesquieu's contemporaries were capable of reading him as either a proponent or a critic of the constitutional system the Venetians had devised, depending on which portion of the text they emphasized.

Conclusion

Much can be learned concerning Montesquieu's methodology as a political philosopher from reflecting upon the glaring differences in tone between his analytical discussions of democratic and aristocratic republics in the early books and his argumentative discussions in Book XI and other parts of *The Spirit of Laws*. His comments disparaging republics in Book XI certainly reveal that he was completely capable of expressing normative judgments, however much such critics as Rousseau and Condorcet complained that he dwelled too much on "is" rather than "ought." It is equally clear, however, that he did not consider the formulation of normative judgments the chief purpose of his work. His intent, rather, was to disassemble each type into its component institutions, laws, and customs in order to show how each type could be rendered stable. It seems clear, then, that we should take seriously Montesquieu's comment in his Preface to *The Spirit of Laws* that his purpose was to explain the rationale of all of the various governments that have existed in order to demonstrate that every man has reason "to love his duties, his prince, his country, his laws." As Auguste Comte, Emile Durkheim, Raymond Aron, Pitirim Sorokin, and others have noticed, there was a degree of objectivity and scientific method in his work presaging the emergence of social science as an academic discipline in the next century.[76]

Montesquieu's most basic goal was to explain rather than criticize, though he left himself ample room to also adopt the role of reformer with the cause of liberty to defend. As we have seen, his criticism of aristocratic republics stemmed from their oligarchical concentration of power in the hands of a narrow patriciate all too likely to govern despotically and in its own class interest rather than in the interest of all. It is interesting to note, however, that he does not introduce the actual word "oligarchy" into his discussion of aristocratic republics prior to Book VIII where in a footnote to chapter 5 he distinguishes between two types of aristocratic republics, those where the ruling class is elected and those where the ruling class is hereditary. The hereditary sort he now labels "oligarchy." Clearly for one versed in Aristotelian political science, oligarchy was a term of opprobrium. Oligarchs, according to Aristotle's time-honored definition, ruled in their own class interest rather than in the common interest. Montesquieu's use of the term, then, constitutes a valuable clue to his negative view of such hereditary aristocracies which he largely suppresses in Books II through VIII of *The Spirit of Laws* and which emerges with a vengeance in Book XI, chapter 6 amidst his discussion of English liberty.

What, then, can be concluded concerning Montesquieu's attitude toward Venice as the epitome of the aristocratic republic conceived as an ideal type? In spite of his negative attitude toward aristocratic republics as compared to such monarchies as England and France, there can be no question that he joins countless other observers in considering Venice clearly superior to other aristocratic republics the world had known. In the very same chapter characterizing hereditary aristocracies as oligarchies prone to corruption, he includes a second footnote stating "Venice is one of those republics that has made the best use of law to correct the inconveniences of a hereditary aristocracy." These are certainly not the words of a man who lacked respect for what the Venetians had achieved. And elsewhere, in a footnote to Book V, chapter 8, Montesquieu remarks that the Venetians "have in many respects conducted themselves very wisely." Certainly the substantial longevity and stability Venice had achieved were apparent to all observers. Hence it was very likely the example of Venice that caused Montesquieu to observe that aristocratic republics are more stable than democratic republics because they more readily achieve the rule of law. "Aristocratic government," he writes, "possesses a certain strength that democracy doesn't have. The nobles there form a body, which through its prerogative and for its particular interest, restrains the people. To ensure that laws are executed, it suffices only to pass them" (III, 4). Hence aristocratic republics can avoid the lawless strife that rendered the classical democracies so unstable and gave democracy a pejorative connotation in both Europe and America in Montesquieu's day.

Given the prevalence of aristocratic republics in his own day, it was perfectly natural for Montesquieu to have thoroughly explored that political type. No empirical observer with any pretense to complete coverage of the subject at hand could have ignored that type of regime. Montesquieu clearly did not believe, however, that such republics could offer any substantial competition to the best that the more modern world had produced. Hence when he was not depicting aristocracy as an ideal type, an activity inclining him toward a stance of objectivity, he was far from complimentary. Certainly Venice had astonished and amazed numerous sixteenth- and seventeenth-century theorists comparing the extent of freedom and stability present there to their own states. Unlike Montesquieu, however, these earlier writers analyzing Venice before 1688, including most prominently Machiavelli, Guicciardini, Gianotti, Seyssel, Harrington, Neville, Milton, and Sidney, did not have the contrasting example of a reformed England at their disposal. Hence they were much more prone than Montesquieu to consider Venice the best constitution that had yet been devised in the whole political history of mankind.

Clearly Montesquieu admired Venice, but he did so in the context of a political outlook which included the recognition that both England and France had developed something better. As we have seen, it is in his justly famous chapter on the English system of liberty that Montesquieu's true attitude toward Venice emerges, and there is no doubt that it heralded a new age in which Venice's reputation would suffer a rapid decline. By the time of the American Founding the very word Venice had become shorthand for despotic tyranny, and one looks in vain among American commentators for favorable reviews of that formerly highly regarded republic.[77] Surely the influence of Montesquieu on the formation of that negative American opinion was substantial. Few theorists were so highly regarded by those who drafted state and national constitutions in America after 1776, and in his widely circulated chapter on English liberty Montesquieu dropped his mask of objectivity with regard to Venice and forthrightly denounced her constitution as producing despotism rather than liberty. It is fitting to conclude this chapter, then, with the observation that however logical and necessary it was for Montesquieu to survey both democratic and aristocratic republics in his epic treatise on laws and governments, neither type of republic receives a very cordial reception in *The Spirit of Laws*.

Notes

I would like to express my appreciation to Rebecca Kingston, Sharon Krause, Catherine Larrrère, Michael Mosher, and Paul Rahe for offering helpful comments on an earlier draft of this chapter.

1. The articles are mentioned in Cecil P. Courtney, "Montesquieu and Revolution," in *Lectures de Montesquieu*, Edgar Mass and Alberto Postigliola, eds. (Naples: Liguori Editore, 1993), 41-61 (at 48).

2. This certainly does not mean, however, that the attempt was not made to "republicanize" Montesquieu's political thought. Certain French patriots attempted to apply his comments on the division of powers in England to France in order to suggest a drastic reduction in the powers of the king. See, for example, the discussion of Saint-Just's *L'Esprit de la révolution* (1791), Marat's *Eloge de Montesquieu* (1785) and *Projet de Déclaration des droits de l'homme* (1789), and Barère's *Montesquieu peint d'après ses ouvrages* (an V-VII) in Roger Barny, "Montesquieu Patriote?" in *Dix-huitième siècle, revue annuelle publiée par la Société française d'étude du 18ème siècle* (Paris: Presses universitaires de France, 1989, 83-95.

3. For Montesquieu's advocacy of revived provincial assemblies in the *pays d'élections* where they had ceased to exist, see his *Memoir on the State's Debts* (1716), in Pléiade, I, 66-71.

4. *The Spirit of Laws*, Book XI, chapter 7. Hereafter cited by Book and chapter number within parentheses inserted in the main body of the text; cf. (XI, 7). This interpretation stressing the potential Montesquieu envisioned for liberty in France, provided that the threat of despotism could be counteracted by sufficiently vigorous intermediary powers and depositories of law, is meant to challenge those accounts of Montesquieu's political thought that overly stress his admiration for England conceived as a modern commercial republic and his disparagement of France as tending irreversibly toward despotism. For a paradigmatic example of this pro-England, anti-France interpretation, see Mark Hulliung, *Montesquieu and the Old Regime* (Berkeley: Univesity of California Press, 1977). For appraisals that take account of Montesquieu's reservations with regard to the English form of government, see chapters 2 and 6 by Rahe and by Courtney in this volume and also Keith Michael Baker, *Inventing the French Revolution. Essays on French Political Culture in the Eighteenth Century* (Cambridge: Cambridge University Press, 1990), 173-85. For an account of Montesquieu's views on monarchy respecting his high level of support for this governmental form, see the essay in this volume by Michael Mosher.

5. For a useful survey of opinions on Montesquieu during the Revolution, see Renato Galliani, "La Fortune de Montesquieu en 1789: Un Sondage," *Archives des lettres modernes* 197 (1981): 31-61. For Montesquieu and Jefferson see David W. Carrithers, "Montesquieu, Jefferson, and the Fundamentals of Republican Theory," *The French-American Review* 4 (fall 1982).

6. Michael Walzer, ed., *Regicide and Revolution. Speeches at the Trial of Louis XVI*, Marian Rothstein, trans. (Cambridge: Cambridge University Press, 1974), 106.

7. *La Noblilmanie* (25 February 1789), 14-15, cited in Galliani, "La Fortune de Montesquieu," 39.

8. For details concerning the pantheonization of Rousseau's remains, see Carol Blum, *Rousseau and the Republic of Virtue. The Language of Politics in the French Revolution* (Ithaca: Cornell University Press, 1986), 278-81. François Furet reminds us that in October, 1790 Rousseau's bust and a copy of *The Social Contract* were installed in the hall of the Constituent Assembly. See his "Rousseau and the French Revolution," in *The Legacy of Rousseau*, Clifford Orwin and Nathan Tarcov, eds. (Chicago: University of Chicago Press, 1997), 168. On May 30, 1791, Prugnon unsuccessfully suggested the pantheonization of Montesquieu's remains, leading Chabroud to protest that Mably had done more for the Revolution. Roger Barny, in "Montesquieu Patriote?" (at 94), concludes that the patriot majority were displeased with Montesquieu's defense of the aristocracy.

9. Montesquieu was hardly alone in thinking that the classical experience was irrelevant to the modern age. As Charles Pinckney remarked at the American Constitutional Convention, "Can the orders introduced by the institution of Solon . . . be found in the United States? Can the military habits & manners of Sparta be resembled to our habits & manners? Are the distinction of Patrician & Plebeian known among us?" Quoted in Carl

J. Richard, *The Founders and the Classics. Greece, Rome, and the American Enlightenment* (Cambridge: Harvard University Press, 1994), 144.

10. On Rousseau's readership, see Louis Trenard, "La diffusion de *Contrat social*," in *Etudes sur le "Contrat social" de J. J. Rousseau*, publications of the University of Dijon 30 (Dijon: University of Dijon, 1964).

11. Pierre Goubert, *The Ancien Régime. French Society 1600-1750*, Steve Cox, trans. (New York: Harper & Row, 1969), 3.

12. David Hume, "Of the Populousness of Ancient Nations," in *Essays Moral, Political, and Literary*, Eugene F. Miller, ed. (Indianapolis: Liberty Classics, 1987), 421. For comprehensive treatment of the general subject of skepticism regarding the prospects of republics in modern times see Paul A. Rahe, *Republics Ancient and Modern*. vol. II. *New Modes & Orders in Early Modern Political Thought* (Chapel Hill: University of North Carolina Press, 1994).

13. "Of the Populousness of Ancient Nations," in *Essays Moral, Political, and Literary*, Miller, ed., 414.

14. "Of the Populousness of Ancient Nations," in *Essays Moral, Political, and Literary*, Miller, ed., 411.

15. *The Theory of Moral Sentiments* V.2.8-9, 15 quoted by Rahe, *New Modes & Orders*, 89.

16. "Of the Populousness of Ancient Nations," in *Essays Moral, Political, and Literary*, Miller, ed., 404-5.

17. Cited by Elizabeth Rawson, *The Spartan Tradition in European Thought* (Oxford: Clarendon Press, 1969), 351.

18. He was, for example, just as concerned about the tendency of democratic governments to self-destruct amidst intense factional struggle as were Madison, Hamilton, and Hume. In a lengthy and remarkable entry in his private notebooks he laid out his grounds for believing that neither the English system of government nor one modeled on the classical republics of Greek antiquity could establish security of life and property as successfully as the monarchical government of France. Democratic republics fail in this regard, Montesquieu asserted, because they are likely to become divided into two factions, and one will become dominant and oppress the other. "A faction that dominates," he asserted, "is no less frightening (*terrible*) than an angry prince." In recent times it was England that showed how destructive of life and property factional struggles can be. Amidst such civil strife as the English had twice experienced in the seventeenth century, Montesquieu observes, "it serves nothing to say that one need only remain neutral. For who can be wise when everyone is mad?" Besides, the moderate man is hated by the two parties. "Moreover," Montesquieu laments, in free States (*États libres*), the insignificant people are ordinarily insolent. . . . There is scarcely an hour in the day when a gentleman (*honnête homme*) has no business with the lower class (*bas peuple*), and however grand a lord one may be, he is always coming into contact with them. For the rest," he concludes, "I consider of very little value either the happiness of furiously disputing State business

and never mouthing more than a hundred words without pronouncing the word liberty, or the privilege of hating half of the citizens." *(Pensée* 1802 [32], in Pléiade, I, 1431.)

19. Recent discussions of the concept of negative and positive liberty owe much to Isaiah Berlin's widely read essay, "Two Concepts of Liberty," reprinted in *Four Essays on Liberty* (Oxford: Oxford University Press, 1969), 118-72.

20. Montesquieu's skepticism regarding political participation as a necessary vehicle for achieving liberty did not go unnoticed in his own time. The author of a work entitled *La Monarchie parfaite, ou l'accord de l'autorité d'un monarque avec la liberté de la nation qui'il gouverne. Discours* (Geneva, 1789) referred specifically to Montesquieu in suggesting that the right of citizens "to concur in the making of defective and unreasonable laws" would be worthless. See Galliani, "La Fortune de Montesquieu," 43.

21. This chapter focuses on Montesquieu's depiction of the democratic republic and the aristocratic republic as ideal types rather than the confederate republic.

22. René Duchac, "Montesquieu et la démocratie: une espèce de la république?" *Cahiers internationaux de sociologie. Nouvelle série* (Janvier-juin, 1970), 32-52. As Cecil Courtney rightly notes in this volume, Montesquieu constructed ideal-types. For similar stress on this aspect of Montesquieu's methodology, see Raymond Aron, *Main Currents in Sociological Thought, Montesquieu, Comte, Marx, Tocqueville, and the Sociologists and the Revolution of 1848* (Garden City: Anchors Books, 1668), 17, 22 and *The Spirit of Laws by Montesquieu, a Compendium of the First English Edition. . .* , David Wallace Carrithers, ed. (Berkeley: University of California Press, 1977), "Introduction," 58.

23. For arguments along the same lines see Hume, "Of the Populousness of Ancient Nations," in *Essays Moral, Political, and Literary*, Miller, ed., 416 and Rousseau, *Social Contract*, Book IV, chapter 4.

24. Rousseau was also critical of the use of the secret ballot in Rome. In Book IV, chapter 4 of *The Social Contract* he remarked: "When the people grew corrupt and votes were bought, it became expedient for the ballot to be cast in secret, so that the buyers of votes might be restrained by mistrust of the sellers, and scoundrels given the chance of not being traitors also." See *The Social Contract*, Maurice Cranston, trans. (Baltimore: Penguin Books, 1968), 167.

25. Until the late eighteenth century, few readers of Plutarch's lives of Solon and Lycurgus treated them as fictional accounts. The most scholarly student of Sparta of the late eighteenth century, C. de Pauw, author of *Recherches philosophiques sur les Grecs* (1788), criticized Montesquieu on precisely this point. See Rawson, *The Spartan Tradition,* 260.

26. *Politics*, Book II, chap. 7 [1266 b].

27. In his history of Rome, published in 1734, Montesquieu had presented a similar argument regarding the importance of censors to retain discipline, morals, and the proper adherence to ancient customs: "They took the census of the people, and, what is more, since the strength of the republic consisted in discipline, austerity of morals, and the constant observance of certain customs, they corrected the abuses that the law had not foreseen, or that the ordinary magistrate could not punish. There are broad examples which

are worse than crimes, and more states have perished by the violation of their moral customs than by the violation of their laws. In Rome, everything that could introduce dangerous novelties, change the heart or mind of the citizen, and deprive the state—if I dare use the term—of perpetuity, all disorders, domestic or public, were reformed by the censors. . . . The censorship was a very wise institution. See *Considerations on the Causes of the Greatness of the Romans and their Decline (1734)*, David Lowenthal, trans. (Ithaca: Cornell University Press, 1965), chap. 8, 86.

28. See the sections below entitled "The Spartan Model" and "The Athenian Model" for discussion of these two sub-types.

29. Aristotle described Phaleas as "the first to suggest regulation of property for the purpose of preventing discord." (*Politics*, Bk. II, Chapter 7 [1266 a.])

30. In his note, Montesquieu cites Book V of Plato's *Laws*, which is incorrectly listed as Book III in the widely used Cohler translation of *The Spirit of Laws* published by Cambridge Univesity Press in 1989.

31. Hence we find General Charles Lee, for example, writing in a letter to Robert Morris that the republican governments of classical antiquity were "defective to absurdity—it was virtue alone that supported 'em." See *The Papers of Robert Morris*, J. Catanzariti and E.J. Ferguson, eds. (Pittsburgh, 1973), VI, 213 cited in Jenniefer Tolbert Roberts, *Athens on Trial. The Antidemocratic Tradition in Western Thought* (Princeton: Princeton University Press, 1994), 185.

32. Robespierre made a similar statement in his famous speech of February 5, 1794 (17 Pluviôse an II): "love of country implies or produces every virtue; for are virtues anything else than the strength of the soul that makes such sacrifice possible?" Quoted in Marc A. Goldstein, ed., *Social and Political Thought of the French Revolution, 1788-1797. An Anthology of Original Texts* (New York: Peter Lang, 1997), 564.

33. This crucial point was made by Thomas Pangle in his *Montesquieu's Philosophy of Liberalism. A Commentary on* The Spirit of the Laws (Chicago: University of Chicago Press, 1973), 57.

34. Manent labels Montesquieu's virtue "a shocking fiction," while also observing: "The virtue Montesquieu speaks of is a truly strange thing that has never yet been met with, in this world or the next. It is an amalgam of ancient political and Christian virtue in which each element loses its specific traits and takes on colors that denature it." See Pierre Manent, *The City of Man,* Marc A. LePain, trans. (Princeton: Princeton University Press, 1998), 24.

35. Robespierre's constant references to terror grossly distorted Montesquieu's language of virtue. In his speech of February 5, 1794 (17 Pluviôse an II) for example, Robespierre remarked to the National Convention: "But what is the fundamental principle of democratic or popular government, that is, what is the basic force that sustains it and makes it work? It is virtue; I am speaking of the public virtue that accomplished so many marvels in Greece and Rome, and that is destined to produce far more astonishing ones in republican France; I am speaking of the virtue that is nothing else but love of country and its laws." Several paragraphs later in the same speech Robespierre added the

important qualification that Montesqueu would never have approved: "If the principle of popular government in peace is virtue, the principle of popular government in revolution is both virtue and terror; virtue, without which terror is fatal; terror, without which virtue is powerless." Quoted in Marc A. Goldstein, ed., *Social and Political Thought of the French Revolution,* 564, 567.

36. It should be readily apparent why Montesquieu's model of the democratic state inspired both Mably and Rousseau, and, later, numerous French revolutionaries to conceive of republics as the proper vehicle for achieving human perfection. It is also apparent why some have read him as seeking to satirize and deride monarchy while suggesting the superiority of republican mores, customs, and morals. See, for example, an extended version of this anti-monarchy argument in Mark Hulliung, *Montesquieu and the Old Regime* (Berkeley: University of California Press, 1977). It can by no means be readily established, however, that merely by contrasting monarchy with a government based on purer mores, morals, and intentions Montesquieu meant to cast aspersions on a governmental type better suited to the more self-interested instincts of the modern age and better suited to the extraordinary territorial expanse of modern states.

37. *Pensée* 598 (221), in Pléiade, I, 1127.

38. Voltaire, "Thoughts on Public Administration," in Voltaire.*Political Writings* David Williams, ed. (Cambridge: Cambridge University Press, 1994), 222.

39. Voltaire, "Thoughts on Public Administration," in Voltaire, *Political Writings,* Williams, ed., 222.

40. Montesquieu praises ostracism in Athens and also Roman legislation aimed at individual citizens together with English bills of attainder on the grounds that "there are cases where it is necessary for a moment, to draw a veil over liberty, as one hides the statues of the gods" (XII, 19).

41. Letter 11 of *Cato's Letters,* quoted by Thomas Pangle in his *The Spirit of Modern Republicanism. The Moral Vision of the American Founders and the Philosophy of Locke* (Chicago: University of Chicago Press, 1988), 31.

42. Montesquieu says surprisingly little, however, about this war-time duty except in the fourth book which deals with educating citizens for republican government.

43. Montesquieu's recognition of the crucial role of education in republican government reflects a classical viewpoint expressed, for example, in the opening lines of Book VIII of Aristotle's *Politics*: "No one will doubt that the legislator should direct his attention above all to the education of youth; for the neglect of education does harm to the constitution. The citizen should be molded to suit the form of government under which he lives." (*The Politics,* Everson, trans., 185 [1337a10-14]).

44. For a forceful interpretation of the need to educate republican citizens, see William A. Galston, "Civic Education in the Liberal State," in *Liberalism and the Moral Life,* Nancy L. Rosenblum, ed. (Cambridge: Harvard University Press, 1989), 89-101.

45. Montesquieu was well aware that the Spartan state was unique and that it was organized around war. "Lycurgus," he writes, "did all that he was able to do to render the citizens more war-like," just as Plato and Thomas More aimed at more virtuous men, So-

lon at more equal men, Jewish legislators at religious men, the Carthaginians at wealthy men, and the Romans at more magnanimous men. (*Pensée* 319, in Pléiade, II, 1076.)

46. Montesquieu, *Considerations,* Lowenthal, trans., chap. 9, 98-99.

47. For Plutarch's comments on these aspects of Spartan life, see *Plutarch on Sparta*, Richard J. A. Talbert, ed. and trans. (Baltimore: Penguin Books, 1988), 8-46.

48. Chastity was nonetheless preserved according to Plutarch. "There was nothing disreputable," Plutarch wrote, "about the girls' nudity. It was altogether modest, and there was no hint of immorality." Furthermore, such displays of nudity functioned as what Plutarch called an "inducement to marry." (Talbert, ed., *Plutarch on Sparta*, 24-25).

49. Aristotle, *The Politics* (1270a).

50. Quoted by Rawson, *The Spartan Tradition*, 253.

51. *Histoire de Lacédémone*, in *Œuvres complètes de Jean-Jacques Rousseau*, Pléiade ed. (1964), III, 545-46 in Rawson, *The Spartan Tradition*, 233. Rousseau's perspective was later shared by Saint-Just who in his *Esprit de la révolution et de la constitution de France* (1791) lamented that it was to be expected that ancient institutions would appear strange to corrupt minds. See Saint-Just, *Œuvres complètes*, ed. C. Vellay, II, 282, cited by Rawson, *The Spartan Tradition*, 276.

52. *Fragments politiques* in *Œuvres complètes*, Pléiade ed. (1964), XIII, 545.

53. Rawson, *The Spartan Tradition*, 234 recounts that a correspondent informed him that remains of a theater had indeed been found. We now know, however, as Rousseau could not have, that those remains were of later, Roman origin.

54. Rousseau, *The First and Second Discourses*, Roger Masters, ed. and trans. (New York: St. Martin's, 1964), 90. Rawson observes (at 235) that Rousseau greatly idealized Geneva and that some residents of that city wrote to him to say he knew nothing of the place and that, contrary to Rousseau's conclusions, it bore no resemblance to Sparta.

55. Rawson, *The Spartan Tradition*, 256.

56. Turgot, *Discours*, in *Œuvres*, G. Schelle, ed. (1913), I, 194 cited by Rawson, *The Spartan Tradition*, 257.

57. Benjamin Constant, "Liberty of the Ancients," in *Political Writings*, Biancamaria Fontana, trans. and ed. (Cambridge: Cambridge University Press, 1988), 311-12. Drawing on Xenophon, Constant later compares Sparta, where "citizens quicken their step when they are called by a magistrate," to an Athenian who "would be desperate if he were thought to be dependent on a magistrate" (at 316).

58. Following the Athenian victories over Persia and the creation of a maritime empire, Athens was heavily engaged in commerce to obtain overseas foodstuffs, including grain. The silver mines at Laurion were mined, small factories arose in Athens, and a huge fleet was mounted in the Aegean. The result was what Victor D. Hanson describes as an influx of "resident alien businessmen, bankers, and traders, an enormous shadow city of outsiders who had no formal political rights in the polis." By the fifth century, he notes, there were in Athens between 10,000 and 40,000 metics (adults and children) and 80,000-150,000 slaves. See Victor D. Hanson, "Hoplites into Democrats: The Changing

Ideology of Athenian Infantry," in *Dēmokratia. A Conversation on Democracies, Ancient and Modern,* Josiah Ober and Charles Hedrick, eds. (Princeton: Princeton University Press, 1996), 292-93.

59. See also *Pensée* 598 (221), in Pléiade, I, 1127.

60. Montesquieu enumerated his objection to the expansionist militarism of the Roman empire with particular perspicacity in his *Reflections on Universal Monarchy* (1734), in Pléiade, II, 19-38.

61. The relevant text is in *The Politics,* Book II, chapter 10 (1272 a).

62. See, in particular, Condorcet's "Observations on the 29th Book of *The Spirit of the Laws,*" in Destutt de Tracy, *A Commentary and Review of Montesquieu's* Spirit of Laws, Thomas Jefferson, trans. (Philadelphia, 1811).

63. "Of the Populousness of Ancient Nations," in Hume, *Essays Moral, Political, and Literary,* Miller, ed., 416.

64. Plato, *The Republic,* Book VIII (557c).

65. This section of this chapter on republics is based on my previous publication, "Not So Virtuous Republics: Montesquieu, Venice, and the Theory of Aristocratic Republicanism," *Journal of the History of Ideas,* 52, no. 2 (April-June, 1991), 245-68 reused here by permission of that journal. For previous recognition of the importance of Venice to Montesquieu's theory of aristocratic republicanism see Jean Brethe de La Gressaye, ed. *De L'esprit des loix,* 4 vols. (Paris: Belles Lettres, 1950-1961), I, 244 and Robert Derathé, ed., *De L'esprit des lois,* 2 vols. (Paris: Garnier Frères, 1973), I, 425, 429. As important as Venice was to the construction of Montesquieu's theory of aristocratic republicanism, Derathé exaggerated when he asserted "For aristocracy, Montesquieu sticks to the sole example of the government of Venice." (I, 425) Rome and Sparta as well as Genoa, Lucca, and Ragusa also informed Montesquieu's views on aristocratic republics, although all to a lesser extent than Venice.

66. Montesquieu's main source on Venice was Amelot de La Houssaye's detailed and disparaging *Histoire du gouvernement de Venise* (Paris, 1676). So critical a perspective did Amelot offer that the Venetian ambassador to France at the time demanded that he be imprisoned for his efforts. See Zera Fink, *The Classical Republicans. An Essay in the Recovery of a Pattern of Thought in Seventeenth-Century England* (Evanston: Northwestern University Press, 1962), 143.

67. Amelot de La Houssaye had included a detailed account of the Venetian ballot within his discussion of the Grand Council (9-14), and many other observers were equally fascinated by the secret, multi-stage procedure employed for the election of all magistrates in Venice and by the secret ballot used when votes were taken in the Great Council and the Senate. Giannotti, for example, devoted over twenty pages of his *Repubblica de' Veneziani* (c. 1527; published 1542) to the subject of Venetian voting, and Harrington in his *Oceana* (1651) declared the complex Venetian system of secret balloting "of all others the most perfect." See J. G. A. Pocock, *The Machiavellian Moment. Florentine Political Thought and the Atlantic Republican Tradition* (Princeton: Princeton University Press, 1975), 284 and Fink, *Classical Republicans,* 64. Both Harrington

in his *Oceana* and John Milton in his *The Ready and Easy Way to Establish a Free Commonwealth* (1660) stressed that the use of randomly selected electors for choosing magistrates and the use of the secret ballot in legislative voting precluded the factional strife and intensely partisan campaigning so prevalent in other states. (Fink, *Classical Republicans*, 181.) Montesquieu's sole allusion to the Venetian secret ballot appears in his Book II, chapter 2 on the institutions of democratic republics where he suggests that the Venetian secret ballot is appropriate both for aristocratic republics and for the Senate in democratic republics as a device to minimize factions.

68. For an engaging study of the problem of designing adequate executive power, see Harvey Mansfield, Jr., *Taming the Prince. The Ambivalence of Modern Executive Power* (New York: The Free Press, 1989).

69. For commentary on this point, see Frederic Lane, *Venice. A Maritime Republic* (Baltimore: Johns Hopkins University Press, 1973), 403-5.

70. For stress on the importance of Venetian residential patterns, see Dennis Romano, *Patricians and Popolani. The Social Foundations of the Venetian Renaissance State* (Baltimore: Johns Hopkins, 1987). The literature on Venice with which Montesquieu was demonstrably familiar abounded in assertions of the truly extraordinary extent to which the nobility mixed with and blended in with the disenfranchised commoners. Amelot de La Houssaye asserted that the custom of allowing the *cittadini*, or citizen class of Venice, to dress like the nobility was intended to mask the small size of Venice's ruling class in order to make its oligarchical nature less apparent. (*Histoire*, 59.) Saint-Didier remarked "nothing renders the Subjection of this People more easy, than to see there is (sic) no Diversions at Venice, which is not in common between them and the Nobility; for they mingle themselves with those of that Illustrious Body at all Ceremonies, and other Publick Rejoycings . . . and these Gentlemen on their sides require no sort of external Respect from them." See Limojon de Saint-Didier, *The City and Republick of Venice. In Three Parts* (London: Printed for Char. Brome, 1699), Part III, 45. For further evidence that Montesquieu paid careful attention to Venetian laws imposing modest behavior on Venetian nobles, see *Spirit of Laws*, VII, 3.

71. This is an example of Montesquieu's too careless use of his sources. While it is true that in his discussion of the laws of Venice Amelot de La Houssaye first asserted that noblemen were barred from trade so that their private business would not interfere with the conduct of public business (*Histoire*, 24), he later indicates that Venetian noblemen nonetheless involved themselves in trade through secret agreements with commoners and that the Senate ignored this situation since such commercial ventures provided noblemen with the economic resources required for holding many important Venetian offices. (*Histoire*, 60) In his footnote to Houssaye's text Montesquieu cites just "Part III" rather than a specific page, and this seems to indicate that he was relying on memory rather than going back to the text prior to publication. In actual fact, Part III of Houssaye's treatise dealt with the Inquisition at Venice. For other comments of Montesquieu on Venetian commerce, see *The Spirit of Laws*, XX, 4, 5 and XXI, 21.

72. Here, in a footnote, Montesquieu cites pp. 30 and 31 of Houssaye directly. In this text Houssaye suggested that unequal inheritances among the nobility would have turned younger brothers into enemies of their country while also causing certain wealthy individuals to become too powerful.

73. For Montesquieu's early enthusiasm for republics, see *Persian Letter* 89, in Pléiade, I, 263-65 and *Pensée* 598 (221) in Pléiade, I, 1127. For his early distrust of monarchy as inherently tending either to despotism or mob rule, see *Persian Letter* 102, in Pléiade, I, 281.

74. *Voyage de Gratz a La Haye*, in Pléiade, I, 546, 548, and 557.

75. *Voyage*, in Pléiade, I, 715.

76. For his influence on the gradual emergence of social science, see David Carrithers, "The Enlightenment Science of Society," in *Inventing Human Science*, Christopher Fox, Roy Porter, and Robert Wokler, eds. (Berkeley: University of California Press, 1995), 232-70.

77. See, for example, "Centinel" in *The Complete Anti-Federalist*, Herbert J. Storing, ed., 7 vols. (Chicago: University of Chicago Press, 1981), II, 157; "A Democratic Federalist," in *Complete Anti-Federalist*, III, 59; and "A Newport Man," in *Complete Anti-Federalist*, IV, 252. Much more work needs to be done on the attitude of American theorists to the much fabled serene republic.

Chapter Four

Monarchy's Paradox:
Honor in the Face of Sovereign Power

Michael A. Mosher

Most explications of this subject start with a simple definition of monarchy, one that at once pulls together the two dimensions of Montesquieu's understanding of it. The standard account begins by saying that monarchy is the rule of one under fundamental law. That sets out in a provisional way its juridical structure. Then one adds that it is also a regime animated by honor. This hints at the role of an aristocratic culture in making monarchical government work well. Accurate as far as it goes, such a definition rushes us along too quickly. It covers up the tensions between these two dimensions, between the "nature" of this government and its "principle." To conceptualize this tension we begin by separating the two domains. After first taking up a few historical issues, we explore in subsequent sections the institutional questions of monarchy while striving hard not to admit the topic of culture into the discussion. Readers who become impatient with my reasons for initially distinguishing institutional and cultural issues may wish to juxtapose them more directly by turning to the section, "The Juridical Discourse of Sovereignty," and then to "Honor: Sovereignty's Supplement" and "Honor's Orbit."

Which line on monarchy did Montesquieu want his reader to remember? He evidently insisted upon this uniquely stressed line, which was, unfortunately, all that the nobility could remember on the eve of the Revolution: *"Point de monarque, point de noblesse; point de noblesse, point de monarque"* (no monarch, no nobility; no nobility, no monarch, Montesquieu's emphasis, II, 2).[1] At one level, this aphorism simply states a juridical ideal. It urges the striking of the right balance between the organization of sovereign authority in a large territorial state and the subordinate authority exercised by those elites who occupy "intermediate" channels of power (II, 4; VIII, 15, 17-18). Nevertheless, the frank defense of inequality that such celebration of local elites entails has enflamed otherwise admiring critics. Louis Althusser offers the typical complaint. The codependence of monarch and nobility seems to describe a sovereign who, far from achieving balance between center and periphery, instead undermines state authority by ceding it to a feudal aristocracy.[2]

Yet it would have been unduly prescient for Montesquieu to offer a preview of the Revolution in his reflections on monarchy and anachronistic on the part of the reader to suppose that Montesquieu should have wished away the inequalities that had characterized the European heritage up to that point. But since we readers are the heirs of the Revolution, let us consider Montesquieu's juridical model in the light of those insurrectionary events that changed Europe forever. Do the new models allow a comparison with the old? Raymond Aron thought so. Monarchy without the landed nobility and even without the king describes a more general problem of governance in large-scale states. Montesquieu raises the issue whether some sort of "social inequality" is not a condition for stable liberty, whether in the ancien régime or today. Montesquieu's monarchy points toward future dilemmas of contemporary pluralist orders: "However history may judge the specific institutions to which [Montesquieu] referred, his ultimate opinion was that the social order is essentially heterogeneous and that the condition of liberty is the balancing of social powers and the powers of government by the *nobility*—the sense in which nobility embraces the best citizens of an egalitarian democracy" (Aron's emphasis).[3]

Monarchy was not to have much of an historical future. But if these observations are correct, his understanding of the problems of governance under monarchy casts light on the issues which successor regimes confront. This suggests a more than antiquarian interest in reconstructing what Montesquieu has to say. In this chapter, our task is to isolate three languages or idioms, historical, juridical, and cultural, for describing monarchy in its European setting. These idioms for taking the measure of political things may appear alien to contemporary democratic usage, but not I think irrelevant to judgements we are still required to make.

In the following section, we set out monarchy's European history as this can be reconstructed from *The Spirit of Laws* and from Montesquieu's early texts. The stages in monarchy's development are the stages in the evolution of a European political identity. In contemplating the sweep of Montesquieu's version of this story, one can see where Jean-Jacques Rousseau could have gotten a narrative model. This history self-consciously appropriates for itself an origin among primitive peoples. It reaches an apogee in a golden age of "well-tempered monarchy" that disappears 200 years before Montesquieu begins to write. It then moodily considers the majestic but disturbing story of *puissance absolue* (absolute power), which may or may not have an unhappy denouement.

From European history we turn in the succeeding section to the abstract juridical discourse of monarchy found in *The Spirit of Laws*. At stake are two institutional questions. The first concerns the meaning of unitary state authority and the doctrine of "sovereignty" that philosophers since Bodin have sought to identify with this authority. I shall challenge the notion that Montesquieu's pluralist understanding of politics is designed to undermine all expressions of unitary authority. In the next section, we look at the second key dimension of Montesquieu's juridical doctrine: the "intermediary bodies," which include three kinds of courts that administer ecclesiastical, seigneurial, and royal justice, the last being the responsibility of the famous Parlements. Pursuing these institutional questions leads in the following section to a consideration of the ideological uses of Montesquieu's political ideas in the years 1748-71, and to a path considered but not ultimately taken in French history.

In the three final sections we come to the main issue: to show how Montesquieu's anthropological notion, a culture of honor, pulls together the disparate parts of his legal and political doctrines. The doctrine of sovereign authority designed by the legal theorist to be *sui generis* is instead radically insufficient and requires a supplement, which the author supplies by inventively reformulating the ancient class code of the nobility. Without understanding honor, the political theorist of juridical structure will be misled about how monarchy actually works. Honor affords its possessors an epistemological perspective that fundamentally alters their relationship to authority. We conclude with a word about the historical bearers of this collective mentality, the eighteenth century French nobility who were suspended between two radically different understandings of themselves in the years leading up to the Revolution.

Monarchy's European History

After the first discussion of the "liberties" promoted by the English constitution (XI, 6), Montesquieu asks "why the ancients had no clear idea of monarchy" and cites Aristotle's "awkwardness . . . in [the] treatment of monarchy" as confirmation of this gap in ancient political thought (XI, 8-9). We should not misinterpret this criticism. Montesquieu was indebted to Aristotle. Both philosophers stress how a rightly ordered diversity of perspectives contributes to a flourishing public life and how, above all, moderation in political judgement comes first. Montesquieu and Aristotle seem to share a vision of the imperfections inherent in any regime. Note that equality and inequality are the organizing principles of Montesquieu's republic and monarchy respectively. In this respect, these two types correspond to Aristotle's imperfect regimes, democracy and oligarchy, each characterized as in the grip of a partial understanding of justice, one leaning too much to equality, the other too much toward inequality.[4]

Nevertheless, Aristotle was embarrassed, Montesquieu thinks, by the idea of monarchy because this great philosopher of nature never quite grasped the nature of this state, the proof being that he mistook despotisms and republics for monarchies. But why should it matter that Montesquieu's predecessor went astray on this subject when Aristotle captured so much of political value about that compelling alternative to monarchy, the republic?

It makes a difference because for centuries Europeans lived under monarchical regimes. French history is the history of its monarchy. The very first line in the chapter directly following the discussion of England reads: "The monarchies we know do not have liberty for their direct purpose as does the one we have just mentioned," thereby affirming plainly that for Montesquieu contemporary England is also a monarchy of some sort, despite his other famous declaration that somehow a republic hides behind the throne (XI, 7; V, 19, 304). It would be a humbling confession of failure in a theory with such large explanatory ambitions to acknowledge an inability to comprehend the central moral and political issues in a thousand years of European history.

It is easy to miss the drama latent in *The Spirit of Laws*. If we place it back in its context, however, the text invites us to reflect on the relationship between a typology of governments (monarchies, despotisms, and two kinds of republics) and the commercial and moral transformations in the Europe of Montesquieu's day. Many of these changes were self-consciously articulated and welcomed as the consequence of "enlightenment." This raised an overarching regime question of which type of government, republic, despotism, or monarchy, was best suited to express as well as contain such changes.[5] It was an open question with no settled answer.

Two later stories of mythical proportions preempt Montesquieu's drama of regime choices: French and American republicanism. The self-justifying genealogies of both seem to require the construction of a story about their prehistory in which ancien régime, absolutism, monarchy, and despotism become nearly interchangeable terms. Both stories suppose that the republic is the only plausible response to social change. In the French story, 1789 is the "ground zero" and "absolute beginning" for the France that simultaneously invents and enters into "modernity." This history of national origins posits as its Book of Genesis the Revolution which in this and all subsequent versions has a standard plot line: it shattered the archaic and repressive shell of ancien régime monarchy in order to unleash the spirit of a republican people open to change and self-transformation.[6] This account raises the question of how such an open and independent spirit could have been nourished for so long under a form of rule, monarchy, which was evidently wholly inimical to it?

By contrast, the story of American experience focuses less on what was destroyed by revolution and more on what republican "founders" created, thereby making an issue out of republics, ancient and modern, whose relationship to the American Constitution has become a subject of intense study.[7] The notion that the American constitutional spirit may owe something to the civil order fostered by European monarchy will not naturally occur to those absorbed in these distinguished alternatives that have proven so fruitful since the eighteenth century. Despite the power of these two narratives, we cannot presuppose that in 1748 Montesquieu was prepared to dismiss the norms of a monarchical order, however much he questions the political direction taken by the French state.

From Montesquieu's contrast between two monarchies, "the one we have mentioned," England, whose object is liberty, and France, the pre-eminent example of "the monarchies we know" that pursue glory, the reader could readily conclude that "liberty" is intrinsic to England but not to monarchical government *per se*. In the very next line, however, Montesquieu insists that French glory fosters a "spirit of liberty" that compares favorably to the liberty directly targeted by the English regime (XI, 7). Nevertheless, we are still left with the option of thinking that this spirit of liberty is but a fortuitous by-product of the French case alone. Before reaching this conclusion, let us consider a comment about monarchy and the distribution of powers that concludes this chapter from Book XI.

The issue of the distribution of powers is a vexed one for the interpreter. Many readers seem almost to abridge Montesquieu's big book into a short treatise on the English constitution (with an appendix in praise of commerce). This smaller book offers the counsel that in order to moderate the effects of power, one might well consider the distribution among different political constituencies of the legislative, executive, and judicial powers Montesquieu believes could be found in England. As an aside, I note that it is proper to refer only to the "distribution" or "division" of powers, phrases Montesquieu actually uses, and not the "separation of powers" which not only does he never use, but which subtly distorts the doctrine he espouses.[8] Be that as it may, those inclined to abbreviate the argument are left with the impression that England is twice over unique. Its constitution aims uniquely at liberty, and the instrument for accomplishing this end is a distribution of powers that the English singularly possess. In this account, England is wholly different from surrounding polities. This reading is too restrictive, however. On the fundamental issue of achieving an equilibrated political system in which power holders check other power holders, England and the Continental monarchies are not different. "The three powers are not distributed and cast on the model of the constitution [England] we have just mentioned," but in France and "in each instance" of monarchical rule, we will find "a particular distribution of [these powers]." Each case "approaches political liberty." This is necessarily so; for if it did not, Montesquieu warns, "the monarchy would degenerate into despotism" (XI, 7).

It appears that every European monarchy remotely worthy of its name "approaches" liberty because every such monarchy exhibits a particular distribution of powers. The argument has taken an interesting turn. We earlier learned that monarchies were not always stable. They were prone to despotism. England under Oliver Cromwell was no exception. The English, now free, could become "one of the most enslaved peoples on earth" (III, 3; VI, 2). Nevertheless, on top of this warning another palimpsest is laid. The idea of Europe and that of monarchy are now linked in a complex way to the theme of political liberty.

The argument presupposes that England and France were historically connected by common genealogy to a "beautiful system [that] was found in the woods" (XI, 6, 407). The common link was to "our fathers, the Germans" (VI, 18). England is free, Montesquieu suggests, because "the English have taken their idea of political government from the Germans" (XI, 6, 407). France, too, was formed by the "Germanic nations who conquered the Roman Empire" (XI, 8). Writers like Dubos and the earlier writers of providentialist history trace French civilization through Roman imperial law. Montesquieu rejects these Romanist claims. He celebrates the civilization recalled by the *thèse nobiliaire* and takes the barbarian side in the Roman-barbarian standoff.

"Barbarian" conveys the standard prejudicial connotation, but it has as well another sense which describes "pastoral peoples" that could be admired (XVIII, 11). Montesquieu seems torn between showing how bloody the barbarian conquest of Roman territory was and explaining why barbarian nations deserve our sympathy. Their moral habits gesture toward a future for self-government that the civilized Romans had lost centuries earlier. "These peoples enjoy a great liberty; for as they do not cultivate the land, they are not attached to it . . . if a leader wished to take their liberty from them, they would immediately go and seek it from another leader or withdraw into the woods to live there with their family" (XVIII, 14).

Through an effort of anthropological recovery (Montesquieu commends here the relevant works of Caesar and Tacitus), one may perceive the origins of human freedom in the life of the European borderlands. In these reflections, which owe much to predecessors like Herodotus and Montaigne, one sees the origins of a thoroughly modern anxiety. Montesquieu poses the question whether, in a contrast of civilization and the "primitive," the former lacks for all its advantages something which only an earlier way of life could have conferred. This theme is picked up by authors of innumerable works in diverse traditions, including Jean-Jacques Rousseau, *Discourse on the Origins and Foundations of Inequality Among Men* (1755), Denis Diderot, *Supplement to Bougainville's Voyage* (1772), François-René de Chateaubriand, *Les Natchez* (1826), Henry David Thoreau, *Walden (1854),* and Frederick Jackson Turner, *The Significance of the Frontier in American History (1892).* Even Nietzsche returns to this scene in *The Genealogy of Morals* (1887). Claude Levi-Strauss, *Tristes Tropiques* (1955) provides a contemporary example.[9]

In Montesquieu's take on these issues, liberty lies in a wandering people's possibilities of exit from all organized claims upon them. Later, civilization raises the cost of exit. Its material temptations, wholly attached to staying in one place, are greater. Less of a premium is placed on cultivating habits of resistance to rule. This is a pity since without the practices of exit in the early history, there is no possibility of voice at the end: "Among these peoples, the liberty of the man is so great that it necessarily brings with it the liberty of the citizen" (XVIII, 14). This becomes a central issue in Enlightenment debates. How can the liberty displayed naturally in humanity's earliest habitats sustain itself when "civilization" evolves? Montesquieu's genealogy also states the risks for a secular teleology. In possession of liberty from the beginnings, humans are meant for citizenship, but more often than not liberty is suffocated before the possibilities of citizenship arrive on the scene.

This brings us to the political problem of Gothic government among German tribes. Unlike any other, such a regime exhibited two novel characteristics that "the ancients did not at all know." First, it was "government founded on a body of nobles." Second, this was "government founded on the legislative body formed by the representatives of a nation" (XI, 8). The baron de La Brède says nothing about why founding government on the nobility is an advantage. Unlike allies who also support the *nobiliaire* thesis, he does not whitewash these events: the barbarian conquest was a nasty, unpleasant business. The advantage he draws from this primal scene is obvious, however. The contemporary French nobility is not required to acknowledge that its privileges are dependent upon an historical grant from a Roman *imperium* that Montesquieu and other *nobiliaire* writers regarded as a thinly veiled despotism.

Let us adopt for a moment the Romanist perspective. If a continuous Roman *imperium* could be established as the source of the authority granted to German ancestors, then the privileges of the French nobility who stand in this line of succession could be modified or removed by the crown that now stakes its legitimacy upon representing this *imperium*. Whether valid or not, this line of argument supported centralizing monarchical governments laboring to control aristocratic factions which, as popular indictments suggest, were little better than irresponsible gangs of ruffians. This view lies at the core of the exultation of executive authority that goes under the name of "enlightened despotism." Take simply the example of Voltaire, who was once beaten with impunity by a minor lord's armed retinue because Voltaire had challenged the man but was not thought worthy enough to do so. Voltaire supports crown powers over noble privileges and provincial rights alike because he sees in central state authority an instrument for reform that is stifled by all these intermediary powers.

Montesquieu does not dispute the authority of the crown. Rather he thinks that the crown's authority would diminish, not expand, if the privileges of the nobility and provincial courts were removed. In any event, Montesquieu does not favor rule by nobles. The original case of a government founded upon a nobility was manifestly unjust and the source of its gravest defect. The Gothic "mixture of monarchy and aristocracy" made the "common people" into "slaves" (XI, 8). We must distinguish Montesquieu's position from that of Boulainvilliers with whom it seems allied by common sympathies. "[Boulainvilliers'] work," Montesquieu says, "is written with no art . . . [but] he speaks with that simplicity, frankness, and innocence of the old nobility. . . . He had more spirit than enlightenment and more enlightenment than knowledge" (XXX, 10). Both authors agree that the French nobility are justified in tracing their roots to the barbarian conquest of Gaul, but Boulainvilliers insists that this fact is pre-scriptive and gives eternal title for noble blood successors to rule. By reifying once and for all who was "noble," Boulainvilliers' argument has a racist aspect to it.[10]

In Montesquieu's history, the liberties of the German nobility were slowly extended to the subject population. The failure adequately to extend these rights to the commons was a great defect in this government. However, the history of the first three lines of French Kings, *les trois races* of Merovingians (481-751), Carolingians (751-986) and Capetians (987-1328), embodied the up and down story of the affirmation of local customs that simultaneously extended privileges more widely and established civil law and rights. The story of these affirmations and extensions could be continued into the Valois line (1328-1589), but they evidently ceased with the ascension of the Bourbon kings.

If, in order to correct the defects of aristocratic domination, "letters of eman-cipation" were constantly issued, why did not the whole political system evolve into a republic, albeit a large republic where representative government replaced monarchical rule? This question points to the difference between the evolution of the English and French constitutions from their common origins *dans les bois*. The national assemblies that characterized original German rule were pre-served and strengthened under English government. In France they were not. The two cases differ because early on the English state was stronger and more united than the French state. In England kings "forced into existence the repre-sentative institutions that could help [them]." By contrast, when the French state belatedly consolidated its authority, it "took over [regions] where laws, customs, and identities had hardened." As a consequence, assemblies "were difficult to convoke" and remained exercises in "public relations" as few ever felt bound by decisions such assembles took.[11]

Montesquieu chose not to signal his awareness of the many occasions in which the French did assemble in both national Estates General and provincial assemblies. The latter continued to meet in Montesquieu's day. After reciting the facts of the national assemblies under the Merovingians and Carolingians (481-986), however, there is not a word to be found on this subject in the rest of *The Spirit of Laws*. He adds only the remark that in this era, it was "not yet a question of the commons," leaving open the possibility that he intends this as an agenda for the modern French as it is for the English (XXVIII, 9). To put Mon-tesquieu's silence on this matter in perspective, we should ask how important the Estates General actually was. One historian suggests it "did not, as usually supposed, lose its powers in the sixteenth and seventeenth centuries owing to the rise of absolutism. It never had any."[12] Montesquieu may have agreed. This does not, however, preclude the reader from seeking in *The Spirit of Laws* effective substitutes for such assemblies.

French rule shares with English rule the common trait of Gothic government, "the capacity to become better" (XI, 8). The original aristocratic oligarchy could be transformed. At a certain point, a new form of rule emerged, the "well tempered" monarchy. "The civil liberty of the people, the prerogatives of the nobility and of the clergy, and the power of the kings, were in such concert that there has never been, I believe, a government on earth as well tempered as that which prevailed in each part of Europe during the time this government continued to exist." Montesquieu subscribes neither to a providentialist nor a determinist view of these developments. On the causes of this novel form of government, he contents himself with another smiling irony: "It is remarkable that the corruption of the form of government of a conquering people should have formed the best kind of government men have been able to devise" (XI, 8).

From Montesquieu's notebook, the *Pensées*, we can venture to date the end of well-tempered monarchy. Two high points were reached among the Valois kings. The first occurred in the reign of Charles VII (who ruled 1422-61), though his son and successor, Louis XI (1461-83), destroyed its achievements. The second came at the turn of the century under Louis XII (1498-1515).[13] The era before the ascent of Charles VII to the throne was one of disaster for the French. The English at Agincourt (1415) humiliated French armies while the crown was in constant struggle and civil war with Burgundian and Orleanist grandees. Charles's reign illustrated a grim maxim: "after the most disastrous of civil wars, a state suddenly finds itself at the highest degree of power."[14] With serene disregard for costs, Montesquieu notes approvingly that civil war turns all men into soldiers. From its turmoil "great men" arise. "What does not destroy the state makes it stronger."[15] An adviser to Charles VII, Count Dunois, was such a figure of grandeur, "a man whom we can regard with as much title as Pharamond [a legendary Frankish Chief] and Clovis [the first of the fifth century Merovingian kings] as the founder of *our* monarchy."[16] Montesquieu expresses his admiration more succinctly in *The Spirit of Laws*. With the advent of Charles VII: "*Voici la grande époque*" (XXVIII, 45, 864, my emphasis).

Montesquieu does not always reject the claims of royal power. His respect for Charles VII's consolidation of authority suggests very nearly the opposite: "France was in a state it had not been since the days of Carolingian rule" (from the eighth to the tenth century). The English were gone; France was at peace with neighbors; and more importantly, given the recent history of civil war, "the Dukes of Burgundy showed respect and the other feudal lords feared the crown." France was now well governed because: "the estates of the principal seigneurial lords were practically all surrounded by royal power. Most of the great fiefdoms were reunited to the crown; others were about to be reunified. The limits of authority and obedience were well enough understood; reciprocal rights well enough established."[17]

Temperate monarchy may point to cooperation and concert among partners but it is the crown that directs this concert. Montesquieu's two medieval heroes, Philip Augustus (1180-1223) and Saint Louis (Louis IX, 1226-70), were reforming kings who proclaimed charters that freed the serfs and promulgated civil law. Charles VII was a third reforming champion of civil rights (XXVIII, 45). Montesquieu's description of his legacy is an encomium to royal authority: "it would have been easy for the successor to Charles VII to ally justice with grandeur and to make himself dreaded even in his moderation, to be in the end the prince the most beloved of his subjects and the most respected by foreigners in all Europe."[18] Alas, this happy balance was destroyed, also by royal authority. For Montesquieu there is no guarantee that even the best polity will survive the accidents of succession: "The death of Charles VII was the last day of French liberty. In an instant one saw another king, another people, other policies, another sort of patience. The passage from liberty to servitude was so great, so quick and rapid, the means so strange, so odious to a free nation that it seemed as though the whole kingdom had tumbled into a dizzying vortex."[19]

It is comparable, Montesquieu assures us, "to the change in the spirit of the Romans after Caesar."[20] Well-tempered monarchy was almost finished. It enjoyed, however, a brief revival under Louis XII (1498-1515) of whom Montesquieu claims, "France has never had a better citizen."[21] In the autumnal glow of this reign, Montesquieu's nostalgia swells into a crescendo: "Here we fall upon the reign which good people will always remember with pleasure, where virtue finds its history, where one is pleased to write, in order to make one's fellow citizens see that there are also happy ages for monarchies and that subjection [to kings] has its advantages, as liberty its inconveniences."[22] Louis XII is the recipient of such praise despite the objections that could be lodged against a policy that led France to invade Italy for a second time. Machiavelli's *The Prince* was written in the shadow of this invasion. Foreign conquest does not evidently detract from admiration for Louis XII. At least in these earlier writings, the baron de La Brède is not immune to the military dimensions of the aristocratic ethos of honor that *The Spirit of Laws* inserts into the fabric of monarchy.

Perhaps however, it was only a monarch and not the monarchy that was well tempered. Montesquieu can think of little to commend in the successors to Louis XII. Under Catherine de Medici and her three sons, France falls into factional dissension and religious civil war. Montesquieu is surprisingly cool toward Henry of Navarre who became Henry IV (1589-1610). This Protestant who converted to Catholicism reunified the country and imposed toleration of Protestants on its Catholic majority. Though Montesquieu admires unification in an earlier era and is a friend of toleration, none of Henry's achievements earns his esteem.

While Montesquieu evinces great dislike for the Sun-King, Louis XIV, he directs his fiercest condemnation to Louis XIII's powerful adviser, Richelieu, one of the "nastiest citizens France has had." Richelieu was "a private man who had more ambition than all the monarchs in the world; . . . the whole universe was for him but a theater for expressing his ambition, his hatred, or vengeance; . . . he governed as a master, not as a minister [and] . . . made slaves for the pleasure of it."[23] Even under better conditions, court life was for Montesquieu a necessary, if regrettable weakness in the structure of monarchical government. "The wretched character of courtiers . . . are not matters of speculation, but of sad experience" (III, 5). In the *Persian Letters*, Montesquieu has Rica, one of his Persians, claim to admire the French monarch because he is so much like the Turkish or Persian despot: "one often hears that of all the governments in the world that of the Turks or that of our august Sultan pleases him most, such is his admiration for oriental policies." Rica also suggests that the king "has more statues in his garden than citizens in a great city," slyly implying that, under Louis, Paris had few citizens.[24]

In likening the political system of Louis XIV to an "oriental despotism," Montesquieu evokes an ancient European prejudice about lands to the East that dates from Herodotus. To pick an early modern example of it, Michel de Montaigne cited approvingly Plutarch's witticism that Asians suffer from the despotism "of one single man because they cannot pronounce one single syllable, which is No."[25] The *Persian Letters* picks up this theme. Can the French say no, or are they more like the wives and eunuchs in Usbek's despicable seraglio, the scene of servile subjection? Usbek, the "oriental" despot, is modeled on Louis XIV. The one fictional and the other real, they govern their subjects from a great distance, both geographical and psychological. Neither is remotely well informed about conditions in their realms. In the case of Usbek, his wives pursue their own interests while only pretending to conform to the ideological platitudes that serve to buttress their husband's fragile self understanding. In the last letter we learn that Roxanne can say "no." Considered all along by Usbek as the most "virtuous" of his many wives, she is instead simply the most daring. Years earlier she was evidently the leader in suborning the eunuch guards, whom we should regard as either priests or *intendants*, and in introducing lovers of various description into the absent husband's household.

Owing to the window of cultural relaxation that opens briefly under the Regency of Philip of Orleans (1715-22), Montesquieu somehow gets away with this satirical lampoon of the monarchy. In 1926 Paul Valery wrote a highly poetic preface to an edition of the *Lettres persanes* which captures the atmosphere of Regency France (1715-22), as well as the uncertainties of post World War I France: "That moment between order and disorder is a delicious moment. Every possible advantage to be had from the regulation of powers and duties has been acquired, and now the first relaxations of the system are to be enjoyed. The institutions still stand. They are great and imposing. But without showing any visible alteration, their splendid presence is nearly all they are. . . . The social body quietly loses its futurity. It is the hour of enjoyment and consummation."[26]

The French, Montesquieu hints, are ruled in an alien manner. Their kings are no different than despotic men from the East. By attaching this prejudice to the political system constructed by Richelieu and Mazarin, Montesquieu contributes inadvertently as much as anyone to the slow delegitimization of the French monarchy in the eighteenth century.[27]

We have yet to mention any of the apologists for the government of Louis. One seventeenth-century ecclesiastical writer stands out, Jacques-Bénigne Bossuet. He is the most successful and learned of those seeking to refurbish a traditional form of address, *le roi très chrétien*, into something altogether more grandiose. In sermons and essays, and especially in *La Politique tirée de l'Écriture sainte* (Politics Drawn from Holy Scripture), composed in 1679 and published posthumously in 1709, this Bishop of Meaux elevates the faint suggestion of royal piety in this traditional appellation, "the very Christian king," into a theocratic justification for absolute rule by divine right. For Bossuet and his audience, all royal authority is sacred, paternal, and absolute. According to the Bishop, "the royal throne is not the throne of a man, but that of God himself." Kings becomes Christ-like figures: "Majesty is the image of the greatness of God in a Prince."[28]

To these imposing and widely circulated theocratic metaphors, *The Spirit of Laws* has seemingly no response despite the fact that it aims generally at a realistic understanding of the norms that undergird European kingship. Montesquieu refuses to engage Bossuet's justification of state power, however standard such conceptions were.[29] Of course, Bossuet's appeal had diminished by mid-century. Montesquieu is apparently determined to finish off this religious conception of kingship for good by applying a strictly secular approach to the subject. He is pleased to hear Bossuet called a "pedant." He has no confidence in the man's judgment: "M. de Meaux has the mannerisms of a seminarian. He calls a bundle of sticks a gaudy delight."[30] Though silent on Bosssuet's political theory, Montesquieu takes up the cudgels on behalf of a history freed of divine intervention. For Bossuet, history is providentialist and Augustinian, "a corollary of faith." This is too mystical for a resolute rationalist. Montesquieu's *Considerations on the Causes of the Greatness of Romans and of their Decline* (1734) is a reply to providentialism of all kinds. "Independently of the secret ways God has chosen, which only he knows," there is, Montesquieu argues, a secular explanation for the success of Christianity. In general, "it is not fortune which rules the world ... [since] every accident is submitted to causes."[31] He insists upon secular causes. History—even the history of kings—is not improved by appealing to the sacred.

Historians hunting down the origins of the French Revolution point to the desacralization of the French kings as though the monarchy could never have survived without remaining in possession of divine support lifting it, so to speak, above mere empirical description. The eminent historian of Jansenist radicalism, Dale Van Kley, sees the seventeenth-century sacralization of royal authority as a self-protective strategy that, in response to the French wars of religion, elevates the monarchy above religious conflict and "immunize[s] the royal conscience against the judgment of priests and pastors alike." Bodin, the original theorist of absolute power, does not suffice because his argument will not place kings on God's throne. But Van Kley does not think it likely that the monarchy could have climbed down from its Bossuetian heights in the eighteenth century because its mechanisms of governance were now inextricably linked with a "propertied and privileged church." Catholic monarchies cannot stop the process of turning "religious dissent into political challenge." The French monarchy might have reinvented itself, but the odds were against this. Keith Baker is on the same page as Van Kley. "Bossuet's impulse . . . to place absolute monarchy beyond the bar of merely historical argumentation," is an appropriate, if desperate, strategy.[32]

Montesquieu is determined to show the opposite: desacralization equals the normalization of a monarchy that ought always to have been a secular enterprise. In those quarters where this latter argument prevails, the history of monarchy can be narrated in terms of a discursive reasoning no longer dependent on divine authority. As Daniel Gordon has shown, a civil life now appears that is capable of nurturing the norm of rational political discourse. The geographical locations for such discussion are illuminated in the descriptions the *Persian Letters* offers of coffeehouses, salons, academies, law courts, and theaters where a public of relative strangers equipped with *politesse* and sociability was able to meet for an empirically oriented consideration of their situation.[33] This is "civil society," or the beginning of it, a space which, when it is elaborated, creates by century's end the fateful dialogue between the nation and the state. Here we have an explanation for the heat generated by the seemingly erudite debate between Romanists and Germanists. According to Mona Ozouf and François Furet, the early eighteenth century spectacle of French writers rejecting the Roman claims of central government in favor of Germanic style decentralization was but a symptom of "civil society's drive toward power . . . and legitimacy."[34]

Despite the existence of a national parliament in England, civil society seems to have almost a greater potential in France, "a nation," Montesquieu says, with "a sociable humor, an openness of heart, a joy in life, a taste, [and] an ease in communicating its thoughts" (XIX, 5). "One is less communicative," Montesquieu argues, "in countries where each . . . exercises or suffers an arbitrary power, than in those where liberty reigns in all conditions" (XIX, 12).[35] If so, on Montesquieu's own account, the communicative French do not suffer from the consequences of *pouvoir arbitraire*, however much the history of *pouvoir absolu* may hold the threat of arbitrariness over its subjects' heads.

What is the import of this history for Montesquieu's political theory? Three narrative moments stand out. Two illuminate a possible future. The first recalls the presence of a natural liberty in the lives of barbarian predecessors that is "so great" it illuminates the way forward to "the liberty of the citizen." The second appeals to the portrait of fifteenth-century "well-tempered" monarchy, which becomes the standard for a distribution of powers that guarantees "civil liberty"

(XVIII, 14; XI, 8). The third narrative moment, the rise of *pouvoir absolu* under Bourbon kings, seems to show why that future will be frustrated.

This denouement suggests two contradictory interpretive strategies in coming to terms with *The Spirit of Laws*. First, we can take the book as a subversive text whose explicit declarations are not to be trusted. It is an historicist discourse that knows that monarchy is an unstable transitional moment on the road to somewhere else. This instability will be foretold in the failure of any effort to judge the possible compatibility of *pouvoir absolu* with the two standards of natural and civil liberty. By contrast a second strategy asks only that we take Montesquieu as meaning what he says. It supposes *The Spirit of Laws* is a work of synthesis meant to reconcile its immediate French readers with who they are and what they might become. It does not require any unnatural prescience by the author about future events. If, for Montesquieu, *pouvoir absolu* in France were somehow or another to satisfy the standards of a liberty that gestures toward citizenship and a constitution that is well tempered, we may regard him as engaged in an altogether different process, "reinventing monarchy." This reinvention will be, however, secular in accordance with the high enlightenment's Olympian detachment from the public display of religious passions. As though Bossuet never existed, it will not take into account the sacral pretensions of French kings nor, therefore, the sacral demands made upon them by the eighteenth century Jansenist-Jesuit replay of the sixteenth-century wars of religion.

The Juridical Discourse of Sovereignty

The political theory of monarchy consists of two separate elements that may not easily mesh with one another. First, monarchy is a set of offices which falls under a distinctive understanding of authority, identified with great understatement as the rule of one according to fixed and established law (II, 1). Montesquieu also calls this fundamental law (II, 4). This is the *nature* of monarchical government. Second, this juridical ideal is related to a stylized understanding of a distinctive mode of conduct among the persons associated under its authority. This is the *principe* of monarchy, its hidden spring of action. With equally great understatement, it is identified simply as honor (III, 5-7; IV, 2; V, 9-12). In this section we focus only upon the nature of monarchical rule leaving the difficult issue of its principle until later.

The nature and principle of monarchy are contrasted to two other norms of authority, despotism and republic. Montesquieu defines the "fact" of despotism as "the rule of one without law and rule in accordance with will and caprice" (II, 1). Its *principe* is fear (III, 9; IV, 3; V, 13-16). The republic comes in two types; either a people as a whole in a democratic republic has sovereign power or a part of the people in an aristocratic republic exercise it (II, 1). The principle of action in the former is called virtue, ostensibly meaning neither Christian nor any other species of personal virtue. Republican virtue manifests itself in a public love of equality (III, 3; IV, 4-8; V, 2-7). Since an aristocratic republic is defined by the inequality between rulers and ruled and yet requires a similar love of equality to function, its manifest principle of action must be moderation. This presupposes a willingness among its leaders not to take advantage or to display their power with too much publicity (III, 4; V, 8).

Moderation, the principle of the aristocratic republic, is also a fundamental divide that distinguishes generally between "moderate" and despotic government (III, 10). In making this distinction, Montesquieu refers only to monarchical government as moderate, leaving the reader to assume that he also includes republics. This assumption is later tested, though not necessarily defeated, when he claims that "democracies and aristocracies [i.e., republics] are not free states by their nature" (XI, 4).

Before monarchy disappeared in the nineteenth century as a government presiding over a way of life understood to have a distinctive ethical content, there were in a thousand years of European experience with this form of polity only two or three philosophers who grasped its nettle. Montesquieu was one. Bodin, the theorist of *pouvoir absolu*, is the great predecessor. Bossuet, discussed above, is also an influential figure, though his arguments, where secular, are derived from Bodin. Here I ignore the other great figure, Hobbes, except to say that the Bodinian theory of sovereignty announced in *Les six livres de la république* (1576) is an important element in French intellectual life by the time Hobbes went to Paris in the 1640s to work out his own theory of sovereignty. Both are theorists of the new political concept of sovereignty. Montesquieu was sufficiently fascinated with Bodin to own two editions of *Les six livres de la république*.[36]

For Bodin "absolute" describes the extent of the power held by those who are "sovereign" in a state or *république*, whether that consists in the whole body of the people, a part, or a king: "Majesty or sovereignty is the most high, absolute, and perpetual power over the citizens and subjects in a commonwealth [*république*] . . . that is to say, the greatest power to command."[37] To be sure, "the absolute power of princes and sovereign lords does not extend to the laws of God and nature."[38] Nevertheless, the prince "is not bound by the laws of his predecessors, still less can he be bound by his own laws."[39] We further learn that the "attributes of sovereignty are peculiar to the sovereign prince, for if communicable to the subject, they cannot be called sovereignty." The sovereign is above all else a lawgiver: "law signifies the right command of that person, or those persons, who have *absolute* authority over all the rest without exception . . . the first attribute of sovereignty is to give law to all in general and each in particular" (my emphasis).[40]

This becomes a more forbidding doctrine if we overlook three sets of crucial qualifications. First, though Bodin defends monarchy, he calls it a species of "republic," thereby appealing to Greek and Roman political theory that highlights the importance of *politeia* and *res publica*, regimes devoted to the common or general interest. For Aristotle *politeia* carries an additional implication, one with which Bodin is also in curious agreement. Whether in the form of the right kind of oligarchy, i.e., aristocracy, or the right kind of democracy, identified by the generic term *politeia*, the notion necessarily incorporates a diversity of perspectives. Bodin embraces this perspectival diversity as one of the commanding features of a well-ordered regime. Since this diversity may not have been a dimension of Aristotle's idea of monarchy, which appealed instead to the Platonic ideal of the philosopher-king who simply governed alone, Bodin may have corrected the ancient notion of monarchy by extending to it this perspectival dimension of *politeia*. Though the king who enjoys sovereign power rules alone, he is never, Bodin claims, rightly alone in ruling.

The second qualification explains how one who rules alone accommodates this diversity. "Many have been led astray," Bodin insists, "by confusing the laws of the prince with the covenants entered into by him." When the prince enters into a covenant with his subjects, Bodin still insists there is always a juridical center of ultimate decision in the person of the sovereign. But now the sovereign is not the sole political power in the community, though he or she is the sole source of this power. Bodin is not intent upon negating constitutional arrangements, but he does intend to subordinate them to a sovereign lawgiver. Thus, it is no surprise when Bodin declares: "the sovereignty of the king is in no wise qualified or diminished by the existence of Estates. On the contrary, his majesty appears more illustrious when formally recognized by his assembled subjects, even though in such assemblies *princes*, not wishing to fall out with their people, *agree to many things which they would not have consented to*" (my emphasis).[41] Prudence is sovereign duty. The power of the sovereign (whether it consists in the rule of one, the few, or the many) is enhanced when it refrains from interfering with the subordinate offices it establishes. Self-denial through constitutional self-restraint preserves power. Self-disablement establishes stable spheres of personal liberty, which elicit initiative and cooperation and permit a polity to prosper. Less rule equals more power.

The language of Bodin is redolent of the *Social Contract*. Rousseau's treatment of republican sovereignty owes much to the author of *The Six Books*. He makes good use of Bodin's distinction between "the form of the state and the form of the government." This distinction is the third critical qualification to Bodin's argument. To explain it, Bodin offers this example: "A state may be a monarchy, but it is governed democratically if the prince distributes lands, magistrates, offices, and honors . . . without regard to the claims of either birth or wealth or virtue."[42] Rousseau adopts this language (while inverting its political intent) in distinguishing between a sovereign republic, the sole legitimate source of all political power, and the administrations or governments, (democratic, aristocratic, or monarchical) to which the sovereign republic delegates power.[43]

What Bodin and Rousseau call "the government" describes a distribution of offices or roles the source of whose power lies with another entity, the sovereign. For Montesquieu, a government also consists in a distribution of powers. Now we come to the critical issue. Does Montesquieu, like Bodin and Rousseau, hold a doctrine of sovereign authority in which there is an ultimate source of political and civil power that presides over a given distribution of powers? Or out of fear of absolute power lodged in the crown, does Montesquieu insist upon the prior and prescriptive rights and privileges of those intermediary bodies (the nobility, Parlements, Church, and cities) which constitute the social bases for the distribution of powers in a government? Either Montesquieu holds a doctrine of sovereignty or he does not. If not, *The Spirit of Laws* becomes a purely pluralist treatise that rejects locating sovereign authority in any single or collective body. It would then reflect an ancient tradition of mixed government in which, instead of there being an ultimate authority, there is only shared responsibility for rule parceled out between rival claimants. Surprisingly enough, *The Spirit of Laws* neither disputes nor challenges the Bodinian claim for the state's absolute powers. Instead, Montesquieu forthrightly declares it: "*in a monarchy the prince is the source of all political and civil power*" (II, 4, my emphasis).

This could not be plainer. Absolute sovereignty, the ultimate power to decide, rests with the holder of royal authority. The significance of this declaration is easy to miss, however, as it is packaged into a sequence of anxiously repetitive sentences that introduces for the first time *les pouvoirs intermédiaires*, widely conceded to be the instrument for breaking the grip of the Bodinian absolute sovereign. Here are the first lines of Book II, chapter 4. "The intermediate, subordinate, and dependent powers constitute the nature of monarchical government, that is to say, the government where one alone governs by fundamental laws. I said intermediate, dependent, and subordinate powers: in effect, in a monarchy the prince is the source of all political and civil power." As the intermediate powers are defined as subordinate to the prince, and therefore presumably subject to his or her will and pleasure, it is not clear, at least juridically, how far the institutions encompassed by these powers can challenge the sovereignty of the prince. Evidently Montesquieu wanted to reinforce the idea of subordination to the sovereign. The intermediary powers are clearly intended to complement the exercise of sovereignty, but they do not in this passage claim to override it. Let us assume that the words mean what they say. The king is the holder of sovereignty that is "absolute," i.e., "the source of all political and civil power."

The acknowledgment of this Bodinian sovereign suggests a rupture with the language of the *Pensées* and *Persian Letters,* which describes *pouvoir absolu* in tones that are either regretful or satirical. From these works we would conclude that France was headed in the direction of Spain and Portugal, countries where *pouvoir absolu*, restrained only by an illiberal clergy, has already fallen into despotism (II, 4, 248). Here Montesquieu's anticlericalism is overt. The clergy are an evil (*un mal*). But as an intermediary body, the clergy are often the last barriers to tyranny in monarchies heading toward despotism. In *The Spirit of Laws*, Montesquieu is prepared to give French *pouvoir absolu* a second chance. If he believed that France was about to fall into despotism, he would have reconciled himself to the clergy playing a bigger role *faute de mieux* in France. There is no evidence that this was his wish, and some evidence, which we will consider, that he favored narrowing the jurisdiction of the Church.

To buttress this unconventional "statist" image of Montesquieu, consider how closely he aligns despotism and monarchy. They both consist in the government of one alone, the only difference being that the monarch governs according to fundamental laws. This is on the face of it a critical distinction. The elaboration of the norm of the rule of law is one of the finer things in Montesquieu.[44] But if, juridically speaking, the one who rules, the monarch, is the source of all power, would it not tend to become the decision of this monarch what fundamental law meant? Montesquieu appears to admit this: "Though the way of obeying is different in these two governments [despotism and monarchy], the power is nevertheless the same. In whatever direction the monarch turns, he prevails by tipping the balance and he is obeyed" (III, 10). The power is the "same," and apparently so is the "turning." The prince may turn toward or favor this faction or that one, this interpretation of fundamental law or another one. But the prince prevails in the end. Neither Bodin nor Hobbes thought differently.[45]

Montesquieu appends to this conclusion a second, at first glance strange, effort to distinguish between the two forms of rule. "The whole difference is that, in the monarchy, the prince is enlightened and the ministers are infinitely more skillful and experienced in public affairs than they are in the despotic state" (III, 10). It is rare in this famous enlightenment text to see such a bold appeal to the force of enlightenment alone as a way out of a difficulty. But saying, in effect, that educated, intelligent people run things in monarchies and that this is how you tell the difference, seems like a wholly empirical proposition which on the face of it could as easily be false as true. In the *Persian Letters*, Montesquieu works hard to establish that it is false. The hero, Usbek, runs a kind of court, and he thinks he is unique in being one of the few people there interested in becoming enlightened. But to the surprise of first-time readers, the enlightened Usbek also turns out to be a horrible despot. So what is Montesquieu up to in now asserting the contrary view?

A classic Bodinian and utilitarian argument lies behind the appeal to enlightenment. The one who has ultimate power has both a need and a duty to preserve it. Through trial and error the sovereign discovers, counter-intuitively, that delegating rights and responsibilities to others preserves power. This encourages the creation of wealth and the growth of the arts and sciences, which redound in turn to the benefit and power of the sovereign ruler. The best way to earn the trust of subjects is to enact a set of self-denying ordinances—otherwise called constitutional restraints—that reduce the likelihood of succumbing to the temptation of interfering in every matter. Yielding to temptation is shortsighted. It deprives the sovereign of the intelligence and initiative of subjects, and in the long run reduces the sovereign's power. The security of the monarch is tied to the security of the subject, which Montesquieu asserts is another name for political liberty (XI, 6, 397; XII, 1). Though a monarch has the ultimate power to decide on anything whatsoever, including the shape of the famous intermediary powers, any monarch interested in conserving power will be glad for the rights and privileges that subjects invoke precisely in order to restrain kings into enlightenment. Kings will be grateful for all the consultative devices that not only inform them of options but also prevent them from taking ill-considered decisions.[46] Usbek is a despot not because he seeks enlightenment, but because the political incentives his situation offers him reinforce instead his despotic impulses, which are incompatible with any mental effort to see things from a broader horizon. Despots cannot achieve enlightenment, Montesquieu suggests, thus refuting Voltaire's and others' preference for enlightened despotism.

These ideas receive a reformulation in *The Spirit of Laws* in its famous rejection of "Machiavellianism," considered by Montesquieu a species of short-term opportunism that is in the long run self-defeating. When we have been "cured" of these habits, there will be "more moderation in councils [of state]." The subject comes up in a discussion of the invention of "letters of exchange" by Jewish merchants trying to facilitate cross-border commerce. By accelerating the rapid flight of capital, these letters create greater solicitude on the part of otherwise shortsighted and predatory princes to treat their merchants better. Montesquieu generalizes the maxim derived from this specific situation into a general rule: "happily, [in properly organized polities] men are in a situation such that, though their passions inspire in them the thought of being wicked, they nevertheless have an interest in not being so" (XXI, 20, 641). One can reconcile a doctrine of absolute sovereignty with the importance of the distribution of powers by showing how the latter defeats the wicked and short-term calculations of the sovereign Prince, which would ultimately defeat the Prince himself if they were to prevail. This is a fate that awaits uninformed and unenlightened despots.

Bodin agrees with Montesquieu. There is no reason to do away with intermediary orders: "sovereign power is in no wise qualified or diminished by the existence of Estates."[47] Sovereign power is enhanced by their existence. In addition, Estates, which may be internally divided or have rivals in other assemblies, also find advantage in the existence of a sovereign power that can bring closure to its affairs. In a Bodinian appeal to closure, Montesquieu proclaims: "Monarchical government has a great advantage over republican; as public business is led by one alone, execution is more prompt" (V, 10).

Promptness must for Montesquieu be balanced against the intelligence of decision making accompanying deliberation. "The bodies [the Parlements] that are the depository of the laws never obey better than when they drag their feet." For only then do they "bring into the prince's business the reflection that one can hardly expect from the absence of enlightenment in the court concerning the laws of the state and the haste of the prince's councils" (V, 10). This suggestion, that the court shows "an absence of enlightenment," does not contradict the claim in Book III, chapter 10 that "the prince is enlightened." The prince becomes enlightened when and because the intermediary bodies act as they should. By resisting, negotiating, and compromising, they make sure the prince is informed: "In order to form a moderate government, one must combine powers, regulate them, temper them, make them act; give one a ballast so to speak so that it can resist another" (V, 14, 297).

The critics of this image of pluralist political bargaining assume there is no closure. The results will then lead to evasion, obfuscation, and open-ended paralysis that constantly defeat reform and even governance. But what if, on one not insignificant detail, this assumption is wrong? What if a sovereign stands on the horizon of this bargaining and presides over it, without necessarily always intervening in it? The closure that this assures is not a panacea, but it stands in contrast, Montesquieu says, with "despotic government" which depends only upon "passions" (V, 14, 297). Bargaining factions are passionate, too, but the passions that typify despotic government are unstructured. They can neither fear nor anticipate closure. Passions unstructured by constitutional relationship are hence irresponsible. Pluralist bargaining without a sovereign is the making of decisions that never arrive. The passions continue to plot coups against any decisions intended to represent the last word. Knowing this in advance, no one has any stake in thinking there can be closure.

Monarchies can become despotic. Richelieu is a "despot" because he "wishes for monarchies to avoid the bristles and thorns (*épines*) of corporate bodies (*compagnies*) which create difficulties on every matter" (V, 10). Bodin, too, recognizes a category of despotic as opposed to "royal" monarchy.[48] The drawbacks for any of these types of deviancy from legitimate monarchy is that the intelligence and enlightenment of its decisions decline and along with that, the royal despot's wealth and power. Bodin does not suppose that subjects owe any less obedience to a seigneurial or tyrannical monarch. Nor does Montesquieu suppose that French subjects owed any less obedience to Louis XIII because of the despotic Cardinal's behavior. Although neither Bodin nor Montesquieu would be surprised by rebellion, neither finds a place for just disobedience in their juridical theories. Montesquieu could be said, however, to have approached the topic from another direction, which we will come to in a moment when we take up the issue of honor.

Regarding Montesquieu from Bodin's horizon provides a corrective to several interpretive tendencies. Suppose that Montesquieu's arguments somehow converge in one of two directions: toward someone like François Hotman, the sixteenth-century defender of Huguenot rights, for whom sovereign power in a monarchy lies with the people rather than with a king; or toward someone like

Henri de Boulainvilliers whom we met before as *nobiliaire* controversialist. When readers are persuaded that Montesquieu's sympathies are allied with either one of these figures, they become irritated at what then looks like his timidity and spinelessness. If either the people or the nobility should rule under monarchy, or if monarchy itself along with its "absolutist" doctrine of sovereignty is not a legitimate form of government in the eyes of the author, should not Montesquieu say so more forthrightly? But if Montesquieu is prepared to play either of these assigned roles, everything he says about monarchy is a sham, since the traditional monarchy he describes puts sovereignty squarely in the hands of the king.

It is out of neither timidity nor coyness that Montesquieu begins with an argument about "*la soveraine puissance*" lodged in the royal prerogative (II, 1; III, 2). Bodin and Montesquieu are in agreement. No one prior to them has understood sovereignty. "Aristotle, Polybius, and Dionysius Halicarnassus alone among the Greeks discussed the attributes of sovereignty," says Bodin, "but . . . they did not really understand the principles involved."[49] Montesquieu is on the same page: "The ancients . . . did not know of the distribution of the three powers of one alone" (XI, 9). These are at first glance odd claims. When taken separately, the ancients obviously understood both the distribution of powers and the government of one alone. What they did not understand is that monarchy is a package deal. The rule of "one alone" is despotic without a distribution of powers; but with it, despotic power becomes royal authority. Correspondingly, without the procedures of an authority that is sovereign, the distribution of three powers is merely a power struggle.

Neither Bodin nor Montesquieu knew the word "absolutism." Like almost all words with the pertinent suffix, e.g., "liberalism," it is a child of the nineteenth century. Absolutism was coined in 1823 by Hyde de Neuville to describe his abhorrence at the coup d'etat of the Spanish King Ferdinand VII that overthrew a relatively liberal constitution. The subsequent popularization of this term has had the peculiar result of undermining the pre-Revolutionary understanding of the role of "absolute power" in monarchy. As Nicholas Henshall concludes, "absolute and shared power which operated side by side in the same ancien régime now became opposed types of government."[50] Nineteenth-century historians projected this understanding of absolutism, now denuded of any notion of shared power, back onto the monarchies of the preceding centuries.

Henshall also claims that British and French authors define absolutism differently. "When the English called a monarch absolute they meant he could do what he liked and take what he wanted. When the French used the appellation they meant that, in certain matters, he had the last word."[51] Whether this is correct or not for the English and French, let us invoke Henshall's distinction to explore Montesquieu's usage. Are *pouvoir arbitraire* and *pouvoir absolu* synonyms? Or does the former mean, doing as one likes, while the latter carries the sense, having the last word? A king in possession of sovereign power is expected to consult with the intermediary bodies and to respect the traditional rights of subjects in order to avoid arbitrary power. "Having the last word" is not inconsistent with "doing what you like," but the former presupposes the likelihood of extensive consultation while the latter projects the possibility of a decision maker, like Usbek, Montesquieu's stand-in for Louis XIV, who was wholly isolated and out of touch, and therefore arbitrary. The presumption of having only the last word carries with it, in addition, the notion that consultation will inject a dose of rationality into decision making.

Since absolute power always has the potential to be exercised in an arbitrary way, Montesquieu sometimes distinguishes the terms, but sometimes, in moods of greater anxiety, he melds them together. When the pejorative is meant, Montesquieu often uses a qualifying adjective like "most" or "extremely." Hence he claims the English tax their subjects more heavily than even the "most absolute prince" would dare (XIX, 27, 577). If he intends by *absolu* that this power is despotic, it is telling that Montesquieu cannot bring himself in this example simply to use the term *absolu* in an unqualified sense as a pejorative term. Similarly in the next to last paragraph of the chapter, he insists that it is not absolute monarchies, but only "extremely absolute monarchies" where writers dare not tell the truth (XIX, 27, 583). The unadorned use of *absolu* is always used in association with *pouvoir arbitraire* and signals what absolute government could become. In one example Montesquieu claims that absolute government in imperial Rome produced laziness, which in turn led to a combination of *politesse* and arbitrary government: "The epoch of Roman politeness is the same as the establishment of arbitrary power" (XIX, 27, 582). The French are polite without being lazy, however, because they have "ambition," which always "has good effects in monarchy" (III, 7).

The other usage of the pair *absolu* and *arbitraire* in this chapter has puzzled interpreters. England, Montesquieu says, was once under an "arbitrary power" that has left traces in the "style" of government one sees there now. He then draws a conclusion that seems at first highly paradoxical: "On the foundations of a free government [in England] one may often see the form of an absolute government" (XIX, 27, 580).

The contradictory quality of this citation is removed, however, if one takes it as further evidence that Montesquieu has adopted a version of Bodin's theory of sovereignty. If so, England has more in common with the absolute monarchies of the Continent than is usually thought. England, like France, subscribes to a doctrine of sovereign power. *Puissance* is *absolu* in the sense that the buck stops in an office whose holder has the final word, exercisable through the royal veto. Rather than standing opposed to sovereign authority, liberty may well require its "foundations" in order to flourish.

But where in England does sovereignty lie? Perhaps the mark of a well-governed nation is that sovereign power is so mediated by the intermediary bodies that its existence is barely visible, its exercise rare. Sovereign power must exist, but it need not always act. The identity of the sovereign is juridically clear in France though, as we shall see, that clarity disappears when the cultural claims of "honor" are rehearsed. The identity of the holder of sovereign office is juridically unclear in England. It would be best, however, to keep it that way. Sovereignty cannot be divided. If the mediation that keeps it invisible or quiet should fail, a test of wills could have fatal consequences.

Suppose that England were an updated version of an ancient polity of shared powers that stands in contrast with Continental absolute government. There would then be no need to declare that English liberties were fragile and constantly threatened just because Parliament had abolished "the prerogatives of the lords, clergy, nobility, and towns" (II, 4). For on Montesquieu's own account in Book XIX, chapter 27, the loss of these intermediary powers was compensated for by the emergence of what looks like political parties that act as the functional equivalents of these powers. Each party represents different, if overlapping, constituencies and attaches itself either to "executive power" or to "legislative power." This would seem to supply England with all the pluralist balance required, especially if the operative understanding is the Aristotelian one that power was simply shared.

But Montesquieu believes instead that shared powers require a sovereign who presides over them. It is the question of the uncertain identity of this sovereign that signals the potential for despotic outcomes in England. From Bodin on, sovereign power must be uniquely located. Either crown or assembly may possess this authority but not both. In the compromise of 1688 and after, the English Parliament makes law even though the English king has not fully ceded the rights of a sovereign. The king's representative in Parliament, Robert Walpole, successfully buys off the opposition, thus fudging the issue. But in any kind of showdown between a legislative majority and the king, the instability inherent in this historical compromise would emerge. Either the collective lawmaker will become sovereign or the king will. If forced to decide, the pretense of sharing power will collapse. An England governed by a sovereign Parliament was far from a mere hypothetical consideration in Montesquieu's mind. Such were the inroads on royal authority that very early on "Elizabeth was the last monarch of England."[52]

If the English king were sovereign, then Parliament would constitute an intermediary power. It would be consulted by the king in a way not dissimilar to how the French king was expected—especially, we shall claim, after the publication of *The Spirit of Laws*—to consult the Parlements who registered his edicts. But suppose, Montesquieu says, there were no sovereign monarch in England, and "executive power were entrusted to a certain number of persons drawn from the legislative power." Then "there would no longer be liberty" (XI, 6, 402). Montesquieu appears to distrust a sovereign parliament. Perhaps this is because a proper distribution of powers would be lacking where the king was wholly dependent upon parliamentary authority. Parliament would then have arrogated to itself two functions, making and administering law. Only with luck and over time might a polity establish a new and now subordinate executive, one neither too subversively independent nor too agreeably compliant to every manifestation of legislative will.

In the eighteenth century, England was spared this test of wills until it became clear that Parliament ruled and not the king. The king became an executive whose advisers the Parliament now merely consulted. Famously, the test of wills that led to the discovery that a king was not sovereign occurred instead in France during the Revolution, but the principle involved was the same. In both countries the governments were underwritten by a concept of sovereign power. In the absence of entrenched barriers to the easy exercise of this sovereignty, it could fall into the hands either of a king tempted to act as a despot or of a people whose representatives were similarly tempted. Montesquieu never denied sovereign power its right of command, but he did deny that it should be easily exercised.

When sovereignty is self-consciously understood to have slipped into the hands of the representatives of "the people," it unveils "the republic [that] hides under the form of monarchy" (V, 19). This birth of a democratic sovereignty gives a new lease on life to the notion of *pouvoir absolu*. Tocqueville picks up where Montesquieu left off. The *pouvoir absolu* that emerges in free government is a harbinger of modern democracy. The latter is in itself neither more nor less dangerous than the original doctrine of sovereignty, which lodged *pouvoir absolu* in the monarch. Before having the last word, the monarch is expected to consult widely through the traditional channels of public communication. But what if the monarch refuses to do so. This "what if" lies at the heart of the anxieties about the sovereignty of the people as well. It explains Montesquieu's formula, "No monarch, no nobility; no nobility, no monarch" (II, 4). Its democratic equivalent is "no sovereign majority, no minority rights; no minority rights, no sovereign majority." The privileges of nobility become the rights of democratic minorities.

There is yet another ground for objecting to the idea that England avoids *pouvoir absolu*, or sovereignty, because a republic is somehow hiding under the monarchy. Upon Montesquieu's understanding of the republic, it, too, is a machine with a sovereign built into it. Montesquieu, again following Bodin, quietly slips this novel doctrine, which "the Ancients did not know," into the definitions of both republic and monarchy. Far from sharing power in a loose, Aristotelian sort of way, Montesquieu's two types of republic are tightly organized exemplars of "sovereign power." In the democratic republic there is no doubt that sovereignty lies with *le peuple en corps*; in an aristocratic republic there is no doubt that sovereignty lies in *seulement une partie du peuple* (II, 1). There are no mixed cases of "polity" because polity possesses no doctrine of sovereignty and no answer to the question: who has the last word?

Yet perhaps *only* republics possess Bodinian "sovereignty." Upon this interpretation, monarchies do not because in the classical definition we cited, Montesquieu avoids using the word "sovereignty" when referring to the prince as the "source of all political and civil power" (II, 4).[53] It may have been prudent not to cite the Bodinian term openly. For this would have raised the question whether the other pillar of monarchy, "fundamental law," limits the power of monarchs who rule in accordance with it, or whether, as Book III, chapter 10 openly asserts, "in whatever direction the monarch turns, he prevails." In addition, omitting to call the monarch sovereign could indicate how Bodinian Montesquieu is. After attributing "sovereign power" in a republic to "the people as a whole," he concludes, "the people" are in this respect "the monarch" (II, 2). It evidently follows that a monarch who enjoys the equivalent of republican sovereignty is a Bodinian sovereign.

The monarchical prince desires not only to prevail, but also to see before he prevails. "The laws are the prince's eyes; he sees with them what he could not see without them" (VI, 6, 215-16). With this image goes the implied threat of blindness (a symbol of the ultimate failure of power) that hangs over the monarch who abuses sovereignty. Montesquieu, who was himself going blind, once again teases out the pluralist perspectives hidden in the Bodinian dogma of sovereignty. For in Bodin also, "the prince depends for his information on the eyes and ears and reports of others."[54] This is why it was prudent for sovereign princes "to agree to many things they would not have consented to." If they did not, they would have neither trust nor intelligence. Thus, sovereign authority must spread itself out over the many institutions that not only moderate but make possible its actions. This leaves the prince at the center as a court of ultimate appeal, one which need not always act to be effective and one which, if it acts too much, sees too little.

Parlements and Intermediary Bodies

In our effort to understand what Montesquieu means in claiming the prince is "the source of all civil and political power," we should not forget the "intermediary powers" and consultative mechanisms, which together establish a distribution of powers under *pouvoir absolu*. The most important of these were those administrators of royal justice, the Parlements. They consisted in the Parlement of Paris and eleven (on some counts, fourteen) provincial courts in the regional capitals, including Bordeaux where Montesquieu once occupied the office of *président à mortier*.[55] Of these, the Parlement of Paris was the "epitome of the kingdom's judicial institutions."[56]

In *The Spirit of Laws*, Montesquieu carefully distinguishes these institutions from rival power centers. "It is not enough to have intermediate ranks in a monarchy. There must also be a depository of laws" (*depôt de lois* II, 4). Without law and its *depôts* serving as the institutionalized memory of judicial precedents, the other intermediary powers do not suffice. The most dangerous rivals of the Parlements were the royal councils. Though the Parlements were the highest ranking appellate courts in a royal system of justice, their decisions could be overruled by royal councils including "the *Conseil d'En-haut*, the *Conseil des Dépêches*, and the *Conseil Privé*, all of which could evoke a case [to another tribunal] or quash a judgment."[57] Such a right to overrule results in worse judgments. Royal Councils cater too much, Montesquieu writes, to the uninstructed will of the prince and to the rapidly changing political winds that sweep across Versailles: "The prince's council is not a suitable depository. By its nature it is the depository of the momentary will of the prince. . . . Moreover, the monarch's council constantly changes; it is not permanent" (II, 4).

Confronting strong rivals on one front, the Parlements faced weaker ones in the courts that administered seigneurial and ecclesiastical justice. The Parlements had the right to take appeals from both courts and, subsequently, the right to change decisions and even jurisdictions. Montesquieu urges the magistrates to restrain themselves in these maneuvers. While his defense of seigneurial justice seems straightforward, he becomes more coy and evasive about ecclesiastical justice. I am not, he says, a "head-strong" partisan (*entêté*, a stubborn defender) of ecclesiastical privilege (II, 4). The cool detachment of this remark sidesteps almost forty years of heated religious controversy over the papal bull *Unigenitus* (1713) which, when enforced by ecclesiastical authorities, tried to suppress within the Church a popular, quasi-Protestant or Augustinian current known as Jansenism.

Though in the past an opponent of perceived Roman transgressions against French authority and against the liberties of a Gallican Church, the crown after 1713 joined with Rome in suppressing the Jansenist "heresy." Whether because the Parlements were animated by zealous Jansenist reformers in their midst—the voices of Dale Van Kley's "judicial Jansenism"—or whether they were simply responding to constituents and subjects who believed their liberties were at risk, French magistrates throughout the century typically opposed both king and pope on the *Unigenitus* issue.[58] This added a dangerous religious dimension to the constitutional quarrels between the Parlements and the king. They threatened to replay in another register the creedal battles of the sixteenth century. If the passage cited above from *The Spirit of Laws* was meant to signal a desire to remain neutral, Montesquieu's evasion satisfied no one. Both Jesuit and Jansenist journals attacked the book. Barring taxation and fiscal questions, the issue of religious conformity was the most important issue faced by both king and Parlements. It deeply affected any constitutional settlement between them.

Turning to seigneurial justice, we see at once that Montesquieu confirms the suspicions of those who dismiss him as a throwback defender of archaic feudal order. The baron de La Brède is outspokenly enthusiastic about seigneurial rights granted to the owners of real property to judge local cases of law and cus-

tom that arise on it. Although such rights were usually associated with noble estates, technically the status of the owner of this property did not matter. Nobles,
commoners, and ecclesiastical communities could all own *seigneuries* with
powers of justice attached to them.[59] In listing the intermediary orders Montesquieu distinguishes between *seigneurs* and *noblesse*, which may indicate acknowledgment of the social changes that, increasingly, were conferring seigneurial office on non-noble land owners (II, 4). In any event, the French nobility
was not an exclusively landed aristocracy. By purchasing a judicial office in a
Parlement, one could become noble without owning land. According to historian
David Bien, a magistrate's office was "a secure form of property . . . [that
avoided] the inconvenience of having to buy and to manage land."[60] Nevertheless, in his most intransigently *nobiliaire* statements, Montesquieu suggests
there was reason to fear spreading these privileges too broadly. "One can
scarcely separate the dignity of the noble from that of his fief. [Its] prerogatives
[including seigneurial justice] are the particular possession of the nobility and
will not pass to the people, unless one wants to shock the principle of government and diminish the force of the nobility as well as that of the people" (V, 9,
288).

It is not on its face a convincing argument, but if we turn to the historical record, perhaps one can begin to understand the sense of this remark. According to
Roland Mousnier, seigneurial courts blanketed all of France. They were not only
everywhere in the countryside, they were well represented in the cities, too.
Their numbers reached 80,000, a figure twenty-five to thirty times as many magistrate courts as France had in 1914. Upholding both rural and urban order in
eighteenth-century France, these myriad local mini-institutions took up under
civil law, issues such as rent disputes, guardianship of minors, payment of bills,
and (of course) feudal dues. Under criminal law, their jurisdiction extended to
crimes of violence and to "morals" issues like bigamy.

Seigneurs could be litigants in their own courts, and in something like 8 percent of the cases they were. We may be surprised that the number is not higher,
but even this many is provocative since it so clearly violates the maxim that persons should not be judges in their own cases. By way of compensation, perhaps,
decisions could be appealed to the royal courts, especially to the *présidial*
courts, which heard appeals from the *bailliage* and *sénéchaussée* courts. Appeals
to the higher-ranking Parlements were less frequent. When made, the latter
tended to reduce the severity of sentences issued at lower levels. The cost to seigneurs in maintaining these courts was high, and there was no short-term profit
from them. By assuring that feudal and other estate dues were paid and that local
order dominated by seigneurial owners was maintained, these courts were in the
long run advantageous to those who maintained them. Moreover, in the view of
one commentator they served the interests of litigants as well. Their justice was
"equitable, inexpensive, easily accessible, and rapid."[61] Montesquieu's fellow
parlementaires were nevertheless bent on the destruction of this localized pat-

tern of administering justice: "The tribunals of a great European state have been for several centuries striking down the patrimonial jurisdiction of the seigneurs" (II, 4). This is not a reform he supports. The question is why.

There were two alternatives to this system for maintaining public order. First the crown or its *intendants*, the commissioners directly dependent on the crown, could set up a uniform and universal system of justice, much as Napoleon and later the Third Republic set in motion. Second, the magistrates eager to dismantle these feudal arrangements could replace them with courts that the Parlements and not the *intendants* would supervise. The latter "federal solution" might guarantee that local interests and cultural diversity were taken into account, but the king would never have granted so much power to the *parlementaire* magistrates. So we are left with the alternative of a uniform justice defined and administered by the crown, and also with several issues that still trouble liberal governments. For example, ought one to seek a balance between support for cultural diversity (in the provinces) and the search for fairness in a uniform code of justice? Respect for local custom and different ways of living are at cross-purposes with the conviction that equality means equal treatment under a common law and the suspicion that what passes as local culture too often excuses the mistreatment of one group by another.

Once it may have been possible to count upon nearly every reader being more or less "pro-modern" or "pro-enlightenment." Then, if the central state institutions of the monarchy were identified with progress, such readers would not be expected to see why practices that stood in the way of such a state should be tolerated. What force this argument still has depends upon whether it recognizes the very point Montesquieu's argument urges: the enlightenment with which reform from above can proceed depends upon the access it has to information and perspectives that necessarily come from below or further afield. When enlightenment is taken to be equivalent simply to well-educated bureaucrats, and not also to the perspectives that those outside the bureaucracy may offer, all is lost. Today the critic is much more likely to regard the enlightened as merely uprooted. What the latter regard as progress is to the critic a despotic steamroller crushing ancient traditions. With their hands upon the media of money and power, mobile elites bludgeon subalterns into conformity while destroying the latter's ecologically delicate "life-worlds" that sustain them in their habitual rounds.[62] This Habermasian account would seem to confirm Montesquieu's perspective: the importance of local justice for balancing against national imperatives.

In seeking ways to sustain local meanings, however, Montesquieu could have raised the issue of whether too much "communication" might itself undermine traditional self-understandings. He was among the first to use the word "communication." The word points to the heightened sociability that he thought monarchy, especially the French monarchy, encouraged. The result was universal change against which no one was insulated: "The more communicative peoples are, the more easily they change their manners" (XIX, 8). Such a potential for spontaneous change suggests that, however favorable a habitat for resisting power from the center, seigneurial rural order could not have endured. If maintaining local diversity through seigneurial justice was important, why should the nobility alone defend it, as Montesquieu seems to urge, despite the fact that bourgeois owners already exercised this prerogative? Three considerations suggest themselves. The first raises questions about rootlessness and mobility that pit Montesquieu against those lacking long-standing memories attached to land and region. Money made in the city but consumed in the country is an economic boon, but the cultural dispositions of its owners become a source of suspicion insofar as they claim now to represent rural order.

The second consideration focuses upon the "dignity" that Montesquieu says is, or should be, associated with the nobility. He means political dignity. The intelligence and self-confidence required to become a local political operator or regional leader tend to atrophy under any rule from the center. In the absence of local competencies, the rule of law under one alone degenerates into the rule of one without law. But judicial decree or feudal right cannot alone uphold dignity. It requires the nourishment of a collective mentality, honor. As we shall see, Montesquieu was of two minds about whether honor could be communicated to others who possess no seigneurial tenure.

The issues of noble identity and honor are important in any theory of how the Parlements might operate precisely because they are, though Montesquieu rarely mentions it, royal institutions and therefore subject to all the manipulation, persuasion, flattery, and coercion a king can apply. For them to function well requires a mentality that neither conforms too much to the king's wishes nor regards itself as wholly justified in subverting sovereign will. If the special temper of this mentality cannot be sustained, one is left with a disposition that prompts either cowardly conformity or rash rebelliousness.

A third consideration suggests that, while lending support to regional governing elites who resist the court bureaucracy, Montesquieu may sense that only long-standing prescriptive right permits toleration of the privileges such groups enjoy. When newcomers begin to exercise the same rights without the weight of tradition behind them, these privileges lose their legitimacy, which then passes to central power. To this one response might be, well and good, the old nobility should lose its legitimacy, but such a transformation raises a question about elites under any form of government. In changing the constitution in the direction of universal access and democracy, has one altogether lost the need for leaders, local or national, who are secure in their material and psychological circumstances and visibly attached to the people they represent?

Montesquieu is never nostalgic about the nobility and their talents for local preservation. When considered as rivals to his favored Parlements, Montesquieu is quick to dismiss his fellow aristocrats. They succumb to "natural ignorance." If it were left up to the indolent nobility, their "contempt for civil government" would leave the laws "buried" in the "dust." No modernizing reformer would have disagreed. This is why a monarchy needs *"political* bodies which announce laws when they are made and recall them when they are forgotten" (II, 4, 249, my emphasis). The Parlements will address themselves to the errors of the uninstructed nobility quite as much as to the errors of the crown.

The political value of the intermediary bodies is purely a function of their sheer passive existence. Just being there, like vegetation along a riverbank, they check the erosion caused by the floodwaters of royal authority and power. Monarchical ambition is quietly stopped by the contours of the constitution within which it operates. "Just as the sea, which seems to want to cover the whole earth, is stopped by the grass and the smallest pebbles one finds along the shore, so monarchs, whose power appears unlimited, are halted by the smallest obstacles, and submit their natural pride to pleas and prayers" (II, 4, 248).

Pleas and prayers do not sound robust, but these are the voices of the Parlements. As the origin of their name in the verb *parler*, to speak, might suggest, the Parlements are the only intermediary bodies (barring the Church, which Montesquieu ignores) to talk back to the king, the source of all power. To reiterate the earlier argument, one finds in Montesquieu a theory of sovereign power that supposes that it exercises sufficient self-restraint to allow "subordinate and dependent" institutions to provide the information, the intelligence, and the resistance it needs to govern well and to rule in conformity with law. At the level of high office only the Parlements (again barring the Church) are not utterly dependent upon the king, as the royal councils are. Therefore, only these courts can become the privileged set of consultative and corrective links in the kingdom. As J. H. Shennan once wrote, *The Spirit of Laws* was "the last and the greatest defense under the ancien régime of the ideal of legitimate royal authority exercised under and not outside the law."[63] The Parlements were the privileged interlocutors in this process. Even the royalist writer Jacob-Nicolas Moreau argues in 1775: "Counsel is of the essence of monarchy . . . . Power is absolute, but its force is tempered." He defends the crown, but in doing so he reiterates, perhaps unwittingly, Montesquieu's justification for the political role of Parlements, which as the preeminent givers of "counsel" distinguish monarchy from despotism.[64]

The Parlements were judicial bodies and appellate courts of last appeal. This was their first source of power because Parlements could threaten to bring the system of justice to a halt. When they went on judicial strike, the king had to bargain with them. Second, the Parlements played an active role in maintaining public order. They did not conform to the standard Anglo-American model, which require courts to wait passively for cases to adjudicate before they can interfere in public affairs. Through their ability to issue *arrêts de règlement* (regulatory orders), the Parlements maintained streets and highways, assured the provision of food and firewood, and supervised merchants, guilds, hospitals, prisons, academies, and universities. They had powers of arrest in emergencies.

They imposed curfews and held hearings on the conduct of other public officials. With the police, they upheld public morals, which included the surveillance and censorship of the theater and literature. In pursing these duties the magistrates regularly burned the books of the *philosophes*. But, according to Julian Swann, "the judges nevertheless borrowed extensively from their writings and above all, from Montesquieu," their fellow magistrate.[65] Many of these *arrêts* were directed against the policy of the crown's commissioners, the *intendants*. The King's Privy Council could quash them, but the king never disputed the right of Parlements to issue such orders.[66]

The courts also assumed the politically explosive responsibility of "registering" the king's edicts and laws. Without registration with the courts, royal decrees did not have the force of law. In earlier times when a Parlement refused to register an edict, it offered the king its opinions in the form of private, indeed secret, remonstrance. But in the eighteenth century, all the Parlements acquired their own printing presses. Though publication was illegal, the jurists nevertheless printed and publicly distributed their remonstrations. This initiated a contest between Parlement and king to win over public opinion, a new phenomenon in itself. This was later re-conceptualized as "civil society." Typically, however, remonstrance, and other confrontational acts like the judicial strike, were avoided in favor of milder *supplications* to the king and, at a calibrated higher level of protest, "representations" to him.[67]

In response to a refusal to register his edicts, the king had a variety of strategies available to him. He could issue a *lettre de jussion*, which ordered the immediate registration of an edict. If this did not work, the king might appear in person at the Parlement of Paris or order the judges to attend him at Versailles. In both instances he would be surrounded by the peers of the realm witnessing the grandiose ritual of a *lit de justice*. The lineaments of this political ceremony stretched back several centuries. As Sara Hanley explains, in the sixteenth and seventeenth centuries *lits de justice* were the occasions for negotiation and the formation of a constitutional consensus between crown and Parlement. "The Crown employed ritual to vest sovereign authority in the monarch, separate legislative (royal) and judicial (*parlementaire*) functions, and provide a consultative, not deliberative body of orders. . . . Parlement bent ritual to vest sovereign authority in the monarch but insinuate co-legislative capacity."[68] By contrast, in the eighteenth century *lits de justice* were more often one-sided assertions of power by either Parlement or crown. In 1715 the Parlement of Paris asserted legislative capacity in breaking the will of Louis XIV and favoring Orleans as Regent. Thereafter, however, the *lit de justice* became the king's means for enforcing edicts against the will of Parlement. Although the king could force the registration of an edict, he could not do this too readily or too often without running the risk of appearing despotic. Under the Regent there were two *lits de justice* in 1715 and 1718. Under Louis XV there were four more in Montesquieu's lifetime, in 1723, 1725, 1730, and 1732.[69]

The king could also exile a Parlement for an indefinite period to regions remote from its traditional seat. He could threaten to reorganize the courts and to eliminate offices. At the worst, he could use a *lettres de cachet* (sealed royal orders) to imprison designated magistrates. Although each of these threats was carried out from time to time, the issuance of a royal threat (or similarly the delivery of a judicial remonstrance) was more often the signal for bargaining and adjustment of position between crown and Parlement. There was risk on both sides in an escalating war because of the growing influence of public opinion in these matters. One experienced contemporary observer Cardinal de Bernis considered public opinion preeminent: "Parlement has only the force that the public voice lends it. . . . As soon as Paris says that the King is right and that Parlement must obey, its resistance is not only useless, it becomes as objectionable as that of the Court itself."[70]

According to William Doyle, the Parlements had four political strengths, "*arrêts de règlement*, registration, *remonstrance*, and tenure." The last the magistrates enjoyed because of "venality," the peculiar practice, unique in Europe to France, of buying public offices. Treated as an inheritable property right, it guaranteed lifetime tenure for judges. Venality, Doyle sardonically comments, gave French judges independence 234 years ahead of the English.[71] In addition, the Parlements possessed other strengths. First, already mentioned, their extensive jurisdiction in maintaining public order added weight to any threat to strike. Second, up to 1774, the Parlements were popular with both the general and the learned public. For instance, the approval Voltaire extended to Chancellor Maupeou's attack on Parlements in 1771 isolated the great free thinker. Diderot and others thought Maupeou's move augured a new despotism.[72]

A third additional strength of the Parlements may well have been the esteem accorded *The Spirit of Laws,* a book that makes these institutions central to the functioning of the monarchy. Montesquieu never alludes to the greater importance of the Parlement of Paris compared to the other provincial institutions. His silence might suggest that he believed nothing should interfere with mutual cooperation among the courts. If this is a consciously thought-out consideration, it fits in well with an ideology that arose in the years after the publication of *The Spirit of Laws*. In the crises of the 1750s, a theory of *parlementaire* unity, the idea that each Parlement is only a division of a single royal Parlement, gained support. As early as 1751 French jurists cited *The Spirit of Laws* itself as support for this view of Parlements as a unified *dépôt de lois* for the nation.[73]

Exactly what role did Montesquieu expect these courts to play in the political life of the nation? This matter is still not exactly settled. Let us look at four possibilities. First, the courts could defend the crown itself against inroads upon its power. Second, the courts could resist the encroachment of royal authority. Third, the courts could go beyond either of these essentially passive roles and, by elevating themselves above the fray, become the impartial arbiters between sovereign and subjects. This leads naturally to a fourth position as the magistrates begin to understand themselves as representatives, albeit "subordinate" to the crown, of the nation as a whole. Durand Echeverria, from whom we draw this list of possible functions, thinks Montesquieu's position coincides with the second one. The courts are passive protectors of local prerogatives.[74] But there is ample evidence for the other possibilities as well. In favor of the first and most conservative interpretation of the courts' role, Montesquieu suggests that their task must be to "enlighten" (*éclairer*) the people in "difficult times" and "to return them to obedience" (II, 4, 249). Montesquieu's sympathies also draw him to the third claim, Parlement as an active arbiter:

> The Parlement judged *in the last resort* on almost *all* the business [*toutes les affaires*] of the kingdom. It had formerly judged only those which were between dukes, counts, barons, bishops, abbots, or between the king and his vassals, though more in the relationship they have with the *political order* than the civil order. Later one was obliged to make this a sitting Parlement and to keep it *permanently assembled* (XXVIII, 39, 855, my emphasis).

This last passage is drawn from a consideration of the role of Parlement in medieval France, but it is an open question whether, in Montesquieu's eyes, these lessons from history did not have prescriptive authority for the present as well. Gathering these passages together reveals just such a prescriptive theory of Parlementary authority. The reader is easily led to the fourth interpretation of the role of these courts. The courts are the only institutions that are expected to earn the people's "trust" (*confiance*). This is the reason the court might also expect "to enlighten them and return them to obedience" to the king (II, 4). Note that it is Parlement and not the king who earns this trust. A Parlement could earn *confiance* only by representing grievances and aspirations.

In the years leading up to the publication of *The Spirit of Laws* the Parlement of Paris took tentative steps in each of the directions corresponding to the four interpretive possibilities mentioned above. When in 1705 the papal bull *Vineam Domini* was submitted to the Parlement, it restricted itself to making sure that the bull contained nothing inimical to the rights of the crown in accordance with an interpretation of its role as defender of sovereign authority. When in 1732 a royal edict closed St Médard Church, a focal point for Jansenist gatherings, the Parlement remonstrated and, after the arrest of six magistrates, went on strike in accordance with the second interpretation that has the Parlement defending the rights of subjects. Court dealings with financial issues generally suggest the third, or neutral arbiter, role. The Parlement's attitude toward taxes in the first half of the eighteenth century was, we are told, "unenthusiastic yet not irreconcilably hostile."[75] It took into account both the state's needs and the nation's burdens. During the John Law era, a royal edict was issued forbidding Parlement from meddling in financial affairs unless instructed to do so by the Regent. This suggests that the magistrates had the ambition to become arbiters, whether neutral or not.

Finally, the Parlements represented the nation, not on economic, but on cultural grounds. The Parlement of Paris was the defender of Gallican liberties and the opponent of Church and Jesuit suppression of Jansenism. It aspired to become the cultural voice of the nation every bit as much as the English Parliament in 1688 sought out this role in chasing a Catholic king out of England. A political revolution in France preceded the new assertiveness of the Paris Parlement. The Regency of Philip of Orleans would not have been possible had the Parlement not overturned the last will and testament of Louis XIV that favored a Spanish regent. In the vacuum created by the death of the king, the Parlement of Paris stepped into the breach with an assertion of authority hitherto restricted to the sovereign. "At one bound, J. H. Shennan observes, it "regained the center of the political stage."[76]

The Birth and Death of an Ideology, 1748-71

In putting together Montesquieu's views on the authority of Parlements, I had only to consult the references under the entry Parlement in the "Analytical and Alphabetical Table of Materials Contained in *The Spirit of Laws* and in the *Defense*."[77] (In the Pléiade edition, it is simply called an *Index*.) The *Table* has never been included in any English translation of these texts. It was not supervised by Montesquieu, but by François Richer, who established the 1757 and 1758 editions along with M. Moreau, a printer and former secretary of Montesquieu, all supposedly under the guidance of Montesquieu's son, Jean-Baptiste de Secondat.[78] François Richer later edited a 1767 version of these works to which he attached a preface demonstrating his great devotion to the authority of Montesquieu. Elie Carcassonne calls him one of Montesquieu's "disciples."[79]

If we consult the histories of Jansenist resistance to the bull *Unigenitus*, we find that François Richer (1718-90) was more than an editor and disciple of Montesquieu. A lawyer at the Parlement of Paris and likely a member of the heavily Jansenist influenced Paris Order of Barristers, Richer was counted among the principal Jansenist and *parlementaire* ideologues.[80] To be sure, Edmond Préclin insists that personally François Richer was "not at all" Jansenist but then concedes that his political writings conformed in every respect to Jansenist demands.[81] For Dale Van Kley, Richer occupied a conceptual twilight zone between Gallican Jansenist and Enlightenment worlds.[82] According to David Bell, Richer was a "protégé" of one of the most famous parlementary ideologues, the barrister Louis-Adrien Le Paige.[83] Le Paige was the author of *Lettres historiques sur les fonctions essentielles du Parlement* (1753) which rivals or outshines the influence of *The Spirit of Laws* among those looking to expand *parlementaire* influence. In 1765 François Richer penned a defense of the civil magistrate's role in regulating ecclesiastical authority: *On the Authority of the Clergy, and of the Power of the Political Magistrate in the Exercise of the Function of Ecclesiastical Ministry.* This accorded with Jansenist positions because it attacked the ultramontane authority of Rome to supercede the Gallican Church and the French state. Richer declared that "the prince's promise to protect the Church's doctrine and discipline . . . entitled him . . . to oppose any novel doctrine—the bull *Unigenitus*—that an ecclesiastical cabal might attempt to foist upon the Church."[84]

All this leads to the question whether an interpretation that relies upon Richer's index is a reliable guide to Montesquieu's thought on these explosive political issues. But we could put the question the other way around. For Richer's access to the author's manuscripts and family circle may suggest that his views are a not wholly unsound guide to the thinking of Montesquieu and his friends between 1750 and his death in 1755. This is after the publication of the *Defense of The Spirit of Laws* and during the Parlementary crisis provoked by the Church's order to refuse the sacrament of absolution to those who had not pledged allegiance to the bull *Unigenitus*. The moment is important because it allows us to ask whether Montesquieu thought there was anything in the 1748 text that could legitimately be used to intervene in the controversy that arises five years later.

In recent histories there is a tendency to characterize the figures of the high Enlightenment, such as Montesquieu, as great writers without influence. This justifies concentrating attention on another group, partisan writers familiar with political intrigue, such as Le Paige. An older tradition mentions the two types of writers in the same breath. Guy Chaussinand-Nogaret recalls this latter manner of speaking in a comparison of Le Paige and Montesquieu that allies their intentions: "With more spirit and talent and, in addition, written under the discipline of a prudent self censorship, *L'Esprit des lois* affirms the Parlement claims" that one finds more self-evidently dramatized in Le Paige.[85]

Richer's index might serve as testimony to the manner in which a Le Paige could have found—at least in carefully selected passages—something of a tactical ally in Montesquieu. Whether any such partisan alliance taps into the philosophical depths of Montesquieu's thought one may doubt. But let us remain on the surface of things for the moment and look closely at a few of the passages from Montesquieu's text that, for his own purposes, Richer brings together under the index entry "Parlement." Parlement is referred to in the singular, thus ignoring the plurality of bodies attached to the name. This emphasis may signal agreement with the ideological currents circulating in the 1750s that uphold a claim for Parlementary unity. Richer begins the index entry with a self-effacing injunction: "the Parlement ought never to strike out at either seigneurial or ecclesiastical jurisdictions." One notes that the prohibition does not tell us how narrow or broad seigneurial or ecclesiastical jurisdictions ought to be. Richer next refers to the manner in which Parlement asserts itself under *pouvoir absolu*: "The Parlement is necessary in monarchies; the more it deliberates on the orders of the Prince, the more it obeys him. Often the Parlement by its firmness, preserves the kingdom from decline; its attachment to law is the surety of the prince in the movements of monarchy."

Richer insists on the importance of Book XXVIII, chapter 39 of *The Spirit of Laws*. Earlier we cited from it the passage where Montesquieu speaks of a "permanently assembled" Parlement. Following this is another incendiary line that might give hope to a judicial or Jansenist rebel: "Sometimes many centuries must pass to prepare for changes; events ripen, and then there are revolutions."

The Richer index entry next proclaims an ambitious national project of reform directed against the Church: "Parlement is to reform the intolerable abuses of ecclesiastical jurisdiction." In so doing, "Parlement . . . limits the greed of the clergy." The index then advises the reader to consult Book XXVIII, chapter 41, concerned with "the ebb and flow of ecclesiastical and lay jurisdiction." Turning to the Montesquieu text, we see that the medieval Church is credited as the source for the procedural rules of good governance imbibed by the Parlements. The Church was able to extend its jurisdiction and hence its instruction because "civil power" was too split by an "infinity of *seigneurs*." Here is a warning from the theorist of plural bodies himself that, when faced with a determined theological rival, too much pluralism is not always a good thing. Nevertheless, Montesquieu explains, now that it was armed with procedures taught to it by an expanding Church, Parlement reversed this expansion and reduced the abusive authority of the clergy. This is a dramatic claim. It invites us to reconsider the opening lines of the Richer index entry that seem to counsel non-interference with ecclesiastical power. It may be a good thing to fix the boundaries of church jurisdiction once and for all, but Book XXVIII, chapter 41 suggests that the boundaries should narrow rather than broaden clerical authority.

Also in chapter 41 Montesquieu writes this curious sentence: "When in a century or a government, one sees the various bodies of the state seek to increase their authority, one would often be mistaken if one saw their enterprises as a sure mark of corruption" (XXVIII, 41). "In *a* century or *a* government" means that such an event could happen in *any* century, including Montesquieu's own. When it does, we should not equate Parlement ambition with corruption. Though Montesquieu admits, "great men who are moderate are rare," in such cases we ought to tolerate excess in favor of their greatness. Thanks to Richer's index, which highlighted these obscure texts from *The Spirit of Laws*, activists could easily have interpreted this call to *grandeur* as warrant to expand the authority of Parlements at the expense of the ecclesiastical domain.

The last line under the Richer Index entry "Parlement" simply says, "see *legislative bodies*," and then slyly refers the reader to Book XI, chapter 6—the chapter on English representative government. Such is the remarkable conclusion to the Richer Index's mini-essay on Parlement. Each line offers an increasingly expansive understanding of the political identity and potential of an increasingly unified Parlement. This reaches a climax by sending the reader's

imagination racing across the English Channel to confront the politically mo-
mentous equation: Parlement equals the Parliament of a "free state," as the entry, "legislative bodies," dubs England.

Could Montesquieu have intended something like the above reading that
would have put him in tactical alliance with Jansenist activists? It is difficult
imagining him very sympathetic with the strict morality of the Jansenists, who
leave us, he once wrote, with only the pleasure to scratch ourselves.[86] His thinking is more in tune with the Jesuit's Pelagian or rather Molinist sympathies,
which embrace not only free will but also a worldly tolerance of human vices
that the Jansenists excoriate. On the other hand, though never a partisan of Jansenism, Montesquieu resented the despotic character of the attempted suppression of this popular religious movement: "the Jesuits defend a good cause, Molinism, by bad means."[87]

We have more precise knowledge of Montesquieu's attitude toward these
quarrels. 1752-53 brought "the last great conflict" over *Unigenitus*, the refusal
of sacraments controversy that once again targeted Jansenist heresy. By order of
the Archbishop of Paris, priests were ordered to deny last sacraments of suspect
penitents who refused to give the names of prior confessors who may have been
Jansenist opponents of *Unigenitus*. The Parlements resisted the order and threatened priests "with imprisonment, exile, and loss of goods" if they obeyed
Archbishop and Church.[88] The famous author was invited by Louis XV to offer
advice on the explosive issue. Montesquieu's advice was consistent with a portrait of a thinker who recognizes that the king is sovereign. The time has come to
exercise this sovereignty, he suggests, but in a way that makes this exercise invisible. He offers a pragmatic solution based upon the fact that the king has already accepted *Unigenitus*. That being the case, the next step is to order that "all
disputes stop." A veil of "silence" must fall on the issue.[89] This approach appears to entail opposition to the Jansenist cause, but it does not. The effect of officially accepting the bull is that no queries can be made about whether anyone
really accepts it. The parishioner who declares his or her opposition to it and the
priest who interrogates his parishioners about their acceptance shall both be regarded as disturbers of the public peace.

Montesquieu shows his Gallican sensibility in warning the king against permitting even the pope to introduce new quarrels.[90] His general message is that
no one should trust theologians on either side of the issue. By accepting a few
simple precepts, most believers are better Catholics than "all the theologians together." Far from sympathizing with one side or the other, he reminds the king
of the personal self-interest that drives these disputants. Without this controversy most of these scribblers would lack any reputation whatsoever. Montesquieu restates for the king a doctrine of *raison d'état*. Let "the Council [of State]
be uniquely your Council of Conscience."[91] The clergy should have no influence
on his majesty. He reminds the king of the facts of sovereignty: "the safety of
the state is the supreme law," but a "state where half the population hates the

other half is in a situation where no one is safe."[92] By means of an acceptance of the bull that undermines any attempt to enforce it, Montesquieu effectively reduces the competence of ecclesiastical jurisdictions whose interest would lie in enforcement. But this also pulls the teeth out of Jansenist programs since any effort to take aggressive advantage of effective tolerance for Jansenism is stymied by a precedent which commits Parlement to the opposite policy, acceptance of the bull that officially suppresses it. This is Montesquieu at his most Machiavellian.

One may conclude that Richer is not wholly wrong in thinking he had an ally in Montesquieu, but the ideology that might be constructed from the materials we considered earlier ignores Montesquieu's central insight about monarchy: it is not a republic underwritten by virtue. It is, therefore, potentially capable of a tolerance which the spectacle of a still sacralized monarchy, pressed by two theological rivals, would seem to deny. Despite this inconvenience for the religious parties of public virtue, it was not implausible to think that *The Spirit of Laws* could be used to lend support to the hope of expanding the power and jurisdiction of the Parlements. In this sense, there was a certain sort of "Montesquieu-ism" that flourished in the *parlementaire* opposition of the 1750s and 1760s.

Attesting to his own growing activism, Montesquieu once more inserts himself into the heady atmosphere of the 1753 crisis. After remonstrating against the king's support of Church policy, the Parlement of Paris was exiled in 1753. On this occasion Montesquieu writes a long letter to one of its members, *le président* Durey de Meinières. Far from expressing sympathy for his colleague's position, the letter is sharply, almost rudely critical. It is far more bluntly Bodinian than his advice to the king! It is all very well to remonstrate, Montesquieu writes, but you have made your point. Now your actions threaten the constitution. To both Louis XV and Durey de Meinières he writes: "The safety of the State [sic] is the supreme law." To the jurist alone, however, Montesquieu draws out the chilling consequences. "To say that you do not anticipate the ruin of the State and that you will perish before it, is not a reason, for your ruin counts for very little compared with that of the State. Think carefully about yourselves, examine things as they are; *in comparison with the State, you are nothing*" (my emphasis). A few paragraphs later he reiterates this Bodinian sentiment. "The State is a great machine of which you are but one of the springs. You bring this machine to a halt, and yet, it is necessary that it continues to function."[93] Jean Ehrard justly concludes, "Montesquieu has a sense for the state."[94] Liberal thinkers do not evidently seek to frustrate *every* expression of sovereign power.

By choosing exile the Parlement runs the risk of losing the battle of public opinion. For Montesquieu, one should always attend to the survival of Parlement itself as a functional part of the monarchical constitution. "All those who dispute at present and the subjects of these disputes themselves will pass away." The ex-president then adds, but *"the Parlement must be eternal"* (my emphasis).[95] With this line Montesquieu proves himself a worthy defender of Montesquieu-ism, that stream of thinking which held that Parlement might itself become, if its officials could manage to avoid discrediting it, the political future of the monarchy projected in *The Spirit of Laws*.

The year 1771 marks, however, the last hurrah of this *parlementaire* ideology. Its demise occurs exactly as Montesquieu predicted in his 1753 letter to Durey de Meinières. Maupeou, a former magistrate elevated to Chancellor, crushes the Parlements. He exiles the magistrates, reorganizes the courts, and finds pliant characters to sit on them. He maintains this policy for the four years he holds onto power. Only the death of Louis XV and the accession to the throne of Louis XVI reverses Maupeou's policy. By then it is too late. The old Parlements return, but they have now definitively lost the battle of public opinion. The public can no longer see in them an instrument for their aspirations. The institutions have proven to be too fragile. The magistrates become even more bogged down in the narrow pursuit of place and prerogative. Montesquieu-ism comes to an end at this moment. In William Doyle's judgment: "it was no theorist, but Maupeou, who really demolished Montesquieu. He demonstrated the practical weakness of the intermediary powers by showing how easily the government might override them."[96]

By reason perhaps of newly felt fragility, the Parlements after the Maupeou exile reversed course and drifted into alliance with an episcopacy that they had previously fought. This conservative alliance of Church and Parlement nobility has been construed as a Montesquieu inspired "aristocratic reaction," but such an alliance was a betrayal of *The Spirit of Laws*.[97] Montesquieu's text supposed opposition, not alliance, between Parlements and Church. Moreover, the text was ominously silent on those occasions when it could have legitimated the Church as the underpinning of monarchy in France.

As a potentially radical ideology, Montesquieu-ism reigns for twenty-three years from 1748 to 1771. A whole generation of French readers, magistrates, and others, use it to consider the possibilities for public transformation based upon the Parlement strategy one finds in *The Spirit of Laws*. Having influence upon the political imagination of readers over this stretch of time is not a bad run as such things go. Doyle concludes, "it was from this time that men began to turn their thoughts to more tangible and permanent checks on governmental power."[98] At this very moment there is a call for that ancient assembly, the Estates General, which last met in 1614. When one thinks, however, about the fate of the Estates General in the Revolution, the description Doyle employs, of the Estates representing "more tangible and permanent checks," does not come to mind. It is permissible to wonder whether there exists any doctrine of tangible and permanent checks that would not look ephemeral in the face of unanticipated events hostile to it.

While echoing Montesquieu in praise of the French Constitution ("you had all that combination and all that opposition of interests"), Edmund Burke notori-

ously blamed the revolutionaries for undermining it.[99] But Maupeou's preliminary "revolution" had already sapped whatever strength Montesquieu and his allies could find in it. What if the Maupeou Revolution never happened or fizzled
out early because, in accordance with the advice given to Durey de Meinières,
magistrates knew how to outwit their adversaries and to preserve their institutional legitimacy? Would this *parlementaire* political theory then have seemed
necessarily so intangible and implausible? No abstract juridical theory can with-
stand the force of events that make it seem an impossible route to the actors who
must take some route or another. But in the absence of such events, what would
have prevented actors from continuing down this road?

Honor: Sovereignty's Supplement

Failing to see that *The Spirit of Laws* displays a juridical doctrine not unlike
Bodin's has led readers to overlook or to under-appreciate another novelty in the
text. This consists in showing that the abstract rights and powers that make up
the juridical picture of the state are radically insufficient. They require a supplement that cannot be provided by juridical discourse itself. Without this supplement we can have no understanding of how monarchy actually operates. In
this manner Montesquieu appears to address a complaint that is sometimes heard
about contemporary theories of rights and other political concepts discussed at
high levels of abstraction: a juridical discourse does not tell us much about how
a politics informed by this discourse actually works. The rights on tap in a treatise and what happens after citizens in an ongoing history tap them are two different things. I offer one example of this from Tocqueville, a great student of
Montesquieu. Despite his awareness of the rights-suffused atmosphere of
American life and of the importance of legal formalities in preserving these liberties, Tocqueville knows that rights fall short in application. Concerning the
treatment of the Indians he says with devastating understatement that their "expulsion . . . takes place at the present day in a regular and, as it were, almost
legal manner," and concludes sarcastically, "it is impossible to destroy men with
more respect for the laws of humanity."[100]

    The same issues arise in the juridical doctrines on display in Bodin and Mon-
tesquieu. After the consequences of *pouvoir absolu* have been stated and as well,
its complex relationships with intermediary institutions filled in, what do we
know about how monarchy worked or for that matter how it might have worked
under altered circumstances? Historical analysis provides useful clues, but it
also suggests a new problem: understanding the intentions and motives of actors.
Typically one discovers motives by projecting one's own dispositions into the
lives of historical characters. We decide that they acted on economic and political "interests" or responded to psychological "strains" and anxieties, but sometimes without wondering how they interpreted interest or how the concepts of

actors channeled their experience of anxiety. The alternative approach, which Montesquieu helps to pioneer, suggests we must try to understand historical characters from within their own culture and with the interpretive concepts they adopt to explain that culture.[101]

Attributing importance to cultural explanations leads to a not uncommon methodological fear. Despite the availability of bridges between cultures, we may have limited imaginative access to one another. Only from within specific and differentiated local contexts do many actions make sense. Epistemological gaps could separate one *esprit* from another, *esprit* being taken as either an individual "mind" or a "collective mentality," i.e., a culture. These notions sometimes tempt the great theorist of *esprit*. In speaking about the consciousness of honor which informs the European nobility, Montesquieu comes right up to the edge of an impasse: "Honor, mingling in everything, enters all the modes of thought and all the ways of feeling and even directs the principles" (IV, 2). This statement threatens to restrict the access of outside observers to the culture of honor since evidently only those who live in the light of honor will have the appropriately directed "principles" for understanding it. Such vertiginous thoughts occur, but unlike later thinkers Montesquieu is for the most part untroubled by these epistemological problems among his communicating *esprits*. "*Un Anglois, un François, un Italien: trois esprits*," Montesquieu writes, but then he leaves it at that.[102]

Beyond the many particular ways people have invented for understanding their situations, there are also paradigmatic political cultures that require study. Montesquieu's descriptions of them are ideal typifications of many and varied cases. The mentalities they pick out, despotic fear, republican virtue, and monarchical honor, are meant to provide readers with only a point of entry into more complex situations. For instance, China, a "despotic" country he admires, functions more like "a republic or a monarchy" (VI, 9). The Bordeaux magistrate thus supplements the juridical analysis of monarchy by embedding it in an account of the prevailing moral and emotional dispositions of those agents who operate its levers. This describes "the human passions that set it in motion" (III, 1).

Honor is the class code of the European nobility described in a highly stylized way. There is nothing here about private duels between swashbuckling dandies, young men fantasizing about heroic war, or any of the other topics that excite the popular or macho imagination.[103] To be sure, as a prominent member of the *noblesse de robe*, or the judicial aristocracy, Montesquieu is ambivalently aware of differences between his values and those held by the *noblesse d'épée*, the military aristocracy. The nobility of the sword are "altogether warlike," or at least, he adds, tongue in cheek, "they go to war so that no one will dare to say they did not go" (XX, 22). But, if anything, the understanding of honor that Montesquieu deploys diminishes the gap between robe and sword. On occasion it even reaches out to embrace others as well.

Honor is a supplement in a double sense, first because it is a *principe* that supplements an inadequate juridical discourse and second because of what honor supplants. As a *principe*, honor is compensation for an inadequacy in the representation of "monarchy." This is an inadequacy in *nature*: "that which makes it what it is." Describing what something is—for instance, that it is identical to or different from some other representation in political space—is now understood to fall short of knowing what "makes it act" (III, 1). To contrast this to the standard Aristotelian understanding, knowing the "nature" of something includes for the Greek thinker knowing the purposes and actions by which it becomes what it is. For Montesquieu, however, actions are motivated by "passions" that in some significant sense cannot be represented within the matrix of *nature*. Succumbing to the changing interpretations of the actors themselves, the passions have become too mobile to be accommodated by Aristotle's nature. To be sure, when Montesquieu is done incorporating "principles" into the different "natures," he has a familiar enough looking taxonomy. These representations are deployed in a kind of geography of political space. The map of this space exhibits republics that function well only if they remain small, despotisms whose characteristic horrors are exacerbated by the empire or excessive extent over which they typically preside, and monarchies whose problems of governability require them to be neither too small nor too large (VIII, 15-20).

Nevertheless, understanding how the "passions" attached to these forms are variously interpreted by historical actors is now an enterprise that has separated itself from an understanding of the institutional forms alone. This is brought out more clearly when we recognize that what Montesquieu calls a *principe* is a critical ingredient in that other puzzling notion, *esprit*. *Esprit* is, in effect, the dialogue that manners and customs have with law, history, and physical circumstance. The assembly required by this dialogue designates no physical space. If what constitutes *esprit* (spirit or mind) could be represented in space, that is to say in *nature*, Montesquieu would never have invoked it with a term which in both religious and philosophical usage points to that which cannot be seen, an invisible force that can only be felt. It is not too extreme, therefore, to connect Montesquieu with the author whose praise of *De l'esprit des lois* concealed only its enormous influence upon him. For Hegel's *Phenomenologie des Geistes*, that history of consciousness that culminates in and fashions a collective identity called "Europe," owes a debt to the possibilities conceptualized in *esprit*.[104] *Esprit* has partially abandoned the territory of spatial representation and is subsequently more fully exposed to the pressure of time and the temporal. Honor, the *principe* of monarchy, has no steady substantive meaning, but is open to the caprice of the actors who interpret and adapt it to evoke their own identity in changing historical time.

For Montesquieu, there is something that cannot be fully represented, but which nevertheless figures (noumenally, so to speak) in understanding the forces acting upon representations. After Kant, these notions were to have an illustrious history in the disputes over methodology in the human sciences. This is a discussion as well about that other elusive concept, power. Starting with his *Considerations* on Roman history, Montesquieu connects *esprit* with power: "there is in each nation *un esprit général* on which *puissance* itself is founded."[105] Both those who think of this *esprit/ puissance* as a "force" capable of being represented in a comparative and universal social science, and those who think of it as a "mentality" whose particularity or temporality might defeat representation, may look back to a predecessor in the baron de La Brède.

Honor is a supplement in a second sense. This constitutes not methodological, but political originality. The title of Book III, chapter 4 announces the subject negatively: "That virtue is not the principle of monarchical government." Without yet identifying it, chapter 5 quite literally offers honor as the supplement: "*Comment on supplée à la vertu dans le gouvernement monarchique.*" *Supplée (suppléer)* means supply, but also to make up for, to fill in, and to compensate. Can honor compensate for the absence of virtue? Here Montesquieu plays with the reader. "I make haste, I lengthen my step so that none will believe that I satirize monarchical government." Some readers nevertheless suspect it. They cannot believe that good government might require the absence of virtue. It depends, of course, on the virtues on offer whether their absence is commendable. "No," Montesquieu declares, "if one *ressort* [this can mean spring, but also spirit, motivating force, even jurisdiction] is absent, there is another: Honor."

Montesquieu's opening definition of honor may not inspire confidence. Honor is "*the prejudice of every person and each condition*" (III, 5, my emphasis). This is at least a democratic definition. There is something here for everyone. Consequently, honor is also highly subjective. With the help of the concept of honor Montesquieu announces a kind of society fearful moralists never tire of denouncing, one that finds a place for everyone's "subjective" or "individual" opinions, which is to say, everyone's "prejudices."

Montesquieu is concerned enough about misunderstanding (or possibly about being understood only too well) to append an "Author's foreword" where he explains that the "political virtue" he discusses is neither Christian nor moral virtue. In addition, he adds, all three virtues can be present in monarchies; it "would be outrageous" to deny that "in every country of the world morality is desired." This acknowledgment seems to provide him with the protective cover he needs. But then he adds that only honor is the "spring" (*ressort*) of monarchical government. The virtues he has spoken of are like gears that have nothing to do with making a watch move. The implication seems clear enough. No attempt to enforce robust virtue, whether moral, Christian, or political, seems consonant with what monarchical government is or promises to become.[106] There seem to be two reasons for this. First, it is in the interest of the sovereign to avoid attaching the throne to the moral ambitions of any one group (whether Jesuit or Jansenist). No group's moral ambitions possess any stability. The very Christian king's troubles in choosing which Christianity that phrase intends to protect are indicative of the problem. Second, if such stability could be maintained, those who speak for legally enforced moral consensus would rule and not the king. Honor will not insist, as virtue does, upon conformity to a singular substantive moral or religious consensus. It could not because honor is the "prejudice" of each.

If Montesquieu is right and the unfolding *telos* of monarchy implies that it requires little or no "virtue," then we must immediately recognize that this resembles very little the regime of Louis XV. To live solely in accordance with "honor" as the supplement for legally enforced virtue would require at least three significant changes. First, Louis XV would have to ignore his coronation oath to uphold the Catholic religion. Louis personally paid little attention to this unless he had to, but his monarchy was hostage to its own divination at the hands of Bossuet and others. The monarchy would need to become secular and "desacralized."[107] Second, Jesuit and Jansenist adversaries would have to stop deluding themselves in thinking it somehow important to get everyone to agree on a common substantive morality. Third, law courts would have to stop thinking of themselves as supplying their own virtue laden "supplement" by supervising the censorship of books, theater, and private life generally.

With these examples in mind, the absence of virtue begins to look like a blessing. The result, a secular monarchy, would still support, at least officially, legally sanctioned social inequality, but such a regime would also paradoxically look more like individualistic contemporary societies ostensibly underwritten by liberal norms that presuppose legal equality. From Montesquieu's account of monarchy, we see the emergence of an ideal of diversity among persons freed from a thick agenda of state-enforced moral conformity. Montesquieu's religious critics are not wrong to complain. The monarchy whose lineaments he traces to latent meanings in the European idea of honor offers a conceptual revolution. The consequence is to narrow the legal jurisdiction over which the mutually exclusive passions of moral critics can have public sway.

Given the commitment of powerful groups mentioned above to the enforcement of virtue in monarchy, is Montesquieu's uncoupling of virtue from the monarchical state only a philosophical fantasy? Before the *philosophes* abandon the monarchy, Montesquieu's version of it is possibly its best defense. But could support for this vision of its possibilities extend beyond the *philosophes* who, in any event, were not unanimous in their opinion about its worth? A response might be found in Daniel Roche's ambitious *France in the Enlightenment* where Montesquieu's model of a new monarchy is so ubiquitous as almost to become a leading character in the drama. Roche shows how the Bordeaux magistrate made the stakes clear to the wider public: "Montesquieu took a crucial step with implications that extended beyond the aristocracy; at stake was the liberty of all which only a composite elite could guarantee." Such a conception of monarchy "permit[ted] hope of reform . . . [and] made it possible to think about the heritage of the past, the weight of tradition, and the still vital forces that existed within the old landed kingdom while simultaneously doing justice to the new society in which there was room for trade, wealth, and talent." Monarchy was "the state for modern times."[108]

Honor's Orbit

Having discussed the broader implications of Montesquieu's reworking of honor, let us return to address more narrowly how precisely Montesquieu construes the result. Honor has both an ethical and a political character. The political dimension of honor focuses upon how those who live within its orbit understand obligation and disobedience to public authority and how their ambitions are related to public purposes. Concerning the connection to public purpose, Montesquieu leaves us in no doubt: "Ambition has good effect in monarchy; it gives life to that government" (III, 7). Montesquieu is careful, however, not to specify the purposes of living an honorable life. This would be an unacceptable invasion of the honor seeker's turf. One of the conditions of living honorably is demonstrating the self-guided character of one's actions. This would include choosing a life, or self-consciously acknowledging that a life is one's own, however much one inherits its circumstances and responsibilities. One may be required, Montesquieu suggests, to accept public employment in a republic, but no sovereign in a monarchical state would dare to make such a demand. "Such is the eccentricity of honor that it is pleased to accept only when it wants and in the manner it wants" (V, 19, 303).

Honor cannot exist except within the social fabric of a lawful state: "honor can be found only in states whose constitution is fixed and whose laws are certain" (III, 8). For Montesquieu, honor has little to do with individuals who live wholly outside juridical norms and substitute their manly codes for the law. Honor conforms to rules. "Honor has its laws and rules which it cannot bend." It is at the same time capricious. The rules of honor can change. Inventive personalities discover new twists and turns in the older rules of community. Honor "depends on its own caprice and not on that of another" (III, 8). "Honor is naturally subject to eccentricities" (III, 10). Sovereign governments cannot control the ever-shifting meanings of honor.

In a monarchy, honor first reveals itself as obedience to sovereign authority. Explicitly, obedience is without conditions (hence it is *pouvoir absolu*). Implicitly, obedience is attached to an understanding of dignity whose meaning neither the sovereign nor any group can fully control. Obedience is also implicitly attached to an understanding of a rule of law upheld by the consultative relationships between the sovereign and the royal courts. Honorable obedience is not itself a goal, but merely a prior condition for having goals, which are left to the discretion and initiative of the holder. To be sure, adhering (or not) to the norms of a specific community at a given time and place provides an ethical content to the sense of honorable attachment. But as adherence is, according to the rules of honor, always given freely, and occasionally fiercely, it may also be withheld freely and fiercely.

The content of honor will vary significantly depending on local context. As each situation is different, it could be argued that on methodological grounds, no linkages centered upon an explication of "honor" could possibly do justice to the many varieties of honor. There is something to be said for this sort of nominalism, but there would be little to be nominalist about if there were not first maps of the overall landscape, typifications of the sort the text invokes.

There is, however, a bigger obstacle standing in the way of recapturing the meaning of honor. This is the moral objection motivated by indignation at class and gender inequalities. That "honor" reinforced inequalities in the European monarchies is generally true, but honor also moderated the resulting power imbalances. In the case of gender inequality (see note 35), honor gave aristocratic women a status they and all other women lost to "egalitarian" male citizens in the early history of the French revolutionary republic. In any event, Montesquieu simply says at the outset that the political type "monarchy" presupposes that power and wealth are unequally distributed. The problem in such polities is how to moderate the domination such concentrations of power afford their holders and consequently how to prevent a country from being ruled despotically. The other non-despotic type, "republic," presupposes equality, albeit only for a male elite. The problems republics have in achieving and sustaining public equality, the compromises its citizens must make in their private lives, and the disappearance of "diversity" in such polities are, if Montesquieu's political science of the republic is remotely applicable, the three difficult issues for contemporary egalitarians.

One could describe honor as providing the ethical content of monarchical life, except that the word "content" would be wrong. Honor's first task is simply to reconcile individual dignity and submission to authority. In the name of honor, one freely accepts authority. At the same time, in the name of honor, one is ready to resist dishonorable commands. There is no public content here, no agreement about what honorable men and women should seek other than that, whatever they seek, the terms of their communal life and subjection to authority should preserve the dignity and liberty of each "honorable" person. Honor provides free subjects with the terms of conformity to sovereign rule. It carries the presumption (not always borne out in practice) that each has a certain kind of moral independence and can find a civic space in which to pursue or explore a diversity of individual or group goals. On principle these are not determinable by government. As such, honor establishes the ethical "proceduralism" of those subject to monarchical government.

This analysis owes something to the reflections of Michael Oakeshott. The moral discovery which fits the facts of the "modern European nation state" is that one can be joined together with others "in acknowledgment of an authority of a practice," but without the added imposition or attraction of sharing in a common substantive purpose. Honor, the authority it subscribes to, and the distinctiveness that it cultivates exemplify such a civil relationship. Republican virtue by contrast is a joining together in pursuit of a common public goal. Whatever their other differences, Hobbes, Bodin, Montesquieu, and Hegel are agreed on the character of this civil relationship.[109]

This is not the commitment to procedure or due process of a constitutional democracy, but neither is it wholly dissimilar. If, as George Kateb suggests, in duly established democracies, "the electoral system promotes energy . . . [while] due process promotes restraint," one can see parallels in the promotions of monarchy. This is not to say that those ancien régime monarchies—even Montesquieu's reform version—and contemporary democracies are morally equivalent. They are not. Both the noble subject and the democrat have means of saying, "I count . . . I take part guiltlessly . . . I press myself forward without feeling shame." But uniquely the democrat says, "I count only as one."[110] Aristocrats only know that some are free. But acting in accordance with these partial and biased convictions maintains precedent for a subsequent claim: all are free. The latter ideal introduces an equality that is literally incompatible with the legal structure of a monarchical society, but not necessarily with a certain interpretation of its spirit. As we shall see, Montesquieu's text is poised between two interpretations. In one, honor is socially exclusive. In the other, it attempts to universalize itself. The latter effort could not avoid undermining the juridical structure of monarchy. But it also provided successor regimes with an aristocratic source for the liberal heritage.

Montesquieu compares the relationship of subjects and sovereign to Newtonian forces that sustain planets in their revolutions. "It is just like the system of the universe, where there is a force constantly repelling all bodies from the center and a force of gravitation attracting them to it. Honor makes all the parts of the body politic move; it ties them together by its very action" (III, 7). Strictly speaking, however, mechanistic explanations are suitable only to despotic states where "the prince's will, once known, should produce as fallibly its effect as one ball thrown against another" (III, 10). The metaphor of a monarchical solar system invokes subtler ideas. Honorable individuals obey a sovereign who is presupposed to require that they will live in dignified freedom. Such subjects feel a compulsion to deserve that honor. This exerts centripetal force. But succumbing to the pull of this gravity would be too servile. Individuals can only exhibit honor by differentiating themselves from one another and by resisting the pull of dishonoring temptations offered by the very sovereign whose presence animates them. This sustains centrifugal force. Such competing centripetal and centrifugal ambitions lead individuals into every kind of eccentric orbit. But they also lead to public service (another route to distinction) and to remonstration with superior authority, if honor requires it. There is an implied critique of the Versailles Court contained in the solar system imagery. Honor accrues only to the orbiting "planets," i.e., the regional political actors, not to those who fall into the embrace of life at the center of the political universe in the court of the "sun-king" himself.

Solar system imagery yields one further implication. Subjects can hurtle through the vastness of social space and sustain themselves through sheer personal ambition at a great distance from a sun-king without threatening the latter's authority or efficacy. This suggests that monarchies capable of accommodating individualistic ambitions create a more expansive space for public and private activities than do those political systems (despotisms *and* republics!) that discourage or are threatened by such ambition. The despot, for instance, or a king contemplating becoming one, collapses the solar system of honorable ambitions into something altogether different. "A monarchy is ruined when the prince, referring everything to himself exclusively, reduces the state to its capital, the capital to the court, and the court to his person alone" (VIII, 6).

Montesquieu makes a similar point in turning to the language of the sovereign court. "In monarchies one sees the subjects around the prince receive his light; there, as each one has, so to speak, a larger space, he can exercise those virtues that give the soul not independence but greatness" (V, 12). The gushy faux-grandeur of this remark seems out of character. It is redolent and even in sly imitation of the chatter of courtiers: "one sees the subjects around the prince receive his light." There is nevertheless a serious argument here, and it is the same one Montesquieu makes earlier in Book III. A political system that can tolerate ambition and even call upon it creates, like the movements of the planets around the sun, a wider sphere, not only for the diverse endeavors of everyone, but for the possibility of political grandeur that had previously been restricted to the republic. To be sure, people who measure their personal ambitions within the orbit provided by their honorable conformity to lawful rule have only the illusion of independence, and for two reasons in particular. First, their ambitions "can constantly be repressed" by the sovereign (III, 7). Second, the psychological mechanism of honor makes its bearers other-directed. They are highly dependent upon the praise of others who watch and judge their actions. This scarcely constitutes real moral independence, but it suitably binds the ambitious while at the same time freeing them.

In a purely functionalist sociology, the moral dispositions of agents will harmoniously fill the roles the juridical structure has prepared for them. This is not quite the way Montesquieu conceives of honor, however. Honor may resonate sympathetically with the juridical structure established by monarchy, but it fundamentally transforms how that structure works. On the face of it, honor directly contradicts *pouvoir absolu* whose fundamental rule of sovereignty is "in a monarchy the prince is the source of all political and civil power" (II, 4). But there is a shadow court hidden in every part of the kingdom unknown to the juridical mind. In this court, honor not only makes law, but also, like the prince, it obeys only its own caprice. In fact, "honor . . . reigns like a monarch over prince and people." In an unanticipated reversal of roles, honor supplements and tempers the juridical structure of *pouvoir absolu*. Yet another form of the distribution of power, honor cannot alter juridically the role of sovereign authority. But it can modify how the government and society actually work, thus moderating the claims of power: "In monarchical and moderate states, power is limited by that which is its spring, I mean honor" (III, 10).

There is no use in sovereigns and their counselors lamenting these effective limits on their power. Honor is the very *ressort* (spring or jurisdiction) of the authority kings exercise. Honor is the source of the energy a monarchy can draw upon. Although there is no republican virtue here, "in well-regulated monarchies, everyone is nearly a good citizen" (III, 6). Obedience is voluntarily given when it signifies that the giver is a free subject. In a democratic society personal dignity, which attaches itself to the idea of individual rights, accomplishes the same task. To be sure, the culture of democratic dignity in a formally egalitarian society is far removed from the inegalitarian atmosphere of a European monarchy. Nevertheless, because the monarch's privileged subjects understood that they lived in honor, they created a political culture based upon the idea of a "free" obedience to authority, i.e., obedience to authority on the terms of the freedoms it guarantees. The liberalism of an absolute monarchy arose from the dissonance between its juridical structure and the culture it creates but cannot control.

Elie Carcassonne captures this idea of a connection between honor and juridical structure as follows: "With ingenious capriciousness, honor conciliates independence and fidelity: it commands service to the prince; and prohibits treason; but it inspires, when necessary, generous resistance." To illustrate this species of resistance, Carcassonne cites Montesquieu's two examples: "Crillon refuses to assassinate the Duke of Guise; the Viscount of Orte opposes massacring the Huguenots," (referring to IV, 2).[111] These illustrious names recall the civil wars of religion of the late sixteenth century. Montesquieu wants us to understand individual actions where refusal is accompanied by respect and continued fealty. "Generous resistance" reminds kings that they are sovereigns over free people. "Disobedience was a normal element of the monarchical state," Carcassonne concludes, and "an illegal means of maintaining the law."[112] In contemplating this respectful resistance, a disobedience that is civil, as it were, we have slipped away from the Bodinian doctrine of sovereignty.[113]

Who Are the Honorable?

Honor would seem to require exclusivity. It justifies the ranks of an inegalitarian society and differentiates its holders from the less honorable and those without honor. Montesquieu admits as much. "The nature of honor is to demand preferences and distinctions" (III, 7). The honorable person is concerned with "what one owes to oneself." The honorable community is concerned with "what distinguishes us from them" (IV, 2). One can see, however, two countervailing tendencies in Montesquieu's thoughts about honor. The first pushes against exclusivity; the other intransigently reinforces it.

Montesquieu appears to democratize honor when he declares that it is "the prejudice of each person and each condition" (III, 6). The nobility does not have an exclusive lock on honor. There are imitators in other social ranks, e.g., among merchants, lawyers, and intellectuals. The sway of honor reaches and rules over "*le peuple*" itself (III, 10). As the culture of honor spreads, it legitimizes social differentiation. Universal norms of conduct are blurred and, as it were, particularized by each group taking pride in its own manner of adapting to them. In addition, bourgeois merchants imitate the nobility because they have legitimate hopes of becoming noble. Montesquieu is enthusiastic about the constant renewal of the nobility from below. "Traders are not nobles, but they may become nobles. They can have the expectation of becoming noble without the drawback of being nobles" (XX, 22). But Montesquieu is equally fervent about maintaining the distinction between merchant and noble. This is the "drawback." Once ennobled, merchants can no longer engage (openly) in the commerce that permitted them to buy into the nobility. One could enter the nobility through a marital union of two families; or one could simply purchase land that carries with it noble title. One could be awarded a title by the government for meritorious service; or through a practice called "venality," one could purchase from the government a judicial office that carries a title. Montesquieu, who inherited and then sold his judicial office, commends this practice, much to the dismay of some of his "enlightened" readers.

The desire to keep the ruling class separate from the earning class is motivated in part by the anxiety of an economic liberal. Ennobled office-holders who continue to engage in commerce will use the state much as the prince uses the market, to create monopolies and private rents that drive out competition and lower trust (XX, 19-22). It is also motivated by a concern that the state has higher interests than the mercantile demands brought to bear on it. Quoting Cicero, Montesquieu declares, "I do not like a people to be both the rulers and the clerks of the universe" (XX, 4). Even though modern democracies recognize no legally privileged class, the problem of the relationship between an economic and a political elite has not gone away. A law that requires disclosure and divestiture of economic assets before assuming public office responds to the same anxieties that push Montesquieu to seek to alienate the wealthy from their economic interests even as he elicits their talents for public office.

Purchasing public offices is a good practice for two reasons. It is an incentive to work: "this manner of self-promotion by means of wealth inspires and maintains industry." It keeps the choice of public office out of the hands of the court aristocracy, which is always the weak point in monarchical government. "If the posts were not sold by a public regulation, the courtier's indigence and avidity would sell them all the same, [but] chance will produce better subjects than the choice of the prince" (V, 19, 305-6).

One sees here the germs of three liberal ideas. First, decentralizing the procedures for selecting public posts resists the centralization of all public activities in the state. The state legitimately concentrates authority in itself, since sometimes acts of sovereign will are required; but always concentrating public activities there would destroy both the initiative and liberties of citizens. Second, as on this view chance chooses better than the state, this lends further justification to Montesquieu's praise of another lottery, exemplified in the English jury whose considerable advantage is that "the power of judging, so terrible among men [becomes] . . . invisible and null" (XI, 6, 398). Third, relying upon the market may carry risks with it, but they are no greater than relying upon interested politicians who will end up selling offices at their disposal even when they are officially excluded from the market. Venality of office is one of the first instances of privatizing public functions, although tax farming, which is another, Montesquieu somewhat inconsistently condemns as a regrettable loss of public authority (XIII, 19).

According to historians of the ancien régime, Montesquieu was right. It was not unrealistic in the eighteenth century to think one could become noble. C. B. A. Behrens offers the classic description of what was at work in France: "Anyone with enough money could prove that he had the appropriate ancestors . . . . Money earned in commerce, and particularly in finance, seems to have exercised [an] . . . immediate influence on social and official status."[114] William Doyle concurs: "Throughout ancien régime society, wealth could overcome almost any social barrier."[115] Citing the work of François Bluche and Jean Meyer, Daniel Roche argues that "wealthy bourgeois in a hurry to achieve nobility could purchase royal secretaryships." David Bien describes these posts as factories for "manufacturing nobles."[116] Roche concludes, "most of the eighteenth century nobility consisted of families ennobled in the modern era."[117] The very rootlessness of these noble offices reminds one of David Bien's generalization: "The striking thing is how little the French nobility was attached to the soil."[118] Julian Swann draws out the implications of this new research: "there has been a growing awareness of the social, cultural, and economic ties that bound the *noblesse* and members of the wealthier bourgeoisie together."[119]

The seminal work of Guy Chaussinand-Nogaret points to a bolder claim. On his account, the French nobility was the most progressive force in the kingdom, open to the intellectual life of the Enlightenment and in the vanguard of pre-Revolutionary industrial development. "Nobles, either alone or in association with members of the greater business bourgeoisie, showed their dynamism, their taste for invention and innovation, and their ability as economic leaders." As a consequence, he concludes, "there was no incompatibility between the monarchical society of the eighteenth century and the development towards industrial capitalism, and there was no need for the Revolution to free the productive forces of a bourgeoisie supposed to be the sole possessor of initiative."[120]

Montesquieu pins his hopes for elite renewal upon upwardly mobile traders. He wants the boundaries to be crossed, but not erased. But Chaussinand-Nogaret raises another issue: "In the last decades of the old order, thanks to the greater nobility's lack of prejudice, there came together a composite class," a new proto-industrial business and professional elite.[121] About this prospect, Montesquieu would have been ambivalent. His writings sometimes evince anxiety at the blurring of cultural or class boundaries. At other times they seem open to such transgressions.

Montesquieu's ambivalence was not unlike that of many other members of the eighteenth-century French nobility. One could argue that the latter underwent an identity crisis while exploring a two-track strategy to resolve it. First, in not wanting to let go of older more comfortable self-understandings, it offered up a political justification of its "difference" from the nation. As the embodiment of ancient liberties, the nobility claimed it was uniquely positioned to protect the subjects of a nation increasingly abused by a centralizing government. But later ideological currents probed another strategy, the one Chaussinand-Nogaret alerts us to, noble reintegration with the nation. Pursuing the dynamic possibilities of alliances with other elites, the nobility attempted to forego its old allegiances and to open its arms to new egalitarian criteria of selection based upon personal distinction, merit, and talent. Too late, on the eve of revolution many of its members, overcome with nostalgia for an abandoned past, disgust with what they had become, or fear of the coming disorder, tried to retreat into an older identity with disastrous results.[122] This account may or may not be accurate as the psychological biography of a collective subject. Its interest for us lies in how it aligns with tensions and strains in *The Spirit of Laws*. Montesquieu's conception of honor splits apart and faces in two directions, toward intransigent pursuit of exclusivity and toward democratizing itself.

On the one hand, the affiliation with Germanic liberties, which stress the role of memory and antiquity, reinforce the old noble identity and carve out a special political role for the aristocracy. A definition of honor that emphasizes a passion for distinguishing oneself also reinforces the pursuit of exclusivity. The apotheosis of this quest for "difference" can be found in the invidious comparisons that Montesquieu offers up in Book 4, chapter 2. Honor, we are told, instructs one in a frankness of speech and manner that allows one "to scorn that of the people." A noble education teaches one to judge actions by the criteria of whether they are beautiful, great, or extraordinary. This stands in contrast with another way of judging, one that regards the same actions in the light of whether they are good, just, or reasonable (IV, 2).

In these lines, as in many others, the author holds himself back. We cannot tell whether he is smiling indulgently at a way of life that still affords nostalgic comfort, grimacing politely at the folly of it all, or earnestly instructing the reader in matters that have been up to now caste secrets. In any event, here we have the intransigent strategy that requires nobility to insist upon exclusive privileges. Foregoing the psychological democratization of honor, Montesquieu requires its legal entrenchment. The nobility must be hereditary. "Noble lands, like noble persons, will have privileges . . . one can scarcely separate the dignity of the noble from that of his fief. All these prerogatives will be peculiar to the nobility and will not transfer to the people" (V, 9).

On the other hand, the French history Montesquieu invokes, one in which the nobility gradually extends civil rights to others, suggests an expansive, open-ended sense of honor. This generous version of honorableness communicates itself literally to everyone. It eventually evolves into personal dignity, which is what Montesquieu's noble peers in England think about such matters. Having lost their ancient prejudices for "war," "birth," and "good fortune," the English "esteem only two things: wealth and personal merit."[123] This democratized version of honor defines the second prong of the French strategy. It reconciles nobility and nation not by proclaiming exclusive aristocratic leadership of the nation, but by inviting the nation to assimilate the cultural norms of the nobility. When the nobility lends its *esprit* to national development, only then will honor genuinely rule over "prince *and people"* and become "the *prejudice* of *each* person and *each* condition" (III, 6, 10, my emphasis).

"Prejudice" sounds, however, a note of warning. It recalls the claim that "speaking philosophically," honor is "false" (III, 7; V, 14; V, 19). Social convention decides what is honorable. Montesquieu contrasts the "false honor" of monarchies with the "principles of Christianity" (XXIV, 6). He distinguishes between Christian institutions, which always distort Christian feeling, and Christian principles among which the demand for "truth" and for "unconditional charity" are the most important. This account of Christian morality is not wholly remote from the virtues celebrated in his beloved stoic authors. In invoking "false honor," Montesquieu may ultimately have in mind Montaigne's essay, "On Glory," where false honor relies on "external appearances" and puts "one's life . . . in the keeping of others." True honor requires only that one live within oneself. The reader will be immediately reminded of Rousseau's contrast of "civilized" and "natural man" in the "Discourse on Inequality."[124]

These scruples not withstanding, for Montesquieu the society born under European monarchy flourishes when the respect for the idiosyncratic implicit in the idea of honor discovers wider constituencies. Subject to the order maintaining tasks of the sovereign, such widening of the scope for subjective standpoints gestures toward the future in which democracies sponsor diversity as an ideal. But in what directions will diversity point? Will each group "scorn" others, much as the nobility in the old monarchy "scorns the people," or will each group discover a generosity of spirit that permits it to see something of itself in the lives of others? A democratized honor also has a two pronged strategy: either toward exclusivity and group intransigence or toward respect for diversity and interpretive idiosyncrasies. The aristocratic spirit inherited from the ancien ré-gime is always condemned for its snobbery and praised for its toleration of ec-centricity (except by those who like the snobbery and are frightened by eccen-tricity). It should entail no surprise that democracies that have inherited these mentalities should produce democratic versions of their problems and prospects.

Ultimately, honor contemplates the possibility of personal grandeur that has, in addition, the potential for being publicly redemptive. But in what direction does grandeur point: toward scorn or generosity of spirit? Nowhere does Mon-tesquieu contemplate this issue more deeply than in the strange and paradoxical passage already cited, where under the reign of honor, "one judges men's ac-tions not as good but as beautiful; not as just but as great; not as reasonable but as extraordinary" (IV, 2). What is this comparison about?

There are two hypotheses. First, it sets out the internal tensions between the two branches of nobility by distinguishing between the military aristocracy, the *noblesse d'épée*—who are the original bearers of honor—and the judicial nobil-ity, the *noblesse de robe*. The members of the former would judge their actions as they once judged their ancestors' military exploits, by the standard of whether they were great or extraordinary. A beautiful action would be worth more than a merely reasonable one. Montesquieu refers to the "brilliance" of this "warlike nobility who think that, whatever degree of wealth one has, one's fortune is yet to be made, but that it is shameful to increase one's goods if one does not begin by dissipating them." These values are not designed for survival. The military nobility are inevitably "ruined. " This is a story of the circulation of elites. A ru-ined nobility "give their place to others who will serve with their capital again" (XX, 22). By contrast, the judicial nobility does not require individual distinc-tion; its glory attaches to Parlement and the law. "*Cet état laisse les particuliers dans la médiocrité tandis que le corps dépositaire des lois est dans la gloire*" (XX, 22). That is to say, the condition of the judicial nobility requires in its indi-vidual members a modesty without which the institution and the law they serve would not appear in all their glory. This is a service that would require the *no-blesse de robe* to become, or affect being, reasonable and just, if not necessarily good. The advantage for the nobility as a whole in this interpretation is evident. It shows them able collectively to incorporate two desirable but difficult to com-bine sets of standards, one requiring an appreciation of the impartial virtues that lead to justice and reasonableness, the other attuning its holders to the distinctive and individual.

But if honor belongs to the whole nobility and not just to a part, the first in-terpretation might not quite work. Let us turn to a second hypothesis. On this ac-count, the impartial virtues belong to ordinary subjects, but more relevantly, to the trader and merchant—the bourgeois in later parlance—who seek noble status. On this interpretation, the passage under consideration offers all such as-pirants instruction in becoming noble. Honor does not necessarily require the abandonment of old standards of judgment (e.g., being reasonable or just). But it does urge the reconsideration of a range of human actions where these standards miss the mark. A noble education teaches a kind of withdrawal from the sentiments that lead to mutual accommodation, to getting along and going along, the better to attend to what these dispositions may neglect, actions whose "beauty," "grandeur," or exceptionality are missed by the merely rational or "reasonable."

Montesquieu may have been attentive to the cost of such an aesthetic stance. If focusing upon great, beautiful, and exceptional things literally means abandoning the language of reasonableness and justice, this would require the nobility to sacrifice access to the very idiom of a common public life. The sacrifice might be commended upon a pretense that the values of a public life founded upon the commercial endeavors of trader and merchant are inadequate preparation for the different task of political leadership. But leaders unable to invoke the political language of reason, goodness, and justice are only preparing themselves for their marginalization from the nation.

This is exactly what happened to the nobility in the French Revolution. It is somehow poignant to see in these lines from 1748 an expression of a tragedy and a road not taken for not just one, but two classes, forty years later. Book IV, chapter 2 appears to commend two intransigent identities, one bourgeois and the other noble. The former may become the latter, but the boundary of value and disposition between the two must always be maintained. Quite possibly Montesquieu intended this; but if he did, his words are symptomatic of the leadership crisis that developed in 1788.

Perhaps there is another way of looking at these passages. Understood with sardonic intent, the comparison is a *reductio ad absurdum* that demonstrates the folly of abandoning the vocabulary of justice in pursuit of "distinction" and "difference." In this construing of the passage, Montesquieu implicitly calls for the reintegration of bourgeois and noble idioms of conduct. Such a composite discourse would recognize a justice cognizant of grandeur and a reasonableness that accommodates the exceptional. Why would this have been an accomplishment? A class in possession of such sentiments could have conducted the Revolution to a successful conclusion. Alas, no class possessed these attributes either during the Revolution or after. Only by relinquishing or relaxing a noble social identity could the nobility have contributed their values to the life of a nation. Instead the nobility became the obstacle that stood in the way of the birth of the nation. Its members opted for an identity that marginalized them on the eve of the Revolution. Too many noble leaders turned against the project of blurring ancient differences and memories and against the earlier experiments with a new criterion of merit. This retreat into an older self-understanding discredited the aristocracy.

The aristocratic radicalism one sees in Montesquieu's lyrical description of scornful aristocrats in pursuit of beauty, grandeur, and the extraordinary became in the nineteenth century a bohemian and artistic radicalism that contrasted its sensibility to the cowardly and philistine style of men who made only money.

We can see this all too well in Flaubert's *Madame Bovary*. Montesquieu's paean to the extraordinary seems so familiar since it survived under the heraldry of romantic art. This aristocratic aestheticism reached an apogee in Nietzsche. Nor should we neglect recent incarnations of this spirit albeit in a more benign form, for example, in Foucault for whom regimes of "normalization" founded on that old bourgeois virtue "reason" were once again indictable for allotting no space to the extraordinary.

There is, however, another route for aristocratic values, which leads to their being incorporated into liberal democracy. It is entirely appropriate that among the writers who effect this intellectual move in Europe are the two friends, John Stuart Mill and Alexis de Tocqueville. Together they symbolize, however imperfectly, the composite class that was almost forged at the end of the ancien régime. Their works in the service of democracy are replete with aristocratic ideas in democratic dress. They seek by these lights to save democracy from low ambitions, dull complacency, and a majoritarian neglect of the exceptional, while nevertheless defending popular rule against all its political rivals. Every liberal or democrat who today takes a stand in favor of "diversity," and against majorities that threaten it, is indebted to those collective mentalities, no doubt inadequately summarized in the word "honor," which once provided a cultural space for the initial appearance of diversity.[125]

"Each Has, So To Speak, a Larger Space"

Let us conclude on a few comparative notes. Though Montesquieu has considerable affection for the Aristotelian ideal of friendship cultivated in small republican communities, he is able to set this to one side and to conceptualize what is radically different about European monarchy.[126] Such a society, characterized by social differentiation and not moral unity, had never before existed. When Montesquieu describes its dominant features in *The Spirit of Laws*, he meets with moral outrage from groups (ecclesiastical and others) who think that civil authority requires a deeper ethical consensus. In the raging debate over his book, this issue surfaces in the irritation many feel about the claim that virtue is neither the *principe* of monarchy nor of any large scale territorial nation state.[127] Republican virtue presupposes people who in small states live together in recognition of common goals. But Montesquieu's many critics want monarchy to be something similar, a large republic that yet preserves the habits of collaboration of the small republic.

Monarchy is not a republic and is not governed by republican virtue. It cannot be. Monarchy presides over a highly differentiated, not to mention unequal, social order. The condition for differentiation, and for the attendant possibility that each might have "a larger space" (V, 12), is first a prior agreement to conform to sovereign authority and second the adoption of a proceduralist mentality. The latter inhibits each person's censorious habits sufficiently to permit the recognition of a potential dignity or honor inherent in nearly everyone's "eccentricities" and "prejudices." Such a monarchy is underwritten by a "proceduralist" consensus, but it is not necessarily thin as opposed to thick. The procedures are intended to frame a morality of both self-restraint and ambition. This calls for a moral discipline able to submit to lawful authority and to recognize the potential value in the projects of others. It calls for the moral energy to undertake one's own project and to fabricate from it a shared public life that leaves room for considerable self-invention.

However, the very lack of a moral consensus about whose project is best (a judgment that exposes itself to the withering criticism of the "prejudice of each," III, 6) might entail destabilizing consequences for the juridical order of monarchy. Since honor inclines toward individual subjective judgement, it runs the risk of tearing itself away from its mooring in inherited family fortune and status. By its own logic of relying on each individual's judgment, this concept of honor turns its face toward achievement, toward "careers open to talent" and later, "equality of opportunity." But this points to the weakness of monarchy, whose restricted elites tend to allot these opportunities wholly to themselves. Where this exclusivity breaks down, monarchy is evidently a structure whose support for "diversity" commends it to the pluralistic democracies of our own times. But long before that moment was reached, the juridical structure of monarchy presented itself as archaic. Its legal structure of inequality was simply unsuitable for the regime of equal opportunity to which the democratization of honor unerringly pointed.

One may as well recognize what is remarkable about monarchy, Montesquieu seems to suggest, and pursue the intimations of this vision of it. He has a nice way of capturing the distinctiveness of monarchy as a tolerant regime. In a republic, which must act through moral consensus, even "private crimes were public" (III, 5). Montesquieu notes the prevalence of family legislation and institutions concerned with domestic surveillance in classical republics. As the principal objects of this surveillance are the sexual mores and behavior of women, he concludes that women could not be free under republics (IV, 5, 8; V, 7-8; VII, 8-17; VIII, 2, 11-12). By contrast, in a monarchy even "public crimes are more private" (III, 5). There is hope, he thinks, for release from surveillance and for decriminalizing "private" behavior in a society that accommodates itself so well to the centrifugal force of people busy distinguishing themselves from one another. In such a society women could be freer than they had ever been (XIX, 5-6, 8-9, 13-15, 25-27). Montesquieu goes into this subject in great detail though this is a topic one cannot address here. (But see note 35.) Suffice it to say that when the *philosophes* abandon the task of improving the monarchy, by desacralizing it while acknowledging its libertarian potential, in order to embrace revolutionary republican ideas, the state as *surveillant* and shaper of private and family life returns as well. This has the consequence, according to one scholar, that "an entire set of practices that before 1789 were left to personal preference and lay out of the reach of monarchical authority, were invaded and devoured by state decrees."[128]

There are, however, distinguished commentators who would deny the force of these claims for monarchy. Let us acknowledge their objections. Mark Hulliung and Thomas Pangle reject the claim that Montesquieu ultimately invites us to appreciate what is remarkable about monarchy. Hulliung hates monarchy and its ethos in all its forms. He believes that a radical and civic republican Montesquieu does so as well. His Montesquieu subjects the aristocratic ethos to a "pitiless" critique and finds honor "embarrassingly diminutive" compared to the grandeur of civic virtue. Although we disagree, Hulliung is correct to say that, "when viewing England, Montesquieu dreamed of nothing less than a national republic." But I add the proviso that for Montesquieu it would be adequate for the republic to remain "hidden" as it can do its work better behind the throne. Pangle opts for a version of "liberal republicanism" founded on a critique of the classical understanding. Like Hulliung, he sees in Montesquieu a kind of whiggish history whose *telos* is some kind of "republic" that looks remarkably like the United States either as it exists or (for Hulliung) as it might become. I agree with Pangle that "there is a possibility in France for some kind of imitation of England," but with the proviso that this is because of the similarities between France and England. Alan Gilbert's Aristotelian Montesquieu is similarly hard on monarchy. Gilbert observes that "individuality" can be pursued under monarchy, but, unlike my account, the latter is a rarely tolerant regime whose honor seekers discover only a "busy emptiness." By contrast, "genuine self-realization" is possible only in the English "Republic." Monarchical life is apparently comparable to the "emptiness of public life" that afflicts contemporary democracies. Whereas for Gilbert this similarity is regrettable, it is for me the deliberate effort of an early modern author to conceptualize subjective freedom in its proper setting, civil society.[129]

Montesquieu's European monarchy has passed from the scene, but it bequeathed to its successor forms of government a rich agenda of unresolved issues. The first is the one Raymond Aron raised about political science. In establishing the relations between sovereignty and the offices and rights it authorizes, constitutions sanction forms of privilege not on grounds of strict justice, but as a form of prudence necessary to protect liberty. Yet as the history of European monarchy demonstrates, the appearance of injustice in inherited status threatens the very liberty for which (the appearance of) justice was sacrificed. One must add that, alas, even regimes of equal opportunity have means of perpetuating new kinds of inheritable status.

For polities floating in the midst of global economies that are constantly churning up human relationships, we can still ask the question the debate over the landed aristocracy first raised. In order to preserve free communities whose leaders have an inbred sense of responsibility and *gravitas*, should groups actively seek to entrench their privileges, much as the contemporary French do when they appeal in an almost Burkean manner to their *droits acquis* or acquired rights? Without an "exception" in their favor, such acquired rights might be lost to the forces of impartial market rules that challenge every status quo relationship. For Phillipe d'Iribaine, French industrial relations still seek an alternative to rule by the market in something like Montesquieu's understanding of aristocratic honor. This is opposed equally to the arms length contractual relations of "equals" in America and the consensual agreements found in Holland.[130]

Second, Montesquieu's description of monarchy also demonstrates the inadequacy of "abstract" juridical discourse. This points political theorists to anthropology and to the other human sciences. The dispositions of the human agents who give life to juridical projects are the indispensable supplement to understanding them. This leads, however, to the recognition of the inadequacy of "nature." Montesquieu is still Aristotelian enough to rely on a certain understanding of "nature," one that leads to a geography of regime types. But nature is no longer the only guide to what the constantly renovated *esprit* of men and women will make of what they inherit and transform through what they are now pleased to identify as their "history." The surprise is the philosophical hope that Montesquieu expresses: nature and *esprit* still have much about which to communicate.

The third issue is "absolutism" and its relation to honor. Montesquieu is juridically an absolutist, but only in the sense that prevails before the nineteenth century invention of the word, when the existence of someone in the polity with the last voice is not inconsistent with sharing in rule. Montesquieu is justly famous for emphasizing sharing, but not to the point of denying either the existence or the legitimacy of sovereignty. Honor tempers sovereignty but not in any juridically comprehensible way.

The germ of this theory is already on display in Montaigne's *Essays*. The first chapter of Book Three announces the theme, "The Useful and the Honorable." Sovereignty is useful, especially when the subordinate powers are distributed so as to put the sovereign in the intelligent service of his own interests, as Bodin would have instructed. For once agreeing with Machiavellian reason of state, Montaigne admits that the "prince" must sometimes yield to necessity: "Vice it is not, for he has abandoned his own reason to a more universal and powerful reason." But these situations represent "misfortune." and are "sickly exceptions to our natural rules." We must remind ourselves "that not all things are permissible for an honorable man in the service of his king, or of the common cause, or of the laws." Honor is not usefulness: "we poorly argue the *honor and beauty* of an action from its *utility*" (my emphasis).[131] Book IV, chapter 2 of *The Spirit of Laws* draws out the implications of this thought. As the two categories of moral assessment, the reasonable and the beautiful, tend to contaminate one another, the typical carriers of these distinct moral codes should not blur their identities.

We have claimed that Montesquieu thoroughly understands the reasons why Bodin argues for there being a final voice. Like other theorists of sovereignty, he thinks that someone's having a last word is a necessary part of a well-ordered constitution. Unlike them, he suspects that speaking the last word is not always wise or necessary. There should be practices that discourage the exercise of sovereignty, but none that deny its legitimacy. Honor may oppose sovereignty, but only by acknowledging its authority. Montesquieu could have found lots of examples of rebellion; but the two acts of disobedience he chooses to illustrate honor demonstrate not rebelliousness but respect. There is a corollary to the new doctrine of sovereignty in the even newer doctrine of a disobedience that is civil.

Notes

The following read all or part of earlier versions of this chapter and offered helpful (often extensive) comments: David Carrithers, Cecil Courtney, Daniel Gordon, Catherine Larrère, Fiona Miller, Paul Rahe, and Dale K. Van Kley. Both the Institute for Advanced Study, Princeton, 1998-1999 and Yale University, 1999-2000, were congenial settings for completing this project.

1. Montesquieu, *The Spirit of Laws (De l'esprit des lois*, 1748) in *Œuvres complètes de Montesquieu*, ed. Roger Caillois, vol. 2 (Paris: Pléiade, 1951), Book II, chapter 2, 247. Hereafter references to *The Spirit of Laws* will be abbreviated in the body of the text by book and chapter number in parenthesis, e.g. (II, 4). Pages provided for longer chapters refer to vol. 2 of the Pléiade edition, e.g. (V, 19, 304). I have also consulted the two standard translations of *L'Esprit des lois*. The first is the Thomas Nugent version still available in an abridged edition by co-editor David Carrithers: *The Spirit of Laws by Montesquieu . . .* , David Wallace Carrithers ed. (Berkeley: University of California, 1977). The second is the Cambridge University Press version: Montesquieu, *The Spirit of the Laws*, Anne M. Cohler, Basia Miller, and Harold Stone, trans. and eds. (Cambridge: Cambridge University Press, 1989).

2. Louis Althusser, *Politics and History: Montesquieu, Rousseau. Hegel, and Marx*, Ben Brewster, trans. (London: New Left Review, 1972), 106. An influential American liberal historian, Franklin Ford, adopted a position close to that of Althusser in claiming that Montesquieu was indistinguishable from Boulainvilliers and that Montesquieu was "destined to serve the most reactionary groups in France." See Franklin L. Ford, "The Restatement of the *Thèse Nobiliaire*," chap. 12 in *Robe and Sword: The Regrouping of the French Aristocracy After Louis XIV* (Cambridge: Harvard University Press, 1953), 242-44. In their notes, both Althusser and Ford show they were indebted to Albert Mathiez, "La place de Montesquieu dans l'histoire des doctrines politiques du XVIIIème siecle," *Annales historiques de la Révolution française* 7 (1930): 97-112, deemed by Judith Shklar "an unscholarly but extremely influential article showing Montesquieu to have been a reactionary member of his class." See Judith Shklar, *Montesquieu* (Oxford:

Oxford University Press, 1987), 130. Mathiez endeavored to demolish the claims of Elie Carcassonne's *Montesquieu et le problème de la constitution française au XVIIIème siècle* (Paris, 1927; Geneva: Slatkine Reprints, 1978). Nevertheless, for any sort of liberal recuperation of the political theory of Montesquieu, Carcassonne's book is the essential beginning.

3. Raymond Aron, *Main Currents in Sociological Thought*, 2 vols. (New York: Basic Books, 1965), I, 60.

4. Aristotle, *Nichomachean Ethics*, V, 3; *Politics*, III, 9. For Montesquieu as theorist of Aristotelian moderation and pluralism, see Bernard Manin, "Montesquieu et la politique moderne," *Cahiers de philosophie politique* (Reims: Centre de Philosophie politique de l'Université de Reims, 1985), 157-229; and Harvey C. Mansfield Jr., *Taming the Prince: The Ambivalence of Executive Power* (Baltimore: Johns Hopkins University Press, 1993; orig., 1989). Alan Gilbert pursues a notion of Aristotelian eudaemonism in "Internal Restlessness: Individuality and Community in Montesquieu," *Political Theory* 22, no. 1 (February 1994): 45-70.

5. Daniel Roche, *France in the Enlightenment*, Arthur Goldhammer, trans. (Cambridge: Harvard University Press, 1998), 251-82.

6. François Furet comments sardonically on the mythology of the Revolution in his *Interpreting the French Revolution,* Elborg Forster, trans. (Cambridge: Cambridge University Press, 1981; orig ed., 1978), 83. To be sure, he also subscribes to a version of this story: "the Revolution was a language . . . invented by the French [that constituted] . . . the origin of democracy," 203-4. Furet and Mona Ozouf also remind readers that "the French Revolution, before it became the zero point of French history, the myth of origins of our contemporary society, was once [considered] the culmination of our remotest past." See Mona Ozouf and Francois Furet, "Two Historical Legitimations of Eighteenth Century French Society: Mably and Boulainvilliers," in Francois Furet, *In the Workshop of History*, Jonathan Mandelbaum, trans. (Chicago: University of Chicago Press, 1982), 139.

7. In a magisterial book, Paul Rahe explains what "led the Founders of the first and paradigmatic modern republic to deliberately turn their backs on the ancient model." Rahe is also attentive to the classic temptation that blinds us to those dimensions of the past that were to have no future: "the way that human beings read the past is for the most part decisively shaped by the regime in which they live." See Paul A. Rahe, *Republics Ancient and Modern: Classical Republicanism and the American Revolution* (Chapel Hill: University of North Carolina Press, 1992), 8.

8. According to Simone Goyard-Fabre, citing Léon Duguit, the phrase "separation of powers" cannot be found in *The Spirit of Laws*. Simone Goyard-Fabre, *La Philosophie du droit de Montesquieu* (Paris: Librairie C. Klincksieck, 1973), 322. See also Jean Ehrard, *L'Esprit de mots: Montesquieu en lui-même et parmi les siens* (Geneva: Droz, 1998), 160, 316-17. The jurist Charles Eisenmann argues that there is no "separation" doctrine in *Laws* XI, 6. Instead Montesquieu argues for two rules. First, a negative rule: a given authority should not accumulate the whole of two functions. Second, the positive rule: the

power to legislate must be attributed to a complex organ consisting in as many as three overlapping elements. Thus, English law required the consent of two houses of parliament with the approbation of the king. This interpretation has the advantage of at least describing English parliamentary government, a regime of shared executive and legislative powers. Since the establishment of the U.S. Constitution, Montesquieu's constitutional thought has been identified uniquely with both the strength and the weakness of American style "presidential" regimes as opposed to English style parliamentary governments. This recovery of Montesquieu's intent shows there is a "distribution of powers" doctrine at work in both of these standard models of democratic government. The original articles are Ch. Eisenmann, "*L'Esprit des lois* et la séparation des pouvoirs," in *Mèlanges Carré de Malberg* (Paris: Sirey, 1933) and "La Pensées constitutionnelle de Montesquieu," in *Recueil Sirey du Bi-Centenaire de L'Esprit des lois* (Paris: Sirey, 1952). These articles are reprinted in *Cahiers de philosophie politique* (Reims: Université de Reims, 1985), 3-66. My summary of Eisenmann's two rules relies on Michel Troper, "Charles Eisenmann contre le mythe de la séparation des pouvoirs" in the same volume, 67-79.

9. For a discussion that concludes with two chapters on Montesquieu, see Tzvetan Todorov, *On Human Diversity: Nationalism, Racism, and Exoticism in French Thought*, Catherine Porter, trans. (Cambridge: Harvard University Press, 1993), 353-82.

10. For a full account, see Harold Ellis, *Boulainvilliers and the French Monarchy* (Ithaca: Cornell University Press, 1988). Ellis concedes the aptness of François Furet's advice not to engage in a "Manichean" treatment of these issues, 9-10, 208-9. Nevertheless, throughout he invokes the Manichean label "reactionary" to describe nobilist thought. Moreover, like Boulainvilliers, Montesquieu is evidently a "reactionary" thinker, the evidence for which is partially that he is an "aristocratic" thinker. Even the notion of *esprit général* might be reactionary! See Harold A. Ellis, "Montesquieu's Modern Politics: *The Spirit of the Laws* and the Problem of Modern Monarchy in Old Regime France," *History of Political Thought* 10, no. 4 (winter 1989): 698-99. For an account of Boulainvilliers and Montesquieu that makes them into heroes of the liberal enlightenment, see Guy Chaussinand-Nogaret, *Les citoyens des lumières* (Paris: Editions Complexe, 1994), 17-40. For a supporting view, see Gail Bossenga, "Review Article: Rights and Citizens in the Old Regime," *French Historical Studies* 20, no. 2 (spring 1997): 233.

11. David D. Bien, "Old Regime Origins of Democratic Liberty," in *The French Idea of Freedom: the Old Regime and the Declaration of Rights of 1789*, Dale Van Kley, ed. (Stanford: Stanford University Press, 1994), 33, 37-38.

12. Nicholas Henshall, *The Myth of Absolutism: Change and Continuity in Early Modern European Monarchy* (London: Longman, 1992), 13. This text surveys the sea change in historiographical attitudes that has overtaken the study of ancien régime monarchy. On this account, "absolutism" has been consistently misunderstood.

13. For the adoption of a similar nomenclature in describing the history of the French monarchy, see Emmanuel Le Roy Ladurie, "Temperate Monarchy in Its Last Incarna-

tion," chapter 1, *The Ancien Regime: A History of France, 1610-1774*, Mark Greengrass, trans. (Oxford: Blackwell, 1996), 1-26.

14. *Pensée* 1480 (187), in Pléiade, I, 1355.

15. *Pensée* 1481 (463), in Pléiade, I, 1356. *The Spirit of Laws* may found a new and "impartial" science of politics, but that does not mean, as his notebook shows, that Montesquieu always thought one should ignore issues of character. For a contrasting view, see Judith Shklar, *Ordinary Vices* (Cambridge: Harvard University Press, 1984), 214-15.

16. *Pensée* 595 (1302) in Pléiade, I, 1099. This is a long note on the history of French kings. In tracing monarchy's history through the *Pensées*, I ignore Montesquieu's two essays, *De la politique* and *Réflexions sur le caractère de quelques princes*. See David Carrithers' discussion of them in "Montesquieu's Philosophy of History," *Journal of the History of Ideas* 47, no. 1 (1986): 61-80.

17. *Pensée* 595 (1302), in Pléiade, I, 1100.

18. *Pensée* 595 (1302), in Pléiade, I, 1101.

19. *Pensée* 595 (1302), in Pléiade, I, 1099-1100.

20. *Pensée* 1541 (195), in Pléiade, I, 1372.

21. *Pensée* 609 (1258), in Pléiade, I, 1132.

22. *Pensée* 595 (1302), in Pléiade, I, 1106-7. The reference to "virtue" in a monarchical state might suggest that this was written before, as Montesquieu put it, "I discovered my principles," which assigned virtue to republics and honor to monarchies (*The Spirit of Laws*, Preface).

23. *Pensée* 595 (1302), in Pléiade, I, 1117-18, 1120.

24. Persian Letter 37, in Pléiade, I, 184-85.

25. Montaigne, *The Complete Essays of Montaigne*, Donald M. Frame, trans. (Stanford: Stanford University Press, 1957), Book I, chapter 26, 115; cited hereafter as I, 26, 115.

26. Paul Valery, *Varieté* I et II, (Paris: Gallimard, 1978), 171-86. For a study of Montesquieu's first book that explores many of its other subtleties, see Diana Schaub, *Erotic Liberalism: Women and Revolution in Montesquieu's Persian Letters* (Lanham: Rowman & Littlefield, 1995).

27. Melvin Richter, "Montesquieu's Comparative Analysis of Europe and Asia: Intended and Unintended Consequences," in *L'Europe de Montesquieu*, Alberto Postigliola and Maria Grazia Bottaro Paulumbo, eds. (Napoli: Liguori, 1995), 331. For the prehistory of the term "despotism," see Roger Boesche, "Fearing Monarchs and Merchants: Montesquieu's Two Theories of Despotism," *Western Political Quarterly* 43, no. 4 (1990): 741-42.

28. Jacques-Bénigne Bossuet, *Politics Drawn From the Very Words of Scripture*, Patrick Riley, trans. and ed. (Cambridge: Cambridge University Press, 1990), Book III, Article 1, Sole Proposition 57; Book III, Article 2, 58; Book V, Article 4, 1st Proposition, 160.

29. Simone Goyard-Fabre, *La Philosophie du droit de Montesquieu* (Paris: Klincksieck, 1973), 40; and Nannerl O. Keohane, *Philosophy and the State in France:*

The Renaissance to the Enlightenment (Princeton: Princeton University Press, 1980), 403.

30. *Spicilège* 604 in Pléiade, II, 1390.

31. Simone Goyard-Fabre, *Montesquieu: la nature, les lois, la liberté* (Paris: Presses Universitaires de France, 1993), 32. The cited passages are in chapters 16 and 18 of *Considerations* in Pléiade, II, 158, 173.

32. See Dale K. Van Kley, *The Religious Origins of the French Revolution: From Calvin to the Civil Constitution, 1560–1791* (New Haven: Yale University Press, 1996), 33, 371, also 191–248 and 290-302 (which explores the possibilities for monarchical reinvention after 1774); and Keith Michael Baker, *Inventing the French Revolution: Essays on French Political Culture in the Eighteenth Century* (Cambridge: Cambridge University Press, 1990), 84 and also 113–14, 225-26. Much depends upon what is meant by "absolute." There are three possibilities. First, "absolute" is best understood by invoking Bodin plus Bossuet, but not Montesquieu. Second, it requires only Bodin. Third, "absolute" is adequately invoked by Bodin and Montesquieu without Bossuet, a thesis that this chapter defends.

33. For an informative discussion of many aspects of this "sociability," see Daniel Gordon, *Citizens Without Sovereignty: Equality and Sociability in French Thought, 1670-1789* (Princeton: Princeton University Press, 1994). However much Montesquieu worried that the French monarchy could become despotic, he would not have agreed with Gordon that the French lived under an "authoritarian regime" which threatened their "dignity," (5). For Montesquieu, neither the monarchy's constitutional structure, where intact, nor its fundamental mentality, honor, encouraged authoritarianism or servility. Also see Jürgen Habermas, *The Structural Transformation of the Public Sphere: An Inquiry into a Category of Bourgeois Society*, Thomas Burger and Frederick Lawrence, trans. (Cambridge: MIT Press, 1989; orig. German ed., 1962). On grounds of historical accuracy, one is tempted to substitute "aristocratic" for "bourgeois" in the subtitle.

34. Mona Ozouf and Francois Furet, "Two Historical Legitimations of Eighteenth Century French Society," in Furet, ed., *Workshop of History*, 137.

35. There is an important missing element in this discussion, namely, how on Montesquieu's view gender relations, specifically an allegedly greater access to public life for French women and greater relative equality for them, positively affected the spirit of openness and liberty in French life. See my "The Judgmental Gaze of European Women: Gender, Sexuality, and the Critique of Republican Rule," *Political Theory* 22, no. 1 (February 1994): 25-44.

36. One was published in Lyon, 1579, the other in Paris, 1583. See Louis Desgraves, *Catalogue de la bibliothèque de Montesquieu* (Geneva: Droz, 1954), 169-70, 184, 189.

37. Book I, Section 8, page 25 in the abridged English translation, Jean Bodin, *Six Books of the Commonwealth*, M. J. Tooley, trans. and ed. (New York: Barnes & Noble, 1967, hereafter cited as follows: Bodin, *Six Books*, Tooley, I, 8, 25. Most of the passages cited from Tooley can also be found in Jean Bodin, *On Sovereignty: Four Chapters from The Six Books of the Commonwealth*, Julian Franklin, ed. and trans. (Cambridge: Cam-

bridge University Press, 1992), I, 8, 3; hereafter cited as Bodin, *On Sovereignty*, Franklin, I, 8, 3. Citations from Tooley and Franklin have been compared to the French in Jean Bodin, *Les six livres de la république*, 6 vols. (Paris: Fayard, 1986).

38. Bodin, *Six Books*, Tooley, I, 8, 29; Bodin, *On Sovereignty*, Franklin, I, 8, 13. There is a continuing dispute in the literature about whether Bodin's thought can be extricated from his theological obsessions. In a commendable article, Dan Engster proclaims that to eliminate God from Bodin's theory of the state is like eliminating references to whales in the novel *Moby Dick*. But in another fine piece Denis Richet proclaims "I think there is in Bodin, despite its Christian vision, a certain secularization and rationalization of the notion of the state." I agree with the latter. (There may be lots of whales in *Moby Dick*, but is it really about whales?) See Dan Engster, "Jean Bodin, Scepticism, and Absolute Sovereignty," *History of Political Thought* 17, no. 4 (winter 1996): 477, 491; and Denis Richet, "La Monarchie au travail sur elle-même," in Keith Baker et al, eds., *The French Revolution and the Creation of Modern Political Culture*, vol. I, *The Political Culture of the Old Regime, Keith Baker, ed.* (Oxford: Pergamon Press, 1987), 34.

39. Bodin, *Six Books*, Tooley, I, 8, 28; Bodin, *On Sovereignty*, Franklin, I, 8, 12.

40. Bodin, *Six Books*, Tooley, I, 10, 42-43; Bodin, *On Sovereignty*, Franklin, I, 10, 49, 51, 56.

41. Bodin, *Six Books*, Tooley, I, 8, 30, 32; Bodin, *On Sovereignty*, Franklin, I, 8, 14, 23.

42. Bodin, *Six Books*, Tooley, II, 2, 56.

43. In the *Social Contract*, Book II is devoted to sovereignty which is, following Bodin, "inalienable," ch. 1, and "indivisible," ch. 2. Chapter three introduces the "general will," a concept borrowed from Montesquieu who invokes it in the first essay on England, *The Spirit of Laws* Book XI, ch. 6. Rousseau waits until Book III, ch. 1 of the *Social Contract* to introduce "government." It matches the Bodinian distinction between the sovereign lawgiver and a dependent government that has only a "borrowed and subordinate life." See Jean-Jacques Rousseau, *The Social Contract and Other Writings*, Victor Gourevitch, ed. and trans. (Cambridge: Cambridge University Press, 1997), 86.

44. Judith Shklar, "Political Theory and the Rule of Law," in Judith Shklar, *Political Thought and Political Thinkers*, Stanley Hoffmann, ed. (Chicago: University of Chicago Press, 1998), 22-25.

45. Some interpreters find in Montesquieu relief from the "statist" implications of Bodin, while others find in Bodin relief from a Montesquieu who defends "feudal privilege" against properly constituted state authority. For the latter, see Blandine Kriegel, especially *The State and the Rule of Law*, Marc A. LePain and Jeffrey C. Cohen, trans. (Princeton: Princeton University Press, 1995), 17-23, 35; and "L'Idée républicaine sous l'Ancien Régime," *Philosophie Politique*, 4 (1993): 41. Though Bodin is less opposed to "*les ordres privilégés*" and Montesquieu less opposed to sovereign authority than her view allows, there is much to commend in this work.

46. This interpretation of Montesquieu is indebted to Stephen Holmes's work on Bodin. See "The Constitution of Sovereignty in Jean Bodin," in Stephen Holmes, *Pas-*

sions and Constraints: On the Theory of Liberal Democracy (Chicago: University of Chicago Press, 1995), 100-33. Another text to which I am indebted on these issues, though for different interpretive reasons, is Pierre Manent, "Les théoriciens de la monarchie: Bodin et Montesquieu," in *Les Monarchies*, Emmanuel Le Roy Ladurie, ed. (Paris: Presses Universitaires de France, 1986), 91-99. Nannerl Keohane points as well to Montesquieu's Bodinian argument without linking it explicitly to Bodin. See Keohane, *Philosophy and the State in France*, 405.

47. Bodin, *Six Books*, Tooley, I, 8, 32; Bodin, *On Sovereignty*, Franklin, I, 8, 23.

48. Bodin, *Les six livres*, Fayard (French) edition, II, 2, 34-35. Also see Richet, "La Monarchie au travail sur elle-même," *The Political Culture of the Old Regime,* Keith Baker, ed., 34.

49. Bodin, *Six Books*, Tooley, I, 10, 40, 42; Bodin, *On Sovereignty*, Franklin, I, 10, 47, 50.

50. Henshall, *The Myth of Absolutism*, 209. Despite *absolutisme* entering into general usage only after 1823, it can be found, Dale Van Kley suggests, as early as 1788 in Condorcet (personal communication).

51. Henshall, *The Myth of Absolutism*, 205.

52. *Pensée* 595 (1302) in Pléiade, I, 1113.

53. On the cognate expressions for sovereignty, see See Jean Ehrard, *L'Esprit des mots*, 147-60.

54. Bodin, *Six Books*, Tooley, I, 8, 32; Bodin, *On Sovereignty*, Franklin, I, 8, 23.

55. On the eve of the revolution, Bailey Stone explains, the high court of Nancy was only "recently" designated a Parlement, thus bringing the number of provincial Parlements up to twelve. In addition, the sovereign councils in German-speaking Colmar on the eastern border and in Roussillon in the Pyrenees were "Parlements in all but name." See Bailey Stone, *The French Parlements and the Crisis of the Old Regime* (Chapel Hill: University of North Carolina Press, 1986), 17-18, 161.

56. Le Roy Ladurie, *The Ancien Régime*, 97.

57 . Julian Swann, *Politics and the Parlement of Paris under Louis XV, 1754-1774* (Cambridge: Cambridge University Press, 1995), 19. See also Stone, *The French Parlements*, 18.

58. Dale Van Kley, *The Religious Origins of the French Revolution,* 108-14. See also Rebecca Kingston, chapter 9 in this volume.

59. Roland E. Mousnier, *The Institutions of France Under the Absolute Monarchy 1598-1789*, Brian Pearce, trans. (Chicago: University of Chicago Press, 1979), 482-83, 534, 544; and François Furet, "Feudal System," in François Furet and Mona Ozouf, *A Critical Dictionary of the French Revolution,* Arthur Goldhammer, trans. (Cambridge: Harvard University Press, 1989), 687.

60. David D. Bien, "Offices, Corps, and a System of State Credit: The Uses of Privilege under the Ancien Regime," in *The Political Culture of the Old Regime*, Keith Baker, ed., 95.

61. Mousnier, *The Institutions of France*, 517-28. Each local situation was potentially so different that one must use caution and not assume too quickly that such a sketch applies uniformly throughout France and in every time period.

62. Jürgen Habermas, *Theory of Communicative Action*, vol. II: *System and Lifeworld: A Critique of Functionalist Reason*, Thomas McCarthy, trans. (Boston, Beacon Press, 1987).

63. J. H. Shennan, *The Parlement of Paris* (London: Eyre & Spottiswoode, 1968), 308.

64. Cited in Richet, "La monarchie au travail sur elle-même?" *The Political Culture of the Old Regime*, Keith Baker, ed., 37. Richet believes that Montesquieu would have resisted this formula whereas it seems to me that, if counsel is understood as what Parlements provide, the royalist Moreau's statement is perfectly compatible with Montesquieu's argument.

65. Swann, *Politics and the Parlement of Paris*, 35, 23-24; Stone, *The French Parlements*, 19. The bad reputation of these judges stems not solely from their censorship of enlightenment texts but also from notorious cases such as the false condemnation, torture, and execution of Calas (which aroused Voltaire's protests) and the execution of the chevalier de La Barre for sacrilege.

66. William Doyle, "The Parlements," in *The Political Culture of the Ancien Régime*, Keith Baker, ed., 158.

67. John Rogister, *Louis XV and the Parlement of Paris, 1737-1755* (Cambridge: Cambridge University Press, 1995), 21.

68. Sarah Hanley, *The Lit de Justice of the Kings of France: Constitutional Ideology in Legend, Ritual, and Discourse,* (Princeton: Princeton University Press, 1983), 342. I thank Joan Scott for bringing this work to my attention.

69. Swann, *Politics and the Parlement of Paris*, 73. The year after Montesquieu's death in 1755 saw a renewal of the practice. During the remainder of Louis XV's reign, *lits de justice* were held in August and December, 1756, and in 1759, 1761, 1763, 1768, 1770, and 1771.

70. Cited in Doyle, "The Parlements," in *Political Culture of the Ancien Régime*, Keith Baker, ed., 162.

71. Doyle, "The Parlements," in *Political Culture of the Ancien Régime*, 158.

72. William Doyle, *Officers, Nobles and Revolutionaries: Essays on Eighteenth-Century France* (London: Hambledon Press, 1995), 22.

73. Shennan, *The Parlement of Paris*, 311; and Roger Bickart, *Les Parlements et la notion de souveraineté nationale au XVIIIème siècle* (Paris: Felix Alcan, 1932), 89, 101.

74. Durand Echeverria, *The Maupeou Revolution: A Study in the History of Libertarianism, France, 1770-1774* (Baton Rouge: Louisiana State University Press, 1985), 87-89.

75. Rogister, *Louis XV and the Parlement of Paris*, 33, 52.

76. See Shennan, *The Parlement of Paris*, 282, 286, 290, 298, and 305.

77. So named in the Garnier as well as in the Nagel edition. See below and as well, Montesquieu, *De l'esprit des lois*, Robert Derathé, ed. (Paris: Garnier, 1973), II, 561.

78. Robert Shackleton, *Montesquieu: A Critical Biography* (Oxford: Oxford University Press, 1961), 87 note. The first volume of the Nagel *Œuvres* is a facsimile of the 1758 edition. André Masson observes that the 1757 and 1758 editions of the collected works neither explain how Richer, Moreau, and Secondat collaborated nor say anything constructive about their claim to have followed the last instructions and corrections of the deceased author. What little information we have comes from the 1767 edition and from the Plasson edition of 1796 (see Nagel, I., D-E). That Montesquieu left detailed instructions for an index seems unlikely. There is no index in the first edition (1748) of *The Spirit of* Laws. A 1749 edition, or rather the reprint of 1750 (*De l'esprit des* lois, Genève: Barrillot & Fils, 1750, Firestone Library Rare Books Collection, Princeton University) has a limited index in which one finds under "Parlement" only brief references to XXVIII, 39, and not the long essay one finds in the *Table analytique*.

79. Carcassonne, *Montesquieu et le problème de la constitution française,* 142, 154, 179, 191, 388.

80. Dale K. Van Kley, *The Damiens Affair and the Unraveling of the Ancien Regime, 1750-1770* (Princeton: Princeton University Press, 1984), 202, 210 and Van Kley, *The Religious Origins of the French Revolution*, 237-40.

81. Edmond Préclin, *Les jansenistes du dix-huitième siècle et la Constitution civile du clergé: Le developpement du richerisme, sa propagation dans le bas clergé* (Paris, 1929), 416, 432. Richerism refers to the doctrines of Edmond Richer, not to François Richer.

82. Dale Van Kley, personal communication, June 2000.

83. David A. Bell, *Lawyers and Citizens: The Making of a Political Elite in Old Regime France* (New York: Oxford University Press, 1994), 130.

84. Van Kley, *The Religious Origins of the French Revolution*, 239.

85. Chaussinand-Nogaret, *Le citoyen des lumières*, 82.

86. *Pensée* 1337 (852), in Pléiade, I, 1321.

87. *Pensée* 1326 (730), Pléiade, I, 1320.

88. R. W. Greaves, "Religion," in *The Old Regime, 1713-63*, Volume VII of *The New Cambridge Modern History*, J. O. Lindsay, ed. (Cambridge: Cambridge University Press, 1957), 116.

89. "Memoir on the Constitution," in Pléiade, II, 1221, 1217. On Montesquieu's interview with Louis XV, see Rogister, *Louis XV and the Parlement of Paris*, 198, 206 and Shackleton, *Montesquieu*, 384-85.

90. Pléiade, II, 1221.

91. Pléiade, II, 1220.

92. Pléiade, II, 1219, 1217. See also Rebecca Kingston, chapter 9 in this volume.

93. Montesquieu to Durey de Meinières, July 9, 1753, in Nagel, III, 1467-68.

94. Ehrard, *L'Esprit des mots*, 153.

95. *Œuvres complètes de Montesquieu*, Nagel, III, 1468.

96. William Doyle, *The Parlement of Bordeaux at the End of the Old Regime, 1717-1790* (London: Ernest Benn, 1974), 217. For a more recent work on the topic, see Kingston, *Montesquieu and the Parlement of Bordeaux* (Geneva: Droz, 1996).

97. For the post 1775 conservative interpretation of Montesquieu, see Ford, *Robe and Sword*, 242-44, and Van Kley, *Religious Origins of the French Revolution*, 297-99, 302.

98. Doyle, *The Parlement of Bordeaux*, 217.

99. Edmund Burke, *Reflections on the Revolution in France*, J. G. A. Pocock, ed. (Indianapolis: Hackett, 1987), 31-32.

100. Alexis de Tocqueville, *Democracy in America*, Phillips Bradley, ed., 2 vols. (New York: Knopf, 1994), I, 340, 355.

101. For a contemporary analysis of the inadequacies of the theories of "interest" and "strain" in comparison with the deployment of the "concepts" that people themselves use to interpret their actions, see Clifford Geertz's classic essay "Ideology As a Cultural System" in Geertz, *The Interpretation of Cultures* (New York: Basic Books, 1973), 201 ff., 229. The pleasures of interacting with Cliff Geertz in seminar discussions at the Institute for Advanced Study, 1998-99, led me to the dubious thought (for a political theorist) that perhaps juridical discourse always requires a supplement.

102. *Pensée* 1382 (376) in Pléiade, I, 1327.

103. For the popular history of honor, see Robert A. Nye, *Masculinity and Male Codes of Honor in Modern France* (New York: Oxford University Press, 1993).

104. See my "The Particulars of a Universal Politics: Hegel's Adaptation of Montesquieu's Typology," *American Political Science Review* 78, no. 1 (March 1984): 179-188.

105. *Considerations*, chap. 2, in Pléiade, II, 203.

106. When Montesquieu speaks of virtue, "it can be demonstrated," Pierre Manent concludes, "he means the virtues we call moral or Christian." See Pierre Manent, *The City of Man*, Marc A. LePain, trans. (Princeton: Princeton University Press, 1998), 22.

107. See Jeffrey W. Merrick, *The Desacralization of the French Monarchy in the Eighteenth Century* (Baton Rouge: Louisiana State Press, 1990).

108. Roche, *France in the Enlightenment*, 254-55.

109. Michael Oakeshott, *On Human Conduct* (Oxford: Clarendon Press, 1975), 246-51. For another effort to theorize the civil character of European monarchies and their relevant successor states, see my "Civic Identity in the Juridical Society," *Political Theory* 11, no. 1 (February 1983): 117-32.

110. George Kateb, "Remarks on the Procedures of Constitutional Democracy," *The Inner Ocean: Individualism and Democratic Culture* (Ithaca: Cornell University Press, 1992), 62, 68. Despite significant differences in sensibility, George Kateb provides the "progressive" and Michael Oakeshott the "conservative" interpretation of those liberal ideals for which *The Spirit of Laws* is a classic text.

111. Carcassonne, *Montesquieu et le problème de la constitution française*, 81. Also cited by Manent in "Les théoriciens de la monarchie," 98.

112. Carcassonne, *Montesquieu et le problème de la constitution française*, 81.

113. For another discussion of honor, see the well-argued case of Sharon Krause, "The Politics of Distinction and Disobedience: Honor and the Defense of Liberty in Montesquieu," *Polity* 31, no. 3 (Spring 1999): 469-99.

114. C. B. A. Behrens, *The Ancien Regime* (New York: Harcourt Brace Jovanovich, 1967), 71-74.

115. Doyle, *The Ancien Regime*, (London: Macmillan, 1986), 24.

116. David D. Bien, "Manufacturing Nobles: the Chancelleries of France to 1789," *Journal of Modern History* 61 (1989): 445-86.

117. Roche, *France in the Enlightenment*, 411. Citing Roland Mousnier, William Doyle says that "the original number of fifty-nine had swollen to 506 by 1655." See also W. Doyle, *Venality: The Sale of Offices in Eighteenth-Century France* (Oxford: Clarendon Press, 1996), 12-13.

118. David Bien, "Aristocracy," in *A Critical Dictionary of the French Revolution*, François Furet and Mona Ozouf, eds., Arthur Goldhammer, trans. (Cambridge: Harvard University Press, 1989), 620.

119. Julian Swann, "The French Nobility, 1715-1789," *The European Nobilities in the Seventeenth and Eighteenth Centuries,* vol. I, *Western Europe*, H. M. Scott, ed. (London: Longman, 1995), 142.

120. Guy Chaussinant-Nogaret, *The Nobility in the Eighteenth Century: From Feudalism to Enlightenment*, William Doyle, trans. (Cambridge: Cambridge University Press, 1985), 87. See also Swann, "The French Nobility, 1715-1789, " 142-43.

121. Chaussinant-Nogaret, *The Nobility in the Eighteenth Century*, 114. See also Simon Schama, *Citizens: A Chronicle of the French Revolution* (New York: Knopf, 1989), 116-19.

122. G. Chaussinant-Nogaret, *The Nobility in the Eighteenth Century*, 22, 170.

123. *Pensée* 1420 (767), in Pléiade, I, 1334; *The Spirit of Laws* XIX, 27, 581.

124. Montaigne, *The Complete Essays*, II, 16, 474 and Jean-Jacques Rousseau, *The Discourses and Other Early Political Writing*, Victor Gourevitch, ed. (Cambridge: Cambridge University Press), 187. For Montesquieu's understanding of Christian morality, see Shklar, *Ordinary Vices,* 239-40.

125. For another discussion of "diversity" in Montesquieu, see C. P. Courtney, "Montesquieu and the Problem of 'la diversité'" in *Enlightenment Essays in Memory of Robert Shackleton* , Giles Barber and C. P. Courtney, eds. (Oxford: Voltaire Foundation, 1988), 61-81. See also Courtney, chapter 1 in this volume.

126. *Pensée* 604 (1253); 551 (1675) in Pléiade, I, 1062-66, 1129-31. See also Shklar, *Montesquieu*, 77.

127. Anthony J. Lynch, "Montesquieu and the Ecclesiastical Critics of *L'Esprit des lois*," *Journal of the History of Ideas* 38, no. 3 (1977): 487-500.

128. Roger Chartier, *The Cultural Origins of the French Revolution*, Lydia G. Cochrane, trans. (Durham: Duke University Press, 1991), 195-97; and David A. Bell, "The 'Public Sphere,' the State, and the World of Law in Eighteenth Century France," *French Historical Studies* 17, no. 4 (fall 1992): 925-26.

129. Mark Hulliung, *Montesquieu and the Old Regime* (Berkeley: University of California, 1976), ix, 29, and more generally 25-53; Thomas L. Pangle, *Montesquieu's Philosophy of Liberalism: A Commentary on* The Spirit of the Laws (Chicago: University of Chicago, 1973), 107-60, 298; and Alan Gilbert, "Internal Restlessness: Individuality and Community in Montesquieu," 45, 47, 51, 56-57, 66.

130. Philippe d'Iribaine, *La Logique de l'honneur: Gestion des enterprises et traditions nationales* (Paris: Seuil, 1989).

131. Montaigne, *The Complete Essays*, III, 1, 607, 609-10.

Chapter Five

Despotism in *The Spirit of Laws*

Sharon Krause

The concept of despotism provides a key that opens *The Spirit of Laws* and il-luminates the sometimes shadowy contours of Montesquieu's political philoso-phy. Despotism has been characterized as "the basis"[1] and "the cutting edge"[2] of Montesquieu's political theory, and as the unifying theme of his corpus as a whole.[3] It is the one phenomenon that is categorically disparaged in a work that otherwise resists categorical judgments,[4] so that while readers may disagree about which regime Montesquieu prefers,[5] there can be no doubt about which one he most despises.[6] Besides being one type of regime, with a particular insti-tutional structure and motivating principle, despotism refers to the universal tendency of political power to overreach its bounds, a tendency that runs through governments of all types and that has roots in human nature itself.[7] In-deed, it is because "the soul has such a taste for dominating other souls" (XXVIII, 41) that anyone who has power is led to abuse it, continuing until he finds limits (XI, 4).[8] Despotism as a common tendency of politics and persons thus inspires Montesquieu's greatest contribution to liberalism, the separation of powers.

The concept of despotism also provides clues to Montesquieu's view of the ends of politics and the nature of the human good. His reluctance to specify di-rectly a comprehensive conception of human nature, including human ends, is well known. He resists doing so partly because he believes that human diversity runs deep, as the influence of particular cultural traditions "can be so great that it changes, so to speak, the whole genius of human nature. This is the reason that man is so difficult to define."[9] In part, too, he is skeptical about the human capacity to know metaphysical essences,[10] and wary of the practical implications of perfectionism in politics.[11] Montesquieu largely accepts the early modern view that the purpose of politics is political liberty understood as security, not the realization of a human *telos*. For him, liberty rests on the protection, not the perfection, of the individual.[12] Yet Montesquieu does not simply replace the ancient idea of a human *telos* with the modern idea of natural rights. Although he mentions natural rights occasionally in *The Spirit of Laws*, he remains as reluctant to prescribe universal standards of natural right as to dictate universal human ends. Without such a standard, however, Montesquieu's liberal philosophy as a whole is difficult to justify. Why is a constitution of separate powers better than the rule of an unlimited will, after all? What justifies the liberty that moderate government provides? Because he does not give a defense of universal natural rights or offer an explicit statement of human ends, Montesquieu has been faulted for failing to justify his preference for moderate government.[13] His description of the human condition under despotic government implicitly contains the needed justification, however. By showing us what despotism denies and debases in human beings, Montesquieu inspires us to think about the talents and the ambitions, the courage, the artistry, and the knowledge of which we are capable—even "those virtues that give greatness to the soul" (V, 12). The *summum malum* of despotism therefore functions as a negative model that contains positive implications for understanding human nature and human ends, and so suggests a justification for political liberty and for Montesquieu's political philosophy as a whole.

This chapter examines the meaning and the significance of despotism in *The Spirit of Laws*. Following a brief account of the background of the term, Montesquieu's treatment of the government of despotism is elaborated, including its nature, principle, limits, and corruptions. A tension between the nature of despotism and its principle sets the most forceful limit on despotic governments and causes their inevitable corruption. Additionally, Montesquieu's association between despotism and the empires of the East is considered in light of recent critiques of "Orientalism." Although Montesquieu uses the travel literature selectively and exaggerates the links between despotism and the governments of Asia, he is no advocate of European imperialism, the justification of which is thought to be a central purpose of "Orientalism." Ironically, Montesquieu's exaggeration of the specific connections between despotism and the East makes it possible for him to show that despotism poses a *universal* danger. Finally, the relationship between despotism and nature is examined, including nature understood as climate and physical terrain and nature understood as human nature. Although Montesquieu regards despotism as an assault on human nature, he also shows it to be the most natural form of government, not least because it expresses fundamental features of human nature. By illuminating the features of human nature that despotism expresses and those it denies, Montesquieu shows us why political liberty is worth pursuing, and so gives us reason to study the spirit of laws.

Sources of "Despotism"

Montesquieu did not invent the term "despotism," but he systematized it and established the definition of despotism that came to predominate in the eighteenth century.[14] In doing so, he both drew on and departed from traditional interpretations of the word. The Greeks had applied the term *despotes* to the head of the household, despotic rule being the command of household slaves. As such, it was not itself a term of derision, as despotic rule could be legitimate if exercised over the class of persons regarded as "natural" slaves.[15] Aristotle did use the word derisively in his *Politics*, however, in describing the degenerate stage of each of the three regimes, including the rule of tyranny in the third book, that of the overbearing *demos* in the fourth book, and that of oligarchy in the fifth book. Each of these political degenerations was tied to the abandonment of law, as when "the multitude has authority and not the law."[16] Under such circumstances, the citizens, by nature free, were treated as though they were slaves because subjected to an unregulated ruling will.[17] Thus, despotic rule acquired a negative connotation when it was applied to the rule of free men rather than "natural" slaves. In this way, the legitimate place of the despot was limited to the private sphere.[18] The *political* despot for Aristotle was by nature disreputable, and a king ruling as a despot was considered a tyrant. Tyranny, which was spoken of in the political context more frequently than despotism, could be remedied by removing the tyrant because the malady was in him, not in the people or in the institutional structure of the regime. For although a tyrant ruling with despotic power might treat his subjects as slaves, they were not by nature slaves, and so were capable of resistance and could resume the role of citizens or subjects after the tyrant's expulsion.

Hobbes rejected the Aristotelian distinction between free persons and natural slaves on the grounds that "when all is reckoned together the difference between man and man is not so considerable as that one man can thereupon claim to himself any benefit to which another may not pretend as well as he."[19] The consequence of natural equality, however, was not so much to discredit the private rule of despots as to make the political despot reputable. All persons, being equal, were equally in need of the protection of an absolute sovereign, and despotic government was just one particular manifestation of this general form. What Hobbes called "despoticall" government originated in conquest, but was legitimated by the covenant of obedience given by the vanquished to the victor.[20] The consent of the vanquished was in principle indistinguishable from the consent of the parties to a Commonwealth by Institution. Despotic rule was no different from the rule of a government "by Institution of the people assembled," because in both cases consent was driven by fear—in the one case the loser's fear of the winning army, in the other case the individual's fear of other persons. Both instances of consent were the products of a state of war, "which is necessarily consequent . . . to the naturall Passions of men."[21] The only solution to the state of war was the establishment of a single sovereign sufficiently strong to make his subjects too afraid of him to be dangerous to each other. The fear of one another or of external enemies, which made individuals consent to be ruled, was replaced by fear of the king, which made them obedient. This fear required unlimited power for the sovereign, as any limitation on his power, including the limitations imposed by laws, would limit his capacity to terrify and so to protect his subjects. The fear engendered by the sovereign's unlimited power had an emancipatory effect on individuals because it produced tranquillity where there had been war, and so established security. "Despoticall" rule, although absolute, was not fundamentally distinct from political rule in general, and not to be disdained. Hobbes thus made political despotism reputable and legitimate by detaching it from the idea of slavery, while preserving the older notion of rule not limited by laws, and introducing the element of fear.

In France, the term *despotique* came into use during the reign of Louis XIV, and was employed most often by his aristocratic opponents, with strongly negative connotations. Among the first to use the word were the pamphleteers of the Fronde (1648-53), an aristocratic uprising occasioned by the minister Mazarin's attacks on the claim of privileged bodies, especially the Parlements, to refuse obedience to the crown and to control royal administration at the local level.[22] The *frondeurs* accused Mazarin of attempting to make France into a *monarchie despotique*,[23] which they associated with both arbitrary rule and the servitude of subjects. This usage combined the idea of rule over slaves, derived from the Aristotelian definition, with Hobbes' idea of political absolutism. In 1689-90 the Huguenot publication, *Les soupirs de la France esclave, qui aspire après la liberté*, drew on the criticism of the earlier pamphleteers, faulting the king for "the oppression of the church, the parlements, the nobility, and the towns," and giving prominent place to the term "despotic power" (*pouvoir despotique*).[24] The anonymous author went further than his predecessors had gone, however, expanding the definition to include religious intolerance, the bureaucratic centralization of political authority, aggressive foreign policy, and mercantilist mismanagement of financial affairs.[25] Shortly thereafter the noun, *despotisme*, indicating a system of government, rather than a quality of personal rule, was given currency by Pierre Bayle in his *Réponse aux questions d'un provincial* (1704).[26] The new term was used widely in the final years of Louis XIV's reign by opponents of his absolute power, such as Fénelon, St. Simon, and Boulainvilliers, to indicate a political order characterized by the qualities enumerated in *Les soupirs*.[27] By the middle of the eighteenth century, then, the central features of the concept of despotism included the arbitrary rule of a single sovereign who was limited by neither law nor intermediary bodies, the political slavery of the ruled, the centralization of power, financial mismanagement, religious intolerance, and military aggressiveness.

Montesquieu systematically elaborated these features of despotism in *The Spirit of Laws*. In doing so, he established its meaning so definitively in the new public mind of the *lumières* that d'Alembert asked him to contribute an entry on despotism to *l'Encyclopédie*.[28] Montesquieu's concept of despotism preserves Aristotle's association between despotic rule and lawlessness, but makes lawlessness a quality of the political order as a whole rather than the ruler. He likewise draws on the Aristotelian link between despotic rule and slavery, but because he rejects the idea of natural slavery he regards all forms of despotic rule as illegitimate. Whereas for Aristotle despotic rule was called for by the presence of natural slaves, Montesquieu believes that despotism *creates* slaves where there should be none. And while Aristotle believed that tyranny could be remedied by removing the corrupt tyrant, for Montesquieu the correction of despotic rule is more complex because corruption permeates the system of despotism as a whole, its institutions and its subjects, as well as its ruler. To slavery and lawlessness, Montesquieu adds the Hobbesian principle of fear, a principle that earlier treatments of despotism in France had not emphasized. Montesquieu acknowledges the unifying and the tranquilizing force of fear, which for Hobbes legitimated its use, but he does not equate unity or tranquillity with liberty.[29] He rejects Hobbes' identification of liberty with power and shows not the emancipating effect of fear but its debasement of human beings and politics. Finally, Montesquieu transforms the polemics of the French pamphleteers into political philosophy. Seeking to explain rather than simply to accuse, he shows the causes and the consequences of despotism, illuminating its particular instances by means of his general principles.

The Nature of Despotism

Montesquieu elaborates three types of government in Books II-VIII of *The Spirit of Laws,* distinguishing the "nature" of each government from its "principle."[30] The nature of a government is the particular institutional structure that "makes it what it is." The principle is the "human passions that make it move" (III, 1). The nature of republican government is that the people as a body, or a portion of the people, has sovereign power. Monarchical government is that in which one alone governs by fixed and established laws. In despotic government, one rules alone, but by his will and caprices, rather than by law (II, 1). Montesquieu's typology of regimes distinguishes between forms of rule on the basis of the number of rulers and the presence or absence of fixed, established laws. By contrast, Aristotle had classified regimes on the basis of the number of rulers together with the presence or absence of virtue.[31] Montesquieu's standard of classification departs from that older one by replacing the virtue of rulers with the legality of the system. He criticizes Aristotle's classification for making distinctions on the basis of "accidental things (*des choses d'accident)*, such as the virtues or vices of the prince" (XI, 9).[32] Virtues and vices are accidental in the sense of being contingent, and therefore not to be relied upon. Even when present, the virtue of a ruler does not predict the outcome of his rule as reliably as does the structure of the government. To predict how a monarch will rule, it is better to know the institutional channels through which power flows than to know the content of his character. The structure of the regime and the laws, not the character of rulers, is the most reliable basis for classification.

One implication of Montesquieu's revised typology is that good government is possible without the cultivation of virtue, or the perfection of the soul. This justifies removing the care of souls from the province of political authority, and so erecting a boundary between the public and the private spheres, a purpose that Montesquieu shares with earlier liberals such as Locke.[33] At the same time, by discounting the role of virtue, Montesquieu's typology suggests that immoderate government is not simply the product of vice. Despotism does not result from the presence of a particularly vicious ruler, but instead poses a more general threat. For if personal vice is not a precondition of despotic rule, then the pool of potential despots is much increased, even unlimited. It is not only the vicious, but *anyone*, Montesquieu says, who is led to abuse power when he has it. Anyone who has power will continue to expand it until he finds limits (XI, 4). Consequently, despotism cannot be dismissed easily as the specific corruption of a particular regime, but instead represents an entrenched possibility of politics. And if despotism is not produced by the vice of the ruler, then it may be possible for despotism to occur even in the regime of a benevolent prince. Thus, a monarch's public displays of benevolence would not be sufficient to distinguish him from a despot.

For Montesquieu's contemporaries, his typology also raised a question as to the status of France. France was ruled by "one alone," but since the typology includes two regimes in which a prince rules alone, one was forced to consider whether the French monarch ruled by law or merely by capricious will. Throughout *The Spirit of Laws,* Montesquieu explicitly associates France with monarchical government, but implicitly he calls to mind the resemblances between French monarchy and despotism. Ironically, by distinguishing monarchy from despotism Montesquieu makes us think about them together, and for the Frenchmen of his day this inevitably meant thinking about them together in relation to France.[34] The fact that Montesquieu's typology invites this association explains in part why Voltaire objected so strongly to it. Voltaire, a defender of royal absolutism, regarded despotism not as a separate regime, but as a corrupt form of absolute monarchy because for him it was not unlimited rule that was dangerous but *unenlightened* rule.[35] The ideal government would not limit power but rationalize it. Accordingly, the proper standard for distinguishing a monarch from a tyrant was reason rather than law. Because he rejected external limitations on sovereign power, Voltaire also opposed the claims of the nobility to mediate the crown's authority. And he considered Montesquieu's suggestive associations between despotism and the French crown incendiary and responsible for stirring up a rebellious spirit among the Parlements.[36] Thus the typology of regimes presented in Book II introduces legality as a new standard for distinguishing forms of rule, implies that despotism poses a general threat to all regimes, and raises questions about the potentially despotic character of monarchy in France.

After defining the nature of the three regimes, Montesquieu discusses the laws relative to each one. Not surprisingly, the description of the laws relative to the nature of despotic states is brief, since despotism is the regime that by definition lacks fixed, established laws.[37] There *is* one "fundamental law" (*une loi fondamentale*) in this state, however, which is that the one who exercises power has it exercised by another (II, 5). The establishment of a vizir is a fundamental law because despots naturally abandon the public business, preferring instead the business of their private pleasures. The unlimited political power of a despot makes everything that is desirable available for his personal use, and the plethora of pleasures that results proves distracting. If he is to devote himself to his pleasures, the despot must put someone else in charge of governing. And it must be one person, because if the public business were entrusted to several different persons, disputes would arise between them and he would be called back to administration. Thus the despot is compelled by the power of his passions to appoint a deputy. The inevitability of the establishment of a vizir results from the equally predictable effects of the unlimited pursuit of sensual and material pleasures. The "fundamental law" of despotic government is fundamental in the sense of being irresistible, even necessary.

It differs in this respect from the fundamental laws of republics and monarchies. In republican government, for instance, the laws establishing the right to vote are fundamental because they constitute the regime as a republic, and as a particular type of republic depending on what portion of the population is accorded the vote. These laws result from the choices of legislators (II, 2). Similarly, a fundamental law of monarchy is the balance of power established between the intermediary bodies and the crown (II, 4), a balance that is in no way inevitable but rather represents "a masterpiece of legislation that circumstance rarely produces and that prudence rarely is permitted to produce" (V, 14). The fundamental laws of republics and monarchies are the products of human art and deliberation. But despots, being "intoxicated with pleasures" and having "given themselves up to the most brutal passions," act mainly on impulse rather than deliberation or art (II, 5). There the fundamental law is fundamental in the sense of being unavoidable. It calls to mind the "invariable" laws of the physical world, of which Montesquieu speaks in Book I, and which he distinguishes from the civil and political laws found in the "intelligent world" (I, 1). That is, the fundamental law of despotism resembles the general laws of motion that govern the material world more closely than the laws by which human beings govern themselves. In this sense, it expresses the necessity that permeates despotic governments, rather than the art and deliberation that shape moderate regimes.[38] Thus, in moving from the fundamental laws of republican and monarchical regimes to the fundamental law of despotism in Book II, Montesquieu effects subtle shifts in the meaning of both "fundamental" and "law."

The Principle of Despotism

The "principle" of despotic government, or the human passion that sets it in motion, is fear. The despot's subjects fear him because he can destroy them instantly (III, 9), while *he* fears his army (V, 14) and the loss of his pleasures.[39] The fear that permeates despotism arises naturally, even automatically, from threats and chastisements (III, 5). For while fear may be a rational response to the raised arm of the despotic prince, there is more impulse in it than deliberation. Fear has no need of education because it is so well supported by instinct, and consequently education "is in some fashion null" in despotism (IV, 3). Education is not only unnecessary, but potentially dangerous, since an education in ideas would "elevate the heart," which could bring down the despot (IV, 3). The spread of knowledge is dangerous to a despot because it could dispel his subjects' fear. The extreme obedience that the despot requires rests on the ignorance of his subjects (III, 3). The subjects, who are "timid, ignorant, and worn down" (V, 14), aim only for the most meager existence. Too insecure to think of living well, they have mere living as their sole purpose. And without education, their actions lack principled ends, such as honor, virtue, even liberty itself. Thus, fear produces the other main motive that operates in despotism, a desire for the satisfaction of material needs, or "the conveniences of life" (V, 17-18; XV, 1).[40]

Fear not only arises automatically in despotism, but also has automatic effects. Fear compels compliance, so that "the prince's will, once known, must have its effect as infallibly as a ball thrown against another ball must have its effect" (III, 10). Hobbes was correct to count fear as "the passion to be reckoned on,"[41] for it imposes pressures on human actions that make them predictable, in contrast to the uncertainties that result from deliberation and choice. As against Hobbes, however, who regarded the predictability of human behavior as a precondition of the "science of natural justice" that established individual security and thus liberty,[42] Montesquieu associates perfectly predictable behavior with the mechanistic responses of beasts and the forced compliance of slaves.[43] Thus, the despot rules his subjects as though instructing a beast (V, 14), for in despotism "the portion of men, like that of beasts, is instinct, obedience, and chastisement" (III, 10). There, too, "men are all slaves" (III, 8), which means that they are the property of the despot, and so the instruments of his will (XV, 1). As a result, "almost no one has a will of his own" (VI, 1). Human behavior under despotism consists in responding to the will of another, rather than in deliberate, intentional action, which is why this society operates as a series of "infallible" reactions. Even the despot is not free, since no one is a tyrant without at the same time being a slave (IV, 3). The despot is a slave to his appetites, reacting "infallibly" to his impulses and his own caprice.[44] If he is slavish like his subjects, he is also something of a beast. His portion, like theirs, is mainly instinct not reason. "The idea of despotism," Montesquieu says, is illustrated by "the savages" of Louisiana: "when they wish to have some fruit, they cut down the tree to the base and gather the fruit. This is despotic government" (V, 13). The immediacy of instinctual appetites calls for immediate solutions and prohibits the mediation of reason, which in this case might have resulted in a plan for cultivating the fruit, thus ensuring a future supply, perhaps even increasing it, rather than eradicating its source.

In part, too, the mechanistic quality of the despot's own actions results from the absence of an opposition. Without opposition, "he does not have to deliberate, to doubt, or to reason; he has only to want" (IV, 3). Montesquieu means for us to notice the difference between *wanting*, which is an impulse, and *choosing*, which implies deliberation, doubt and reason. Because a despot has no opponents, there is no one to demand a reason for his actions and therefore no reason for him to have a reason. But without deliberating about an action, without being able to provide a reason for it, distinguishing a choice from an unchosen impulse proves difficult. Ironically, the despot's perfect power of choice undermines his capacity for intentional, self-initiated action.[45] The "tempering, modification, accommodation, terms, equivalents, negotiations, remonstrances" (III, 10) that result from a strong opposition mediate the will of the sovereign in moderate governments, and by doing so they force the sovereign's will to be more reasoned and deliberate, and therefore more free, than is the case under despotism. The mediation of an opposition interrupts the infallible operations of despotic government because it interrupts the prince's unreflective responses to his appetites. Without an opposition, the despot as much as his subjects lacks deliberate intention, even a will of his own. When Montesquieu describes despotism as a system in which "man is a *creature* that *obeys* a creature that *wants*," he means to convey that everyone is part beast and part slave there (III, 10; emphasis added). Indeed, the despot's *wants* reflect an obedience to his appetites that is as extreme as the obedience that he compels in his subjects.[46]

The simple structure of despotic government, which lacks the complexity that results from a differentiated social order and a constitution of balanced powers, is reflected in the simplicity of civil laws (VI, 1). As all subjects are slaves under despotic rule, everyone is equal. No differences exist in rank, origin, and condition that would require variations or exceptions in the laws. Moreover, because the prince is master of the estates of all his subjects, no private property exists, and therefore few if any laws are needed to regulate the ownership of land. The same is true for commerce. Since all commodities belong to the despot, the many laws that regulate commerce in moderate regimes are rendered useless. Nor are marriages regulated by civil laws since they are "contracted with female slaves" who have no legal standing.[47] In principle, civil laws operate at the intersection of the public and private spheres. They regulate and protect by public authority the private enterprises of individuals, such as landholding, trade, marriage, associational activities, and contractual obligations. The dearth of civil laws under despotic government points to the ambiguities that permeate the categories of public and private there.[48] On the one hand, in the absence of private property one is tempted to conclude that everything is public. From the standpoint of the individual subject, this surely is the case, as neither one's goods nor even one's person are one's own possession, and no activities or opinions are protected from government intrusion. Everything is a part of a common estate. Yet the common estate is the personal holding of a single individual. Consequently, while there is no private sphere from the standpoint of the subject, neither is there a public sphere. Indeed, *everything* is private in despotism for everything is the private property of the despot. All is contained within the private sphere of his personal, if extensive, household. Thus, "the preserving of the state is only the preserving of the prince, or rather of the palace in which he is enclosed" (V, 14). There are no real interactions between public and private of the sort that civil laws are established to regulate, because the separation between public and private has collapsed, and the simplicity of the civil laws reflects this fact.

The prince's personal privatization of the public sphere not only simplifies the civil laws but actually depoliticizes the state. No politics is possible there, since politics presupposes the existence of public matters, along with the opposing views of these matters that sustain public deliberation.[49] Since everything in the state is the personal property of the prince, all matters are by definition his private affairs, and thus subject only to his prerogative. With nothing held in common, no one besides the prince has a legitimate claim to an opposing opinion, or to any opinion. But without multiple opinions about common matters, the tempering, modification, accommodation, and remonstrances that facilitate deliberation are impossible. Thus, "politics with its springs and laws here should be very limited," for "everything comes down to reconciling political and civil government with domestic government, the officers of the state with those of the seraglio" (V, 14). It is true that the prince's household is full of intrigue and petty rivalries. But these rivalries are not strictly political because they do not represent contests of principle or opinion. They are simply squabbles over the comforts of life, the main motive that operates in despotic countries besides fear.

Montesquieu conveys the loss under despotism of the animation that marks politics with a reference to Charles XII of Sweden, who, on receiving word of resistance in the Senate of Sweden while he was out of the country, wrote that he would send one of his boots to command it. The boot, Montesquieu says, would have governed like a despotic king (V, 14). Despotic authority is inanimate, like a boot, because it lacks the *animus* of politics—both the animating spirit of reason that sparks deliberation and the courageous opposition, even animosity, that sustains it. But in despotism everyone—the prince as much as his subjects—lacks the animating forces of reason and courage, and consequently, "less is communicated" there (XIX, 12). Montesquieu's criticism of the inanimate, apolitical quality of life under despotic government does not rest on a glorification of political participation, however.[50] It is true that the principle of divided power requires political participation by different groups within society, but for Montesquieu participation is only a means to liberty, not the definition of liberty or an end in itself.[51] The purpose of participation is not so much to deliver the good of self-government to each group as to prevent any one of them from endangering the personal security of members of the other groups, for, he says, "I do not attach much value to the delights of furious disputation about affairs of state to the endless repetition of *liberty* and the privilege of hating half of one's fellow-creatures."[52] Similarly, he prefers modern representative government to the direct democracies of antiquity in which the people had immediate power (XIX, 27). If disputation about the affairs of state is not the end of politics, however, it is a crucial component of politics and a check on despotic authority. Thus in free governments, while it does not matter whether individuals reason well or badly, it is crucial that they reason; whereas in a despotic government, any reasoning at all runs counter to the principle of the government (XIX, 27). Reason gives rise to deliberation, which engenders the principled clashes between opposing viewpoints that animate political life. By suppressing the reason and the courage that animate politics, despotism depoliticizes the state.

The apolitical character of despotism recalls Aristotle's concept of despotic rule because of its association with the non-political sphere of the household. Aristotle considered despotic rule tyrannical when imported from the household into politics because he thought it ill-suited to the nature of politics. But Montesquieu's despot forces a fit between his manner of ruling and the nature of the political sphere. It is not just that he rules in the public sphere *as though* he were still in the household, as Aristotle's tyrant did. Instead, Montesquieu's despot transforms the public sphere into a household and the populace into slaves in order to accommodate his masterly rule, as when Louis XIV eroded the intermediary bodies of the French monarchy. The transformation of the public sphere permeates society at every level. For example, the arbitrary, lawless character of despotic rule runs through the entire regime because "where law is only the will of the prince, although the prince may be wise, how could a magistrate follow a will that he does not know? He must follow his own" (V, 16). The lawless rule of will is ubiquitous in despotism because no local authority can supply a principled standard of rule that is missing at the top. Every mayor and magistrate inevitably becomes a petty tyrant. Similarly, where property is insecure, trade dominated by the prince, and offices dispensed at his discretion rather than sold or inherited, important men "will be driven to a thousand misdeeds because they will believe that they possess nothing except the gold or silver that they can steal or hide" (V, 14). Therefore embezzlement is natural in despotic states (V, 15). And if a prince declares himself owner of all the land and heir to all his subjects, no one has an incentive to make repairs or improvements on his holdings, or to take up industry and the cultivation of land (V, 14). Consequently, the prince's subjects come to resemble him in being lazy (II, 5)[53] and are satisfied simply with "subsistence and life" (XV, 1). Whereas the despotic rule of Aristotle's tyrant is ill-fitted to the nature of political life, Montesquieu's despot makes political life conform to the nature of his unlimited rule. His transformation of society results in a system and a population ill-equipped for the deliberation and the disputation that animate politics and that make the public sphere political.

Constraining Despotic Rule

Despite the absence of fixed and fundamental laws independent of the prince's will, one thing that sometimes can counter his will is religion. Thus, "one will abandon one's father, even kill him, if the prince orders it, but one will not drink any wine even if the prince wants it and orders it. The laws of religion are of a higher precept, because they are imposed on the head of the prince as well as those of his subjects" (III, 10). The laws of religion can provide grounds for resisting the will of despots. Religion also can be a source of intimidation to the prince (II, 4). Indeed, even if it were useless for subjects to have religion, "it would not be useless for princes to have one and to whiten with foam the only rein that they who fear no human laws can have" (XXIV, 2). Thus, religion can constrain despots both from below and from above. On the one hand, laws of religion can give a despot's subjects reason to disobey him. When his commands violate the laws of religion, his subjects have legitimate grounds, and a powerful motive, to resist him. The piety of the populace can be an obstacle to the boundless power of the prince, which like the sea "seems to want to cover all the earth" (II, 4). At the same time, by positing an authority more powerful and more ferocious than himself, religion gives the prince something to fear, and therefore a motive to restrain himself in the exercise of his will. His subjects' piety constrains him from below and the threat of divine vengeance constrains him from above.

Commerce provides another potential limit on despotic authority. The establishment of commerce requires the establishment of exchange, and exchange, which provides the means of transferring silver from one country to another, "constrains despotic states" (XXII, 14). The exchange sets limits on the authority of kings (and "theologians," too) by putting commerce, "in some fashion, out of their power" (XXI, 20). Commerce is an extrapolitical source of power that can check the abuse of political power and "limit great assertions of authority, or at least the success of great assertions of authority" (XXII, 13). In this sense, Montesquieu regards commerce as an auxiliary of constitutional safeguards (especially the institutional balance of powers), functioning as a bulwark against despotism.[54] Commerce also incites and rewards the ambitious, with the result that commercial men are more "daring" than others (XX, 4). The daring that commerce inspires counteracts the debilitating fear inspired by the despotic regime. It gives rise to pride and confidence, which are dangerous for despots because "any people capable of esteeming themselves very much would be in a position to cause revolutions" (III, 9). More generally, commerce animates society, stirring up the rivalries and the personal ambitions that support politics. For whereas "the laws that order each man to remain in his profession and to pass it down to his children are and can be useful only in despotic states, where no one can or ought to have a rivalry" (XX, 22),[55] commercial societies encourage rivalries by equalizing opportunities, or providing a relative equality of opportunity. And "the political world," Montesquieu says, "is sustained by the inner desire and restlessness that each one has for leaving the place where he has been put."[56] Besides establishing countervailing sites of authority, then, commerce engenders daring and ambition, which animate the public and counteract the deadening effect of fear and the passivity of a populace that could be ruled by a despot's boot.

If commerce and religion *can* set limits on a despot's power, however, they do not always do so. On the one hand, commerce is difficult to establish and sustain under despotic government. Never knowing when his commodities might be confiscated or the currency devalued, a merchant lives from day to day, too insecure to take the risks required to make a commercial enterprise succeed (V, 15). Indeed, in despotic states, Montesquieu says, one works more to preserve than to acquire (XX, 4). And as lending is risky, usury is "naturalized," which makes financing large-scale enterprises difficult. Consequently, one cannot engage in much commerce under despotic government (V, 15). Moreover, although commerce establishes independent sites of influence, which can provide resources for contesting encroaching political power, the influence produced by commerce also can be used to support despotic authority. After all, it never has been difficult to find merchants and financiers willing to collaborate with despotic regimes for the sake of filling their pockets. Then, too, commerce can be forcefully co-opted by despots. This explains why Montesquieu so strongly opposed the policies of John Law, who had promoted the idea of a national public bank to be financed by commercial enterprises but overseen by the monarch. In Montesquieu's view, such a system would appropriate the resources of commerce that should be used to check the power of the sovereign and turn them instead to his aggrandizement. In addition, the excessive currency manipulation central to the system undermined the potential power of commerce as a check on the crown by depriving individual citizens of what one scholar calls a "gauge with which to make rational determinations of value on their own and thereby prevent[ing] them from resisting the designs of the state."[57] For this reason, Montesquieu refers to Law as "one of the greatest promoters of despotism ever seen in Europe"[58] (II, 4).

Besides being difficult to establish under despotic government, and vulnerable to co-optation, the power of commerce to check despotism is further limited by the effect it has on individual motivations. Commerce keeps individuals occupied and satisfies their desires. This has the potential benefit of preventing what one commentator describes as "an unnaturally powerful fixation with political power,"[59] but in the extreme it can cause individuals to prefer their profits, or their comforts, to their liberties. For example, if restrictions on his political liberties did not threaten his commercial activities, would the ambitious merchant stand up to a despot to defend them? Montesquieu expresses some doubts, remarking in his "Notes on England" that "the English do not deserve their liberty" because they "sell it to the king."[60] Similarly, he tells us that England "has always made its political interests give way to the interests of its commerce" (XX, 7). Indeed, "many" Englishmen willingly abandon the one nation in the world whose constitution has liberty for its direct purpose in order to "search for abundance," and they do so "even in countries of servitude" (XIX, 27). The motive of material interest that commerce supplies does not contain a principled standard for preferring political liberty to personal profit, and thus may be an insufficient spring for resisting despotic power. In fact, it may be perfectly consistent with despotism, since in despotism individuals act, if not from fear, then in anticipation of the comforts of life, as we have seen. In a commercial society, where the motive of material interest predominates, subjects may be gratified into submission by a despot who successfully supplies their needs even while denying their liberties. For this reason, some have seen in Montesquieu's remarks on commerce "a new despotism . . . founded not on fear but on gratification."[61] So while commerce has the potential to check despots, it also may support despotism.

Religion, too, may as easily enhance despotic power as constrain it.[62] If the despot can succeed in putting himself at the head of his people's religion, he can use their religious piety to his own advantage. Under such conditions, religion is "a fear added to fear," and "it is from religion that the people derive, in part, the astonishing respect they have for their prince" (V, 14). Moreover, religion tends to make individuals heedless of worldly perils and disdainful of worldly goods.[63] Faith, like fear, may give rise to passivity, which partly explains Montesquieu's mistrust of the contemplative life that religion promotes (XXIV, 10).

Religion "makes us hope for a state that we believe in, not a state that we feel or that we know" (XXIV, 19), and the promise of heavenly rewards can make the abuse of political power easier to abide, which is why the effectual truth of the city of God too often supports this-worldly despotism.[64] By contrast, what one feels and knows in this world keeps one interested in politics, and inspires vigilance in resisting the abuse of power. And while the other-worldly orientation of religious faith may seem to contradict the mechanistic materialism of despotic government, their effects are similarly fatalistic. The fatalism of religion,[65] according to which every outcome is the result of a single omnipotent will, parallels the fatalism that permeates despotism, in which everything happens in response to the will of the sovereign, a resonance that is enhanced by the blind fatality that Montesquieu associates with the despot's slavish pursuit of pleasures and his subjects' unreflective grasping for gratification. So religion, like commerce, may limit a despot's power, but cannot be relied upon to do so.

Nor does Montesquieu regard reason as a dependable barrier to despotism. He is more skeptical than some other Enlightenment thinkers, such as Voltaire, about the power of individual reason to limit the exercise of political power. It is true that *The Spirit of Laws* aims to enlighten us on political matters by disclosing to us the fruits of Montesquieu's reasoning, and by engaging our reason. And Montesquieu believes that political power cannot be limited without reason, since a constitution of separate powers is the product of reason, even a "masterpiece" of reason, as we have seen. Yet in his view the proper role of reason is to clarify the most effective external constraints, or mechanisms, for limiting power. Reason cannot replace these mechanisms, as Voltaire thought it should do, because reason works better as a guide for great legislators than as a check on individual action. When reason is left alone to check individual actions, as it was for Voltaire's enlightened despot, the overwhelming tendency, according to Montesquieu, is for enlightenment to lose out to despotism.[66] Human reason is easily swayed by the human will, and so our reasonings can be difficult to distinguish from our rationalizations.[67] Even the reasoning of philosophers is not immune to the influence of will, but may be colored by "passions and prejudices," as in the case of Aristotle, "who wanted to satisfy sometimes his jealousy of Plato, sometimes his passion for Alexander," or Plato, who "was indignant at the tyranny of the people of Athens," or Machiavelli, who "was full of his idol, Duke Valentino" (XXIX, 19). Reason on its own is as contingent as virtue, and like virtue has need of limits (XI, 4). The rule of reason without limits on reason, as in enlightened despotism, turns out to be just another form of tyranny, not the solution to it. Whether the rule of reason takes the form of Plato's philosopher-king, or the *phronesis* of Aristotle's "best man," or the "natural reason" of Hobbes' sovereign, or even the "communicative rationality" of today's deliberative democracy, for Montesquieu it never can be, on its own, a reliable limit on political power.

In addition to being vulnerable to the will, reason, like religious faith, has a tendency to become too "contemplative." The contemplative reason of philosophy is as much a problem for politics as religious contemplation, and for the same reason. The "speculative sciences," Montesquieu says, "render men savage (*sauvages*)" (IV, 8). Contemporary usage of the term *sauvage* carried the meaning of ferocious (*féroce*), as well as uncultivated and shy (*farouche*). *Sauvage* meant something asocial.[68] Too much speculation causes individuals to "turn their backs on everything that pertains to this world" (XXIV, 11). The problem with turning one's back on this world is that the limitation of political power requires constant vigilance.[69] Power continually seeks to augment itself and a people that is not continuously on guard against encroaching power surely will be overwhelmed by it (XI, 4). Reason as "detachment" thus may support despotism, rather than check it (XXIV, 11), and consequently the excess of reason is not always desirable (XI, 6). Too much reason, or reason of a speculative sort, makes human beings heedless of the pressures that bear on them in the material world and delivers them too easily into the hands of despots.

The Corruption of Despotic Regimes

Neither commerce nor religion nor reason itself constitutes a reliable limit on despotic authority. Once despotism has been established, it seems, one can only wait for its inevitable decline. The decline of despotic governments is inevitable because unlike other regimes, which are corrupted by particular violations of their principles, despotism is corrupted by its own nature (VIII, 10). It is self-destructive. One reason is that in states where there are no established laws, the inheritance of dominion cannot be fixed. Fixed laws of succession cannot be reconciled with the despot's inclination to identify his person with his state. If the state *is* the prince then it cannot outlive him, but must dissolve on his death, and thus despotic governments have a natural life span of a single generation. And without fixed laws of succession, rivalries among potential successors constantly disrupt the state during its short life, compounding its instability, and giving it additional reason for a faster dissolution than other states (V, 14). In addition, because the despot can make his subjects fear him only through the threat of force, despots are dependent on their armies. Yet the military force that sustains the despot's state is dangerous to his person, for the stronger his army becomes the more easily it can destroy him. This presents a paradox, since the despot's person and the despot's state are conceived to be the same thing, and consequently despotic governments prove to be unsustainable over an extended period. The fact that any particular despotic government is in principle unsustainable over time, however, does not mean that despotism in general is likely to disappear. When one despot falls because of his army, a new one rises in his place. Despotism in general is persistent because while "a free nation can have a liberator, a subjugated nation can have only another oppressor" (XIX, 27). Consequently, the destruction of any one despotic regime typically is followed by the establishment of another. Still, the dependence of despots on their armies constitutes a weakness that makes particular despotic governments unstable and short-lived.

Another problem that despots face is a natural devaluation in the currency of fear. Severe penalties suit despotic governments (VI, 9), but over time penalties must become more and more severe to achieve the same effects. Subjects who are "accustomed to be checked only by a cruel penalty" eventually force the regime to "become more cruel than itself," as "souls that are everywhere overawed and made more atrocious can be guided only by a greater atrocity" (VI, 13). The problem is that penalties that are so atrocious as to be thoroughly terrifying are difficult to execute. Montesquieu reports that the Japanese are known to hide the crimes of their fellows, for example, because the punishments would cause so much bloodshed (VI, 13). With penalties that "impose terror upon men's spirits" no one can be found to accuse or condemn (VI, 14). But the result of crimes going unpunished is a rising disdain on the part of the people for the authority that prosecutes, which is the despot himself. Thus, the need to preserve the mechanism of fear through increasingly severe penalties ultimately undoes the mechanism of fear, replacing it with the unruly sentiment of disdain.

Yet another cause of the corruption of despotic states is that they tend toward expansion by military means. The despot's unlimited desire expresses itself in foreign policy as much as in domestic affairs. The result is an unwieldy empire, prone to fragmentation from within. Subjects who are faithful because punishment is at hand, Montesquieu points out, tend not to remain faithful when the threat of punishment is distant (IX, 6). The expansion of states also exposes new sides from which they can be taken, and thus large states are difficult to defend at the borders. And since much of the territory has been annexed through conquest, little of it will be of personal concern to the despot, much less to his subjects. Consequently, despotic governments tend to "provide for their security" by "separat[ing] and hold[ing] themselves, so to speak, apart. They sacrifice a part of the country, ravage the frontiers, and leave them deserted" (IX, 4). In other words, they defend themselves by dissolving themselves. Thus, the size of despotic states also contributes to their dissolution.

When Montesquieu speaks of the "corruption" of despotism he means something different from what is entailed by the "corruption" of monarchies and republics. Corruption in relation to despotic government simply means disintegration. In relation to monarchies and republics, however, the corruption of the regime also refers to a violation of what *ought to be*. What Montesquieu calls the "nature" of the government in these cases implies a standard of right and even carries moral weight. When a democratic people gives its vote for silver (VIII, 2), for example, or a monarch removes the privileges of the intermediary bodies (VIII, 6), one can say that a *wrong* has been committed. Such actions constitute violations of the fundamental laws of these regimes. Moreover, when democratic citizens sell their votes and monarchs attack the intermediary bodies, particular forms of human excellence are eroded–deliberation in the one case, moderation in the other. The same cannot be said of despotism. Its corruption is its destruction and nothing more. There is no violation of what ought to be because in despotism no standard of right exists that would give meaning to *ought*. There the fundamental law expresses what is unavoidable, not what ought to be. Force replaces right, and so *ought* gives way to *is* and *must*. And there is no human excellence that is particular to despotism, in which both the ruler and the ruled exist merely as the instruments of their own and others' fears and appetites. Despotic rule rests on the debasement of human beings and the erosion of human excellence. Therefore in the context of despotism, the term "corruption" loses all moral significance. It no longer implies a violation of what ought to be but refers simply to the collapse of the government, a shift that parallels the shift in the meaning of fundamental law under despotic government.

Much as deliberation and choice have little to do with the fundamental law of despotism, so human art can do little to prevent the corruption of despotic governments. The corruption of despotism is so unavoidable, in fact, that no purely despotic government can endure.[70] Despotic government "maintains itself only when circumstances . . . force it to follow some order and to endure some rule. These things force its nature without changing it; its ferocity remains; it is, for some time, tamed" (VIII, 10).[71] China is the example most often cited in this regard, but virtually every other despotic regime that Montesquieu mentions departs in some way from the type, as he acknowledges.[72] The despot is impotent when it comes to preserving his regime because he is so artless and lacking in the capacity for reason and deliberation. By contrast, the art of legislators in republics and monarchies can have significant effects in preserving the regime, in restraining each one's tendency to depart from its nature and principle, a tendency that affects every regime. Legislators have greater influence in monarchies and republics because the fundamental laws of these regimes are the products of human art, unlike despotism, where the fundamental law stems from necessity.

The despot's inability to arrest the decline of his regime reveals a fundamental tension between the nature of despotism and its principle. The nature of despotism, which is the rule of will, runs counter to the principle of despotism, which is fear and the anxious appetites that accompany it. The despot's fear of his army and the loss of his pleasures disables his will, much as his subjects' fear of him deprives them of any will of their own. And his concupiscence is all instinct and reaction, a slavish obedience to his appetites, rather than a willful assertion of his intention. The mechanistic materialism resulting from the principles of fear and appetite suggests a loss of will at the foundation of despotism. The despot as much as his subjects acts as he *must*, not

The despot as much as his subjects acts as he *must*, not as he chooses. So while the nature of the regime implies the despot's absolute choice, its principle implies his necessity. The regime of despotism proves to be incoherent, and this becomes a powerful argument against despotism, one that is meant to be more persuasive to despots and potential despots than moral exhortation ever could be. Montesquieu offers a way of criticizing the one regime that does not recognize any *ought* by showing that even by the one standard that despotism does recognize—the rule of will—despotic governments are bound to fail, because the rule of will cannot be maintained in the absence of limits on will. And the incoherence at the heart of despotism has personal as well as political implications, since it suggests that for individuals as much as for governments there is more liberty to be found in living within principled limits than in living without them.

Montesquieu Orientalist?

Montesquieu draws a special connection between despotic government and the empires of the East where, he says, "despotism is . . . naturalized" (*naturalisé*) (V, 14). Throughout *The Spirit of Laws*, the large empires of the East, such as Persia, Turkey, India, and China, provide illustrations for his theory of despotic government. In these countries, he maintains, the climate, terrain, religion, and mores all support the unlimited rule of one. The association between despotism and the Orient precedes Montesquieu. Aristotle had remarked on the despotic kingships that existed among "some of the barbarians," particularly in Asia.[73] Despotism predominated in Asia, he thought, "because barbarians are more slavish in their character than Greeks (those in Asia being more so than those in Europe) [and] they put up with a master's rule without making any difficulties."[74] Aristotle's associations between Asia and the slavish subjects of despotism survived into the modern period, illustrated, as one commentator has noted, in sixteenth-century maps depicting the continent of Asia as a horse, "ill-defined but ungainly, and of course being the servant of man."[75] Montesquieu's treatment of despotism drew on these conventional associations and increased their force in the public mind. For this reason, he has been faulted for contributing to the Orientalist standpoint sometimes invoked to justify Europe's imperialist policies throughout Asia and Africa in the nineteenth century, and that even today is thought to contribute to Western disregard for non-Western persons.[76]

Montesquieu's portrait of Eastern countries may seem to exemplify the prejudicial standpoint associated with Orientalism, not least because of his departures from the empirical evidence. His portrait of despotism relies heavily upon the newly available travel reports that had emerged early in the eighteenth century. References to this literature abound in his footnotes to *The Spirit of Laws* and even take center stage from time to time, as in Book XVII, chapter 3,

"On the climate of Asia," which opens with long quotations from the collected *Recueil de voyages au nord* and Father Jean-Baptiste Du Halde's *Description de l'empire de la Chine*. Montesquieu's use of the travel literature has been carefully scrutinized.[77] There is broad consensus among interpreters that he used it when and how it suited him, emphasizing reports from travelers that supported his theory of despotism while not infrequently ignoring those that did not.[78] Although he classified Persia as a despotism, for example, in fact the Koran provided a fundamental law that could set limits on the will of the sultan. In addition, the shah's military officials, as well as lawyers, merchants, and artisans operated as limited intermediary bodies, not unlike the corporate orders of monarchical France. And while direct challenges to the sultan's authority might elicit extraordinarily severe penalties, most crimes among the people themselves were tried in accordance with clearly defined procedures and penalized according to established rules.[79] Similarly, fear was noticeably absent from most of the travel reports from China, or mixed with other motives.[80] Because of such discrepancies Montesquieu's portrait of China was criticized by François Quesnay as early as the mid-1760s, and his portrait of Persia was attacked by Abraham-Hyacinthe Anquetil-Duperron in 1778.[81]

Some have interpreted Montesquieu's selective use of the travel literature as an effort to force a fit between his typology of regimes and the empirical data presented by European travelers to Asia.[82] Yet Montesquieu's typology of governments is not meant to be absolute. England, for example, does not fit easily into the typology, since it constitutes something of a hybrid between a monarchy and a republic strengthened by commerce. The important role that the English constitution plays in *The Spirit of Laws* suggests that regimes that depart from his typology do not represent a fundamental threat to his political philosophy as a whole. Even China, which Montesquieu describes as "a despotic state the principle of which is fear," (VIII, 21) also represents "a case of a republic or a monarchy" with respect to the moderation of its civil and criminal laws (VI, 9, note 25). Because perfect despotism is impossible, actual despotic governments always are impure, the power of the despot being limited in some way, if only (as in China) by external forces (VIII, 10). Such fortuitous limits make particular despotic governments possible even as they render them impure from the standpoint of the typology. Thus Montesquieu's selective use of the travel literature cannot be explained by a supposed desire to preserve the strict integrity of his typology of regimes.

A more plausible explanation for the distortions that exist is that Montesquieu meant to correct what he regarded as existing distortions in contemporary French treatments of the Orient. Many notable men and women of Montesquieu's day were favorably impressed by reports of Persia, for example, which enjoyed a significant measure of respectability by the middle of the eighteenth century both culturally and politically.[83] China, too, enjoyed a growing reputa-

tion for wisdom and prosperity.[84] Voltaire in particular had praised the government of China as ideal.[85] He admired the absolutism of Chinese rule and recommended it as a model for European monarchs.[86] His admiration fueled the
public fascination with the empires of the East, with their mystery and exoticism, which already was being nourished by the travel literature and by new
French translations of Asian folk tales and fables, such as *The Thousand and
One Nights*. Montesquieu regarded the popular fascination with Asian absolutism as dangerous, and his *Persian Letters* exploited this fascination for the purpose of correcting it. In *The Spirit of Laws*, he presents a more sober, scientific
argument against the faddish romanticizing of the East, and more generally
against the romanticizing of absolutism. There is thus a polemical element to
Montesquieu's selective use of the travel literature insofar as part of his purpose
is to counter such French polemicists of the *thèse royale* as Voltaire.[87] Diderot,
who shared Montesquieu's anti-absolutist sentiments, later pursued the same
purpose, treating China as a despotism so that he could prevent enemies of liberty from using China as a model for French government.[88] Thus, one reason
that Montesquieu distorts the travel reports is that he means to counter the distortions of those who romanticized absolute government in general and who
admired China, Persia, and other Eastern regimes as instances of it. He exaggerates the despotic features of these regimes to counter the romanticized accounts
of them advanced by others.[89]

Montesquieu's selective use of the travel literature aims not only to correct
popular misconceptions of the East, but also to illustrate universal aspects of
despotic rule. His purpose is to identify political developments that Europeans
should be wary of at home. Given this purpose, there would be little value in
specifying the various contingencies that mitigate the actual practice of despotism in different Asian countries. Europeans would not learn how to prevent despotism by examining all the particular ways that Asian governments depart from
despotism, and so Montesquieu largely leaves them out, highlighting instead the
Asian practices that exemplify despotic government. One should not conclude,
however, that Montesquieu's picture of Oriental despotism is purely imaginary.
On the contrary, he clearly believes it to be based on the facts of the matter,
even if it does not include all the details.[90] Details complicate the picture, which
can be a good thing if it advances understanding of a particular government. But
the details also can obscure from view the significant features of the general
form of the government. So Montesquieu proceeds much as contemporary political scientists do when they "model" interactions between select variables by
systematically excluding the effects of other complicating factors, or details.
Like them, Montesquieu is "more attentive to the order of things than to the
things themselves" (XIX, 1).[91] Besides its polemical purpose, then, Montesquieu's selective use of the travel literature has a didactic end. And the governments of Asia serve his didactic purpose well, since the actual and metaphorical

distance between East and West makes the East a safe foil for his indirect critique of despotism nearer to home.[92]

Preserving this distance is crucial to his project, because only by doing so can he risk the deeper, broader critique that he intends. One part of the critique is to show the despotic tendencies of the French monarchy. This is not to say that Montesquieu regards France as an example of a full-blown despotism, either under Louis XIV or later. France is not despotic, in Montesquieu's view, but like every monarchy it tends in that direction (VIII, 17). Montesquieu mentions Cardinal Richelieu in this regard, minister to Louis XIII.[93] Richelieu, Montesquieu says, "wants one to avoid, in monarchies, the spines of the assemblies, which form difficulties at every point. Even if this man did not have despotism in his heart, he had it in his head"(V, 10).[94] Later, Louis XIV too fully identified the state with his own person, as a despot will do, "relating everything to himself uniquely, reduc[ing] the state to its capital, the capital to the court, and the court to his person alone"(VIII, 6).[95] One can see in this passage Montesquieu's methodical use of the Orient to buffer his criticism of more local concerns. The chapter containing the veiled critique of *le roi soleil* is entitled, "On the corruption of the principle of monarchy" and opens by noting that monarchies approach despotism when the prerogatives of the established bodies or the privileges of the towns gradually are removed. Montesquieu illustrates the point with a reference to the Chinese dynasties of Tsin and Sui, in which the monarch attempted to govern without any intermediaries. Having deflected attention away from the French monarchy with this reference to the government of China, Montesquieu returns to speaking of monarchy in general terms in the following paragraph, warning against the destruction of the intermediary bodies that ruins monarchical government, and for which Louis XIV had been so much criticized by others. Here as elsewhere in *The Spirit of Laws*, Oriental despotism serves as a device for carefully introducing a criticism of France.

Montesquieu's use of the Orient to illuminate and warn of despotism has even wider implications, however. Commentators have also seen in his remarks on despotism implicit criticism of the Christian Church.[96] Christianity, like despotism, is characterized by the absolute rule of One who is not bound by any external limits, together with the fear and perfect obedience of His subjects. It is true that Christianity emphasizes "the felicity of the other life" (XXIV, 3) as much as the fear of divine vengeance, but even the promise of future rewards carries with it the threat of future punishments. Consequently, Christian piety is inextricably tied to fear. The Christian God has His vizir in the pope and His eunuchs in the priests.[97] He rules absently, much as the despot described in Book V, chapter 12, who is hidden from his subjects. The Christian faithful, like despotic subjects, remain in ignorance of their Master's condition, but "are such that they need only a name to govern them." The awesome displays of symbolism in Christian churches in this respect are not unlike the boot of Charles XII, sent to command the senate of Sweden in his place. Similarly, the Christian faithful are conceived of as God's servants. They are most virtuous when, like the subjects of despotic government, they have no will of their own, but rather seek to serve the will of God. There are parallels between Christianity and Islam, the religion that supports Persian and Turkish despotism.[98] Christianity "leads us to spiritual ideas" (XXIV, 19), much as "Mohammedans become speculative by habit" (XXIV, 11). In both cases, the contemplative life produces passivity, and its "detachment" makes tolerable the abuse of political power. And the religious fatalism that is based on "the dogma of a rigid destiny" (XXIV, 11) parallels the blind fatality of despotic government, as we have seen, in which everything happens with invariable effects in response to a single will. The use of Islam and despotic Asian governments to suggest the despotic features of Christianity protects Montesquieu much the way it makes possible his critique of the French monarchy. Beyond that, it suggests that Montesquieu's view of despotism ultimately transgresses the boundary between East and West. Christianity, after all, was Eastern in its origins but has played its defining role in the West. The implication is that despotism permeates, or threatens to permeate, the West as well as the East. The East/West divide is drawn by Montesquieu, and emphasized, only to be elided. In fact, the emphatic contrast between them is precisely what makes possible the elision, because by accusing the East Montesquieu disarms the despots and would-be despots of the West, and warns us without offending them.

Another example of how Montesquieu's treatment of despotism transcends the putative Orientalist standpoint is his discussion of the "despotism of all" that is one form of corruption in republican government.[99] The despotism of all arises "when the people strip the senate, the magistrates, and the judges of their functions" (VIII, 6) and reduce their representative government to direct democracy. In doing so, they remove the institutional obstacles that mediate the ruling will. Republican government is vulnerable to the unlimited rule of will, albeit a collective will rather than a solitary one, because the nature of republican government does not include the rule of fixed, established laws sustained by the presence of intermediary bodies. The despotism of all parallels the despotism of one that results from a monarch's destruction of the mediate channels through which power flows. Montesquieu alludes to it briefly when he criticizes the English parliament for having "taken away all the intermediate powers that formed their monarchy," and warns that because of having eradicated the intermediary bodies the English "have good reason to preserve [their] liberty; if they should come to lose it, they would be one of the most enslaved peoples on earth" (II, 4). For the same reason he characterizes England as having "the form of an absolute government," which refers to the absence of intermediary bodies, "over the foundation of a free government," which means a legal separation of powers (XIX, 27). The threat of a despotism of all, which lurks behind the constitutional balance of powers that Montesquieu so much admired in England, explains in part why one commentator has seen in Montesquieu's account of England a "concern about unlimited democracy," while another argues that Montesquieu regarded England as "precariously close to despotism."[100]

The despotism of all that potentially threatens England differs somewhat from despotism in the republics of antiquity, which has been characterized by one scholar as a "despotism of virtue."[101] What Montesquieu calls "political virtue," the principle of republican government, is "self-renunciation," the "sacrifice of one's dearest interests" for the sake of the common good (III, 5). It requires a complete identification of the individual with the collective and even requires the individual to prefer the collective, since citizens may be expected to show that they love the state more than themselves by sacrificing themselves in battle to defend the homeland. In this respect, republican virtue resembles Bossuet's description of the loyal subject under absolute monarchy who "will love the king even more than his own life."[102] Because republican virtue also resembles Christian obedience, Montesquieu illustrates political virtue by describing the self-sacrifice of Christian monks (V, 2). Political virtue is a form of obedience in which one's particular self is made to obey the general "self" of the political community, and the good republican displays an obedience as perfect as that of a despot's subjects. And while fear is less visible among republican citizens than among the subjects of despotic government, virtue is not inconsistent with fear in the same way that it is incompatible with honor, the principle of monarchy. The compatibility of virtue and fear explains why Montesquieu says only that virtue "is not necessary to" despotic government, whereas honor "would be dangerous" to it (III, 9). Virtue is not necessary to despotism, but could be present in a despotic government. By contrast, honor could not be present in despotism because the ambition and the courage it entails could not be "endured" (*souffert*) by a despot (III, 8).[103] In fact, during the French Revolution the Jacobins actually did unite virtue and fear under the direction of Robespierre, who regarded virtue without terror as impotent.[104] The Jacobins brought together other aspects of despotism, as well, such as the destruction of intermediary bodies, a scorn for the rule of law, and a centralized, bureaucratic authority.[105]

We have seen that although Montesquieu associates despotism with the empires of the East, and even exaggerates this association, the reach of despotic authority and the dangers of despotic rule extend well beyond that region. In this sense, Montesquieu is not a true Orientalist, even if Orientalist conclusions could be drawn from his analysis. For him the Orient is not Europe's "Other" so much as Europe's mirror. Because Montesquieu means for us to see ourselves in Oriental despots and their subjects his treatment of Eastern despotism cannot rightly provide the justification for European imperialism in Asia that is thought to be so central to what is called the Orientalist project. Of course, his treatment of Asia could be misappropriated and put to the Orientalist use of "dominating, restructuring, and having authority over the Orient," and it may well have been misappropriated in this way by some.[106] But there is an irony in such misuse. Instead of confirming that Montesquieu believed the East a deserving subject of Western imperialism, the Orientalist position inadvertently confirms the real point that Montesquieu meant to convey, which is that the tendency toward despotism is universal.[107] Imperialism, after all, is a fundamental feature of despotic government as Montesquieu presents it, and the imperialist impulse of the Orientalist is a despotic one. Far from being an Orientalist, Montesquieu's treatment of despotism shows him to be the first critic of Orientalism. He used the Orient to prudently express and to make vivid the meaning and the consequences of despotic government, to enlighten us about how despotism haunts every regime and how it has roots in the natural world around us and in the human nature within us.

Despotism and Nature

Montesquieu's contention that despotism is related to the natural conditions of climate and physical terrain has proven to be one of the most controversial aspects of his theory. Throughout *The Spirit of Laws* he maintains that despotism arises more naturally in hot climates (V, 15; XIV, 3; XIV, 10; XVII, 2-3). In part, he says, the torrid weather enervates the populace, making persons less vigorous, both in their actions and in their reasoning. In part, too, the difficulty of manual labor in hot climates makes the possession of slaves seem desirable to anyone who can afford it, thus producing a higher prevalence of slavery, which supports the political slavery of despotism. Additionally, the physical terrain of Asia, characterized by "greater plains," facilitates the creation of expansive empires, which then require a despotic authority to maintain them. In contrast, the terrain of Europe is characterized by natural divisions that "form several states of modest expanse," suitably sized for moderate rule (XVII, 6). At times Montesquieu seems to attribute a determinism to these material conditions, as when he concludes from the description of Asian terrain that "therefore power always should be despotic in Asia" (*la puissance doit donc être toujours despotique*) (XVII, 6). The notion of natural determinism calls to mind the inevitability of the despot's appointment of a vizir, which is an unavoidable consequence of his unlimited pursuit of pleasure. The idea that despotic government arises on the basis of a natural necessity, rather than human art, is consistent with the idea that the "fundamental law" of the despotic state is necessitous, rather than the product of deliberation and choice, and that its corruption is inevitable.

Determinism runs counter to the spirit of Montesquieu's political philosophy, however. Human agency cannot be depicted along the lines that the Newtonian laws of physics predict the motions of material bodies. Instead of being determined, Montesquieu says, "man . . . must guide himself" (*il faut qu'il se conduise*) (I, 1). In his *Pensées* he rejects efforts to explain human action in terms of the laws of causality that govern the material world:

> A great genius [Spinoza] has promised me that I will die like an insect. He is looking to flatter me with the idea that I am only a modification of matter. He employs a geometrical order and some reasons that are said to be very strong, and that I have found very obscure, to elevate my soul (*l'âme*) to the dignity of my body, and, in place of the immense space that my spirit (*l'esprit*) embraces, he gives me to my material body alone and to a space of four or five feet in the universe.[108]

Human actions cannot be explained on the basis of the same causal relations that determine the flights of "insects," because human beings, Montesquieu says, possess *l'âme* and *l'esprit*. It is because of *l'âme* and *l'esprit* that "the intelligent world . . . does not follow its laws as consistently as the physical world follows its laws." Although "particular intelligent beings are limited by their nature and are consequently subject to error" (I, 1), the indeterminacy of human behavior does not result from errors alone. For even if human beings were perfectly rational, their actions would not be perfectly predictable, since "it is in their nature to act by themselves" (I, 1). Because we have reason, our actions cannot be strictly subject to the same mechanistic materialism that determines the motions of physical bodies. Montesquieu calls the effort to subsume human behavior under a mechanistic-materialist framework an attempt "to destroy liberty in me" (*détruire en moi la liberté*).[109] Similarly, the moderate government in which powers are combined and put in a position to resist one another is not natural, as we have seen, but a masterpiece of legislation that chance rarely produces. Indeed, the philosophical insights presented in *The Spirit of Laws* would be useless if political societies were merely the products of natural necessity. Thus, the suggestion of a natural determinism at the foundation of despotic government is inconsistent with the indeterminacy of "the intelligent world."

By emphasizing the material causes of despotism, then, Montesquieu may seem to have abandoned his convictions about the indeterminacy of the intelligent world and about the power of human reason to produce masterpieces of legislation. Yet the mechanistic quality of despotism is itself the product of human choice. In particular, it results from the choice to relinquish the power and responsibility of deliberative reason. It is the choice to be guided—whether by one's appetites or by a sovereign master—rather than to guide oneself. Montesquieu affirms that man must guide himself while at the same time asserting that it is human nature to forget this fact. For "man is a flexible being . . . equally capable of knowing his own nature when it is shown to him, and of losing even the feeling of it when it is hidden from him"—or when he hides it from himself

(Preface). The failure to establish institutional limits on political power produces a situation in which nature overwhelms art and necessity undercuts choice. The result is the mechanistic materialism of despotism, in which the power of material causes is much increased, both in the form of climate and physical terrain, and in the form of the natural impulses of appetite and fear.

The idea that despotism results from an abdication of human art also explains how despotism can be both more natural than the other regimes and more destructive of human nature. Despotism is more natural insofar as nature (understood as climate and terrain, as well as material instincts) has more immediate effects there than in the other types of government. Despotism "leaps to view" because "only passions are needed to establish it," not art. And since no art is required, everyone is "good enough" for despotism (V, 14), which makes it natural in the further sense of being common, for while "it would seem that human nature would constantly rise up against despotic government" in fact "most peoples are subject to it" (V, 14). Thus, in reading historical examples of despotism, Montesquieu says, "we feel with a kind of sadness the ills of human nature" (VI, 9). The fact that despotic tendencies are fundamental to human nature explains why it has eternally been observed that any man who has power is led to abuse it (XI, 4). It also explains why Montesquieu does not regard despotism as the result of vicious character. Anyone could become a despot if given unlimited power because the seed of despotism is in human nature, which is common, not in a particular form of vice. It is true that despots have "many faults" (V, 14). They are, for example, "lazy, ignorant, and voluptuous." But a despot becomes lazy, ignorant, and voluptuous because his "five senses tell him incessantly that he is everything and that others are nothing" (II, 5). His faults arise from the interaction between his situation of unlimited power and common aspects of human nature; they do not presuppose any special flaws.

Montesquieu also characterizes despotism as a violation of human nature, and in this sense it is *unnatural*. Despotism, he says, "causes appalling ills to human nature" (II, 4), "insults human nature" (VIII, 21), and causes it to suffer (VIII, 8). We have seen some of the ways in which despotism undermines the human capacities for deliberation and ambition, reducing individuals to "beasts" and "slaves" who merely react to the given rather than acting deliberately and with purpose. And the insecurity that despotism engenders hinders the development of commerce and other arts, such as industry and the cultivation of land. Beyond that, Montesquieu points out that despotism erodes the attachments and obligations that contribute to elevating human lives above mere life, such as "respect for a father, tenderness for one's children and women, [and] laws of honor . . ." (III, 10). The possibility of acting on principle, rather than on the basis of unreflective wants and fears, is out of the question. By showing what despotism denies in human beings, Montesquieu indicates indirectly the qualities he most values in human beings. Ambition, deliberation, knowledge, social attachments, obligations, and principled action are features of the "human nature" that despotism assaults. They are aspects of what Montesquieu calls the "greatness" (*grandeur*) of "soul" (*l'âme*) that moderate government makes possible (V, 12). It is these qualities, or possibilities, that are lost under despotic government, where the "soul . . . constantly is constrained to be debased" (XV, 13).[110]

These qualities do not amount to a substantive conception of the human good, it is true. For example, Montesquieu suggests that living ambitiously is better than living passively, but he does not specify the ends of ambition, and therefore leaves open its substantive content. Similarly, Montesquieu clearly believes that it is better to act on the basis of principles, rather than simply to react to impulse or external pressure, as do beasts and slaves, but he does not specify the content of the principles that should direct human action. Montesquieu has good reasons to resist presenting the perceived essentials of human nature as a justificatory standard for his liberal theory of government. He well knew that such standards could be co-opted to justify less liberal regimes, much as ancient virtue had been appropriated and adapted by the Christian Church and used to solidify what he took to be its oppressive power. Beyond that, Montesquieu's own treatment of human nature shows it to be an unreliable standard. The fact that despotism is in some respects natural to human beings, that the despotic tendency is a fundamental feature of human nature, suggests that nature is not in itself a fully reliable guide for politics or an indisputable source of moral and political standards.[111] As a result, human nature understood in the fullest sense as the collection of characteristic possibilities or ends that distinguish human beings from other creatures has only a ghostly presence in *The Spirit of Laws*. It haunts the perimeters of the argument, surfacing briefly from time to time (as in V, 12), but never taking definitive shape. Yet it is crucial to Montesquieu's liberal project as a whole because without the standard it provides, liberty itself is difficult to justify. And only on the basis of such a standard does Montesquieu's uncharacteristically universal disparagement of despotism make sense.

So despotism is closer to nature than either republican or monarchical government because it involves less art. Despotic government gives immediate expression to some common features of human nature, including the instinctual drives for pleasure, gratification, and domination. And the lack of art involved in establishing despotic governments contributes to the strength that nature wields within them. Yet even though despotism is in some respects the most natural of the three types of regime, it also results in the greatest shocks to human nature. And by showing how despotism violates human nature Montesquieu provides indirectly the closest thing to a universal standard of right that exists in *The Spirit of Laws*.

Conclusion

Montesquieu's idea of despotism as a total system of government, rather than just a quality of personal rule, remains a crucial component of classificatory schemes in political science even today.[112] His innovative articulation of the concept of despotic government emphasizes the interaction between political institutions and human motivation and its impact on the exercise of political power. There are ambiguities inherent in such an interactive model of causality, but they reflect the real ambiguities that characterize the collective lives of beings who are so constituted that they must "guide" themselves but frequently "forget" themselves. Our reason gives us the ability to act, rather than simply to react, and so to be our own causes. But our instincts and impulses continually respond to external causes, which have their own independent effects on our actions. In despotic governments the unlimited power that marks the nature of despotism interacts with the fear and the instinct for gratification that characterize its principle. Predictability, simplicity, and a loss of political animation result. Religion and commerce may set limits on despotic rule, but cannot be relied upon to do so. Ultimately, despotic governments are limited only by their inevitable declines, which result from the incoherence of rule on the basis of unlimited will. This incoherence can be seen in the tension between the nature of despotism and its principle. The fears and appetites of the despot and his subjects transform the rule of will into mechanistic necessity. The necessity implicit in the principle of despotism contradicts the unlimited will in its nature.

Montesquieu's explicit identification of despotism with the empires of the East conceals his implicit warning about the dangers of despotic rule in the West. His treatment of despotism is said to have been appropriated by others with the Orientalist purpose of disparaging the people and governments of Asia so as to legitimate European imperialism there, but this is not Montesquieu's own purpose. For him such an aim would be self-refuting, as the imperialist impulse is itself despotic. In the end, what makes Montesquieu's concept of despotism so powerful is that he shows how common the despotic tendency is in human societies and in human beings as individuals. He shows us that the tendency to abuse power is universal and cannot be written off as the vice of particular persons or regimes. Without accusing us, he makes us aware of this tendency even within ourselves, and aware of our responsibility to limit it by establishing liberal constitutional governments. The universal threat of despotism therefore provides a negative justification for Montesquieu's liberal theory of government. It also contains implicitly a positive justification for liberty, as the government of despotism indirectly illuminates what is best in human beings and so worth protecting by means of moderate government. Even as it shows us the ills of human nature, despotism makes us think of the "grandeur" of the human soul, and so reminds us of the reasons for studying the spirit of laws.

Notes

A version of this chapter was presented at the 1999 Annual Meeting of the American Political Science Association and I thank Sankar Muther for his incisive commmentary in that forum. David Carrithers and Paul Rahe also provided extensive and illuminating suggestions on earlier drafts. The chapter was completed with the assistance of a John M. Olin Foundation Faculty Fellowship and the generous support of Wesleyan University in administering that grant.

1. Muriel Dodds, *Les Récits de voyages: Sources de* L'Esprit des Lois *de Montesquieu* (Paris: Librairie Ancienne Honoré Champion, 1929), 149.

2. Melvin Richter, "Montesquieu's Comparative Analysis of Europe and Asia: Intended and Unintended Consequences," in *L'Europe de Montesquieu,* Alberto Postigliola and Marie Grazia Bottaro Paulumbo, eds. (Napoli: Liguori Editore, 1995), 347.

3. Diana J. Schaub, *Erotic Liberalism: Women and Revolution in Montesquieu's* Persian Letters (Lanham, Md.: Rowman and Littlefield, 1995), 19.

4. Robert Shackleton, "Les mots 'despote' et 'despotisme,'" in *Essays on Montesquieu and on the Enlightenment,* David Gilson and Martin Smith, eds. (Oxford: Voltaire Foundation, 1988), 483; Shackleton, *Montesquieu: A Critical Biography* (Oxford: Oxford University Press, 1961), 269; and Albert Sorel, *Montesquieu,* Melville B. Anderson and Edward Playfair Anderson, trans. (Chicago: A. C. McClurg & Co., 1888), 104.

5. There is a reasonable debate between those who regard Montesquieu as favoring republicanism and those who see him as a defender of monarchy. Mark Hulliung defends the former position in his *Montesquieu and the Old Regime* (Berkeley: University of California Press, 1976). Representatives of the latter position include Marc Duconseil, *Machiavel et Montesquieu: recherche sur un principe d'autorité* (Paris: Les Éditions Denoël, 1943), 169; Jean Ehrard, *Politique de Montesquieu* (Paris: Armand Colin, 1965), 35; Emile Faguet, *La politique comparée de Montesquieu, Rousseau et Voltaire* (Paris: Société française d'Imprimérie et de Librairie, 1902), 46f; and see the chapters in this volume by David Carrithers, C. P. Courtney, and Michael Mosher.

6. Françoise Weil, "Montesquieu et le despotisme," in *Actes du congrès Montesquieu réuni à Bordeaux du 23 au 26 mai 1955* (Bordeaux: Impriméries Delmas, 1956), 191. On the same point, see Tzvetan Todorov, *On Human Diversity,* Catherine Porter, trans. (Cambridge, Mass.: Harvard University Press, 1993), 362 f.

7. Alain Grosrichard, *Structure du sérail: La fiction du despotisme asiatique dans l'occident classique* (Paris: Éditions du seuil, 1979), 59f. On the same point, see Anne M. Cohler, *Montesquieu's Comparative Politics and the Spirit of American Constitutionalism* (Lawrence, Kansas: University Press of Kansas, 1988), 71.

8. These and other bracketed citations refer to Charles-Louis de Secondat baron de La Brède et de Montesquieu, *The Spirit of Laws* in his *Œuvres complètes de Montes-*

quieu, Roger Caillois, ed., 2 vols. (Paris: Pléiade, 1949-51), II 225-995. Roman numerals indicate the book number and Arabic numerals indicate the chapter number. Translations are my own although I have consulted previous translations in my work, including those of Anne Cohler, Basia Miller, and Harold Stone (Cambridge: Cambridge University Press, 1989) and Thomas Nugent (New York: Hafner, 1949). Henceforth references to *The Spirit of Laws* will be inserted parenthetically in the text, with Roman numerals indicating the book and Arabic numerals indicating the chapter.

9. See *Pensée* 579 (1622), in Pléiade, I, 1075. See Schaub, *Erotic Liberalism*, 94. Manent agrees that "human nature itself remains undetermined or underdetermined" in *The Spirit of Laws*. See his *La cité de l'homme* (Paris: Fayard, 1994), 110. That Montesquieu resisted the idea of a single, absolute standard of right based on a universal conception of human nature still is the most widely accepted interpretation of his view, and the one best supported by the evidence that his words provide. See, for example, Georges Benrekassa, *Montesquieu: La liberté et l'histoire* (Paris: Librairie générale française, 1987), 175; Simone Goyard-Fabre, *La philosophie du droit de Montesquieu* (Paris: Librairie C. Klincksieck, 1973), p. 54; Robert Alun Jones, "Ambivalent Cartesians: Durkheim, Montesquieu and Method," *American Journal of Sociology* 100, no. 1 (July, 1994): 13, 29f; Emile Durkheim, *Montesquieu and Rousseau: Forerunners of Sociology*, Ralph Manheim, trans. (Ann Arbor: University of Michigan Press, 1966); Phillip Knee, "La question de l'appartenance: Montesquieu, Rousseau et la révolution française," *The Canadian Journal of Political Science* 22, no. 2 (June, 1989): 285-311; Michael Mosher, "The Particulars of a Universal Politics: Hegel's Adaptation of Montesquieu's Typology," *American Political Science Review* 78, no. 1 (March, 1984): 178-188; Shackleton, *Montesquieu*, 250ff; Cohler, *Montesquieu's Comparative Politics*, 48; and Ehrard, *Politique de Montesquieu*, 10f. Notable exceptions to that interpretation are Mark Waddicor, who characterizes Montesquieu as a natural law theorist in *Montesquieu and the Philosophy of Natural Law* (The Hague: Martinus Nijhoff, 1970), and Cecil Courtney in chapter 1 of this voulme.

10. Montesquieu criticized ancient philosophy in his *Pensées* for not seeing that "[t]he terms beautiful, good, noble, great, perfect are attributes of objects which are relative to the beings who consider them" (*Pensée* 2062 [410], Pléiade, I, 1537). By that he did not mean to deny the possibility of metaphysical truths, but rather to assert their limits. Thus "when one says that there is not at all an absolute quality, that does not mean that there is nothing at all but that . . . our spirit cannot determine them" (*Pensée* 2063 [1154] , in Pléiade, I, 1537).

11. Politics should not be in the business of perfecting souls, Montesquieu says, because "perfection does not concern the universal in men or things," *Spirit of Laws*, XXIV, 7.

12. There is broad consensus among interpreters as to Montesquieu's liberal conception of liberty. Keohane, for example, notes that while he "greatly admired the extraordi-

nary virtue and patriotism that made self-government possible, he did not greatly admire self-government *per se,"* because "the exercise of political responsibility is not itself, for Montesquieu, a part of the good life." See Nannerl O. Keohane, *Philosophy and the State in France* (Princeton: Princeton University Press, 1980), 418. See also her "Virtuous Republics and Glorious Monarchies: Two Models in Montesquieu's Political Thought," *Political Studies* 20, no. 4 (December, 1972): 392. For further discussion of Montesquieu's liberal conception of liberty, see David W. Carrithers, "Montesquieu's Philosophy of Punishment," *History of Political Thought* 19, no. 2 (summer, 1998): esp. 221-6; Norman Hampson, *Will and Circumstance: Montesquieu, Rousseau and the French Revolution* (London: Duckworth, 1983), 10; Franklin Ford, *Robe and Sword: The Regrouping of the French Aristocracy after Louis XIV* (Cambridge, Mass.: Harvard University Press, 1953), 20; and Knee, "La question," 303.

13. John Plamenatz, *Man and Society* (New York: McGraw-Hill, 1963), I, 274.

14. On this point, see Grosrichard, *Structure du sérail*, esp. 8-11; Lucette Valensi, *The Birth of the Despot: Venice and the Sublime Port*, Arthur Denner, trans. (Ithaca: Cornell University Press, 1993), 2-3; Roger Boesche, "Fearing Monarchs and Merchants: Montesquieu's Two Theories of Despotism," *Western Political Science Quarterly* 43, no. 4 (December, 1990): 741; Robert Koebner, "Despot and Despotism: Vicissitudes of a Political Term" in *Journal of the Warburg and Courtauld Institutes* (London: Warburg Institute, 1951), vol. 14, nos. 1 and 2, 302; Bertrand Binoche, *Introduction* à De l'esprit des lois *de Montesquieu* (Paris: Presses universitaires de France, 1998), 208-13; and Shackleton, "Les mots 'despote' et 'despotisme,'" 483.

15. See Schaub, *Erotic Liberalism*, 20. For further discussion of Aristotle's idea of despotic rule, see Grosrichard, *Structure du sérail*, 11-25.

16. Aristotle, *Politics*, Carnes Lord, trans. (Chicago: University of Chicago Press, 1984), 1292a14.

17. Koebner, "Despot and Despotism," 277.

18. Schaub, *Erotic Liberalism*, 20.

19. Thomas Hobbes, *Leviathan*, Edwin Curley, ed. (Indianapolis: Hackett, 1994), Part I, chapter 13, paragraph 1.

20. Hobbes, *Leviathan*, II, 20, 11-14.

21. Hobbes, *Leviathan*, II, 17, 1.

22. Koebner, "Despot and Despotism," 293. For a thorough treatment of the Fronde and the events leading up to it see Geoffrey Treasure, *Mazarin: The Crisis of Absolutism in France* (London: Routledge, 1995), esp. 103-229.

23. Harold Ellis, *Boulainvilliers and the French Monarchy* (Ithaca: Cornell University Press, 1988), 38. See also Koebner, "Despot and Despotism," 293ff; and Boesche, "Fearing Monarchs and Merchants," 741.

24. Koebner, "Despot and Despotism," 298.

25. Koebner, "Despot and Despotism," 299; and Richter, "Montesquieu's Comparative Analysis," 334f.

26. See Binoche, 224; Franco Venturi, "Oriental Despotism," *Journal of the History of Ideas* 24, no. 1 (January-March, 1963): 134; and Koebner, "Despot and Despotism," 300f.

27. Koebner, "Despot and Despotism," 301; and Shackleton, "Les mots 'despote' et 'despotisme,'" 482f.

28. Montesquieu declined. See Weil, "Montesquieu et le despotisme," 191.

29. "Although the principle of despotic government is fear, its end is tranquillity; but this is not at all a peace, it is the silence of those towns that the enemy is poised to occupy" (*Spirit of Laws*, V.14). Berlin remarks that, according to Montesquieu, "only those societies are free that are in a state of agitation . . . and unstable." Isaiah Berlin, "Montesquieu," in *Against the Current* (New York: Viking, 1980), 158. On the same point, see Judith Shklar, *Montesquieu* (Oxford: Oxford University Press, 1987), 59; David W. Carrithers, "Introduction" in *The Spirit of Law, a Compendium of the First English Edition . . .*, David W. Carrithers, ed. (Berkeley: University of California Press, 1977), 15; Cohler, *Montesquieu's Comparative Politics*, 83; and Keohane, *Philosophy and the State in France*, 398.

30. Montesquieu actually enumerates four types of government, insofar as he notes that a republic can be either democratic or aristocratic. He classifies them together because in both cases the people (whether the whole or a part) are sovereign (*Laws*, II, 2). See chapter 2, above.

31. *Politics*, 1289a128-33. For accounts of how Montesquieu's idea of despotism differs from tyranny in Plato and Aristotle, see Badreddine Kassem, *Décadence et absolutisme dans l'œuvre de Montesquieu* (Paris: Librairie Minard, 1960), 107; Thomas Pangle, *Montesquieu's Philosophy of Liberalism* (Chicago: University of Chicago Press, 1973), 70; Koebner, "Despot and Despotism," 291, 299; Richter, "Montesquieu's Comparative Analysis," 333; and Schaub, *Erotic Liberalism*, 23.

32. For a discussion of Montesquieu's criticism of Aristotle in this respect, see Pangle, *Montesquieu's Philosophy*, 70.

33. For a discussion of Montesquieu's appreciation of the importance of the private sphere, see Carrithers, "Montesquieu's Philosophy of Punishment," esp. 221-35.

34. Thus Richter notes in "Montesquieu's Comparative Analysis" that "more than anyone else, it was Montesquieu who, by reclassifying political regimes, makes it possible to call the French monarchy despotic and the king a despot" (331). Levin also remarks on the significance of Montesquieu's treatment of despotism as a separate type of regime, comparing it to ancient classifications. See Lawrence M. Levin, *The Political Doctrine of Montesquieu's* Esprit des Lois: *Its Classical Background* (New York: Columbia University Press, 1936), 62.

35. See Koebner, "Despot and Despotism," 275; and Weil, "Montesquieu et le despotisme," 191.

36. On this point, see Venturi, "Oriental Despotism," *Journal of the History of Ideas* 24, no. 1 (Jan.-Mar. 1963), 135; Weil, "Montesquieu et le despotisme," 191; and Koebner, "Despot and Despotism," 275. For a rich account of Voltaire's position in the battle between the *thèse royale* and the *thèse nobilaire*, see Peter Gay, *Voltaire's Politics: The Poet as Realist* (Princeton: Princeton University Press, 1959).

37. Weil notes that it seems strange for Montesquieu to speak of fundamental law in a regime that by its nature lacks fixed, established laws. See "Montesquieu et le despotisme," 198f.

38. On the fatalism that pervades despotic government, see Paul Vernière, *Montesquieu et L'Esprit des lois ou la raison impure* (Paris: Société d'Édition d'Enseignement supérieur, 1977), 179, 184f; Kassem, *Décadence et absolutisme*, 127; and Shackleton, "Asia as Seen by the French Enlightenment," in *Essays on Montesquieu and on the Enlightenment*, 232.

39. Boesche points out that every despot is a slave to the providers of his pleasure, and afraid of their leaving. See his "Fearing Monarchs and Merchants," 744. Todorov also notes the despot's fear in *On Human Diversity*, 362. For a comparison between the fears of Montesquieu's despot and the fears of Plato's tyrant, see David Spitz, *Essays in the Liberal Idea of Freedom* (Tucson: University of Arizona Press, 1964), esp. 24f.

40. Boesche presents the two motives of fear and gratification as in conflict with one another, thus understating the connections between them.

41. Hobbes, *Leviathan*, I, 14, 31.

42. Hobbes, *Leviathan*, II, 31, 41.

43. Simone Goyard-Fabre notes that Montesquieu rejects the mechanistic materialism of Hobbes. See her *Montesquieu adversaire de Hobbes* (Paris: Lettres modernes, 1980), 16. Binoche also notes the mechanistic qualities of despotic government, 227-30.

44. Kassem emphasizes that the despot is all appetite. See his *Décadence et absolutisme*, 93. Althusser, too, remarks on the absence of reason under despotism. See his *Politics and History* (London: Verso, 1982), 76.

45. For an account of the ways in which the perfect power of choice undermines the capacity for intentional, self-initiated action, see Charles Taylor's interesting discussion of how "radical choice . . . fades into non-choice" in "What is Human Agency?" in his *Human Agency and Language* (Cambridge, England: Cambridge University Press, 1985), esp. 28-35.

46. Montesquieu's conviction that the unlimited power of despots prevents them from transcending the particular standpoint of their desires contradicts the standard view of absolutists, such as Bossuet, who believed that a king who had everything would have nothing more to desire and therefore would rule in a disinterested fashion. See Keohane, *Philosophy and the State in Modern France*, 275f.

47. For accounts of the standing and significance of women in relation to despotic government, see Schaub, *Erotic Liberalism*; Mosher, "The Judgmental Gaze of European Women: Gender, Sexuality and the Critique of Republican Rule," *Political Theory* 22, no. 1 (February, 1994): 25-44; Boesche, "Fearing Monarchs and Merchants," 749; and Vernière, *Montesquieu et la raison impure*, 182.

48. On the absence of a public/private divide in despotism, see Ellis, *Boulainvilliers and the French Monarchy*, 38f.

49. Richter also notes the absence of politics in despotism, in "Montesquieu's Comparative Analysis," 338.

50. For references to liberty as security, see *Laws*, XI, 6; XII, 5; XII, 12; XII, 23; XIII, 7; and XIX, 6.

51. On this point, see Henry J. Merry, *Montesquieu's System of Natural Government* (W. Lafayette, Ind.: Purdue Research Foundation, 1970), xiii; Gabriel Loirette, "Montesquieu et le problème, en France, du bon gouvernement," in *Actes du congrès*, 225; Faguet, *La politique comparée*, 15; and Ehrard, *Politique de Montesquieu*, 38.

52. Montesquieu, *Cahiers*, II, 209, cited in Hampson, *Will and Circumstance*, 10, n. 30.

53. Boesche points out that in despotic governments, the character of subjects mirrors the character of the ruler. See his "Fearing Monarchs and Merchants," 749. On the same point, see David Young, "Montesquieu's View of Despotism and His Use of Travel Literature," *Review of Politics* 40, no. 3 (1978): 397.

54. For a discussion of the role of commerce in limiting despotism in Montesquieu, see Albert O. Hirschman, *The Passions and the Interests* (Princeton: Princeton University Press, 1977), 78.

55. See also *Laws*, III, 8.

56. Montesquieu, *Pensée* 69 (5), in Pléiade, I, 993.

57. Thomas E. Kaiser, "Money, Despotism, and Public Opinion in Early Eighteenth-Century France: John Law and the Debate on Royal Credit," *Journal of Modern History* 63 (March, 1991): 22.

58. See also *Laws*, XX, 10 for Montesquieu's description of Law's system.

59. Richard Myers, "Christianity and Politics in Montesquieu's *Greatness and Decline of the Romans*," *Interpretation* 17, no. 2 (winter, 1989-90): 233.

60. Montesquieu, "Notes on England," in Pléiade, I, 880.

61. For a description of this aspect of despotism, see Boesche, "Fearing Monarchs and Merchants," esp. 743-59. Although Boesche illuminates an important aspect of despotism that has been too much neglected, he errs in attributing to Montesquieu a nostalgia for ancient virtue, claiming that Montesquieu longed for the greatness of the past (757). For further discussion of the significance of the desire for the comforts of life as a motivation in despotism, see also Young, "Montesquieu's View of Despotism," 398.

62. Young, in "Montesquieu's View of Despotism," also notes that religion can both reinforce and limit a despot's power, 399.

63. Recall the emphasis on the zealotry of the Christian monks and republican citizens in *Spirit of Laws*, V, 2. See also Montesquieu, *Considerations on the Causes of the Greatness of the Romans and their Decline* in Pléiade, II, chap. 11: "It was a dominating love of the homeland which, leaving behind the ordinary rules of crimes and virtues, listened only to itself and saw neither citizen nor friend nor benefactor nor father: virtue seemed to forget itself in order to surpass itself, and, an action that one formerly could not approve because of its atrocity was made to be admired as divine."

64. As Augustine had suggested when he remarked that "as for this mortal life, which ends after a few days' course, what does it matter under whose rule a man lives, being so soon to die." Augustine, *City of God*, Henry Bettenson, trans. (New York: Penguin, 1984), Book V, chap. 17, 205.

65. At least Montesquieu associated fatalism with the Christian and Muslim religions with which he was most concerned.

66. Shklar, *Montesquieu*, 33. See also Todorov, *On Human Diversity*, 365. In this respect, Montesquieu's skepticism about the power of reason to limit political power contrasts equally with the views of royal absolutists such as Voltaire and the later Jacobins, such as Robespierre, who believed that public reason could be a guarantor of liberty. On Robespierre's faith in reason, see Keith Michael Baker, *The Old Regime and the French Revolution* (Chicago: University of Chicago Press, 1987), 370. The similarities between the despotism of one and the democratic despotism of many is discussed later in this chapter.

67. Mosher remarks in "The Judgmental Gaze of European Women" (at 28) that "Montesquieu was only too aware, before Foucault, before Nietzsche, before Rousseau, how the theoretical impulse itself may mask despotic desire."

68. See R. Richelet, ed., *Dictionnaire françois* (Geneva: Jean Herman Widerhold, 1680), 350; and Montesquieu, *The Spirit of the Laws*, Anne M. Cohler, et al., eds. And trans., IV, 8, editor's note j, 41.

69. Albeit not, as we shall see, constant participation.

70. On this point, see Grosrichard, *Structure du sérail*, 47; Cohler, *Montesquieu's Comparative Politics*, 71-3; Weil, "Montesquieu et le despotisme," 201; Melvin Richter, *The Political Theory of Montesquieu* (Cambridge: Cambridge University Press, 1977), 83; and Kassem, *Décadence et absolutisme*, 247.

71. It is true that Montesquieu mentions "the genius of the people" as one of the "circumstances" that may preserve a despotic regime. Yet the examples he gives in this regard do not indicate much in the way of reason or deliberation. The genius of the Chinese people in limiting despotic power is illustrated by the "great fertility" of the women, which leads to large populations, the tendency of the peasants in search of scarce food to form bands of robbers multiplying into large armies, and their "tireless" labor, which re-

sults from a lack of productive land. In other words, the "genius" of the Chinese people is itself forced, the product of biological contingencies and material necessities, not deliberation and choice. And Montesquieu acknowledges as much, saying that "causes drawn for the most part from the physical conditions of the climate have been able to force the moral causes in this country, and to give rise to some sorts of miracles" (*Spirit of Laws*, VIII, 21).

72. See, for example, *Spirit of Laws*, XXV, 8: "The king of Persia is head of the religion, but the Koran rules the religion; the emperor of China is the sovereign pontiff, but there are books, which are in the hands of everyone, and to which he himself should conform. In vain did an emperor wish to abolish them; they triumphed over tyranny."

73. Aristotle, *Politics*, 1285a117.

74. Aristotle, *Politics*, 1285a119-21. On Aristotle's associations between despotism and Asia, see Koebner, "Despot and Despotism," 277f; Richter, "Montesquieu's Comparative Analysis," 337f; Venturi, "Oriental Despotism," 133; and Schaub, *Erotic Liberalism*, 20f.

75. Shackleton, "Asia as seen by the French Enlightenment," 231. Valensi also provides a particularly interesting account of the "forefathers" of Montesquieu's idea of oriental despotism, noting the use of the term as early as 1637 by a Venetian ambassador to Constantinople. See Valensi, *The Birth of the Despot*, 2-4.

76. Edward Said, *Orientalism* (New York: Pantheon, 1978), 119. On Said's rendering, Orientalism is characterized as a Western effort to give intellectual legitimacy to Western domination of the Orient (at 3). Said maintains that the Orient is the "cultural contestant" of Europe, "one of its deepest and most recurring images of the Other," and for that reason has helped to define Europe (or the West) as its contrasting image (at 1f). Orientalist authors use Asia as a counterpoint to clarify the particular ideas of European politics and society that they wish to promote. The portrait of Europe's "Other" is based as much on European projections of its fears and aspirations as on actual Oriental peoples, politics, and cultures, however (at 2). Consequently, it may portray qualities that are not actually present, and obscure from view aspects of Asian politics and society that should be appreciated. At the same time, by attributing a host of negative characteristics to Asians and characterizing their political systems as corrupt and inept, Orientalist authors are thought to provide a justification for those who wish to dominate the Orient culturally, economically, and politically. Said's analysis has been debated by scholars but that debate is beyond the scope of this study. For present purposes it is enough to note the disagreement, since the truth or falsehood of Said's thesis is immaterial to the argument advanced here.

77. For more extensive analysis of Montesquieu's use of travel literature, see Ali Behdad, "The Eroticized Orient: Images of the Harem in Montesquieu and His Precursors," *Stanford French Review* 13, no. 2-3 (fall-winter, 1989): 110f; Dodds, *Les récits des voyages*, esp. 139, 147, 150; Young, "Montesquieu's View of Despotism," 394f;

Goyard-Fabre, *La philosophie du droit de Montesquieu*, 148; Kassem, *Décadence et absolutisme*, 120, 133.

78. See, for example, Elie Carcassonne, "La Chine dans *L'esprit des lois*," in *Revue d'histoire littéraire de la France* (Paris: Librairie Armand Colin, 1924), 198-205; Richter, *The Political Theory of Montesquieu*, 72; Shackleton, "Asia as seen by the French Enlightenment," 239; Weil, "Montesquieu et le despotisme," 193; Sorel, *Montesquieu*, 104; Vernière, *Montesquieu et la raison impure*, 186-88; Young, "Montesquieu's View of Despotism," 401; and Jonathan Spence, *The Chan's Great Continent: China in Western Minds* (New York: Norton, 1998).

79. For a discussion of the various limits on Persian despotism see Young, "Montesquieu's View of Despotism," 401f.

80. Carcassonne, "La Chine," 202. Other discrepancies between travel reports of China and Montesquieu's idea of despotic government are noted by Kassem, *Décadence et absolutisme*, 130; Dodds, *Les récits de voyages*, 149f; and Shackleton, "Asia as Seen by the French Enlightenment," 239.

81. Richter, "Montesquieu's Comparative Analysis," 340; Venturi, "Oriental Despotism," 137.

82. Kassem, *Décadence et absolutisme*, 111.

83. Young, "Montesquieu's View of Despotism," 394; Richter, "Montesquieu's Comparative Analysis," 338f.

84. Carcassone, "La Chine," 194.

85. For discussion of Voltaire's approval of China, see Spence, *The Chan's Great Continent*, esp. 95f; Kassem, *Décadence et absolutisme*, 142; and Richter, "Montesquieu's Comparative Analysis," 339. Grosrichard provides an interesting account of the disagreement between Voltaire and Montesquieu over China and its connection to their different positions in the contemporary French constitutional debates. See his *Structure du sérail*, esp. 40-45. On Voltaire's objections to Montesquieu's definition of despotism, see Binoche, 237-8.

86. Richter, "Montesquieu's Comparative Analysis," 338.

87. Young, "Montesquieu's View of Despotism," 404.

88. Richter, "Montesquieu's Comparative Analysis," 345.

89. Those who romanticized Eastern absolutism were not limited to the defenders of the *thèse royale*, but also included Christian missionaries, who themselves authored many of the travelogues. Montesquieu calls into the question the reliability of the missionaries' judgments of China in *Spirit of Laws*, VIII, 21, saying, "Could it not be that the missionaries were deceived by an appearance of order; that they were struck by this continuous exercise of the will of one alone by which they themselves are governed, and which they love so much to find in the courts of the kings of India?" For additional discussion of Montesquieu's treatment of China, see Spence, *The Chan's Great Continent*, esp. 87-95.

90. Montesquieu states his methodological approach to "details" in the Preface to *Spirit of Laws*: "The more one will reflect on the details the more one will feel the certainty of the principles. The details themselves, I have not given them all; for who could say everything without a fatal boredom?"

91. See Kassem, *Décadence et absolutisme*, 135.

92. In his *Pensées*, Montesquieu complains about "the censors whom princes have established, who direct all pens." (*Pensée* 1456 [1525], in Pléiade, I, 1342). Indeed, he says, "since the discovery of the printing press, there is no longer any true history. The princes used not to be attentive, and the police did not concern themselves about [books]. Today, all books are submitted to the inquisition of this police, which has established rules of discretion. To violate them is an offense. One has learned from this that princes are offended by what one says about them. In other times, they did not concern themselves with it; one then spoke the truth." (*Pensée* 1455 [1462], in Pléiade, I, 1342). Thus Montesquieu clearly indicates that he wrote with censors in mind. He had good reason to worry about offending the king and the Church, as much because he wanted his book to be read as out of fear for his safety. Still, safety was a concern. There is evidence that friends advised him not to publish *The Spirit of Laws*, fearing repercussions (George Saintsbury, *French Literature and its Masters* [New York: Alfred A. Knopf, 1946], 88). When he did publish it in 1748, Voltaire had already been incarcerated, and Diderot would be imprisoned the following year at Vincennes. See Solange Fricaud, "Pour qui est écrit *l'Esprit des lois?*" in *Analyses & réflexions sur Montesquieu* (Paris: Edition Marketing, 1987), 181. Montesquieu took the precaution of publishing his book anonymously, and in Geneva rather than France, but even so, he was reprimanded by the Sorbonne for his "disparagement" of the crown, and the book was placed on the *Index* of works proscribed by the Church. For a listing of passages censured by the religious authorities in France, see Carrithers, ed., *The Spirit of Laws*, Appendix I, 466-67. Today we expect and reward transparency in writing, and are suspicious of anything else, but Montesquieu neither expected transparency nor expected to be rewarded for it, as he himself tells us, and he wrote accordingly.

93. See Young, "Montesquieu's View of Despotism," 404f.

94. This remark illustrates the fact that despotism is not the result of a vicious soul, or "heart," but rather can be the objective even of those who lack a despotic heart. It also points to the inadequacy of reason as a limit on despotism, since Montesquieu associates Richelieu's despotic tendency with his "head," the seat of reason.

95. Shackleton agrees that this remark is directed against Louis XIV. See his *Montesquieu*, 272.

96. For example, Schaub, *Erotic Liberalism*, 23, 63.

97. Schaub, *Erotic Liberalism*, 72.

98. On this point, Schaub notes that in *Persian Letters* 35, Usbek says of France that "everywhere I see Mohammedanism, though I cannot find Mohammed." See her *Erotic*

Liberalism, 71. On the parallels between Christianity and Islam, see also Young, "Montesquieu's View of Despotism," 403; and Mosher, "The Judgmental Gaze," 28.

99. Binoche points out that what Montesquieu calls the "despotism of all" should be understood as an analogy to despotism proper, rather than being taken literally, since Montesquieu defines despotism, strictly speaking, as the rule of one not many (at 205).

100. Merry, *Montesquieu's System*, 313; Baker, *The Old Regime*, 178. For additional discussion of the potential for despotism in England, see C. A. Sainte-Beuve, *Portraits of the Eighteenth Century*, Katharine P. Wormeley, trans. (New York: G.P. Putnam's Sons, 1905), 132; Sharon Krause, "The Spirit of Separate Powers in Montesquieu," *The Review of Politics* 62, no. 2 (spring 2000), 231-65; and consider the argument advanced in chapter 2 of this volume.

101. Schaub, *Erotic Liberalism*, 19.

102. Cited in F. J. C. Hearnshaw, *The Social and Political Ideas of Some Great French Thinkers of the Age of Enlightenment* (New York: Barnes and Noble, 1931), 61.

103. For further discussion of honor as a source of resistance to potentially despotic authority, see Mosher, "The Judgmental Gaze," 38-40 as well as Chapter 4 in this volume; and Sharon Krause, "The Politics of Distinction and Disobedience: Honor and the Defense of Liberty in Montesquieu," *Polity* 31, no. 3 (spring 1999): 469-99.

104. Baker, *The Old Regime*, 374. On same point see Knee, "La question," 305 and chapter 3 of this volume. For a rich account of the Jacobin cult of Graeco-Roman antiquity and its debt to Mably, see Johnson Kent Wright, *A Classical Republican in Eighteenth-Century France: The Political Thought of Mably* (Stanford: Stanford University Press, 1997).

105. For more extended discussion of the despotic features of Jacobinism, see François Furet, "Révolution française et tradition jacobine," in *The French Revolution and the Creation of Modern Political Culture*, Keith Baker, Colin Lucas, François Furet, and Mona Ozouf, eds., vol. II, *The Political Culture of the French Revolution*, Colin Lucas, ed. (Oxford: Pergamon, 1988), esp. 332-34.

106. Said, *Orientalism*, 3. For a fine treatment of the complex relationship between Montesquieu's intentions in associating despotism with Asia and the unintended consequences of that association, see Richter, "Montesquieu's Comparative Analysis."

107. Along these lines, Todorov argues (at 377) that Montesquieu sees despotism as a translation on the social level of features that characterize every human being.

108. Montesquieu, *Pensée* 615 (1266), in Pléiade, I, 1138.

109. Montesquieu, *Pensée* 615 (1266), in Pléiade, I, 1138.

110. Weil in "Montesquieu et le despotisme" notes that despotism destroys talents (201f). On the same point, see Kassem, *Décadence et absolutisme*, 20, 92.

111. Mosher in "The Judgmental Gaze" (at 31) notes that this fact should make one "regard with skepticism the claim that [Montesquieu] is an ordinary natural law thinker."

112. See, for example, Juan Linz, "Totalitarian and Authoritarian Regimes," in *Handbook of Political Science,* Fred Greenstein and Nelson Polsby, eds. (Reading, Mass.: Addison-Wesley, 1975), III, 191-357; Samuel P. Huntington, *The Third Wave: Democratization in the Late Twentieth Century* (Norman, Okla: University of Oklahoma Press, 1991), esp. chap. 1-4; Guillermo O'Donnell and Philippe Schmitter, *Transitions from Authoritarian Rule:Tentative Conclusions about Uncertain Democracies* (Baltimore: Johns Hopkins University Press, 1986), esp. 3-72; and Giuseppe DiPalma, *To Craft Democracies: An Essay on Democratic Transitions* (Berkeley: University of California Press, 1990), esp. chap. 1.

Chapter Six

Montesquieu and English Liberty

C. P. Courtney

Montesquieu's biographers remind us that he was born in the year of the Revolution Settlement when, by drawing up a Bill of Rights, followed by later constitutional enactments, the English Parliament set out to define the main features of that system of government which would one day be described in the *The Spirit of Laws* as a system of liberty. This is certainly a useful piece of information, not however because of any "necessary relation" ("*rapport nécessaire*") between Montesquieu's birth in 1689 and his later intellectual career, but because it reminds us that he belongs to a generation for whom, at least during their early years, the image of England and the English, as seen from France, was by no means that of a country which had very much to recommend itself to the rest of Europe.[1]

It is easy for us to forget that in the seventeenth century the French considered England a small, remote and uncivilized island where the climate was abominable and the language incomprehensible. The story is told that Corneille, when he received a translation of *Le Cid* into English, regarded it as a curiosity which he kept in a cupboard along with a translation of the same work into two other strange and exotic languages, Turkish and Slavonic; and Louis XIV, usually a well-informed monarch, once asked his ambassador in London whether the English had any writers or men of learning.[2] No doubt by 1689 the French had become somewhat better informed about their neighbors on the other side of the Channel, but this information was not necessarily to the advantage of the English. The French could hardly be expected to admire a nation where one king had been executed and another dethroned, Roman Catholics persecuted, Huguenot refugees welcomed and even encouraged to publish pamphlets against the French monarchy and where, after the expulsion of the Catholic James II, his disloyal subjects had replaced him with William III, a Dutch Protestant who, before leaving Holland, had led his army against that of Louis XIV and in 1702, with the outbreak of the the War of the Spanish Succession, would once again take sides against France.

With the Quadruple Alliance of 1718 relations between England and France improved, at least until the War of the Austrian Succession, which began in 1740 and ended in 1748. Even during the period when the two countries were at peace, however, French writers had to tread carefully when speaking of the English political system; Montesquieu, as we shall see, was very much aware of this when in 1734 he published the *Considerations on the Causes of the Greatness of the Romans and on their Decline.*

The Image of England in Montesquieu's Early Writings

A convenient starting point for any discussion of Montesquieu's views on England is the *Persian Letters,* published in 1721. In Letter 104 Usbek speaks of the "impatient temper" (*"humeur impatiente"*) of the English, who resent having to obey those who govern them, and we find in the same letter a reference to the political theory (contract and the right of resistance) which was frequently invoked by the English to justify the Glorious Revolution:[3]

> But, if a prince, far from making his subjects happy, wants to overwhelm and destroy them, the basis for obedience ceases: nothing binds them, nothing attaches them to the prince: and they re-enter the state of natural freedom.

However, in what immediately follows, Usbek has recourse to sarcasm in order to dissociate himself from the English:

> The crime of high treason is nothing else, according to them, than the crime that the weaker commits against the stronger by disobeying him, in whatever manner. So the English people, finding themselves stronger in their struggle against one of their kings, declared that the prince was guilty of the crime of high treason in waging war against his subjects.

Later, in Letter 136 there is an account of England as portrayed by historians:

> Here are the historians of England, where you see liberty emerging endlessly from the fires of discord and sedition; the Prince forever reeling on his unshakeable throne, an impatient nation, wise even in its fury and which, master of the seas (something unheard of until then,) mixes commerce with imperialism.

This is a somewhat ironic and not exactly flattering portrait, especially if read alongside Letter 102, where Usbek, after noting that most European states are monarchies, writes of this form of government:

> It is a violent state, which always degenerates into despotism or republic: power can never be equally shared between the people and the prince; the balance is too difficult to preserve.

He adds in this same Letter 102 that, when there is any imbalance of power between the prince and the citizens, the former has the advantage, since he has control of the army.

There is nothing very new or original here, and it seems that, at this stage, Montesquieu had no special interest in the English form of government and no particular admiration for English liberty.[4] On the contrary, what he admires most is ancient republicanism, particularly the republicanism of classical Greece. Thus, in Letter 131 we read: "The love of liberty, the hatred of kings, preserved Greece in independence and spread afar republican government, and this spirit of freedom was passed on by the Greeks to their colonies. These Greek colonies brought with them a spirit of freedom to which it had become accustomed in this mild country."

This enthusiasm for classical republics seems to have diminished during the period from 1728 to 1731, when Montesquieu undertook an extended tour of Europe and found himself singularly unimpressed with some modern republics, especially Venice. On the other hand he took a close interest in the English form of government, which he had the opportunity of studying during his stay in that country from November 1729 until early in 1731. During this visit he kept a journal, of which all that survives is the *Notes on England*. In this fragment there are a number of passages devoted to English liberty, for example:

> In London, liberty and equality. Liberty in London is the liberty of respectable people, in which it differs from that of Venice, which is the liberty to live obscurely and with prostitutes and to marry them: equality in London is also the equality of respectable people, which differs from liberty in Holland, which is the liberty of the riff-raff of the people [*la canaille*].[5]
>
> England is at present the country in the world where there is the greatest freedom. I do not make an exception for any republic; I say free, because the prince does not have the power to harm anyone in any way, because his power is limited by an act.[6]

In his *Notes*, Montesquieu goes on to refer to the separation of the executive power from the legislative in a way which anticipates the *The Spirit of Laws*:

but if the lower chamber became dominant, its power would be unlimited and dangerous, because it would have at the same time the executive power; whereas at present unlimited power is in the parliament and the king, and the executive power in the king, whose power is limited.[7]

There is also a dark side to the picture, however:

England is a country where money is more important than honor or virtue and the people are coarse, unsociable and, worst of all, corrupt: The English are no longer worthy of their liberty. They sell it to the king; and if the king gave it back to them, they would sell it to him again.[8]

Notwithstanding these unfavorable remarks about the English, there can be no doubt that Montesquieu was impressed with their form of government, and when in 1734 he published the *Considerations on the Causes of the Greatness of the Romans and on their Decline,* he included an extremely flattering reference to England, which is particularly interesting because the general picture he gives in that work of ancient Rome and its decline can hardly be considered favorable to classical republicanism:

The government of England is one of the wisest [*un des plus sages*] in Europe, because it has a body [i.e., the British Parliament] which examines it continually, and such are its mistakes that they never last long, and, consequently, by the spirit of attention which they give to the nation, its mistakes are often useful.[9]

However, having written this and had it printed by his Dutch publisher in the copies of the work ready for distribution, Montesquieu had to make arrangements for a different text to be inserted, by means of a cancel, into the copies to be sold in France, altering the passage to read, instead of "The government of England is one of the wisest in Europe," to "The government of England is wiser" [than various ancient governments and the Italian republics],[10] a very minor change, but indicative of how sensitive the censorship was at this time concerning anything which praised the English system of government. There were also other changes to the text of the copies distributed in France. For example, Montesquieu suppressed two passages which could be read as shocking religious susceptibilities by justifying suicide. One of these passages referred explicitly to two of the Stuart monarchs, whose adherence to the Roman Catholic religion, it is suggested, prevented them from finding an honorable solution to their dilemma by taking their own lives: "If Charles I and James II had been members of a religion which had allowed them to kill themselves, they would not have had to bear, the first such a death, the other such a life."[11]

What led to the need for these changes was no doubt the furor caused by the publication a month or two earlier of Voltaire's *Lettres philosophiques*.[12] This work's somewhat extravagant praise of everything English, including passages which seemed to condone regicide and dethronement, was unacceptable to the French authorities, who issued a *lettre de cachet* against the author and ordered his book to be publicly burned. Montesquieu had no desire to see his work on the Romans suffer a similar fate and, if it is true, as is suggested by a contemporary source,[13] that by this time he had already written a draft description of the English constitution (which would later find its way into the *The Spirit of Laws*), it is understandable that he should have decided to delay making any decision with regard to the possibility of having it published.

Quite apart from these bibliographical considerations, the fact that Voltaire and Montesquieu, each in his own way, had discovered English liberty is of considerable interest. Voltaire, at this stage, at least in his publications, was ahead of Montesquieu in seeing England as one of the wonders of the modern world: in England citizens are free to practice whatever religion they please, the government places no obstacles in the way of philosophical and scientific enquiry, there is nothing to debar noblemen from taking part in trade, men of letters are appreciated at their true worth and the system of government is such that all classes are represented in Parliament and the power of the king is strictly limited by the law.

A striking aspect of this slanted and idealized picture is that Voltaire turns his back on the traditional reverence for classical antiquity. He portrays England as in the vanguard of progress and makes a point of demonstrating that the English form of government is vastly superior to anything found in the ancient world. Thus, rejecting any facile comparison between the English Parliament and the Roman Senate, he points out that whereas the latter had no scruples about riding roughshod over the citizens, in England the citizens are protected from this kind of abuse thanks to a political system in which power is shared by King, Lords, and Commons. He acknowledges that the English, like the Romans, have had their civil wars; but the outcome in Rome was slavery, whereas in England it is freedom.[14] As for the image of England as a country in constant disorder, he writes:

> The French think that the government of this island is stormier than the sea which surrounds it, and that is true; but that is when the king begins the storm, when he wants to take over the vessel of which he is only the first pilot. The civil wars in France have been longer, more cruel, more fertile in crimes than those of England; but of all these civil wars none has had a wise freedom [*une liberté sage*] as its object.[15]

And, continuing to reject the traditional French view of England as an uncivilized regicide nation, Voltaire dismisses the execution of Charles I in a way
which was bound to be condemned by the French authorities: "What the English are most reproached with by the French," he writes, "is the suffering of
Charles I, who was treated by those who conquered him as he would have
treated them if he had been the victor." He concludes by inviting his French
readers to compare this execution, which took place after a trial, and where what
was at stake was liberty, with the indiscriminate assassinations of which the
French kings Henri III and Henri IV were the victims.

We shall find in Montesquieu a more sober picture of the English form of
government; but, like Voltaire, he presents it as superior to anything known to
classical Greece or Rome. In fact, for Montesquieu, it was a system which had
come down to the English, not from classical antiquity, but from the ancient
Germans:[16]

> In perusing the admirable treatise of Tacitus on the manners of the Germans, we
> find it is from that nation the English have borrowed the idea of their political
> government. This beautiful system was invented first in the woods (XI, 6, 407).

The Image of England in *The Spirit of Laws*

It is to the *The Spirit of Laws* that one turns for Montesquieu's mature views on
English liberty, especially to Book XI, chapter 6 ("Of the constitution of England") and to Book XIX, chapter 27, ("How the laws contribute to form the
manners, customs, and character, of a nation").[17] It is tempting to read these
chapters as if they formed an independent work (and indeed, they were published in this way in English translation in the eighteenth century);[18] however, it
is important to see them in the context of Montesquieu's general approach to the
study of laws and political institutions.

The description of the English constitution in Book XI, chapter 6 is closely
related to the sections of *The Spirit of Laws* devoted to typologies of different
forms of government, especially Books II to VIII, where Montesquieu describes
republic, monarchy, and despotism. In a republic power is in the hands of the
many (democracy) or the few (aristocracy); in a monarchy it is in the hands of
one man, but there are fixed laws, and the power of the monarch is restrained by
the existence of intermediary powers and a repository of laws; in despotism
power is in the hands of one man who rules according to personal whim. Each
form of government has what Montesquieu calls its "principle": in republics it
is virtue (a sense of civic responsibility which gives priority to the interests of
the community over those of the individual); in monarchy it is honor (respect
for rank and distinctions); and in despotism it is fear. As for England, which is
not quite a monarchy and not quite a republic, but a curious hybrid "where a re-

public is hidden under the form of monarchy" (V, 19), it is described separately as a form of government which has as its object the liberty of the citizen.

It is important to stress that these descriptions, although obviously inspired by Montesquieu's information about real republics, monarchies and despotisms, have the status, not of factual accounts or descriptive generalizations, but of abstract models or ideal types. Thus, he writes at the end of Book III:

> Such are the principles of the three sorts of government: which does not imply, that, in a particular republic, they actually are, but that they ought to be, virtuous: nor does it prove, that, in a particular monarchy, they are actuated by honor; or, in a particular despotic government, by fear; but that they ought to be directed by these principles, otherwise the government is imperfect (III, 11).

Similarly, he writes toward the end of chapter 6 of Book XI:

> It is not my business to examine whether the English actually enjoy this liberty, or not. Sufficient it is for my purpose to observe, that it is established by their laws; and I inquire no farther (XI, 6, 407).

Having defined these ideal types, Montesquieu's procedure is to hold them up to reality, to use them as models to explain and evaluate the different regimes which exist in his own day or have existed in the past. Thus in Books II-X he examines various republics, monarchies, and despotisms, past and present, in the light of his definitions of the three forms of government. In Book XI, chapter 5 he refers to the English model, which will reveal to the reader the principles of the system of liberty:

> One nation there is also in the world, that has, for the direct end of its constitution, political liberty. We shall presently examine the principles on which this liberty is founded: if they are sound, liberty will appear in its highest perfection (*la liberté y paraîtra comme dans un miroir*).

Then, in the remaining chapters of this same book, he seeks to establish to what extent these principles, essential to liberty, were understood, or at least applied by legislators (consciously or unconsciously), in the ancient world.

Much has been written about the alleged inaccuracy of Montesquieu's description of the English constitution,[19] a description which says nothing about the cabinet or political parties and which attributes to the monarch the right to veto the resolutions of the two chambers of the legislative power by withholding his assent. In a sense, such criticisms are based on a misunderstanding, since Montesquieu is describing an ideal model, that is to say, the theory rather than the practice of the constitution, and by theory he means (as we have seen in the passage quoted) what is established by the laws, the relevant laws being presumably the various constitutional enactments such as the Bill of Rights (1689) and Act of Settlement (1701) which define the role of the executive as well as the legislative and judicial powers. The Bill of Rights makes it clear that the king cannot rule without Parliament: it leaves him neither suspending nor dispensing power. Nor can he raise taxes or keep an army without the consent of Parliament. In fact the only real part in legislation left to him is to give or refuse his assent to bills. But his power as head of the executive power is left intact, though Lords and Commons can impeach his ministers. As for the judiciary, the Act of Settlement specified that judges were to be appointed *quamdiu se bene gesserint*, which meant that, though they were appointed by the king, they could no longer be dismissed at pleasure. These constitutional arrangements meant that there was, in fact, a very high degree of separation of powers, especially between executive and legislative, so much so that there was always a danger of deadlock between king and Parliament.[20]

If we accept that in Book XI, chapter 6 Montesquieu's purpose is to describe the English form of government in terms of theory rather than practice, that is to say according to existing constitutional enactments, we shall find that his model reflects remarkably accurately the laws relevant to the constitution. The points on which he can be accused of inaccuracy by a literal-minded reader are the following: first, his omission of any mention of professional judges, thus giving the impression that the judiciary consists solely of juries; secondly, his statement that the upper chamber has the power to "modify the law in favour of the law, in pronouncing less harshly than it does" (*modifier la loi en faveur de la loi même, en prononçant moins rigoureusement qu'elle*, XI, 6, 404); and thirdly, in overlooking that the duration of parliaments was not simply a matter for decision by the king, but that this had been settled by Act of Parliament, limiting the duration first to three years (1694) and then to seven (1716). On the other hand, he remains close to the actual constitution in his description of the powers attributed to king, Lords, and Commons, and if he speaks of the monarch's right to withhold his assent from bills, this was (and in theory still is) constitutionally correct. As for the absence of any reference to the cabinet or political parties, there was in fact at this time no cabinet in the modern sense and, as for parties, no constitutional enactment had ever as much as mentioned their existence. That is to say, they belonged to the practice rather than to the theory of the constitution. It should also be mentioned that in Montesquieu's account of the executive, legislative, and judicial powers, there is no question of each power being in a watertight compartment.[21] The upper chamber has certain judicial functions, since noblemen have the right to be tried there, and it is also the highest court of appeal. In addition, the Lords and Commons have a judicial function in cases of impeachment; and the monarch, as has been seen, has a share (if only a negative one) in legislation.

The explanation of why the English system makes for liberty is that it is a highly complex piece of constitutional machinery embodying the principle that "To prevent this abuse [of power], it is necessary, from the very nature of things, power should be a check to power" (XI, 4). This protection of the citizens against the abuse of power is achieved in two ways. The first is by the functional separation of the executive, legislative and judicial powers, a separation which, as has been seen, admits of certain clearly defined exceptions, and which in its simplest form is expressed as follows:

> There would be an end of everything, were the same man, or the same body, whether of the nobles or of the people, to exercise those three powers, that of enacting laws, that of executing the public resolutions, and of trying the causes of individuals (XI, 6, 397).

The second way in which protection against the abuse of power is secured is by a system of checks and balances within a mixed form of government: this is summarized as follows:

> Here, then, is the fundamental constitution of the government we are treating of. The legislative body being composed of two parts, they check one another by the mutual privilege of rejecting. They are both restrained by the executive power, as the executive is by the legislative.
>
> These three powers should naturally form a state of repose or inaction: but, as there is a necessity for movement in the course of human affairs, they are forced to move, but still in concert (XI, 6, 405).

This account of how the English constitution guarantees liberty is not entirely original. However, it is impossible to attribute Montesquieu's ideas to any one source, for both the theory of the separation of powers and that of checks and balances within a mixed constitution had been developing in an unsystematic way during the struggle between king and Parliament in the seventeenth century.[22] Elements of these theories can be found in such diverse documents as *His Majesties Answer to the XIX Propositions* (1642), the Bill of Rights, the Act of Settlement, and the pamphlets of a multitude of minor political writers, as well as in Locke and Bolingbroke.[23] References to the balanced constitution had long been commonplace. The theory of separation had not been fully developed, but the elements which Montesquieu brought together were already there: the independence of the judiciary, the fierce independence of upper and lower chambers from interference from the monarch who, however, was sole head of the executive and had the right to refuse his assent to bills. Montesquieu's achievement was to make a brilliant synthesis of these dispersed elements. His success in England was immediate, and nobody, not even such an authority as Blackstone,[24] disagreed; readers had somehow heard all this before, but no one had ever said it quite like this or brought out its full significance.

The Character and Political Customs of the English

As has been seen, in Book XI, chapter 6, Montesquieu is concerned with theory rather than practice, with the constitutional system of liberty rather than with the question of whether the English actually enjoy liberty. To discover his views on this second question we must turn to chapter 27 of Book XIX. This often neglected[25] chapter belongs to that part of *The Spirit of Laws* where Montesquieu, after defining different forms of government, examines how laws are related to such factors as environment, commerce, and religion. The English climate, we learn in Book XIV, chapter 13, is responsible for the high rate of suicide in that country. It is also responsible for the fact that the English live in a constant condition of physical and mental agitation, an unhappy condition which has at least one important advantage in that it creates an atmosphere highly uncongenial to the establishment of tyranny:

> This temper, in a free nation, is extremely proper for disconcerting the projects of tyranny, which is always slow and feeble in its commencements, as in the end it is active and lively; which at first only stretches out a hand to assist, and exerts afterwards a multitude of arms to oppress.
>
> Slavery is ever preceded by sleep. But a people, who find no rest in any situation, who continually explore every part, and feel nothing but pain, can hardly be lulled to sleep (XIV, 13).

There is a further development of this theme in Book XIX, where Montesquieu examines the interplay between laws and the character of the citizens (the "general spirit") of different countries. It is here, in the final and longer of his two chapters on England, that he returns to the English system of government and describes how it works in practice.

Before examining chapter 27 of Book XIX in any detail, it should be noted that the perspective adopted by Montesquieu is not that of an historian. He never mentions England explicitly by name and throughout he uses the conditional. It might be supposed that this is an attempt to avoid censorship, but it seems more likely that it is simply the application of the method referred to in the second paragraph of the chapter:

> I have spoken in the eleventh book of a free people and have given the principles of their constitution: let us now see the effects which follow from this liberty, the character it is capable of forming and the customs which naturally result from it (XIX, 27, 574).

In other words, chapter 27 is written as if it were a series of deductions or geometrical demonstrations because Montesquieu wishes to show that the working of the English system of government is the logical consequence of the form of the constitution of this country (as described in Book XI, chapter 6) or, more precisely, the consequence of the interaction between this constitution and the English "general spirit."

Montesquieu identifies as the most important feature of the working of the English parliamentary system the relation between the executive and legislative powers, describing in terms which were transparent to contemporaries, the party struggle between "ins" and "outs," that is to say between Court and Country or Whigs and Tories:

> As there would be, in this state, two visible powers, the legislative and executive, and as every citizen would have a will of his own and might at pleasure assert his independence, most men would have a greater fondness for one of these powers than for the other, the multitude having commonly neither equity nor sense enough to show an equal affection to both.
>
> And, as the executive power, by disposing of all employments, could give great hopes and no fears, every man, who obtained any favour from it, would be ready to espouse its cause; while it would be liable to be attacked by those who would have nothing to hope from it.
>
> All the passions being unrestrained, hatred, envy, jealousy, and an ambitious desire of riches and honors, appear in their full extent: were it otherwise, the state would be in the condition of a man weakened by sickness, who is without passions because he is without strength.
>
> The hatred which arises between the two parties will always subsist, because it will always be impotent.
>
> These parties being composed of freemen, if the one becomes too powerful for the other, as a consequence of liberty, this other is depressed; while the citizens take the weaker side, with the same readiness as the hands lend their assistance to remove the infirmities and disorders of the body (XIX, 27, 575).

It is obvious from these passages that Montesquieu understands how, for practical reasons, the King uses his patronage to give offices to those supporting the Crown's "interest" in Parliament. In this way the theoretical separation of executive power from the legislative, which meant there was a risk of deadlock, was overcome by a system which to the "ins" was simply carrying out the King's business, but which to the "outs" was "corruption." This was the same system that David Hume described as follows in his essay *On the Independency of Parliament* (1741):

The Crown has so many offices at its disposal, that, when assisted by the honest and disinterested part of the House, it will always command the resolutions of the whole, so far, at least, as to preserve the ancient constitution from danger. We may, therefore, give to this influence what name we please; we may call it by the invidious appellation of corruption and dependence; but some degree and some kind of it are inseparable from the very nature of our constitution and necessary to the preservation of our mixed government.[26]

Montesquieu also understood that one important result of the party struggle was that unscrupulous pamphleteers or orators would seek to stir up fear among the people:

As we are afraid of being deprived of the blessing we already enjoy, and which may be disguised and misrepresented to us, and as fear always enlarges objects; the people would be uneasy under such a situation, and would believe themselves in danger even in those moments when they are most secure.

As those, who, with the greatest warmth, would oppose the executive power, dare not avow the self-interested motives of their opposition, so much the more do they increase the terrors of the people, who could never be certain whether they were in danger or not. But even this would contribute to making them avoid the real dangers to which they may, in the end, be exposed (XIX, 27, 575-76).

The picture may not be entirely edifying, but it would be a mistake, on account of the use of the words "fear" and "terror" in the passages quoted, to seek a link between the English system and despotism. The "fear" to which reference is made is surely nothing more than a temporary reaction of the people to the kind of fiery rhetoric which was commonly used in pamphlets and in Parliament, and which Montesquieu himself had read or heard when he was in England.[27] Thus, immediately after the last passage quoted above, he writes:

But the legislative body, having the confidence of the people, and being more enlightened than they, would be able to calm their uneasiness, and make them recover from the bad impressions they have entertained (XIX, 27, 576).

And he sees this as one of the ways in which the English system is superior to that of classical republics:

This is the great advantage which this government could have over the ancient democracies, in which the people had an immediate power; for, when they were moved and agitated by the orators, these agitations always produced their effect (XIX, 27, 576).

This is followed by a passage where he sums up the good effect of this rowdy practice:

> But, when an impression of terror has no certain object, it could produce only clamour and abuse: it could have, however, this good effect, that it could put all the springs of government into motion, and fix the attention of every citizen (XIX, 27, 576).

The system described by Montesquieu and Hume would be replaced in the nineteenth century by the modern parliamentary system of party and cabinet government, in which the monarch was gradually pushed out of active politics. In the eighteenth century, however, a cabinet composed of a committee of the legislative body would have been considered an unconstitutional usurpation of the executive power and destructive of the traditional balance of power. On this important principle Montesquieu, who is in agreement with Hume, had written in chapter 6 of Book XI:

> But if there were no monarch, and the executive power were committed to a certain number of persons selected from the legislative body, there would be an end to liberty; by reason the two powers would be united, as the same persons would actually sometimes have, and would moreover be always able to have, a share in both (XI, 6, 402).

Conclusion

In all this we seem to have traveled a long way from Book XI, chapter 6, from the tidiness of a theory or ideal type to what looks like the picture of an improvised squabble between unprincipled factions. However, the important point is that the model enables us to see how the political behavior of the English makes sense. That is to say, it only makes sense if we can see that what it amounts to is the balance and relative independence of the executive and legislative powers and those other features essential to liberty described in the earlier chapter. At the same time, in order to make sense of the behavior of the English, we need to understand their character, particularly the reasons for their commitment to liberty and impatience with any form of authoritarian regime.

Toward the end of chapter 6 of Book XI Montesquieu had stated that the English constitution would perish when the legislative power became more corrupt than the executive.[28] It was essential, therefore, that the representatives should be careful not to sacrifice their independence to the Crown. Montesquieu makes an interesting comment on this point in a letter written to William Domville in which the latter had inquired about the possible long-term effects of corruption on the English Parliament. Montesquieu's reply expresses his faith, less in the members of Parliament, than in the ordinary English people:

> I think, Sir, that what will preserve your government is that, basically, the people have more virtue than their representatives. I do not know whether I am mistaken, but I think I saw that in your nation the soldier is better than his officers and the people than their magistrates and those who govern them. . . . It seems that you wanted to corrupt your magistrates and your representatives. It is not the same with the general body of the people, and I think I saw a certain spirit of liberty which always lights up and is not ready to be extinguished; and when I think of the spirit of this nation, it seems to me that it appears more enslaved than it really is because that which is most enslaved shows itself more openly and that which is free less openly.[29]

This is followed by remarks on parliamentary and electoral corruption, the importance of which Montesquieu thinks should not be exaggerated, provided the ordinary people remain honest and retain their love of liberty: "I say then that, whilst the ordinary people preserve their principles, it will be difficult to subvert your constitution."[30] He also makes the point that in England liberty is related to the fact that it is a commercial nation: its wealth comes from trade and not, as in ancient Rome, from pillage or taxes imposed on conquered nations:

> After all, the sources of your wealth are commerce and industry, and these sources are of such a nature that anyone who draws on them cannot enrich himself without enriching many others. The sources of the wealth of Rome were profit in raising taxes and in the pillage of conquered nations. Now these sources cannot enrich an individual without impoverishing an infinite number of other people. Thus there were in this state and in those which in this repect are like it, only extremely rich and extremely poor people. There could not be people of the middle station (*gens médiocres*), as with you, nor a spirit of liberty, as with you. There could only be, on the one hand, a spirit of ambition and, on the other a spirit of despair and consequently no liberty.[31]

In the final analysis the liberty enjoyed by the English does not depend simply on constitutional engineering. The importance of the laws supporting any constitution is not to be underestimated, but without the underlying principle (virtue, honor, fear), it will not function. The underlying principle in the English form of government is not defined in the same way as for republic, monarchy, or despotism; however, whatever this principle may be in theory, it is clear that in practice it is a whole complex of factors to be found in the "general spirit" of the English: their somewhat unstable and impatient character, their devotion to commerce and trade and various other characteristics which, all taken together, make them fiercely independent, proud of their liberty, and impatient of any kind of authoritarian rule.

The Spirit of Laws offers the reader two different images of England which may seem contradictory, but which in fact are complementary. The first, consistent with Montesquieu's aim to construct abstract models of different forms of government, is based on the theory of the constitution, where liberty is shown to depend on separation and balance of powers. The second shows how the system of separation and balance appears when it is embodied in practice, and once one takes into account all those factors which make up the "general spirit" of the English. Liberty cannot be reduced merely to a matter of constitutional engineering; it must be related to the character of the citizens. This character is of exceptional importance in a country where, the intermediary powers of the monarchy having been abolished,[32] the maintenance of liberty is a matter of precarious balance, being constantly threatened on the one side by the ambitions of the executive power and on the other by the legislative. Whether this balance could be maintained, or whether the English form of government would tip over toward republic or absolutism, was in the eighteenth century a matter of speculation. Hume was among those who feared it might be absolutism.[33] Montesquieu, while apparently accepting the inevitablility of the decline of the English system, was more ambiguous, believing that "in Europe the last gasp of liberty would come from an Englishman" and that the example of England in resisting tyranny might even help to retard the decline of the other European countries.[34]

Notes

References to Montesquieu are, unless otherwise specified, to the Pléiade edition; references to *The Spirit of Laws* are given simply by book and chapter number, except for the two extremely long chapters (XI, 6 and XIX, 27), where page references are given to the Pléiade edition. For *The Spirit of Laws* translations are from the classic Thomas Nugent translation of the eighteenth century, although I have occasionally altered or corrected the text as necessary. Translations from Montesquieu's other works, and from other authors quoted, are my own.

1. For the image of England in seventeenth- and eighteenth-century France see the following works: Joseph Texte, *Jean-Jacques Rousseau et les origines du cosmopolitanisme littéraire; étude sur les relations littéraires de la France et de l'Angleterre au XVIIIe siècle* (Paris: Hachette, 1895), translated by J. W. Matthews as *Jean-Jacques Rousseau and the Cosmopolitan Spirit in Literature* (New York: Burt Franklin, 1899); Georges Ascoli, *La Grande-Bretagne devant l'opinion française au XVIIe siècle*, 2 vols. (Paris: Gamber, 1930); Gabriel Bonno, *La Culture et la civilisation britannique devant l'opinion française de la Paix d'Utrecht aux "Lettres philosophiques" (1713-1734)*,

Transactions of the American Philosophical Society, New Series 328, no. 1 (1948); Frances Dorothy Acomb, *Anglophobia in France, 1763-1789; an Essay in the History of Constitutionalism and Nationalism* (Durham: Duke University Press, 1950); Josephine Grieder, *Anglomania in France, 1740-1789: Fact, Fiction, and Political Discourse* (Genève: Droz, 1985).

2. Texte, *Jean-Jacques Rousseau and the Cosmopolitan Spirit in Literature*, 7, 13-14.

3. See the notes to this letter in the following edition: Montesquieu, *Lettres persanes*, Paul Vernière, ed. (Paris: Garnier, 1960), 215-16.

4. Montesquieu, during this period, moved in Jacobite circles; see, for his friendship with the Duke of Berwick (natural son of James II), the Duke of Liria (Berwick's son) and Bulkeley (related to the Berwicks), Shackleton, *Montesquieu*, 19-20, 46-47; however, documentation is thin and it is not clear what conclusions one should draw from such friendships.

5. *Notes on England*, in Pléiade, I, 876.

6. *Notes on England,* in Pléiade, I, 876.

7. *Notes on England*, in Pléiade, I, 884.

8. *Notes on England*, in Pléiade, I, 880.

9. Montesquieu, *Considérations*, Camille Jullian, ed. (Paris: Hachette, 1912) 92 and notes (chapter 8, penultimate paragraph). The Pléiade text (II, 116) does not give this variant.

10. *Considérations*, Jullian, ed., 92, note.

11. *Considérations*, Jullian, ed., 131-32 and notes (end of chapter 12).

12. See Shackleton, *Montesquieu*, 154.

13. Jean-Baptiste de Secondat, *Mémoire pour servir à l'éloge historique de M. de Montesquieu*, in Louis Vian, *Histoire de Montesquieu d'après des documents nouveaux et inédits*, seconde édition (Paris: Didier, 1879), 401; Shackleton, *Montesquieu*, 285.

14. See Letter VIII: "This is the most essential difference between Rome and England, which gives the advantage to the latter: the result of the civil wars in Rome was slavery, and in England it was liberty. The English nation is the only one in the world which has succeeded in regulating the power of kings by resisting them and which, after much exertion, finally established this wise government where the prince, all-powerful to do good, has his hands tied when it comes to doing harm, where the nobles are great without being insolent and without vassals, and where the people have a share in government without any disorder coming about."

15. Letter VIII.

16. See, for Montesquieu's views that modern monarchies (including the French) were Germanic in origin, *Laws*, XI, 8.

17. There is a vast literature on the topic of Montesquieu's views on English liberty as expressed in *The Spirit of Laws*. See particularly Joseph Dedieu, *Montesquieu et la tradition politique anglaise en France; les sources anglaises de l'Esprit des lois* (Paris: Lecoffre, 1909); Gabriel Bonno, *La constitution britannique devant l'opinion française*

de Montesquieu à Bonaparte (Paris: Champion, 1931); Lando Landi, *L'Inghilterra e il pensiero politico di Montesquieu* (Padova: Cedam, 1981); Alberto Postigliola, "Sur quelques interprétations de la 'séparation des pouvoirs' chez Montesquieu," *Studies on Voltaire and the Eighteenth Century,* 154 (1976): 1759-75 and "En relisant le chapitre sur la constitution d'Angleterre," *Cahiers de philosophie politique et juridique de l'Université de Caen,* 7 (1985): 9-28; *The Spirit of Laws by Montesquieu, a Compendium of the First English Edition, . . .* David W. Carrithers, ed. (Berkeley: University of California Press, 1977), 75-82; Montesquieu, *Selected Political Writings,* Melvin Richter, ed. and trans. (Cambridge University Press, 1990), 38-42. See also Shackleton, *Montesquieu,* and C. P. Courtney, *Montesquieu and Burke* (Oxford: Blackwell, 1963; reprinted, Newport: Greenwood Press, 1975). The following studies are particularly valuable: M. J. C. Vile, *Consititutionalism and the Separation of Powers* (Oxford: Clarendon Press, 1967) and W. B. Gwyn, *The Meaning of the Separation of Powers* (New Orleans: Tulane University; The Hague: Nijhoff, 1965). See also the introductions and notes to the following editions: *De l'esprit des loix,* Jean Brethe de La Gressaye, ed., 4 vols. (Paris: Les Belles Lettres, 1950-1961), Robert Derathé, ed., *De l'esprit des lois,* 2 vols. (Paris: Garnier, 1973),

18. *Two Chapters of a celebrated French work entitled De l'Esprit des loix, translated into English. One treating of the constitution of England; another of the character and manners, which result from this Constitution* (Edinburgh: Hamilton and Balfour, 1750).

19. See, for example, Boris Mirkine-Guetzévitch, in an article which is frequently quoted: "Qu'y avait-il de commun entre l'Angleterre de Montesquieu et l'Angleterre du milieu du XVIIIe siècle?. . . . Rien ou à peu près rien; à l'exemple de tant d'autres écrivains du XVIIIe siècle, Montesquieu fait un voyage dans un pays imaginaire; l'Angleterre de Montesquieu, c'est l'Utopie, c'est un pays de rêve," *La Pensée politique et constitutionnelle de Montesquieu: bicentenaire de l'Esprit des lois, 1748-1948* (Paris, 1952), 161-81. See also Brethe de La Gressaye, in the introduction to his edition of the *Esprit des lois:* "Les hommes politiques anglais ont été reconnaissants à Montesquieu d'avoir voilé les réalités du parlementarisme, et c'est peut-être pourquoi ils ont tant loué "l'exactitude" du tableau qu'il a brodé de la constitution anglaise."

20. This separation would have been increased if the following provision of the Act of Settlement had come into effect: "That no person who has an office or place of profit under the king, or receives a pension from the Crown, shall be capable of serving as a member of the House of Commons." In fact, this clause was abrogated in 1707 by 6 Anne c.7. For a useful discussion of place bills during the late seventeenth and early eighteenth century see Betty Kemp, *King and Commons, 1660-1832* (London: Macmillan, 1957).

21. This was understood by Madison in *The Federalist,* no. 47: "[Montesquieu's] meaning . . . can amount to no more than this, that where the whole power of one de-

partment is exercised by the same hands which possess the whole power of another department, the fundamental principles of a free constitution are subverted."

22. See the studies of Vile and Gwyn cited above, note 17. See also Courtney, *Montesquieu and Burke*, 59-62.

23. The relevant works are Locke, *Second Treatise of Civil Government* (1690), Bolingbroke, *A Dissertation upon Parties* (1735) and *The Craftsman* (1730); see particularly the studies by Vile and Gwyn. See also, on Locke, Shackleton, *Montesquieu*, 286-88 and (not very convincingly) on Bolingbroke: "Montesquieu, Bolingbroke and the Separation of Powers," *French Studies* 3 (1949): 25-38.

24. On Montesquieu and William Blackstone's *Commentaries on the Laws of England* (1765-1769) see F. T. H. Fletcher, *Montesquieu and English politics (1750-1800)* (London: Arnold, 1939).

25. The only recent discussions are by Keith Michael Baker, in his *Inventing the French Revolution* (Cambridge: Cambridge University Press, 1990), 173-78, and by Pierre Manent, in *An Intellectual History of Liberalism*, Rebecca Balinski, trans. (Princeton, 1994), 53-64; for an earlier discussion see Courtney, *Montesquieu and Burke*, 64-67.

26. Hume, *Political Essays*, Knud Haakonssen, ed. (Cambridge: Cambridge University Press, 1994).

27. Cf. Montesquieu's account of a debate in Parliament recorded in his *Notes on England*: "Mr Chipin [Shippen] spoke in the House of Commons on the subject of the army; he said that only a tyrant or usurper needed the support of soldiers . . . . At the words tyrant and usurper all the members of the House were astonished. Shippen repeated the same words a second time; he then said that he disliked Hanoverian principles. . . . The session was so stormy that the House was afraid it might come to a debate; everyone therefore shouted 'Let the House divide,' in order to bring the proceedings to a close" (Pléiade, II, 878).

28. "As all human things have an end, the state we are speaking of will lose its liberty, will perish. Have not Rome, Sparta and Carthage perished? It will perish when the legislative power shall be more corrupt than the executive" (XI, 6, 407).

29. "A Monsieur Domville," in *Pensée* 1883 (1960), in Pléiade, I, 1447.

30. "A Monsieur Domville," in *Pensée* 1883 (1960), in Pléiade, I, 1449.

31. "A Monsieur Domville," in *Pensée* 1883 (1960), in Pléiade, I, 1449.

32. This point is made by Montesquieu in II, 4 of *The Spirit of Laws*. "The English, to favor their liberty, have abolished all the intermediate powers of which their monarchy was composed. They have a great deal of reason to be jealous of this liberty: were they ever to be so unhappy as to lose it, they would be one of the most servile nations upon earth."

33. "Absolute monarchy . . . is the easiest death, the true euthanasia of the British constitution"; see his essay, "Whether the British government inclines more to absolute monarchy, or to a republic," *Political Essays*, Haakonssen, ed., 32.

34. Montesquieu to Domville, 22 July 1749, in Nagel, III, 1245.

Chapter Seven

Montesquieu and the Liberal Philosophy of Jurisprudence

David W. Carrithers

Whether government is conceived on the Hobbesian model of protecting individuals from their fellow citizens, or on the Lockean-Montesquieuian model of shielding citizens from potentially oppressive governments, the fundamental tenet of the liberal perspective is the need to safeguard individuals from unwarranted losses of life, liberty, or property. Hence for a liberal theorist desiring to reduce the degree of fear generated by arbitrary and oppressive government, there is no aspect of a regime more important than its criminal laws and its criminal justice system. It is at the crucial point of conjunction of police, prosecutors, magistrates, and the accused that any political system demonstrates its level of interest in protecting the security of its citizens, including those accused of crime. On the conduct and outcome of criminal trials hinges the people's confidence in the basic fairness of their government. Hence a liberal system of crime and punishment will strive to establish procedural safeguards enabling the innocent to clear themselves of false charges as well as sentencing procedures that avoid punishing those guilty of crimes more severely than they deserve, or more severely than is required in order to deter others.

Viewed from this perspective, there was no more important figure in the emergence of the philosophy of liberalism than Montesquieu. If Locke had crucial things to say regarding the need to create limited governments acting only pursuant to the consent of the governed, Montesquieu substantially extended Locke's arguments on the need for moderate government by focusing attention in *The Spirit of Laws* on the need for fairness and restraint in matters of criminal law. Trained in law at the University of Bordeaux, and experienced as a judge in the Parlement of Bordeaux where he was assigned for more than ten years to its criminal section, *La Tournelle*,[1] Montesquieu was well positioned to weigh the issues posed by criminal investigations, trials, sentencing, and punishment. Long before the sensational miscarriages of justice in the trials of Calas, Sirven, and the Chevalier de La Barre in the 1760s and 1770s—cases that galvanized Voltaire into becoming the pre-eminent *philosophe*-advocate of judicial reform in France—Montesquieu was quietly raising the issues that would contribute to what would become, in the half century following his death, a veritable flood of treatises addressing the inadequacies of the unreformed French criminal law procedures codified in the Criminal Ordinance of 1670.

Montesquieu saw no reason to fundamentally alter the French inquisitorial system of criminal justice that, unlike the Anglo-American accusatorial systems, does not presume the innocence of the accused and does not require proof beyond a reasonable doubt by a unanimous jury for conviction. He did focus public attention, however, on the critical need to protect those wrongly accused. "When the innocence of the citizens is not secure," he proclaims, "neither is liberty."[2] Later French reformers went much farther than Montesquieu in their criticisms of pre-Revolutionary French jurisprudence, particularly where procedural safeguards for criminal defendants were concerned, but it was nonetheless Montesquieu who became the *philosophe*-initiator of discussions of crucial criminal law matters instrumental to the achievement of liberty defined as security of life, liberty, and property.[3] It certainly comes as no surprise, therefore, that Cesare Beccaria was very substantially influenced by *The Spirit of Laws* in formulating his own views on legal procedures and on punishment and that, in tribute to his mentor, he referred to "the immortal Montesquieu" in the preface to his *On Crimes and Punishments* (1764).[4]

Two Types of Liberty

Montesquieu drew a sharp distinction between the political liberty of the constitution and the civil liberty of the individual, devoting Book XI of *The Spirit of Laws* to political liberty and Book XII to civil liberty. Though the two types of liberty will very often co-exist, Montesquieu posits no necessary connection between the two. A constitution whose political institutions are free does not automatically give rise to laws and a legal system ensuring that the rights of innocent individuals will be safeguarded. For citizens to be fully secure in the preservation of their liberties, there must be codes of laws and also court procedures that are fully protective of individual security (VI, 1; XII, 2). Even states that are wholly despotic in their political structures may actually achieve a degree of security for individuals, if they substitute for non-existent civil and criminal codes a religious code contained in a sacred book that provides guidance to judges, as with the cadis in Turkey who consult the mullahs (XII, 29). Furthermore, merely respecting the right of emigration will provide a measure of security—even in despotisms—since where such a right exists, as in Persia, "fear of the flight or retreat of debtors checks or moderates the persecutions of pashas and exactors" (XII, 30).

Montesquieu's views on how best to achieve political liberty of the constitution are well known. As exemplified in his famous portrait of the English constitution in Book XI, chapter 6 of *The Spirit of Laws*, he believed that governments desiring to possess political liberty will establish competing centers of power so that no one individual or group will be able to exercise unfettered rule. "In order that power not be abused," he observes, "it is necessary that by the arrangement of things power stop power" (XI, 4). He regarded the division, or partitioning, of power as the essential guarantee of liberty where the constitution is concerned, and he therefore rejected the "legal despotism" favored by the physiocrats and the enlightened despotism advocated by Voltaire. The necessary division of powers, he contends, may be achieved under various governmental forms. Thus in Book XI he carefully refrains from associating liberty with any single form of government. "Democracy and aristocracy," he asserts, "are not free states by their nature. Political liberty is found only in moderate governments. . . . It is present there only when power is not abused" (XI, 4). Such moderate governments, Montesquieu believed, may be either republics or monarchies, or mixed forms provided that there is proper attention to partitioning power.

Civil liberty depends on safeguards quite distinct from those measures producing political liberty. For citizens to be free, there must be a close approximation to what we now commonly term the "rule of law." Certainly Montesquieu does not employ this now common English phrase, but in his discussions of civil liberty in both Books VI and XII of *The Spirit of Laws* he approximates the concept by vilifying despots who regard their transitory whims and desires as a substitute for standing laws. He uses despotism as a foil to liberty. Had there been no real-world despotism, it almost seems that he would have had to invent the concept to assist him in his rhetorical defense of liberty.[5]

It is Montesquieu's opinion that where proper laws and rules exist, even those condemned to die for the crimes they have committed must be judged free (XII, 2). To the extent that criminal laws and judicial regulations embodying justice are arrived at by the people as a whole, or their representatives, a measure of democracy will accompany the rule of law. Popular participation in the making of laws and legal rules, however, is not essential to achieving such a rule of law. The question of who can legitimately make and impose legal rules stands logically apart from the issue of the fairness of those rules.

The primary meaning of civil liberty, for Montesquieu, is freedom from arbitrary or unlawful arrest or detention and protection from loss of liberty under judicial processes unfair to the accused. Montesquieu believed that the key component of individual liberty defined as security is a properly constructed code of judicial procedures protecting the rights of the accused. "The knowledge that has been already acquired in some countries and will be acquired in others," he

opines, "concerning the safest rules that one can adhere to in criminal judgments, concerns mankind more than anything else in the world. It is only on the
practice of this knowledge that liberty can be established" (XII, 2). The security
of the citizen is to be achieved, however, not exclusively by means of legal procedures—though the importance of such procedures is paramount—but also by
means of appropriate customs, manners, and even religion.

With Montesquieu's discussions there first entered into French discourse of
the Enlightenment era that passionate concern for the rights of criminal defendants that has since become one of the key features of modern liberal theory. In
actual fact, however, as will be developed later in this chapter, Montesquieu
took exception to very few of the existing procedures of French criminal law as
codified in the Criminal Ordinance of 1670, the last wholesale re-working of
criminal law procedures prior to the Revolution. Nonetheless, his discussions of
key crime and punishment issues raised liberal concerns that greatly inspired
other reformers later in the century who frequently referred to Montesquieu's
importance on the general subject of crime and punishment while at the same
time criticizing him for being too supportive of existing procedures. However
conservative and cautious he was compared to later reformers, one commentator
has nonetheless termed Book XII of *The Spirit of Laws*, "the Magna Carta of
liberty."[6] Rather than defining liberty along classical republican lines as the right
to participate in political deliberations, he instead focuses his discussion on the
protection of individuals from the state's enormous power. His primary emphasis
is on "security, or at least in the opinion one has of one's security" (XII, 2)—an
intriguing formulation indicating his keen sensitivity to the psychological dimensions of human existence.

It is not just the *opinion* of security that must be cultivated, however. Real as
opposed to imagined security must be the goal of all liberal systems of criminal
justice. But since no government can positively guarantee a condition of perfect
security for its citizens owing to the impossibility of preventing all miscarriages
of justice, there is much to be said for establishing a system that gives citizens
an "opinion" of security. Without such a feeling of security, individuals will not
trust the system and will resort either to vigilante justice when they are the ag-
grieved party, or flight when they are the accused party. Legal chaos will no
doubt ensue should large numbers of individuals become completely disenchanted with the legal system as a result of losing the conviction that they are
basically secure in their rights and property.

Judicial Process in Montesquieu's Moderate State

What, then, are the fundamental safeguards of security of life, liberty, and property according to Montesquieu? First of all, there can be no security without an
independent judiciary protected from political pressures and influences. This
may be regarded as Montesquieu's fundamental premise serving for him as the

veritable foundation stone supporting civil liberty. Without an independent judiciary, judges will be corruptible and unable to speak truth to power. The formula for attaining an independent judiciary will vary depending on the governmental form. In monarchies, judging should be done by a trained group of professional judges insulated from political pressures and corrupt influences because they have purchased their positions from the Crown in the system known as venality of offices. In republics, on the other hand, judging will be in the hands of lay jurors whose independence is guaranteed by the random nature of their selection and by the brevity of their terms of service. As will be seen below, however, Montesquieu had little confidence in juries (VI, 3, 4).

A second premise of liberal jurisprudence for Montesquieu is that judicial power must always remain in the hands of those legally vested with the powers of judging under a regime's fundamental laws. When judging is transferred to those not legally entrusted with such powers, or not properly trained in its exercise, injustice—and even despotism—will result. "Judgments rendered by the prince," Montesquieu observes, "would be a perennial source of injustices and abuses; the courtiers would extort his judgments by their pleadings. Some Roman emperors," he continues, "insisted on judging; no reigns stunned the universe more by their injustices" (VI, 5).[7] Montesquieu draws a sharp distinction between the different temperaments required for political and judicial decision making. "Passion," he notes, should characterize the ministers of the Crown in their political decisions whereas judges must display "self-control" and remain "neutral" (VI, 6). Hence ministers of the Crown, or special commissioners, ought never to be entrusted with judging (VI, 6; XII, 22). Speaking of France, he asserts that if the king himself were to judge cases, "the constitution would be destroyed and the intermediate dependent powers reduced to nothing; one would see all the formalities of judgments cease; fear would invade all spirits; one would see pallor on every face; there would be no more trust, honor, love, security, or monarchy" (VI, 5). Since in monarchical states the king, as head of state, is indirectly entrusted with prosecuting cases through his officials known as *procureurs de roi*, making him also the judge in civil and criminal cases would combine executive and judicial powers to the detriment of liberty. Exercise of judicial power by the king would also make a mockery of the pardoning power. The king "would lose the finest attribute of his sovereignty which is that of pardoning. It would be absurd for him both to make and unmake his own judgments; he would not wish to be in contradiction with himself" (VI, 5).[8]

Beyond providing for an independent judiciary insulated from political tampering and protected in its exclusive right to try cases, the attainment of security requires a particular method of judging by those entrusted with judicial power. Judges must regard themselves as caught up in a web of judicial decisions linking past and present so that precedents will enjoy due weight, thereby reducing arbitrary discretion. Judges must not be empowered to act arbitrarily. Rather than relying on their own interpretations, they must consult the body of prior de-

cisions handed down by judges previously confronted with similar cases. Without such a precedential approach, akin to the common-law method of judging,
there will exist insufficient protections for the security of life, liberty, and property (VI, 1). There must be, as Montesquieu asserts in explaining the crucial role
of the Parlements of France, a body of courts functioning as a "depository of the
laws" to recall past laws when they are forgotten so that continuity of judicial
decision making can be assured (II, 4).

Another key aspect of Montesquieu's liberal jurisprudence is the stress he
places on the need for complex, even painstakingly slow procedures. Legal matters defy simplicity, and a degree of complexity and slowness must not only be
tolerated but consciously cultivated if individual liberty is to be protected.[9]
Moderate states, he counsels, avoid precipitous judicial decisions. In all moderate states—whether republics or monarchies—the formalities of justice will be
substantial, and civil and criminal trials will involve many complex stages and
procedures. In cases of criminal law, "the troubles, costs, length of proceedings,
and the risks even of danger are the price each citizen pays for his liberty" (VI,
2). The very same formalities that make it difficult to recover property when it is
stolen are what protect liberty when it is threatened in criminal law proceedings
(VI, 2). "Thus," Montesquieu asserts, "when a man becomes more absolute, the
first thing he thinks about is simplifying the laws," as Caesar, Cromwell, and
countless others had done. Despots will see only the inconveniences of complex
laws and care not a whit about the protection such laws offer liberty (VI, 2). The
more emphasis that is placed in moderate governments, however, on "honor,
fortune, life, and liberty," the more complex the formalities of justice will be
(VI, 2).

Both republics and monarchies, Montesquieu contends, are capable of being
moderate states where personal liberty is protected, and in such states maximum
safeguards need to be available whenever the state moves to reduce individual
liberty, invade property, or, more drastically, seeks to take the life of one of its
citizens accused of a capital crime. Particularly in monarchies where inequalities
in rank, origin, and condition purposefully abound, sorting through various types
and distinctions of property will be a complex matter, and civil cases involving
property will be time-consuming to resolve (VI, 1). Furthermore, in moderate
monarchies where custom and tradition are not obliterated and uniformity is not
desired or required, the king will tolerate different laws for different provinces
and also allow different customs to exist in different regions, thereby further
complicating the nature of judicial decision making. Even within the same province, in fact, different individuals, depending on their rank, will be able to plead
their cases before different tribunals (VI, 1).

In moderate states the criminal law will be clear and readily intelligible so
that all persons will know in advance the rules they must not break. A key aspect
of the rule of law, as envisioned by Montesquieu, is the presence of fair, clear,
and well-publicized laws and judicial procedures that define in advance of actual

unlawful conduct how alleged infractions of the law will be handled. "The laws," Montesquieu writes, "must not be subtle; they are made for people of middling understanding. They are not an art of logic but the simple reasoning of a father of the family" (XXIX, 16). Furthermore, in the drafting of laws no attempt should be made to enter into such prolixity that all circumstances will be foreseen. "When exceptions, restrictions, modifications, are not necessary in a law," he observes, "it is much better not to put them there. Such details hurl one into new details" (XXIX, 16). The style of the laws, Montesquieu asserts, "should be concise. The laws of the Twelve Tables are a model of precision; children learned them by heart. The *Novellae* of Justinian are so diffuse that it was necessary to abridge them." (XXIX, 16). In addition, "the style of the laws should be simple; straightforward expression is always better understood than indirect. . . . When the style of the laws is inflated, they are regarded only as a work of ostentation." Furthermore, "it is essential that the language of the laws give rise to the same ideas in all men" (XXIX, 16), and this will be most readily achieved through simple and direct laws.

In addition to being clear and readily intelligible, criminal laws must be narrowly drafted to avoid what we now term "overbreadth." Overly broad statutes have the malign effect of criminalizing conduct that should be considered legal. Montesquieu's chief examples of overbreadth were presented in the context of his painstaking analysis of the issues surrounding the crime of treason. He devotes no less than seven chapters of Book XII to this important subject, which was so much more important in his day than in ours because of the broad definitions applied to treason. Like accusations regarding sorcery, heresy, and homosexuality where prosecutorial abuse is also rampant, the greatest precaution must be taken against concluding that actions that are merely criminal are wrongly considered treasonous and therefore subject to extreme, capital punishment. "Vagueness in the crime of high treason," Montesquieu asserts, "is enough to make government degenerate into despotism" (XII, 7). He singles out China for particular criticism in this regard since in that country anything that may be deemed to show "lack of respect" for the emperor could be judged treasonous and warranting death (XII, 7). Also completely indefensible, Montesquieu observes, was the provision of the Roman *Corpus Juris civilis* that elevated to the level of sacrilege criticisms of a prince's judgment, or criticism of those persons he had appointed to accomplish certain tasks (XII, 8). Montesquieu also singles out as destructive to liberty declaring counterfeiters guilty of treason, as was common in most countries of Europe in his day (XII, 8). Also completely detrimental to liberty was the English law passed during the reign of Henry VIII that made it treasonous to predict the king's death even should he suffer an injury, or become seriously ill (XII, 10).

Though China was his chief example of a despotic country too broadly defining treason, Montesquieu did not refrain from criticizing prosecutions for treason in France during the period of Richelieu's influence whom he considered an architect of despotism. Though it had been forbidden by the Estates General in 1579 to name special commissioners to try exalted persons who might be accused of treason, this had not deterred Cardinal Richelieu from doing precisely that in his proceedings against La Valette in 1639 and against Cinq-Mars in 1642. In Cinq-Mars' trial, the judges wrongly allowed Roman law to be quoted to the effect that attacking a minister of the Crown (in this instance Richelieu whose influence Cinq-Mars wished to diminish) was regarded as no different than attacking the king himself (XII, 8).[10] Another abuse of judicial authority in France involving the creation of special commissioners outside the normal channels of the monarchical constitution was the use of periodic *Chambres de justice* designed to squeeze money out of officials caught up in the complex web of the realm's finances.[11]

Discussion of treason enables Montesquieu to draw crucial distinctions between protected speech and unprotected actions that can be legitimately criminalized. Only when speech crosses the line into treasonous action does it become subject to prosecution (XII, 11-13).

> The words that are joined to an action take on the nature of that action. Accordingly, a man who goes into the public square in order to urge the subjects to revolt becomes guilty of high treason because the speech is joined to the action and participates in it. It is not speech that is punished but an action that is committed in which speech is used. Speech becomes criminal only when it prepares, accompanies, or follows a criminal act (XII, 12).[12]

Since speech contains so many subtle messages and is so nuanced by inflection and tone, it would be impossible, Montesquieu concludes, to list in advance what speech acts might be judged treasonous even if one happened to think that *any* speech could ever be considered tantamount to treason (XII, 12). The same goes for the written word. "Writings contain something more permanent than speech, but when they do not prepare the way for high treason, they are not material to the crime of high treason" (XII, 13).

In addition to avoiding overbreadth in the drafting of criminal laws, vagueness must also be avoided. As an example of vagueness, Montesquieu singles out the law of the barbarian chieftain Honorius that "punished by death any one who bought as a serf a freed man and any who wished to harass him." What would constitute harassment, Montesquieu notes, would "depend entirely on the degree of his [the freed man's] sensitivity" (XXIX, 16). Similarly, Montesquieu singles out for rebuke the Julian law that had labeled as treasonous the melting down of the statue of a Roman emperor or some similar action, leaving wholly unspecified what might constitute such "similar action" (XII, 9). Still another example of a law Montesquieu judged indefensible on account of vagueness was a provision in the French criminal code of 1670 adding to what was otherwise an "exact enumeration of royal cases" the hopelessly broad and vague formula, "and those the royal judges have judged in all times" (XXIX, 16).[13]

All of the fundamental safeguards of security thus far analyzed are applicable to both monarchical and republican states seeking to achieve political moderation. Not surprisingly, however, Montesquieu also has a number of things to say that are specifically relevant to monarchical constitutions. Placing heavy emphasis on the king's need to trust his subjects, Montesquieu stresses the need to avoid the use of spies and other underhanded tactics in evidence gathering when prosecuting crimes in monarchical states. What kings must realize, he observes, is that "When a man is faithful to the laws, he has satisfied what he owes to the prince. He must have his house as an asylum at least and feel safe about the rest of his conduct" (XII, 23). Hence the king must not invade the privacy of subjects in order to seek out information regarding their conduct. Eavesdropping, spying, or reading a person's mail—all these acts of internal surveillance characteristic of the paranoid police state—must be rejected. Instead, the king must display complete trust in his subjects and banish from his mind all "anxieties, suspicions, and fears" (XII, 23). In moderate monarchies kings have no need for the tactics of the police state because their subjects love them. And why should this not be so, Montesquieu asks? "He (the king) is the source of almost all the good that is done, and almost all punishing is on account of the laws. He presents himself to the people only with a serene countenance; his very glory is communicated to us and his power sustains us" (XII, 23).

Later in the century, many French criminal law reformers bitterly protested the use of *lettres de cachet*—the secret letters used by the king to imprison individuals without trial. Montesquieu, however, does not choose to attack the use of these letters which were loosely analogous to English Bills of Attainder, although such attainders had to be voted by Parliament and signed by the king whereas the *lettres de cachet* were simply issued by the king or one of his ministers.[14] Perhaps owing to fear of reprisal, Montesquieu removed all references to *lettres de cachet* during the course of the printing of *The Spirit of Laws*. Even in the texts he finally deleted, however, he had not called for the outright abolition of these letters. Instead he had only recommended that their use be modified. Originally part of Book XII, chapter 22, the suppressed texts suggested that no longer should a single minister of the Crown be empowered to imprison an individual without trial. Rather, only the Royal Council should be able to incarcerate individuals with *lettres de cachet*, and only for a year at a time. Furthermore, Montesquieu asserted, the grounds for such incarceration should be stipulated so that the affected party could respond to all allegations and appeal his or her detention to another minister of the Crown.[15]

Clearly such reforms as Montesquieu recommended in his suppressed texts would at least have blunted an instrument of repression often destructive of security. Even later in the century, however, there was no strong consensus on the need to suppress such secret letters since many families found them beneficial in incarcerating a relative who was about to run seriously afoul of the law and suffer an even worse penalty. The concept of shared guilt in French criminal law, and also the confiscation of the property of anyone judged guilty of a capital crime, made families eager to avoid having one of their own members prosecuted for a serious offense.[16]

Unlike Beccaria who concluded that the need for punishments to function as deterrents requires that pardons never be granted, Montesquieu has a good deal to say on the subject of granting clemency to those who may have been wrongly convicted of crimes. Kings, he contends, should increase the level of security present in monarchical states by continually making available the prospect of clemency following judgment of guilt in criminal proceedings. The channels through which pleas for forgiveness may be sought must be kept open so that the king can step in at rightful moments and dispense justice when it has been denied in court proceedings (XII, 30).[17] Montesquieu may well have thought that royal mercy was an essential aspect of criminal justice in pre-Revolutionary France because all homicides were tried without attention to such extenuating circumstances as their involuntary or accidental nature, or their origin in self-defense.[18] Almost one-fourth of the 413 death sentences rendered by the Parlement of Paris between 1735 and 1749 were commuted by Royal letters of *grâce* ratified by the Parlement because those convicted had acted accidentally, or in self-defense, or following intense provocation, or in transient rage.[19] We can readily appreciate, therefore, why Montesquieu would judge wholly despicable and suited only to the vilest sort of despotism the rule under Peter I of Russia, as reported by John Perry, that an individual denied justice could appeal his case to the czar, with the proviso that if proven unwarranted, the penalty for such an appeal would be death (XII, 26). Far from weakening his powers, the exercise of mercy by a king, Montesquieu asserts, has the effect of augmenting the love his people rightfully display for him. In a moderate monarchy, the king will almost never be blamed for anything. The trust of his people will be so great that it will be assumed that the prince was uninformed and that any failing or shortcoming of the monarchy was the fault of a subordinate minister rather than of the king himself.

> Even during public calamities, the people do not blame him personally. They complain that he doesn't notice them or that he is plagued by corrupt persons. If only the prince had known! say the people. These words are a kind of invocation and a proof of their trust in him (XII, 23). In our monarchies, all felicity lies in the people's opinion of the gentleness of the government. . . . In a certain way, command is easy: the prince must encourage, and the laws must menace (XII, 23).

The more the king is perceived as a benign figure looking out for the welfare of his people, the more trusting his subjects will be. Furthermore, it is this public trust, rather than some presumed arbitrary power, that will legitimize and hence augment the Crown's power. Just as Bodin had earlier counselled, less actually becomes more, to put the matter very colloquially, where monarchical power is concerned.[20]

Assessing Montesquieu's Views on the Criminal Ordinance of 1670

Recently, revisionist views have been dramatically altering our beliefs about the true nature of crime and punishment in pre-revolutionary France. Whereas it was once quite typical to encounter in the scholarly literature on the subject the same tones of pained indignation, violent protest, and palpable outrage found in Beccaria's and Voltaire's radical denunciations of ancien régime practices, a number of revisionist scholars have complained of distorted caricatures in the secondary literature on the subject. These revisionist scholars doubt the accuracy of what Richard Mowery Andrews has termed "the black legend" of pre-revolutionary justice, and they stress the extent to which rights and liberties were protected under the Criminal Ordinance of 1670, the last wholesale revision prior to the Revolution of the French criminal law procedures governing all stages of French investigations and trials.[21] Any proper assessment of the true state of criminal justice in pre-revolutionary France and of Montesquieu's views on that subject must take into account the rules of this ordinance and the nature of his reaction to them insofar as that reaction can be known.

Drafted in large part as a result of the influence of Louis XIV's great minister, Jean-Baptiste Colbert, the 1670 ordinance was not meant to be a criminal code linking specific punishments to specific crimes. Punishment issues, in fact, were largely ignored. Available penalties were listed in order of severity, but there were no stipulations as to precisely what offenses should receive what punishments. The whole matter of recommending specific punishments for specific crimes was left either to royal edicts dealing with particular acts of crime or was simply left up to the discretion of judges trying individual cases. When it came to procedural matters, on the other hand, the ordinance was painstakingly thorough, so much so, in fact, that Montesquieu acknowledged in one of his *Pensées* that he despaired of ever mastering all of its rules.[22] All of the complex stages of the criminal process were governed by the ordinance from the initial inquiry through trial, judgment, and appeals. There were no less than 407 specific articles apportioned among twenty-eight different titles. So comprehensive were its procedures that the ordinance covered even such arcane matters as how to prosecute or receive testimony from deaf-mutes, how to try rebellious guilds, villages, or towns, and how to prosecute an accused person who had died soon after committing a crime.[23]

The goal of the 1670 ordinance was to provide France with a uniform criminal law system to aid in the process of centralization so greatly favored by Louis XIV. Even the seigniorial courts of manorial lords were required to follow the procedures of the ordinance in the few cases left to their disposition under the law.[24] Such seigniorial courts retained jurisdiction only over certain relatively minor crimes, however, and even in those cases jurisdiction was forfeited if the formal inquiry into the crime and the summoning of both the accused and witnesses was not completed before twenty-four hours had elapsed. In addition, even when a seigniorial court did successfully retain jurisdiction of a case, its decision had to be reviewed by the Parlement in its region before it became final.[25]

As mentioned above, revisionist scholars have contended that the procedures under the ordinance were not the travesty of justice many have alleged. "To describe the 1670 Ordinance as repressive is fallacious," writes Richard Andrews.

> It was foremost an investigative system that contained rules for the determination of penalty should proof of guilt emerge from the investigation. . . . A crime and a defendant were made objects of quasi-scientific inquiry for a long period before judgment occurred. Convictions were then reviewed by Parlements. Punishment, when it occurred, was at the end of a long intellective process, at considerable temporal remove from the crime—even if the crime had been notorious—and generally moderate.[26]

Andrews is far from being the only revisionist scholar to question the accuracy of contemporary accounts of pre-revolutionary criminal justice penned by Beccaria and Voltaire. Following an exhaustive study of crime and punishment in the Auvergne and Guyenne regions of France, Ian Cameron concluded that "In the eighteenth century, as in the twentieth, rules of competence, procedure and evidence were firmly established. As in the twentieth century, these rules involved a certain class bias in the administration of justice, but at least they were applied consistently and with an evident degree of rationality." According to Cameron, it is easy to exaggerate the extent of unfairness under the procedures of the ancien régime. "The reputation of ancien régime criminal justice," he contends, "has never recovered from the Calas Affair. It is easy . . . to overdramatise the clash between the 'enlightened' principles of our own day and the barbarism of a benighted ancien régime." In his detailed researches, Cameron discovered no bias to wrongly convict. He found only three cases, in fact, of all those handled by the prévôtal courts of the Auvergne and Guyenne regions from 1720 to 1790 where the trial transcript seems not to prove beyond a reasonable doubt the guilt of the party convicted.[27]

Focusing specifically on the Parlement of Bordeaux, Rebecca Kingston has reached similarly revisionist conclusions. Kingston has reviewed the entire record for the period 1716-1726 during which Montesquieu served first briefly as *conseiller* and then as *président à mortier*. She concludes that the Parlement of Bordeaux normally refrained from imposing the death penalty except for crimes of homicide even though under a royal edict of 1682, modified only in 1724, death could also be the punishment for sacrilege, rape, theft, and judicial fraud. Of the 117 death sentences automatically appealed to the Parlement of Bordeaux from lower royal courts between 1716 and 1726, twenty-nine were reduced to galley service for either limited or life terms. Similarly, numerous galley sentences handed down by lower courts were reduced, on appeal, to banishment or whipping. Hence Montesquieu was the veteran of service on a Parlement whose criminal chamber was likely to lessen the severity of punishments meted out by the lower royal courts in its jurisdiction, a fact that is certainly significant considering his strong pleas to reduce the severity of punishments in France.[28]

One of the intriguing aspects of Books VI and XII of *The Spirit of Laws* is Montesquieu's relative detachment from the procedural issues posed by the 1670 ordinance, issues later routinely raised by other *philosophes* and by numerous attorneys and magistrates involved in the reform movement of the criminal law that gradually gathered momentum as the century progressed. Montesquieu refers to the ordinance only once, in Book XXIX, chapter 16, and although he strongly opposed the excessively severe punishments employed in ancien régime France, he was far less critical of the procedural aspects of French criminal law as set out in the 1670 ordinance. He appears to have brought to this subject not only his distrust of radical change but also years of experience as a magistrate applying the complex rules of the ordinance. An important characteristic of the later reformers is that those who had experience as judges within the system tended to be substantially more accepting of the established procedures than those who had not been part of the system.[29] Hence it seems likely that Montesquieu's involvement in the French system as a judge on the Bordeaux court biased him in favor of the inquisitorial rules and procedures.

Whatever the precise reasons, there was much in French judicial procedure that Montesquieu chose not to contest. He was not, of course, focusing his attention specifically on France in Books VI and XII of *The Spirit of Laws* but was instead employing a much broader approach to questions of criminal law. He nonetheless makes it a point to praise certain French practices while ignoring the rest, thereby leaving the distinct impression that there was much that met with his approval. In Book XII he presents a broad historical view of the evolution of criminal procedures in Europe from antiquity to the present. He observes that "criminal laws were not perfected all at once" and suggests the superiority of modern developments to ancient practices in general by drawing all of his examples of imperfections from classical and early medieval time frames. His procedural concerns are expressed in very general terms, and there is no pointed criticism or even commentary on existing French procedures codified in the 1670 ordinance. Instead, we are treated to a few very general prescriptions for avoiding procedural unfairness. Relatives of the accuser, we are told, must not be allowed to be witnesses. Kings must not be allowed to render judgments against personal enemies or their families. Accused parties must have opportunities to offer defenses of their conduct, and individuals who give false testimony must be punished. Montesquieu links all these points to the critical need to avoid wrongly convicting the innocent. "When the innocence of the citizens is not secure," he concludes, "neither is liberty" (XII, 2).

Such very general observations by Montesquieu shed little light on his views regarding the details of existing criminal law procedures in France. To arrive at proper conclusions on this subject it is necessary to examine the stages of French trials in some detail, while assessing, where possible, Montesquieu's biases. It should be stated at the outset that a number of procedural rules that Montesquieu refrains from criticizing made it very difficult for the accused to mount an adequate defense. Almost all trials were conducted secretly, for example, which shielded judges from public scrutiny. Thus the interrogations of the accused normally took place in secret, as did the recording of depositions from witnesses. Only those trials involving minor infractions could be conducted in accordance with "ordinary" procedures that involved open trials and the possibility of bail.[30] Outrage at such secrecy escalated steadily during the second half of the eighteenth century. More and more critics of the system came to agree with Condorcet that an attempt was being made, through secrecy, to protect judges from public censure.[31] Voltaire made his position known in his *Prix de la justice et de l'humanité* (1777) by asking: "Must justice be secret? This is the jurisprudence of the Inquisition."[32] Although such complaints later became routine, Montesquieu lodged no protest against the secrecy enveloping French trials. Rather, in Book XXVIII, chapter 34 of *The Spirit of Laws,* in keeping with his well-known penchant for explaining the causes for what exists, he carefully explains how and why formerly public trials had become secret. At a time when very few individuals could read or write, he explains, written trial records were of little use, and interested parties were therefore invited to be present when either witnesses or the accused were being interrogated or confronted one another. Gradually, however, as literacy increased, transcripts of such proceedings sufficed, and it made more sense for trials to be closed. Far from objecting to the evolution toward closed, secret trials, Montesquieu concludes that "The first [public] form of procedure suited the government of that time as the new one was proper to the government that was later established" (XXVIII, 34).[33] Hence we have a perfect example of Montesquieu's famous penchant, so much decried by Condorcet and others, for providing reasons for what exists rather than proposing root and branch reform based on perceived universal truths of justice.

In the French inquisitorial system there were no grand juries. Instead, criminal investigations were conducted by an examining judge supervising the case from the initial investigation down to final judgment. The first stage of the trial was the *instruction préparatoire*, which began with the *information*, involving both investigation of the crime and the interviewing of witnesses designated to the judge by the prosecutor, (*procureur du roi*) or the plaintiff.[34] Such witnesses received compulsory summonses and were paid fixed amounts for travel and the giving of testimony. Each witness was heard, not by the full panel of judges who would later reach a verdict in the case, but rather by the single examining judge in secret. Title VI of the 1670 Ordinance prohibited interrogation of witnesses by the judge. Instead the judge simply read the text of the complaint, and the witness recounted everything he or she knew about the crime in question, while a clerk recorded the testimony. This testimony was then read back to the witness, and the deposition was signed by the witness and labeled a *charge*, if it incriminated the defendant, or a *décharge*, if it did not incriminate the defendant or provided evidence of innocence.[35] Once the witnesses had given their depositions, they could not alter their version of events without being prosecuted for perjury, even if they were reminded by the accused, during the later *confrontation* stage of the trial, of certain matters they had overlooked.[36] This inability of witnesses to change their testimony and also the failure of French law to entitle the accused to cross-examine witnesses as they gave their testimony were both frequently criticized by later criminal law reformers. Montesquieu, on the other hand, lodges no such protest. He does not appear to have found anything inherently prejudicial to the defendant in this procedure. In fact, he finds it completely rational to threaten prosecution witnesses with perjury should they alter their testimony since there may be no witnesses for the defendant, and, in such instances, the judges deciding the verdict will have to rely only on the testimony of the government's witnesses. Therefore such testimony must be as credible as possible, and witnesses should know in advance of providing such testimony that giving false testimony and later changing it will prompt charges of perjury (XXIX, 11). Once again, then, Montesquieu was moved, not to criticize the existing procedures, but rather to explain their rationale in keeping with his professed goals in the Preface of his work to offer reasons to his readers to love the governments responsible for their welfare.

When the prosecution was unable to produce sufficient witnesses to prove its case, *monitoires* could be read out in churches by parish priests on three successive Sundays urging those with evidence to come forward and give testimony. Often these *monitoires* contained highly prejudicial information containing allegations as to events leading up to the crime being investigated, but the names of possible suspects could not be mentioned. Those who had evidence of a suspect's guilt and did not come forward were threatened both with civil penalties and excommunication. If parishioners spoke directly to the parish priest instead of contacting the secular authorities, such information would be transcribed by the priest outside the confessional and sent to the court with jurisdiction in the case.[37] Montesquieu neither criticizes nor approves this blending of secular and ecclesiastical authority in the prosecution of crimes in France. If he had any objections to this aspect of the criminal ordinance of 1670, he kept them to himself.

After all the witnesses had been examined, the judge transmitted the results of his investigation, including the testimony of any respondents to any *moni-toires* that had been issued, to the public prosecutor, the *procureur du roi*. Then, following the receipt of the views of this prosecutor, the judge would either drop the case for lack of evidence or issue a warrant for the accused requiring his appearance in court. If the accused party did not appear following the issuance of such a warrant, and gave no excuses, then the judge would issue an arrest warrant. The *information* stage of the trial involving both the investigation and the hearing of witnesses could be waived altogether if the crime in question had been in flagrant delict or involved public dueling, or if the *procureur du roi* filed charges against vagrants, or if masters filed charges against their servants. Unless the defendant was apprehended for a minor offense and the "ordinary" procedure was used, there was no bail granted.[38]

Upon surrendering himself to the authorities following the issuance of a subpoena to testify, or subsequent to receiving a warrant for his arrest, the defendant was questioned by the examining magistrate without being informed of the charges against him. The goal was to elicit facts concerning his behavior on the day or days in question without alerting him to any facts that would aid him in formulating responses that might provide an alibi for his conduct.[39] Neither guilt nor innocence was to be assumed at this stage, and no torture could be applied during this initial questioning. When there was more than one suspect, each was questioned separately and in secret. The whole of the interrogation of accused parties was transcribed for the use of the panel of judges who would later decide guilt or innocence and punishment for parties found guilty. After a defendant had been interrogated, his testimony was read back to him, and both he and the judge signed the written record along with the transcribing clerk. Suspects might be interrogated on more than one occasion during this *instruction préparatoire* phase of the trial.

Substantially disadvantaging the accused, as compared to accusatorial systems of justice, was the rule that except where the crime in question was quite minor, the accused was not allowed to be represented by an attorney during court proceedings. Criminal suspects accused of serious crimes could hire defense counsel prior to their arrest, but, once apprehended, contact with this attorney was forbidden, although, through the connivance of their jailers, this rule was sometimes broken, as happened, for example, in the notorious and much studied Calas case.[40] In cases involving non-capital crimes, the situation with regard to defense attorneys was slightly better. In those cases, judges could allow, at their discretion, some consultation between attorney and the accused, after the defendant's preliminary interrogation. Furthermore, under the Criminal Ordinance of 1670, the assistance of counsel, even in capital cases, was not "absolutely forbidden" at the appeals stage, though many defendants were unable to afford such counsel.

Montesquieu nowhere states or implies that defendants must enjoy right to counsel if criminal law procedures are to be judged fair on their face. Although this was a contention advanced so frequently later in the century as to become a commonplace, he does not appear to have believed that the absence of counsel prevented the accused parties from properly defending themselves. He must have felt that ample opportunity was provided for defendants to state their own cases before an examining magistrate, who was, theoretically, just seeking to develop the facts of the case as objectively as possible. Under the inquisitorial system of justice it was not just defense counsel who were barred from trials. The public prosecutor was similarly excluded. Hence rather than involving a contest of words between prosecutor and defense attorney, as in the Anglo-American accusatorial system, French trials were conducted under the supposedly objective gaze of an examining magistrate who elicited information from both witnesses and defendants in order to get as full and accurate an account as possible of the crime in question so that justice might be served.

Although defense counsel could not represent their clients in court, they could argue a case for innocence in the broader world of public opinion by writing *Mémoires judiciaires*. In certain sensational trials these *Mémoires* became best sellers and proved instrumental to clearing the accused of all charges.[41] In composing these *Mémoires,* however, defense counsel were provided no access to trial records unless court clerks leaked documents for a price, a practice more common in some jurisdictions than in others. As mentioned, one does not find in Montesquieu's texts in *The Spirit of Laws* any objections to these French practices relegating defense attorneys to writing tracts intended to mobilize public opinion. There is no evidence that he believed the rules of the ordinance on these points were in need of change. If the accusatorial system in use in England required attorneys to speak for the accused, the French inquisitorial procedure was presumed to have other safeguards ensuring that defendants received fair trials before neutral magistrates.

In nearly all criminal trials, the preliminary *instruction préparatoire* was followed by the *instruction définitive* involving confrontation of the witnesses by the accused. If the crime could be punished only with defaming penalties, however, or if the accused requested judgment without the definitive instruction and the prosecutor concurred, the case could proceed to judgment immediately after the preparatory instruction was finished. Under the terms of Title XV of the 1670 ordinance—though the matter of actual conformity to the law is obviously another question—the defendant had the opportunity, during the definitive instruction, to confront all witnesses whose testimony was hostile to him. As mentioned previously, however, no witnesses could alter their earlier testimony without being charged with perjury. Furthermore, the ordinance did not automatically give the defendant the same opportunity as the examining judge to present an appropriate list of his own witnesses. Unless the judge decided to grant what was called a *fait justificatif,* the defendant would not be allowed to present any witnesses at all.[42] And if such a *fait justificatif* were granted, the defendant had to name his witnesses immediately with no subsequent opportunity to make additions to his list. Should the *fait* be denied, then the only witnesses who would be heard would be those selected by the public prosecutor. Defendants were not allowed to cross-examine witnesses as they presented information against them in their original testimony. They were instead restricted to rebutting, in this later *instruction définitive* stage of the trial, specific points made by the witnesses in their prior depositions. Furthermore, if they wished to challenge a witness on specific points, they had to state such challenges directly to the judge who would then decide whether to question the witness on those points. After confronting all hostile and neutral witnesses, however, defendants could also submit written challenges to the evidence, and this is perhaps one reason why Montesquieu chose not to cast aspersions on the procedural details of the conduct of French trials under the Criminal Ordinance of 1670, though we can only infer what his attitude may have been to such details of French criminal law policy.

Once the defendant had been given the opportunity to hear and confront the testimony of all witnesses against him, the case was sent to the public prosecutor who could recommend, in death penalty cases, the application of torture to gain a confession. Torture, however, was much more rarely utilized in French trials than is often thought, and its use required not only extremely strong indications of guilt but also the approval of the particular regional Parlement, which had jurisdiction over a lower court.[43]

In reaching a verdict the judges relied on the written records at their disposal, which were often lacking in accuracy, supplemented by what they might learn in their own final interrogation of the accused. Each of the judges voted for either conviction or acquittal, and only a simple majority was required for conviction. Each of the judges voting for conviction also recommended a penalty. Sometimes penalties had been specified in royal edicts, but usually there were no such guidelines. After the first vote, if the verdict was guilty, there was a second round of balloting to choose between the two penalties most frequently recommended. A majority of two judges was required for the most severe penalty to be imposed.[44] Without such a two-vote majority, the penalty imposed would be the lessor of the two recommended. This rule of a two-vote majority for the infliction of the harshest penalty had the effect of adding a strong statistical bias against infliction of death as a punishment.[45] The death penalty by no means fell into complete desuetude, however, even though the Parlements of France, in reviewing cases appealed to them from lower courts, often saw fit to reduce such penalties to galleys for life, or some lesser term. If the judges thought the accused party was guilty but were not fully convinced of such guilt, they could vote for a verdict of *plus amplement informé*, which required the gathering of further evidence before a final verdict could be reached. Today we would likely consider this verdict a form of double jeopardy, but in the thinking of the time it was considered a humane measure designed to ward off a rush to judgment.

As mentioned, there was very little in these French criminal law procedures under the 1670 Ordinance that Montesquieu saw fit to criticize in either Book VI or Book XII of *The Spirit of Laws*. He by no means impugns the fundamental fairness of French trials, even though they were conducted in secrecy against defendants who were not informed of the charges against them and who could not be represented in court in capital cases by defense counsel prior to the appeals stage. Nor did he criticize the system of proofs then in use in France which enabled judges to cobble together various semi-proofs, and light proofs in order to arrive at the complete proof necessary for conviction. Montesquieu did protest mightily, however, the use of torture to extract confessions, and his plea that convictions be reviewed thoroughly on appeal so that pardons could be issued if justice had been miscarried implies his opposition to that portion of the 1670 ordinance calling for the infliction of punishment within twenty four hours of the sentence being handed down.

Montesquieu's protest against the use of legal torture in criminal trials is contained in Book VI, chapter 17 of *The Spirit of Laws*. His comments are quite brief. Rather than engaging in an extended argument against the use of legal torture, he simply suggests that so many others have spoken eloquently on the subject that extended commentary is not required. There can be no mistaking his strong opinion however. "The voice of nature," he asserts, "cries out against the use of legal torture even in despotic governments" (VI, 17). He begins his chapter by referring to the French system of legal proofs adopted from Roman law (VI, 17). With regard to eye witnesses, he acknowledges somewhat begrudgingly that the law is obliged to "believe them as if they spoke with the mouth of truth." This is a necessary legal presumption, he observes, similar to the legal presumption that children born to married women are legitimate, rather than being bastards. In his view, however, there exist no conceivable justifications whatsoever for torture in cases where eye-witness testimony is unavailable. Though the law is forced to assume the veracity of eye witnesses, "it is not forced to use the *question* in criminal cases" (VI, 17). Based on the example of England where torture was expressly forbidden, he concludes that the use of legal torture is "not necessary by its nature" (VI, 17). In the notes to this chapter he praises the Athenians for restricting the use of legal torture to cases of high treason—the position Voltaire, incidentally, felt appropriate for France—and also the Romans for excluding torture where the well-born or those in the militia were concerned, unless the case involved high treason.

With the exception of his strong protest against the use of torture as part of the French system of legal proofs, Montesquieu does not incorporate in Books VI or XII of *The Spirit of Laws* criticism of any of the many aspects of French trial procedures so routinely pilloried by later criminal law reformers writing before and during the Revolution. Clearly, his view of the ordinance was closer to that of such current revisionist scholars as Richard Andrews than to the opinion of numerous radical Enlightenment critics of the ordinance. Montesquieu's stated requirements where witnesses were concerned were minimal. He only insists that no one be condemned without an opportunity for the witness to see him up close for purposes of identification and an opportunity for the accused to say, "It is not me of whom you speak" (XXVI, 3; XII, 2). Beyond that, he only suggests that witnesses ought not to be blood relatives of the accuser and that there ought to be penalties for false witnesses who perjure themselves, as was the case under French law (XII, 2). The cross examination of witnesses by defense counsel representing the accused was not, in his view, required to guarantee a fair trial.

Should Montesquieu, then, be rebuked for failing to criticize basic aspects of ancien régime justice that were routinely attacked later in the century? Clearly, the more one agrees with recent revisionists, the more understanding one will be of Montesquieu's complacency with regard to many basic elements of the pre-revolutionary system of criminal justice. Revisionists will likely conclude that he was correct in thinking there were sufficient safeguards of the security of defendants built into the system. On its face, the Criminal Ordinance of 1670 assumed neither the guilt nor innocence of the accused.[46] Andrews has suggested that if the whole point of the trial was to arrive at the truth rather than employ clever lawyers capable of obfuscating the truth, then there was no reason to conclude that French criminal law procedures were unfair. It is only in systems presuming the innocence of all persons charged with crimes that the rules need to favor the defendant. Where neither guilt nor innocence is assumed, a more neutral set of rules can be employed. Andrews, for one, believes that neutrality is fully sufficient and that the presumption of innocence makes it too difficult to convict a guilty defendant.

Andrews also believes that there is a danger of exaggerating the power of ancien régime judges. The procedural rules were complex, and no less than forty-seven Articles in the Ordinance specified penalties for judges who failed to follow them.[47] Careful note was taken of this fact by several important commentators on the French criminal law of the pre-revolutionary period. Daniel Jousse, for example, asserted that "In their review and judgment of criminal trials judges must adhere exactly to the Laws of the Realm." If they did not do so, harsh penalties could be imposed on them. "They must conduct and examine with integrity and all possible care," Jousse continues, "the criminal trials entrusted to them; the life, liberty, honor, or reputation of the accused, and sometimes of his entire family, often depends on their judgments."[48] Whether or not judges adhered to the rules of the ordinance with the scrupulosity Jousse here implies is altogether another matter, however.

As we have seen, no decision for guilt could be made in the French system by a single judge. Instead, verdicts were arrived at by a panel of judges, a procedure that Montesquieu singles out for praise in *The Spirit of Laws* as appropriate to monarchies where trained, professional judges decide the fate of defendants through consultation and negotiation as compared to republics where untrained lay jurors, who are little capable of fashioning proper punishments, render verdicts of guilty or innocent with the actual punishments for guilty parties decided ahead of time and written into law. "In monarchies," he concludes, it is most appropriate that "judges take on the behavior of arbiters; they deliberate together, they communicate their thoughts to one another, they agree among themselves; one modifies his opinion to make it conform to that of another; opinions with the least support are cast aside in favor of the two most widely held" (VI, 4). In republics, on the other hand, the punishments that are to be inflicted are to be written into law so that the sole role of the jury is to determine guilt or innocence. "It was a vice of the republic of Sparta," he writes, "that the ephors decided cases arbitrarily without having any laws to guide them." In England, on the other hand, which Montesquieu judged "a republic disguised as a monarchy" (V, 19), the penalties are imposed by the laws rather than by juries or judges (VI, 3).

Unlike a good many later reformers in France, we do not find Montesquieu advocating jury trials as a necessary corrective to any perceived defects in French criminal law procedures. He did not fully trust lay jurors to reach proper verdicts. Hence, in commenting on the use of juries in Athens, he praises the decision of Solon to have the Council of the Areopagus review all jury verdicts and order new trials where necessary both in cases of acquittal and in cases of conviction where the Council believed justice had not been served by the jury. This was, he asserts, "an admirable law, which subjected the people to the censure of the magistracy they most respected" (VI, 5). His skepticism as to the ability of lay jurors to reach proper legal decisions is also transparent in his assertion that "(i)t will be beneficial to introduce some slowness into such matters (of criminal trials), especially after the accused is imprisoned, so that the people can calm down and judge objectively" (VI, 5).

As is characteristic of his discussions of the relative merits of republics and monarchies in Books II through VIII of *The Spirit of Laws*, we do not find Montesquieu disparaging monarchies and favoring republics in his discussions of criminal law. He does not appear to have believed that the procedures of French, monarchical justice were in any way inferior to those that had existed in Athens, Sparta, or Rome. He saw no reason to prefer the jury system employed by republics to the system of professional judging used in France, an attitude that may be judged typically French considering the decline in jury use following their brief period of popularity during the Revolution.[49] He concluded, in fact, that the lack of sophistication of lay jurors often means that issues of law have to be drastically simplified. In Rome, for example, the *praetors* stated the legal issue in one sentence precisely in order to reduce the complexity of the legal issues posed for the laymen on the juries (VI, 4). Even following the simplification of the issues posed in a case, Montesquieu was skeptical of the ability of lay jurors to reach correct decisions. Thus he praised Roman laws permitting those accused of crimes to go into exile before judgments were handed down and also those Roman laws protecting the property of the condemned from confiscation by popular juries (VI, 4). Trained as a professional judge himself, he was fully prepared to see the advantages monarchical governments have in being able to draw on the expertise of well-trained judges when it comes to adjudicating guilt or innocence. As will be apparent in the section that follows, Montesquieu believed the punishments from which French magistrates could choose should be greatly reduced in severity. He does not appear to have believed, however, that the procedures of French criminal trials were seriously flawed except for the continuing availability of torture to extract confessions.

Punishment

A liberal philosophy of jurisprudence is by no means restricted to concern for the procedural aspects of criminal trials. Nowhere does Montesquieu's liberal viewpoint emerge so clearly, in fact, as in his discussions of the need to decriminalize certain offenses considered crimes under existing French law. Actions that are simply distasteful to some, or disfavored by those in power, he contends, should never be criminalized. It is only where real harm exists or is threatened that punishment should be forthcoming. "It is rare," he announces as an axiom of criminal law drafting, "that it will prove necessary to prohibit something that is not bad under the pretext of some perfection that is imagined" (XXIX, 16). Actions merely offensive to the sentiments or views of others do not warrant punishment. Hence manners and customs, he believes, should be regarded as completely outside the domain of the law. They should only be changed by "introducing other manners and other customs" rather than by imposing criminal sanctions on those who cling to them (XIX, 14). We encounter, then, in Montesquieu's classification of types of crimes the workings of the liberal mentality eager to protect a sphere of individual freedom from state intervention. If he outlines a zone of privacy by no means as protective as that later advocated by Mill in his *On Liberty* (1859), he nonetheless suggests the decriminalization of religious offenses such as magic, blasphemy, and heresy, while also contending that where actions or behavior merely disturb the public tranquillity, without actually threatening the security of lives or property, only modest penalties are appropriate.

Montesquieu divides all possible offenses into four distinct categories, running from the least serious of offenses such as religious misconduct, which he believed should be completely decriminalized, to the very most serious crimes threatening lives and property. In so doing, he makes an important advance over existing criminology.[50] Aside from allowing him to pursue a decriminalization agenda, this classification system saves him from the nearly impossible task Jeremy Bentham later tackled of classifying every conceivable sort of crime and suggesting a corresponding analogical punishment. Montesquieu could instead suggest a range of appropriate penalties for whole categories of crimes.

The lowest category of offenses in Montesquieu's punishment scale are those against religion (XII, 4). He argues for the decriminalization of religious offenses substantially before Beccaria in Italy, or Voltaire in France, or Jefferson in America took up the same crusade. He vigorously opposes conflating the religious notion of sin with the secular concept of crime. Sins, he suggests, are an offense to the Deity and to the religious community. Crimes, on the other hand, pose real and tangible threats to the security of individuals or the government. Since sins are between man and God, "there can be no criminal matter; all passes between man and God, who knows the proportion and timing of his vengeance." Governments must refrain from all attempts to avenge the deity since allowing men to adopt the role of fighting God's battles will unleash sentiments nearly impossible to control (XII, 4).

Montesquieu did not regard sacrilege or blasphemy—or even heresy, though here the case is a bit more complex—as crimes per se. Such religious offenses were unholy from the vantage point of the faithful, but this did not raise them to the level of crimes. Therefore nothing more than excommunication through ecclesiastical courts, combined with contempt for the offender and refusal to associate with him, should be considered just penalties where offenses against religion are concerned (XII, 4).[51] He does include a caveat, however, where heresy is concerned, remarking "I have not said here that heresy must not be punished; I say that one must be very wary in punishing it" (XII, 5). In other texts on heresy Montesquieu strikes a much more liberal note. In a scalding and justly famous chapter denouncing the Spanish Inquisition, for example, he summons the most exquisite irony to mock the Christian sense of rectitude in expunging Jewish infidels from the face of the earth. This could only have the effect, he was convinced, of displeasing the very God in whom both Jew and Christian alike professed to believe (XXV, 13). Furthermore, Montesquieu contends that prosecutions for heresy can only prove problematic since advocacy of theological positions often involves "an infinite number of distinctions, interpretations, and limitations" (XII, 6). Hence the more ignorant the people are, the more likely they are to bring false accusations of heresy (XII, 5).

Anticipating a line of argument made prominent in both Jefferson's *Bill for Religious Freedom* (1777) and John Stuart Mill's *On Liberty* (1859), Montesquieu suggests that religious truths must triumph, not by means of the power of the state to enforce them, but rather by winning over the hearts and minds of men. Imposing orthodoxy through such drastic measures as burning perceived infidels at the stake can only have the effect of suggesting that, unaided by the cruelties of power, truth is impotent (XXV, 13).

Montesquieu's conclusion on the subject of supposed crimes against religion is bold and uncompromising: "It is necessary to avoid penal laws where religion is concerned. . . . In a word, history teaches us well enough that penal laws (regarding religion) have never had any effect other than destruction" (XXV, 12).[52] Such penal laws, he acknowledges, do indeed produce the sort of fear that can guide human actions, but where religion is concerned such fear of secular punishment is effaced by the even greater fear of eternal damnation should one fail to conform to God's law. Hence harsh penalties in matters of religion will not only be ignored but will also produce a "hardening of the soul" (XXV, 12).

According to Montesquieu, religious law and civil law should be regarded as residing in wholly separate spheres. Religious laws will seek to govern the actions of individuals as they seek perfection in their personal lives, but civil laws must direct the conduct of persons considered in their roles as citizens. "There are then different orders of laws, and the sublimity of human reason consists in perfectly knowing to which of these orders the things that are to be decreed ought to be chiefly related. . . . We ought not to decide by the divine laws what should be decided by human laws, nor regulate by human laws what should be determined by divine laws" (XXVI, 2). The Romans rightly punished thefts from sacred places like other thefts, leaving to canon law the punishment for the sacrilege involved (XXVI, 8). Just as Jefferson and others were later to conclude, Montesquieu understood that there is protection for religion in such a separation. Only when religious laws actually conflict with civil laws will there ever be a proper case for laws of the civil realm to impinge on the laws of religion (XXVI, 10).

The second category of crimes in Montesquieu's classificatory scheme consists of offenses against a society's moral code where the moral conduct in question is between consenting adults and where no one's security is threatened (XII, 4). For these sorts of crimes, as for example for adultery, polygamy, and incest, there were no royal edicts governing punishment in the France of Montesquieu's day, and judges therefore possessed substantial latitude in these sorts of cases.[53] Where such offenses against morals are concerned, Montesquieu stops short of arguing for complete decriminalization, as he had done for crimes against religion. He was clearly appalled, however, that the offense of homosexuality had been punished with burning at the stake, particularly since, as Beccaria was also later to observe, false charges would be difficult to disprove (XII, 6-7). Here, as always, Montesquieu indicates that the penalties should be "drawn from the nature of the thing." The goal in the area of controlling sexual offenses should be moderate measures "to repress the temerity of the two sexes." Appropriate penalties for offenses in this second category would be "forfeiture of the advantages society has attached to the purity of morals, fines, shame, compulsory concealment, public infamy, (or) expulsion from home and society"[54]—penalties, in other words, much less severe than those sometimes employed in pre-revolutionary France for offenses involving immorality (XII, 4).

Clearly it would be incorrect to interpret Montesquieu's sharp distinction between morals that govern "inner conduct" and civil laws that are designed to govern the conduct of men as citizens (XIX, 16) as suggesting that he believed there should be no criminal sanctions where morals are concerned. He draws no bright line between private acts involving morality and public acts that involve one's actions as a citizen. Acts of private immorality may indeed be regulated by criminal sanctions on the assumption that such conduct may have implications for public order, or even for the stability of government, particularly in republican governments where lack of purity in morals will weaken the willingness of individuals to place the needs of the commonwealth above their own selfish desires (V, 7; VII, 10). Offenses against morality, however, provided they are consensual, should never be punished as severely as those that harm, or threaten harm, to life or property.[55]

The third class of crimes in Montesquieu's punishment scale are those acts that disturb the public tranquillity, by which he meant offenses encompassing "a simple disruption of public order" (XII, 4). This category of offenses had not been addressed under the French Ordinance of 1670, which divided all crimes into the four categories of *lèse-majesté divine*, *lèse-majesté humaine*, crimes against public security and crimes against public morality. Montesquieu included in Book XXVI of his work, "Of Laws in Relation to the Order of Things Which They Determine," a ringing denunciation of any system of justice that conflates simple breaches of the peace with truly serious crimes that threaten the security of individuals, or society (XXVI, 24). The offense of disturbing the peace, or being a public nuisance was ordinarily punished by the Lieutenant Generalcy of Police rather than by a royal court.[56] According to Montesquieu, the penalties for disturbing public tranquillity should be "drawn from the nature of the thing" and should be "connected to this tranquillity. Hence appropriate punishments would include imprisonment, exile, floggings, and punishments which restore restless (*inquiets*) spirits and cause them to fall back under the established order" (XII, 4).

Montesquieu's fourth class of crimes consisted of the very most serious offenses warranting capital punishment. These were crimes injurious to life or property. Unlike Beccaria, Montesquieu does not reject the death penalty, although he recommends drastically restricting its use, as compared to current practices, by making it apply only to treason, murder, attempted murder, and certain large scale crimes against property where the offender has no property with which to make restitution (XII, 4).[57] Using explicitly retributive language, he opines that "A man deserves death when he has so far infringed the security or another person as to deprive, or to attempt to deprive him of his life." The penalty of death for crimes directly threatening the security of individuals or the state is "derived from the nature of the thing, and drawn from reason and the sources of good and evil" (XII, 4).

Montesquieu does not restrict himself to such retributive justifications of the death penalty. Supplementing his avowedly retributivist explanation with a utilitarian rationale, he concludes that the penalty of death is actually very favorable to the liberty of the citizen since the deterrence provided by this ultimate punishment is what protects the liberty of all citizens, including the life of the murderer (XV, 2). Montesquieu clearly believed that the death penalty, positioned at the summit of a properly graduated scale of punishments, has a crucial deterrent function to perform. Sharply contrasting laws establishing capital punishment with laws establishing slavery, he approves the former while rejecting the latter, since laws creating slavery could never be useful to those subjected to them. Laws inflicting capital punishment, on the other hand, are designed for the protection of all, and anyone who shows callous disregard for the safety of others by breaking the pattern of deterrence aimed at by laws designed to protect life and property deserves capital punishment (XV, 2). Confident that the death penalty is readily justifiable for certain heinous crimes, Montesquieu concludes his discussion of the four categories of crime and the ascending scale of penalties and punishments commensurate with these crimes with the assertion, "All that I say, is founded in nature and is very favorable to the liberty of the citizen" (XII, 4).

Those familiar with Montesquieu's massive treatise, composed over the course of some twenty years, are well aware that what he asserts in one text he sometimes appears to take back in another. Thus it comes as no surprise that, although he must be read as a proponent of the death penalty for a few of the most serious crimes, and although he refers explicitly to the law of the *talion* in his justification, he took care to cast aspersions on blatantly retaliatory punishments by linking them to despotic states. Despotic states use retaliation, he asserts, because they love simple laws. Moderate states use retaliatory punishments only infrequently, on the other hand, and they nearly always moderate their use by making pardons available in appropriate cases. In the European monarchies of modern times, Montesquieu cautions, princes wishing to avoid despotism must moderate the harshest retaliatory penalties, particularly where noblemen, motivated by honor, have found it necessary to do what the laws prohibit (VI, 21). He believes there will be no lessening of deterrence if punishments are made less severe and mercy is sometimes shown, since in monarchical governments the shame of being punished strikes as deeply as do more physical punishments in despotic states where human sensibilities have been hardened by brutal punishments (VI, 21). Hence Montesquieu praises the Romans for abandoning the death penalty, while noting that they loved moderation in penalties, a fact he attributes to the nurturing impact of their republican constitution prior to the civil war period. Republics, Montesquieu observes, must not only strive for "gentleness of penal laws, but also allow the accused to depart to escape punishment" (VI, 15).

Punishment in Ancien Régime France

Recently, a number of revisionist scholars have contended that just as the procedures employed in French trials were less prejudicial to defendants than has often been contended, so, too, were the punitive excesses of French punishments less severe than is often thought. The use of bloody, corporal punishments, Richard Andrews seeks to demonstrate, has been grossly exaggerated. Shaming and incarceration—not direct bodily assault—were the chief repressive tools of the criminal law.[58] "Physical chastisement (including the death penalty)," he writes, "was but one, and a carefully limited, sphere in the versatile Old Regime penal system." Thus, "shaming and humiliation, not physical suffering, formed the essence of Old Regime legal punishment. The overarching goal of punishment was moral correction, even salvation."[59]

> Crime required punishment, just as sin required expiation. But punishment, like expiation, was apportioned to both the malefactor and the offense. Even in cases involving capital offenses (many of which were mortal sins), penal retribution was not usually implacable or extreme, for the character, motives, and moral and social being of the offender, as well as the circumstances of the crime counted in judgment and in the assessment of penalty. . . . Equity in judging persons, not merely crimes, required consideration of aggravating and mitigating circumstances and also discretionary penalties.[60]

Some of this emphasis on moderation in punishments is no doubt wishful thinking. It is difficult to square Andrews' benign gloss on Old Regime jurisprudence even with some of his own reporting. He covers certain cases involving punishments that must strike us today as completely barbaric. He mentions, for example, the case of one Nicolas Bara, a seventeen-year-old, unemployed stonemason who committed fraud and burglary compounded by alleged sacrilege. He was convicted of the sacrilege of several times feigning sickness and asking for Extreme Unction while also stealing from those who cared for him during his pretended sickness. A recidivist whose punishment for his previous theft of a suit jacket had been to be branded with a "V" for "voleur" and to be banished from the locale of his crime, he chose this time to confess his new crimes. Following three rounds of balloting among seven judges in a provostial court from which there was no right to appeal under the 1670 ordinance, Bara received, as his punishment, death by hanging and the burning of his corpse to ashes following the standard public shaming that involved kneeling in the portal of Notre Dame Cathedral while wearing a placard inscribed "thief, recidivist, impostor, and profaner of sacraments."[61] Such a punishment of death for a non-violent crime suggests that contemporary criticisms of the pre-revolutionary criminal justice system were certainly not completely overblown. As shown by the notorious cases involving Calas, Sirven, and the Chevalier de La Barre, the law was quite capable of baring its teeth as ferociously as any pack of wolves in search of tender prey, particularly where crimes against religion were concerned. Hence one needs to be cautious in reviewing revisionist assessments of the system of crime and punishment in pre-revolutionary France. We must not ignore the extent to which, in some cases, particularly those involving sacrilege, the black legend of Draconian punishment does not seem to distort the truth of what transpired.

Whether or not some of the recent revisionist work goes too far in reversing previous conclusions regarding the brutality of punishment in ancien régime France, we can certainly conclude that Montesquieu was in the forefront of the Enlightenment movement to moderate the severity of the punishments then in place. In fact, he posits a direct correlation between moderate punishments and liberty. "It would be easy to prove," he asserts, "that in all or nearly all the states of Europe, penalties have decreased or strengthened to the extent that they have drawn closer to or farther from liberty" (VI, 9). In the opening chapter of Book XXIX, devoted to the composition of laws, he remarks that his whole purpose in writing *The Spirit of Laws* has been to prove that "the spirit of moderation" should prevail since "the political good, like the moral good, is always found between two limits" (XXIX, 1). On this principle of the mean alone, absent all the other considerations inclining him toward moderation, Montesquieu was moved to oppose excessively brutal punishments. In reviewing that portion of the Roman law of the Twelve Tables allowing a creditor to cut an insolvent debtor to pieces, he remarks, "Shall the cruelest laws, therefore, be the best? Shall excess be judged the good, and all the relations between things be destroyed?" (XXIX, 2).[62]

Lenient punishments, Montesquieu was convinced, as Beccaria would also later conclude, can be just as effective as deterrents as extremely severe punishments, since it is the certainty of punishment rather than the severity of punishment that best deters crime (VI, 12). Even the invention of breaking on the wheel, Montesquieu asserts, only reduced the incidence of highway robbery for a very short time, just as the introduction of the death penalty for desertion from the French military did little to stop that offense. Considering the soldier's fear of shame, a more effective punishment, Montesquieu contends, would have been to slit the deserter's nose and cut off his ears in order to brand him with infamy for life—a suggestion reminding us not to exaggerate the humanitarianism of such Enlightenment era reformers of the criminal law as Montesquieu (VI, 12). Brutal punishments, Montesquieu generally believed, debase those subjected to them while also having the perverse result of encouraging individuals to commit crimes by causing them to retaliate against the wrathful punisher.[63] The deterrent effects of punishment depend on the *mentalités* of those subjected to them.[64] Among peoples not brutalized by the specter of such cruel and barbarous punishments as the rack or the wheel, the thought of something far less painful, such as even the loss of status in one's society, or the humiliation of being labeled a wrongdoer, can serve as just as effective a deterrent as the threat of painful injury (VI, 12). Among the early Germans, Montesquieu observes, it was considered such a mark of shame "to leave one's buckler behind in combat" that several individuals "killed themselves after this misfortune" (XXVIII, 21).

Montesquieu considered a society's system of punishment nothing less than an index to the "character of the human spirit" present in that society (XXV, 12). He had nothing but loathing for the cruel Japanese system, which he judged the height of barbarism, and which may well have functioned in his analysis as a stand in for French punishment trends he may not have been comfortable attacking directly.[65] The Japanese had introduced a brutal system of punishments because they wrongly regarded all crimes, no matter how insignificant, as direct affronts to the emperor. Since the emperor was deemed the proprietor of all goods, all violations of law were considered a threat to his personal interests. Hence the Japanese sought to avenge the emperor by means of their criminal laws, which could only lead to the same sort of excessive punishments produced in other countries such as France where the goal was to avenge the Deity following offenses against religion. Vengeance carried out in the name of defending either extreme political or religious authority, Montesquieu concludes, knows no limits.

The Japanese, Montesquieu observes, criminalized actions stemming even from the fundamental human instinct of self-preservation. Lying to a magistrate, for example, was made a capital crime in Japan. Risking one's money at the gaming table was also a capital offense. In Japan, Montesquieu concludes, despotism had surpassed even itself in cruelty! These horrid laws did not produce their desired effect, however. Such laws had "more fury than force." They were so excessive that people shuddered at the thought that they might actually be carried into effect (VI, 13). This will always be the case, Montesquieu suggests, where punishments are not properly scaled to the crimes committed. Ways will be found to avoid the enforcement of excessively punitive laws. Montesquieu argues this point in various historical contexts. He notes, for example, that at one point in Roman history the senate opposed a law designed to check popular intrigues on the argument that although it might "terrify men's spirits," the actual result would be that no one would bring an accusation "whereas, with moderate penalties, there would be both judges and accusers" (VI, 14).

Montesquieu considered excessively brutal punishments contrary to nature. "Let us follow nature," he counsels, "who has given shame to man for his scourge; and let the heaviest part of the punishment be the infamy attending it. But if there are some countries where shame is not a consequence of punishment, this must be owing to tyranny," he concludes, "which has inflicted the same punishment on villains and honest men" (VI, 12). He acknowledges that despotic governments will likely resort to severe punishment since the principle of such governments is fear. "In moderate governments," however, "the love of one's country, shame and the fear of blame, are restraining motives capable of preventing a great multitude of crimes. Here the greatest punishment of a bad action is conviction. The civil laws have therefore a softer way of correcting, and do not require so much force and severity" (VI, 9). One cannot impose "great punishments" in republican states, Montesquieu continues, without inadvertently bestowing on the punishers more power than is consistent with republics (XII, 18).

Montesquieu could find no historical evidence that harsh punishments serve as better deterrents than moderate ones. There had been, he observes, no increase in crime in Rome as a result of the replacement of the immoderate Law of the Twelve Tables first by the Valerian law and then by the Porcian law (VI, 11). Furthermore, he believed that harsh punishments fail to rehabilitate. Instead, severity often produces a hostile reaction among the populace that threatens the stability of the government itself, particularly in despotic states where all hope of pardon is denied. The goal of vengeance, he notes in one of his *Pensées*, is making offenders wish they hadn't offended. In actual fact, however, vengeance can never produce that result. Instead, vengeful punishments make offenders wish to offend again.[66] It is not the wrath of the punisher, but rather the executive's exercise of the pardoning power that is most likely to result in repentance. Forgiveness, not wrath, will produce the proper penitence on the part of the wrongdoer and return errant souls to the political community.

Conclusion

How, then, are we to assess Montesquieu's contributions to the exploration of crime and punishment issues in ancien régime France? Certainly we can conclude that if he seems quite conservative on procedural issues as regulated by the Criminal Ordinance of 1670, he was nonetheless in the forefront of enlightened opinion on the matter of reducing the severity of punishments while also decriminalizing religious offenses and certain consensual moral failings that he believed should be treated as sins rather than crimes. Later criminal law reformers in France had a good deal of respect for Montesquieu's pioneering efforts in stressing the importance of protecting the innocent and reducing the severity of punishments. Many were understandably critical, however, of his complacency with regard to procedures they identified with the despotic oppression one might expect of the Inquisition. As David Jacobson rightly concluded, "he provided . . . neither a systematic critique of criminal law, a systematic program of reform, nor even a call to reform."[67] And this was well understood by reformers later in the century. Both Charles Valazé and J.-E.-D. Bernardi, for example, criticized the lack of a criminal law reform program in *The Spirit of Laws*.[68] They still considered the proper label for that treatise "immortal," however. Montesquieu's importance on the subject of crime and punishment is related to his argument that nothing is more crucial to the achievement of civil liberty than fair criminal law procedures, and he made this point in a weighty tome whose stance was unrivaled in France as an authoritative dispensation of political wisdom. It would certainly be an exaggeration to suggest that without Montesquieu there would have been no criminal law reform movement later in the century, but it is nonetheless true that all the reformers were familiar with and inspired by his liberal perspectives on protecting the innocent, decriminalizing offenses that pose no real threat to individuals or property, and reducing the severity of punishment while restricting the use of the ultimate punishment of death to only a few crimes of the very most serious sort.

As previously mentioned, French writers on the criminal law who, like Montesquieu, had served as judges on any of the various Parlements of France tended to be much more accepting of the existing criminal law procedures than lay reformers. Not surprisingly, then, all four of the major reformers in the generation after Montesquieu who believed the inquisitorial system should be improved but retained rather than being replaced by trial by jury (Jean Blondel, A.-J.-B. Boucher d'Argis, Guillaume François Letrosne, and Nicholas-Joseph Philpin de Piépape) were judges.[69] Even though they published their views late in the century (three of the four, in fact, published their reform tracts in 1789 and one in 1779), they continued to believe that the ordinance of 1670 provided a solid basis for fair criminal trials. They acknowledged that legal education might be improved, and even that the abolition of venality of offices might improve the quality of judging. And they also called either for the abolition of seigniorial justice or its improvement, and also for improvement in the conditions in the jails holding defendants awaiting trials, but they did not see any need for a fundamental transformation of the inquisitorial system to resemble the accusatorial system in use in England. All four of these late century reformers who had been professional magistrates did indeed favor procedural changes to enable defendants to more skillfully confront the witnesses against them and ensure that they could present their own witnesses by making *faits justificatifs* mandatory rather than subject to the judges' discretion. Furthermore, they believed the right to defense counsel should be granted in all cases, though they differed on how early in the disposition of the case such counsel should be allowed to intervene and actually participate in the proceedings. None of these four major reformers, however, who, like Montesquieu, had served as judges in the existing inquisitorial system, concluded that the inquisitorial system was beyond repair or rotten through and through. And certainly their basic support of the system outlined in the 1670 ordinance, even late in the century when other lay participants in the system were calling for much more fundamental changes, including trial by jury and full representation by counsel at all stages of questioning, makes it not at all surprising that Montesquieu, writing substantially earlier, displayed a similarly supportive attitude toward the basic design of French procedures under the ordinance of 1670.

It will be helpful in assessing Montesquieu's conservatism with regard to existing French criminal law procedures to note that he was far from being alone in believing French procedures were basically fair to defendants. It was only in the mid-1770s that the tide of French opinion first turned to a contrary view stressing the need for fundamental reforms.[70] Thus we find Jean-Baptiste-Jacques Elie de Beaumont taking the position in his 1767 *Mémoire judiciaire* on behalf of Pierre-Paul Sirven that, in the summary of David Bell, "the existing laws of the French kingdom incarnating a sort of immemorial wisdom, provided all the guarantees that the defendants needed."[71] According to Bell, it was only after the Maupeou strike against the authority of the Parlements that lawyers even began to argue for reform on the basis of a natural rights philosophy since it was no longer possible for the Parlements, now vanquished, to protect rights by resisting royal abuses of power. And this natural rights development transpired more than twenty years after Montesquieu had published his treatise. Bell concludes that Montesquieu's attitude of strong support for an autonomous judiciary, which he deemed capable of guaranteeing individual rights, was quite typical of legal thinking in France up to mid-century. In the latter half of the century, however, substantially greater stress began to be placed on legislative guarantees emanating from an enlightened monarch or from an enlightened legislature. With this shift came substantially less reliance on the robe nobility functioning as depositories of the laws and substantially more emphasis on enlightened "public opinion" as the safeguard of individual liberties.[72]

Many authors rightly stress the influence of Cesare Beccaria's *On Crimes and Punishments* (1764) as the key development fueling the reformist climate in France and igniting the thoughts of Voltaire and others on the subject of necessary reforms. Beccaria provided a brief, sharply focused text that seconded Montesquieu's notions on the need to reduce the severity of punishments. Also stressed as influences on the shaping of a reform climate in France during the 1760s and thereafter are Voltaire's various writings and activities following the sensational trials of Calas, Sirven, and La Barre. Whatever the various influences may have been, the frequent reformist calls for new legislation and radical change in French criminal law procedures date mainly from the mid-1770s, and they steadily picked up steam as the impact of reformist literature was increasingly felt.[73] By the late 1780s, discontent with French legal procedures had reached critical mass. Thus we find Arthur Young commenting in his travel book on France,

> I have, in conversation with many very sensible men, in different parts of the kingdom, met with something of content with their government, in all other respects than this, but on the question of expecting justice to be really fairly administered, everyone confessed that there was no such thing to be looked for.[74]

Young was writing very close to the outbreak of the Revolution, however, and we should not expect to encounter the same attitudes he detected among the populace in 1787, or shortly thereafter, in a work by Montesquieu published in

1748. The author of *The Spirit of Laws* was a moderate rather than a radical reformer, and, as he stressed in the Preface to his work, he set out primarily to explain rather than censure every nation's laws. Even on the subject of punishments, where he was most inclined to call for radical reform, he by no means called for an end to the differential treatment of *noblesse* and commoners in France since the honorific distinctions that define monarchy will lead quite logically to different rights and privileges even where crime and punishment are concerned (VI, 15). In the ancient French laws, he concludes, "the spirit of monarchy" is readily discovered since in lesser offenses involving pecuniary punishments noblemen paid more than commoners whereas in criminal cases involving serious crimes a nobleman lost his honor and his influence at court whereas a villein was punished corporally (VI, 10).[75]

However moderate his reformist posture where judicial procedures were concerned, Montesquieu provided a solid platform of concern for the rights of the innocent on which later reformers could build. If writers of the next generation certainly advanced well beyond his views on many of the procedural elements of French criminal law outlined in the Criminal Ordinance of 1670, this was in part a logical product of a more strident reform atmosphere to which Montesquieu had himself greatly contributed by pointing out the risks of despotism in excessively harsh and brutal punishments not only in *The Spirit of Laws* but in his earlier *Persian Letters* as well. As we have seen, Montesquieu wrote prior to several key developments that added substantial fuel to fires of reform. Hence it would make little historical sense to fault him for not advancing the more radical reformist arguments that became typical later in the century. In his generation he led the way to reform, and the high regard in which he was held by Beccaria and also many French reformers writing after mid-century remains a testament to his very substantial importance as the initiator of reform discussions of the criminal law in ancien régime France.

It was only the French Revolution with its relentless purpose of remaking France in a new image that brought wholesale revision of the 1670 ordinance. Prior to the epoch making events of 1789, changes had indeed been contemplated—not just by reformers but even in official circles—but they constituted only minor tinkering with the details of the inquisitorial procedure. Six edicts of criminal law reform were approved by Louis XVI's royal council in May 1788, but the sum total of these recommended changes left the basic structure of ancien régime justice in tact.[76] The *sellette*, or low stool, on which the accused sat during questioning was to be banished. Torture to extract the names of accomplices (the *question préalable*) was to be outlawed, following the earlier abolition of the *question préparatoire* by royal edict in 1780. Appeals in cases of riot or sedition were to be facilitated by postponing executions for a month's time rather than carrying them out immediately, and all courts handing down sentences were to state the grounds for conviction in order to facilitate appeals. Finally, a majority of three votes in capital cases, rather than a two vote majority, was henceforth to be required for conviction. The reform edicts of 1788, even had they been put in place, would have left much unchanged. The secrecy of French trials, the denial of effective defense counsel, the rule against witnesses changing their accounts on penalty of perjury, the failure to allow the accused to confront witnesses as part of the initial examination and reporting of evidence, the failure to arraign defendants and pronounce charges against them—all these more basic problems went unmentioned by the six jurists Louis XVI appointed as a commission to recommend what became the modest proposed reforms of May 1788, all of which were postponed in the aftermath of the decision to convene the Estates General.

Even during the Revolution, reform arrived slowly. First to go were the *lettres de cachet* outlawed in Article 7 of the Declaration of the Rights of Man and the Citizen of 1789. Then a decree passed by the National Assembly in October, 1789 abolished the *sellette* and the use of torture to obtain names of accomplices while also mandating the assistance of legal counsel. The use of juries in criminal cases was approved in April, 1790, although it was some time before this reform was implemented. A new penal code was finally passed by the Legislative Assembly in October, 1791, adopting many of Montesquieu's proposals for reducing the severity of punishments.[77] We may justly conclude, then, that in the area of criminal law reform involving both the definition of criminality and the scale of punishments, Montesquieu was not without influence on revolutionary outcomes. If he proved too supportive of the status quo on procedural questions to be of much use in guiding later revolutionary reformers, his insightful discussion of punishment issues certainly had a lasting impact.[78]

Notes

I would like to express my appreciation to Rebecca Kingston for her comments on an earlier draft of this chapter.

1. Montesquieu was first assigned to *la Tournelle*, the criminal justice section of the Parlement as a *conseiller* entrusted with the duty to summarize cases for the magistrates who were to interrogate accused persons with cases pending on appeal before the Parlement. After becoming a *président à mortier* in 1716, he served another ten and a half years in this criminal justice section, longer than anyone else in this period of time and much longer than the usual system of rotation allowed. The reasons for his continual reappointment to serve in that section of the Parlement appear to be unknown. See Rebecca Kingston, *Montesquieu and the Parlement of Bordeaux* (Geneva: Droz, 1996), 102.

2. *The Spirit of Laws*, Book XII, chapter 2. Hereafter cited by Book and chapter number in the main body of the text; e.g. (XII, 2). All translations are my own.

3. There exists strong consensus on this point. Hence John Mackrell in his "Criticism of Seigniorial Justice in Eighteenth-Century France," in J. F. Bosher, ed., *French Gov-*

ernment and Society 1500-1850 (London: Athlone Press, 1973), 123-44 remarks: "The first eighteenth-century writer who can be said to deal with criminal law both comprehensively and in a philosophical way was Montesquieu" (at 134).

4. For the substantial influence of Montesquieu on Beccaria, see Catherine Larrère, "Droit de punir et qualification des crimes de Montesquieu à Beccaria," in *Beccaria et la culture juridique des lumières. Etudes historiques*, Michel Porret, ed. (Geneva, 1996), 89-108.

5. Starting in the eighteenth century, a good many commentators concluded that he did indeed present an exaggerated caricature of despotism. See, for example, Franco Venturi's analysis of the views of Anquetil-Duperron in his "Oriental Despotism," *Journal of the History of Ideas* 24, no. 1 (January-March, 1963): 133-42 and David Young, "Montesquieu's View of Despotism and His Use of Travel Literature," *Review of Politics* 40, no. 3 (1978): 392-405.

6. Peter Gay, *The Enlightenment: An Interpretation. The Science of Freedom* (New York: Norton, 1969), 428.

7. A justly notorious instance in France of the despotic evocation by Louis XIV of a Parlementary case to the king's royal council was his moving the appeal of six priests from Reims for not approving the papal bull *Unigenitus*, designed to stamp out Jansenism, from the Parlement of Paris to his own council. It was moved back to parlementary jurisdiction after Louis XIV died and Philippe d'Orléans became regent. See David A. Bell, "Safeguarding the Rights of the Accused: Lawyers and Political Trials in France, 1716-1789," in Dale Van Kley, ed., *The French Idea of Freedom. The Old Regime and the Declaration of Rights of 1789* (Stanford: Stanford University Press, 1994), 242-43. Louis XIV's decision prompted sharp criticism from some quarters. Claude-Joseph Prévost, for example, protested that "to evoke an *appel comme d'abus* to the king's own person is in a way to destroy the foundation, the very idea of justice which so to speak, has engendered the *appels*." See Prévost, *Mémoire pour les trois docteurs et curez de Reims . . .* (Paris, 1716), 11-13, in Bell, "Rights of the Accused," 246.

8. Montesquieu's advocacy of the pardoning power is in sharp contrast to Beccaria's position. See Beccaria, *On Crimes and Punishments* (1764), chapter 46, "Pardons."

9. In at least some cases, however, justice was far too slow, and individuals awaiting trial were kept in dank and inhumane jails much too long before being tried. One cause of the excessive slowness in many cases was the confusion of jurisdictions in France. There were provisions in the Criminal Ordinance of 1670 for resolving jurisdictional disputes, but the process was often agonizingly slow. J.-E.-D. Bernardi criticized this aspect of the French system in his *Discours sur les loix pénales . . .* (Paris, 1781), 19, as did J.-M.-A. Servan in his *Réflexions sur quelques points de nos loix . . .* (Geneva, 1781), 199, 201. See David Jacobson, "The Politics of Criminal Law Reform," Dissertation, Brown University, June 1976 and John A. Carey, *Judicial Reform in France before the Revolution of 1789* (Cambridge: Harvard University Press, 1981), 114. In his *Discourse concerning Equity regulating Judgments and the Execution of Laws* (1725) Montesquieu stressed the

inequity of prolonging the disposition of cases in order to increase the magistrates' fees. See Kingston, *Montesquieu*, 70. It bears noting that the Sixth Amendment to the U.S. Constitution guarantees not only a public trial by an impartial jury but also a "speedy" trial.

10. Under existing French law treason was divisible into two types, one more serious than the other: crimes against the king, and treasonous acts directed, not against the king himself, but against his ministers or principal offices. Both categories were forms of lèse majesty. See Jean Brethe de La Gressaye, ed., *De L'esprit des Loix*, 4 vols. (Paris: Les Belles Lettres, 1950-61), II, 378 (note 51) citing Muyart de Vouglans, *Institutes au droit criminel, ou principes sur ces matières, avec un traité particulier des crimes* (Paris, 1757), Part VIII, Titre II.

11. Such a special court had last been convened in 1716, and Montesquieu had taken a strong stand against its establishment in drafting his youthful "Memoir on the State's Debts" (1715). On this subject see Jean Ehrard, "À la découverte des finances publiques: le *Mémoire sur les dettes de l'État*," in *Montesquieu, les années de formation* (1689-1720), Catherine Volpilhac-Auger, ed. (Société Montesquieu, 1999) and David Carrithers, "Montesquieu and the Spirit of Modern State Finance: An Analysis of his *Mémoire sur les dettes de l'État* (1715)," in *Montesquieu and the Spirit of Modernity*, David W. Carrithers and Patrick Coleman, eds. (Oxford: The Voltaire Foundation, 2002 forthcoming).

12. Montesquieu came very close to formulating the current doctrine under the First Amendment of the U.S. Constitution as enunciated in *Brandenburg v. Ohio* (1969). In that case, the Supreme Court devised the "incitation test" for seditious speech not protected by the First Amendment. When speech is linked to specific calls for action against the government, and the hearers are urged to act illegally rather than just listen and agree or disagree with an abstract idea, a speaker is no longer protected from the crime of seditious speech.

13. As Anne Cohler, Basia Miller, and Harold Stone point out in their note to this text in XXIX, 16, this was Montesquieu's gloss on the ordinance, rather than actual words quoted from it. See Montesquieu, *The Spirit of the Laws*, Anne Cohler et. al., eds. (Cambridge: Cambridge University Press, 1989), 613.

14. Bills of attainder were outlawed in the English Bill of Rights of 1689. The *lettres de cachet* were outlawed in Article 7 of the French Declaration of Rights of 1789.

15. The suppressed texts are printed in Brethe de La Gressaye, ed., *Loix*, II, 381. Montesquieu asserts that banishment from the king's presence and from the capital would be a better way of dealing with those who offend the king than incarceration by means of *lettres de cachet* since the substantially milder punishment of banishment would be more in accord with the true spirit of monarchical government. In 1784 the king's minister, Breteuil, brought about a review of all cases involving incarceration by *lettres de cachet*, and many imprisoned individuals were set free. In addition, the use of such letters was restricted in 1784 to serious offenses, and the length of incarceration was restricted to two

or three years. See Alfred Cobban, *A History of Modern France. Volume I: 1715-1799* (Baltimore: Penguin Books, 1957), 110. Though the "black legend" of Old Regime criminal justice includes the belief that these secret letters were universally despised, their use was not always unwelcome. For discussion of their popularity see, in particular, Brian E. Strayer, *Lettres de cachet and Social Control in the Ancien Régime, 1659-1789* (New York: Peter Lang, 1992) and Richard Mowery Andrews, *Law, Magistracy, and Crime in Old Regime Paris, 1735-1789* (Cambridge: Cambridge University Press, 1994), 367-69. Montesquieu qualified his argument in the texts he suppressed for reforming the use of these *lettres de cachet* by suggesting that there might be situations of public danger when even these new safeguards he was recommending would have to be waived in order to preserve liberty, just as he had suggested in defending the use of Bills of Attainder in England that "there are cases where a veil has to be drawn, for a moment, over liberty" to protect a government from danger (XII, 19).

16. Hence Shelby T. McCloy has remarked that although the *lettres de cachet* "violated justice," they "in the great majority of cases . . . no doubt served a useful purpose." More generally McCloy concludes that "through most of the century they had been popular throughout France, as is attested by the abundant demands for them, especially by the clergy, the nobility, and the bourgeoisie." Some individuals even asked that they be used to bring about their own incarceration for various purposes. Eventually, however, the cause of justice trumped mere convenience, and the Declaration of the Rights of Man banned their use. See Shelby T. McCloy, *The Humanitiarian Movement in Eighteenth-Century France* (Lexington: University of Kentucky Press, 1957), 140-42.

17. Under the rules of the French Criminal Ordinance of 1670, however, sentences were to be carried out on the day they were pronounced, and there was, therefore, little or no time for the king to exercise his powers of clemency. Title XXV, article 21 specified: "The judgments will be executed the same day that they are rendered." Only in cases involving automatic appeals was this stipulation inapplicable. The reason for such prompt execution of sentencing was stated by the Regent, the Duke of Orleans, in a letter to the Parlement of Bordeaux on July 23, 1716 stressing the effect of such swift punishment in maximizing "the effect on the people's minds." It is by no means true, however, that, in practice, all sentences could be carried out so promptly. See Kingston, *Montesquieu*, 110, note 34.

18. Andrews, *Law, Magistracy, and Crime*, 395.

19. Richard Mowery Andrews, "The Death Penalty in Old Regime France," in Andrews, ed., *Perspectives on Punishment. An Interdisciplinary Exploration* (New York: Peter Lang, 1993), 76-77.

20. See Stephen Holmes, "The Constitution of Sovereignty in Jean Bodin," in Holmes, *Passions and Constraints: On the Theory of Liberal Democracy* (Chicago: University of Chicago Press, 1995), 100-33 and also the general argument of Michael Mosher in chapter 4 of this volume,

21. See Andrews, *Law, Magistracy, and Crime*, 420 (note 6) for references to recent studies of actual trials and punishments that refute the black legend of French criminal justice.

22. See *Pensée* 1102 (29) in Pléiade, I, 1286.

23. Andrews, *Law, Magistracy, and Crime*, 417. The impetus for changes in the criminal law had come from Jean-Baptiste Colbert and his uncle Henri Pussort, a member of the Royal Council. In 1655 they persuaded Louis XIV to appoint a Council of Justice, which solicited suggestions for procedural reforms from the Parlements of France and from other superior courts. Working simultaneously with this Council of Justice was an independent commission of Parlementary magistrates chaired by Guillaume de Lamoignon, first president of the Parlement of Paris. In January of 1667 Lamoignon convinced Louis XIV that the two groups should work together, which produced a drafting body consisting of thirty-nine individuals. This group issued a Civil Ordinance in 1667 and finished the Criminal Ordinance in June of 1670. See Andrews, *Law Magistracy, and Crime*, 418.

24. Andrews, *Law, Magistracy, and Crime*, 419.

25. This is a description of the law, however, rather than of existing practices with regard to seigniorial justice.

26. Andrews, *Law, Magistracy, and Crime*, 419.

27. Ian Cameron, *Crime and Repression in the Auvergne and the Guyenne 1720-1790* (Cambridge: Cambridge University Press, 1981), 133, 152, 154.

28. For details, see Kingston, *Montesquieu*, 121-22.

29. Jacobson points out that all four of the major reformers (Blondel, Boucher d'Argis, Letrosne, and Piépape) who believed the inquisitorial system should be improved, but nonetheless retained, were magistrates with substantial experience as judges under the existing system. The example of Charles-Marguerite Dupaty, however, suggests the possibility that a professional magistrate could indeed favor scrapping the ordinance rules altogether in favor of jury trials. This was an unusual stance for a judge serving within the existing system, however, whereas lay persons who had been attorneys rather than judges were much more likely to favor root and branch abolition of the inquisitorial system. See Jacobson, " Politics of Criminal Law Reform," 200.

30. Roland E. Mousnier, *The Institutions of France under the Absolute Monarchy 1598-1789*. Volume II. *The Organs of State and Society*, Brian Pearce, trans. (Chicago: University of Chicago Press, 1979), 404; Adhémar Esmein, *A History of Continental Criminal Procedure with Special Reference to France,* John Simpson, trans. (New York: Augustus M. Kelley, 1968), 227-32; Andrews, *Law, Magistracy, and Crime,* 432.

31. John Lough, *The Philosophes and Post-Revolutionary France* (Oxford: Clarendon Press, 1982), 149.

32. Lough, *The Philosophes and Post-Revolutionary France*, 152.

33. Even the Constituent Assembly, in its law of October 8-9, 1789, did not alter the secrecy of the investigatory stage of French trials, although the investigating judge was to

be joined in his efforts by two ordinary citizens appointed by local authorities. Following the investigation, however, all that followed was henceforth to be conducted in public. See Lough, *The Philosophes and Post-Revolutionary France*, 152.

34. Andrews, *Law, Magistracy, and Crime*, 425. Ian Cameron has observed that "witnesses should not be understood in too literal a sense. It was exceptional for the 'witness' to produce concrete evidence that contributed materially to the case; their usual role was to suggest a suspect, and establish his reputation. If two or three witnesses agreed on a suspect, he would be arrested. Almost always these suspects," Cameron continues, "were individuals of low reputation. It was also common for the authorities to arrest a number of individuals some of whom were not so much suspected as perpetrators of the crime as they were judged potential sources of useful information on the persons the court was genuinely interested in." See Cameron, *Crime and Repression*, 310 and also Kingston, *Montesquieu*, 141-42.

35. Andrews, *Law, Magistracy, and Crime*, 426.

36. Roland E. Mousnier, *Institutions of France*, II, 404; Esmein, *Continental Criminal Procedure*, 227-32; Andrews, *Law, Magistracy, and Crime*, 432.

37. Mousnier, *Institutions of France*, II, 404.

38. Andrews, *Law, Magistracy, and Crime*, 428-29.

39. Andrews, *Law, Magistracy, and Crime*, 428.

40. In his study of the Calas case, David Bien notes that access by attorneys to court records was common in Languedoc and that when the Parlement of Toulouse heard the famous Calas case, Calas' attorney did gain such access prior to writing his *Mémoire* in the case. The ability to craft a proper *Mémoire*, however, was very different from being able to defend one's client in court and cross-examine witnesses, which was never allowed in capital cases. See David Bien, *The Calas Affair: Persecution, Toleration and Heresy in Eighteenth-Century Toulouse* (Princeton: Princeton University Press, 1960), 96-97. In conformity with his revisionist views, Andrews defends this aspect of the system so sharply criticized by criminal law reformers in France in the decades leading up to the Revolution. "Permitting defense counsel," he writes, "would have introduced obscurantism, prevarication, and mendacity into the proceedings. Procedure was so constructed that if the suspect or defendant was innocent, or guilty only in a limited degree, judges would be capable of determining that from evidence, depositions, interrogations, and confrontations of accused with accusers during the last stage of trial. . . . He (the suspect) was not informed of the specific charges against him, their sources, or the extent of the judge's knowledge of the crime and of him. The entire situation was contrived to deprive him of guile, to incline him toward responsiveness and candor from the onset of questioning." See Andrews, *Law, Crime, and Magistracy*, 429. Speaking elsewhere in more general terms, Andrews suggests that ample opportunities for self-defense were made available to defendants. "The system also made defendants active protagonists in their trials," he writes. "The ordinance gave them successive opportunities to state their case: in interrogations; in confrontation with witnesses; in allegation of justificative facts; before

original judgment; before final judgment on appeal." See Andrews, *Law, Magistracy, and Crime,* 497.

41. See Sarah Maza, *Private Lives and Public Affairs. The Causes Célèbres of Pre-revolutionary France* (Berkeley: University of California Press, 1993), 35-36 and *passim.*

42. Dupaty and other reformers, and also Louis XV's own chancellor, d'Aguesseau, strongly objected to this rule as suppressing evidence that should have been allowed into trials. See Dupaty, *Lettres sur la procédure criminelle de la France* (1788), 156-57 cited in Jacobson, "Politics of Criminal Law Reform," 176-77.

43. Andrews, *Law, Magistracy, and Crime,* 445-46. Ian Cameron asserts that "(h)owever systematic its use in the fight against group banditry, torture made a minimal contribution to eighteenth-century judicial processes in less critical areas. The prévôtal court in Perigueux resorted to the 'question' in only nine cases between the 1720 Reform and the Revolution and not at all after 1772. Those unfortunate prisoners who were put on the rack were not convicted on the strength of evidence or confessions extracted under torture, for in virtually every case the decision to use torture was made at the same time as the decision to convict, when judges were already convinced of the accused's guilt by a heavy weight of circumstantial evidence. . . . In only one case did the authorities resort to torture in an attempt to make up for lack of evidence from other sources." See Cameron, *Crime and Repression,* 145.

44. Louis XVI's edict of May 8, 1788 revised the rule to require a majority of three votes before a defendant could be sentenced to death, but the Parlement of Paris refused to register the edict. See Mousnier, *Institutions of France,* II, 407.

45. Andrews, *Law, Magistracy, and Crime,* 476-79. For information on the reduction of death penalties by Montesquieu's own Parlement of Bordeaux during the years from 1716 to 1726 when he was associated with the criminal chamber of that court, see Kingston, *Montesquieu,* 121-30. Andrews reports that "(b)etween 1735 and 1789, the death sentence was statistically rare within the jurisdiction of the Parlement of Paris, comprising only 4 to 8 percent of all final penal sentences in *grand criminal.*" See *Law, Magistracy, and Crime,* 384.

46. Andrews, *Laws, Magistracy, and Crime,* 420.

47. Andrews, *Law, Magistracy, and Crime,* 494. In her detailed researches of the criminal court records of *la Tournelle* of the Parlement of Bordeaux for the period of 1716-1726 Rebecca Kingston unearthed a number of instances where judges of the lower royal courts were disciplined for breaches of the ordinance. One presidial court judge was found guilty of assaulting individuals in court with a cane, falsely registering court judgments, and charging fees where none were due, activities that had already gained him a year's suspension prior to the Parlement of Bordeaux sending out a *conseiller* to further investigate his behavior. Kingston's conclusion is supportive of revisionist views: "To recognize this is to cast doubt on those theses which would see the pre-revolutionary jus-

tice system in France as a monolithic enterprise, whose parts were all concerted and geared to identical methods of repression." See Kingston, *Montesquieu*, 119-20.

48. Andrews, *Law, Magistracy, and Crime*, 495 citing Jousse's *Traité de la justice criminelle de France*, 4 vols. (Paris, 1771), II, 574-77.

49. See James Donovan, "Magistrates and Juries in France, 1791-1952" *French Historical Studies* 22, no. 3 (summer, 1999), 379-420 who asserts (at 381-82): "Despite the magistrate's advice, Napoleon kept the jury system. But he severely curtailed it in the 1808 Code of Criminal Procedure, which maintained the jury system for the trial stage of felony prosecutions but restored most of the elements of the old inquisitorial system for the pretrail phase. By granting magistrates a monopoly over the investigation and indictment process, the code gave them the means to eventually remove many cases from the juries' jurisdiction through the process of correctionalization. One of these was the stipulation that only *procureurs* could initiate criminal proceedings. Another was the abolition of grand juries and their replacement by *chambres des mises en accusation*, composed entirely of judges taken from the *cours d'appel*." Later, the *juges d'instruction* played an important role in determining which cases went to jury. See also Frederic R. Coudert, "French Criminal Procedure," *Yale Law Journal* 19 (1910): 326-40 and James W. Garner, "Criminal Procedure in France," *Yale Law Journal* 25 (1916): 255-84.

50. Concerning this aspect of Montesquieu's theory of crime and punishment, Leon Radzinowicz has observed that "Montesquieu's classification, although somewhat rudimentary, is important, inasmuch as it was one of the first attempts to divide criminal acts into groups in accordance with their gravity and to devise the scale of punishments. It constituted a valuable point of departure for future legislators." See Radzinowicz, *A History of the English Criminal Law and its Administration from 1750*. Vol. I, *The Movement for Reform* (London, 1948), 273-74. For more extensive commentary on Montesquieu's views on punishment, see David W. Carrithers, "Montesquieu's Philosophy of Punishment," *The History of Political Thought* 19, no. 2 (summer 1998): 213-40.

51. Montesquieu's recommendations were a far cry from existing policy. A royal edict of 1682 had called for the death penalty for sacrilege, and this harsh penalty was only moderated by a subsequent edict of 1724 substituting service in the galley fleet for men and service in a workhouse for women. The crime of blasphemy had been regulated by ordinances of 1510, 1651, and 1666 and, depending on the circumstances, could trigger a punishment of the *carcan*, or banishment, or fines, or some combination of all three. See Kingston, *Montesquieu*, 122, 125. Montesquieu's viewpoint regarding decriminalizing offenses against religion was widely reflected in the *Cahiers* drawn up before the meeting of the Estates General in 1789, which frequently called for distinguishing sin, or vice, from real crimes deserving secular punishment by state authorities. The Penal Code of September, 1791 decriminalized both heresy and magic, along with all other religious crimes. See Antoinette Wills, *Crime and Punishment in Revolutionary Paris* (Westport, Conn.: Greenwood Press, 1981), 42.

52. Some of that destruction was very close at hand. In 1716 the Parlement of Bordeaux had punished one Jean Martin, a brewer and one Jean Miller, a merchant, who had organized a meeting of Protestants to serve on the galleys for life. See Kingston, *Montesquieu*, p. 111.

53. On this point, see Kingston, *Montesquieu*, 105.

54. Montesquieu's recommendations for punishments for moral offenses were actually quite close to what was already in place in the system of French criminal law. Under Article 13, Title 25 of the Criminal Ordinance of 1670, such offenses warranted "defaming" penalties rather than "afflictive" or "capital" penalties. Such defaming punishments could include fines, a severe reprimand, the forced witnessing of punishment (usually capital punishment), or public shaming, with discretion available to the authorities in the choice and combination of these penalties. Adulterers were often given a ride in full public view on a donkey, facing rearward with ankles and feet bound with rope and with a placard displayed stating the crime committed. In addition, this penalty might be supplemented with whipping, or banishment. Legal infamy accrued to all defaming punishments as it did also to afflictive and capital punishments. Hence the defamed individual became perpetually ineligible to testify in either civil or criminal cases, perpetually ineligible for any public office or commission, and immediately and perpetually unable to exercise any office the convicted individual might hold at the time of conviction. See Andrews, *Law, Magistracy, and Crime*, 308-11.

55. There was very good reason to stress this point. Rebecca Kingston mentions a sentence of ten years on the galley ships for one Jean Coustard for impregnating his sister-in-law. See Kingston, *Montesquieu*, 114.

56. Kingston, *Montesquieu*, 111.

57. "This penalty of death," he asserts, "is like the remedy of a sick society" (XII,4). Voltaire also wished to restrict the use of capital punishment without abolishing it. See his *Commentary on the Book* "Of Crimes and Punishment," (1766). Beccaria did not actually rule out the death penalty altogether. He reserved its use for situations where it might be needed to avert a revolution, or where there might be no other way to "dissuade others from committing crimes." See Cesare Beccaria, *On Crimes and Punishments* (1764). Translated from the Italian. With Notes and Introduction by David Young (Indianapolis: Hackett Publishing Company, 1986), p. 481.

58. Andrews, *Law, Magistracy, and Crime*, 307.

59. Andrews, *Law, Magistracy, and Crime*, 307.

60. Andrews, *Law, Magistracy, and Crime,* 498. Andrews notes that under the 1670 ordinance there were no less than twenty-seven mitigating factors that needed to be taken into account in fashioning penalties as compared to only seven aggravating circumstances. The Parlements played a constructive role in correcting lower courts within their jurisdiction should they deviate from the rules of the ordinance by failing to justify a sentence, or carrying out a sentence of banishment before an appeal could be heard, or

wrongly sentencing a woman to the galleys instead of to service in a workhouse (*hôpital*). See Kingston, *Montesquieu*, 118.

61. Andrews, *Law, Magistracy, and Crime*, 290-91.

62. Montesquieu acknowledges in a footnote to this text that the reporting of this aspect of the law of the Twelve Tables by Aulus Gellis was in error and that the law actually refers to dividing up the sum of money gained by the sale of the debtor into slavery (XXIX, 2).

63. See *Pensée* 1102 (29), in Pléiade, I, 1286.

64. Montesquieu had become convinced of this fact long before he made the point in *The Spirit of Laws*. In Persian Letter 80 Usbek remarks to Rhedi, "Our imagination adapts itself to the customs of the country in which we live, and eight days in prison or a fine impresses the mind of a European, raised in a mild-mannered country, as much as the loss of an arm intimidates the Asiatic. . . . A Frenchman will be overcome with despair at the disgrace of a punishment that would not disturb a quarter-hour of a Turk's sleep. Furthermore, I do not see that the police regulations or the principles of justice and equity are any better observed in Turkey, Persia, or in the lands of the Mogul, than in the republics of Holland and Venice, or even in England. I see no fewer crimes committed there, no evidence that men, intimidated by the magnitude of punishment, are more submissive to the laws. On the contrary, I notice a source of injustice and vexation within these very states." See *The Persian Letters*, George R. Healy, trans. (Indianapolis: Bobbs-Merrill, 1964), 136.

65. For this point, see Mark Waddicor, *Montesquieu and the Philosophy of Natural Law* (The Hague: Martinus Nijhoff, 1970), 138.

66. See *Pensée* 1102 (29), in Pléiade, I, 1286.

67. See Jacobson, "Politics of Criminal Law Reform," 69.

68. See Jacobson, "Politics of Criminal Law Reform," 142, citing Bernardi's *Principes de loix criminelles suivis d'observations impartiales sur le droit romain* (1788), 73 and Valazé's *Loix pénales* (1784), 12.

69. See Jacobson, "Politics of Criminal Law Reform," 200.

70. John Mackrell reminds us that there were extremely few published demands for reform of the criminal law down through the first two-thirds of the eighteenth century. Of the nearly 10,000 works reviewed by the Jesuits in their *Mémoires de Trévoux* between 1701 and 1775, only about a dozen were devoted to the subject of legal reform. He speaks of "the hurried development of an interest in law reform" in the late 1770's. See Mackrell, "Criticism of Seigniorial Justice," 128-29.

71. Elie de Beaumont, *Mémoire . . . pour Pierre–Paul Sirven* (Paris, 1767), in David Bell, "Rights of the Accused," in *French Idea of Freedom*, 255.

72. David Bell, "Rights of the Accused," in *French Idea of Freedom*, 263.

73. For a useful listing of these reform tracts showing dates of publication, see Jacobson, "Politics of Criminal Law Reform," 103. Only three works, two by Guillaume-François Letrosne, and one by A.-J.-M. Servan, appeared as early as the 1760s.

74. A. Young, *Travels in France during the years 1787, 1788, and 1789*, C. Maxwell, ed., (Cambridge, 1929), 333, cited in John Mackrell, "Criticism of Seigniorial Justice," 123.

75. Except in the very most infamous of crimes rendering a guilty nobleman unworthy of noble status, the method of execution for those of such high rank and station was death by decapitation by the executioner's sword rather than death by hanging or death by burning or breaking on the wheel, forms of execution always employed for non-nobles. See Andrews, *Law, Magistracy, and Crime*, 384 and Andrews, "The Death Penalty in Old Regime France," 77-78.

76. None of the six edicts went into effect, in any case, because the Estates General convened in July, 1789 and it was decided to submit all such reform measures to that body. See McCloy, *The Humanitarian Movement*, 200-1.

77. See McCloy, *The Humanitarian Movement*, 202-7.

78. It is also quite striking that opposition to the ordinance of 1670 is much less evident in the Napoleonic period. Therefore, the *Code d'Instruction criminelle* (1808) of Napoleon represented a return to many of the principles and practices of pre-revolutionary criminal justice. See Frederic Coudert, "French Criminal Procedure," 330-40.

Chapter Eight

Montesquieu on Economics and Commerce

Catherine Larrère

The fourth part of *The Spirit of Laws* (Books XX-XXIII) is rather homogenous, concerned with issues about commerce (XX, XXI), money (XXII), and population (XXIII). Indeed, it is not the first time, in the whole book, that such issues are approached. But, in the first nineteen books of *The Spirit of Laws*, when Montesquieu speaks of commerce, he speaks of commerce as a "profession" (V, 8), as a private activity conducted by individuals, who are subjects, or citizens, of a specific governement, and who are subjected, as such, to the laws of their country. Hence, while speaking of "commerce" in these first nineteen books, he mostly speaks of "those who engage in commerce," of the "*commerçants*" or merchants, or traders. In Books XX-XXIII, on the contrary, Montesquieu speaks of "commerce" as an entity sufficiently independent, general and homogenous, to be the subject of a whole part of *The Spirit of Laws*. What is truly significant is that Montesquieu considered commerce as just as important and deserving of treatment in a separate section of his work as the more traditional topics with which the whole book was concerned, including the purpose and nature of laws and the "diversity of laws and manners," which was, according to his Preface, the object of *The Spirit of Laws*, and of which commerce was only a part.

The very use of the word "commerce" to speak of what is now known as "political economy" is revealing of some ambiguity, or rather of a transitional situation. As soon as the physiocrats conceived the knowledge of wealth as a "new science," the word commerce, which previously had been much more often used than the outdated *Œconomie politique*, was relinquished, and *économie politique*, or political economy, came into more common usage.[1] Can it be said, then, that Montesquieu was bringing an era to a close (that of mercantilism, when commerce was understood as an instrument of politics) and opening a new one (that of liberalism conceiving of the economy as a self-subsisting process), without fully belonging to the new epoch? This is certainly chronologically true. Montesquieu wrote after the main lines of mercantilism were elaborated in France as well as in England,[2] and before the development of economic liberalism by Gournay, Quesnay, and their schools in France, and by David Hume and Adam Smith in England. It is also true that we cannot find, in *The Spirit of Laws*, a full-fledged economic theory resembling the systems of Quesnay or Smith. Montesquieu's more scattered historical remarks on commerce are closer to the political pragmatism of mercantilist observations and analysis.[3] Could Montesquieu, then, be both mercantilist and liberal? If these two streams of economic thought conflict, to assume such an hypothesis would be to presuppose that Montesquieu is incoherent.

Montesquieu's originality lies nonetheless not in his being at a transition point but in the originality of the questions he poses. To mercantilists, he poses not the question of efficiency, but that of liberty. This enables him to develop a critique of mercantilism while putting forward some of the main arguments of liberalism, that is the idea of economics as a self-regulating process. His critique is based on the viewpoint of political liberty, which he has studied in the second part of *The Spirit of Laws*, and this explains why he was not inclined to consider the liberty that commerce requires as pertaining to a unified natural system, as Quesnay would conclude later with his physiocratic "natural order," or Smith would conclude with his "system of natural liberty." Having studied political liberty for its own sake, Montesquieu well knew that it was much too fragile to be entrusted to the guardianship of nature, that is, to self-regulating, untrammeled processes alone. He was aware that if liberty was to flourish, or even exist, a certain arrangement of political institutions was required. Hence, Montesquieu never treated commerce as completely autonomous and never stopped studying its relationships with politics as well as with other more global social processes.

Rather than attempting to depict Montesquieu's economic thought as it could have been, had he written a special, separate work about it, we will rely on the fact that his books about commerce form a part of *The Spirit of Laws*. Analyzing how commerce is treated in the first nineteen books allows us to understand how Montesquieu comes to consider commerce as a general process, and what kind of generality belongs to such a process. Hence we will first examine how he moves, in Books I-XIX, from "*les commerçants*" to "*le* commerce," from the individual activities of those who are engaged in commerce, to the processes which result from such activities. We will then be able to understand that Montesquieu's method is not so much to separate commerce from government, as it is to study commerce, as a general process, in its relationships both with government and with society. That is the reason why, in Books XX-XXI, he continues to study the relationships between wealth and power, and, in Books XXII-

XXIII, never severs the economic processes from their political and social embodiments. Hence, Montesquieu's approach to political economy is political and embedded. It is neither mercantilist (because it is not state-driven), nor classically liberal (because it is socially embedded), and is not separate from government.

The Conceptualization of Commerce

In the first part of *The Spirit of Laws*, Montesquieu studies the different forms of government, from the point of view of what can maintain the constitution of each government. Seen in such a perspective, commerce does not specifically fit any form of government better than others. In ancient republics commerce suffers from the general contempt for arts involving labor or money, and is considered too "servile" for the free citizen of a free republic (IV, 8). Since commerce generates wealth and inequality, it threatens the equality and frugality on which democracies are based, while also exposing aristocracies to excessive inequality (V,8). In aristocracies, as well as in monarchies, the nobility should be barred from commerce (V, 8 and 9). Commerce, however, is not completely excluded from any government. In despotic governments, especially, where poverty reigns and property is very uncertain, no merchant is capable of "carrying on a great trade" (V, 15), but this does not mean that there is no trade at all.

The most extreme case that Montesquieu envisions is that of democracies, where, because of the contempt in which commercial activities are held, a community of goods may be established and commerce may be conducted by the city rather than by individual merchants, as in the *Republic* of Plato (IV, 6). But this is hardly a real possibility. Commerce, for Montesquieu, is first of all an individual activity, a private profession, which may either threaten, or support, the government. The result depends on the way each government combines wealth and power, on the one hand, and on the distinction between the private and the public spheres on the other hand. In addition, it depends on the extent to which the particular government requires equality or inequality in order to function properly.

Like Hobbes, as well as Smith,[4] Montesquieu is convinced that "wealth is power." This is the reason why he considers private wealth dangerous in a democracy. It "gives a power that a citizen cannot use for himself, for he would not be equal" (V, 3). Montesquieu does not criticize the conflation of wealth and public power in democracies, however, when the city itself undertakes the commerce. In such situations, the public good is literally the "common wealth." In other cases, when the rulers and the ruled are not the same persons, when the private and the public spheres are distinguished, that is in aristocracies, and in "governments by one alone," the confusion of wealth and political power must be avoided by all means possible: "the poorest (*misérables*) despotic states are those whose prince is a merchant" (V, 8). This is the reason why Montesquieu states that individuals of noble rank (in aristocracies as well as in monarchies) should be prohibited from engaging in commerce (V, 8, 9). The nobles would employ their rank and power to set up all sort of monopolies, thus disrupting the equality that commerce requires, since "commerce is the profession of equal people" (V, 8).[5]

Hence commerce displays a rather complex relationship with equality. Commerce generates wealth, luxury, and inequality,[6] and for that reason it subverts equality and frugality on which democracy is based. In a governement where every citizen should be satisfied with only what is necessary for himself and for his family, commerce enhances the desire for private enjoyments and diverts the citizens from committing themselves to the public good (V, 3). In short, commerce corrupts virtue. But commerce conducted on a certain model may also be the profession of equal people, in an uncorrupted republic. In such situations, commerce may be seen as having a "spirit" of its own, which "brings with it the spirit of frugality, economy, moderation, work, wisdom, tranquillity, order and rule" (V, 6). In republics like Athens, then, it is not necessary, in order to maintain equality, to equally divide land and goods, and to make sure that everybody has only a small part of it, yielding no more than what is necessary for each. It is enough to give to all children an equal portion of the inheritance of their father. Equality, then, is no longer the strict equality of frugal democracies. It is rather equal access, through work, to fortune.

Even in commercial republics however, excessive inequality of wealth must be avoided, and the expenses of the rich must be diverted from private consumption, and turned toward public expenditures and enjoyment. In examining in Book VII how sumptuary laws can reduce luxury or divert the profits of commerce towards public expenditure, Montesquieu clearly states that such laws are made "in the spirit of the republic." Even in "commercial republics," the general pattern remains that of classical republicanism. Equality must be maintained, or at least, excessive inequalities must be avoided.

Monarchical government presents a wholly different situation. Monarchy is based on inequality, and for that reason, commerce supports the structure of monarchies. Montesquieu explains this conclusion in such a way as to leave his readers ill at ease, however, because it is not always clear whether, in stating his point, he is bluntly cynical, slightly ironical, or completely candid and sincere in his concern for justice. In a monarchy, he asserts, "the laws must favor all the commerce that the constitution of this government can allow, so that the subjects can, without being ruined, satisfy the ever-recurring needs of the prince and his court" (V, 9). One can surmise, then (according to Montesquieu's idea that the reader's part is to complete what has not been fully elaborated), that it is better that such needs be satisfied through a regular exchange which profits both parties, rather than through some form of pillage, as is often the case in despotic governments. Similarly, Montesquieu explains that, because monarchies are based on inequality, there is an "absolute necessity" for luxury.

Were the rich not to spend their money freely, the poor would starve. It is even necessary that the expenses of the rich should be in proportion to the inequality of fortunes; and luxury, as we have already observed, should increase in this proportion. The augmentation of private wealth is owing to its having deprived one part of the citizens of their necessary support; this must therefore be restored to them (VII, 4).

Montesquieu's argument proceeds at two levels: the factual level, reflecting the circumstance that monarchies are based on inequality, and the moral level, on the other hand, which Montesquieu explained in the opening chapter of Book I. Luxury and commerce should conform to a moral pattern, which is a pattern of justice. Justice may conflict with inequalities, which does not entail that any particular inequality should automatically be eradicated, but suggests that inequalities require justification. Montesquieu provides such a justification, and the half-cynical, half-moral tone of it indicates that it comes from Mandeville. In the *Fable of the Bees* (1714), Montesquieu found the scheme of "private vices" (indulging in satisfying "ever-recurring needs") and "public benefits" (the poor will be fed). More specifically, he finds in Mandeville the very argument which makes inequality tolerable, and even renders such inequality a form of justice, the idea that the expenses of the rich make up the wages of the poor.[7] According to Montesquieu, the poor should be "restored." The word restore clearly indicates an idea of restitutive justice while, at the same time, suggesting the idea of a circular process, a kind of circular flow of money from the rich to the poor. The factual necessity of this flow supports the moral assessment of its consequences.

Moreover luxury can be calculated, as a "proportion" between several variables, "the wealth of the state, the inequalities of the fortunes of individuals, and the number of men gathered together in different places" (VII, 1). By speaking of luxury as a "compound ratio," by stating that luxury "increases" proportionally to this "compound," and by giving the arithmetical ratio of such an increment (0, 1, 3, 7, 15, 31, 63, 127), Montesquieu shared the taste for "political arithmetic" which had been characteristic of the development of economic thought since the seventeenth century. "Everything is reducible to calculation: calculation extends even down to purely moral things,"[8] Melon exclaims in his *Essai politique sur le commerce* (1734), while expressing his admiration for William Petty's work in "political arithmetic."

This ambition to extend to social studies a quantitative approach already successful in the natural sciences was based upon the empirical progress of economic calculation in two main areas : the calculations of the merchants, and those of the state, involving the first attempts at statistical fiscal inquiries.[9] The results were very primitive and limited (nobody knew, for example, the real magnitude of the French population until the end of the eighteenth century), but it was enough to suggest several assessments, largely hypothetical, but well designed, like Vauban's conclusions in the *Dîme royale* (1698). The projected goal of economic thought was thus to understand society as a set of quantitative relations, and this perspective led, in the second part of the century, to its most striking achievement, François Quesnay's *Tableau économique* (1758).

Hence we can say that Montesquieu contributed to one of the main lines of development in economic thought of the eighteenth century. While he first speaks of commerce in *The Spirit of Laws* as a private profession, engaged in by individuals for their own sakes, he comes eventually to assess some more global effects of such activities, by perceiving luxury as a process, as a circular flow of money and wealth throughout the country, in a way which can benefit the less advantaged, a process which can be assessed in quantitative proportions. It was this same concern for the global effects of economic policies which was at the very core of Montesquieu's reflections about taxation in Book XIII of *The Spirit of Laws*.

Taxation

Montesquieu viewed taxation as that point at which the state's finances meet the people's wealth (or their lack thereof). Therefore taxation, like commerce, implicates concerns of justice. Scholastic writers based the justice of taxation upon necessity, and Jean Bodin even quoted a Roman senator saying that "there is nothing more just than what is necessary" to authorize royal taxation.[10] Hence it is not surprising that Montesquieu writes about "necessity" when dealing with taxation in Book XIII. But the way he approaches necessity, indicating that one needs to consider "both the necessities of the state and the necessities of the citizens" (XIII, 1), suggests that he is critical toward some ways of understanding "necessity." The literature of absolutism equated "necessary" and "arbitrary," assuming that the amount of taxation was limitless and left up to the free will of the prince. To this effect Cardin Le Bret quotes the adage "*Necessitas non habet legem.*"[11] One should not hesitate to tax the subjects heavily, added Richelieu, since it benefis the state as well as the subjectgs: "All the astute politicians agree that if the People were too comfortable, it would be impossible to contain them within the rules of their duty. They must be compared to mules which, being used to the task, are more weakened by a long repose than by work."[12]

Montesquieu objected to such absolutist theorizing. Stating that far from inducing subjects to work harder, an "arbitrary power" renders subjects lazy (XIII, 2), he added to the argument regarding the public benefits of private expenditures on luxuries the assumption that lesser levels of taxation are preferable since, in those cases where subjects do not pay enough, "their convenience and ease turn to the public advantage," while, "if some private people pay too much, their ruin redounds to the public detriment" (XIII, 7). Montesquieu gave both an anti-absolutist and anti-mercantilist spin to the luxury argument. That the expenses of the rich make the wages of the poor is a commonsensical enough idea that

Mandeville had clearly expressed but did not invent, and it can be found in the mainstream mercantilist literature, in such authors, for example, as Montchrestien, or Pottier de la Hestroye. The latter expresses the argument in favor of luxury in terms very close to Montesquieu's own formulation in Book VII, although it is highly unlikely that Montesquieu could have read Pottier's manuscript:

> if the rich and those who enter most into luxury reduce their wealth in this way,
> it is certain that they also support at the same time an infinity of poor families,
> who, without work, would die from starvation, and become rich by their indus-
> try.[13]

The difference between such mercantilist authors and Montesquieu lies in the way the monetary flow is considered.

The comparison between money and blood is a very ancient one, existing long before William Harvey's discovery of the circulation of blood.[14] Such a comparison conveys the idea that, just like blood in animal bodies, money irrigates the political body, distributing life wherever it flows. Mercantilist authors emphasized the role of the state, and especially of taxation revenues, in such a life-advancing circulation. Melon advocated allowing the local tax-collectors (*receveurs particuliers des provinces*) to lend the money they had collected, because it would benefit commerce.[15] Forbonnais, in his polemic with the physiocrats in the 1760s, still maintained the mercantilist arguments that the state was a very important economic agent and that the financial circuit could initiate and enhance the economic flow.[16] Those were perspectives favoring high taxes, since attracting money into the financial circuit would augment prosperity. Hence the development of a financial state whose resources come from the revenues of the subjects rather than from the prince's estates is strongly connected with the development of the mercantilist thought, and Montesquieu's position on taxation is an important indication of his anti-mercantilist position. "Will the state begin by impoverishing its subjects in order to enrich itself?" Montesquieu asks, "Or will it wait for its subjects to enrich it at their own pace? Will it begin by being rich or will it end by doing so?" (XIII, 7) Montesquieu favored the liberal position. The state must adjust to society, not the society to the state.

Montesquieu highlighted this choice, at the very beginning of Book XIII, by distinguishing between the "real needs of the people" and the "imaginary needs of the state" (XIII, 1). The latter are bloated by "the sick envy of vain glory," an inappropriate passion underlying the military adventurism of the European kings. Book XIII contains an extract from Montesquieu's *Reflections on Universal Monarchy* (1734), an historical and critical survey of the unsuccessful attempts of successive states to rule hegemonically over Europe, in a fashion similar to the Roman Empire. Focusing his criticism most specifically upon Spain

and on the France of Louis XIV, Montesquieu eloquently denounced the catas-
trophic consequences of past and present European military policies.

Wars, Montesquieu explained, entail massive escalations of governmental
expenditures, leading to burdensome loans and mushrooming public debt, followed by higher taxes to provide money to make interest payments on the ac-
cumulated debt. Wars thus trigger a vicious circle of poverty including impoverishment of the people because of increasingly heavy taxes and impoverishment
of the state in search of money that it can never possess in sufficient quantities.
Thus "a new distemper has spread over Europe," writes Montesquieu, a war-
oriented Europe, where more and more money is spent in preparations for wars
nobody can win. "Each monarch keeps as many army on foot as if his people
were in danger of being exterminated; and they give the name of peace to this
general effort of all against all" (XIII, 17). Since considerations of war dominate
policy making even in times of peace, the state's behavior is thoroughly irrational. Montesquieu compares the European states, engrossed by imaginary needs,
to an "extravagant young spendthrift" who, having spent all his revenues, mort-
gages his capital. Such practices cannot help but ruin those who engage in them.

Melon and other mercantilists[17] argued that private and public spending had
little in common. "The private individual regulates his expenditures according to
his revenues but the King regulates his revenues based on what he needs to
spend to preserve the state."[18] Needs of the state allowed mercantilists to justify
the public debt and all the "extraordinary means" to which kings and their ministers resorted to meet their needs. For Montesquieu, such extemporaneous or
extraordinary means were deprived of any rationality. To the prodigal son, he
opposed the prudent father, suggesting as a model for the king the wise management of the household—what he called, according to its etymology, "economy," the rule of the house, good husbandry: "the administration of a good father
of a family who levies his revenues himself with economy and order" (XIII, 19).

Montesquieu used this image of the prudent father to assert the superiority of
the "*régie*" (the direct administration of the revenues by the prince) to tax-
farming, the prevailing system, where the levy of the taxes was auctioned to private persons. These "*traitants,*" or more generally, the financiers, are one of the
main targets of Montesquieu's criticisms of the French system of taxation in
Book XIII. He charges them with being no less than blood suckers, greedy as
well as immoral. *Traitants* flourish amidst deceit. When taxes on a commodity
greatly exceed the actual value of what is to be consumed, the people will defraud the tax collectors who will then be given "extraordinary means of har-
rassment" so that "the more opportunities a people are given to defraud the *traitant*, the more the latter is enriched and the former are impoverished" (XIII, 8).
He also accuses them of disrupting the social order. By seeking, with their
wealth, to be as honored as the true nobility, they jeopardize the social distinction on which the monarchy is founded (XIII, 20). Montesquieu's criticism,
then, of the wealth generated for *traitants* by the system of tax-farming was po-

litical. Excessive importance and power given to them leads to despotism. In Book XI, Montesquieu contended that the role of the *traitants*, in ancient Rome, was one of the reasons for the demise of liberty (XI, 18).

Hence, for Montesquieu, the criticism of mercantilism overlapped the critique of absolutism. He judged the tax system of the French monarchy counterproductive to the prosperity of the realm and a threat to the liberty of its citizens. Richelieu had defined taxation as a "mark of servitude." Montesquieu, on the contrary, presented taxation as an exchange between the citizen and the state that had to be consensual. Taxation did not pertain to necessity, but to contract. The proper question to ask was not what "the people can give" but what "they should give" (XIII, 1). Montesquieu propounded the paradoxical thesis that the magnitude of the taxation is proportional to the liberty the citizens are enjoying. The greater the liberty, the higher the taxes can be. Paradoxically, it is in despotic governments that the subjects are the least heavily burdened with taxation. Montesquieu reminds the king and his advisers, who are always seeking financial resources, that the money they have from their people is a mark of confidence, and if they abuse their power, they will encounter disappointment, for "the effect of servitude is to produce a decrease in taxes" (XIII, 15). Far from taxation being a "mark of servitude," the wealth it yields "is a kind of reward to the prince for his respect of the laws" (XIII, 13).

Montesquieu prefers taxes on merchandise to direct taxes on persons or on lands because excise taxes are more conducive to liberty. Direct taxes originated in the late Roman Empire as attached to serfdom, and they remained marked by their origin. To pay them is to be reminded of the power of the state. On the contrary, taxes on merchandise are easily paid, without even being noticed. For Montesquieu, part of being free is the opinion that we are free, and such an opinion can be partly delusional. In several of his *Pensées*, he compares the citizens with fish in a net. If the net is large enough, the fish feel free.[19] If those taxes are "wisely managed . . . the people will be almost unaware that they pay them" (XIII, 7); they will not be reminded of their servitude by excessive and unreasonable taxes (XIII, 8). Such a view of taxes was directly opposed to the idea Richelieu had of them.

Between taxes on persons (or lands) and taxes on merchandise, there is a difference not only between servitude and liberty, but also between war and peace. In a war-mongering state, driven by its "imaginary needs," the Prince and the *traitants*, are in a "state of war"[20] with the subjects. In contrast to such an irrational situation stands the picture of a well-ordered state where the subjects or citizens enjoy freedom and security so that there is trust and confidence between the rulers and the ruled. The merchant is central in such a relationship. Though the taxes on merchandise are really paid by the buyer, in a well-ordered society they should first be paid to the state by the seller. In such a situation, the merchant, who pays the tax, is the go-between, acting as the "debtor" of the state and the "creditor" of the individuals: "He advances to the state the duty the buyer will eventually pay, and he has paid, for the buyer, the duty he has paid for the commodity" (XIII, 14). Therefore the merchant takes the place of the *traitant*, and it contributes to peace and confidence, instead of war and distrust.

Throughout Book XIII, Montesquieu rejects the "imaginary needs" of the state in favor of the "real needs" of the people, castigating a state-centered, mercantilist conception of finances and praising a society-centered conception of economics and commerce in which the merchant is a key figure. This liberal inflection of Montesquieu's thought is based upon a new anthropology. Absolutist thought, such as Richelieu's, had relied on a traditional, pessimistic, Christian (especially Augustinian) anthropology stressing that men are sinners who need to be corrected by the state authority. Labor, in such a view, is a punishment, a painful activity which must be forced on reluctant, lazy subjects. This is the basic philosophy of those who pretend that "there must be heavy burdens in order to make the people industrious" (XIII, 2). Such an Augustinian view is misguided, Montesquieu objects. Wealth motivates people to work, and they are deterred from work by poverty. Work, in such a view, ceases to be a painful burden. Rather work becomes part of prospective enjoyment, part of a self-induced enterprise.

One can find here in Montesquieu's thought the liberal idea that individual interest is the best guide for each person's conduct and that no repressive authority is needed, along with a special emphasis on the need for, and right of everyone, for ease and wealth, which is common to French critics of mercantilism. Quesnay will echo Montesquieu on these points, stigmatizing the "maxims of these wild men maintaining that one must reduce the common people to destitution in order to force them to work."[21] Like Montesquieu, Quesnay thinks that it is wealth that incites individuals to work: "men are all inclined to ease and wealth and are never lazy when they can succeed."[22] And as Quesnay would also later contend, Montesquieu thinks that the possibility of wealth originates in the first profitable exchange between man and nature: "Nature is just toward men. She rewards them for their pains; she makes them hard workers because she attaches greater rewards to greater work" (XIII, 2). The model of justice must be sought on nature's side to which Montesquieu opposes the "arbitrary power" which "removes nature's reward." The seminal economic idea of society as a set of quantified relationships has its original model in the relationship between man and nature. Because he understood this fact, Montesquieu certainly belongs in the pantheon of the history of economic thought.[23]

Commerce, Society, and Sociability

It is clear, then, that the third part of *The Spirit of Laws*, beginning with Book XIV, marks a shift in emphasis. The first two parts were concerned with given political orders, or constitutions, first described as distinctive types and then analyzed from the standpoint of their relations to political liberty. Part three be-

gins with the differences in the natural environment of human societies, including variations in climate, topography, and soil. Montesquieu contends that human societies differ in their complexity, as in their legal institutions, "in relation
to their ways of procuring subsistence" (XVIII, 10-17). This enables him to
sketch a progression from savage peoples (hunters), to barbarous peoples (pastu-
rage), to agricultural peoples (farming), and finally to commercial peoples, a
schematization which greatly influenced Turgot and Rousseau[24] in France as
well as figures of the Scottish Enlightenment. Dugald Stewart, for example,
congratulated Montesquieu for contending that laws have their origins mainly in
social determinations. The hunter-sheperd-farmer-merchant progression was to
become, in Ferguson and Smith, the well-known "four-stages theory" which has
been considered one of the seminal dynamic schemes of political economy.[25]

Whereas Stewart or Smith could feel indebted to Montesquieu, there was
still a gap between their point of view and his outlook. Montesquieu's standpoint, in Book XVIII of *The Spirit of Laws,* was not oriented toward "natural
history," but rather remained a comparative study, an inquiry about the correlation between political situation and the nature of the soil (chs. 1-7) on the one
hand, and between the kinds of the laws and ways of subsisting (chs. 8-18) on
the other hand.[26] But Montesquieu certainly shared with his Scottish followers a
common interest in a science of "civil society,"[27] concerned not so much with
the forms of political obedience as with the relationships between men as a
consequence of their relationships with their natural environment.

Defined in this fashion, society becomes the level at which the effects of
commerce can be studied. The subject of luxury, analyzed in Book VII, is resu-
med in Book XIX, but from a new standpoint. Commerce and luxury are no
longer to be studied in relation to the form of goverment alone. Rather, their effects on the whole society are to be considered. Women, who, according to widespread opinion, are especially prone to luxury should be the main targets of
sumptuary laws, which aim to keep them virtuous by imposing on them a rule of
frugality, simplicity, and chastity This was the reason why the Roman republic,
and other republican governments, were so keen on requiring "a certain gravity
in the mores of the women" (VII, 8). Legislators might attempt the same thing
in France, Montesquieu mentions in Book XIX. "They might lay a restraint
upon women, make laws to correct their manners, and limit their luxury" (XIX,
5). But it is not necessary in a monarchy, and Montesquieu again resorts to
Mandeville, quite explicitly this time,[28] to explain the "public benefits" of "private vices." The prince and the legislators should cast a blind eye on the women's lack of austerity, since their luxury, and the taste which accompanies it, is
"the source of the riches of the nation" (XIX, 5).

Restraining women would change the "general spirit" of a "sociable nation."
Acting contrary to this spirit, would embody the sort of tyranny Montesquieu
dubs "tyranny of opinion" (XIX, 2). He advises the legislator to know the difference between laws and mores, and hence to learn how to adapt the laws to the

mores, and how to avoid making "laws that run counter to the general spirit" (XIX, 11). Legislators must allow people to live freely and are advised to respect the "general spirit." Montesquieu thus speaks the language of liberty, that is the language of "*laissez-faire*," suggesting that in a nation such as France which is naturally "full of gaiety," it is best to "let it do frivolous things seriously, and serious things frivolously" (XIX, 5). At the same time, he speaks the language of nature, which favors spontaneity as opposed to constraint so that the "natural genius" of the nation can emerge. "Nature repairs everything" (XIX, 6), Montesquieu observes. The vivacity stemming from the "natural genius" of a "sociable nation," for example, is "corrected by the politeness" it displays (XIX, 6). The "public" benefits, which result from this process of natural correction are "social" benefits as well.

Once women are allowed to be frivolous in the context of a monarchical state, everyone is reminded that such frivolity is a source of state wealth since it increases "the branches of commerce" (XIX, 8). In order to see commerce flourish, the government need only sit back and allow frivolous, light-headed women the freedom to seek to live in luxury. Women will control an area which is well beyond the grasp of government. In such an emancipation, commerce finds its own independance, since commerce and women's sociability expand together. And sociability can be called *commerce*, since Montesquieu, as was usual among eighteenth-century authors, speaks of commerce in a much broader sense than we currently do, applying it not only to the moneyed exchange of goods, but to all sort of other exchanges, spiritual as well as material, between persons as well as between things. He envisions the society of women as well as the commerce of merchandise as forms of communication, part of a dynamic web of relationships in which things and people are continually changing. To the static stance of the state, firmly enclosed within its boundaries, Montesquieu opposes the constant mobility of all forms of communication, including all forms of commerce (XIX, 8).

Montesquieu advances from consideration of the activities of the individuals to the analysis of a general commercial process by studying the effects of individual actions. He does so in two contexts, first within the political frame, then within society. In both cases, he finds in Mandeville the general pattern of the public benefits flowing from privates vices, as having unintended, but greatly beneficial global effects. In the context of government, the general pattern is mainly that of the circular flow of luxury as the expenditures of the rich create the wages of the poor. This economic scheme is enclosed within the limits of the state and is oriented toward justice. In the case of society, the general pattern is that of communication, of an unlimited set of extending relationships. In both contexts, to take these patterns into consideration is to limit the control of the state upon society in order to rely on the capacities of social relationships to provide for the common good. The second pattern, that of communication, is much more independant of the government, because it extends beyond its boundaries. But this does not mean that Montesquieu considered commerce as embodying completely autonomous, independant processes. Commerce is embedded in society and participates in more general form of communication, which gives to commerce its language of sociability and manners.

Commerce, on the other hand, though a general process, is all the more embedded in specific governments or societies, since, as we become fully aware in Book XIX, Montesquieu does not fully endorse Mandeville's pattern of unintended positive efffects. In *The Spirit of Laws*, the private vices/public benefits scheme is valid only in monarchies, where there should be luxury. It is not valid in republics where sumptuary laws are necessary. And, as we see in Book XIX, the scheme is particulary relevant to a very specific monarchy, which is home to a very "sociable nation," France. When, at the end of Book XIX, Montesquieu comes to a special examination of England, the combination of commerce and of the English constitution results in a very different outcome. Instead of a "society of women," there is separation of genders. Instead of politeness and luxury, there is rudeness and relative frugality. Thus, in Book XIX, Montesquieu seems not at all prepared to conceive of commerce as being generally independant of the political, as well as social, forms, to which it is related. He was instead sceptical, or wary, of such an idea.

Contexts and Goals of Distinctive Forms of Commerce

Montesquieu presented a contrasting conception of the independence of commerce from direct political influences, however, at the beginning of Book XX, which opens with his most famous statement about commerce: "The natural effect of commerce is to lead to peace" (XX, 2). He here pronounces a universal judgment about the general character of commerce, no matter how commerce can be combined with various constitutions. Commerce is portrayed as an activity that brings peace to the whole of humanity, fulfilling the ends of sociability. Commerce is now depicted as possessing such a general and common nature that Montesquieu can compare the way the ancients considered it, who, like Plato, thought that it "corrupts pure mores," to the way moderns conceive it, who contend that "it polishes and softens barbarous mores" (XX, 2). Such differences are not attributable to the differences between the governments in which commerce exists (dangerous in republics, it would be tolerable in monarchies) but to its intrinsically ambiguous nature. For the positive effects of commerce are global ones, however much it turns individuals to self-interest, depriving them of virtue. Emphasizing one of these two aspects—the one global and the other personal—leads to opposite judgments.

Soon after his initial general statement regarding the beneficial consequences of commerce for peace, Montesquieu returns to the distinction between a "commerce of luxury" and "economical commerce" (XX,4), contending that the first is appropriate for monarchies and the latter for democracies. What is remarkable, however, is that the distinction between the two forms of commerce is not really an economic one. In both forms, "everything is exchanged," as he remarked in one of his *Pensées*.[29] The difference relates to the ends sought in the two forms of commerce. For nations engaged in economical commerce (*commerce d' économie*), commerce itself is the object, and the success of such commerce depends on the ceaseless repetition of the same commercial operations, for it is "founded on the practice of gaining little" in each exchange (XX, 4). The commerce of luxury (*commerce de luxe*), however, is a means to other ends: "its principal object is to procure for the nation engaging in it all that serves its arrogance, its delights, and its fancies" (XX, 4).

Therefore, the distinction between economical commerce and commerce of luxury originates directly from the conclusions drawn in Books V and XX about the relationships between commerce, luxury and the different governmental forms. It is no surprise that Montesquieu assigns economical commerce mostly to "the government of many," and the commerce of luxury to "the government by one alone." All the features of the "spirit of commerce" proper to commercial republics, as discussed in Book V, chapter 6, are to be found in ancient Marseilles, a city—and a republic as well—which displayed the archetypal form of economical commerce. Its citizens were "hardworking." "just," "moderate," and "finally of frugal mores" (XX, 5).

Clearly economical commerce is related, in Montesquieu's mind, to a political and social context of equality, whereas a commerce based on luxury goods is connected to political and social inequality. The two sorts of commerce also display different relationships between wealth and power. That is the reason why the same institutions do not suit both types of commerce. Indeed, Montesquieu's main purpose in proposing this distinction in forms of commerce seems to be to suggest that such commercial institutions as "great commercial enterprises," or "banks," "commercial companies," and "free ports" are not suitable for both kinds of commerce. The potential value of such institutions, or policies will depend on the political context in which they are situated. Taking this position allows him to directly oppose the policies favored by the Scotsman John Law who gained substantial influence in France in the years following the death of Louis XIV in 1715. When Law presented his project for a bank to the French Regent, Philippe d'Orléans, he suggested that the form of the government is not important to the success of the enterprise: "In every country where the people wanted to establish a bank, the project has always succeeded whether in monarchies or republics."[30]

Montesquieu believed such an argument had despotic implications since it reduced to insignificance differences between governments. Thus Montesquieu could contend that "M. Law, equally ignorant of the republican and of the monarchical constitutions, was one of the greatest promoters of despotism that had until then been seen in Europe" (II, 4). Clearly Montesquieu's purpose in assessing the value of various commercial institutions based on the crucial differences between governmental forms, as reflected in the difference between economical commerce and a commerce of luxury, was to avoid the use of commercial institutions that would result in governmental despotism.

In a republic, private wealth and public power may be properly entwined since every citizen participates in the exercise of political power. Trading companies supporting economical commerce are appropriate in such republican governments since "the nature of these companies is to give to individual wealth the force of public wealth" (XX, 10). If individuals can achieve their goals without resorting to conglomerates, trading companies are not necessary. But they are tolerable, whereas in monarchies they must be avoided because banks must also be avoided in monarchies. Were such banks private, they would be either a threat, or a temptation, for a prince always in need of financial resources: "wherever there is a treasury, as soon as it is excessive, it immediately becomes the prince's" (XX, 10). Were such a bank public, it would not be successful, for the prince should not be a merchant, and his people are expecting his "justice," not his "opulence" gained through monopolizing trade which would reduce everyone else to poverty (XX, 19). In monarchies, political and economic functions must be kept well apart. Confusing wealth and power as would be the case if the nobility were allowed to engage in commerce would lead to despotism, and a despotic government whose prince is a merchant is the worst kind of despotism. Furthermore, there is no doubt in Montesquieu's mind that this would have been the outcome of Law's system, had it succeeded.

Therefore such institutions typical of mercantilism as trading companies, banks, and free ports belong to commercial republics, not monarchies. Judged from this perspective, England is certainly an enlightening case. English commerce is not a typical example of economical commerce, for England is a monarchy, with a large territory, while economical commerce is typically carried on by small republics like ancient Marseilles, a city without any real territory. However, English commerce is economical commerce rather than a commerce of luxury. Montesquieu describes the English as hardworking, while also indicating that they do not indulge in excessive luxury and are busy with their own interests so that the prosperity of the nation depends on numerous small profits. England, however, is not, strictly speaking, a pure monarchy. There are clearly republican features in England's constitution. Montesquieu insists on the republican aspect of "a nation where each man in his own way would take part in the administration of the state" (XIX, 27). England also moved in the direction of republicanism by permitting its nobility to engage in commerce, which should never be permitted in a monarchical state (XX, 21).

Thus the spirit of commerce thoroughly permeates England, even its government, England being the nation which "has always made its political interests give way to the interests of its commerce" (XX, 7). Hence England is peaceful by principle and seeks to gain not to conquer (XX, 8; XIX, 27).[31] England does not cease being political, however, since it is "jealous" of its commerce (XX, 7), which is a very political passion indeed, and it cherishes its political independance, that is, its sovereignty. It makes commercial treaties with some other nations (XX, 7), which entails that in international relationships, and even in matters of commerce, England is ruled by the political principle of the distinction between friends and enemies. Similarly, its merchants are not free to do what they want, and are submitted to the constraints of the laws: "Liberty of commerce is not a faculty granted to traders. . . . What hampers those who engage in commerce does not, for all that, hamper commerce" (XX, 12). Political interests may "give way to the interests of its commerce" (XX, 7), but the state takes steps to protect commerce by avoiding disadvantageous treaties. Furthermore, English law prohibits wool exports and exports of ungelded horses and strictly controls the trade of her colonies (XX, 12). Clearly, in international relationships, including those involving commerce, England is ruled by the political principle of the distinction between friends and enemies.

This is a very mercantilist outlook. The interests of commerce coincide with those of the state, which in turn coincide with the public interest. Since commerce serves the public interest, the government is allowed to enforce constraints on individuals engaging in commerce for the sake of the commonwealth. The state is able to "hamper" the individual merchants' freedom in order to develop commerce as a whole. Montesquieu could have found a similar viewpoint in Melon, who wrote that "liberty of commerce must not consist of imprudent license for merchants to ship and receive all sorts of merchandise without any controls being applied."[32]

Melon contrasted "liberty" and "license," contending that men's immoral desires must be constrained and that obedience defines the proper political relationship between subjects and the government. Montesquieu, by way of contrast, juxtaposes "independence" and "liberty." "Liberty of commerce," he writes, "is not a faculty granted to traders to do as they wish; this would rather be the servitude of commerce" since commerce thrives best amidst some state imposed restrictions (XX, 12). Thus it is, paradoxically, in the freest countries as far as political liberty is concerned, that one encounters the most burdensome import duties and the strictest enforcement of anti-smuggling policies, including the confiscation of all contraband (XIII, 11). To make better use of its commerce, a government may decide to enforce constraints on its subjects, and these constraints are tolerable if they are self-imposed, which presupposes political liberty. In Book XIII, however, liberty concerns mostly security, and the connection of liberty and taxation could exist in monarchies as well as in republics, provided they are moderate governments. As far as commercial regulations are concerned, in Book XX liberty is clearly more specifically related to republican forms of participation in the administration of the state and to a form of political representation allowing political interests to be subjected to economic interests. Commercial regulations suit only economical commerce, which is carried on by republican governments. They do not suit the commerce of luxury, located in monarchies.

Mercantilist regulations in commercial republics (or countries like England) presuppose a virtue of sorts. They are self-imposed constraints advancing the public interest. No such constraint can be expected from the subjects of a monarch. Montesquieu is not so much advocating free trade, as a principle, as he is advising the government to stop bothering the merchants with constraints and demands, like those entailed by the English Acts of Navigation (XX, 8) that French mercantilists admired and would have liked France to imitate. To Colbert, who inclined toward such a policy, the French merchant Legendre allegedly replied "*laissez-nous faire*" (leave us alone).[33] Gournay's and Quesnay's *laissez-faire* philosophy originates in such an answer, which is typical of the merchants' opposition to Louis XIV.[34] Montesquieu, who advocated that "we be left as we are" (XIX, 6), certainly belongs to this French genealogy of *laissez-faire*.

Therefore when he states that, in a monarchy, "the laws must favor all the commerce that the constitution can allow" (V, 9), he is not recommending mercantilist regulations which hamper the individual liberty of the merchants in order to favor commerce generally. He is referring rather to the presence of civil laws that govern the exchange of commodities through complex commercial agreements (XX, 18). Such laws, characteristic of a moderate government, should establish security of property and preclude those "great strokes of authority" (*grands coups d'autorité*) which ravage commerce. Proper laws will provide for consistency and predictability in the commercial area.

Far from enclosing private wealth within the boundaries of the state, as was the case with landed property, such commercial laws should allow the new form of wealth, which is a deterritorialized one, to thrive. Montesquieu was fully aware of the imporance of what he termed "*effets mobiliers*" (movable stocks) to national wealth. Such moveable, or fluid, wealth that is readily exchangeable includes money, notes, bills of exchange, stocks, and all the goods produced by domestic industries. It is by exchanging these fluid forms of wealth in a healthy balance of payments environment that a nation further augments its wealth and raises the standard of living of its people (XX, 23). When a nation has very few commodities or goods to offer for sale to others, it will be better off not engaging in foreign trade. Poland, for example, would have been better off if the small amount of grain offered for sale abroad had been retained for internal distribution to those in need of it. This would have made the populace more energetic and able to provide for themselves in becoming independent proprietors of land given them by grandees no longer deriving advantages from large estates. In addition, domestic industries would be encouraged as a source for the luxuries the grandees could no longer obtain from abroad. Poland, a nation with very little to offer to world commerce was the prototype, then, for Montesquieu, of a nation that would be better off not engaging in foreign trade at all. At the opposite extreme stood Japan.[35] The abundance of Japanese exports (since supply of such goods exceeded domestic demand) meant that they received from foreign consumers the currency needed to buy the imports they wished to have. Exports and imports existed in a state of equilibrium productive of prosperity and power. Unlike a poor country which would need to buy so much abroad that its currency would remain abroad and never come back, Japan could benefit from high levels of consumption and employment and also a balance of payments situation ensuring that imports purchased with Japanese currency would be balanced by exports purchased with foreign currency. Foreign trade would generate prosperity, power, and wealth for a country like Japan, whereas a country like Poland would only be impoverished by such trade. In need of everything, Polish currency would remain abroad and never return.

Poor countries cannot reciprocate by selling their own merchandise abroad, and the money which has left them never comes back, while wealthier countries are engaged in reciprocal exchanges, and the money comes back. Commerce between two wealthy countries is a win-win game. With such a claim, Montesquieu completely breaks with mercantilism since mercantilists considered commerce a zero-sum game. If one side wins, the other loses. Hence mercantilists considered commerce a kind of war, and the maxims of mercantilism were maxims of war. Nations were expected to seize, or capture the commerce of other nations; the increase of wealth (that is of power) of another nation must be dreaded and avoided by all means; manufacturing techniques must be kept secret; exportation of domestic raw materials useful for manufacturing must be prohibited; foreign manufactured goods which could compete with domestic ones must be banned. Clearly, the aim of mercantilist commercial policy was to ruin the other countries, as if one country could actually monopolize the whole commerce of the world. In the *Pensées* that accompany *The Spirit of Laws*, Montesquieu thoroughly criticizes such maxims, contending that, on the contrary, "a state that ruins the others ruins itself" and that "it is often useful to peoples who cultivate the arts that others cultivate them also."[36] Similar arguments concerning the reciprocity of wealth among wealthy trading nations were central to Hume's thinking in his essay "Of the Jealousy of Trade."

Montesquieu does not universalize such a remark, however. Not all countries profit from reciprocal exchanges. This is because Montesquieu combines two patterns in analyzing commerce: the pattern of the unlimited web of extending commercial relationships, and the pattern of the circular flow of expenditures and wages. Although commercial exchanges are deterritorialized, they are not to be separated from their domestic effects. External exchanges bring domestic prosperity for "there will be more consumption, more things on which the arts can be exercised, more men employed, more means of acquiring power"(XX, 23). Thus two basic aspects of commerce (the network of communication and the luxury circuit) are combined. As soon as goods are exchanged, they share a common nature, and the traditional hierarchy of goods is erased since "the nature of commerce is to make superfluous things useful and useful ones necessary." If this refers to the communication pattern, this assumption is a utilitarian one, and it could be argued that commerce destroys all traditional values, based on this hierarchy of goods. But it can also be argued, according to the luxury pattern, that this is the way that the expenses of the rich make the wages of the poor. This is the conclusion that Montesquieu eventually draws: "Therefore the state will be able to give the necessary things to a greater number of its subjects" (XX, 23). With Montesquieu, commerce becomes a subject relevant to political philosophy. It emerges as a matter of general interest. If communication and luxury are merged, there is no reason that the distinction between the two kinds of commerce should be maintained. But such a perspective supposes that commerce is really widespread over the whole world, which is an historical outcome.

The History of Commerce

Book XXI, dedicated to the history of commerce, develops a kind of universal history, spanning ancient as well as modern ages and including the whole universe. This universal history contrasts with Montesquieu's usual comparative method, which consists in constructing abstract or ideal types by relating relevant features in diverse historical situations. Here he treats commerce as an autonomous process, spanning history and comparable only to itself. One must ask why Montesquieu bestows such importance on the history of ancient commerce (eleven chapters about antiquity, versus seven about modern commerce), whereas he had suggested in Book XX (and stated in some accompanying *Pensées*) that commerce is essentially a modern phenomenon.[37] We cannot assume that he was writing history designed to explain why commerce did not prevail in antiquity since he makes numerous comparisons between ancient and modern commerce, implying that they are not so different after all.

On the history of commerce, Montesquieu has very few forerunners, and in Book XX, he draws almost exclusively from ancient sources, mostly Greek geographers. His only modern reference is to Pierre Daniel Huet, bishop of Avranches.[38] Huet's design was to find in ancient commerce, and more especially in Roman commerce, a glorious antecedent of modern French commerce with the Indies in pursuit of mercantilist goals. Such a mercantilist justification of French commercial policy is precisely Montesquieu's target. He begins Book XXI by contending that, although commerce is generally subject to "revolutions" (that is important changes), European commerce with the Indies will, for specific reasons, always stay the same: "in all times those who deal with the Indies will take silver there and not bring any back" (XXI, 1). Beyond contesting the proposition that commerce will always serve mercantilist goals, Montesquieu rebutted Huet's notion that "the Romans greatly encouraged and honored commerce" (XXI, 14).

"The Roman spirit was not commercial," Montesquieu writes (XXI, 15). Neither Roman genius nor Roman glory, neither militarism nor governmental form inclined them toward commerce. The Romans did not respect their agreements, and they did not recognize the principle of reciprocity. In short, their spirit was that of conquest, not commerce. Whereas commerce unites, "Roman policy was to remain separate from all nations that they had not yet subjected; fear of conveying to them the art of conquering led them to neglect the art of enriching themselves" (XXI, 15). Against the received ideas of mercantilism contending that commerce and conquest could be mutually supportive, Montesquieu presents Rome as a counter-example, showing the radical incompatibility between Roman conquest and commerce. If Rome displayed no strong regard for commerce, the outcome was not so much that it kept its pure mores, as the republican tradition would imply, but rather that it remained barbarous, for lack of the civilizing effects of commerce. Montesquieu had stated in his Roman history that "Rome being a city without commerce and without industry, pillage was the sole means available to private individuals to increase their wealth." Resorting to pillaging had been common among all peoples in their early history as with "the first Greeks" who "were all pirates" (XXI, 7). But the Greeks did not remain pirates, and to study Greek history is to follow the development of its commerce. Hence Montesquieu's criticism of the mercantilist ideological justifications has heuristic consequences. It causes him to focus not just on non-commercial Rome, but rather on all the often overlooked or underestimated commercial peoples of antiquity.

Most of these peoples were carrying on an economical commerce, which made "them necessary to all the nations in the world" (XX, 6), while at the same time they were not interested in conquest. This much can be said for Rome. Being deprived of the spirit of commerce, she partook of none of its faults, just as she reaped none of its benefits. The Romans displayed no "jealousy" of the commerce of other peoples (XXI, 14). They feared nothing from trading peoples and encouraged the growth of commercial cities even when such cities were not under their command.

The example of Athens suggests the inadequacy of the Roman policy. Athens, too, had been an "empire" inclined to conquest. But this did not completely hinder Athenian commercial development which developed simultaneously with empire. So, too, is the inadequacy of the Roman model demonstrated by the career and exploits of Alexander the Great. Unlike the Romans who "conquered all to destroy all," he wanted to "conquer all in order to preserve all" in order to increase both the prosperity and the power of the conquered countries (X, 14). Furthermore, Alexander aimed at "uniting" peoples by bringing them together and establishing new connections and routes of communication. Paradoxically, Alexander thus becomes the image of modernity found in the midst of ancient ages, just as Montesquieu, while reading Xenophon on Athens, thinks that one "might say that he was speaking of England" (XXI, 7).

Such a reversal of the usual historical analysis erases the difference between ancients and moderns. As long as one focuses ancient history on Rome, ancient and modern ages may be opposed, the one favoring conquest and the other commerce. That was still Montesquieu's position when he wrote his *Reflections on Universal Monarchy* (1734) as the last chapter of his Roman history. Inquiring whether there could be something similar to the Roman empire in the modern era, he answered in the negative. The spirit of modernity being the spirit of commerce, power was now based on wealth rather than on military force, and a military hegemony was increasingly unlikely. In *The Spirit of Laws*, Montesquieu goes further in his debunking of the Roman model.[39] He makes it clear that Rome is not representative of the broader scope of ancient history, which was characterized not just by conquest, but by commerce as well. Granted, modern commerce differs greatly from that of ancient times (XXI, 4), but commerce may nonetheless be studied as an activity with a continuous history.

"The history of commerce is that of communication between peoples" (XXI, 5), Montesquieu writes. In the wake of what he said in Book XIX, he inserts commerce into a broader category of communication so that commerce refers not only to a transportation of goods, but also to a process that brings people together. Thus, correctly understood, commerce belongs to the history of civilization and culture. Contrary to many of his contemporaries, who considered the knowledge of merchants biased and narrow-minded, Montesquieu praises their knowledge, precisely because it is practical. "Having their eye on all the nations of the earth" (XX, 4), merchants offer reliable narratives of their travels, of "the climate, the terrain, the mores and the manners of the inhabitants" (XXI, 11). Montesquieu dubs Hanno's account (which Huet had criticized, doubting it was genuine) "a fine piece of antiquity," neither bombastic, nor fabulous. The *Odyssey*—a maritime travelogue—is deemed "the finest poem in the world" (XXI, 6), second only to the Bible, but superior to the *Iliad*, a war epic. In modern ages, Camoens' poem, which describes Portuguese discoveries in "Mozambique, Melinde and Calicut" is comparable to Homer and Virgil (XXI, 21).

Although commerce is equated by Montesquieu with the highest achievements of human poetry, commercial culture remains practical, being based on mostly geographical as well as technical knowledge, which requires "infinite observations" and which, for that reason is exposed to many flaws and failures: "Most of the reasoning of the Ancients lacks accuracy, owing to their not possessing the ideas that modern discoveries have given to the world." For Montesquieu, the history of commerce includes the history of all the techniques which develop navigation, like the compass, a decisive discovery in the history of modern commerce. In the seventeenth century, the mechanics of ship maneuver had become a very complicated and extensively debated issue in applied physics taken up by such prominent scientists as Huyghens, Bernoulli, and Leibniz. Montesquieu relies on such technological assessments to compare ancient and modern navigation in regard to their "mechanism" (XXI, 6), that is, the mechan-

ics of hull construction as related to the depths of the waters in the ports fre-
quented by various ancient and modern vessels.

Unlike Christian, Providential history, encompassing universality and unfolding in accordance with Divine pattern, commerce is the outcome of a fragile
history. Knowledge gained by man can be lost, and one cannot accurately speak
of "ancient knowledge" of commerce in general, since different peoples knew
different things. Ancient knowledge was necessarily scattered since there was no
printing to aid communication of useful truths. Bringing the history of commerce into the history of Enlightenment, as Montesquieu did, entails stressing
the material dimension of such a history. The progress of commerce overlaps
the material, physical discovery of the Earth.

In the comparative examination of such progress, Montesquieu refers to the
geographical and climatic oppositions already highlighted in the third part of
The Spirit of Laws, the great North/South opposition. Ancient commerce, he notes, was "almost entirely in the South," whereas "Today the commerce of Europe is principally carried on from north to south" (XXI, 4). With the
North/South polarity comes the liberty/servitude opposition, and Montesquieu
compares the natural bounty, laziness, servitude linkage typical of the South,
with the natural sterility, labor, liberty linkage of the North (XX, 3). But this
does not lead to such a sharp opposition between Asian servitude and European
liberty, as in Book XVII, since as far as the "needs" of differently located people
are concerned, an equilibrium may be the outcome of such differences. While
conquest separates, commerce once more unites, all the more so since it operates
through concentric circles, in a manner of speaking, relying on an extensive
network of relationships which grows larger and larger, while conquest proceeds
in a linear way. Eventually, the progress of commerce is liberated from this rigid
North/South opposition, to become an East-West trend or drift. The most significant difference between ancient and modern commerce is that, once the Americas were discovered, "Italy was no longer at the center of the commercial
world; it was in a corner of the universe, so to speak, and it remains there today"
(XXI, 21). The progress of commerce is mostly a decentering one, and this is
the reason why, when Montesquieu speaks of Europe as carrying on the commerce of the whole world (XXI, 21), he was not transferring to Europe the mercantilist idea, or ideal, of one state conducting all the commerce. Europe is a society of nations, not a unified government. Political unity and commercial progress no longer coincide.

Being the history of "communication among peoples," the record of commerce chronicles the emancipation of societies from their governments. A history of civilization, a history of enlightenment, a history of technological progress,
the history of commerce is not related to political history. Rather commerce
creates a history of its own, which replaces the boundaries of states with an unlimited network of commercial ways of communication. Viewed from this perspective, the most conspicuous revolution of commerce is the complete reversal,

from ancient to modern times, of its relationships with governments and political power. Book XXI begins with the striking picture of a timid commerce threatened by political and military powers: "Commerce, sometimes destroyed by conquerors, sometimes hampered by monarchs, wanders across the earth, flees from where it is oppressed, and remains where it is left to breathe" (XXI, 5). By the end of Book XXI, the tables have been completely turned. Modern governments are depicted as powerless toward ever more mobile forms of commerce, which escapes their grasp. Far from submitting commerce to their will, governments must regulate their passions, and act, just like commerce does, according to their interests (XXI, 20).

Apropos of the invention of letters of exchange, Montesquieu thus qualifies his initial statement concerning the pacifying effects of commerce upon political power. He now distinguishes between economics and politics, and between society and government, without suggesting their complete separation, or independence. Commerce and war intersect since they have a common origin in pillage. The history of commerce, he observes, has been "formed by their various destructions and certain ebbs and flows of population and of devastation" (XXI, 5) a comment equally descriptive of the history of wars. Therefore political history and the history of commerce, although distinct, remain interconnected, and Montesquieu's design, in Book XXI, is not so much to oppose conquest and commerce, as if the two were completely separate, as to study the still existing relationships between wealth and power.

A "great navigation" is the source of a "great power" (XXI, 16), and the difference between Rome and Athens was not so much a sharp contrast in their military power and commercial wealth as between their contrasting forms of empire, one territorial and the other maritime. Though generally critical of the despotism inherent in large empires, Montesquieu clearly favors maritime empires over land based empires. In *Persian Letter* 136 he marveled at the way England (the modern replica of Athens) had mastered the sea. Indeed, the general statement that "a large empire presupposes a despotic authority" does not apply to maritime empires, such as the Athenians and the English developed. Whereas Rome conquered only to destroy what lay in its path and ruled despotically over conquered countries, Athens associated conquest with prosperity, as Alexander the Great also did in antiquity and as the English were doing in modern times. Contrary to the example of Rome, England is capable of "communicating" its government to its colonies (XIX, 27), which links prosperity with power.

As the Roman example clearly indicates, prioritizing territorial domination impedes commercial prosperity, while maritime empires successfully link political domination with commercial prosperity. Therefore a sea-based empire suits a country like England, which subordinates its political interests to its commercial ones. Furthermore, the modern English maritime empire is superior to the ancient Athenian empire since Athens' domination, though largely maritime, was partially territorial, and Montesquieu wonders whether "one must conquer a

country in order to trade with it?" (XXI, 8) Greek colonization was aimed at populating conquered lands, while the less aggressive, less military goal of modern
European colonization is "to extend commerce not to found a town or a new
empire" (XXI, 21).

Montesquieu's analysis of modern commercial colonization may look like a
justification of mercantilism since he explained that the privileged relationships
between the homeland and its colonies are protected by the policy that governments can hamper individuals in order to extend commerce. Quesnay was later
critical of this perspective, arguing that the difference between the home land
and the colonies should be considered purely political. Hence colonies should
not be treated any differently as far as economic policy is concerned than any
other states. Neither monopolies nor privileges should be granted. Trade should
be free. There is certainly a strong political dimension, however, to Montesquieu's handling of the colonial question. The reciprocity he envisions and justifies between the colonies and the home land is political. The colonies lose the
right to trade freely, but they gain the protection of the mother country. Montesquieu is not arguing on behalf of a mercantilist position however. The "wisdom"
of European policy is that the governments delegate their privileged sovereignty
to commercial companies, restraining themselves from political interference in
commercial interests. In the same spirit, Montesquieu concludes that Spain, if
unable to itself engage in commerce with the Indies, would open that area to foreigners (XXI, 23). Free trade, he concludes, would have many advantages for
all who are involved. Hence Quesnay's and Montesquieu's practical conclusions
converge, but Quesnay states as a universal law what Montesquieu still thinks of
as pertaining to the area of political decision making. Commerce for him is not
thoroughly separated from politics, though he remarks: "I shall say that it is suitable for it to put the fewest obstacles in the way of commerce that its policy can
permit" (XXI, 23).

Spain was not likely to adopt such a moderate and wise policy, since she
considered her American territories as "objects of conquests," and not as more
"refined" people were to do, as "objects of commerce" (XXI, 21). Spain, in
other words, subscribed to the need for territorial domination, like Rome, and
even worse than Rome, since Rome expanded at a time when victory necessarily
derived from military virtue and strength whereas Spain was establishing colonies in South America at a time when "it is wealth that establishes power." Explaining the modern history of the discovery of the new worlds, and its consequences, Montesquieu inserted fragments of what he had already written on
such issues in his *Considerations on the Wealth of Spain* (1728) and his *Reflections on Universal Monarchy* (1734), where he had tried to explain the paradox
of Spanish American gold. The gold of America had made Spain fabulously
rich, as no state had been before, but this wealth in gold, far from making Spain
more powerful, had decreased her power. In *The Spirit of Laws* Montesquieu re-

sumes his inquiry into "the cause of the powerlessness of Spanish wealth" (XXI, 22).

The answer is very simple. These riches are not true riches: real wealth is to be found in the "industry of the nation, the number of its inhabitants, the cultivation of its lands" (XXI, 22), not in these "conventional" riches consisting or gold or silver. "Gold and silver are fictional wealth, or a sign" (XXI, 22), and multiplying the signs does not increase wealth, but only the expression of wealth. If a country suddenly has twice as much gold as before, it will require twice as many gold coins to buy the same things. Prices, not wealth, will increase. Such ideas were not new. Melon began his *Essai politique sur le commerce* (1734) with a similar assessment of the difference between genuine wealth (land, grain, and men), and fictional or conventional wealth (gold or silver). The idea that money is a conventional sign of value and not wealth can be traced back at least to Aristotle, who states in his *Nicomachean Ethics* (V, 5) that money is so named (*numisma*) because it is conventional, not natural (deriving from *nomos*, not *phusis*). Similarly, Montesquieu's "quantitative" explanation of the inflation following the arrival of the American gold wasn't novel either. In his *Response to the Paradoxes of Monsieur Malestroit* (1568), Jean Bodin had already provided a similar explanation of a problem which was puzzling and worrying Europe, namely, how to amass gold and avoid economic decline.

Montesquieu's originality lies in the way he relates the weakness and "internal vice" of Spanish wealth to its military policies. Chrysohedonism, or believing that only gold and silver constitute true wealth, is a typical delusion of states engaged in wars. They do need "treasure," or cash, to pay for troops, allies, supplies, and so on. Such expenditures do not return. Such money flows out to others and does not come back. The gold amassed by Spain did not enter into commercial exchanges. Unlike the situation in Hungary or Germany, where the work of mining, which is designed to procure precious metals, employs many people who live from local supplies and make the land worth cultivating, the Spanish gold was taken out of the American mines by overworking the natives. It was then brought back to Spain where it did not stay because it was needed to buy commodities from elsewhere in Europe. Hence, the king of Spain was a "very wealthy individual" in a "very poor state" (XXI, 22). It is precisely because money is but a sign that it needs to be part of the commercial flow of goods in order to be useful. Therefore to study money is to study the commercial processes in which it "performs its office," as Book XXII concerned with money is intended to demonstrate.

Money and Its Worth

Among all the books of the fourth part of *The Spirit of Laws* dedicated to com merce, Book XXII, whose subject is money, must have been the least read and studied. It is full of rather complicated comments about foreign exchange, about operations performed by governments on currencies, about public debt, and about private usury. Furthermore, these matters are all the more difficult to understand since most of these practices (like the distinction between real and ideal monies) disappeared after the French Revolution and the adoption of the gold standard. As mentioned above, Montesquieu considers money a sign (XXII, 2), and, after him, this explanation was soon replaced (especially with Turgot[40]) by the theory of money as merchandise. Turgot's theory is considered liberal because it equates money and goods, locating the measure of worth among the things themselves, making money part of a realm not subject to the arbitrary power of the prince. Montesquieu's view of money was deemed mercantilist and has been rather forgotten or overlooked.

The gold standard has disappeared as well, however, and the idea of money as merchandise currently looks as quaint as viewing it as a sign, all the more so since economists are no longer interested in inquiring about the nature, or essence, of money, and prefer to deal with its functions, so that the sign versus merchandise debate is out of fashion. This has not prevented Michel Rosier, however, from contending that there is no substantial opposition between treating money as a sign or as merchandise since money cannot be conceived as uniquely one or the other.[41] Rather, each explanation overlaps the other one, both in theory and in practice.

By suggesting that money is a sign Montesquieu meant to show that it does not correspond to real wealth, as the Spanish case shows. Money is not intrinsically desirable. It is of no use except when it is exchanged for goods whose value it represents. That money is a sign entails, according to Montesquieu, a reciprocity between the signifying sign and the signified value: "just as silver is the sign of a thing and represents it, each thing is a sign of silver and represents it" (XXII, 2). Being a sign refers to the universal exchangeability of money for commodities, and it could be argued that, already with Montesquieu, the function money performs is more important than its nature. The reason why gold or silver are generally elected as signs of value is that they are durable and easily divisible into small equal amounts, and these properties are directly related to its function as a counting unit and a means of exchange. A country will be prosperous, Montesquieu asserts, when money is readily exchangeable for goods, and goods are readily exchangeable for money, and no one feels so threatened that specie is hoarded. Prosperity will require a moderate government and one that pursues wise policies. For example, "if the laws favor an unjust debtor, the things belonging to him do not represent silver and are not a sign of it." Conversely, political "art" may enhance the circulation, as in England where, thanks to its laws, "all the goods of an Englishman represent silver" (XXII, 2).

In Montesquieu's day governments frequently manipulated currencies as part of their presumed sovereign powers. Montesquieu actually states that it is part of the prince's power to establish what he calls "the positive value" of the currency. This will be done by regulating the nature, weight, and fineness of the coins in circulation and even by determining which coins may circulate. In ancien régime France a distinction was drawn between "real money"—the actual coins—and "ideal money" or "*monnaie de compte,*" its monetary price. It was the king who established the relationship between coins and their value by saying that a coin—a *louis* or an *écu*—was worth so many *livres*. Such power enabled the king to arbitrarily manipulate the value of money without even re-coining it. It was also possible to change the weight of coins by calling them in for re-minting, the consequence of such a practice being that the money, whose name originally indicated a weight (like the *livre*, or the pound), is no longer equivalent to that and becomes an "ideal" money. Fixing the "*monnaie de compte*" was usually a way to devalue the currency. Montesquieu considered all such operations as "abuses of power," asserting: "Nothing should be as exempt from variation as that which is the common measure of everything"(XXII, 3).

Conceiving of money as a "fiction," or a "sign," or a "convention" does not prevent Montesquieu from analyzing money as being part of a mechanical process, whose effects can be studied. According to Montesquieu's quantitative theory, prices vary according to the relation between the quantity of "wealth in signs" and the total quantity of the commodities available for purchase so that "the prince or magistrate can no more assign the value of commodities than he can establish by an ordinance that the relation of one to ten is equal to that of one to twenty" (XXII, 7). "Just" prices are not a matter of political manipulation. They automatically adjust themselves in the many encounters between traders in a market: "It is competition that puts a just price on goods and establishes the true relations between them" (XX, 9).

There is no reason to oppose the theories of money as sign and money as merchandise as bringing about different practical or theoretical results. Both Montesquieu and Turgot actually take into account both the sign and the merchandise aspects of money, even though they do not acknowledge this fact.[42] When Montesquieu contends that interest rates dropped after the arrival of American gold in Europe because gold had become more abundant, he bases his explanation on a comparison between the supply and demand for gold, which suggests that he considers gold as merchandise in its monetary function.

The only difference (and it is an important one) between money as sign and money as merchandise is epistemological. In order to consider money explicitly as merchandise, Turgot reconstructs, in an abstract and imaginary manner, the process which leads to select merchandise becoming money. Montesquieu on the other hand, does not attempt to go behind the monetary veil. He keeps to the phenomenological description of things, the way they appear. That is the reason why Book XXII is sometimes so difficult to understand. Using money is a very complicated matter, requiring the very sophisticated techniques of bankers, or of financiers. But this is the technicity of art, of empirical practice, not of science. Montesquieu does not construct a scientific explanation which can make us understand the true nature of money. He describes the technical management of money, and he speaks of exchange as it actually takes place in real countries.

Foreign exchange is the way the value of a currency is expressed in another currency. To illustrate, Montesquieu takes Holland and France as examples of two trading countries. French traders buying in Holland need Dutch currency, just as Dutch traders need French currency to buy goods in France. The rate of exchange, according to Montesquieu, will depend upon the relative demand for Dutch currency or French currency, or vice versa, which will in turn reflect the balance of trade between the two countries. The exchange is said to be "at par" "when the same grade and the same weight of silver in France give me the same weight and the same grade of silver in Holland" (XXII, 10). When more Dutch funds are needed in Holland by the French than French funds are needed in France by the Dutch, the exchange rate of the French currency in the Dutch currency is said to be "high." When France is losing in the balance of trade, we speak of a declining rate of exchange, while, in the other case, when France is gaining, we speak of a better rate of exchange. The effect of a loss in the exchange rate is to diminish the value of the French exports, as expressed in the Dutch currency, widening the trade gap between Holland and France. Hence the lowering of the rate of exchange should have aggravating effects: "with the ill continuing to exist because such a debt would lower the exchange rate still further, France would in the end be ruined" (XXII, 10).

Montesquieu demonstrates, however, that a shifting exchange rate triggers compensatory mechanisms which counteract this plummeting process. First, when the exchange rate does not favor France, French prices will decline as measured in Dutch currency, and French traders may raise their prices without the Dutch traders losing all their profit. The profits of the French traders thus increase, and "the profit will be spread between the Frenchman and the Dutchman." Second, in the same situation, Dutch prices expressed in French currency are going to increase and the French traders "will feel the loss" and buy less, which will decrease the French loss: "the loss will then be spread between the French merchant and the Dutch merchant. Eventually, the combination of the effect of a declining exchange rate and its effect on quantities purchased should bring the price of commodities back to equilibrium: states tend to bring themselves into balance and liberate themselves" (XXII, 10).

Such compensating mechanisms are based on the merchants' interests, and they occur within the commercial competition because it is made up of reciprocated acts. This is not the case with the money of the government: "a prince who sends to foreign countries only silver that is never to return always loses" (XXII, 10). Montesquieu thus proceeds to explain how non-commercial variations of the exchange rate do not have re-equilibrating effects. Law's system, once more the target of Montesquieu's criticism, causes such non-commercial variations in the exchange rate. In France a bank note of one *livre* was supposed to have the same value ("positive values" are fixed by the state) as a silver *livre*. But since the notes were constantly multiplying, each one owning notes "would seek to secure his fortune, and as the exchange provides the easiest route for changing its nature or for sending it where one wants, one could continually remit a part of one's effects to the nation that regulated the exchange" (XXII, 10). The rate of exchange would decline lower and lower, as long as paper would be presented to exchange: "This went so far that one gave no more than eight *groschen* [the Dutch currency], and finally there was no longer an exchange" (XXII, 10).

This was the way Law's system collapsed. The exchange, which belongs to commerce, that is to the communication of peoples, won over government and its attempted "violent operations" and *"grands coups d'autorité."* The study of exchange gives the effective confirmation of Montesquieu's statement, in Book XXI, that the invention of the letters of exchange had liberated the merchants from the arbitrary power of the governments, rendering Machiavellian coups d'état ineffective. Modern traders (merchants and bankers) are not only mobile, they are also well informed, having the knowledge which allows them to avoid being fooled or impressed by government secrecy. If princes can conduct politics secretly, commerce is a public matter, and money is part of commerce, no longer of politics: "The exchange has taught the banker to compare all the monies of the world and set them at their just value; the grade of monies can no longer be kept secret" (XXII, 13).

In his study of Roman examples of monetary operations, Montesquieu seeks to confirm what he has been stating in his chapter about exchange, a venture not without irony since he warns his readers "that an example will not be made of something that is not one," before crediting the Romans with a "remarkable wisdom" (XXII, 11). Montesquieu intends to draw attention to the French government's lack of wisdom in similar circumstances. Rome is praised for having devalued its money so that it "gained half on its creditor," and the state was given "a great jolt." In his youthful *Memoir on the State's Debts* (1715), Montesquieu advised the Regent to opt for a partial bankruptcy under the ægis of an assembly of notables, a solution which would have had effects similar to the Roman devaluation. Such a decision would certainly have been preferable to Law's debt reduction scheme. Indeed Montesquieu praised Rome for having aimed at liberating "the republic from the citizens" without liberating "the citizens from themselves," whereas Law's system confused what the Romans distinguished, i.e., public debt and private fortunes.

In his chapter "on public debts" (XXII,17) Montesquieu overtly criticizes Melon's optimistic assertion that "The state's debts are what the right hand owes to the left, and the body does not find itself weakened if it has the necessary quantity of food, and it knows how to distribute them."[43] In criticizing Melon, Montesquieu resumes his criticism of Law's system, arguing again that it wrongly confused private wealth and public finances: "there has been a confusion," Montesquieu observes, "between a circulating paper that is the sign of the profits a company has made or will make in commerce, and a paper that represents a debt" (XXII, 17). Law's scheme was precisely to create a state bank which would buy the public debt and issue shares to an equivalent amount. These shares could be purchased with gold or silver, and only these shares (not metal coins) could be used to buy shares of a state-backed trading company. A new circulating medium would then emerge, a circulating paper issued by the bank, which would be the only way to buy shares in the trading company, and which would be used as well to pay the interest on the debt.[44] Assessing the "advantages" of such a scheme of public indebtedness, Montesquieu reminds us that we are not looking for the prince's opulence but for his justice, and he draws our attention to the negative social effects of such a process of state debt. Since the state will have to pay interest on money loaned by its creditors, public debt "takes the true revenues of the state from those who are active and industrious to transfer them to idle people" who have invested in the state's debts (XXII, 17). The passive class of *rentiers*, however, idly living off the state's interest payments should be "protected" nonetheless by the state, because they are always threatened by the government's projects, and because it is necessary to maintain "public confidence." If the state abuses its creditors, then obtaining loans from such wealthy individuals will be all the more difficult in the future. So Montesquieu is capable of using the usual mercantilist argument of "protected liberty," as far as social interests are concerned and in consideration of public interest.

This does not entail approving state interference with private interests as a principle. On the question of private loans between individuals Montesquieu argues that laws aimed at forbidding usury to protect the people have unintentional effects contrary to their goal. As an example, he turns to republican Rome and the way laws which were made to abolish debts or protect the people from abusive interest rates had effects contrary to what was intended. Such laws "naturalized usury in Rome" because the people were not only debtors but legislators and judges as well, and every tribune who wanted to be popular brought up the abolition of debts. This eventually destroyed any trust in contracts so that "all honest means of borrowing and lending" were abolished in Rome, and those who needed to be loaned money, were subjected to "frightful usury"(XXII, 21).

In Book XXI, Montesquieu charges the scholastic theologians with falsely drawing arguments from Aristotle in their condemnation of lending at interest, with the consequence that usury was equated with bad faith (XXI, 20).[45] In Book XXII, he is more discreet in criticizing the Church's ban on loaning money at interest. He reverts to Grotius' distinction between perfect obligations (commutative justice), which can be rightly enforced and imperfect obligations (of charity) which cannot,[46] to assert that lending money without interest "can be only a religious counsel not a civil law," and therefore cannot regulate civil contracts (XXII, 19). But one can presume that his criticism of Roman policy about banning usury can be applied to the Church's argument that such a prohibition was made to protect the poorest people. In showing how trying to protect the people actually "naturalized usury" rather than destroying it, Montesquieu was using an argument about unintended consequences, which he was to draw upon again in Book XXIII, where he argues that charitable institutions often tend to create the poverty that they want to remedy.

Labor and Productivity

In the developing countries of Europe in the modern age, human labor was a key factor to productivity, and population a central concern. Hence Book XXIII, while dealing ostensibly with population issues, addresses the whole problem of real wealth, as opposed to the ideal "wealth in signs," a real wealth which depends on the "industry of the nation" and "the cultivation of its lands" as well as on "the number of its inhabitants." Montesquieu was well acquainted with Fenelon's thought (as the Troglodytes' story in the *Persian Letters* shows), and he had some of Boisguilbert's writings in his library.[47] Both writers were involved in the opposition to Louis XIV which permeated Montesquieu's years of intellectual formation. One finds, however, no hint, in *The Spirit of Laws*, either of Fenelon's "Christian agrarianism,"[48] or of Boisguilbert's eulogy of the free exportation of grain, which was later championed by Quesnay in the "Grains" article of the *Encyclopédie*. Montesquieu certainly deemed agriculture a very important, and respectful, activity, and he praises the Chinese emperors for duly honoring it (XIV, 8), but he did not think of it as a central object of commerce, or as yielding a "net product," the way the physiocrats would conceive of it some ten years after *The Spirit of Laws* was published. Doubtless, as he stated in Book XIII, "nature is just toward men" (XIII, 2) and provides more to those who labor. But Montesquieu did not favor societies based on an agrarian order. He did not praise the ancient republics which artificially maintained equality with agrarian laws reducing everybody to their subsistence share. Nor did he think that the feudal agrarian order based on landlords and serfdom was sufficient to produce wealth. In modern states where those engaged in agriculture produce more than they consume, there must be a corresponding group of artisans and workers who can sell what they make in order to have income to purchase the surplus food that is grown. Only this situation can create a balanced economy functioning properly (XXIII, 15).

Montesquieu shared this idea that industry "enlivens" the land, by making "cultivating the land worthwhile" (XXI, 22), with the mercantilists who did not (as they were falsely accused of) sacrifice agriculture to industry, but who thought that industry alone could bring prosperity to the country, by stimulating trade and the circulation of wealth and by increasing the population. This was certainly more commonsensical than the physiocratic idea of the exclusive productivity of agriculture. It was not specifically a mercantilist idea either.

It could be argued that, for Montesquieu, agriculture cannot entirely pertain to commerce since its primary function is to provide for vital human needs of consumption. In the "three-stages" history of humanity that Montesquieu sketches in Book XVIII, the hunters he begins with are somewhat akin to the animals they are hunting. They live in small groups, rather like herds instead of organized societies, wandering in a natural environment on which they are entirely dependent. This close dependence on the land is still true of agrarian societies, and this is the reason why farmers are easily subjected to despotism (XVIII, 2), unlike men of industry who carry their skills with them. The history sketched in Book XVIII chronicles the emerging human artificialization of laws and the refinement of civilization out of an originally animal condition. Commerce, whose nature is "to make superfluous things useful and useful ones necessary" (XX, 23), conceals the animal roots of the human quest for subsistence by making everything equal. But although commerce enhances artificialization, it does not separate human workmanship from its natural environment. In Book XVIII Montesquieu praises men who, "by their care and their good laws, have made the earth more fit to be their home" (XVIII, 7). But while he thus celebrates human power to modify natural conditions (even to modify climate as he wanted to show in his youthful project of a *Physical History of the Earth, Ancient and Modern*, [49] he did not think that it made men autonomous makers of their own world. Their workmanship was still part of the natural environment, immersed in it and activated by natural processes. Speaking of the way men can make water flow by draining marshlands (a process highly appreciated in the eighteenth century because it was supposed to be especially healthy), he adds "it is a good that nature did not make but which is maintained by nature" (XVIII, 7).

Hence the "general spirit" is an emerging entity in a history which is continuous from natural animality to complex human social organization, and artifice achieves or perfects nature, rather than opposing it. This is the reason why Montesquieu cannot speak of economic processes as "natural laws." Commerce, as well as human industry, requires man-made "laws." Thus, Montesquieu did not consider commerce entirely "natural," the way the physiocrats will speak of the economy as a "natural order" and suggest that human societies cease making artificial laws and respect the natural laws. Nature and artifice are interactive, and the economy is not ruled by autonomous processes, like nature. There is no reason to draw the borderline between nature and artifice. They are continuous, and there is no reason, either, to think that nature can by itself establish liberty. But Montesquieu knows too well that there is no liberty without human laws. He does not speak of a "system of natural liberty," the way Adam Smith does to signify that government must not interfere with individuals acting on behalf of their own interest.

Like agriculture, population growth is a concern which is rooted in animality but carried on by humanity. Like any animal society, human societies must take care of the preservation of the species, and for this reason, they develop complex strategies of reproduction. Being also religious, however, they make reproduction an object of veneration (as the quotation of Lucretius' hymn to Venus at the beginning of Book XXIII on population reminds us). Furthermore, being animals capable of industry as well as capable of submitting themselves to law, these strategies are not only spontaneous, but also a matter of art, and of law. The laws and mores concerning marriage are the way human societies regulate their reproduction, enhancing it or thwarting it (XXIII, 2-10). Reproduction is a natural process which is highly dependent on its environment. Therefore the fertility of women is related to the climate, and the strategies for the preservation of the species vary accordingly: polygamy in the south, monogamy in the north. Population strategies vary, as well, according to the social environment. If available food and means of sustenance are extremely significant to population growth, it is nonetheless true that "countries are not cultivated in proportion to their fertility, but in proportion to their liberty" (XVIII, 3). As was commonly believed in the eighteenth century, Montesquieu was convinced that a great population was a sure sign of prosperity and of a happy people ruled by a good government. On the contrary the "harshness of the government" (XXIII, 11) does not induce poor people to have children. Montesquieu thus reminds the followers of Richelieu that their policy of low wages, and their views on the utility of poverty, run counter to the avowed mercantilist desire to have a large population, producing wealth (because of labor) and power (because of soldiers).

Achieving a large population may not require setting a deliberate policy goal with this end in mind. "Where nature has done everything" (XXIII, 16), no special legislation on the propagation of the species is required. But such laws can be necessary wherever depopulation threatens or is developing. Montesquieu partook of the "beneficial error"[50] common to many in the eighteenth century, regarding the supposed modern depopulation of areas which had been more populated in antiquity. But, as usual, Montesquieu does not stick to a rigid historical opposition. Depopulation was not unknown to antiquity, and Rome had to make laws inducing people to marry and have children, since it was losing citizens because, first, of wars and later because of the corruption of mores (XXIII, 21). As a modern threat, Montesquieu connected depopulation to religion. Like many of his contemporaries, he accuses the Catholic Church of threatening population growth by imposing celibacy on its clerics. But for him, population growth or decline is mostly related to the size of the government. Greek republics were so populated that they tried to limit their population, or sent people to populate new cities (XXIII, 17); feudal Europe was much more populated than Europe in the present day, as "the prodigious armies of crusaders" in the Middle Ages indicate (XXIII, 24). This is because Europe was divided into small cities, or into small sovereignties. Each lord lived close to his subjects whose number only made him secure, so that "each one strove with a singular attentiveness to make his country flourish" (XIII, 24), whereas a widening empire leads to depopulation.

As Rousseau would later say, "man clings to everything that surrounds him,"[51] and Montesquieu noticed in *Persian Letter* 121 that men are attached to local conditions and cannot be so easily transported from one place to another. In *The Spirit of Laws*, he states that while it was extending its navigation, Europe did not increase its population since overseas voyages are hazardous and since some among the voyagers will decide to remain in foreign climes. Of Dutch sailors sent to the Indies every year, says Montesquieu, "only two-thirds return" (XXIII, 25). There are two conflicting forces at work: the universal force of commerce making for dispersion and the local attachments of men, who still depend upon natural conditions and attachments.

This polarization between the global and the local finds a solution at the national level. Even though local care is of very great importance for population growth, the laws encouraging it must be general ones, adopted by the state to achieve a general purpose. If a large population is a sign of prosperity, enhancing population is fighting against poverty. The demographic and the social concerns converge, and Montesquieu brings Book XXIII to a close with a chapter about "poorhouses" (*hôpitaux*). Melon had already suggested the difference between religious care and political concerns for the poor, by saying the "charitable man provides alms; the statesman gives work."[52] Montesquieu adopts this distinction between religious charity and political-social obligations by stating that the state's duties are not fulfilled by "a few alms given to a naked man." The state must provide employment for those who are capable of working. Therefore Montesquieu's definition of poverty is a very secular one. The poor are not those who are in need, the necessitous, that is; rather the poor are those who do not work. Montesquieu is very careful to specify that only the needs of those who cannot work—"the old, the sick, and the orphaned"—must be provided for. All the others are no longer poor, as soon as they can work, and there are available jobs (XXIII, 29).

Montesquieu thus engages in a very serious criticism of the Church's charitable institutions, its "perpetual establishments." He not only accuses these institutions of being unable to cure poverty, but also of maintaining and even developing poverty: "the spirit of laziness that poorhouses inspire increases general poverty." The undiscriminating definition of poverty upon which charitable poorhouses are based enhances poverty because it creates an interest in being poor; one can live better in a poorhouse than by having a job, as in modern day Rome (XXIII, 29).

In his *Encyclopédie* article on "Foundations," Turgot used exactly the same argument to criticize the Church's "perpetual establishments," and it became a central argument in the liberal criticism of the obnoxious, unintentional effects of political or social interference with free competition. Montesquieu thus seems to contribute to this liberal onslaught against governmental assistance. He does not, however, go so far as to say that economic prosperity will itself provide for all people's needs. He clearly states, on the contrary, that even though a country has reached prosperity it still needs poorhouses (or alternative measures designed for the same end), to provide for those who face the consequences of temporary economic disturbances. The economic equilibriums are long-term and general; the momentary movements of such processes are quite shaky; there are ups and downs in each branch, and employment conditions are pretty uncertain. The people's needs may at times be urgent; and social and economic temporalities do not always coincide. It is the duty of the state to adjust the two temporalities in order to protect the poor against the untoward consequences of economic freedom.

And these state duties are far reaching. Some commentators consider that by contending that the state owes "all the citizens an assured sustenance, nourishment, suitable clothing, and a kind of life which is not contrary to health," and by adding that the state should give work and teach work, Montesquieu was far ahead of the 1789 property-centered Declaration of Rights and was anticipating the 1848 claim for social assistance, and more important still, "right to work."[53] What validity is there to such an assertion?

Montesquieu's ambiguous position (if compared to our own standards) at the end of this fourth part of *The Spirit of Laws* is very representative of all his thought about commerce and economics. He surely made many assertions about commerce as a self-regulating process which were to be central in late eighteenth-century economic liberalism, and he surely criticized mercantilism very firmly. But his criticism was mainly a political one, centered on the relationships between the government and society. Thus, he opposed mercantilist views on the utility of poverty and advocated political involvement in matters of economics.

To understand Montesquieu's position, Keynes' judgment about Montesquieu being the "greatest French economist"[54] could be very useful. Keynes' specific attention to Montesquieu's interest theory, however, is hardly convincing. Montesquieu contends in XXII, 19 of *The Spirit of Laws* that a low interest rate will be advantageous to commerce, which was a rather commonplace view in the eighteenth-century French and English literature on commerce. One must be Keynes himself, or, at least, be impregnated by Keynes' ideas, to find that, in such a chapter, Montesquieu insightfully perceived that "the role of interest is to preserve the equilibrium not of demand and supply of new capital goods, but the demand and supply of money, that is to say the demand for liquidity and the means for supplying it."[55] But it is true that Montesquieu, precisely because he did not distinguish between money circulation and the capital market (a distinction which was to be one of Turgot's main contributions to economic analysis), did not separate productive expense from non-productive consumption, and this made it possible to think of cash flow supply and demand the way Keynes does. It was possible to conceive of a policy of general expenditure, at once social and economic.

Montesquieu thought of commercial processes as being socially embedded, as well as politically accessible, even though as little political interference as possible was the best policy. It allowed him to combine a call for leaving individuals free to act on their own initiatives—a call based on an optimistic secular anthropology—with the advocacy of a welfare state, based on a genuine social concern. Therefore rather than saying that Montesquieu anticipates Keynes (which is unconvincing), one could rather say that Keynes tried to find inspiration in Montesquieu's approach to economics, an approach that was at once empirical and historical while also involving political and moral analysis. For Montesquieu economics was not a purely deductive science. It is because commercial enterprises are so uncertain, that no general science, on the model of natural sciences can exist and that economics still pertains to human history.

Notes

I would like to thank especially David Carrithers, who helped me greatly in putting this chapter into English.

1. Montchrestien, in his *Traicté de l'Œconomie politique* (1615), is supposed to have coined the phrase. Initially, it was not a very successful coinage, perhaps because it sounded too Aristotelian. The phrases "political arithmetic" or "commerce" were much more frequently employed.

2. E. F. Heckscher, *Mercantilism*, Mendel Shapiro, trans., 2 vols. (London: 1935).

3. Very few studies have been devoted, since 1950, to Montesquieu's economic thought as a whole (we will cite more specific studies later). See Nicos E. Devletoglou, "Montesquieu and the Wealth of Nations," *The Canadian Journal of Economics and Political Science* 29, no. 1 (February 1963): 1-25; Devletoglou, "The Economic Philosophy of Montesquieu," *Kyklos; Internationale Zeitschrift für Sozialwissenschaften* 22, no. 3 (1969): 530-41; See, besides Devletoglou's articles, M. Garrigou-Lagrange, "Montesquieu et les économistes," *Actes du congrès Montesquieu* (Bordeaux, 1956): 282-84, Alain Cotta, "Le développement économique dans la pensée de Montesquieu," *Revue d'histoire économique et sociale* 35, no. 4 (1957): 370-415; Claude Morilhat, *Montesquieu, politique et richesses* (Paris: PUF, 1996); Eluggero Pii, "I libri sull commercio nell'Esprit des lois," in *Leggere L'Esprit des lois, Stato, societa e storia nel pensiero di Montesquieu*, Domenico Felice ed. (Napoli: Liguori editore, 1998), 165-200. Although in his Preface to the French edition of the *General Theory of Employment, Interest and Money*, Keynes refers to Montesquieu as "the greatest French economist," more often than not, general histories of economic thought overlook Montesquieu, or say very little about him. See, for instance, Joseph A. Schumpeter, *History of Economic Analysis* (Oxford : Oxford University Press, 1954).

4. Adam Smith, *Wealth of Nations* (1776), I, 5 where he quotes Hobbes' assertion "Wealth is power."

5. Equality, here, must be understood as equality of power, or rights, rather than equality of wealth.

6. See XXI, 6 of *The Spirit of Laws*: "The effect of commerce is wealth; the end product of wealth, luxury, that of luxury, the perfection of the arts."

7. Mandeville, *The Fable of the Bees*, 1714, 10, line 12.

8. J. F. Melon, *Essai politique sur le commerce*, in *Collection des économistes et financiers*, Eugene Daire ed. (Paris: Guillaumin, 1847), 809.

9. Jean-Claude Perrot, "Economie politique" and "Les économistes, les philosophes et la population," in J. C. Perrot, *Une histoire intellectuelle de l'économie politique* (Paris: éditions de l'EHESS, 1992), 63-96, 143-94.

10. Jean Bodin, *Les six livres de la république* (Paris, 1583), 878 (VI, 2). For coverage of the main ideas regarding taxation, see *Systèmes économiques et finances publiques*, Richard Bonney, ed. (Paris: PUF, 1996).

11. Cardin Le Bret, *De la souveraineté du roy* (1632).

12. Armand Jean du Plessis, cardinal de Richelieu, *Testament politique* (Paris: 1688),179-80 (Part I, chap. 4).

13. Jean Pottier de la Hestroye, 1698, bibliothèque municipale de Poitiers, MS 548, quoted and translated by Lionel Rothkrug, *Opposition to Louis XIV* (Princeton: Princeton University Press, 1965), 104-5.

14. The comparison can be found in the *Leçon sur la monnaie*, written in 1588 by the Florentine financier Davanzati. See Simone Meyssonnier, *La Balance et l'Horloge. La genèse de la pensée libérale en France au XVIIIe siècle* (Paris: Les éditions de la passion, 1989), 45.

15. Melon, *Essai politique*, 797, 818.

16. François Véron de Forbonnais, *Principes et observations économiques* (Amsterdam: Rey, 1767).

17. Like Sonnenfelds, for example, an Austrian cameralist, and author of *Principes de police* (Vienne, 1765-1776). See R. Bonney, ed., *Systèmes économiques et finances publiques*, 179.

18. Melon, *Essai politique*, chap. 16.

19. *Pensée* 1798 (943) in Pléiade, I, 1430. See also *Pensée*, 1800 (597) and 1801 (828), in Pléiade, I, 1431.

20. "In Europe's present situation," Montesquieu writes in one of his *Pensées*, "the creditors and the debtors of the State are engaged in a perpetual war. The landed proprietors and proprietors of companies are at war with the State's creditors, and the creditors of the State are also at war with themselves because they must pay to themselves a portion of what the State has paid them and what they have paid by means of the taxes that it has levied on them." (*Pensée* 2018 [255], in Pléiade, I, 1509)

21. Quesnay, "Hommes," in *François Quesnay et la physiocratie,* 2 vols. (Paris: INED, 1958), II, 541.

22. Quesnay, "Hommes," 549.

23. Louis Dumont's thesis, argued in *From Mandeville to Marx. The Genesis and Triumph of Economic Ideology* (Chicago: University of Chicago Press, 1977), is that economic thought is modeled on the relationship between man and nature prior to the development of social relations.

24. Turgot, *Discours sur l'histoire universelle* (1751, published in 1808); Rousseau, *Essai sur l'origine des langues*, chapter 9.

25. R. L. Meek, *Social Science and the Ignoble Savage* (Cambridge: Cambridge University Press, 1976).

26. See Bertrand Binoche, *Introduction à De L'esprit des lois* (Paris: PUF, 1998), 327-31.

27. See David Carrithers, "The Enlightenment Science of Society," in *Inventing Human Science*, Christopher Fox, Roy Porter, and Robert Wokler, eds. (Berkeley: University of California Press, 1995), 232-70.

28. He quotes Mandeville (XIX, 8, note) while distinguishing between "political" and "moral vices" (XIX, 11). In a suppressed part of the manuscript he expresses his agreement with Mandeville. See *Pensée* 1978 (1553), in Pléiade, I, 1489.

29. *Pensée* 336 (1694), in Pléiade, II, 1080.

30. John Law, *Mémoires sur les banques présentés à Mgr le duc d'Orléans, régent de France*, premier mémoire, in *Collection des économistes et financiers*, Daire ed., 562.

31. Montesquieu does not explicitly name England here, but one can surmise, with enough certainty, that he is speaking of the English navigation acts (designed to deprive Holland of its commerce) and is clearly indicating that England is the only nation able to successfully adopt such laws.

32. Melon, *Essai politique*, 456.

33. Turgot, *Éloge de Vincent de Gournay* (1759), in *Écrits économiques* (Paris: Calmann-Lévy, 1970), 103.

34. See Rothkrug, *Opposition to Louis XIV*, chapters 4 and 7.

35. The reference to Japan is somewhat surprising, since Japan was not an especially commercial state. Some commentators think that Japan may stand for France.

36. *Pensées* 336 (1694) and 337 (1800), in Pléiade II, 1080-81.

37. *Pensée* 1228 (810), in Pléiade, I, 1306: "it is the spirit of commerce that dominates today."

38. Pierre Daniel Huet, *L'Histoire du commerce et de la navigation des anciens*, 1716. Montesquieu had one of his secretaries take notes on this book (Bordeaux: BM, Ms 2526).

39. About Montesquieu's criticism of the received ideas regarding Rome, see Jean Ehrard, "Rome enfin que je hais," *Storia e ragione*, Alberto Postigliola, ed. (Napoli: Liguori Editore, 1987), 23-32 and Georges Benrekassa, "La position de la romanité dans *L'Esprit des lois*: l'État moderne et le poids de son histoire," *La politique et sa mémoire* (Paris: Payot, 1983), 257-358.

40. Turgot, "Réflexions sur la formation et la distribution des richesses"; "Valeurs et monnaies," in *Écrits économiques* (Paris : Calmann-Lévy, 1970), 121-88, 221-30.

41. See Michel Rosier, "Les marchandises et le signe: Turgot versus Montesquieu" and Maurice Lagueux, "A propos de Montesquieu et de Turgot: Peut-on encore parler de la monnaie comme d'un 'signe'?" in *Cahiers d'économie politique*, 18, *Monnaie métalli-*

que et monnaie bancaire, études présentées par M. Thérèse Boyer-Xamben, Ghislain De-
leplace, et Lucien Gillard (Paris: L'Harmattan, 1990): 81-96; 97-107.

42. In his article, Michel Rosier explains that Turgot contends that money is only a
form of merchandise, a point he is not able to argue completely, and this "analytical failure" leads him to a normative position. Since he cannot explain why money *is* also a
sign, he contends that money *should not* be a sign. Liberal doctrine clung to the money
as merchandise creed, and since this became the prevailing ideology, it explains why
considering money as a sign has been so much out of favor.

43. Melon, *Essai politique*, in *Collection des économistes*, Daire, ed., 802.

44. See Michael Sonenscher, The French Fiscal Deficit (Part I), *History of Political
Thought* 28, no. 2 (Summer 1997): 71-75.

45. This chapter was censured by the Sorbonne.

46. Grotius, *The Laws of War and Peace* (1625), Prolegomenon, §XLV.

47. See *Catalogue* n° 2442; Montesquieu owned the *Détail de la France*, 1695 and
the *Factum de la France* (sent to the *Contrôleur général* in 1705), collected under the title *Testament politique de M. de Vauban. . .* , which had been written by Boisguilbert in
1707, but was published under Vauban's name since he was much the better known figure. See *Pierre de Boisguilbert, ou la naissance de l'économie politique*, 2 vols. (Paris:
INED, 1966), I, 499.

48. Rothkrug, *Opposition to Louis XIV*, 234-98.

49. See comments in Rolando Minuti, "Ambiente naturale e dinamica delle società
politiche: aspetti e tension di un tema di Montesquieu," in *Leggere L'Esprit des lois*, 137-
63.

50. It was beneficial because it initiated an important debate, which enhanced economic and demographic questioning. See Jean-Claude Perrot, "Les économistes, les philosophes et la population," in *Une histoire intellectuelle de l'économie politique*, Perot,
ed., 143-92.

51. Jean-Jacques Rousseau, "L'Influence des climats sur la civilisation," in *Œuvres
complètes*, 5 vols. (Paris: Gallimard, 1966), III, 530.

52. Melon, *Essai politique*, 737.

53. Jean Ehrard, "Individu et Citoyen," in Ehrard, *L'Esprit des mots, Montesquieu en
lui-même et parmi les siens* (Geneva: Droz, 1998), 167.

54. In his Preface to the French edition of the *General Theory of Employment, Interest and Money* cited in the footnote below.

55. J. M. Keynes, *Théorie générale de l'emploi de l'intérêt et de la monnaie* (Paris,
Payot, 1966), 12.

Chapter Nine

Montesquieu on Religion and on the Question of Toleration

Rebecca E. Kingston

Traditional natural law theory developed a picture of social and political order based on a singular notion of human fulfillment. By the seventeenth century, after years of religious conflict, it became apparent to some that this teleological stance could no longer be compelling given the diversity of religious persuasions and ensuing skepticism over what constituted the good life. Against this background, Hugo Grotius and Samuel von Pufendorf, the founders of the modern school of natural law, set out to uncover a set of principles intended to restore peaceful coexistence. The strength of these basic principles, such as the law and the right of self-preservation, was purported to be their relative immunity from theological dispute. They were principles intended to be acceptable to individuals of multiple religious persuasions to reestablish civil order and domestic peace in Europe in the wake of civil wars.[1]

While Grotius and Pufendorf grounded their arguments in theological frameworks, the principles they advanced for the establishment of public order and the advancement of toleration became the foundation for modern liberalism in that the essentially secular understanding of the roots and purposes of political power came to be seen as separate from any purpose of human life disclosed by revelation.[2] This arrangement was intended not only to preserve the political order from the disputes and conflicts associated with the appearance of religious diversity, but also to preserve religion from corruption and from being used solely for political ends.

The modern natural law approach, however, harbored certain ambiguities. On the one hand, in order to foster domestic peace, the sanctity of religion and toleration, public life was seen as devoid of religious justification and sectarian identifications. In this view, religion was relegated to the private sphere. On the other hand, it came to be generally recognized that within the polity, religion could play an important role in promoting public ends, not least the inculcation of civic virtue. The problem, then, was to find a system in which public life would foster the religious life (given its valuable political effects) and yet be seen as independent and fully separate from religion in order to promote toleration and public peace. This ambiguity has led to continued theoretical difficulties as witnessed by ongoing confusion and criticism of the notion of the separation of religion and the state.[3]

In the light of these difficulties, it is useful to return to a moment in the development of modern political thought when toleration was beginning to be advocated as a public virtue. Montesquieu offers us a picture of a thinker whose commitment to values of toleration and individual freedom link him to the development of the liberal tradition, yet who did not adopt a strictly separationist approach in his discussion of the relation between religion and the state. Instead of building a theory of politics on principles distinct from sectarian differences as in the modern natural law approach, Montesquieu constructed a broader social theory in which the ends of religion and politics are reconciled under common principles. By examining Montesquieu's position in the context of his day, we will come to a better understanding of a road not followed in the history of ideas while gaining insight into how one can provide a better account of the interrelatedness of religion and politics than that provided by the separation of church and state while still preserving a commitment to religious diversity and toleration.

Montesquieu lived at a time of intense interest in how best to accommodate concern for the public good and the needs of diverse religious interests. The persecution of French Protestants by the state, culminating in the Revocation of the Edict of Nantes in 1685 denying them all political and civil rights, combined with a practical accommodation of other religious minorities, such as Jews, and the rise of new radical movements within Catholicism itself all served as subjects of commentary. Also, while the French monarch had traditionally been regarded as a defender of the Catholic faith sanctified by God, there was increasing pressure from various parties in the late seventeenth and early eighteenth century to emphasize the king's independence from the church hierarchy. The issues debated in this climate included: the basis of the *right* of secular authority to adjudicate matters of religion, the *means* by which a government can legitimately intervene in matters of religion, and the *limits* to the State's ends of promoting the public good while preserving a certain autonomy for the (dominant) church. By examining Montesquieu's remarks on religion in *The Spirit of Laws* (1748) as in part a working out of these issues, we can build a picture of an early-modern alternative to the views flowing from the modern school of natural law.

In doing so this chapter is divided into three parts. I begin with a discussion of Montesquieu's conception of religion and the relation of religious to political law as he develops it in particular in the first book of *The Spirit of Laws*. I then show how he develops his argument for the independence of religious and political spheres in the context of the eighteenth-century debate concerning the bull *Unigenitus*. In a third section I show how his call for a practical toleration in sectarian debates in France, as expressed in *The Spirit of Laws* and his *Memoir on the Constitution* (1753), provides a unique combination of arguments for toleration.

The Nature and Grounds of Religious Belief in *The Spirit of Laws*

There is no clear scholarly consensus on the meaning of Montesquieu's ideas concerning religious beliefs and institutions. While some have seen in his work a defense of deism, Erastianism, or Machiavellianism, others have seen a clear defense of Christian principles.[4] Interpreters are faced with the challenge of piecing together disconnected and at times inconsistent observations made by Montesquieu in various works and across a long life span. In addition, in a climate of ongoing censorship from both state and church, it may also be an issue whether some observations should be explained more as an expression of prudential irony than as a matter of conviction. Montesquieu's claim in Book XXIV that he wished to bracket questions of the truth or falsity of metaphysical claims and instead focus on the social and political effects of various religions is sometimes interpreted in this light, that is, as a ruse to placate the censors while opening the door for subversion.[5]

   Given these difficulties in interpretation, it is a challenging task to uncover a coherent theory of religion in his work. Some commentators have attempted to reveal Montesquieu's personal religious beliefs through a study of the debates ensuing on the publication of *The Spirit of Laws* and Montesquieu's *Defense of "The Spirit of Laws"*[6] However, Montesquieu's own personal convictions are likely to be a continuous matter of dispute, and focusing on degrees of theological orthodoxy may in fact obfuscate the intended message of his discussions. This chapter will instead focus on the broader issue of how Montesquieu envisions the relation between political and religious power and on his argument for religious toleration. It will show that in *The Spirit of Laws* Montesquieu presents a strong argument for the distinct nature of religious and positive law while at the same time suggesting their ultimate compatibility and indeed rootedness in a common origin. It is this sense of their underlying compatibility that shapes his commitment to toleration.

   At the beginning of *The Spirit of Laws* Montesquieu presents a metaphysics to ground his theory of law. At one level, he recognizes that all beings have their laws, including the divinity, a view which rids the world of all forms of contingency and arbitrariness. According to this view, there is a natural equity or justice which pervades the universe, providing a natural, though non-teleological, order or relationship among things as they exist. Positive law, including political, civil, and religious law, is regarded by Montesquieu as playing a restorative role. The physical world does not contravene its laws. The intelligent world, however, as a condition of its freedom, is subject to error. Seen from this perspective, the moral dictates of philosophy, law and religion are codes designed to restore a basic practice of justice factored into the order of the world at the time of its creation.[7]

Religious law differs from other forms of positive law insofar as its basic tenets, such as belief in a creator and the notion of a duty of worship are set by the divinity. "As an intelligent being he constantly violates the laws God has established. . . . Such a being could, at any time, forget his creator; God has called him back to him by the laws of religion"[8] (I, 1). Still, religious law remains distinct from natural laws governing the material world, as expounded upon by Newton and others, as they share with other forms of positive law this status of *restoring* order and not directly instilling it. Herein lies much of Montesquieu's originality. Narrowly perceived, religion for Montesquieu plays the role of responding to one feature of human behavior, namely the tendency of humans to forget their creator and to neglect the duties associated with this relation. However, insofar as in Montesquieu's system God also acts according to laws to conserve the universe, the laws of religion will indirectly have a relation to the preservation of the whole, but again not as natural law directly establishing order but as a particular form of law meant to respond to tendencies of human behavior. It is this ambiguity in religion as a code of laws geared toward the specific purpose of worship and the ends which it serves in relation to preserving the universe which will allow Montesquieu to recognize the independent sphere religion occupies while asserting that its ends should be compatible with those guiding positive law, morality, and other codes of law.

Still, what is the source or origin of religious law? Montesquieu refers to multiple levels or modes by which religious law is generated. At one level, he subscribes to the view that there is a natural basis for belief in a Creator: "The law, that by impressing upon us the idea of a creator, brings us towards him, is the first of the natural laws in importance, but not in the order of these laws" (I, 2). This natural basis of belief, however, develops in conjunction with the development of speculative powers in the human mind, and religious conceptions therefore will not be the first set of ideas experienced by humankind. This point of view rules out the possibility of some traditional accounts of the state of nature relying on some basic belief in a divinity to guarantee moral rules. Instead, Montesquieu traces the development of human society from the state of nature to organized society without reference to God, owing to the belief that it is only with the development of speculative notions in society that a religious sense could be cultivated.[9] Still, the fact that Montesquieu provides no theological basis for entry into society does not mean that he accepts the Hobbesian alternative of a social order based solely on calculations of rational self-interest. In an interesting way, Montesquieu subtly subverts the natural law tradition by having social existence suddenly appear as a fact of existence. It is in the thought processes put in motion by this social experience that sociality, as a retrospective recognition of the gains achieved in association with others, can provide a grounding for the duties necessary to preserve society, including religious duties. For Montesquieu, then, religion, as an institution serving divine ends though instituted by human effort, stands ultimately accountable to (though not limited by) the demands of sociality as its necessary condition. This allows him to recognize that while religion is governed by certain principles specific to its nature, it must also be judged by its capacity to reinforce the demands of sociality, that is, the natural social condition of human beings and the obligations flowing from this recognition.[10]

Being rooted in sociality, religious movements will develop in conjunction with the general development of the intellectual and cultural life of a society, and the particular qualities of religious association will be shaped by those features. Drawing on Porphyry, Montesquieu states that in earliest times rites were simple and could be performed by all. As society developed, however, and tasks became more specialized and rites became more complex, a priestly class was established and notions of sanctity shaped collective understandings of the specialized places of worship (XXV, 4). In more developed societies, Montesquieu argues, the extent of formality and pomp in the ceremonies of worship has links to the collective values of the community (XXV, 7). In Book XXV, chapter 2 he refers to various cultural motives for religious beliefs and explains how these may affect the strength of our religious convictions, such as how disdain for the primitive nature of idolatry will reinforce identification with more spiritual religions. Varying religious movements will, he asserts, take on qualities particular to the context in which they developed. "When Montezuma persisted in saying that the religion of the Spanish was good for their country and that of Mexico for his own, he was not saying an absurd thing, because in fact the lawmakers were not able to avoid taking into consideration what nature had established before them" (XXIV, 24). Montesquieu recognizes that the rites of religion may be linked to (though not determined by) climate. For example, in warm climates habits of frequent bathing are developed and in turn have been integrated into the practices of Islam and Hinduism. It is because of the cultural rootedness of religion that Montesquieu suggests it is inappropriate to export religion from one country to another (XXIV, 25), masking thereby criticism of the missionary activities of the Catholic Church, particularly in China, which drew the attention of the Vatican censor who called for an amendment to the text. Following this same line of argument, Montesquieu also notes that the division of northern and southern Europe into Protestant and Catholic regions represents an expression of a prior difference in cultural sensibilities between those peoples of the north who have a

strong sense of independence and freedom and those of the south who do not
(XXIV, 5).[11]

Montesquieu does leave some opening for a recognition of revealed religion
in remarking, "Such a being could, at any time, forget his creator; God has called
him back to him by the laws of religion" (I, 1). Still, for the most part, he discusses religion as a cultural artifact whose truths and doctrines are largely fashioned by humans themselves. What, then, is religion exactly for Montesquieu?
From his discussion in Book I it appears that religion is both a type of human association and set of ideas which gives expression to a natural human sentiment
and need to recognize the existence of a divinity and to worship this divinity, a
need which corresponds to a deeper metaphysical truth. Furthermore, this is an
expression which has taken a variety of cultural forms given its rootedness in the
human community. This understanding has caused some commentators to assert
that Montesquieu was a defender of natural religion and a deist, like his friend
David Hume.[12] Montesquieu remarked in a letter to Bishop Warburton subsequent to publishing *The Spirit of Laws*: "natural religion . . . is derived from the
nature of man, which one cannot dispute, and from the internal sentiment of
man, which again one cannot dispute."[13] It is, nonetheless, difficult to prove that
he believed (as deists would) that each established religion expresses a minimal
but adequate set of theological truths discovered through natural religion, a position which would grant all religious expression equal theological legitimacy.[14] In
various passages of *The Spirit of Laws* he does distinguish between 'true' and
'false' religious doctrine in terms of the conventions of his day.[15]

Furthermore, Montesquieu does not always equate religious law with the
rules of basic morality (though he argues they should be compatible), and in this
respect he differs from traditional deists. He notes that religious law requires
unique features; in other words religion develops as a distinct type of human association.[16] For example, while laws should take the form of precepts, religious
law is made to speak to the heart and should, for the most part, take the form of
counsels (XXIV, 7). He goes on to note that religion is more apt to give rules
based on the standard of perfection, a standard which is not attainable by all and
which therefore must not be enforced by immoderate means. He gives the example of celibacy within the Christian tradition, which when imposed by legislative
force only exasperates the legislator and society (XXIV, 7). He states in Book
XXVI that religious laws aim at the goodness of the individual whereas positive
laws have the function of promoting the general good of society. For this reason,
Montesquieu argues, religious law should not be seen as a foundation for civil
law. Thus, "however respectable may be the ideas that spring directly from religion, they should not always serve as the basis for civil laws, because civil laws
have another basis which is the general good of society" (XXVI, 9). Thus he
presents a clear argument for the independence of religious and civil law as
modes of governing conduct.

In addition, Montesquieu remarks that religious law also differs from positive law (*les lois humaines*) in that religion presupposes the unchanging quality of the law. Positive law, in contrast, regulates a variety of human situations and is subject to change according to the changing will of the times. The force of religious laws, Montesquieu observes, comes from the belief which sustains them, whereas positive laws take their force from the fear they inspire (XXVI, 2). These differences allow Montesquieu to argue that religious law and positive law are by their very natures meant to regulate distinct spheres of life, which provides another justification for different forms of jurisdiction and administration.[17] It is not a question of a hierarchical ordering of religious law above positive law, or inspiring other forms of positive law, but rather a matter of two different means to promote the ends of justice.

Thus, in his famous description of the general spirit (*l'esprit général*) Montesquieu notes not only that religion stands as one mode among many of governing behavior, but also that these different modes work to some degree in common toward the same end so that in the event one mode is dominant, others may yield. "Many things govern men: climate, religion, laws, maxims of government, examples of past things, mores, manners; from which a general spirit is formed. In each nation, as one of these causes acts more forcefully, the others yield"(XIX, 4). This notion can be more easily understood in the context of Montesquieu's theory of sociality as shown and with a better understanding of how, in Montesquieu's eyes, religion can work to further the general good. Because the laws of morality, those of religion and positive law all seek to reinstate or restore an order of justice written into the structure of the world, they can be seen as working in some concerted fashion towards the same end. In this sense Montesquieu avoids a conceptual framework which makes them fully separate. Still, the distinctiveness of these forms of law as instruments influencing human behavior ensures their relegation to relatively independent spheres of jurisdiction and hence their susceptibility to conflict in institutional terms.[18]

Montesquieu's *Spirit of Laws* and the Politics of Religion in Early Eighteenth-Century France

What was the significance of this view of religion? By exploring Montesquieu's position as he worked it out in *The Spirit of Laws* against the background of the debate over the Papal decree called *Unigenitus* (also called the 'Constitution'), we will be able to come to a better understanding of the strands of argument he employed. In particular, it may be possible to read Montesquieu's remarks as in part a response to those individuals and groups in France, including the magistrates of the Parlement of Paris, who sought to protect religious freedom (or at least to protect a religious minority from oppression within the church) through increased legislative regulation of the church. Montesquieu's position demonstrates that the argument for distinct spheres for religion and politics united in the king as head of the Gallican Church and state is a more appropriate model, but one which in fact would not serve the cause of absolutism as much as promote political freedom and serve as a check on absolutist rule. His arguments, then, may be read as a form of warning to the magistrates of Paris, who saw in their interference in the ecclesiastical courts the best strategy for protecting the Jansenist cause and for promoting opposition to the absolute power of the king which they saw as favored by monarchical predominance in religious matters.

The accommodation of religion and politics in early-modern France rested on a complex balance of responsibilities with no clear separation of church and state. According to the theory of divine right, the king was held to be directly appointed by and accountable to God. Called the Most Christian King, he was deemed by official doctrine to be a representative of God on earth and participated in the sacredness of the divine through the expectation of healing scrofula by his touch on special calendar days. In addition to his participation in divine qualities he had more specific sectarian ties and duties. His coronation oath included a promise to defend the Catholic Church and clergy (as the first estate of the realm) and to chase heretics from the kingdom. As head of the Gallican Church, the king also exercised the ecclesiastical powers of appointing bishops and abbots as instituted by the Concordat of Bologna (1516.)[19]

While ultramontanism (the doctrine supporting the pope's absolute authority and suggesting that the pope had temporal as well as spiritual power in Catholic nations) enjoyed periods of strong influence in France, the revival of Gallicanism in the late seventeenth century gave rise to a new understanding of church-state relations and raised new areas of dispute in the factional battles characteristic of French politics at this time.[20] In the Gallican articles passed by the Assembly of Clergy in 1682 it was acknowledged that the kings of France, with respect to their temporal government, were to be independent in their exercise of power and not subject to the pope. Furthermore, even in matters spiritual, the pope's decrees, while deemed of primary importance in matters of faith, were not to be judged irreversible unless confirmed by the consent of the Gallican Church.[21] While providing a clear negative to any papal pretensions to influence the monarchy in France, the Gallican articles raised new questions as to who spoke for the church of France and what would be the relative power of spiritual and secular authorities. The move to religious Gallicanism thus raised questions of political Gallicanism. For many years after 1682 different bodies such as the theologians of the Sorbonne, the episcopate, the general assembly of clergy of France, the Parlements, and the king had competing claims over who could regulate or speak for the Gallican Church.[22] Throughout these clashes there also surfaced differing accounts of the nature of the relationship of religious to secular power within France and of the power of secular authority to adjudicate religious disputes.

Disputes between secular and religious authorities were most intense in the ongoing debates concerning the status of Jansenism in France.[23] These debates were born in the seventeenth century, and although the Jansenist order was largely squelched by a royal decree of 1709, the theological debates between Jansenist sympathizers and their Jesuit opponents continued into the 1760s. Pasquier Quesnel's *Réflexions morales sur le Nouveau Testament* (1671) was the early focal point of this long dispute. By 1710 bishops were denouncing this work as heresy, sparking tension with the Archbishop of Paris, Cardinal de Noailles, who was sympathetic to Jansenist ideas. While Noailles took measures against the Jesuits for their support of the bishops' denunciation, the Council of State banned the sale of Quesnel's *Réflexions morales*. By December of 1711, Louis XIVth himself, in a pragmatic bending of Gallican principles to weaken a growing number of Jansenist sympathizers within the political elites, demanded that the pope make a ruling which identified and condemned the errors in Quesnel's work. This was the origin of the papal bull *Unigenitus dei filius* promulgated on 8 September 1713 formally censuring 101 propositions from Quesnel's commentary.[24]

The effects of the bull were felt far into the century, setting off an intricate series of moves and countermoves that came to a head in the political crisis of 1730-33. In the course of the struggles two parties emerged offering differing interpretations of Gallican traditions. Supporters of the papal bull (called *acceptants*) defended the power of the king to enforce the ruling. A strand of Gallicanism had been emerging in the late seventeenth century through the work of such writers as Lebret, de Marca, and Dupuy which recognized the absolute authority of the king as head of the Gallican Church to impose orthodoxy within his kingdom.[25] According to Lebret, the king who was granted power by divine right exercised a monopoly of indivisible sovereignty. "The king belongs to God," he wrote, "and . . . laws belong to the king."[26] Similarly, de Marca in his 1641 treatise *De Concordia sacerdotii et imperii, seu de libertatibus ecclesiae gallicanae* argued that political power came to the king directly and not through the church or society so that the king was not bound by any social contract but was responsible only to God.[27] These arguments gave the crown the prerogative to use its power to enforce religious orthodoxy as defined by the king and his advisors, along with its longstanding power to nominate ecclesiastics.[28]

Alongside this support for the absolutist power of the king, however, the *acceptants*' position also rested on an argument for separate and protected spheres for church and state. In particular, the *acceptants* stressed that ecclesiastical tribunals were to be essentially self-regulating and that their decisions were unappealable to the Parlements. This was a call for the careful restriction of use of the famous *appel comme d'abus*, the means by which recalcitrant clergy could appeal the rulings of their ecclesiastical superiors by appealing to secular authorities.[29] In 1732 the king prohibited all interference by the civil courts in church matters. All alleged ecclesiastical abuses were to be referred to the Council of State.[30] Thus, the *acceptants*' position carried with it a separationist argument, in the sense of keeping the civil courts separate from the ecclesiastical jurisdiction,

in the service of what was largely a defense of the modern monarchical understanding of absolutist government, with a strong role for princely prerogative.
The union of church and state in the view of the *acceptants* could only be put
into effect by the king himself, the sole authority to proclaim the bull a law of
both church and state, as Louis XV proceeded to do in 1730.

In contrast, the *appellants*, so-called because of their support for the formal
appeal of the *Unigenitus* made by four bishops in the spring of 1717 to a General
Council of the Church, defended the right of the Parlements to serve as a court
of appeal for lower clergy opposing the bull and its sanctions imposed by the ecclesiastical hierarchy.[31] In the name of political liberty writers such as LePaige
expounded constitutionalist theories of the Parlements dating back to the sixteenth century in order to criticize the imposition of the bull by the king as an act
of despotism.[32] In religious terms, the *appellants* perceived the defenders of the
monarch's position on *Unigenitus* as ultramontanist, particularly since in its 91st
proposition the bull called for the condemnation of Quesnel's notion that "fear of
an unjust excommunication ought never to deter us from doing our duty." The
bull's position could, it was argued, bolster the power of the pope in relation to
the king and Parlement as well as to the Gallican Church.

The *appellants* saw themselves as the true Gallicans in their appeal to the
body of the church as the sole legitimate ecclesiastical legislative institution
within France. Both La Borde and Le Gros published treatises after the papal
declaration arguing in the tradition of the sixteenth century Sorbonne con-
ciliarists that the legitimate basis of spiritual authority lay in the congregation of
the faithful, both lay and cleric, and not in the church hierarchy.[33] In political
terms, the *appellants* saw that, in the immediate struggle against the bull, the
Parlement of Paris served as a legitimate site of appeal to protect the lower
clergy against the Papal order. Fundamentally, then, the *appellants* defended the
possibility of civil intervention in religious matters. The *appellants* argued that
temporal power was superior to spiritual power and that it should be used to
regulate disputes within the church, though not to independently generate doctrine.[34] These positions as articulated during the crisis of the 1730s became the
standard set of arguments articulated in the dispute which continued on into mid-
century and to which Montesquieu would offer his own solution.[35]

Montesquieu's remarks in the *Persian Letters* show that at an early stage in
the dispute he had no clear allegiance to either party. While referring to religion
in general often in the work, he refers explicitly to the debate over the *Unigenitus* only in letters XXIV and CI. Through the voice of Rica, he portrays the imposition of the bull as a somewhat arbitrary act of papal authority, an act which
was resisted by increasingly large numbers, many of them women who were often more sympathetic to Jansenist theology. Through Usbek, he draws a satirical
picture of a party to the dispute who despite his learned facade, is unable to provide a reasoned and understandable defense of his position. Neither reference
demonstrates clear support for one position over the other. Instead, Montesquieu

mocks the conduct of all the parties involved.

Montesquieu's interest in the debates over Jansenism and the bull *Unigenitus* did not wane after the publication of the *Persian Letters*. His theological sympathies seemed to lie more with the Jesuits than with the Jansenists. As he states in his *Pensées*: "the Jesuits support a good cause, Molinism, by unfortunate means" and "Jansenists would deprive us of all our pleasures, except that of scratching ourselves."[36] He is skeptical of the claims of the *convulsionnaires* and of the doctrine of predestination espoused by the Jansenists.[37] On the other hand, he is critical of some of the methods used on both sides of the debate. He criticizes defenders of the bull who called for the exile of *appellant* doctors of the Sorbonne since he believed force would not be an effective means for bringing about a change of opinion. Still, he also recognizes that the arguments and strategies used to promote Gallican liberty could in themselves backfire and leave the church even more amenable to political control, as the doctrine of Gallicanism could easily be put to the service of absolutism.[38] In writing the *Memoir on the Constitution*, Montesquieu made the recommendation to the Crown and to the Parlement of Paris that the bull be accepted as a law of state, but that the king, as a show of tolerance, not enforce it with any vigor. A reading of passages from writings prior to the *Memoir* offers important clues as to the deeper justification for this stance.

On the basis of the notion previously discussed of how religion, for Montesquieu, works independently but in conjunction with other modes of regulating human conduct to promote the prior ends of sociality, he develops a justification for an independent institutional expression of religion. As we will see, he argues for this in two ways. First, he points out that an examination of political and social reality reveals that such an independence clearly exists, even in the most corrupt of regimes. Second, he argues that the consequences of allowing a merger of political and religious spheres would be destructive of the very principles and ends of political community.

The basis for his first argument can be traced back to some of his earliest writings. In his unfinished *Treatise on Duties* Montesquieu argues against *raison d'état* theorists by showing that political authority is not boundless but always constrained by contextual factors.[39] In his *Considerations* he develops this point further. In chapter 22 in particular he argues that political authority rests on a general spirit, here regarded by Montesquieu as distinct from the laws.[40] This is used specifically to argue against those Roman rulers who worked to merge religion and politics. Montesquieu thereby uses the idea of the general spirit to argue for separate political and religious jurisdictions as a means of constraint on political leaders.

In *The Spirit of Laws*, Montesquieu no longer refers to a separation of religion and politics and instead refers to the natural independent jurisdiction of the church which he sees in the structure of the monarchical regime. "In a monarchy if you abolish the prerogatives of the lords, clergy, nobility and towns, you will soon have either a popular state or a despotic state" (II, 4). He goes on to remark how in France the royal courts have been progressively encroaching on the jurisdiction of the ecclesiastical courts. For Montesquieu, such a development threatens the essential nature of the monarchical constitution. He argues for the need to clearly establish the lines of jurisdiction of the ecclesiastical courts in order to express in administrative terms the intrinsic independence of the religious realm.[41] This can easily be read as a critique of the position of the *appellants* in their call for the expansion of the jurisdiction of the Parlement in allowing them to hear appeals from ecclesiastical courts and adjudicate internal disputes of the church. This call for an independent jurisdiction is distinct, however, from a call for the separation of church and state. For Montesquieu, independent jurisdiction implies that churches will always be subjected to justified political regulation if their actions are clear violations of the demands of sociality.

Religion also enjoys a sphere of independence in despotism, according to Montesquieu, though it is recognized as having a less strongly entrenched institutional basis. He notes that a despot will seek to concentrate all power in his own hands and may attempt to dictate religious law. Still, the texts and traditions of the religion will continue to exert a certain power and will guarantee its identity and continuity. "The king of Persia," he states, "is the leader of the religion, but the Koran regulates the religion: the emperor of China is the sovereign pontiff, but there are books, which are in everyone's hands, and to which he must himself conform. In vain did an emperor want to abolish them; they triumphed over tyranny" (XXV, 8).[42] Even in despotism religion carries some independence from political power. In despotic states religion is the one institution which expresses a certain permanence and continuity and therefore often takes on added importance (II, 4). It is this continued independence of religion in despotic states which allows Montesquieu to place great faith in its ability to contain the will of the despotic prince to some degree, though it may also play the role of increasing the deference of subjects to their ruler.[43] By these remarks Montesquieu distinguishes himself clearly from Machiavelli who regarded religion as a potential and highly effective tool in the hands of rulers to mold social values.[44] Montesquieu regards religion not merely as a set of doctrines to be manipulated, but as a tradition with a history and a following which takes on a reality independent of political power and which may serve to limit that power.

In his second line of argument for a certain institutional independence of the church, Montesquieu shows how a merger of the two spheres of politics and religion would be destructive and would undermine the ends of political community. He advocates the avoidance of penal laws in matters of religion (XXV, 12). He recognizes that there are religious offenses which may contravene religious law, but he argues that those guilty should not be subjected to the penalties of civil law for such acts, but should suffer only the misfortunes allotted by religion itself, such as excommunication and condemnation by the church (XII, 4). [45] The independence of religion as a set of beliefs and practices dictates that the civil magistrate has no legitimate role in seeking to avenge injuries done to the divinity, unless the religious offenses have negative repercussions on public tranquillity or security.[46] Montesquieu is arguing that given the unique quality of religious law, the relinquishing of policing functions to civil courts would have undesirable consequences in that it would open to the magistrate an area of competency which is only fully known by God and therefore open the door to arbitrary judgements which could undermine the principles for which civil authority was established. In other words, one consequence of the merger of religion and politics in matters of penal law would be the corrupting of the political sphere.

In addition, the merging of ecclesiastical and political judgements for crimes of sacrilege would create, according to Montesquieu, the potential for ongoing cycles of vengeance and counter-vengeance corrupting society and undermining the ends of order and peace for which political community was established. The dynamic of corruption is rooted in the fact that by such actions, the state would be overstepping its purpose to judge humans as they are and not according to the laws of perfection.[47] In fact, as Montesquieu sees it, it is the very purpose of human reason to be able to discern the qualitative differences among the codes governing human life and to know when each should apply.

> Men are governed by diverse kinds of law (*lois*); by natural law (*le droit naturel*); by divine law (*le droit divin*), which is that of religion; by ecclesiastical law (*le droit ecclesiastique*), otherwise called canon law, which is that of the policing of the religion; by international law (*le droit des gens*) . . . ; by general law (*le droit politique général*)...; by constitutional law (*le droit politique particulier*) . . .; by the law of conquest (*le droit de conquête*). . . ; by civil law (*le droit civil*)...; finally by domestic law (*le droit domestique*).
>
> There are, therefore, different orders of law, and the sublimity of human reason consists in knowing well to which of these orders the things one must rule on relate principally, and in not putting confusion into the principles that should govern men (XXVI, 1).

In spite of these arguments for the independence of the religious realm from the civil, Montesquieu does not call for a complete separation of the two spheres. As we have seen, the very way in which he conceptualizes the grounds of religion as flowing from the prior fact of sociality suggests a more complex understanding acknowledging the interconnectedness of all forms of law governing human conduct. While religion and politics are seen to work in independent spheres with corresponding institutions, Montesquieu does not see the ends toward which these institutions strive as parallel to a division between private and public, but as complementary public ends. The central question then, both for the interpretation of Montesquieu and for the subsequent history of liberalism, is how he conceptualizes their interconnectedness.

Montesquieu mentions explicitly that his interest lies in seeking what unites religion and politics.[48] However, it is important to recognize that Montesquieu analyzes religion as a cultural artifact comprised of two important elements: doctrine or dogma and an institutional structure through which that doctrine is discussed, interpreted and applied. As he states in Book XXIV, chapter 19: "It is not enough for a religion to establish a doctrine; it must also direct it." Thus, it is not by looking at beliefs alone that one can arrive at an adequate understanding of a religion's public role. One must also come to an understanding of how those beliefs have been interpreted by various churches and the role the church leadership has played in applying them to the lives of the believers. He notes for example that both the Calvinist and Lutheran sects could see themselves as the most perfect, the Calvinists appealing to their strict adherence to the words of Christ and the Lutherans appealing to their strict adherence to the examples of the apostles (XXIV, 5). In the chapter where he first raises this distinction explicitly, he is particularly concerned with the "horrible consequences" which he argues Taoism and Buddhism have spawned owing to their interpretation of the doctrine of the immortality of the soul.[49] He feels that in both, concerns and duties of the present life may come to be ignored or overridden by religious concerns.

By what standard does Montesquieu judge these consequences? He states clearly in his discussion of religion in Books XXIV and XXV of *The Spirit of Laws* that he is concerned largely with the social, political, and economic effects of various religions rather than the truth or falsity of their metaphysical claims, though he does not deny that one can judge these claims.[50] Although controversial in the eyes of the church censors, this stance is grounded in Montesquieu's recognition that since the ends of sociality are prior to the institution of religion, ends of the society can serve as one legitimate measure of the appropriateness of the interpretation of a given religious doctrine.

Montesquieu recognizes that at a basic level religion may have an important impact on the material development of a society.[51] At one level this relates to meeting the basic needs of citizens. According to Montesquieu, religion should respect those needs. He notes that the religious practices of the Abyssians with a fasting period of fifty days left them unable to defend themselves suitably against their Turkish enemies (XXVI, 7), and argues that the demands of religion should not impede the right of self-preservation. This offers a hint of the possibility for secular power to override religious prescription, but only in the circumstance where the basic dictates of sociality are threatened. In addition, Montesquieu notes that religious leaders when seeking to order days of rest for reasons of religious commemoration must give greater consideration to the needs of the people for whom they are legislating than to their sense of the need to worship (XXIV, 23). Thus, in matters relating to meeting the basic needs of citizens, Montesquieu gives an unequivocal argument for their priority over the dogma and direction of a religious group.

Moral law is another type of dictate governing human behavior whose rules may at times conflict with those counsels advanced by religion. At one level, Montesquieu argues that the basic principles of religion should provide strong support for general laws of morality, though religion is not the grounding for those laws. "In a country where one has the misfortune of having a religion not revealed by God, it is always necessary that it be consistent with morality; because religion, even when false, is the best guarantee that man can have of the integrity of man" (XXIV, 8). It is on this basis that he develops his criticisms of Bayle's paradox that it is better to be an atheist than an idolater. Montesquieu argues that in general, though not always, a belief in God or gods serves as a check on our impulses and encourages performance of social virtues. He takes particular note of the manner in which religious belief can act as a force to restrain overbearing princes.[52] He also remarks, however, that dogma can be interpreted by religious leaders in ways that conflict with morality. His main target here is the doctrine of reincarnation in Hinduism, which through its rebuke of bloodletting, encouraged low levels of violent crime and bolstered the precepts of moral law, but was also linked to the practice of *sati* and thereby supported wanton sacrifice (XXIV, 21). In contrast, Montesquieu heaps lavish praise on the Jesuits of Paraguay who in their republican experiment were able to show for the first time in the Americas how religion could be rightly joined with the ends of humanity.[53]

At still another level, that of a particular society where a religion finds itself, Montesquieu shows how religion can serve to bolster public ends. It is from this perspective that he is able to praise Stoicism so highly. "Born for society, they all believed that their destiny was to work for it. It was less burdensome as their reward was all within themselves; happy through their philosophy alone, it seemed that solely the happiness of others could increase their own" (XXIV, 10). It is also in this regard that he praises Christianity. He argues (in anti-Augustinian fashion) that the Christian tenet of brotherly love should be interpreted to imply that Christians should work on perfecting their political and civil laws as this is the highest form of concern for others possible.[54] He argues again against Bayle stating that Christianity can easily be reconciled with earthly ends and that, as citizens, Christians would constitute a vibrant and active republic.[55]

Clearly, Montesquieu sees that religious law can in certain circumstances serve the very same purpose or end as civil law. He cites the example of the early Greeks who lived without any organized civil society but whose religious laws served to provide effective sanctions against those guilty of murder (XXIV, 18). He also shows how in some societies marked by civil disorder because of war, religion brought about a cessation of hostilities so that the people could meet their basic needs and maintain a basic sense of community.[56] In the same way, the religion of the Chinese, according to Montesquieu, mixes with the maxims of morality and law to promote a uniform code of behavior (XIX, 17). In Confucianism, civil, religious, and moral laws all combine to reinforce order and respect for elders (XIX, 19). He also argues that in circumstances where the climate leads citizens to be passive, both religion and civil laws should work to counteract such effects (XIV, 5 and 6).

In fact, Montesquieu goes so far as to suggest that the forming of good citizens is the principal object of religion and civil law, noting that when one of these influences strays from this end, the others should make up for it.[57] For this reason, he is very critical of religious dogma which weakens the force of civil law. He cites the case of the belief in India that having your cremated ashes thrown into the Ganges will absolve you from your evil acts. Montesquieu believed that such a dogma encourages licentiousness and detachment from the demands of civil law: "Men who believe in the certainty of rewards in the next life are beyond the power of the legislator; they will have too much scorn for death" (XXIV, 14).

He uses a similar principle to criticize an overly contemplative life. He argues that excessive religious contemplation may distract individuals from the basic demands of life including self-preservation, nourishment, and an active life in society.[58] He argues that such tendencies in religion can be encouraged by a history of harsh government. While overtly criticizing the practices of Islam in this regard, he is also obviously using this as a foil to criticize the contemplative monastic orders of his day. He had already criticized the excessive inactivity of monastic life in Asia and India in his discussion of climate (XIV, 7). Not surprisingly, these passages were highlighted by the Vatican censor and also censored by the Sorbonne in 1752.[59]

In a more subtle way, Montesquieu criticizes monastic principles of unquestioning obedience and renunciation since these rules, depending on the nature of the religious leadership, could be used to subvert the ends religion should serve. He does this by praising the practices of the ancient Essenes: "The Essenes took an oath to be just towards men; to do no harm to anyone, even by command, to hate unjust men; to keep faith with everyone; to rule with modesty; to always take the side of truth; and to reject all illicit gain" (XXIV, 9).[60] Similarly, in another passage, he praises Henry VIII of England for undermining the monastic system which encouraged laziness in the upper classes and was an impediment to the development of a spirit of commerce and industry (XXIII, 29).[61]

So at one level the independence of the religious jurisdiction from that of the state in Montesquieu's eyes does not imply strict separation but rather a complementarity of means to achieve certain shared ends. The contemporary doctrine of the separation of church and state as developed from its origins in natural law theory holds that religion is a matter for the private sphere and has no claims on the ordering and basic principles of public life. While the contemporary doctrine may hold that both religion and law may play a role in making men moral and good, it does not define religion in these terms nor see its ends as grounded in the same principles that justify the state. In contrast, for Montesquieu, religion is not in essence a matter of private belief, but an alternative form of public regulation. Insofar as religion is a cultural artifact grounded in the prior demands of sociality, it should include a commitment to a beneficial ordering of society. This end should be followed in conjunction with the goals of worship and the perfection of humankind which are particular to religion and which provide the grounds for its status as an independent institution. Some religious practices may indeed be subject to regulation in view of those public ends.

Nonetheless, Montesquieu recognizes that religion can also shape the very political tradition within which it operates as an independent player. He notes for example that in its Biblical advocacy of moderation the Christian religion may be less inclined to a culture of despotism than a religious doctrine advocating vengeance. He argues that the presence of Christianity in Ethiopia allowed the political system to overcome the factors favorable to despotism and establish moderate government. In contrast, he argues that Islam, by advocating polygamy, may encourage the isolation of its rulers from the general population, generate a false sense of invincibility among those rulers, and thereby encourage immoderate and cruel behavior (XXIV, 3). Furthermore he makes the claim that a tradition of moderate behavior by Christian rulers has generated public recognition of the doctrines of constitutionalism and international law serving the ends of human sociality.[62] He recognizes that these principles have not always been followed in the history of Christian nations, but suggests that codes of international law have been generated as a result. In an earlier book he had also observed that Christianity had served to hasten the abolition of slavery in Europe (XV, 8). He is showing therefore that while religion may and should be shaped by the demands of sociality, some religions, through their doctrine and/or leadership, may advance those ends more successfully than others. Some in fact may do so in ways which in turn shape the political traditions of that nation.

He also recognizes the possibility of the opposite dynamic, however, namely that the political leader may take advantage of existing religious doctrine to advance certain public ends. As he states in Book VI: "A wise legislator would have sought to lead men's spirits back by a just balance of punishments and rewards; by maxims of philosophy, morality and religion" (VI, 13). In other words, religion is used as one instrument among others to advance public goods. Unlike Numa, as portrayed by Machiavelli in *The Discourses*, the legislator here does not found or mold religion to serve public ends, but rather uses the independent dynamic of religion to the state's own advantage. It is this stance that helps to explain why Montesquieu can consider religion both as a support for but also as a limit on political power. Religion can serve as a strong barrier, one of the most efficacious of associations, against an overzealous political leader.

We find, then, that, while advocating the independence of religion from politics, Montesquieu does not advocate the separation of religion and politics based on a distinction between private and public spheres. He recognizes that religious law is in essence different from civil law in that it focuses on worship of a higher being and espouses values of human perfection, rather than the more immediate and prosaic demands of order and security. Still, these differences do not render religion a private and civicly neutral activity, for religion both issues from basic human sociality, which also forms a grounding for political life, and has an impact on the quality of collective life. In consequence, he clearly is aware of the manner in which religion may influence politics and the manner in which politics may be justified in regulating religion.

In the context of the debate over *Unigenitus*, the significance of the argument is that Montesquieu shows why the *appellants* side is misguided in defending formal recourse to the Paris Parlement to intervene in matters of dispute over religious doctrine in order to advance the cause of political and civil liberty. To prevent civil authorities from usurping control in unjustified spheres and to preserve the independence of religious law, unless the matter concerns a violation of basic human needs, the civil authority is to be awarded no role in enforcing doctrine through the imposition of penal sanctions. Montesquieu thus accepts the *acceptants* notion of the carefully guarded independence of the ecclesiastical jurisdiction. In fact, he develops a theoretical justification for why the political realm must respect the independence of the religious realm and in what limited circumstances state action in the realm of religious matters is justified. However, Montesquieu differs from the *acceptants* by arguing that it is precisely through this recognition that the ends of political and civil liberty will be best promoted. The *appellants* argued in part that the intervention of the civil courts was needed in order to protect minorities within the church from persecution and that certain procedures should be followed in ecclesiastical decision making to make decisions legitimate. Montesquieu believed, however, that the protection of religious minorities can best be achieved, not by an acceptance of a basic right of intervention, as this was more likely to lead to despotism, but by political leadership promoting a public commitment to toleration. Political authorities, while given license to intervene in religious matters if sectarian actions or doctrines violate basic human needs, must also recognize the legitimacy of established religious groups in the community. This commitment to religious pluralism in Montesquieu's work is protected and promoted precisely through a policy of nonintervention. To argue for the state's active regulation of ecclesiastical courts would threaten to undermine that pluralism which provides a foundation for liberty and an associational check against excessive concentration of power.

Toleration

How then is this spirit of toleration achieved? In the early eighteenth century there existed three dominant lines of argument in favor of toleration: the *politique*, the skeptical, and the inner conscience arguments.[63] The first, which can be traced to various Renaissance theorists, including Bodin, held that in the interests of social peace and the consolidation of power in the state, the ruler should avoid impinging on religious matters and instead tolerate sectarian diversity.[64] From this perspective, toleration was judged to be an effective means to a political end grounded in an overriding need for internal peace. The skeptical argument held that because one cannot be certain about the correct means to salvation, one need be tolerant because of the impossibility of imposing any one sure path. The third line of argument, most directly associated with Locke, asserts that the state and all legal instruments are by nature ineffective in shaping the inner conscience.[65] Toleration is not deemed a means to a prescribed political end, but a necessity flowing from the nature of the conscience itself. Stemming from this position is the juridical point that it is impossible for people to alienate to the state the power to dictate religious belief.[66] Still, while the state cannot determine the content of an inner creed, reasons of public utility do have a place in this argument. Because Locke founds the sanctity of public order on a binding contract guaranteed by divine oath he calls for a policy of state intolerance toward atheists, who cannot be trusted for oaths they would make, and toward Roman Catholics, whose deeper religious allegiances to Rome would undermine the ability of the state to have sovereign sway over its population.

Montesquieu does not fully accept any of these arguments. He had already taken on the *politiques* in his early writings and he was highly critical of maxims bolstering central authority. Nor was he a true skeptic. While he recognized that various sets of religious beliefs were better suited to different cultural contexts, he also distinguished between true and false religions. In addition, the alliance between religious skepticism and toleration is an approach which he associates most clearly with the Orient, that is with regimes identified as despotic (XXV, 15). Montesquieu was aware that toleration based on skepticism and possible indifference may diminish the power of religion as a check on government. Finally he was too aware of how the conscience is fashioned by contextual features to espouse the Lockean argument fully. His dilemma was to construct an argument for toleration which would fortify religion as an associational check on government, while providing a political check on religion to avoid the intolerance which could issue from excessive church power, all in the context of the French state where the establishment of the Roman Catholic Church could not be questioned with impunity.

According to Montesquieu, there are two obvious levels at which toleration can be exercised. On an international level it is clear that he espouses respect for the differing religious systems of other countries as themselves issuing from a complex array of cultural factors. This is rooted in his more basic view of the means by which religious belief is developed. Toleration also occurs within a country, but as Montesquieu implies, a policy of toleration can be compatible with an established church since toleration is not approval [("there is a great difference between tolerating a religion and approving of it" (XXV, 9).][67]

Early in his career, in letter 85 of the *Persian Letters*, Montesquieu offers a defense of toleration contending that toleration is a means by which the social utility of religion can be maximized. In a clear allusion to the experience of the

Huguenots and Jews in France, he notes that religious minorities, given their limited opportunities for advancement, are often very productive and hardworking. He makes the added argument that religion contains precepts useful to society and that the zeal with which these precepts are pursued can in fact be enhanced by competing sects. In this early work, then, Montesquieu makes the argument for a broadly tolerant community. He makes the further point that it is not the diversity of religious sects but rather the spirit of intolerance which has been a major cause of war in Europe.

In *The Spirit of Laws* Montesquieu's defense of toleration is again rooted in what he sees as the prior ends of sociality, but he advances the argument in a more developed way which allows him to place limits on the practice of toleration justified through sociality. In Book XXV, chapter 9 he notes that for reasons of social order not only should the government tolerate existing religious sects, but the government must also ensure that those sects tolerate one another. His most forceful statement in favor of toleration comes in Book XXV, chapter 13 in the form of a letter of remonstration by a Jew sentenced to death by the Spanish inquisition. Here Montesquieu provides an array of arguments against intolerance, including the ineffectiveness of promoting faith with force, its unreasonableness as a means to deal with ignorance, and its hypocrisy given Western criticisms of Eastern persecutions. He suggests that a practice of tolerance is more consonant with Christian values and with the basic values of humanity and justice. He concludes by noting that toleration is also more in tune with the spirit of the age in which there is greater recognition of the rights of humanity. At this point, then, Montesquieu offers a somewhat eclectic defense of toleration. Still, all these arguments are rooted in the more general notion that religious diversity is not a threat and that toleration in fact may be more conducive to the good of the society. It flows from his earlier arguments that religion must be seen as reinforcing basic social goods.

Despite these arguments for toleration, in discussing the means by which civil authorities regulate such a policy, Montesquieu advocates an idea of toleration limited by the very ends which justify it. The limits in his notion flow largely from the fact that both religion and politics, as we have seen, are grounded in the prior ends of sociality, ends which determine what can be deemed acceptable in both. First, he argues that political authorities may have a right to decide what new religions can be established in the country. He argues in Book XXV, chapter 10 that the state, if able to control the establishment of religions in a country, should not allow the introduction of any new religions. The reason for this is that a religion which is seeking to establish itself as a strong presence in another country is likely to be intolerant itself. In other words, intolerance of suspected intolerance is acceptable in the interest of promoting basic social values which should guide both religion and politics.

With regard to the regulation of already existing religious groups, fundamental human needs for life, shelter, and liberty must be respected and promoted.

Civil authorities may have reason to intervene in the event that some of these basic needs are being denied by a religious community. The justification for doing so would lie in the fact that religion is seen by Montesquieu as fulfilling a purpose issuing from those needs being denied and from basic human sociality. In addition, the fact that religion is seen as constituted by both a set of beliefs and by religious leaders leads one to note the possibility of corruption, or a falling away from the basic counsels and purposes of religion as a result of human error. As he states in Book XXIV: "The truest and holiest doctrines can have terrible consequences when they are not allied with the principles of society; and, in contrast, the most false doctrines can have admirable consequences, when they have been linked to those same principles" (XXIV, 19). This possibility of corruption establishes a condition for legislative intervention in these primordial matters, though Montesquieu, as we have seen, does limit what the state can do. For example, he proscribes the imposition of civil penalties for religious crimes. Furthermore, he notes that the state, while allowing the policing of incoming sects, must tolerate them once they are established in the country (XXV, 10).[68] More importantly, his reasoning justifying possible intervention focuses on particular practices or rites which may have detrimental consequences. Nowhere does he suggest, as Locke did, that whole sects or groups, such as atheists and Roman Catholics, ought not to be tolerated in principle.[69] This stems in part from Montesquieu's recognition of the social benefits which all forms of religious belief can bring.

For Montesquieu, it is not enough that the state approve the existence of competing sects if already in existence. It is also important that the state invoke regulations forcing the various religious communities and individual citizens to tolerate each other (XXV, 9). A policy of political toleration would be meaningless in its objective to promote social peace without a realistic means of promoting civil toleration. "It is . . . useful that the laws demand of these various religions, not only that they do not trouble the State, but also that they do not trouble each other" (XXV, 9). This might also imply advocacy of toleration for sectarianism within the religious communities themselves, that is, a suggestion for toleration of Jansenism within the ecclesiastical establishment of France. Montesquieu, then, provides an argument for toleration which is not absolute, but which demands that both the state and religion conform to more fundamental principles, such as self-preservation, and that they promote the general laws of morality.

By these arguments, then, Montesquieu builds a theory of toleration which limits both the state and religion, while still respecting the established relation between the state and the Roman Catholic Church within France. In this way he hoped to overcome the weaknesses of the dominant arguments for toleration in the eighteenth century.

These themes were carried over into Montesquieu's fullest statement on the Jansenist question, his *Memoir on the Constitution,* written as a policy proposal for the king five years after the publication of *The Spirit of Laws*.[70] Montesquieu begins this work by distinguishing between "external toleration" and "internal toleration." By external toleration he means permitting the religious practice and public presence of rites and systems of belief outside the dominant culture with no implication of approval of the religious beliefs being expressed. By internal toleration he means the acceptance and approval of other belief systems in one's own judgement. Montesquieu argues that part of the unrest of the times is rooted in an inability to apply this distinction.

External toleration for Montesquieu involves no clear challenge to a religious group's system of belief and therefore is judged to be more easily attainable. It is based on the need for public peace. In contrast, internal toleration involves a degree of acceptance of the other as a valid expression of religious sentiment, a disposition he felt was not accessible to believers of all sects. "How can the Roman Catholic religion approve of something," he states, "which according to its principles would exclude others from salvation?"[71] He concludes that internal toleration cannot and should not be a goal of public policy.

He notes that the state policy of tolerating the practices of diverse sects, for the sake of public order, does not carry with it the demand that all citizens also practice internal toleration. External toleration is well suited to the needs of French Catholics. "Catholic subjects who live in a state under the laws of external toleration cannot thereby be suspected, nor suspect themselves, to have that internal toleration disapproved of by the Catholic religion."[72] The justification for limiting toleration to its external form is that politics cannot afford to be governed by theology, because it must respond primarily to those distinct principles by which all governments are established. By this line of reasoning Montesquieu seeks to usher in a regime of greater toleration not only for Jansenists, but also for Calvinists and Jews, while not denying or downplaying the distinctly Roman Catholic nature of the monarchy.

While his focus on public order may liken the argument to that of the *politiques*, Montesquieu differs from this line of thinking by devising a broader framework which sees toleration and respect for established religious belief as constitutive and not merely instrumental to that end. In addition, he pays greater attention to the sanctity of the king's conscience. Montesquieu argues that the disputes of theologians or the conflicts among various religious interests should not have direct implications for the state of the king's conscience. By stressing the importance of the inner conscience of the king for his relationship to God, Montesquieu can minimize the degree to which certain public acts, such as granting of toleration, have an impact on that relationship. "Although our kings, up to the revocation of the Edict of Nantes, granted external toleration to the Huguenots, one cannot say that they were not very good Catholics, nor that they had internal toleration for the Huguenots."[73] In this way, the king is freed from the tight control and advocacy pressures of religious elites in certain matters, but still held by the traditional bridle of religion. By this argument, Montesquieu seeks both to hold the king apart from the direct influence of religious elites and the Catholic hierarchy while at the same time not denying the traditional Catholic nature of the monarchy. This strategy preserves religious precepts as an important check on his authority while assuming that he continued to regard the king as a valued head of the Gallican Church.

As a practical response to the questions posed by Jansenism, then, Montesquieu recommends that the king declare *Unigenitus* the policy of the kingdom while curbing all further discussion of the matter, under threat of prosecution. It was a way for the king to uphold the legality of the bull (and thereby reaffirm his leading role in the French Church) while in reality inhibiting the higher clergy from enforcing it. Montesquieu believes this to be the best way to advance public tranquillity and to silence the disputes.

Conclusion

Montesquieu did not support the separation of church and state. He could not deny the reality of the dominance of the Catholic Church within France and its ties to the monarchy. In fact, he saw that tie as an important facet of liberty insofar as religion worked as a constraint on the impulses of rulers overly zealous for power and control. Thus, religion had a public role to play. Still, within these bounds, he sought to devise a theory which also would allow for religious diversity and toleration. His framework which grounded both religion and politics in the prior ends dictated by human sociality allowed him to construct a theory in which the ends of religion and politics were seen as ultimately compatible, even if distinct. This helped to fashion his argument for toleration since he could argue that quite different religious practices can all contribute in their own way to the overall social good.

It may be seen as a naive argument. Still, Montesquieu is well aware of the complexities involved since conviction of the integrity and truthfulness of one's own beliefs may at times conflict with the embracing of any other. For this reason he stresses that toleration is something different from approval. It is a practice of acceptance which for him does not thereby forfeit judgement or require a hearty endorsement of the other in their difference.

While we may hesitate at what appears to be the limited extent of toleration as compared to modern practices, we can still admire the broader framework within which this argument is couched. In particular, Montesquieu offers a way of reconceptualizing the relation between religion and politics in terms of shared ends. While this may run counter to modern democratic intuitions of the need for a separation of religion and politics, as themselves derived from completely distinct principles, a theory with a deeper sense of their interrelatedness may be better equipped to offer some directions in those occasions when their interests clearly overlap and where some guidance is needed.

Notes

I would like to thank the contributors to this volume, and especially David Carrithers, for their helpful comments on an earlier version of this chapter.

1. For this interpretation of the modern natural law tradition I draw from the arguments of Richard Tuck. See in particular his "The 'Modern' Theory of Natural Law," in *The Languages of Political Theory in Early-Modern Europe*, Anthony Pagden, ed. (Cambridge: Cambridge University Press, 1987), 99-119 and *Philosophy and Government 1572-1651* (Cambridge: Cambridge University Press, 1993). For a view of this dynamic in Grotius see Timothy Shah, "Making the World Safe for Liberalism: The Moralization of Christianity and the Roots of Liberal Public Reason in Hugo Grotius (1583-1645)," presented at the annual meeting of the American Political Science Association in Washington, D.C., August 1997.

2. This interpretation has nonetheless been challenged. Eldon Eisenach in *Two Worlds of Liberalism* (Chicago and London: University of Chicago Press, 1981) argues that in fact Biblical religion is an essential component of the liberal creed.

3. The difficulties of solving this conundrum are reflected in current disputes over the meaning of what has in more recent times come to be known as the doctrine of the separation of church and state. Harold Berman in "Religious Freedom and the Challenge of the Modern State," in *Articles of Faith, Articles of Peace*, Os Guinness and James Hunter, eds. (Washington, D.C.: The Brookings Institution, 1990) notes that the modern judicial notion that religion is the private affair of each individual was unknown in the early years of the republic. Michael Sandel in "Freedom of Conscience or Freedom of Choice?" *Articles of Faith*, 78 makes a similar point, tracing the current dominant notion to the 1947 decision of the Supreme Court *Everson v. The Board of Education of Ewing Township*, 330 U.S. 1 (1947).

Stephen Carter in *The Culture of Disbelief* (New York: Basic Books, 1993) has argued that the privatization of religion trivializes religious conviction as legitimate grounds for public argument. He contends that instead of leading to toleration, it constrains religion in general by diminishing the public importance and acceptance of religious conviction. In the interest of keeping religion out of public life, religion itself is diminished.

From another angle, some have argued that the current understanding of the doctrine of the separation of church and state as articulated by the United States courts harbors a particular conception of religion as a purely private affair, one which cannot serve as a self-definition for all religious traditions. For this view see Berman's "Religious Freedom" as well as Stephen Feldman, *Please Don't Wish Me a Merry Christmas* (New York and London: New York University Press, 1997). Feldman charges that the practice of church-state separation has served in the history of the West as a foil for the continued hegemony of Christianity. In addition, the need to favor religion occurred at the expense of toleration. Yet still other scholars question the degree to which this doctrine is a suitable reflection of current practice in the United States. Ronald Thiemann argues through an analysis of court judgments and policy statements that there is no consistent doctrine being applied. Some officials advocate a strictly neutral and secular view of government with regard to religious matters. Others advocate a more active role for government to encourage the protection and flourishing of a diversity of religious groups, or even of what is perceived to be a dominant sectarian outlook. See Ronald Thiemann, *Religion in Public Life* (Washington, D.C.: Georgetown University Press, 1996), chap. 1.

From these debates three important points emerge. The first is that the doctrine of the 'separation of church and state' has served as a general catch-all term subject to a variety of interpretations and applications as well as judgements as to its effects. In addition, the metaphor of separation offers little direction for policy in certain areas such as faith healing cases when the defense of religious rights clashes with the pursuit of public goods. The doctrine leaves us with a dilemma when it is clear that the ends of each cannot be fully 'separate' and that one claim must often be judged to supersede the other. It thus appears at present inadequate to give clear direction for policy in certain matters. Second, then, it may be unclear what toleration means and how it is to be pursued effectively. Third, these problems of interpretation reflect a deeper question as to what the proper relation of religion and politics should be. It seems natural to ask, given the criticisms of present forms of accommodation, whether their claims can all be met with integrity and justice for both sides, particularly in a modern context characterized by a diversity of belief systems. Given these problems, it becomes clear that there may be cause to rethink how best to conceptualize the most suitable link between public goods and religious belief within the liberal tradition, that is while protecting a commitment to toleration and religious diversity.

4. R. P. Lacordaire in his "Discours de réception à l'Académie française, le 24 janvier 1861," noted that *The Spirit of Laws* was "la plus belle apologie du christianisme au XVIIIe siècle." See his *Œuvres* (Paris: Librairie Poussielgue Frères, 1880), vol. viii, 326. In contrast, Emile Faguet and more recently Judith Shklar read Montesquieu as largely an anti-religious thinker. See Emile Faguet, *Dix-huitième siècle* (Paris: Boivin and Compagnie, 1893), 142-43 and Judith Shklar, *Montesquieu* (Oxford: Oxford University Press, 1987), 84. Robert Shackleton argues that Montesquieu was a practicing Catholic with deist convictions and strong sympathies for Christianity. See "La Religion de Montesquieu," in *Actes du Congrès Montesquieu à Bordeaux du 23 mai au 26 mai 1955* (Bordeaux: Imprimerie Delmas, 1956), 287-94. F. T. H. Fletcher in "Montesquieu et la politique religieuse en Angleterre au XVIIIe siècle," in *Actes du Congrès Montesquieu*, 295-304 argues that Montesquieu, like Warburton, can be considered Erastian in calling for an alliance of religious cult and the state. Warburton is also stressed by Shackleton as an influence on Montesquieu in his defense of natural religion. See his *Montesquieu. A Critical Biography* (Oxford: Oxford University Press, 1961). In an analysis of Montesquieu's early writings on religion, Lorenzo Bianchi argues that Montesquieu's position closely resembled that of Machiavelli in positing a central importance to religion as a

means of social control. See "Nécessité de la religion et de la tolérance chez Montes-quieu. La 'Dissertation sur la politique des Romains dans la religion,'" in *Lectures de Montesquieu*, Edgar Mass and Alberto Postigliola, eds. (Napoli: Liguori Editore, 1993), 25-39. His early interest in religion may have been sparked by his reading of the works of Nicholas Fréret. See Lorenzo Bianchi, "Montesquieu et Fréret: quelques notes," *Corpus* 29 (1995), 105-28. Still, Bianchi makes clear that Montesquieu's views on religion changed throughout his life and lost their critical edge in his more mature years. See his "Histoire et nature: la religion dans *L'Esprit des lois*," *Actes du colloque 'Le Temps de Montesquieu,'* Michel Porret ed. (Geneva: Droz, forthcoming).

5. See, for example Thomas Pangle's *Montesquieu's Philosophy of Liberalism* (Chicago: University of Chicago Press, 1973).

6. Passages of the work were censored by both Abbé de La Roche in October 1749 in the *Nouvelles Ecclésiastiques*, a Jansenist publication, and the Faculty of Theology of the University of Paris in August 1752. For a full listing of these censored passages see *The Spirit of Laws, a Compendium of the First English Edition* . . . David Wallace Carrithers, ed. (Berkeley: University of California Press, 1977), Appendix 1, 467-68.

7. For an elaboration of this point see my *Montesquieu and the Parlement of Bordeaux* (Geneva: Librairie Droz, 1996), chap. 5.

8. All translations in this paper are my own, though I have consulted previous translations, and in particular Montesquieu, *The Spirit of the Laws*, Anne Cohler et al., eds. (Cambridge: Cambridge University Press, 1989).

9. For emphasis on the importance of God in the arguments of Locke and Pufendorf, see John Dunn, *Locke* (Oxford: Oxford University Press, 1983) and James Tully, "Introduction" in *On the Duty of Man and Citizen*, by Samuel Pufendorf (Cambridge: Cambridge University Press, 1991).

10. This position was also reflected in letter 46 of the *Persian Letters*: "Indeed, should not the first goal of a religious man be to please the divinity who established the religion he professes? But the most sure means of succeeding is certainly to observe the rules of society and the duties of humanity: because, regardless of the religion that one espouses, as soon as one assumes one, it is also necessary to assume that God loves men as he established a religion to make them happy; and, if he loves men, one can be assured of pleasing him by loving them also, that is in practicing all the duties of charity and of humanity, and in not violating the laws under which they live."

11. Still, such comments may have done no more than perpetuate the prevailing stereotypes of Calvinists. See Geoffrey Adams, *The Huguenots and French Opinion, 1685-1787* (Waterloo: Wilfrid Laurier University Press, 1991), chap. 5. Certain social factors seem to affect religion more than others. In particular, developmental features have more impact on the nature of worship than types of regime. Montesquieu's language about the link between regime types and forms of worship is somewhat muted, though he does note a certain affinity between monarchy and the Catholic religion as well as an affinity between republics and Protestantism.

12. Natural religion has been defined as "the system of conclusions about God's (or

the gods') existence and nature supposedly attainable from evidence and by reasoning accessible to any intelligent person irrespective of any special information conveyed in the Bible, Koran, or other revelatory source." J. C. A. Gaskin, "Hume on Religion," in *The Cambridge Companion to Hume*, David Fate Norton, ed. (Cambridge: Cambridge University Press, 1993), 314.

13. Montesquieu to Warburton, May 1754, in Nagel, III, 1508-10.

14. Shackleton, *Montesquieu. A Critical Biography*, 352-54.

15. See for example Book XXIV, 19.

16. For a discussion of Montesquieu as a defender of 'associational' discourse see my *Montesquieu and the Parlement of Bordeaux*.

17. He also notes early in the work that the distinctiveness of the religious code and the obligations it brings produce in the modern world competing strands of thought unknown among the ancients: "Today we receive three different or competing educations: that of our fathers, that of our teachers and that of the world. That which is told to us in the latter upsets all the precepts of the preceding. The reason for this in part is the contrast that exists among us between religious and worldly commitments, something which the ancients did not know" (IV, 4).

18. As an example, Montesquieu refers to the way in which both religious law and positive law regulate marriage. The need for religion in regulating marriage practices, according to Montesquieu, stems from the need of society to distinguish between necessary and unnecessary causes of things considered illicit or impure. Thus, religion will be concerned with the quality and legitimacy of the contract to sanctify the legitimacy of the union. In contrast, because this contract has an important effect on questions of property and civil responsibility, civil law will also be involved in the regulation of various matters related to its object (XXVI, 13).

19. Jean Barbey et al., *Histoire des institutions de l'époque franque à la révolution* (Paris: Presses Universitaires de France, 1987), 495ff and Jeffrey Merrick, *The Desacralization of the French Monarchy in the Eighteenth Century* (Baton Rouge and London: Louisiana State University Press, 1990), chaps. 1 and 2.

20. See for example Sharon Kettering's *Patrons, Brokers and Clients in Seventeenth-Century France* (Oxford: Oxford University Press, 1986).

21. Rev. Henley Jervis, *A History of the Church of France*, 2 vols. (London: John Murray, 1872), II, 49-50.

22. Friedrich Heyer, *The Catholic Church from 1648 to 1870* (London: Adam and Charles Black, 1969), 18-19.

23. Jansenism was a movement in the French Catholic Church, named for its founder Cornelius Jansen and centered at the convent of Port-Royal. The movement stressed a form of predestination emphasizing the sinfulness of human nature and the inability of believers to attain salvation by their own will.

24. For a detailed account of the events leading up to the declaration and its aftermath see Jervis, *A History of the Church of France*, 202ff.; Dale van Kley, *The Religious Origins of the French Revolution* (New Haven and London: Yale University Press,

1996), 73ff.

25. This served to justify continued persecution of Protestants, culminating in the Revocation of the Edict of Nantes in 1685, under the principle of *cujus regio, ejus religio*. It also justified the Edict of 1695 and Declaration of 1698 diminishing the power of the lower clergy (especially parish priests and their auxiliaries) and increasing the power of bishops over them while deepening episcopal ties to the crown. The Edict of 1695 gave the bishops the sole right to grant (to nonbeneficed priests, most serving as auxiliaries in a parish) all rights and privileges, including the right to preach, to administer the sacraments, and to hear confession. The Declaration of 1698 gave these same bishops the right to incarcerate or send local priests for a forced seminary stay in the event of insubordination. See Dale Van Kley, *The Religious Origins of the French Revolution*, 41.

26. W. J. Stankiewicz, *Politics and Religion in Seventeenth-Century France* (Berkeley and Los Angeles: University of California Press, 1960), 130. Lebret's *De la Souveraineté du roy* was published in 1632.

27. Stankiewicz, *Politics and Religion*, 130.

28. In seeking to enforce the bull *Unigenitus* Louis XIV had it registered in the Parlements and called for a special assembly of bishops from the region of Paris to have it adopted. In the initial stages of the Regency the Duke of Orleans asserted the crown's independence from the Papacy and ordered French clergy to abstain from taking notice of papal documents requiring observance of papal decrees. See Jervis, *A History of the Church of France*, 234. This was short-lived, however. After a formal call for an appeal of the bull was put forward by four bishops, with support from the Theological Faculty of Paris, the Regency Council made the *Unigenitus* a law of state. In face of the refusal of the Paris Parlement to register this decision, Cardinal Dubois sent out *lettres de cachet* to discipline the recalcitrant magistrates. Dubois became Chief Minister in 1722 and issued *lettres de cachet* to rebellious clergy, causing them to lose their benefices, lose their homes, and be fined, exiled, or imprisoned. In 1730 the king sent to Parlement a decree that the *Unigenitus* should be considered and respected as a law of State and that no further talk of appeal was to be tolerated, sparking a political crisis. A *lit de justice* was held in April 1730 to ensure its immediate registration. Faced with the recalcitrance of many magistrates in a subsequent appeal of three parish priests against the rulings of their bishop, Cardinal Fleury, acting on behalf of the king, seized the case from the Parlement, ruled in favor of the bishop and declared that the Parlement was prevented from taking any further action in the case. In the ensuing debates, the Archbishop of Paris defended the independence of the church's judicial structure and their right to legislate in matters of faith and morals.

29. The *appel commme d'abus* emerged in the fifteenth century out of earlier prerogatives of the courts to seek the overturning of clerical decisions which impinged on the lay courts' jurisdiction. By the fifteenth century the courts took upon themselves the authority to annul such rulings whether by their own initiative or on appeal by the crown or particular individuals. See Jean Barbey et al. *Histoire des institutions de l'époque franque à la révolution*, 347-48.

30. One can see, then, how the initial State-building dynamic associated with the French crown was being modified. In the Renaissance period, the power of the crown was increased in part through the expansion of the realm of royal justice and the progressive encroachment of the royal system through the Parlements on other formerly autonomous systems such as seigneurial justice and ecclesiastical justice. By the eighteenth century, this process of consolidation was virtually complete. However, this reality of consolidation in the case of the *Unigenitus* brought to light the possibilities of the independent power of this imposing hierarchy of royal justice, one which could serve in certain matters as a powerful basis of opposition to royal control. Seen in this light it becomes evident why the king in the 1730s was seeking to defend and bolster the separation of jurisdictions for he wished to weaken the power of the magistrates who were using their position to contravene the spirit of royal policy on the Jansenist question.

31. It is thought that at its height in 1719, the party of *appellants* encompassed approximately one tenth of the Catholic clergy of France, including the theological faculties of universities of Paris, Nantes and Reims, the Archbishop of Paris and much of his diocese and about 450 curés. See Dale Van Kley, *The Religious Origins of the French Revolution*, 85.

32. See Peter Campbell, *Power and Politics in Old Regime France 1720-1745* (London and New York: Routledge, 1996), 219. LePaige states in his *Judicium francorum* (1731): "When it is a question of something in which the people has an interest, it cannot be decided in the council of state. The king can only contract with his people in the *parlement*, which, being as old as the crown itself and born with the state, is the representation of the whole monarchy. The king's council, which is a kind of jurisdiction established to the prejudice of the most fundamental laws of the kingdom, has no public character, and when it annuls or modifies the *arrêts* of the *parlement* it commits a clear usurpation" (cited in Campbell, *Power and Politics*, 219).

33. Vivien de La Borde, *On the Testimony of Truth*, 1714 and Nicolas Le Gros, *Memorandum on the Rights of the Second Order*, 1733 and *Du Reversement des libertés de l'église gallicane*, 1716. See Dale Van Kley, *The Religious Origins of the French Revolution*, 78ff.

34. A political crisis was sparked beginning in 1730 when the new Archbishop of Paris, Gaspard de Vintimille, sought to impose the *Unigenitus* by asking the king for an edict requiring all clergy to accept it or lose their benefices. In addition, he demanded that the bull be proclaimed a law of both church and state. The king held a *lit de justice* in April of 1730 to enforce the immediate registration of these edicts by the Paris Parlement. Despite opposition from two thirds of the magistrates, the assent of the chamber was proclaimed by the crown. In response, the next day the Parlement passed a resolution proclaiming essentially that the king did not have the right to declare unilaterally any religious doctrine a law of State without the proper consent of Parlement and that temporal power was superior to spiritual authority. This resolution was quickly annulled by an order of the Council of State.

Shortly thereafter three priests from Orleans appealed to the Parlement after being deposed from their functions by the bishop because of their opposition to the bull. The Parlement ordered that they continue in their functions while their case was being reconsidered. The bishop of Orleans sought the intervention of the crown, but again the magistrates protested, arguing that the civil courts had the duty to protect especially lower levels of the clergy from potential abuse by their superiors and that they had the right to suspend the execution of the bishop's sentences until a final decision was made. The case was brought to the Grand Conseil where it was decided to let the diocesan courts make a final decision. Meanwhile, their positions would be suspended, essentially reinforcing the *acceptant* position. The Parlement was banned from ever reconsidering the case, and those who had signed the earlier resolutions citing the superiority of the civil to ecclesiastical tribunals and stating that no enactment could achieve the force of law without the consent of Parlement would have to retract their support of the resolution or be debarred. Those who had accepted the court's jurisdiction in this matter were labeled heretics and schismatics by a group of powerful bishops, and these pronouncements were in turn called seditious and abusive by the Parlement. The confrontation led to a general strike of the *avocats*. Later, after further matters of dispute and the arrest of Jansenist councillors, almost the whole Parlement threatened to resign. As the conflict continued, the royal council exiled 139 *parlementaires* outside of Paris. By the end of the crisis, the government finally succeeded in having the magistrates accept *Unigenitus* as a law of church and state and in subduing Jansenism as a challenge to religious orthodoxy within France. Still, the political effects of the struggle would be much longer lasting. For discussion of this crisis of 1730-33 see Van Kley, *The Religious Origins of the French Revolution*, 122ff.

35. As noted by J. Carreyre, while there is no record of intensive discussion surrounding the bull *Unigenitus* in Bordeaux in 1713 when it was issued, several incidents did flare up in 1730-31 which divided the clergy and *Parlement* on these matters. See "La bulle 'Unigenitus' et le Parlement de Bordeaux," *Revue historique de Bordeaux et du département de la Gironde* 2 (1909): 196-207.

36. See *Pensées* 1326 (730) and 1337 (852), in Pléiade, I, 1320-21.

37. See *Pensée* 2175 (437), in Pléiade, I, 1565 and *Spicilège* 638-39 and 783-84, in Pléiade, I, 1402 and 1432-33.

38. See *Pensée* 2039 (215) in Pléiade, I, 1520-21.

39. See Montesquieu, "Of Politics," in Pléiade, I, 112-19.

40. Montesquieu, *Considerations*, chap. 22, in Pléiade, II, 203.

41. "I do not insist on the privileges of the clergy, but I would like that their jurisdiction be determined once and for all. It is not a matter of knowing if one was right in establishing it; but if it is established, if it is a part of the laws of the country, and if it is relative to them everywhere: if, between two powers that are recognized to be independent, conditions should not be reciprocal" (II, 4). Note that Montesquieu here sees the ecclesiastical jurisdiction as an "independent" one and not as separate.

42. He also makes a similar point in XII, 29: "Though despotic government is everywhere the same, by its nature, circumstances such as a religious opinion, a prejudice,

precedent, a turn of mind, manners and mores can leave considerable differences among them. . . . It is suitable that there be some sacred book that acts as a rule, like the Koran among the Arabs, the books of Zoroaster among the Persians, the Veda among the Indians, the classics among the Chinese. The religious code takes the place of the civil code and fixes what is arbitrary."

43. "However, there is one thing that one can sometimes use to counter the will of the prince: it is religion. One will forsake one's father, kill him, if the prince commands it: but one will not drink wine, if he wishes and commands it. Religious laws are of a higher precept, because they apply to the prince as well as to the subjects" (III, 10); "In these states, religion has more influence than in any other; it is a fear added to fear. In Mohammedan empires it is from religion that the people derive in part the astonishing respect they have for the prince" (V, 14). Montesquieu also believes religion can provide a sense of order amidst the breakdown of civil order, such as with the Romans after the loss of the battle of Cannes (XXIV, 16 and VIII, 13).

44. I refer here to Machiavelli of *The Discourses* who saw in religion a great tool for the advancement of republican greatness.

45. This notion is an expression of Montesquieu's more general principle that liberty of the citizen is best promoted with a system of criminal law in which punishments are derived clearly from the nature of the crime. "In order that the punishment for simple sacrilege be drawn from the nature of the thing, it should consist in deprivation from all the advantages that religion brings: expulsion from places of worship, deprivation from the society of the faithful for a limited time or forever, shunning them, execration, detestation and exorcism." According to Robert Derathé, Montesquieu was here inspired by Locke's *Letter Concerning Toleration*. See Montesquieu, *L'Esprit des lois*, Robert Derathé, ed., 2 vols. (Paris: Bordas, 1990), I, 485.

46. "For those things that wound the divinity, where there is not public action, it is not a criminal matter: it only concerns man and God, who knows the measure and extent of his vengeance. If the magistrate, in confusing these things, searches also for the hidden sacrilege, he brings inquisition to a kind of action where it is not necessary: he destroys the liberty of citizens, by arming against them the zeal of both timid and bold consciences" (XII, 4). Because of such sentiments it would be impossible to identify Montesquieu as Erastian as argued by F. T. H. Fletcher in "Montesquieu et la politique religieuse en Angleterre au XVIIIe siècle," 297. An eighteenth-century dictionary speaks of the Erastians as follows: "They deny the authority of the church with regard to discipline, and hold that it does not have the legitimate power to excommunicate, exclude, absolve, censor, etc." (my translation). See Joseph Nicolas Guyot et al., *Le Grand vocabulaire français* (Paris: Panckoucke, 1767), vol. 9, 467. In contrast, Montesquieu does allow that the church use its own methods of discipline, such as excommunication, to further its own objectives.

47. "Bad things came from this idea that it is necessary to avenge the divinity. Rather one must make the divinity honored and never avenge it. Indeed, if one was guided by this last thought where would the punishments end? If human laws have the

purpose of avenging an infinite being, they will be measured by his infinity, and not by the weaknesses, ignorance and caprice of human nature. An historian from Provence reports a fact that shows very well what this idea of avenging the divinity could produce in weak spirits. A Jew, accused of blasphemy against the Holy Virgin, was condemned to be flayed. Masked knights, with knife in hand, mounted the scaffold and chased the executioner away to avenge the honor of the Holy Virgin themselves. . . . I do not wish to anticipate the reader's thoughts" (XII, 4).

48. "With regard to the true religion, the slightest fairness will show that I have never claimed to make its interests cede to political interests, but to unite them both; now, in order to unite them, they must be known" (XXIV, 1).

49. "The truest and holiest doctrines can have terrible consequences when they are not allied with principles of society; and, in contrast, the most false doctrines can have admirable consequences, when they have been linked to those same principles. The religion of Confucius denies the immortality of the soul; and the sect of Zeno did not believe in it. Who could guess? These two sects drew from their bad principles consequences that were not only just, but admirable for society. The religion of Tao and Foe believes in the immortality of the soul; but from this saintly doctrine they have drawn frightful consequences. Almost everywhere in the world, and at all times the notion of the immortality of the soul, badly taken, has led women, slaves, subjects and friends to kill themselves in order to serve the object of their respect or love in the other world. . . . It is not enough for a religion to establish a doctrine, it must also direct it" (XXIV, 19).

50. "Just as one can judge the least dark of shadows, and the least deep of abysses, so among false religions one can search for those which conform better to the good of society; those which, while they don't lead men to the felicities of the next life, can contribute most to their happiness in this one. Therefore, I will examine the diverse religions of the world only in relation to the good to be drawn from them in the civil state; whether I speak of the one which is rooted in heaven, or those rooted in the earth" (XXIV, 1).

51. He notes for example that religion can have an important effect on population growth, both in a positive and negative way. "The principles of religion have had an important influence on the propagation of the human species; sometimes they have encouraged it, as among the Jews, the Mohammedans, the Ghebers, the Chinese; sometimes they have run counter to it, as they did among the Romans who became Christians" (XXIII, 21).

52. "A prince who loves and fears religion is a lion who yields to the hand that pats him, or to the voice that appeases him; he who fears and hates religion is like the savage beasts who gnaw the chain that keeps them from throwing themselves on those who pass by; he who has no religion, is the dreadful animal that only feels its liberty when it tears and devours" (XXIV, 2).

53. "It is glorious to have been the first to have shown in these regions the idea of religion joined with that of humanity. By repairing the ravages of the Spanish, it began to heal one of the greatest wounds ever given to humankind" (IV, 6).

54. "The Christian religion, which commands men to love one another, no doubt

wants each people to have the best political and civil laws, because these are, after it, the greatest good that humans can give and receive" (XXIV, 1).

55. "Bayle, after insulting all religions, casts a slur on the Christian religion: he dares to argue that true Christians could not establish a lasting state. Why not? They would be citizens well enlightened about their duties and who would have great zeal to perform them; they would sense very well the laws of natural defense; the more they would see themselves devoted to religion, the more they would think of their duties to their country" (XXIV, 6).

56. "In states where wars are not waged by common deliberation, and where laws do not have any means of terminating or preventing them, religion establishes times of peace or truces, so that the people can do the things that keep the state going, such as harvesting and similar tasks" (XXIV, 16).

57. "As religion and the civil laws should tend chiefly to render men good citizens, one sees that when one of the two shifts from this goal, the other should aim more toward it: the less repressive religion is, the more civil laws should repress" (XXIV, 14).

58. "As men are made to preserve, nourish, and clothe themselves, and to do all the things done in society, religion should not give them an overly contemplative life" (XXIV, 11).

59. *Lois*, R. Derathé ed., 501-2.

60. In his manuscript Montesquieu began this chapter with an explicit criticism of monastic vows prescribing exact obedience and renunciation which he eliminated in the published version. See *Lois*, R. Derathé, ed., 477.

61. This passage was censored by the Sorbonne and was questioned by the Vatican censors also, though Montesquieu made no changes.

62. "If, on the one hand, one envisages the continual massacres of the Greek and Roman kings and leaders and, on the other, the destruction of peoples and cities by Timur and Genghis Khan, the same leaders who ravaged Asia; we will see that we owe to Christianity both a certain political right in government and a certain law of nations in war, for which human nature can never be sufficiently grateful. It is this law of nations in our time which, in victory, leaves to the vanquished these great things: life, liberty, laws, goods and always religion, when one does not blind oneself" (XXIV, 3).

63. This is not to state that toleration was a value 'invented' by the Enlightenment. As Cary Nederman and others have shown, there were arguments for toleration back into medieval times and in the early-modern period. See Cary Nederman and John Christian Laursen, eds., *Difference and Dissent. Theories of Toleration in Medieval and Early Modern Europe* (Lanham: Rowman and Littlefield, 1996). One might also include what Steven Smith calls the 'rationalist strategy,' namely the construction of a form of rational religion to replace Scriptural theology. However, this would issue in toleration largely through the elimination of religious differences and thus could also be seen as a form of intolerance. See Steven Smith, *Spinoza, Liberalism and the Question of Jewish Identity* (New Haven and London: Yale University Press, 1997), chap. 1.

64. A clear proponent of this view, as argued by Stephen Holmes, is Bodin though

the argument preceded his work. See Stephen Holmes, *Passions and Constraint* (Chicago and London: The University of Chicago Press, 1995).

65. See John Locke, *A Letter Concerning Toleration*, James Tully, ed., (Indianapolis: Hackett, 1983).

66. This is a position commonly associated with Pierre Jurieu. See Guy H. Dodge, *The Political Theory of the Huguenots of the Dispersion* (New York: Columbia University Press, 1947).

67. This distinction between toleration and approval had already been recognized by Pierre François Le Courayer in his *Défense de la nouvelle traduction de l'Histoire du Concile de Trente contre les censures de quelques prélats et de quelques théologiens* (Bruxelles: Simont T. Stevens, 1742), 427.

68. "Here, therefore, is the fundamental principle of political law in religious matters. When one is master in deciding whether the state should accept a new religion, it should not be established; when it is established, it must be tolerated" (XXV, 10).

69. For further comparison of Locke's and Montesquieu's theories of toleration see my "Locke, Montesquieu et la tolérance religieuse," in Louis Desgraves, ed., *Actes du Colloque international tenu à Bordeaux du 3 au 6 décembre 1998 pour commémorer le 250ème anniversaire de la parution de L'Esprit des lois* (Bordeaux: Académie de Bordeaux, 1999), 225-34.

70. "Memoir on the Constitution," in Pléiade, II, 1217-21.

71. "Memoir," in Pléiade, II, 1219.

72. "Memoir," in Pléiade, II, 1219.

73. "Memoir," in Pléiade, II, 1219.

Chapter Ten

Montesquieu and the History of Laws

Iris Cox

At the end of *The Spirit of Laws*, Montesquieu presents three books, XXVIII, XXX, and XXXI, in which he describes the development of the civil and constitutional laws of his own country. The three books, taken together, show a picture of a state which has gone through many changes, but whose spirit is that of a "moderate monarchy," one in which the king governs by known laws, and with the help of intermediary powers.

These historical books describe the evolution of the French monarchic state from the time of the barbarian invasions in the fifth century A.D. up to the accession of Hugh Capet at the end of the tenth century, and of the evolution of French civil law up to about the sixteenth century when Roman law was re-established as the law of the land in parts of France and various codes of customary law were established in the rest of the country. They offer one illustration of the theory of monarchy put forward in Book II, chapter 4 of *The Spirit of Laws*. Another illustration is provided by the celebrated description of the constitution of England in Book XI, chapter 6 supplemented by Book XIX, chapter 27, but as this describes the England of Montesquieu's own time, the two constitutions cannot be directly compared. As he explains in the Preface to *The Spirit of Laws,* Montesquieu is writing for a much wider public than France. Consequently in the statements he makes in Book II, chapter 4 and elsewhere about the monarchic state in general, the need for intermediate powers, the role of the nobility and the role of political bodies charged with declaring and upholding the laws, the reader must guard against interpreting these as practical recommendations intended for the actual government of France. Montesquieu was very widely read; he had travelled in Europe and conversed and corresponded with many educated and influential people in his own country and elsewhere.

He had some first hand experience of the workings of government, though his direct experience was restricted to his own Parlement of Bordeaux where he served as a magistrate between 1716 and 1726, apart from a short period as a student in Paris, when in about the year 1711 he observed a number of cases brought before the Parlement of Paris. He intends his conclusions, unless specifically directed at particular targets, to be understood as conclusions of general relevance in relation to different types of states.

Emile Chénon, in the second volume of his *Histoire générale du droit français public et privé* (Paris, 1929), which is still an invaluable source for understanding the evolution of French law, ably described the legal situation after the decline of the feudal system. He likened the theoretical power of the French kings to that of the Roman emperors. Kings were responsible for legislation. They accepted perhaps the existence of certain fundamental laws,[1] ill-defined and mostly relating to the establishment of the monarchy itself, while the Parlements maintained that their own right to register laws, and to make remonstrances before doing so, was itself a fundamental law. Chénon summarizes the situation as follows:

> The king was persuaded that he could not infringe the fundamental laws, and in general he did not do so. Most of them were in any case in his interest or at least in the interest of the monarchy. But if he had wanted to violate them, who could have prevented him? The theory of the fundamental laws was in fact only a moral limit on the power of the king: this limit, amply sufficient when a Saint Louis is on the throne, must have appeared less of a safeguard to the subjects of Louis XIV.[2]

Nevertheless, the system lasted until almost the outbreak of the Revolution, not without problems and dissensions, but in a reasonably effective way. In 1770-71, however, roughly a decade and a half after the death of Montesquieu, a crisis occurred which brought home to parlementaires, whose key role Montesquieu had so stressed, and to others interested in political debate—former parlementaires, other office-holders, nobles, the academies and salons, academics and educated people—the lack of any effective constitutional barriers to the power of the king. While France was in the grip of severe financial and economic troubles, the Parlements refused to register edicts imposing new taxes, repudiating public debts, and suspending payment of interest. They then refused to approve edicts limiting their own powers, and published a remonstrance "alleging the multiplicity of acts of absolute power exercised at that time against the spirit of the laws which constitute the French monarchy," with a reminder to the king that one of these laws preserved his own right to the throne and the succession of his heirs.[3] The chancellor, René-Nicolas de Maupeou, arranged for the edicts to be passed by the king in an official *lit de justice*, but the parlementaires showed their dissatisfaction by refusing to conduct legal business. After this provocation, the chancellor had no difficulty in getting the king's consent by a decree of January 1771 to send the existing members of the Parlement of Paris into exile and set up a new Parlement of Paris and later on new provincial Parlements, with different personnel and new, and more restrictive terms of reference.[4] Although the powers of the Parlements were restored in the two years after Louis XVI came to the throne in 1774, Maupeou's actions had shown how easily they could be overturned by arbitrary action. As William Doyle has commented:

> The events of 1771 clarified matters in the most brutal way. Chancellor Lamoignon declared that the king was a sovereign to whom everything was not permitted but everything was possible. Chancellor Maupeou proved it—there was nothing the king could not do, permitted or not, if he were determined. . . .
> The Parlements could no more prevent their own reformation than Terray's tax increases or anything else. In the view of most magistrates and many others besides, Louis XV had crossed the narrow divide between monarchy and despotism, and it was clear, if it had not been before, that there were no effective regular checks on government in France.[5]

All this of course was in the future when *The Spirit of Laws,* published in 1748, was being composed, but debate on the French constitution had been a live issue long before then. Three works published between the late sixteenth century and the early seventeenth century typify the range of opinion. The first, the *Franco-Gallia* or *La Gaule Françoise,* by François Hotman, was published in Latin in 1573 and French in 1574, at a time when the break-up of Christendom and, in France, the Wars of Religion and particularly the massacre of St. Bartholomew's day in August 1572 were forcing people to consider the nature and location of authority in the state. All three authors accepted the fact of kings at the head of the state, but their different ideas on the succession to the throne, and on the legitimate exercise of authority, set the scene for discussions of the French constitution up to the Revolution. Hotman contended that, by the long tradition of French Gaul, kings should be elected, and deposed if necessary, and laws should be made, by the Estates, meeting in an annual assembly.[6] A much more famous writer was Jean Bodin, whose *Six Books of the Commonwealth,*[7] published in 1576, approached the question of the right organization of the state on general grounds, focusing on the political community as such, rather than from a specifically French angle. His reasoning led him to the conclusion that, to avoid anarchy, the recognition of an absolute sovereign power was essential, though the ruler had an obligation to obey the laws of God. A little later, the discussion, particularly as it concerned the state of France, was taken up by Bernard de La Roche-Flavin in his *Treize livres des Parlements de France,* published in 1617.[8] He argued that, first, the Parlement of Paris, and then all the other Parlements, were the true successors of the early *Assemblées des Grands* which advised the sovereign and had the power, with the sovereign, to make law.

The Dynastic Argument: Boulainvilliers and Dubos

Although in 1748 the Revolution was still some forty years ahead, there was a considerable degree of uneasiness in the Old Regime leading to an ever increasing constitutional debate. I propose here to consider just two of the causes, both relating to constitutional law, which contributed to this unease. In a monarchy in which the king exercises real power, arrangements for the succession are of crucial importance.

Between the death of Henri IV in 1610 and the Regency period of the early eighteenth century, the crown had three times been inherited by a child too young to exercise personal power. This had led to the prolonged regencies of Marie de Medici during the minority of Louis XIII, Anne of Austria during the minority of Louis XIV, and Philip, Duke of Orleans during the minority of Louis XV, accompanied by the often resented influence of first ministers, including the cardinals Richelieu and Mazarin. Many of the high nobility in particular resented and feared the first ministers since they wished to look upon themselves as entitled by birth to be the king's counsellors, though no regular forum was established for that purpose. The Parlements also, led by the Parlement of Paris, resented the first ministers. It was the job of the Parlements to register legislation, and they were able to exercise some influence on the form that legislation, took by using their powers of remonstrance, so that they too regarded themselves as the legitimate advisors of the king.

The two conflicting interests never made common cause, and during the minority of Louis XV the Parlements soon gained an advantage. Orleans' right to act as Regent was itself contentious. The deaths in 1711-12 of both the duc de Bourgogne, grandson and heir of Louis XIV, and of Bourgogne's elder son brought very close the prospect that King Philip V of Spain, younger grandson of Louis XIV, might in the future also claim the throne of France. The heir apparent was Bourgogne's younger son, the future Louis XV, but he was still a very young child when his great grandfather, Louis XIV died, and after him the nearest in blood was Philip of Spain. The prospect of a union of the kingdoms of France and Spain was anathema to the coalition powers, particularly England, which fought against France in the War of the Spanish Succession. Therefore, as a preliminary to the Treaty of Utrecht, they insisted that Philip V renounce any claim to the succession. He did in fact do so in 1712, and Louis XIV issued a decree to this effect, registered by the Parlement of Paris in 1713. The validity of the renunciation was questioned by many in France, however, as a violation of the fundamental law of the royal succession. When Louis XIV died, some argued that Philip V, as the nearest in blood, should be Regent in place of Philip of Orleans during the new king's minority.[9] Nevertheless, Orleans took up the post of Regent and took the precaution of immediately referring the matter to the Parlement of Paris, which duly registered the appointment. The validity of the renunciation by Philip V of Spain of any right to succession to the throne of France was never tested legally, since Louis XV survived to reign until 1774 and provided legitimate heirs in the direct line. The uncertainty of the succession, however, helped to unsettle the nobility and the Parlements, and encouraged political debate. The nobility, taking the view that they, rather than the Parlement, should have been consulted, were now meeting in an unauthorized assembly of their own, as Franklin Ford describes:

> On the peers' side, the strategy of publication and appeals addressed to the Regent was laid out in a long series of meetings which began on the very day of Louis XIV's death. In the Archives Nationales one can still read a thick pack of invitations announcing gatherings at the homes of such leading activists as the Archbishop of Reims, the Duc de la Force, the Duc d'Uzès and the Duc de Tresmes. At these meetings of which no fewer than fifty-five took place between September 1 1715 and February 22 1717 the peers discussed both the parlementary issue and that of the *légitimés*.[10]

Who were the *légitimés*, and why should the peers discuss them? Before his death, Louis XIV had declared his two illegitimate sons by Madame de Maintenon, the duc du Maine and the comte de Toulouse, to be legitimate and had given them an intermediate rank below the legitimate princes of the blood and above the *ducs et pairs de France*. In his will he added them to the line of succession to the throne and in 1715 accorded them the status of princes of the blood. After his death these actions gave rise to a great deal of dissension as people took sides, and a regular war of pamphlets broke out. Again the parties to the dispute were not united in their aims, and all they achieved was to provoke the Regent into action. The unauthorized assembly of high nobles was dissolved by a decree of the Regency Council in 1717, the nobles were denied the right to hold assemblies without the express permission of king or Regent, and, without involving the Parlement, a commission was also set up to look into the claims of the legitimate and legitimated princes. Eventually the Regent issued a decree, registered by the Parlement of Paris on 6 July 1717, which denied any right of Maine and Toulouse to the succession, although they kept their titles and intermediate rank.[11]

Underlying both dynastic arguments was the problem of authority. Did the king have absolute authority, even over his own successors, or was his authority subject to fundamental laws? And what were the fundamental laws? How had they come into being? Could they be altered and if so, by what person or process? Most of the theories put forward in the eighteenth century concerning this problem have been divided by historians into two schools, known as the *thèse royale* and the *thèse nobiliaire.* In general, advocates of the royal thesis maintained that the king's authority was literally absolute, subject only to self-imposed limitations. Advocates of the nobility thesis, however, maintained that other institutions and powers in the state, particularly the nobility, also had the historic right and duty to play a part in the government of France. Montesquieu was quite familiar with the views of the chief expositors of these two schools, the comte de Boulainvilliers,[12] and the abbé Dubos.[13] His own mature view of the succession issue, though he does not specifically relate it to the royal succession in France, was expressed in Book XXVI, chapter 16 of *The Spirit of Laws.* He says that the order of succession is founded, in monarchies, on the good of the state, which demands that there should be a reigning family and that the order of succession should be fixed. This is a matter of political not civil law. Once the order has been fixed, it would be absurd to alter it according to the precepts of a civil law meant for individuals. Also once a family has renounced the succession, it would be absurd to invoke a civil law to restore their rights: "It is absurd to claim to settle the rights of kingdoms, nations, and the universe," Montesquieu asserts, "by the same maxims used to decide a right concerning a drainage pipe disputed between private individuals, to make use of Cicero's expression" (XXVI, 16).

   In the historical books, Montesquieu refers to and quotes from many original sources. He did not seek out manuscript material. If he had wished to do so, his poor eyesight would have been a serious handicap. We know, however, from one or two references and comments that he had access, probably through his Bordeaux friend Barbot,[14] to what represents the third serious effort to publish a comprehensive collection of documents relating to the history of France. This was the *Recueil des historiens*[15] (29 volumes eventually), of which the first five, covering the period from the foundation of the Frankish monarchy, up to and including the reign of Charlemagne, ending in the year 814, were published from 1734 to 1744. Barbot's library contained the first five volumes. Usually, however, Montesquieu gives, as his detailed source on early French history, either a separate edition or the previous official collection, the *Historiae Francorum Scriptores*, edited by André and François Duchesne (Paris 1636-49). Since this collection was in the library at La Brède (cat. 2932), physical access to it was easy, and it also had the advantage that documents such as annals, lives, and histories were usually included in full in one of the volumes, whereas in the later *Recueil* they were divided into chronological parts in different volumes. In any case, although the *Recueil* benefitted from another hundred years of research and collation, documents were often reprinted from the earlier collection with only a small number of very minor amendments.[16] Boulainvilliers, Dubos and Montesquieu all used the documents when they wrote about the constitutional history of France. Montesquieu disagreed with the interpretations put forward by Boulainvilliers and Dubos and arrived at his own independent view of the historical process. A brief look at the conclusions of Boulainvilliers and

Dubos, however will prove instructive as background to Montesquieu's own conclusions.

Henri de Boulainviliers followed in the steps of Jean Le Laboureur, a historian who had been commissioned in 1664 by the *ducs et comtes pairs de France*—the old nobility of the highest rank, to undertake research into the rights and privileges attached to their rank. Le Laboureur's *Histoire de la pairie* was not published until 1740,[17] but it circulated in manuscript and was brought to Montesquieu's attention in 1723.[18] The author equates the barbarian conquerors of France with the nobility and recalls the general assemblies of the first two dynasties in which the *Grands du royaume* deliberated and voted on measures to be taken. According to him, since feudal times the equality of all the nobles has changed, and only those great nobles directly linked to the Crown and equal between each other and superior to all others retain the right to form the king's Council. These conclusions were welcomed by the high nobility, some of whom, including famously the duc de Saint-Simon,[19] had the ear of the Regent and were influential in his decision when he came to power in 1715 to set up the Regency Councils, headed by great nobles, to advise on the conduct of affairs. This experiment, known as the polysynody, lasted but a very short time. By 1718 the secretaries of state again reported directly to the Regent. The polysynody was probably not so much an attempt to put the clock back to feudal times as it was an effort to find a better way of governing France than the centralizing regime of Louis XIV, an effort which failed because it relied on the nobility to act as a governing class, whereas in reality the nobles had not been trained to govern and were no longer accepted by other people in the state as their natural representatives.

Boulainvilliers' *Mémoires historiques* (part of his *Etat de France*) and the *Histoire de l'ancien gouvernement de la France* were the main vehicles for his constitutional theory. Both were first published posthumously in 1727.[20] Like Le Laboureur before him and Saint-Simon after him, Boulainvilliers goes back to the barbarian invasions and claims that the sovereign power was originally shared between the king and the conquering Franks. Unlike the other two writers, however, Boulainvilliers, though not consistent in his views, as Harold Ellis shows,[21] does not recognize any diminution in the rights of the conquerors. For him, all descendants of the Franks are noble and should rightfully share in the sovereignty of the nation while all descendants of the conquered people, the Gallo-Romans, remain non-noble and subservient. No doubt he was influenced by the fact that he himself, though of the old nobility, was not *duc et pair de France*. In any case, in reading his work it has to be remembered that, when he speaks of the liberty and equality of the Franks and claims that their descendants should inherit the same condition, he is speaking for part of the French nation only. He describes the process by which serfs became free and in some cases ennobled, without recognizing this as anything but a corruption of the true position:

More than forty thousand families mostly coming from serfdom, share the honours and rights formerly reserved to the conquerors of Gaul alone. So that, with no attention paid to the truth of facts vouched for by titles and history, it is today taken for certain that all men being born in the condition of workers, there is no difference between them except that they quitted that state earlier or later. To the point where Denis de Salvain, a well regarded author of the previous century, who wrote about feudal matters, even dared to put the question whether it was claimed that the nobility had fallen from the sky and could have any real privilege other than by concession of the prince.[22]

A little later the *thèse royale* was powerfully reasserted by the abbé Jean-Baptiste Dubos. Dubos was an establishment man. He served the government of France, first as a diplomat in the reign of Louis XIV, then as advisor on matters of state during the Regency, and finally, from 1722 until his death in 1742 as perpetual secretary of the *Académie française*. He began his historical researches into the beginnings of the French monarchy during the Regency period when the question of succession in the event of the death of the young Louis XV was, as we have seen, a very live issue. He prepared a treatise, not published at the time, but later developed into the *Histoire critique de l'établissement de la monarchie française dans les Gaules* (Paris 1734). In that work he refutes the aristocratic thesis by claiming to show from history that the Franks had not entered Gaul as conquerors (there was no record of such a conquest as an individual event) but as allies of Rome, and that absolute sovereignty had been transferred peacefully from the Roman Emperor to the Frankish King, with all other inhabitants being subject to him, a state of affairs inherited by all their successors. Where Boulainvilliers had seen an overwhelming conquest of Roman Gaul by the Franks, which established a permanent relationship of superiority of the victors over the vanquished, Dubos saw a peaceful transfer of absolute power which established a permanent dominance of the king and his successors over all his subjects, whether Gallo-Roman or Frank.

Montesquieu's Historical Argument

Montesquieu does not think highly of either Boulainvilliers or Dubos as historians. Boulainvilliers had in his view "more wit than insight, more insight than real knowledge" (XXX,10). He respects the erudition of Dubos but criticizes the use he made of it:

This work [the *Histoire critique*] has persuaded many people, because it is constructed very cleverly (*avec beaucoup d'art*); because it presumes everlastingly what is in doubt; because the more that proofs are lacking, the more probabilities are asserted; because an infinite number of conjectures are invoked as principles, and give rise to other conjectures. The reader forgets his doubts and starts to believe. And as an endless amount of erudition is produced, not as part of the theory, but alongside the theory, the reader's mind is distracted by peripheral matters and does not concern itself with the essential. Besides, it is impossible to suppose that so much research has not found anything; the length of the voyage makes one believe that one has at last arrived (XXX, 23).

Montesquieu's direct attack on Boulainvilliers occupies only a few paragraphs at the beginning of Book XXX, chapter 10, where he argues from the various barbarian laws that as servitude was not a state confined to the Gallo-Romans, nor liberty and nobility confined to the barbarian peoples, Boulainvilliers had failed to demonstrate the essential point of his system. His direct attack on Dubos occupies part of Book XXVIII, chapter 3 and Book XXX, chapter 10, and all of Book XXX, chapters 23, 24 and 25. He argues that Dubos advanced no proof of a peaceful transfer of power and that "when one sees a conqueror enter a state and subdue a large part of it by force and violence, and shortly afterwards one sees the entire state in submission, although history does not describe how the submission occurred, one has good reason to believe that the process continued as it had begun."

Montesquieu concludes that there is considerable evidence for the conquest, though it did not all occur at the same time and not everything in the state was changed by the conquerors. Montesquieu describes the theories of Boulainvilliers and Dubos as, respectively, a conspiracy against the third estate and a conspiracy against the nobility. His own theory is closely argued, with a wealth of documentation, throughout Books XXVIII, XXX, and XXXI. He argues that over many centuries the French monarchy was characterized by a division of sovereign power between the king and other bodies in the state. The balance of power and the composition of the intermediary bodies varied at different times over the period described—about one thousand years. He finds the origin of the French monarchic state in the characteristic organization of the Franks, which was to have a prince surrounded by his trusted followers, who served him and were rewarded by him. This, he says, was the system imported into France with the barbarian invaders. Under Clovis I (481-511) and the Merovingian dynasty, the rewards took the form of grants of land and other advantages (XXX, 3-4). In time the grants of land became hereditary (XVIII, 22; XXVIII, 9). This was the origin of the *seigneurs*, who thus became a landed nobility. These early kings ruled with the help of a Mayor of the Palace, responsible for administration, while the king headed the armed forces. The administrators gradually took over more power, until the two offices were merged under a palace revolution which resulted in a new king, Pepin, and the establishment of the Carolingian dynasty (A.D.751-987).

Montesquieu concludes that assemblies of the "nation" were frequent during the first two dynasties. He explains that only seigneurs and bishops took part, there being no question of commoners yet. Laws enacted by the assemblies were added by the king as capitularies to the codes of law. It was the assembly at Soissons which recognized Pepin as king in 751, and he was consecrated by the pope in 734. Although it is clear that assemblies had a real role during the early history of France, Montesquieu tells us very little about them. He refers to individual capitularies, but scarcely at all to the people concerned or their deliberations. The whole matter is treated almost as an aside in Book XXVIII, chapter 9 as part of the discussion about how the codes of law and the capitularies fell into disuse. He says that once landholding became hereditary, the feudal system extended gradually to all parts of France. Every great or even small seigneur became almost all-powerful in his own little kingdom. National laws almost disappeared because there was no one responsible for enforcing them. The arts of reading and writing almost disappeared also, except within the Church. Written laws were replaced by customs which varied according to each seigneurial domain, and were passed on verbally. This confused system was only gradually and partially brought under control during the Capetian dynasty (987 to the Revolution). The kings gradually gained authority over the whole kingdom, and, as internal peace was established, the learned arts began to flourish again. From about the thirteenth century, Roman law was recognised as the law of the land in parts of the country where its tradition had lingered as a form of customary law, while in the rest of France customs were written down, partially harmonized with each other, and, after being authorised by the regional Parlement, received the royal seal of approval, with Roman law being invoked in case of doubt or in some cases where it brought greater clarity to the situation. The Church meanwhile drew up and administered its own code of canon law.

Montesquieu asserts that the power of judging disputes and crimes had normally and properly accompanied the grants of land. He thought that this was a natural association, not a result of *seigneurs* usurping the royal prerogative as historians of the royal school contended.[23] At the height of the feudal system, an almost infinite number of mostly petty tribunals administered justice in France. This situation had to change with the introduction of Roman law and with settled customary laws and written records that made it possible to compare precedents. Most of the *seigneurs* and their staffs were ill-educated and quite incompetent to handle the work of administering justice, particularly once trial by personal combat or by ordeals by fire and water were no longer acceptable ways of deciding on guilt or innocence. From the thirteenth century and the reign of Saint Louis (Louis XI), procedures gradually changed. Cases were tried in secret instead of openly, the state took over the prosecution of criminal cases, and it became possible to have laws of general application, introduced by ordinances, and to have tribunals with wide authority. The Parlement of Paris, appointed by the king and originally part of the king's Council, at first specialized in appeals in cases involving the king or members of the nobility or higher clergy. Later it became a general court of appeal and sat permanently in Paris. The press of business became such that provincial Parlements were also set up to act as final courts of appeal in their own areas (XXVIII, 39). Montesquieu stresses the gradual nature of the changes in response to changing circumstances: "All this was done little by little by the force of the thing" (XXVIII, 43).

We have seen that Montesquieu had identified in Book II, chapter 4 a need in a monarchy for an intermediary body to act as the "depository of laws," and had said that this could only exist in the political bodies which announce the laws when they are made and recall them when they are forgotten. He had also said that the ignorance of the nobility, as well as their carelessness and scorn for civil government, disqualified them from fulfilling this role. He does not mention here the Parlements, but his readers would reasonably have concluded that in France the Parlements were the appropriate body to act as the "depository of laws." As he continues the story in Books XXVIII, XXX, and XXXI, he traces changes in the way the sovereign executive, legislative, and judiciary powers had been exercised. There had been *révolutions*—changes in the balance of power between the kings and the nobility, changes in the laws, and changes in judicial procedures. Sometimes power had been too much centralized in the monarch which brought the danger of despotism, and sometimes too decentralized, which brought the danger of breaking up the state. The shifts had twice led to a change of dynasty when the titular king had been superseded by the representative of a more powerful family, as when Pepin and then Charlemagne and the Carolingians superseded the Merovingian line in the eighth century, and when Hugh Capet and the Capetian line replaced the Carolingians at the end of the tenth century. Montesquieu does not present a picture of a state with unchanging fundamental laws and institutions, but rather of a country which had evolved from the simple organization of the Frankish conquerors into a complex monarchical state which had preserved a balance of sovereign powers between the king and other intermediary bodies, and thus had preserved a spirit of liberty and moderation. He does not mention the Estates General held in Capetian times, nor explain when and how the Parlement of Paris, and then the provincial Parlements, became not just a final court of appeal but also the bodies responsible for registering the laws, with the power to make remonstrances before registration. This is no doubt because, whereas in Book XXVIII he took the history of French civil law almost up to his own time, Books XXX and XXXI, which deal with constitutional law, the foundation of the monarchy, and subsequent changes in the way in which it operated, take the story only up to the time when the monarchy and the greatest fief were combined in Hugh Capet and the Capetian line from 987 onwards. He may have hesitated to risk offending Louis XV by comments on the monarchy, but it is also likely that he felt that he could not undertake all the extra work needed to bring the story more up to date, especially since so much in the way of collection, collation, and editing remained to be done on the relevant manuscript material. Furthermore, even as he composed the last two books of *The Spirit of Laws,* his printers in Geneva were clamoring for the completed work.

Evaluating Montesquieu's Views

Since Montesquieu was critical of other scholars, we need to ask whether his own understanding of constitutional law and history was soundly based. His interest in the history of French law was not a new development. He was building on foundations laid many years before. He graduated in law at Bordeaux University in 1708, with a view no doubt to his expected career as *président* in the Parlement of Bordeaux in succession to his uncle. We do not have the curriculum at Bordeaux, but it probably resembled the course at the University of Paris, described by Henri-François d'Aguesseau, three times Chancellor of France, in the first (dated 27 September 1717) of four *Instructions* addressed to his sons.[24] We learn that the first year of University study in law was devoted to Roman law, still in daily use in France; the second to Roman and Church law; and the third to French law including ordinances and customs. D'Aguesseau recommended a good deal of supplementary study to prepare his eldest son for the post of king's advocate, which he expected him to take up on leaving the University of Paris.

In Montesquieu's case there was a gap between his University studies and his destined career. The older generation was still active, his uncle in the Parlement of Bordeaux, and his father in charge of the family estates and wine business. He spent the years after 1708 in Paris until called home by his father's death at the end of 1713. There is not much evidence of his life and studies in Paris,[25] except for six notebooks, the *Collectio juris,* which have survived.[26] Up to the middle of the sixth notebook, the contents are devoted to a detailed study of the *Digest,* the *Code,* and the *Novellae,* which, along with an introductory work, the *Institutes,* almost certainly studied earlier at University, make up the *Corpus juris civilis,* the compilation of Roman law authorized by the Emperor Justinian I in the sixth century A.D. The rest of the sixth notebook is taken up by notes on customary law, legal maxims and disputed points of law, and by summaries of nine cases, heard in various courts of the Parlement of Paris, about 1711, at which Montesquieu seems to have been present. His own comments on the *Corpus juris* become more detailed and interesting the farther he advances. In addition to the glosses, dating mainly from the twelfth and thirteenth centuries and often included in editions of the text, such as the Lyon edition of 1612 which was at La Brède (cat.705), he makes full use in the *Code* and the *Novellae* of the extremely detailed commentaries by Antoine Mornac,[27] and also of a work by his own near contemporary, Jean Domat,[28] a very distinguished and influential legal expert, who published a new edition, still highly regarded, of the

Roman law, arranged by topics. Most of the references to other commentators such as Cujas, Dumoulin, Faber, and Boerius, are taken from Mornac, at least in the first instance, but there are also references to such later commentators as Bernard Automne[29] and Claude de Ferrière,[30] who were not known to Mornac. By the time Montesquieu returned to Bordeaux, he had acquired a detailed knowledge of at least one of the major branches of European law. This was followed by about twelve years practice in the courts of the Bordeaux Parlement,[31] and very wide general reading including, as can be seen from *The Spirit of Laws,* many books relating to the development of French law.[32]

Montesquieu has often been claimed as a supporter of the *thèse nobiliaire.* Johnson Kent Wright, for example, says that "the historical books which conclude *De l'esprit des lois* certainly provided a more authoritative and attractive version of the *thèse nobiliaire,* establishing it on far securer grounds than did the quasi-racial, voluntarist account of Boulainvilliers."[33] According to Wright:

> It was Montesquieu, far more profoundly than any of his contemporaries, who recognised that the fortunes of the 'regrouped' French nobility of the eighteenth century now depended more than ever on the absolute monarchy whose highest offices in the state, church and military it occupied. If it bears witness to the ineradicable friction that persisted between aristocracy and absolutism in France, it nevertheless faithfully reflects the broad self-confidence of the eighteenth century nobility, now free to enjoy the fruits of its final rapprochement with the monarchy.[34]

I would suggest, however, that it is difficult to reconcile this assessment with *The Spirit of Laws,* the work of Montesquieu's maturity. The main lines of his theory of monarchy are set out, as we have seen, in Book II, chapter 4, but it seems certain both from this chapter and from comments made throughout Books XXVIII, XXX, and XXXI, that he sees the monarchical state in France as something fluid. It evolves over time and does not depend on any set organization. What is essential to the spirit of monarchy is that the king does not govern alone, but with intermediary powers and through recognized channels. He says, as we know, that the most natural of the intermediary powers is the nobility, but he does not specify that the nobility should be organized in a special way to enable it to participate in government. His concern in Book II, chapter 4 seems to be rather that the nobility, like the *seigneurs,* the clergy, and certain other individuals or bodies such as towns should have a particular status and privileges which would enable them, though subordinate to the king, to share in government. He deprecates the loss of jurisdiction by these subordinate and dependent powers, which has occurred over many centuries in a great state in Europe—no doubt he means France—and he makes a graphic comparison: "As the sea seems to want to cover the entire earth and is held up by the plants and small stones on the shores, so monarchs, whose power seems to have no limits, are held up by

the smallest obstacles, and bow their natural pride to complaints and prayers."
He does specify however, as we have also seen in the same chapter, the need in
a monarchy for an organized body or bodies to serve as the depository of laws,
to register and recall them, and he says that neither the nobility nor the monarch's own Council are fit to fulfill this role—the nobility because of their personal shortcomings and contempt for civil government and the Council because
it is too much under the influence of the changing will of the monarch. It is true
of course that the office holders in the Parlements enjoyed noble status and
privileges by virtue of their offices. Some of these office holders came from the
old nobility but most formed what was known as the robe nobility. It seems that,
when the nobility *as an order in the state* is under consideration by Montesquieu
and other political writers such as Saint-Simon and the various writers mentioned in this chapter, they are not thinking of the *noblesse de robe* but of the
old nobility. It is the old nobility who are stigmatized by Montesquieu as ignorant and careless. And when he speaks of the bodies responsible for the depository of laws, he does not appear to regard them as part of the nobility. Therefore
his silence on the subject of the Estates General may be at least partly explained
by assuming that he realized how unsatisfactory was the representation of the
three orders in the Estates.

In Book XI, chapter 6 of *The Spirit of Laws*, Montesquieu sets out constitutional arrangements designed to preserve liberty in a state. He is describing here,
not such arrangements in general terms, but the actual constitution of England,
as he understood it. We may wish that we had from him a similar description of
the constitution of France, but we have not. Instead, right at the end of the work,
we have what might be called the *thèse évolutionnaire,* a description of how the
French constitution had developed historically. It was not Montesquieu's object
to propose changes in the way in which France was governed. He was already a
successful author when he composed this major work, and no doubt he wished
his greatest achievement to be not only published, but widely circulated in his
own country. Even as it was, he arranged for publication in Switzerland and for
the work then to be imported into France. The censorship was sufficiently re-
laxed by that time to turn a blind eye to such arrangements, but it is likely that
the government censors would have obstructed circulation if the work had contained specific proposals affecting the powers of the king of France. Even if he
had felt free to do so, Montesquieu would probably have been cautious about
making specific proposals. One of his recurring themes is the need to understand
the causes which have led to particular laws and customs. His advice is to move
slowly in making changes. For example, though he admires the liberty established by the English constitution as described in XI,6, he ends the chapter by
saying:

> I do not intend by this to attack other governments, nor to say that this extreme
> political liberty should be a reproach to those who have only a moderate degree

of liberty. How could I say that, I who believe that an excess even of liberty is not always desirable, and that people nearly always adapt better to averages than to extremes?

In the following chapter, Book XI, chapter 7, he goes on to speak of "the monarchies we know," presumably including France, whose object is the honor and reputation (*la gloire*) of the citizens, the state, and the prince, and he says that this quest for *gloire* results in a spirit of liberty which may contribute as much to happiness as liberty itself. In the Preface to *The Spirit of Laws* he says:

> I do not write to censure what is established in any particular country. Each country will find here the reasons for its maxims; and the conclusion naturally suggests itself that the business of proposing changes belongs only to those sufficiently gifted to be able by a stroke of genius to understand fully the constitution of a state. . . . In a time of ignorance people do not hesitate even in perpetrating great evils; in enlightened times they tremble even in bringing about the greatest good. They realize the old abuses, and they see how to correct them, but they also see how the correction may be an abuse. One leaves the evil if one fears something worse, one leaves the good if one is doubtful how to do better. One looks at individual measures in the light of the whole; one examines all the causes in order to assess all the results.

Conclusion

What measures might Montesquieu have favored to improve the government of France had he felt free to consider them? This is very debatable given his opinion about the difficulty of foreseeing the results of changes in the laws. It also needs to be considered that he published his great treatise prior to mid-century. The Parlementary reforms of 1771 were in the future. The king did not see himself as a despot, and in the first half of the eighteenth century, probably most of his subjects did not think of him as such. Though the Parlements were the only intermediary bodies with any legislative functions at the national level, executive power continued to be channelled in many of the traditional ways, often overlapping with the functions of the king's Council, his ministers and/or the recently instituted system of royal intendants. Some provincial governors, such as, in particular, the princes of Condé who held the post of governor of Burgundy in succession from 1632 until 1789,[35] exercised real power in their provinces. Some of the provincial Estates continued to meet, though the extent of their power and influence is a very complex matter.[36] "The crucial point," observes Richard Bonney, "is that estates in one form or another survived in the four great outlying provinces (Brittany, Burgundy, Provence and, above all, Languedoc), and their continued existence was in itself a limitation on the absolute power of the king." He adds, however, that there were still alternative instruments of government available to the crown in each locality (e.g., Parlements, governors, intendants).[37]

A long tradition of municipal self-government also continued. As Gail Bossenga observes:

> in the Old Regime, individuals were able to exercise civic rights and obtain privileges primarily through their membership in a privileged province, estate or corporate body. Cities were one such type of corporate body that conferred privileges on its members. Typically these included tax exemptions, and the political right of certain inhabitants, usually designated members of professional groups, to elect municipal officials.[38]

All these intermediary bodies, however, were subject to the king's influence, partly through the sale of offices and partly through the pressure which could be brought to bear on office holders by the king, ministers, and intendants.

In light of his admiration for the English constitution as he understood it (XI, 6), perhaps Montesquieu would have proposed, had he lived at the time of the Revolution, some version of the division of sovereign powers between king, lords, and commons, with the judiciary separately organized except occasionally as a last court of appeal. He might have thought that an enhanced role for the Parlements would be in accordance with his expressed opinion that the nobility were the most natural intermediary body in a monarchy, since all the officials of the sovereign courts had either inherited or purchased their offices, which conferred noble status. Such a course would have had grave drawbacks. As Richard Bonney says: "The failure of the Estates-General left a power vacuum which could not be filled by the sovereign tribunals."[39] He gives various reasons for this. One is that each Parlement, as well as the other sovereign courts such as the *chambres des comptes* and the *cours des aides,* had its own *ressort*, or area of competence and its own responsibilities, which might overlap with those of its neighbors. The Parlement of Paris had the largest *ressort* but this still amounted to less than half of the country. It was the most important in its personnel and was first in line to receive new legislation for registration and to have the opportunity to remonstrate, but it was never in a position to dictate to other courts. This severely weakened the position of the French Parlements in comparison with the English Parliament whose competence extended to the whole of the kingdom. Again, the legislative function of the Parlements was very limited. Unlike the Parliament of England, they did not initiate legislation but merely reacted to it and sometimes influenced it behind the scenes. Finally the personnel of the Parlements, being composed of those who had inherited or bought their offices, had no real authority to represent the nation, though they often claimed to do so. In any case, Montesquieu might have regarded any combination of the existing judicial powers of the Parlements with either executive or increased legislative functions as prejudicial to liberty (XI,6). As we have already noticed, he does not mention the Estates-General in *The Spirit of Laws,* although it seems from a later perspective that the best hope for the survival of a moderate monarchy in France would have lain in the revival of these Estates on a better constitutional basis, providing for frequent, regular meetings, not depending on a summons by the king when and if it suited him, and providing also for improved representation of the various parts of the nation.

All this is speculation. The accusation of despotism in 1771, after the Maupeou reforms, were instituted sounded the death-knell of the Old Regime, and even the restoration of the powers of the Parlements by Louis XVI in 1774 could not repair the damage. The Parlements themselves were foremost in calling for the summoning of the Estates General, a body which the government would find it difficult to coerce. As it turned out, however, the pressures for change after 1771 very quickly became too great to be contained within the institutions of the Old Regime.

One wonders how Montesquieu would have viewed the Revolution of 1789. Perhaps he could have discerned the repetition of a familiar pattern. However much tempered in practice, the sovereign powers had become too much concentrated in the king. It was time for the balance to swing back, away from the crown, but this time it was not a question of a family or an individual becoming powerful enough to take over the sovereignty. No doubt Montesquieu would have preferred changes to take place peacefully, but the appropriate constitutional machinery for peaceful change did not yet exist, even in the Estates General. The lay orders in the three estates had changed very greatly over the centuries. The second order, the nobility, constantly received accessions from the creation of new offices and office holders. The privileges conferred by noble status were not the reward for service to the state. Everyone knew that offices were bought and sold like commodities. Acquiring noble status was always possible for oneself or one's children if one had the money. In the normal course of affairs, those who had acquired the status earlier tended to despise those who acquired it later, but this did not affect the privileges of the new nobility. The justification for the venal system, in the view of Montesquieu, was that it was a way of ensuring that the state's business was carried on and that it tended to stabilize society (V,19). Meanwhile many of the rest of the inhabitants of France—the third estate, about 95 percent of the population—were themselves often quite comfortably off, even wealthy, well educated, and increasingly practised in political debate, but they had no political role except as one part of an Estates General so rarely summoned (the last time had been in 1614), that in 1789 no living person could remember the last occasion. Furthermore, even if the Estates were convened, the representation of the third estate would by no means correspond to their numbers since voting had always been by order rather than by head. Thus there was built in dissatisfaction in society, even among members of the nobility who were already privileged but even more in the third estate, while at the same time constitutional means of expressing and remedying any grievances were very inadequate. This dissatisfaction combined in 1789 with other grievances, including particularly those relating to taxation, and led to an irresistible demand for constitutional change which took everyone by surprise at the time. The Estates-General finally met on 5 May 1789. François Furet has given a good account of the events which then led the Third Estate to set up almost immediately the first National Assembly in place of the Estates-General: "The great act of revolution was accomplished: the Third Estate had destroyed and created a new authority independent of the king."[40] The sovereignty had once again been transferred, and a new constitutional epoch had begun.

For most of the next two hundred and more years, France has been described not as a monarchy but as a republic. Montesquieu, however, might still recognize in his own country a type of moderate state, governed by known laws and with separate powers which act as a check on each other. He might well feel that the spirit of the laws of France—a spirit of liberty and moderation, was more fully realized in today's *République française* than in the monarchy he knew.

Notes

I would like to thank David Carrithers for helpful comments and suggestions on an earlier draft of this chapter.

1. Fundamental laws had evolved over time and were no more than the statement of certain commonly accepted constitutional principles: (1) that the crown of France was not the personal property of the holder but devolved in accordance with the law and custom of France; (2) women, bastards, and heretics were excluded from the crown; (3) the king could not dispose of the domain belonging to the crown, and any personal property which he owned when becoming king would be added to the domain of the crown; (4) the temporal power was independent of the spiritual power i.e., the king, as king, was not subject to the pope, and the pope did not have the right to depose him. All other laws designated as fundamental by the Parlement or writers such as Bodin, Fénélon, and Saint-Simon, were contested by other parties in the state. See Emile Chénon, *Histoire générale du droit français*, 2 vols. (Paris: Recueil Sirey, 1929), II, 410-12 and Michel Antoine, *Le Conseil du Roi sous le règne de Louis XV* (Geneva: Droz, 1970), 13-15.

2. Chénon, *Histoire générale du droit français*, II, 412.

3. Jules Flammermont, ed., *Remontrances du Parlement de Paris au XVIIIe siècle, 3 vols.* (Paris: Imprimerie nationale, 1888-98), III, 157.

4. Jean Egret, *Louis XV et l'opposition parlementaire 1715-1774* (Paris: A. Colin, 1970); Peter Campbell, *Power and Politics in Old Regime France 1720-1745* (London: Routledge, 1996), 228-29.

5. Archives Nationales, K163, Miromesnil to Louis XVI: 4.1.1787, in William Doyle, "Was there an Aristocratic Reaction in Pre-Revolutionary France?" in *Past and*

Present 57 (1972), 97-122 reprinted in William Doyle, *Officers, Nobles and Revolutionaries: Essays on Eighteenth-Century France* (London: Hambledon Press, 1995).

6. François Hotman (1524-90), *Franco-Gallia*, translated as *La Gaule Françoise* (Cologne, Fayard, 1574). See Franklin Ford, "Restatement of the *Thèse Nobiliaire,"* in *Robe and Sword, the Regrouping of the French Aristocracy after Louis XIV* (Cambridge, MA: Harvard University Press, 1953), 222-45.

7. Jean Bodin (1530-1596), *Les Six livres de la république,* first published 1576. There are many editions and translations, including *Six Books of the Commonwealth* in Blackwell Political Texts (Oxford, 1967). For commentary on Bodin, see Richard Bonney, "Bodin and the Development of the French Monarchy," in *Transactions of the Royal Historical Society*, 5th series 40 (London: Royal Historical Society, 1990), 43-61, reprinted in Bonney, *The Limits of Absolutism in Ancien Régime France* (Aldershot, Hampshire: Ashgate Publishing Limited [Variorum Reprints], 1995).

8. Bernard de La Roche-Flavin (1552-1627), *Treize livres des parlements de France* (Bordeaux, 1617, Geneva, 1621). See Franklin Ford, *Robe and Sword,* 223-24.

9. Richard Bonney, "Was there a Bourbon Style of Government?" in Keith Cameron ed., *From Valois to Bourbon: Dynasty, State & Society in Early Modern France* (Exeter: University of Exeter, 1989), reprinted in Bonney, *The Limits of Absolutism in Ancien Régime France,* 176-78.

10. Franklin L. Ford, *Robe and Sword,* 178-79. A.N., K.648, nos.6-11. Ford says that four of the meetings were termed *assemblées générales,* and for these several of the absent peers sent notarized declarations of proxy.

11. Harold Ellis, *Boulainvilliers and the French Monarchy* (Ithaca, NY: Cornell, 1988), 92-93 and 112-18.

12. Henri de Boulainvilliers or Boulainviller (1658-1722). See Renée Simon, *Henri de Boulainviller: historien, politique, philosophe, astrologue* (Paris, 1941) and Ellis, *Boulainvilliers.*

13. Abbé Jean-Baptiste Dubos or du Bos (1670-1742). See A. Lombard, *L'Abbé du Bos, Un Initiateur de la pensée moderne* (Paris: Librairie Hachette, 1913).

14. Jean Barbot, a friend of Montesquieu, and his colleague at the Academy of Bordeaux. It was to Barbot, Guasco, and his son Jean-Baptiste, that Montesquieu read several chapters of *The Spirit of Laws* on 12 February 1745. See Robert Shackleton, *Montesquieu* (Oxford, 1961), 239.

15. Dom. Martin Bouquet, ed., *Recueil des historiens des Gaules et de la France,* 19 vols. (Paris: Palme, 1738-1904, reprinted 1867-71).

16. The editors of these collections, and of the separate collections of capitularies, Barbarian laws, imperial constitutions, etc., seem not to have seen it as their job to interpret the historical significance of documents. Dom Bouquet, first editor of the *Recueil,* writes in the preface to the first volume: "Our intention here is not to write history , but only to compile the acts which may serve for that purpose" (p.iv).

17. Jean Le Laboureur, *Histoire de la pairie de France et du Parlement de Paris ou l'on traite aussi des électeurs de l'empire, & du cardinalat. Par Monsieur D.B.* (London: S. Harding, 1740).

18. *Correspondance,* Nagel, III, 752.

19. Louis de Rouvroy (duc de) Saint-Simon, (1675-1745). His *Mémoires* were not published until after the Revolution.

20. Henri de Boulainvilliers, *Mémoires présentés à Monseigneur le Duc d'Orléans, régent de France. Contenant les moyens de rendre ce royaume très-puisssant, & d'augmenter considérablement les revenus du roi & du peuple. Par le C. de Boulainvilliers* (La Haye et Amsterdam: Aux dépens de la Compagnie, 1727); *Histoire de l'ancien gouvernement de la France, avec XVII lettres historiques sur les Parlements ou Etats-Généraux* (La Haye et Amsterdam: Aux dépens de la Compagnie, 1727).

21. Ellis, *Boulainvilliers and the French Monarchy.*

22. Boulainvilliers, *Histoire de l'ancien gouvernement de la France,* 318.

23. Abbé Claude Fleury, *Histoire du droit français* (1674); le Père Gabriel Daniel, *Histoire de France depuis l'établissement de la monarchie française dans les Gaules* (Paris: D. Mariette, 1720) and Jean Baptiste Dubos, *Histoire de l'établissement de la monarchie française dans les Gaules* (Paris: Osmont,1734).

24. Henri-François D'Aguesseau, *Discours et Œuvres mêlées, nouvelle édition augmentée de plusieurs discours et de ses instructions à ses fils, 3 vols.* (Paris: 1771), III, 8.

25. Shackleton, *Montesquieu,* 8.

26. The ms is in the Bibliothèque Nationale de France, n.a.f 12837-42.

27. Antoine Mornac (1554-1620), *Observationes in viginti quattuor priores libros Digestorum et in quattuor priores libros Codicis* (Paris, 1656)*; Posteriorum viginti sex librorum Pandectarum Synopsis . . .* (Paris, 1660)*; Posteriorum librorum Codicis synopsis* (Paris, 1660). The observations on the first twenty-four books had been published previously in 1616.

28. Jean Domat (1625-1696), *Les Loix civiles dans leur ordre naturel* (Paris: La Clare, 1689-94).

29. Bernard Automne (1587-1666), *La Conférence du droict françois avec le droict roman, en laquelle les titres, loix & paragraphes des Pandectes & du Code du droict civil sont confirmez, interpretez & abrogez par ordonnances royaux, arrests des cours souveraines & auctoritez des plus grands praticiens de France* (Paris, 1610).

30. Claude de Ferrière (1639-1714), *Jurisprudence du Digeste, conférée avec les ordonnances royales, les coutumes de France, et les décisions des cours souverains; ou toutes sortes de matières du droit romain, & du droit coutumier, sont traitée suivant l'usage des provinces de droit écrit & de l'usage de la France coutumière,* 2 vols (Paris: Chez Jean Cochart, 1667); *La Jurisprudence du Code de Justinien. Conférée avec les ordonnances royaux, les coutumes de France, et les décisions des cours souverains, 2 vols.* (Paris: Chez Jean Cochart, 1684); *La jurisprudence des Nouvelles de Justinien; conférée*

avec les ordonnances royaux, les coutumes de France, et les décisions des cours sou-verains (Paris: Chez Jean Cochart, 1688).

31. Shackleton, *Montesquieu,* 14-20.

32. Françoise Weil , "Les lectures de Montesquieu," *Revue d'histoire littéraire de la France,* 57 (1957): 494-514 and Iris Cox, *Montesquieu and the History of French Laws* (Oxford: Voltaire Foundation, 1983), 71-81.

33. Johnson Kent Wright, *A Classical Republican in Eighteenth Century France, The Political Thought of Mably* (California: Stanford University Press, 1997), 129-30.

34. Wright, *Mably,*129-30.

35. Beth Nachison, "Absentee Government and Provincial Governors in Early Modern France: The Princes of Condé and Burgundy, 1660-1720," *French Historical Studies,* XXI, no. 2 (spring 1998): 265-97.

36. Franklin Ford, *Robe and Sword,* 193-94.

37. Richard Bonney, "Absolutism: What's in a Name?" in *French History* I (1987), 93-117, reprinted in Bonney, *The Limits of Absolutism in Ancien Régime France,* 112.

38. Gail Bossenga, "City and State: An Urban Perspective on the Origins of the French Revolution," in *The French Revolution and the Creation of Modern Political Culture,* 4 vols. (New York: Pergamon Press, 1987-1994), Volume I: *The Political Culture of the Old Regime,* Keith M. Baker, ed. (Oxford, 1987), 116.

39. Richard Bonney, "The English and French Civil Wars," in *History* 65 (London: Historical Association, 1980), 365-82, reprinted in Bonney, *The Limits of Absolutism,* 380-81.

40. François Furet and Denis Richet, *The French Revolution* (New York: Macmillan, 1970), 70.

Index

About the Contributors

David W. Carrithers is Head of the Political Science Department and Adolph Ochs Professor of Government at the University of Tennessee at Chattanooga. He is the editor of *The Spirit of Laws by Montesquieu. A Compendium of the First English Edition* (1977) and the author of articles on Montesquieu in such journals as the *Revue Montesquieu, History of Political Thought, Journal of the History of Ideas,* and the *French-American Review.* A corresponding member of the Académie de Bordeaux, he is currently co-editor, with Patrick Coleman of UCLA, of the forthcoming volume *Montesquieu and the Spirit of Modernity.*

C. P. Courtney is a Fellow of Christ's College, Cambridge. His publications include *Montesquieu and Burke* (1963) and numerous books and articles on French literature, intellectual history, and bibliography. Currently, he is the General Editor of Benjamin Constant's *Correspondance générale* (in progress) and a member of the editorial boards preparing critical editions of the *Œuvres complètes* of Montesquieu and the *Histoire philosophique des deux Indes* of Raynal. He is a corresponding member of the Académie de Bordeaux and a Chevalier dans l'Ordre des Arts et des Lettres.

Iris Cox, an independent scholar in Great Britain, is the author of *Montesquieu and the History of French Laws* (1983) for which she was awarded the Prix Montesquieu by the Académie Montesquieu of Bordeaux. Currently she is editing, with Andrew Lewis of University College, London, Montesquieu's previously unpublished notebooks on Roman law, the *Collectio juris,* for the new critical edition of the complete works of Montesquieu under publication by the Voltaire Foundation.

Rebecca Kingston is Associate Professor of Political Science at Saint Francis College in Pennsylvania. She is the author of *Montesquieu and the Parlement of Bordeaux* (1996), for which she received the Prix Montesquieu awarded by the Académie Montesquieu of Bordeaux, and of articles on Montesquieu and eighteenth-century French history appearing in assorted journals and conference proceedings.

Sharon Krause is Assistant Professor of Government at Harvard University. Her work on Montesquieu and other subjects has appeared in such journals as *The Review of Politics, Polity, Philosophy & Social Criticism,* and *Political Theory.* She previously taught political theory at Wesleyan University.

Catherine Larrère is professor of philosophy at the University of Bordeaux III. She is the author of *L'Invention de l'économie au XVIIIe siècle* (1992) and *Actualité de Montesquieu* (1999) as well as numerous articles in journals and conference proceedings on Montesquieu, Rousseau, natural law, Enlightenment philosophy, and the history of economic thought. Currently she is part of the editorial committee preparing a new critical edition of the complete works of Montesquieu being published by the Voltaire Foundation.

Michael A. Mosher is Chair of the Department of Political Science at the University of Tulsa. He is the author of articles on Montesquieu, Burke, Hegel, Whitman, and Rawls in the *American Political Science Review*, *Political Theory*, and *Political Studies*. A contributor to the forthcoming volume *Alternative Conceptions of Civil Society*, edited by Simone Chambers and Will Kymlicka, he has recently taught at the University of Tokyo and Yale University and has been a Fellow in the School of Social Science at the Institute for Advanced Study, Princeton.

Paul A. Rahe is Jay P. Walker Professor of History at the University of Tulsa. He is the author of *Republics Ancient and Modern: Classical Republicanism and the American Revolution* (1992) and of numerous articles and book chapters dealing with classical antiquity, early modern political thought, and early American history. He has been a fellow at the Center for Hellenic Studies, the National Humanities Center, the Woodrow Wilson International Center for Scholars, and Clare Hall, Cambridge, and he is editor of the forthcoming volume *Machiavelli's Republican Legacy*.